THE **HIST** SOLUTION

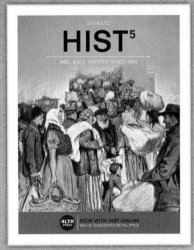

Print + Online

D1560497

HIST⁵ delivers all the key terms and core concepts for the **U.S. History** course.

HIST Online provides the complete narrative from the printed text with additional interactive media and the unique functionality of **StudyBits**— all available on nearly any device!

What is a StudyBit™? Created through a deep investigation of students' challenges and workflows, the StudyBit™ functionality of **HIST Online** enables students of different generations and learning styles to study more effectively by allowing them to learn their way. Here's how they work:

COLLECT WHAT'S IMPORTANT
Create StudyBits as you highlight text, images or take notes!

WEAK

FAIR

STRONG

UNASSIGNED

RATE AND ORGANIZE STUDYBITS
Rate your understanding and use the color-coding to quickly organize your study time and personalize your flashcards and quizzes.

StudyBit™

TRACK/MONITOR PROGRESS
Use Concept Tracker to decide how you'll spend study time and study YOUR way!

85%

PERSONALIZE QUIZZES
Filter by your StudyBits to personalize quizzes or just take chapter quizzes off-the-shelf.

CORRECT

INCORRECT

INCORRECT

INCORRECT

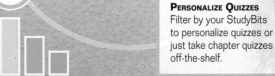

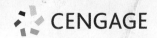

HIST5, Volume 2
Kevin M. Schultz

Senior Vice President, Higher Ed Product,
Content, and Market Development:
Erin Joyner

Product Manager: Joseph D. Potvin

Content/Media Developer: Sarah Keeling

Product Assistant: Alexandra C. Shore

Marketing Manager: Christopher Walz

Sr. Content Project Manager: Colleen A. Farmer

Sr. Art Director: Bethany Bourgeois

Text Designer: Chris Miller, Cmiller Design

Cover Designer: Lisa Kuhn/Curio Press, LLC/Chris
Miller, Cmiller Design

Cover Image: Robert Holmes/Alamy Stock Photo

Back Cover and Special Page Images:
Computer and tablet illustration:
© iStockphoto.com/furtaev; Smart Phone
illustration: © iStockphoto.com/dashadima;
Feedback image: © Rawpixel.com/
Shutterstock.com

Intellectual Property Analyst: Alexandra Ricciardi

Intellectual Property Project Manager:
Reba Frederics

Production Service: MPS Limited

For product information and technology assistance, contact us at
Cengage Customer & Sales Support, 1-800-354-9706

For permission to use material from this text or product,
submit all requests online at **www.cengage.com/permissions**
Further permissions questions can be emailed to
permissionrequest@cengage.com

Library of Congress Control Number: 2017949025

Student Edition ISBN: 978-1-337-29426-3

Student Edition with Online ISBN: 978-1-337-29425-6

Cengage
20 Channel Center Street
Boston, MA 02210
USA

Cengage is a leading provider of customized learning solutions with
employees residing in nearly 40 different countries and sales in more
than 125 countries around the world. Find your local representative at
www.cengage.com.

Cengage products are represented in Canada by Nelson Education, Ltd.

To learn more about Cengage platforms and services, visit
www.cengage.com

To register or access your online learning solution or purchase materials for
your course, visit **www.cengagebrain.com**

Printed in the United States of America
Print Number: 01   Print Year: 2017

SCHULTZ HIST⁵ BRIEF CONTENTS

CONTENTS

MPI/Getty Images

Eon Images

20 Becoming a World Power   372

Naval Parade, held in honor of commander George Dewey (1837-1917) 1898 (oil on canvas), Pansing, Fred (1854-1912)/© Museum of the City of New York, USA/Bridgeman Art Library

Library of Congress Prints and Photographs Division[LC-DIG-fsa-8b29516]

THE ADVERTISING ARCHIVES LTD.

25 The Sixties 484

Hulton Archive/Getty Images

David Paul Morris/Getty Images

Carlos Amarillo/Shutterstock.com

29 Globalization and Its Discontents   558

AP Images/Mark Lennihan

About the Author

Kevin M. Schultz is an award-winning historian and bestselling author. He is currently a Professor of History at the University of Illinois at Chicago (UIC), where he has won several awards for his teaching and writing. He is the author of two other books: *Buckley and Mailer: The Difficult Friendship that Shaped the Sixties* (W.W. Norton & Co., 2015), which was an Amazon #1 New Release in American History; and *Tri-Faith America: How Postwar Catholics and Jews Helped America Realize Its Protestant Promise* (Oxford University Press, 2011), which is used in both graduate and undergraduate classes across the country. He has published widely for popular audiences, too, including having had a journal article appear immediately before one written by the Pope. He received his BA from Vanderbilt University and his PhD from UC Berkeley.

16 | Reconstruction, 1865–1877

LEARNING OBJECTIVES

After reading this chapter, you should be able to do the following:

16-1 Describe the changed world of ex-slaves after the Civil War.

16-2 Outline the different phases of Reconstruction, beginning with Lincoln's plan and moving through presidential Reconstruction to Congressional Reconstruction.

16-3 Explain how Reconstruction evolved at the individual states' level.

16-4 Evaluate and understand the relative success and failures of Reconstruction.

AFTER FINISHING
THIS CHAPTER
GO TO **PAGE 306**
FOR STUDY TOOLS

Confederate soldiers returned home to a devastated South in 1865. While northern trains and cities began to hum with activity, the South's farms and factories, its railroads and bridges—almost its entire infrastructure—had been destroyed by war. Nearly 23 percent of the South's fighting-age men had died in the war. Thousands more bore the physical scars of battle. The physical rebuilding of the region began quickly and progressed rapidly, but reconstructing southern society was a much more difficult process, especially considering (1) the political questions about how to integrate rebel states back into the nation and (2) the social questions about how to integrate 4 million newly freed slaves.

The North was also vastly changed, albeit in another way. Northern politicians seized the opportunity to pass many of the laws that southerners in Congress had long resisted. During and shortly after the war, Congress passed laws supporting internal improvements, outlawing slavery, and expanding the developments of the Market Revolution. Indeed, some historians argue that the Civil War was crucial in turning the Market Revolution of the 1830s, 1840s, and 1850s into the Industrial Revolution of the second half of the nineteenth century. Regardless of the term you use, the North after the Civil War was beginning to resemble what we think of today as a modern industrial society.

But, first, to the era of **Reconstruction**, defined as the country's various attempts to resolve the issues that remained after the Civil War, including: how free could former slaves be in the ex-Confederacy; how could the country re-incorporate the states that had voted to leave; and would the country undertake the dramatic transformations necessary to overturn two hundred years of slavery?

16-1 FREEDMEN, FREEDWOMEN

After the Civil War, black Americans encountered a new world of opportunities. After years of enslavement, or at least the perpetual threat of enslavement if they had been already freed, African Americans confronted a new question: what does it mean to be free? After the passage in 1865 of the Thirteenth Amendment outlawing slavery throughout the land forever, black Americans had to wonder: what does one do after the bonds of slavery have been broken?

The first thing many freed people did was move. They often left the plantations upon which they had labored as slaves, typically to put some distance between them and their former owners. They also moved in search of long-lost family members who had perhaps been sold to another owner during an era when the stability of slave families was always secondary to profits. The freedom of movement was the key.

This new mobility meant that black family life began to stabilize throughout the South. Men and women now had more control over their lives and their familial roles. Reflecting the priorities of nineteenth-century American society, ex-slaves often removed women from the fields so that they could occupy a "women's sphere of domesticity." Most black women still had to work for financial reasons, but they often began working as indoor domestics rather than field hands.

Meanwhile, freed families often desperately sought to purchase land in order to continue the planting life they knew best, sometimes by simply purchasing a piece of the land on which they had labored before the Civil War. In their new communities, African Americans also expressed their religious independence by expanding the independent network of black churches that had been established since the Revolution. During Reconstruction, the number of black churches grew exponentially.

The newly freed people also sought the education that had been denied them during slavery. Schools for African Americans opened all over the South, for parents and for children. Learning to read meant learning to understand contracts, engage in political battles, and monitor wages, new experiences for those who had only recently been deemed chattel.

Politically, African Americans sought to vote. They marched in demand of it. They paraded to advocate bills

> **Reconstruction** The federal government's attempts to resolve the issues resulting from the end of the Civil War in order to reconstitute the nation

◄◄◄ **The process of reconstructing the nation after four years of civil war was long and exhausting, so long in fact that it may have even allowed the South to lose the war but win the peace. Here, new laws are explained at the office of the Freedman's Bureau in Memphis, Tennessee.**

endorsing it. They lionized black Revolutionary heroes in order to establish their credentials as vote-casting Americans. And they held mock elections to show their capacity and desire to participate in the American political process. Life for the newly freed was tumultuous but exciting, filled with possibilities.

16-1a The Freedmen's Bureau

While ex-slaves explored a life based on the free-labor vision, members of the defeated Confederacy sought to maintain as much of the old order as possible. To this end, they worked to prevent ex-slaves from acquiring economic autonomy or political rights. Although they had lost the war, ex-Confederates feared a complete turnover from the lives they had led before it. Indeed, one of the first organizations created after the war in the South was the **Ku Klux Klan**, founded in 1865 by six white Confederate soldiers concerned about the racial implications of black freedom. The Klan and other similar organizations, such as the Southern Cross and the Knights of White Camellia, served as quasi-military forces serving the interests of those who desired the restoration of white supremacy. Nathan Bedford Forrest, a Confederate general, was the Klan's first national leader.

To help mitigate this resistance, in 1865, Congress established the **Freedmen's Bureau**, a government agency designed to create a new social order by government mandate. Under the management of northerner O.O. Howard (after whom Howard

>> **What it means to be free** | After the Civil War, freedom was an expansive concept for African Americans in the South. They demonstrated this new freedom in numerous ways, large and small: many bought dogs and married, some purchased firearms, and several held mass meetings without white supervision. These were all actions often denied them under slavery. Pictured here is a group of "freedmen" in Richmond, Virginia circa 1865.

University is named), Congress designed the Freedmen's Bureau to build and manage new schools, provide food and medical care to needy southern black and white people, and ensure equal access to the judicial system for southerners both black and white. It had some success with this Herculean task: the Freedmen's Bureau built 3,000 schools and expanded medical care throughout much of the South, paying particular attention to the freed slaves and the areas where they had settled.

Its task of redesigning economic relations would prove more challenging. Lincoln's Republicans in Congress succeeded in putting into the bureau's charter a provision that plantations be divided into 40-acre plots and sold to former slaves, thus the origin of the phrase "40-acres-and-a-mule" signifying promises (often broken) made to African Americans. However, that plan was upended by politicians intending to enforce their own plans for reconstructing the South. Because politics were vitally important in determining how Reconstruction would unfold—would wealthy southerners simply get their land back?—it is to politics we must turn.

Ku Klux Klan A quasi-military force formed immediately after the Civil War by former Confederate soldiers in order to resist racial integration and preserve white supremacy; after a temporary decline, the group reformed in 1915 and sporadically returned to prominence throughout the nineteenth and twentieth centuries

Freedmen's Bureau Government agency designed to create a new social order by government mandate; this bureau provided freedmen with education, food, medical care, and access to the justice system

>> "The Secretary of War may direct such issues of provisions, clothing, and fuel, as he may deem needful for the immediate and temporary shelter and supply of destitute and suffering refugees and freedmen and their wives and children, under such rules and regulations as he may direct."—Freedmen's Bureau Bill, 1865. The image shows the old and sick being issued rations at the Freedmen's Bureau.

16-2 POLITICAL PLANS FOR RECONSTRUCTION

Even before the war was over, President Lincoln had pondered what it would take to bring the South back into the nation. Unfortunately for him, many in Congress were more interested in punishment than in reconciliation.

16-2a Lincoln's Plan for Reconstruction and His Assassination

In 1863, while battle was still raging, Lincoln issued his **Ten-Percent Plan**, which offered amnesty to any southerner who proclaimed (1) loyalty to the Union and (2) support of the emancipation of slaves. When 10 percent of a state's voters in the election of 1860 had taken the oath to the United States, they could develop a new state government, which would be required to abolish slavery. Then that state could reenter the Union with full privileges, including the crucial apportionment to the House of Representatives and Senate. Although requiring just 10 percent of the population to declare loyalty to the Union, and sidestepping the issue of preserving rights for the millions of ex-slaves,

it is important to remember that the war was still being fought. Lincoln was simply attempting to drain support from the Confederacy and shorten the war by making appeasement look easy.

CONGRESS BRISTLES

Republicans in Congress, more interested in punishing the South than Lincoln was, bristled at Lincoln's leniency. In opposition to Lincoln's plan, they passed the **Wade-Davis Bill**, which would have allowed a southern state back into the Union only after 50 percent of the population had taken the loyalty oath. Furthermore, to earn the right to vote or to serve in a constitutional convention, southerners would have to take a second oath, called the **iron-clad oath**, that testified that they had never voluntarily aided or abetted the rebellion. The iron-clad oath was designed to ensure that only staunch Unionists in the South could hold political power. Lincoln vetoed the bill, thinking it too harsh, and the battle about Reconstruction continued.

LINCOLN'S ASSASSINATION

As the battle wore on between Congress and the president, the hostilities of the American Civil War finally ended. Although the South had lost the war, a few disgruntled southerners would attempt to get revenge. Three days after Appomattox, John Wilkes Booth, a local actor and Confederate sympathizer, shot and killed Lincoln during a play at Ford's Theater in Washington, D.C. Eleven days later, a Union soldier shot and killed Booth as he tried to escape from a burning barn. In the coming political showdown, Lincoln's deep empathy and political acumen would be missed, as the battle to reconstruct the nation now took place between defiant congressional Republicans and the insecure man who had stumbled into the presidency—Andrew Johnson.

Ten-Percent Plan Plan issued by Lincoln in 1863 that offered amnesty to any southerner who proclaimed loyalty to the Union and support of the emancipation of slaves; once 10 percent of a state's voters in the election of 1860 signed the oath, it could create a new state government and reenter the Union

Wade-Davis Bill Bill that would have allowed a southern state back into the Union only after 50 percent of the population had taken the loyalty oath

iron-clad oath Oath to be taken by southerners to testify that they had never voluntarily aided or abetted the rebellion

Library of Congress Prints and Photographs Division|Currier & Ives./LC-USZC2-1947|

THE ASSASSINATION OF PRESIDENT LINCOLN.
AT FORD'S THEATRE WASHINGTON, D.C. APRIL 14TH 1865.

>> Shown here, in an act of retribution, actor John Wilkes Booth shoots Lincoln in the head just three days after the Civil War had ended.

16-2b Andrew Johnson and Presidential Reconstruction

Upon Lincoln's assassination, Andrew Johnson became president. Johnson was a native southerner, born poor to functionally illiterate parents in North Carolina, before the family moved to Tennessee. He didn't master reading and writing until he was in his twenties, and was trained to be a tailor. It was his wife who pushed him into politics and throughout the war Johnson proved a loyal Unionist. He served as Tennessee's military governor after the state was taken over by the Union Army. And, despite Johnson being a Democrat, in 1864 Lincoln selected Johnson as his running mate because Lincoln hoped to quiet dissent by running with a non-northerner and a non-Republican. While it may have helped him win the election, Lincoln's plan would ultimately backfire.

> Even Robert E. Lee applied to be pardoned.

PRESIDENTIAL RECONSTRUCTION, 1865–1867

Johnson was a lonely man who had a tough time handling criticism. Since his youth, he had looked up to the South's planter aristocracy and constantly sought

black codes Post–Civil War laws specifically written to govern the behavior of African Americans; modeled on the slave codes that existed before the Civil War

its approval. Reflecting these insecurities, within a month of assuming the presidency, Johnson unveiled his plan for Reconstruction: (1) scrapping the "40-acres-and-a-mule" plan suggested in the charter of the Freedmen's Bureau and (2) creating a tough loyalty oath that many southerners could take in order to receive a pardon for their participation in the rebellion. However, Johnson added a curious but vital caveat that Confederate leaders and wealthy planters—who were not allowed to take the standard oath—could appeal directly to Johnson for a pardon. Anyone who received amnesty through either of these measures regained his citizenship rights and retained all of his property, except for his slaves. Under Johnson's plan, a governor appointed by the president would then control each rebel state until the loyalty oath was administered to the citizens. At that point, southerners could create new state constitutions and elect their own governors, state legislatures, and federal representatives. Johnson's plan showed no concern for the future of black people in America.

Southern states made the most of the leeway Johnson afforded them. Even Robert E. Lee applied to be pardoned (although his pardon was never granted during his lifetime). A line of southern planters literally appeared at the White House to ask Johnson's personal forgiveness; doing so allowed the southern elite to return to its former privileged status. In the end, Johnson granted amnesty to more than 13,000 Confederates, many of whom had been combative leaders in the Confederacy. Once Johnson had granted these pardons, he ensured that there would be no social revolution in the South. With pardons in hand, wealthy southerners would not lose their land or their social control of the South.

BLACK CODES

Most of the new southern state governments returned Confederate leaders to political power. These leaders then created **black codes** modeled on the slave codes that existed before the Civil War. Although the codes legalized black marriages and allowed African Americans to hold and sell property, freed slaves were prohibited from serving on juries or testifying against white people in court. Intermarriage between black and white Americans was also strictly forbidden. Some states even had special rules that limited the economic freedoms of their black populations. Mississippi, for example, barred African Americans from purchasing or renting farmland. Most states created laws that allowed police officials to round up black vagrants and hire them out as laborers to white landowners.

In the end, these new laws hardened the separation of black Americans from white Americans, ending the intermingling and interaction that had been more common during slavery. With the rise of post-Civil War black codes, black and white southerners began a long process of physical separation that was not present before the war and that would last for at least a century. These black codes would also begin the process whereby black southerners after the Civil War were left with, in the words of one historian, nothing but freedom.

16-2c Congressional Reconstruction

Johnson did nothing to prevent the South from re-imposing these conditions on the black population. In Johnson's eyes, reconstruction of the Union would be finished as soon as southern states returned to the Union without slavery. Conservative members of Congress agreed. However, a group that would come to be called the **Radical Republicans** heartily disagreed.

THE RADICAL REPUBLICANS

The Republican Party had never been squarely behind Lincoln's plan for Reconstruction, and in fact the Radical Republicans, defined as the wing of the party most hostile to slavery, had opposed Lincoln's plans fiercely. Radicals in Congress, including Thaddeus Stevens of Pennsylvania, Charles Sumner of Massachusetts (of "Bleeding Sumner" fame), and Benjamin Wade of Ohio, had pushed for emancipation long before Lincoln issued the Emancipation Proclamation, and they considered Lincoln's lenient Reconstruction program

>> This print shows a campaign banner for 1864 Republican presidential candidate Abraham Lincoln and running mate Andrew Johnson. An insecure man who had stumbled into the presidency, Johnson found it difficult to reunite the nation.

Library of Congress Prints and Photographs Division [LC-DIG-ppmsca-17562]

outrageous. As they looked toward the end of the war, Radicals hoped to use the Confederacy's defeat as an opportunity to overhaul southern society. At the very least, they hoped to strip the southern planter class of its power and ensure that freed slaves would acquire basic rights.

THE RADICALS VERSUS JOHNSON

As we have seen, Johnson, considering himself somewhat of a moderate, took office intending to wrap up the process of Reconstruction quickly. Granting amnesty to former Confederate leaders and other wealthy southerners demonstrated as much. Radicals in Congress, however, continued to devise measures for protecting the interests of the newly freed black population. With no southerners yet in Congress, the Radical Republicans wielded considerable power.

Their first moves were (1) to expand the role of the Freedmen's Bureau, creating a stronger organization with greater enforcement powers and a bigger budget, and (2) to pass the important **Civil Rights Act**, which was designed to counteract the South's new black codes by allowing all citizens, black or white, the protection of the law, the right to enforce contracts, to sue and be sued, give evidence in court, and hold property. Johnson

Radical Republicans Wing of the Republican Party most hostile to slavery

Civil Rights Act Bill that granted all citizens mandatory rights, regardless of racial considerations; designed to counteract the South's new black codes

vetoed both bills, but Congress overrode the veto on the Civil Rights Act, making them the first laws ever passed over presidential veto. Their willingness to override a presidential veto suggests the importance that Radical Republicans placed on a meaningful reconstruction effort. It was the first of many vetoes the Radical Republicans would override.

THE FOURTEENTH AMENDMENT

Congress's success in circumventing Johnson's veto began a new phase of Reconstruction known as **Congressional Reconstruction** in which Congress wielded more power than the president. Congress introduced a constitutional amendment in 1866 that (1) barred Confederate leaders from ever holding public office in the United States, government (2) gave Congress the right to reduce the representation of any state that did not give black people the right to vote, and (3) declared that any person born or naturalized in the United States was, by that very act, an American citizen deserving of "equal protection of the law." This, in essence, granted full citizenship to all black people; by the power of the constitution, states were prohibited from restricting the rights and privileges of any citizen.

> There was nothing worse than being part of a nation and having no say in how that nation was governed.

To the frustration of Radicals like Thaddeus Stevens and Charles Sumner, the amendment, which became the **Fourteenth Amendment** to the U.S. Constitution, did not also protect the voting rights of African Americans. Nevertheless, Congress passed the amendment and it went to the states for ratification. Tennessee approved it and, in 1866, was invited by Congress to reenter the Union. Every other state of the former Confederacy rejected the amendment, suggesting that the Radicals' hopes for restructuring the South would not be realized easily.

CONGRESSIONAL RECONSTRUCTION, 1867-1877

Despite the strenuous labors of Andrew Johnson, the midterm elections of 1866 gave the Radical Republicans a two-thirds majority in both houses of Congress, and they began to push their program of Reconstruction more vigorously. The election was vicious, as Johnson and his supporters went around the country on what was called the "swing around the circle" to castigate and even threaten the execution of several Radical Republicans.

Despite Andrew Johnson's claim that Reconstruction was over, the Radical-led Congress easily passed (again over Johnson's veto) the **Military Reconstruction Act** in March 1867. This act divided the former rebel states, with the exception of Tennessee, into five military districts. In each district, a military commander took control of the state governments, and federal soldiers enforced the law and kept order (see Map 16.1).

Congress also made requirements for readmission to the Union more stringent. Each state was instructed to register voters and hold elections for a state constitutional convention. In enrolling voters, southern officials were required to include black people and exclude any white people who had held leadership positions in the Confederacy, although this provision proved easy to ignore. Once the conventions were organized, the delegates then needed to (1) create constitutions that protected black voting rights and (2) agree to ratify the Fourteenth Amendment. Only then would Congress ratify the new state constitutions and accept southern state representatives back into the national Congress. Holding a fair state election and agreeing to the Fourteenth Amendment became the litmus tests for reentry to the nation. Without doing so and thereby becoming full-fledged members of the Union again, the southern states would remain without congressional apportionment and under military control.

THE SECOND RECONSTRUCTION ACT

At first, these provisions proved to be both too harsh and too lenient. The Military Reconstruction Act so outraged southerners that they refused to enroll the voters needed

Congressional Reconstruction Phase of Reconstruction during which Radical Republicans wielded more power than the president, allowing for the passage of the Fourteenth and Fifteenth Amendments and the Military Reconstruction Act

Fourteenth Amendment Amendment to the U.S. Constitution passed in 1868 that extended the guarantees of the Constitution and Bill of Rights to all persons born in the United States, including African Americans and former slaves; it promised that all citizens would receive the "due process of law" before having any of their constitutional rights breached

Military Reconstruction Act Act that divided the former rebel states, with the exception of Tennessee, into five military districts; a military commander took control of the state governments and federal soldiers enforced the law and kept order

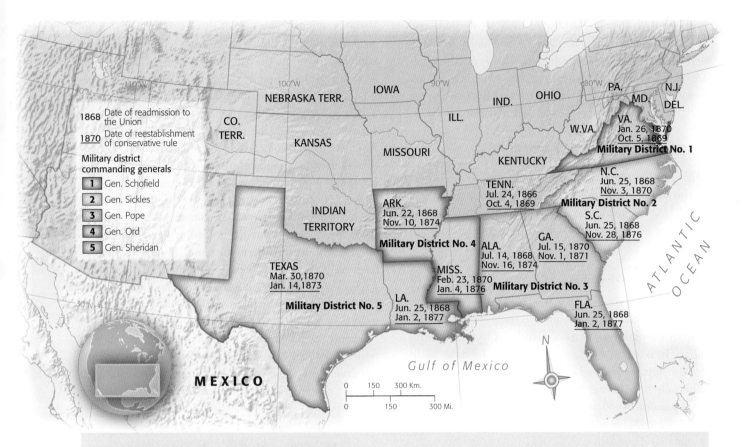

Map 16.1 Reconstruction in the South

>> Reconstruction in the South required continued military involvement, even after the end of formal hostilities. This map shows the five military districts created by the US government in order to keep the southern states in line with the demands of the United States.

to put Reconstruction into motion. But southerners also preferred military rule to civilian control by those hostile to the South. In response to these various objections (and to the South's subsequent foot-dragging), Congress passed the Second Reconstruction Act, authorizing the Union military commanders to register southern voters and assemble the constitutional conventions (since southerners were not eager to do this themselves). The southern states continued to stall, so, in the summer of 1867, Congress passed two more acts designed to force southerners to proceed with Reconstruction, including requiring universal manhood suffrage. President Johnson vetoed all these measures, but his vetoes were all overridden by Radical Republicans in Congress. He was helpless to stop Congress's actions.

Eventually, the southern states had no choice but to follow the Military Reconstruction Act's instructions. There was nothing worse than being part of a nation and having no say in how it was governed.

Southerners wanted congressional representation back, and, in order to get it, they had to acquiesce to Congress's demands. In June 1868, Congress readmitted representatives and senators from six states: North Carolina, South Carolina, Florida, Alabama, Arkansas, and Louisiana. By 1870, the remaining four southern states—Virginia, Mississippi, Georgia, and Texas—had also agreed to the required provisions and they too received permission to send congressmen to Washington. As more and more Confederate states came back into the Union, the Fourteenth Amendment became the law of the land in 1868.

FRUSTRATIONS

Although the Radical Republicans in Congress had considerable successes, in many important ways they did not produce the social revolution they had envisioned: (1) they did not redistribute land to freed slaves; (2) they did not provide black people with guaranteed access to education; (3) they did not forbid racial segregation; and (4) they did not call for absolute racial equality for black and white people. President Johnson's leniency at the outset of Reconstruction, allowing wealthy southerners to retain their land and possessions, had denied Republicans the ability to radically reform the social structure of the South.

16-2d Johnson's Impeachment

Still stung by Johnson's initial act of granting pardons to the southern aristocracy, Radicals were equally stymied by his constant string of vetoes. Frustrated by all this, Congress took steps to limit the president's authority.

THE TENURE OF OFFICE ACT

In 1867 Congress passed the Tenure of Office Act, which required the president to obtain the consent of the Senate before removing certain government officials from office. In essence, the law declared that Johnson could not fire anyone who had earned congressional approvals, especially Republicans who had been appointed by Lincoln. Johnson of course vetoed the act, but Congress once again overrode his veto.

THE IMPEACHMENT

A showdown over the new law occurred in August 1867, when Johnson wanted to remove from office Secretary of War Edwin M. Stanton. Stanton sympathized with the Radicals and had fallen out of favor with Johnson, so Johnson ordered his dismissal. The Senate, however, refused to authorize the firing. Undeterred, Johnson ordered Stanton to resign. When Republicans in the House of Representatives learned that Johnson had defied the Senate's Tenure of Office Act, they drafted a resolution to impeach Johnson. This could be the chance they had sought to eliminate a major obstacle to Congressional Reconstruction. The House made eleven charges against Johnson, stemming mostly from his refusal to heed the Tenure of Office Act, and a majority of the representatives voted in favor of putting him on trial. This made Andrew Johnson the first president in the nation's history to be impeached.

Radical Republicans in the House of Rep-resentatives (especially Thaddeus Stevens) powered the vote for impeachment, but the Constitution dictates that impeachment trials must take place in the Senate and must be judged by the chief justice of the U.S. Supreme Court. Moderate Republicans and Democrats in the Senate refused to join the House Radicals in condemning Johnson, and, by one vote, the Senate lacked the two-thirds majority needed to convict the president and remove him from office.

16-2e The Fifteenth Amendment

In 1868, there was no way the Republicans were going to allow Johnson to run for reelection. Instead, they nominated the war hero Ulysses S. Grant for president, hoping that Grant's tremendous popularity in the North would help them control the White House and propel their Reconstruction plans through the federal government. The Democrats nominated Horatio Seymour, the governor of New York. To the shock of the Republicans, the race between Grant and Seymour was relatively close. Although Grant obtained a majority in the Electoral College, he won the popular vote by only 300,000 ballots. Since an estimated 450,000 black people had voted for Grant, it was clear that a narrow majority of white Americans had cast their ballots for Seymour.

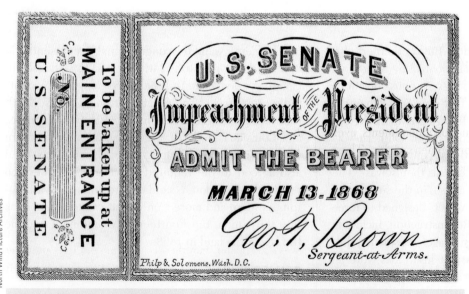

>> Johnson was the first president ever to face an impeachment trial, and he held onto his job by only one vote in the Senate. Tickets, like the one pictured here, were sold at the trial.

Recognizing the importance of their newest support base—and aware that their time in power might be limited—Republicans in Congress moved quickly to create a constitutional amendment guaranteeing the suffrage rights of black males. It became the **Fifteenth Amendment**, which was ratified and adopted in 1870. The Fifteenth Amendment prohibited any state from denying citizens the right to vote on the grounds of race, color, or previous condition of servitude.

16-2f Women's Rights

The Fourteenth Amendment introduced the word *male* into the Constitution for the first time, and the Fifteenth Amendment ratified the notion that voting rights were solely intended for men. Many women, who had often supported the fight for black civil rights, fought back. Historically, advocates for the rights of women have often first fought for the rights of racial minorities, especially black people. This was the case in the 1830s and 1840s, and again in the 1860s and 1870s. Viewing the overhauling of the U.S. Constitution as a moment ripe for extending various freedoms to women, Elizabeth Cady Stanton, Susan B. Anthony, and Olympia Brown, veterans of the struggle to expand women's rights, pushed for a constitutional guarantee of women's suffrage. Using new journals such as *The Agitator* and *The Revolution*, women also pushed for a reform of marriage laws, changes in inheritance laws, and, as always, the vote.

But they were frustrated at almost every turn. Even Republicans declared that Reconstruction was designed solely for black men. Women were torn about whether or not to support the Reconstruction amendments, even if they excluded provisions for women's rights. These bitter differences led to divisions within the women's suffrage movement that would last until the 1890s.

16-3 GRASSROOTS RECONSTRUCTION

With all the political jockeying within the federal government, Reconstruction at the state level was even more rancorous. At the state level, freed slaves exercised more muscle, ensuring that Republicans

The Granger Collection, NYC

>> During Reconstruction, Hiram Revels of Mississippi (on the left in this image of seven African American congressmen) became the nation's first African American senator, while several other southern states voted African Americans to the House.

dominated all of the new state governments in the South. Newly freed slaves steadfastly cast their ballots for the party that had given them their freedom. To support this voter bloc, Republican politicians—from the North and the South—sought dramatic Reconstruction efforts. But at every turn they encountered strong opposition. Before long, it became evident that the process of reconstructing the South would be a process of two steps forward, one step back. And the most substantive change that could have happened—land and economic redistribution to the ex-slaves—remained perpetually frustrated.

16-3a Black Officeholders

Even with the admission of black voters, the proportion of government positions held by black Americans was still smaller than their proportion in the population. They were rarely elected to high positions, and until

Fifteenth Amendment Amendment that extended voting rights to all male citizens regardless of race, color, or previous condition of servitude

>> The Man with the (Carpet) Bags by Thomas Nast, 1872, Harper's Weekly. This political cartoon of Carl Schurz depicted as a carpetbagger, reflected Southern attitudes toward Northerners during Reconstruction. Many Southerners saw carpetbaggers as corrupt and lowly, although many came South with the intention of improving the life of America's black people.

protecting black rights. Some of these new officials were northern-born white men who moved south after the Confederacy's defeat. Southerners called these men **carpetbaggers** because they supposedly journeyed to the South with nothing more than what they could carry in a ratty old carpetbag. The carpetbag was meant to symbolize corruption and lowliness, as supposedly poor and pretentious northerners headed south seeking to capitalize on the region's fall from grace. Not all the so-called carpetbaggers were corrupt, of course. Many of them came to the South with a desire to improve the lot of America's black people.

Southern-born, white Republicans were given the name **scalawag**, originally a term used by cattle drivers to describe livestock that was too filthy for consumption, even by dogs. Although southern Democrats insisted that only the "dirtiest" citizens became scalawags, in reality, many elite southerners joined the Republican Party, including Confederate generals Pierre Beauregard and James Longstreet. Most of the scalawags, however, had been nonslaveholding poor white farmers who worked and lived in the hill country. Many of these scalawags believed that participating in the Republicans' plan was the fastest way to return their region to peaceful and prosperous conditions.

SOUTHERN REPUBLICAN SUCCESSES

Although they faced considerable opposition from the old antebellum elite, southern Republicans managed to (1) construct the South's first public school system, (2) develop a system of antidiscrimination measures, (3) strengthen the rights and privileges of agricultural workers, and (4) begin efforts at internal improvements in the various states. Under the leadership of southern Republicans, for example, every state in the South financed a system of railroads and attempted to lure northern industries to the South. They met with mixed results, but they showed a newfound commitment to greater equality and to bringing the gains of the Market Revolution southward.

16-3c Sharecropping

Despite the new opportunities put forward by southern Republicans, freed slaves had to struggle hard to enjoy their new liberty. There was no serious land

1990 no black person was ever elected or nominated to serve as governor of a southern state. South Carolina was the only state where a black judge served in the state supreme court, and, because the state was 60 percent African American, only in South Carolina did African Americans form a plurality of the legislature. Nevertheless, more than 2,000 black citizens gained political office in the Reconstruction South. Some were policemen, some were sheriffs, some were tax assessors. Their roles were important because they ensured that fairness would be enforced and that the rule of law would be upheld.

16-3b Carpetbaggers and Scalawags

Yet white men held most of the offices in the new state governments, and many were Republicans supportive of

carpetbagger Northern-born white who moved south after the Confederacy's defeat

scalawag Southern-born white Republican; many had been nonslaveholding poor farmers

reform and the Market and Industrial Revolutions were slow to move southward, so most black southerners had no choice but to accept work as agricultural wage laborers for white landholders, many of whom had been slaveholders before the war.

THE BATTLE OF LABOR

Many of these landowners attempted to recreate as much of the slave system as they could, closely overseeing their workers, forcing them to work in gangs, and even trying to use the whip to maintain discipline. The freedmen, however, refused to be reduced to slavery again. They insisted on working shorter hours, and they often refused to work in gangs. To limit the amount of surveillance, freedmen often built their own log cabins far away from the houses of their employers. Unless they were willing to go beyond the rule of law, most landowners could do nothing to stop them.

THE SHARECROPPING SYSTEM

The power struggle between southern whites and the freedmen led former slaveholders to establish and develop the **sharecropping** system. As sharecroppers, families farmed a plot of land owned by someone else and shared the crop yield with the owner of the property. Typically, the farmer and the owner split the yield in half, but the owner often claimed an even larger share if he supplied the seeds or tools necessary for cultivating the crop or if he provided housing and food. Although black farmers had earned the right to work in a familial setting, as opposed to the gang labor system of the slave era, landowners had managed to curtail black freedom by preventing many of them from owning property.

Despite sharecropping's prominent place in southern black history, there were more white sharecroppers in the South than black. It was a sign of the South's poverty after the war. The sharecropping system offered little hope for economic or social advancement. Sharecroppers could rarely earn enough money to buy land, and they were constantly in debt to their landlords. The landlord was always paid first when crops were sold at market, so if crop prices were lower than expected, sharecroppers were left with little or no income. Although sharecropping was not slavery, it was still a harsh and limited form of economic existence that permeated the South after the Civil War. By 1900, 50 percent of southern whites and 75 percent of southern blacks lived in sharecropping families.

CONVICT LEASING

Southern landowners and politicians also began the practice of convict leasing during these years, whereby the state leased out prisoners to private companies or landowners looking for workers after the demise of slavery. Convicts usually were not paid for their labor and were often treated harshly. But the system was good for the state, which earned income from the practice, and the lessees, who exploited the labor of the prisoners. Convicts were used in railroad, mining, and logging operations, as well as on farms. And, although convicts of all colors were exploited by the system, African Americans were particularly targeted. During the three decades after the Civil War, the number of men in prison increased in nearly every state of the South, and the percentage of those prisoners who were black ballooned. Many were convicted on questionable charges, and more than one dirty judge was exposed for fraudulently convicting an innocent black man who would be destined to work as the leased property of the state. Some historians see convict leasing as just an extension of slavery, with only a different name.

 # THE COLLAPSE OF RECONSTRUCTION

Despite the obvious setbacks, the reconstruction of the South did have some significant achievements, including two new constitutional amendments, the passage of the nation's first civil rights law, and the abolition of slavery. These positive achievements could have continued to accumulate, but they did not, for two reasons: (1) growing northern disinterest in the plight of America's southern black population and (2) increasingly violent resistance to Reconstruction from white southerners.

16-4a In the North

On the whole, the eight years of Grant's presidency (1869–1877) were not marked by great strides for African American civil rights. Instead, Grant's term became infamous for economic chicanery and corruption. The president's personal secretary was caught embezzling federal whiskey revenues in the so-called Whiskey Ring, while Grant's own family was implicated in a plot to corner the gold market. Charges of corruption even led to a split in the Republican Party, further draining support for Reconstruction efforts. As more upstanding

> **sharecropping** System in which a family farmed a plot of land owned by someone else and shared the crop yield with the owner

Education Images/Getty Images

>> African American sharecroppers picking cotton during Reconstruction.

political leaders became preoccupied with efforts to clean up the government and institute civil service reform, securing equal rights for black people in the South ceased to be the most pressing issue. Other things seemed to matter more. And, as Reconstruction moved into the background, northerners' racism—always just under the surface—became more visible.

Despite charges of corruption, Grant was reelected to the presidency in 1872, and during his second term, only one major piece of Reconstruction legislation was passed. Even that had key limitations. The **Civil Rights Act of 1875** forbade racial discrimination in all public facilities, transportation lines, places of amusement, and juries. Segregation in public schools, however, was not prohibited. Moreover, there was no effort whatsoever to legislate against racial discrimination by individuals or corporations, so discrimination in the workplace remained legal.

Civil Rights Act of 1875 Act that forbade racial discrimination in all public facilities, transportation lines, places of amusement, and juries; it proved largely ineffective

Civil Rights Cases Cases in which, in 1883, the Supreme Court declared all of the provisions of the Civil Rights Act of 1875 unconstitutional, except for the prohibition of discrimination on juries

Panic of 1873 Financial crisis provoked when overspeculation, high postwar inflation, and disruptions from Europe emptied the financial reserves in America's banks; many banks simply closed their doors; this emergency focused northern attention on the economy rather than on civil rights

In addition to these flaws, the Civil Rights Act of 1875 proved ineffective anyway. The federal government did not enforce the law vigorously, so the southern states ignored it. And in 1883, in what would come to be called the **Civil Rights Cases**, the Supreme Court delivered a final blow to this last act of Reconstruction by declaring all of its provisions unconstitutional, except for the prohibition of discrimination on juries. In 1890, Henry Cabot Lodge, a Republican from Massachusetts, led the House of Representatives in passing a Federal Elections Bill that would have revived protection of voting rights for African Americans, but a Senate filibuster prevented the piece of legislation from becoming law. It would be nearly seven decades before another civil rights bill made its way through Congress.

The failure of the Civil Rights Act of 1875 reflected a larger northern disinterest in Reconstruction. For many northerners, support for black rights had been an outgrowth of their animosity toward the South. In 1865, such feelings burned hotly, and northerners were willing to support federal efforts to guarantee the liberties of former slaves. As the bitterness of war faded, northerners were tired of the antagonism between North and South, so their interest in civil rights faded, too.

Instead, northerners became consumed with economic matters, especially after the United States entered a deep recession in 1873. The **Panic of 1873** erupted when overspeculation, high postwar inflation, and disruptions from Europe, emptied the financial reserves in America's banks. Rather than honor their loans, many banks simply closed their doors, which led to a panic on Wall Street. Although Grant acted quickly to end the immediate panic, many businesses were forced to shut down. The Panic lasted six years and left 3 million Americans unemployed. In the years after 1873, Americans became concerned more with jump-starting the economy than with forging new laws to protect the needs and interests of black citizens.

The Republicans, meanwhile, took the blame for the nation's economic troubles, so, in the congressional elections of 1874, they lost seventy-seven seats, thus losing control of the House. The party that had spearheaded civil rights legislation in America was no longer in a position to control federal policy. Instead, the Democrats were back.

16-4b In the South

The decline of northern support for Reconstruction emboldened southern Democrats, who worked to reclaim political control of their region. In order to create white solidarity against Republican rule in the South, the Democrats shamelessly asserted white superiority.

Racism proved to be a powerful incentive for the Democratic Party, especially to attract poor southerners worried about their economic fortunes. Keeping black people as an underclass in southern society was important to poor white people's sense of self-worth (and economic well-being), and Democrats promised to protect the racial hierarchy as it had been before the Civil War. Democrats earned the backing of the vast majority of white southerners—mostly by championing continued white supremacy.

INTIMIDATION OF BLACK AND REPUBLICAN VOTERS

To control black votes, white Democrats often used economic intimidation. Throughout the nineteenth century, voting was not done by secret ballot, so it was easy to know how every individual cast his ballot. Democratic landowners fired tenant farmers who voted Republican and publicized their names in local newspapers to prevent other landowners from hiring them too. The threat of starvation and poverty thus kept many black citizens from voting for the Republican Party.

More than economic intimidation, however, southern Democrats used violence to control southern politics. A number of paramilitary groups, including the Ku Klux Klan, provided the ground troops. They harassed black and white Republicans, disrupted Republican Party meetings, and physically blocked black southerners from casting ballots in elections. They even assassinated Republican Party leaders and organizers. Their goal was to erode the base of Republican support in the South and to ensure election victories for the Democratic Party. For instance, prior to the presidential election of 1868, 2,000 people were killed or injured in Louisiana alone. In Texas, the federal military commander said murders were so common he could not keep track of them.

TERROR IN THE HEART OF FREEDOM

In addition to these more purely political forms of repression, southern white males also used rape and sexual violence against African American women as a form of political terror. Because black women now had the right to accuse white men of sexual crimes, historians have been able to determine that white men often staged elaborate attacks meant to reenact the antebellum

racial hierarchy, when southern white men were firmly in control. African Americans of course fought back, but as Democrats grew increasingly powerful in the region, the claims made by southern black women often went unheard. Most damningly, these crimes indicated how limited black freedom had become in the decade after the Civil War. Not only were African Americans losing their political and social rights, they were also losing the right to basic safeties, the right to organize their life as they saw fit, and the right to live comfortably in a democratic nation.

GRANT'S RESPONSE

Although not known for its civil rights activism, the Grant administration did respond to the upsurge in southern violence by pushing two important measures through Congress: (1) the Force Act of 1870 and (2) the Ku Klux Klan Act of 1871. The new laws

The Granger Collection, NYC

>> The White League and other similar organizations were founded to use violence and intimidation to keep African American voters from the polls throughout the South. This cartoon from a Northern American newspaper of 1874 depicts the efforts of White League member in Louisiana attempting to intimidate and disenfranchise black voters.

declared that interfering with the right to vote was a felony; they also authorized the federal government to use the army and suspend the writ of habeas corpus in order to end Klan violence. Grant proceeded to suspend the writ in nine South Carolina counties and to arrest hundreds of suspected Klan members. These efforts crushed the Klan in 1871 (although it would resurge in the 1910s and 1920s).

THE MISSISSIPPI PLAN

Southern Democrats, however, did not relent. In 1875, Democrats in Mississippi initiated a policy called the **Mississippi Plan**, which called for using as much violence as necessary to put the state back under Democratic control. Democratic clubs began to function much as the Klan had, terrorizing Republican Party leaders and the black and white citizens who supported them. This time, the Grant administration refused to step in to stop the violence. Most northerners no longer seemed willing to support federal intervention into southern strife.

In 1876, the Mississippi Plan formally succeeded. By keeping tens of thousands of Republicans from casting ballots, the Democrats took charge of the state government. In the vocabulary of the time, Mississippi had been "redeemed" from Republican rule. In fact, it had been tortured into submission; official reports proclaiming as much were generally ignored.

"REDEEMERS" WIN THE PRESIDENTIAL ELECTION OF 1876

The presidential election of 1876 put the final nail in Reconstruction's coffin. Through violence and intimidation, the Democrats had already succeeded in winning control

> Reconstruction was America's unfinished revolution, and a great chance to correct the colossal wrong that was slavery.

of all the southern states except Louisiana, Florida, and South Carolina. Now they intended to use the Mississippi Plan to "redeem" those three states and win the presidency as well. Perversely using the Christian language of redemption, the leaders of these efforts were widely called **Redeemers**.

The presidential campaign pitted Ohio Republican Rutherford B. Hayes against New York Democrat Samuel Tilden, who had a reputation as a reformer and a fighter against political corruption. The election was a mess. Violenceprevented as many as 250,000 southerners from voting Republican, and, as southern Democrats had hoped, Democratic governors triumphed in Louisiana, Florida, and South Carolina. The Democrats in those states reported that the majority of voters favored Tilden for the presidency. Republicans were suspicious, however, and did a canvass of their own. They claimed that the Democrats had used violence to fix the results. Louisiana, Florida, and South Carolina, the Republicans argued, should have gone to Hayes. These disputed states carried enough Electoral College votes to swing the entire election one way or the other.

THE COMPROMISE OF 1877

After receiving two versions of the final tallies, Congress needed help deciding what to do. It created a 15-member electoral commission, with 5 members from the Senate, 5 from the House, and 5 from the Supreme Court. The commission was composed of 8 Republicans and 7 Democrats, and, by a purely partisan vote of 8 to 7, the commission gave the disputed states of Louisiana, Florida, and South Carolina to Hayes, the Republican. The Democratic Party leaders were furious, but, in order to prevent further violence, Republican leaders proposed a compromise that became known as the **Compromise of 1877** (see Map 16.2).

In the compromise, Republicans promised (1) not to dispute the Democratic gubernatorial victories in the South and (2) to withdraw federal troops from the region. The white redeemers would thus be in control throughout the entire South. In return, the Republicans asked the Democrats to (1) accept Hayes's presidential victory and (2) respect the rights of its black citizens. The Democrats accepted these terms, and, with that, Hayes withdrew the federal military from the South. Of course, without a federal military to protect black Americans, Reconstruction was over, and the South

Mississippi Plan 1875 Democratic plan that called for using as much violence as necessary to put Mississippi back under Democratic control

Redeemers A collection of southern Democrats and their supporters who used violence, intimidation, and the law to win political and social control away from those promoting greater racial equality in the region

Compromise of 1877 Compromise in which Republicans promised not to dispute the Democratic gubernatorial victories in the South and to withdraw federal troops from the region, if southern Democrats accepted Hayes's presidential victory and respected the rights of black citizens

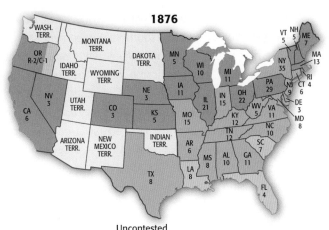

1876

Candidate (Party)	Uncontested Electoral Vote	Electoral Vote		Popular Vote	
Hayes (Republican)	165	185	50%	4,036,572	48.0%
Tilden (Democrat)	184	184	50%	4,284,020	51.0%
Contested					
Territories					

Map 16.2 The Disputed Election of 1876

>> An electoral map of the 1876 presidential election, showing the states that supported Hayes and Tilden, as well as the three contested states, where Democrats likely received more votes but only because of the violent suppression of Republican votes.

was left under the control of the Redeemers who used violence, intimidation, and the law to create the society they envisioned. Freed blacks progressively lost whatever political and social gains they had achieved during the previous twelve years. This failure ensured that racial oppression would continue. In the words of one historian, Reconstruction was America's unfinished revolution. A great chance to correct the colossal wrong that was slavery vanished. For more on why Reconstruction ended in 1877, see "The Reasons Why . . ." box.

>LOOKING AHEAD...

Why did Reconstruction fail? So boldly stated, the question is perhaps unfair. There were major accomplishments. Slavery was abolished. Federal laws were established that provided support for further political gains for America's black population. Following the 2016 elections, there have been only ten black senators ever elected to the U.S. Senate, but two of them were elected during Reconstruction (Hiram Rhodes Revels and Blanche K. Bruce, both from Mississippi). About 10% of the 139 black Americans ever to serve in the U.S. House of Representatives were elected during Reconstruction.

The Reasons Why...

There were three prominent reasons why Reconstruction ended in 1877, before equality could be ensured for southern African Americans.

Northern indifference. After the Panic of 1873, many northerners focused intently on economic matters. The passions inflamed by the Civil War had begun to fade by the early 1870s, and the economic turmoil provoked by the Panic led northerners to focus on their personal fortunes. Plus, with the Industrial Revolution ramping up in the North (see Chapter 17), northerners were even less likely to take big risks on behalf of black civil rights in the South.

Southern recalcitrance. With northern indifference becoming increasingly evident during the second presidential term of Ulysses S. Grant, white southerners increased the level of violence—political, physical, and sexual—they used against African Americans and Republicans more generally. The Democratic Party in the South promised white superiority, and throughout the 1870s it was beginning to deliver.

National political ambivalence. By 1876, northern politicians had more at stake in reviving the sagging economy than in fighting for the rights of African American southerners. When it became clear that the results of the presidential election of 1876 were going to be disputed, northern Republicans willingly negotiated with southern Democrats, securing the Republicans the presidency at the cost of pulling federal troops out of the South. Without northern oversight, southern whites were free to reclaim their social and political power, and that is exactly what they did.

But there was a dramatic decline of black political participation in the South (where a large majority of black people lived) beginning in 1876 and lasting until after the Second World War. There was an even more dramatic increase in physical segregation between America's black and white populations during and after Reconstruction. The causes are many. President Johnson's unwillingness to participate in a wholesale social revolution meant that land would not be redistributed in the South, signifying that, for the most part, the wealthy would remain wealthy and the poor would remain poor. The development of sharecropping as an institution further paralyzed black advancements, especially after the emergence of black codes limited black Americans' abilities to protest economic injustices. Finally, the violence used by the southern Redeemers served as an emblem of the wrongs felt by white southerners, and, when northerners became more focused on the rollicking economy of the Industrial Revolution, there was no one left to monitor the henhouse. Plainly enough, most white southerners strongly opposed racial change, and after 1876, they were left in power to do as they wished.

As this happened, most Americans began to look away, focusing their attentions on another dramatic transformation in American life. It is to the development and ramifications of the great Industrial Revolution that we now must turn.

STUDY TOOLS 16

READY TO STUDY? IN THE BOOK, YOU CAN:

❏ Rip out the Chapter Review Card, which includes key terms and chapter summaries.

ONLINE AT WWW.CENGAGEBRAIN.COM, YOU CAN:

❏ Collect StudyBits while you read and study the chapter.

❏ Quiz yourself on key concepts.

❏ Find videos for further exploration.

❏ Prepare for tests with HIST5 Flash Cards as well as those you create.

❏ Read Lincoln's proclamation on vetoing the Wade-Davis Bill.

❏ View a Library of Congress picture gallery about Lincoln's assassination.

❏ View an oath of amnesty to the Union from Joseph Trimble.

❏ Read a *Harper's Weekly* editorial about the Civil Rights Bill.

❏ Read the Second Reconstruction Act.

❏ Find out more about the impeachment of Andrew Johnson.

❏ Analyze an image of the South Carolina legislature.

❏ Read the Fifteenth Amendment to the U.S. Constitution.

❏ Read the Mississippi legislature's black codes.

❏ Analyze a *Harper's Weekly* cartoon on the Panic of 1873.

❏ Analyze a *Harper's Weekly* cartoon on the Civil Rights Act of 1875.

CH16 TIMELINE

		What Else Was Happening
1863	Abraham Lincoln proposes the lenient Ten-Percent Plan.	
1864	Lincoln pocket-vetoes the stricter Wade-Davis Bill for Reconstruction.	**1865:** *John Wilkes Booth assassinates Abraham Lincoln.*

1865–1867 Johnson's presidential Reconstruction demands loyalty oath from Confederates. Congress establishes Freedmen's Bureau. Congress passes Civil Rights Bill.

1866 The Ku Klux Klan forms in Tennessee.

1867: *Congress enacts Military and Second Reconstruction Act.*

Benjamin Disraeli helps pass the 1867 Reform Bill in Britain, which extends the franchise to all male householders, including, for the first time, members of the working class.

1867–1877 During Congressional Reconstruction Congress enforces its rules for readmission.

1868 Fourteenth Amendment grants full citizenship to all persons born in United States.
North Carolina, South Carolina, Georgia, Florida, Alabama, Arkansas, Louisiana return to Union.

1869: *Opening of the Suez Canal in Egypt connecting the Mediterranean Sea and the Red Sea, allowing water travel between Asia and Europe without having to navigate around Africa.*

1873: *Marketing of Remington typewriter opens clerical positions for women.*

Financial panic causes severe recession and mass unemployment.

Mark Twain patents the scrapbook.

1870 Fifteenth Amendment bans state disfranchisement based on race but not gender.
Virginia, Mississippi, Texas return to Union.

First New York City subway line opens.

1871 Force Act of 1870 and Ku Klux Klan Act permit federal government to respond to Klan violence.

Euphemia Allen, age sixteen, composes simple piano tune "Chopsticks."

1875 Mississippi Plan calls for use of violence to restore Democratic control.
Civil Rights Act forbids racial discrimination in public places.

1877 To overcome election stalemate, Republicans grant Democrats home rule in return for presidency.

1883 In Civil Rights Cases, U.S. Supreme Court declares Civil Rights Act unconstitutional.

17 | The Industrial Revolution

MPI/Getty Images

LEARNING OBJECTIVES

After reading this chapter, you should be able to do the following:

17-1 Describe and discuss the development of the Industrial Revolution in America after the Civil War, concentrating on the major industries and their leaders.

17-2 Describe how the United States' regional and local markets merged into one national market and how this influenced consumer demand for products and services, as well as some of the costs associated with the transition.

17-3 Discuss the functioning of national, state, and local politics during the late 1800s.

17-4 Describe the formation of the early labor unions in the United States, including their goals, activities, and confrontations at the end of the nineteenth century.

AFTER FINISHING THIS CHAPTER GO TO **PAGE 327** **FOR STUDY TOOLS**

As the process of ensuring political, economic, and social rights of African Americans waned during the 1870s, most Americans turned their attention to another transformation brought on by the Civil War: the Industrial Revolution. During the half-century between 1865 and 1915, the United States evolved from a relative economic backwater to become the most powerful economy in the world. Industrialization played a key role in the nation's advances, and both the Civil War and a core group of innovative, aggressive, farsighted, and opportunistic entrepreneurs were the main stimulants of growth. They embodied the optimism and inventiveness of the late nineteenth century, although they often pushed too far and engaged in practices we now see as unethical and corrupt, leaving wide gaps between rich and poor, between black and white, and between immigrant and native.

Like the Market Revolution of the first half of the century (which focused primarily on improvements in communications and transportation to broaden the reach of American agricultural goods), the Industrial Revolution of the second half transformed the nation's economy, its social life, and its politics. During the nineteenth century, the nation's main energy sources shifted from human and animal power to mechanical power. Builders transitioned from using materials one might find on the ground, such as stones and logs, to using manufactured materials, such as lumber, bricks, and steel. Smaller craft shops lost business to large specialized factories. Industrial cities grew dramatically as well, as mechanized public transportation allowed wealthier people to move away from noisy city centers. And railroads made travel increasingly easy—even, by 1869, allowing people and goods to cross the entire continent speedily and safely. During the late nineteenth century, the world that had consisted of small farms, artisans' workshops, and small- or medium-sized factories at the beginning of the century transformed into a full-scale industrial society of large factories, polyglot urban hubs, and a wide range of people working and managing the newly developed industries.

Unsurprisingly, the politics of the era were poorly equipped to handle all these challenges. In a society uncertain about the moral role of politics (especially after the bloody Civil War) and eager not to miss out on the economic possibilities of the new age, politics during the last third of the nineteenth century were characterized by high voter participation, extreme partisanship, and massive corruption.

By the early 1900s, three waves of reformers had emerged to demand that the government curtail the most oppressive practices of big business: (1) the labor movement, (2) the Populists, and (3) the Progressives. The first of these reformers—the labor movement—was the most radical. It emerged concurrently with the Industrial Age and focused on the working classes. During its first years, this labor movement was raucous and provocative, questioning America's commitment to capitalism and democracy. Socialists flourished, as did communists and anarchists. Each challenge to American democratic capitalism stirred fear among the American upper and middle classes, but that, of course, was the point.

This chapter describes and explains the advent of the Industrial Revolution, focusing on the key industries and business developments, as well as the inability or unwillingness of politicians to manage these challenges. It concludes with an examination of the first grassroots demands for reform: the American labor movement.

17-1 THE ADVENT OF THE INDUSTRIAL REVOLUTION

The process of industrialization began well before the Civil War, and indeed, industrialization, along with improved communications and transportation, sparked the Market Revolution during the first half of the nineteenth century. But after the Civil War, American material output increased dramatically, and big businesses extended their reach deeper into American life. Together, these events revolutionized the way Americans lived, no matter which region they called home. Why an Industrial Revolution in America? The Industrial Revolution had been launched in Britain in the 1750s, made its way over to the European continent by the early 1800s, and crossed the Atlantic well before the 1840s. But three reasons figure in its dramatic growth from 1865 to 1915 (see "The Reasons Why . . ." box under 17-1b).

◄◄◄ **Schoolchildren play on the hills above the Carnegie steel mills, symbols of the effects of the Industrial Revolution on Americans big and small, rich and poor, northern, southern, and western.**

17-1a What It Was

The **Industrial Revolution** can be defined as a transformation in the way goods were made and sold, as American businessmen between 1865 and 1915 used continuing technological breakthroughs and creative financing to bring greater efficiency to their businesses, which dramatically expanded their markets and their ability to produce goods. The effects of this transformation were felt outside the business world, resulting in two key social transitions: (1) more and more Americans left farming to work in factories or retail, which spurred the rapid growth of cities; and (2) the American economy became dominated less by family businesses and more and more by large corporate firms. Thus, many historians cite the late nineteenth century as the birth of a modern industrialized America. One historian has pinpointed these years as the time when Americans physically and intellectually left behind the small, localized "island communities" that dotted the United States before the Civil War and confronted the large, polyglot nature of the American nation.

17-1b The Basic Industries

The central industries of the Industrial Revolution were railroads, steel, and petroleum. Each had leaders who took control of their industry's development. These "captains of industry" were also sometimes called "robber barons," depending on the perspective of the observer. Through these industries, Americans created a corporate society.

RAILROADS

The expansion of the railroads was perhaps the one predictable development of the post-Civil War years. With the support of the federal government, between 1860 and 1915 total railroad development leapt from approximately 30,000 miles of track to more than 250,000 miles (see Map 17.1). By the eve of World

>> Here, workers carry the heavy pieces that would become the first transcontinental railroad.

War I in 1914, the national railroad network was basically complete, such that some historians say that all tracks built after 1890 were simply unnecessary. Railroads spanned the nation, making the movement of goods and products easy, cheap, and reliable.

Several ruthless and ingenious businessmen helped make all the growth possible. Leland Stanford, for example, was one of the "Big Four" captains of the railroad industry. With his partners, Collis Huntington, Charles Crocker, and Mark Hopkins, Stanford developed the railroad system in California and made the entire West accessible via train. All four men were New Yorkers who had headed to California during the gold rush that began in 1849. All four were Republicans and supporters of Lincoln during the war. Knowing the Civil War would promote the expansion of railroads, the four invested money and energy in creating a transcontinental network of tracks. Once these railroads were completed, the Big Four controlled much of the access to the West—control that brought great wealth and power.

STEEL

The steel industry made the massive expansion of railroads possible. As early as the Middle Ages, steel had been used to make weapons. But because the process of making steel—by burning impurities out of iron ore—was laborious and expensive, artisans produced only small quantities. In the mid-1850s, British inventor Sir Henry Bessemer crafted a way to convert large quantities of iron ore into steel by using extremely hot air. Mass production of steel did not take

Industrial Revolution Transformation in the way goods were made and sold, as American businessmen between 1865 and 1915 used continuing technological breakthroughs and creative financing to bring greater efficiency to their businesses, dramatically increasing the nation's industrial output

The Reasons Why...

There were at least three reasons why American industrialization expanded when it did:

The Civil War. Production needs during the Civil War stimulated industrial development, particularly in the North. For example, the Union Army's high demand for food fueled the expansion of western farms. Clothing and shoe manufacturers were encouraged to produce more goods faster. And the government offered huge wartime contracts for uniforms, weapons, food, and other commodities, sparking breakthroughs in their manufacture.

Government support. Besides purchasing goods for its troops, Congress took advantage of the absence of southerners in the House and the Senate to pass a series of national internal improvement projects. The most majestic of these was the first transcontinental railroad. In July 1862, Congress offered enormous financial incentives to the Union Pacific Railroad and the Central Pacific Railroad companies to complete the expansive task. This transcontinental railroad was completed in 1869, and, over the next twenty years, legendary business moguls built other transcontinental lines, often with financial incentives from the federal government. The federal government also supported scientific training and research, developed the first national currency and tax system, and made possible the construction of the first land grant universities (such as Michigan State University and Rutgers)—all evidence of the government's willingness to midwife the Industrial Revolution. In the end, government support of the building infrastructure allowed goods and information to travel more quickly and efficiently to wider markets.

Library of Congress Prints and Photographs Division [LC-US262-52310]

>> With guaranteed contracts from the government during the Civil War, factory output increased tremendously. This photograph shows women mass producing manufactured goods in an early industrial factory.

Technological breakthroughs. An abundance of scientific developments also contributed to the expansion of big business, and again, the Civil War was the transitional moment. For example, the need to move meat from one place to another in order to feed Union soldiers prompted the creation of refrigerated railroad cars. By 1878, inventors had perfected the cars, which permitted long-distance transfer of numerous perishable goods. This, of course, allowed for the development of new towns in the West—so long as they were close to the railroad lines.

Mathew Brady/Getty Images

---

off, however, until Andrew Carnegie became interested in the industry. On a trip to Britain in 1872, Carnegie saw the Bessemer process at work in a steel plant, and, amazed at its efficiency, decided to open a steel plant in the United States. Rather than artisans, he could use cheap, unskilled laborers, who were willing to operate the hot, dangerous machines for low wages. By 1900, he had built the largest steel company in the world and produced more than 25 percent of the steel used in the United States. Carnegie's steel was used in many national landmarks, including the Brooklyn Bridge.

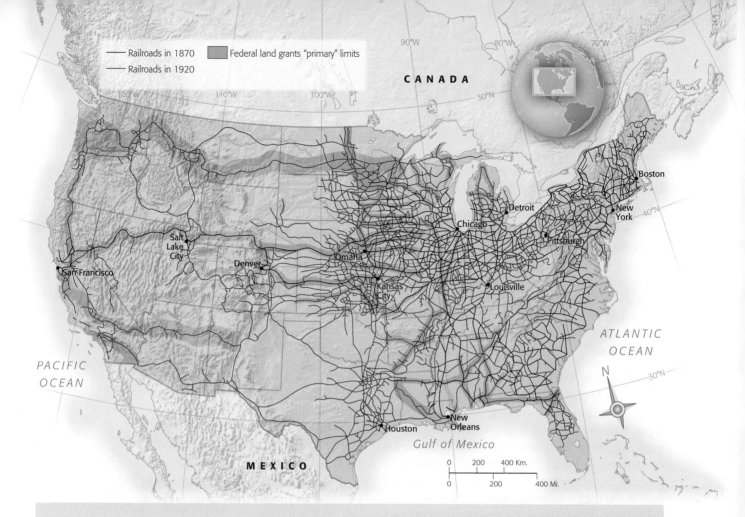

CANADA

San Francisco

Salt Lake City

Denver

Omaha

Kansas City

Chicago

Detroit

Pittsburgh

Boston

New York

Louisville

PACIFIC OCEAN

ATLANTIC OCEAN

Houston

New Orleans

Gulf of Mexico

MEXICO

0   200   400 Km.

0   200   400 Mi.

Map 17.1 Railroad Expansion, 1870–1920

>> This map of the US shows the rapid development of railroads across the country, and the large swaths of land granted to railroad companies by the federal government.

In business terms, Carngie masterfully used the concept of **vertical integration**, which meant placing all aspects of steel production under his control, from the moment iron ore was extracted from mines to the time finished steel was shipped to customers. Carnegie realized that, by integrating all the processes of making and distributing steel, he could avoid working with other companies and thus increase profits. His method worked: in 1901 Carnegie sold his company, U.S. Steel, for more than $400 million—the equivalent of $10.8 billion today.

In 1901 Carnegie sold his company for more than $400 million—the equivalent of $10.8 billion today.

vertical integration The system by which a business controls all aspects of its industry, from raw materials to finished product, and is able to avoid working or sharing profits with any other companies

PETROLEUM

In the mid-nineteenth century, petroleum was increasingly used both as a machine lubricant and as a source of illumination. The breakthrough here came in 1855, when Professor Benjamin Silliman of Yale University discovered that kerosene, a formerly "useless" byproduct of crude oil (unrefined petroleum), was a powerful illuminant. Entrepreneurs then rushed to find greater supplies of crude oil. The Pennsylvania Rock Oil Company hired Edwin Drake, a speculator and promoter, to drill for oil in northwestern Pennsylvania. After two years of searching, on August 28, 1859, Drake successfully drilled for oil in Titusville, Pennsylvania. His find ushered in an American oil boom.

The next challenge was to figure out the best means of extracting crude oil, transporting it to refineries, packaging it, conveying it to cities and towns across the nation, and marketing the finished products. John D. Rockefeller essentially filled all of these niches. He consolidated refining operations in Cleveland, and then, by paying close attention to cost-cutting details, he ruthlessly drove down the costs of producing usable commodities. Much of Rockefeller's success can be attributed to his pioneering efforts at **horizontal integration**. In essence, he took over other oil companies or worked in combination with them to control competition, lower the cost of petroleum, and, of course, maximize profits. He practiced vertical integration as well, much like Andrew Carnegie in the steel industry. But he focused more intently on limiting competition with other businesses in the same industry. His legal advisors created a unique entity called "the trust," which acted as a board of directors for all the oil refiners. Rockefeller intended to provide cheap petroleum and to make himself wealthy. He succeeded at both.

17-1c Technology

In addition to the dynamic developments of business leaders, numerous technological, financial, and legal innovations powered the Industrial Revolution. Indeed, this was the era of many of America's most far-reaching inventions and innovations.

Perhaps no invention had more lasting impact than the incandescent light bulb, created by Thomas Edison in 1879. After years of experimentation, Edison harnessed the power of electricity and transmitted bright light for extended periods of time. The subsequent development of huge electrical power stations made this new form of energy cheap enough to allow middle-class homeowners to purchase it and businesses to operate after dark. Development of the first electric grids spread electricity throughout cities. In addition to light bulbs, Edison also perfected the motion picture camera, the phonograph, the microphone, and more. He set up the first industrial research laboratory in the world, developed solely to invent new things. It worked. In the United States alone, Edison held 1,093 patents. He possessed more abroad.

Separately, Alexander Graham Bell's invention in 1876 of the telephone, which also used electrical power, vastly sped up the flow of communications over long distances and enabled businesses to exchange information more efficiently. In architecture, the Bessemer process of steel production allowed architects to design the first skyscrapers, reaching hundreds of feet into the air. And the mechanized elevator, invented by Elisha Otis in 1853, made all these skyscrapers useable. Before the elevator, few people would rent rooms above the sixth floor. At the

---

horizontal integration The system by which a business takes over its competitors in order to limit competition, lower costs, and maximize profits

>> Bessemer converter in use at a Pittsburgh steel plant.

>> The Brooklyn Bridge. "Hard! I guess it's hard. I lost forty pounds the first three months I came into this business. It sweats the life out of a man."—Steelworker at a Carnegie plant, circa 1893

Hulton Archive/Getty Images

Library of Congress Prints and Photographs Division[LC-USZ62-79048]

same time, the typewriter was invented in the 1860s and marketed by Eliphalet Remington and Sons beginning in 1873. The typewriter created a number of office jobs that opened up to women during these years. In the otherwise patriarchal business world of the nineteenth century, it helped make women earners in an industrializing economy.

Invention bred still more invention. In the seven decades before 1860, the U.S. Patent Office issued 36,000 patent licenses. During the three decades after 1860, that number of patents grew to 144,000.

17-1d Innovative Financing, Law, and Business Practices

Despite all these incredible inventions, perhaps no innovation was more transformative than one that emerged from a new breed of financiers. Such financial giants as Jay Gould and J. Pierpont Morgan specialized in forming groups of rich men (called syndicates) in order to provide huge amounts of capital to fund promising companies and start up new industries. Morgan and a handful of associates gathered investors from around the globe to underwrite and fund various investment opportunities. The advent of pooled funds allowed Morgan to broker the formation of one of the world's first billion-dollar corporations, the Northern Securities Company. In addition to everything else, the latter half of the nineteenth century was also the era of the giant corporation.

Beginning in the mid-1800s, federal and state governments made changes in corporate law that supported these financial schemes and encouraged growth. They provided corporations with the power to acquire and merge with other businesses, thus allowing corporations to accumulate the capital required to finance big businesses. They also provided a significant layer of protection between families' fortunes and the courts. Rather than relying on any single individual's fortune to raise money, corporate officers were allowed to sell their stock on the open market. In that way, the investors who bought shares of the stock would become "part owners" of the company. In the event that a corporation was sued successfully, investors holding stock limited their liability to just the number of shares they owned. During the Industrial

>> In the nineteenth century, petroleum was used as both a machine lubricant and as a powerful illuminant. This photograph shows an oil strike spewing crude oil high into the western air.

©chippix/Shutterstock.com

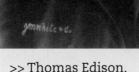

>> Thomas Edison.

Library of Congress Prints and Photographs Division[LC-USZ62-98066]

Revolution, the number of corporations increased dramatically, creating a sizeable number of organizations with large amounts of money that were able and willing to buy up successful smaller companies and develop a national (and even international) market.

Entrepreneurs also worked to streamline their operations. As businesses became larger, managers could not personally supervise all facets of their operations. So entrepreneurs established a hierarchy of managers and supervisors to coordinate schedules, keep track of shipments, and analyze the costs of each facet of the business. This development had two results: (1) it allowed corporations to control shops across a broad stretch of the nation, often centralizing control in one of the growing cities of the Midwest, such as Chicago; and (2) it created a class of managers that would figure prominently in the rapidly expanding middle class.

17-2 THE NATIONAL MARKET: CREATING CONSUMER DEMAND

By the late nineteenth century, with railroads spanning the nation and the process of replaceable parts making more and more goods available to a consuming public, the entire American nation became a marketplace. Americans could buy mass-produced shoes or furniture and have them shipped along rails to wherever they lived. As wise businessmen capitalized on this development, they helped create the modern consumer culture. They also spread the growing pains of industrialization far beyond its central hubs.

17-2a Advertising

One significant development in the formation of a modern consumer culture was a revolution in advertising. Before the Industrial Revolution, businessmen notified people about the availability of goods simply by printing announcements in local newspapers or in leaflets handed out to customers. Because their companies served mostly a local market, such advertising techniques were effective. As the consumer economy evolved after the Civil War, however, businesses began to market goods more aggressively and across numerous regions. In newspapers, multiple-column, even full-page advertisements began to replace the single-column notices of earlier years. Celebrities were featured wearing watches or hats. The number of advertising agencies expanded rapidly. Billboards and placards sprouted up everywhere.

17-2b National Brands

Along similar lines, the first advertising agencies began rudimentary marketing surveys to identify potential consumers' preferences and then applied the results to the marketing of individual products. For example, buying biscuits in the late nineteenth century was often problematic because they were stored in open containers; usually they became stale before they were bought. The National Biscuit Company (Nabisco) test-marketed a rather ordinary biscuit that had one difference from typical biscuits—a new, sealed package. Soon, consumers across the country demanded the product. The combination of technological and transportation innovations allowed the creation of truly national brands.

17-2c Stores and Mail Order

Chain stores quickly followed. Essentially, chains began when successful storeowners decided to reach more customers by opening branches in separate locations. Large chain stores had the advantage of being able to negotiate lower wholesale prices because they could purchase items in bulk; often they passed on a portion of their savings to consumers in the form of lower prices. One of the largest grocery chains was the Atlantic and Pacific Tea Company, known as A&P. Frank W. Woolworth devised another type of chain based on the idea of selling lots of inexpensive goods at cheap, fixed prices. His Woolworth outlets were originally called "five and tens," meaning that almost all of the goods were priced at either a nickel or a dime. The growth of his stores was phenomenal. In 1859, Woolworth founded his first store; by 1915 he and his partners controlled around six hundred outlets.

>> Nabisco's first ads featured a little boy in a rain slicker carrying a box of the specially packaged biscuits unharmed through the rain.

The emergence of advertising and national chain stores helped create a consumer culture in the nation's cities. The wide availability of consumer goods prompted some entrepreneurs to open department stores, which quickly became the greatest symbol of the emerging desire for consumption. In ornate window displays, such as New York's Macy's (founded 1858) and Philadelphia's Wanamaker's (1877), a large selection of items dazzled passersby. The stores also provided employment to thousands of urban Americans, especially women.

Chain retail stores appealed to city and town dwellers, but to reach rural customers, farsighted entrepreneurs used catalogues. In 1872, Aaron Montgomery Ward set up a mail order business. Beginning with a single-page list of items, he expanded his lists until his catalogue was heavier than many magazines. Richard W. Sears and Alvah C. Roebuck were comparative latecomers to the mail order business, but they offered Ward stiff competition. By the late 1890s, the Sears catalogue numbered more than five hundred pages. Next to the family Bible, it was one of the few "books" considered indispensable by farm families.

>> Sears Roebuck catalogue.

Advertising Archives

17-2d Harmful Business Practices

All this innovation and marketing came with significant costs; most significantly they signaled the advent of corporate life in America, a time when businessmen engaged in several harmful business practices to ensure greater control of the market. For most of them, whatever it took to drive out competitors, they did. Thus, while several of the innovations of men like Stanford, Carnegie, and Rockefeller benefited the American population, often these men took things too far.

MONOPOLIZATION

As brilliant an entrepreneur as he was, Rockefeller was involved in many of the harmful practices. In the late 1800s,

"Mr. Rockefeller awakened a general bitterness."

—IDA TARBELL, THE HISTORY OF THE STANDARD OIL COMPANY, 1904

for instance, Rockefeller essentially controlled the drilling, refining, and transporting of most of the nation's petroleum. But that was not enough. He was determined to control the product's wholesale distribution and retail marketing as well. So he established regional outlets that ruthlessly undersold well-established companies for as long as it took to drive them out of business. Rich as he was, Rockefeller could absorb short-term losses much longer than his competitors. Once he had driven his rivals out of business, he was free to charge whatever he wished for his product (although he had to keep prices relatively low to keep international competition at bay). In 1879, his Standard Oil Company controlled 90 percent of all petroleum in the country.

Rockefeller also had his way with railroads. His petroleum shipments comprised the majority of the business of several rail lines. By threatening to take his business to other competitors, he forced several railroad officials to offer him rebates on every barrel he shipped. In this way, Rockefeller paid lower railroad rates than his competitors. Rockefeller also interfered with railroad lines that carried his competitors' products. He convinced officials they were hurting his business whenever they shipped a competitor's products and that they should pay him a refund for each such barrel they shipped. Such business practices tested the limits of how much freedom politicians would allow businessmen to have.

PRICE GOUGING

Railroads also engaged in price gouging. For example, in urban areas where demand was high, usually several railroads operated their lines. These railroads often had to provide competitive rates, and during the occasional price wars between their competitors, railroads sometimes cut prices below their own costs. To make up for these losses, railroads gouged customers in other places—usually small towns that were served by just one line. Railroad officials also increased rates for local service, provoking differences between "long haul" and "short haul" charges. For instance, farmers in the eastern Dakotas complained that it cost more to ship a bushel of wheat 400 miles to Minneapolis than it cost to send

>>John Muir was among the first to recognize the environmental costs of the Industrial Revolution, and became a passionate advocate for conservation. This bronze statue of Muir, sitting with his arm on his walking stick and taking in an expansive view of Yosemite National Park in California, serves to commemorate his efforts.

that same product to Europe, more than ten times as far. Once again, these practices would eventually motivate the government to act—but not for many decades.

ENVIRONMENTAL DAMAGE

A third harmful business practice concerns what the Industrial Revolution did to the environment. Drilling for petroleum damaged the soil. The development of mechanized hydraulic mining in the Industrial Age caused much more damage to the land than any of the mining done by miners in previous centuries. Burning coal for all those railroads and machines gave off damaging gases. And railroad tracks cut through lands that were largely untouched by sustained human development.

Most Americans did not express deep concerns for these types of problems, but a few did. The top preservationist of the period was John Muir, the founder of the American environmental organization the Sierra Club and an influential advocate of preserving the mountain lands between California and Montana. In 1872, the federal government created the first national park, Yellowstone National Park, which comprises parts of Wyoming, Montana, and Idaho. Other parks proliferated shortly thereafter, but the growth of federally preserved lands hardly outpaced the expansion of industry into previously lightly touched terrain.

17-2e Working Conditions

The land was not the only thing transformed by the rise of big business. Workers also faced new challenges. Although they had access to a greater number of goods, workers suddenly found themselves at the mercy of powerful machines that required them to perform the same simple task again and again. Because of a growing pool of laborers, they worked ten to twelve hours a day, six days a week. They repeated the same boring task, hour after hour, until the whistle finally blew at the end of the shift. Between 1880 and 1900 an average of 35,000 workers died each year on the assembly line. The work was grueling.

Even children were not spared. As mechanization continued to decrease the need for skilled labor, and as employers kept searching for workers who would accept low pay, women and children entered factories in increasing numbers. By the turn of the century, 20 percent of the industrial work force was female. The textile industry in particular relied almost completely upon women and children. Many states passed child labor laws by the end of the 1800s, but employers routinely ignored these laws, and the number of child factory workers remained high.

Many employers also callously ignored the basic needs of their workers, most notoriously illustrated by the 1911 Triangle Shirtwaist Fire, in the New York City garment district, near Washington Square Park. Foremen at the **Triangle Shirtwaist Company** had bolted the fire escape door shut to prevent female workers from stealing cloth or taking breaks. When a fire broke out in the front of their **sweatshop**—located several stories above the street—hundreds of employees were trapped in the back of the shop. They faced two choices: sure death from the fire or probable death by leaping from the window to the pavement below. Bystanders had life-long nightmares from the sight of falling bodies thudding to the ground. The final death toll was 146 workers, most of them poor women. The company's two owners were tried for manslaughter, but both were acquitted.

Triangle Shirtwaist Company New York City garment factory; scene of a horrific fire in 1911

sweatshop Crowded factory in an urban setting, often one where workers are exploited

17-3 THE POLITICS OF THE INDUSTRIAL AGE

The dramatic changes that came about as a result of industrialization—including the growing strength of business leaders and corporations and the widening economic disparities in the cities—demanded a new kind of politics. Instead, the politics of the late nineteenth century reflected the Industrial Revolution's devotion to business, not to the needs of the urban poor or the working classes. Indeed, politically, the devotion to the needs of business had two vital consequences: (1) it permitted a dramatic decline in attention to the treatment of African Americans, which had dominated the politics of the Reconstruction era; and (2) it sullied the image of politicians, who sometimes were guilty of blatant corruption as they prioritized the interests of business over those of other groups. Federal, state, and local politicians gave massive land grants to their friends, offered government contracts only to their supporters, and accepted bribes for doing all sorts of "public works."

17-3a Justifications of the Industrial Order

Three intellectual justifications emerged to defend the actions of the leaders of the Industrial Revolution. Often they overlapped. Any reformer would have to overcome, or at least acknowledge, each of them before attempting to reform American politics.

MAINLINE PROTESTANT MORALITY

First, many of the leading industrialists of the late nineteenth century were sons of ministers, and they relied on a hard-line defense of Protestant individualism, arguing that economic problems stemmed from a particular individual's actions (or inactions) and that these problems were therefore not social in nature. There was a good bit of nativism in this argument too, especially considering that the vast majority of immigrants were Catholics and Jews from southern and eastern Europe (immigration will be discussed more fully in the next chapter). Furthermore, the industrialists firmly believed that their actions were improving the lot of humankind, which, despite some obvious contradictions, they were in fact doing. It was easy to argue that power

>> In this photo of victims of the Triangle Shirtwaist Fire, the victims lay exposed, open invitations for onlookers to debate the costs of the Industrial Age.

Hulton Archive/Getty Images

grids, electric light, better transportation, and improved communications had increased the convenience and comfort of modern living.

SOCIAL DARWINISM

The second justification was **Social Darwinism**. Railroad tycoons like Charles Francis Adams, Jr., believed that they were justified in their overbearing behavior because they had shown themselves to be the most successful competitors in an open market. Of course, because they had benefited from the federal government's actions to promote industrial growth through tariffs, subsidies, and cheap land sales, the successful capitalists' wealth was not as independently earned as they believed.

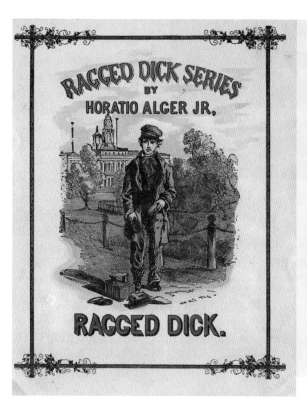

>> "He was above doing anything mean or dishonorable. He would not steal, or cheat, or impose upon younger boys, but was frank and straight-forward, manly and self-reliant."—Horatio Alger, description of the hero from Ragged Dick. The hero was a "bootblack," or shoeshine boy, and is pictured on this cover in "rags" with the tools of his trade.

Bettmann/Getty Images

British philosopher Herbert Spencer promoted this Darwinistic perspective. After reading Charles Darwin's theories on biological evolution, Spencer coined the phrase "survival of the fittest" and applied Darwin's concepts to the contemporary economic environment. Although very few Americans took Darwin's theory as far as Spencer did, businessmen occasionally borrowed those ideas that fit their needs.

Social Darwinism also had a racialist tinge, providing intellectual justification for laws and social practices that kept African Americans, Indians, certain categories of immigrants, and women second-class citizens who were often denied the vote and a basic right to property ownership. This notion of a racial or cultural hierarchy of peoples was widely espoused in late-nineteenth-century America; even the African American intellectual W. E. B. Du Bois relied on it when he argued that the vast majority of African Americans were ill equipped to be full citizens and instead should rely on a "talented tenth" to lead the way.

THE MYTH OF SUCCESS

Finally, successful businessmen also perpetuated the belief that if you worked hard enough, you could become wealthy. This notion was popularized by many writers, none more ardently than Horatio Alger, Jr. An admired and prolific writer (he produced 135 pieces of fiction), Alger wrote virtually all of his stories with the same plot: a good person works hard and, with a little luck, inevitably succeeds. His protagonist, a young man with working-class roots, moves from a farm or small town to the city. Once there, leading a morally upright life, wholly committed to hard work, and, above all, showing loyalty to his employer, the hero literally rises "from rags to riches." Alger's formula was sometimes called "pluck and luck," because the hero always benefits from some fortuitous event (such as rescuing the boss's beautiful daughter from the path of a runaway fire truck). Nonetheless, the notion that through hard work and dedication one could rise above one's social station, sometimes called "the myth of success," was prevalent throughout Industrial America.

17-3b Political Corruption

Supported by these justifications, many businessmen brought their pro-business agenda to politicians. Business interests quickly became the strongest lobby in the nation, and their requests usually came with reimbursements. In order to obtain land grants, protective tariffs, tax relief, and other "favors," many businessmen exchanged cash or

Social Darwinism The theory that "survival of the fittest" extended to the business realm; tycoons believed they were justified in their overbearing behavior because they had shown themselves to be the most successful competitors in an open market

stock options with the era's politicians. The exchange of these favors occurred on both national and local levels. These "exchanges" often erupted in public scandal.

THE CRÉDIT MOBILIER SCANDAL

The most damaging of these scandals was the Crédit Mobilier Scandal. In order to ensure an abundance of subsidies and land grants for their railroad, representatives from the Union Pacific offered federal lawmakers stock in the **Crédit Mobilier Company**. The problem was that

Crédit Mobilier Company A construction company set up by the directors of the Union Pacific in 1867 in order to build part of their transcontinental railroad—in essence, they were their own subcontractors and awarded themselves generous contracts

Tweed Ring Friends and cronies of New York's corrupt "Boss" William M. Tweed

Tammany Hall A political organization known as a "machine," whose members regarded politics as an opportunity to get rich while providing favors to the urban underclass

this construction company had been set up by the directors of the Union Pacific in 1867 in order to build part of their transcontinental railroad—in essence, they were their own subcontractors. In these dual roles, they awarded themselves generous contracts. To avoid any interference from the government, officials at Crédit Mobilier awarded congressmen stock in the company. The corruption was so blatant that company proxies handed out shares on the floor of the House of Representatives. Recipients included the Speaker of the House, the minority leader, and Schuyler Colfax, vice president of the United States from 1868 to 1872. When the scandal became public, it led to a congressional investigation and sullied the image of many of the era's leading politicians.

THE TWEED RING

Urban politics were equally corrupt, and none more so than New York's under "Boss" William M. Tweed. His **Tweed Ring** of friends controlled **Tammany Hall**, a Democratic political organization known as a "machine" whose members regarded politics as an opportunity to get rich while providing favors to the urban underclass. Through his connections at Tammany, "Boss" Tweed was appointed to supervise the dramatic rebuilding of New York City's infrastructure during the formative years of the Industrial Revolution. Tweed profited from this rebuilding because he or his associates owned or had access to many of the subcontractors who did the labor. He also typically overcharged contractors and took tidy sums off the top for himself.

Tweed was eventually exposed as a fraud in 1871 and was subsequently jailed and fined. After a dramatic escape, he was returned to jail, where he died in

WHO STOLE THE PEOPLE'S MONEY? — DO TELL. N.Y.TIMES.   'TWAS HIM.

>> "'Who Stole the People's Money?' 'Twas him." One of cartoonist Thomas Nast's famous cartoons on the corruption of the Tweed Ring, shown here, has each man in the circle pointing to the next. Boss Tweed himself is pictured, far left foreground, with the full beard.

1878. But Tammany Hall continued to exert influence on local politics until the early 1900s.

THE APPEAL OF TAMMANY

Despite its rampant corruption, Tammany appealed to recent Irish, Italian, and Jewish immigrants, who would provide Tammany politicians with their votes in exchange for preference in getting city jobs, free drinks on Election Day, and assorted social services. One way local "bosses" established loyalty was to watch over neighborhoods and take care of short-term emergencies. George Washington Plunkitt, for example, a colorful Tammany boss who came to power a generation after the fall of Tweed, told journalist William Riordan that if a family was made homeless by a fire, he went straight to the scene, found the family a temporary place to live, gave them money for immediate necessities, and ensured that they got back on their feet. What better way was there, he asked, to ensure voters' gratitude and loyalty? And what did it matter if, once empowered by the votes of those he "served," he took a little off the top?

Historians recognize that the machine system had its advantages, both in easing the transition to America for European newcomers and in dealing with short-term crises. But the system's reliance on above-the-law patronage also bred inefficiency, corruption, and cynicism, as unqualified people filled important government positions and as bribes raised prices for consumers.

17-3c Political Divisions

Despite the corruption, or perhaps because of it, politics were vibrant at the national level, political parties dominated, and few major political programs were implemented (the battles were too fierce). Judging from presidential elections, the

> "There's an honest graft, and I'm an example of how it works. I might sum up the whole thing by sayin': 'I seen my opportunities and I took 'em.'"
>
> —GEORGE WASHINGTON PLUNKITT, FROM PLUNKITT OF TAMMANY HALL, 1905

nation was almost evenly divided between Democrats and Republicans. But if the nation was evenly divided, the states were not, with Republicans controlling most of the northern states and Democrats controlling the South. Democrats also did well with urban immigrants. Rarely did the party of the president also control Congress, and between 1876 and 1896, a series of one-term presidents occupied the White House. More than 80 percent of eligible voters turned out for elections, mostly because of the dynamism of the parties and their numerous supporting machines. Nevertheless, for the most part the nation's leaders were incapable of managing, or unwilling to manage, the many problems associated with the Industrial Revolution.

Moreover, after the trauma of the Civil War, the American people often shied away from such deeply emotional issues as social welfare or concern for minorities. In a brutal reminder of the way politics could inspire passion, in 1881, President James A. Garfield

>> Boss Tweed and others like him looked at the immigrant communities of the late nineteenth century and saw votes. Pictured here is a bustling street corner in a Russo-Polish Jewish community in New York City.

was assassinated by a fellow Republican who disagreed with the president over the issue of civil service reform. Spurred to act by the assassination, Congress passed the Pendleton Act in 1883, which for the first time created a class of federal jobs that was not entirely controlled by political patronage. (Garfield's assassin had been fired from his post, not for incompetence, but based on the faction of the Republican Party he had supported during the election of 1880.) The act revealed divisions within the Republican Party, which was split between idealist reformers on the one hand and those supportive of machine politics and the spoils system on the other. Machine politicians mischievously labeled their Republican opponents **mugwumps**, meaning Republicans who supported Democratic candidate Grover Cleveland in the 1884 election only because the Republican candidate, James Blaine, was viewed as a product of machine politics.

17-4 THE RISE OF LABOR

For the first three decades after the Civil War, then, businessmen generally had their way in the political arena. They could count on friendly legislators to provide subsidies for promising new industries, and more mature industries might receive tariff protection against foreign competition. When workers went on strike, the government often intervened on the side of management by ordering troops to protect strike breakers. There were few safety regulations mandated by government, and workers' rights were limited. Job security was nonexistent. Workers who became sick or injured risked being fired, and new inventions in machinery continually made certain jobs obsolete. And pay was minimal. Although the average wage for industrial work rose between 1870 and 1900, that wage in 1900 was still only 20 cents an hour, or less than five dollars today, hardly enough to pay for adequate food, clothing, and shelter. Nevertheless, workers still went on strike and fought for better working conditions, and one of the most important developments of these years was the rise of organized labor.

mugwumps The machine's mischievous nickname for Republicans who supported Democrat Grover Cleveland in the 1884 election only because Republican candidate James Blaine was considered a product of machine politics

17-4a The Railroad Strike of 1877

Tensions caused by these conditions inevitably reached the boiling point, and the first labor conflict to come to national attention occurred in 1877, when railroad workers in West Virginia went on strike and froze most of the country's train traffic. The railroad industry had expanded enormously following the Civil War, and wage cuts during the Panic of 1873 created widespread resentment among workers. When the B&O Railroad announced a second wage cut in the calendar year, workers in Martinsville, West Virginia, went on strike. Almost immediately, the

>> The Great Railroad Strike of 1877 brought the cause of labor to national attention. Pictured on this cover of the magazine "Harper's Weekly" is a drawing of the Sixth Maryland Regiment fighting its way through striking workers in Baltimore, Maryland.

strike extended to Maryland, Pennsylvania, and Illinois. The easy transport brought by railroads moved more than goods; it helped circulate ideas too.

Word of the strike reached President Rutherford B. Hayes while he was dining in a train car with the president of the B&O Railroad, who argued that the strikers posed a serious threat to public safety. Hayes agreed and authorized the use of the National Guard to put an end to the strikes. Violence soon erupted in towns and cities across the country, and battles broke out in Baltimore, Chicago, San Francisco, and Pittsburgh. In St. Louis, striking railroad workers were joined by all other industrial workers in the city, shutting down all manufacturing establishments for four days. The city's industry was at a standstill.

Eventually, the National Guard defeated the strikers, railroad workers took pay cuts, and strike leaders were jailed. But more than one hundred people were killed nationwide, and there was astronomical property damage. Though the strike's carnage evaporated public sympathy for the workers, the conflict brought the issue of labor activism into the national consciousness.

17-4b The Struggle over Union Expansion

As worker discontent grew, emerging unions of organized workers struggled to exert influence. But they faced an uphill battle. Business owners opposed them, had ample resources to do so, and could take advantage of ethnic, religious, and racial divisions among the workers themselves.

OPPOSITION OF BUSINESS OWNERS

On a practical level, employers considered unions bad for business. To stay competitive, business owners were constantly seeking to keep costs down. Labor was one such cost, and a company whose profits were dropping might cut jobs and wages. Most owners also saw their union-busting tactics as a defense of the American way of life. For them, union organizing ran counter to the American virtues of independence and self-reliance, and they often justified the pitfalls of the capitalist system by citing the theory of Social Darwinism or the fact that their industries were propelling the United States toward building the largest economy in the world.

BUSINESS RESOURCES

Regardless of motive, American business owners had several resources at their disposal to fight against unions.

They fired workers who joined unions and denied jobs to union organizers. Many workers had to sign a **yellow dog contract**, in which they promised, upon pain of termination, not to join a union. Employers also used the **blacklist**, a compilation of known union activists in a particular area. Employers shared these lists and refused to hire anyone whose name appeared on them. Also, by hiring a mixture of native-born Americans and immigrants of different backgrounds, employers tried to exploit ethnic divisions to forestall any feelings of worker unity, and they did so with considerable success.

Business owners were often just as successful in breaking strikes as they were in hindering union organization. To keep their factories and mines running, they hired **strikebreakers**, often unemployed immigrant workers from other areas who were hungry for jobs and had no stake in the union struggle.

DIVISIONS AMONG WORKERS

In addition to stiff opposition from business owners, union organizers also faced obstacles within the labor pool itself. Workers did not share the same levels of skill and pay, or the same occupations. More highly skilled workers enjoyed higher wages and better job security; for them, unions did not have much appeal. Immigrant workers also posed a problem to unity. They were isolated from one another by language and sometimes religion, and native-born Americans, who saw immigrants as a threat to their own jobs, often resented them. Many immigrants were in America only temporarily, to earn quick money to send back home; they had families to support and did not stand to benefit from a typical strike's long months of idleness. For these reasons, many labor unionists despised immigrants, seeing them as not committed to the cause.

LABOR SOLIDARITY

Despite the fractured nature of the American work force, union leaders fought to create a sense of common purpose among its members. Arguing that it was the working class, not owners and managers, who produced America's wealth, union organizers tried to

yellow dog contract Contract stipulating that an employee would not join a union

blacklist A compilation of known union activists in a particular area; employers refused to hire anyone whose name appeared on one

strikebreakers Workers who agreed to work while union workers were on strike

instill a sense of pride andcamara-
derie among union members. Some
unions, especially those in urban areas with a large immigrant population,
sought to overcome the inherent
barriers between ethnic groups. The
**International Ladies' Garment
Workers' Union (ILGWU)** of New York
City, for example, often conducted
its union meetings in five different
languages simultaneously.

ROLES OF GOVERNMENT AND THE MIDDLE CLASS

To achieve their goals, union leaders
needed more than solidarity among
workers; they also needed support
from government leaders and the
politically influential middle class. Such
support was hard to find. In the last two
decades of the 1800s, some middle-
class reformers did address labor
issues, and the government did take
some actions to improve worker conditions. For instance, many middle-class
Americans participated in charitable
reform efforts that sought to improve
workers' living conditions. As a result
of these efforts, Congress in 1868
mandated an eight-hour workday for
federal construction projects, and in
1885 it passed the **Contract Labor
Law**, which prohibited employers from
forcing immigrants to work to pay off
the costs of their passage to America.
But these laws were exceptions. For
the most part, the middle class and the
government remained supportive of
industry leaders.

17-4c The Knights of Labor

At the national level, the Knights of Labor was America's first effective union, one that sought to unite all

LEADERS OF THE KNIGHTS OF LABOR.

>> The Knights of Labor, led by Terence Powderly (center),
sought to unite all the nation's "toilers," as indicated by
the variety of laborers (railroad workers, woodworkers,
blacksmiths, and lumberjacks) in each of the four corners
of the image. Encircling Powderly are portraits of other
prominent labor leaders of the time.

**International Ladies' Garment Workers' Union
(ILGWU)** Major New York City union that often conducted its union
meetings in five different languages simultaneously

Contract Labor Law Passed in 1885, this prohibited employers
from forcing immigrants to work to pay off the costs of their passage
to America

of America's "toilers" into a single organization that,
through the power of its vast membership, could deliver workers from their plight. The Knights of Labor
accepted farm hands and factory workers; it welcomed
women, African Americans, and immigrants. (The
union excluded lawyers, bankers, doctors, and liquor
dealers, all of whom, from the union's perspective, were
not toilers but white-collar workers.)

Founded in 1869 by a Philadelphia tailor named
Uriah Stephens, the Knights of Labor rose to

prominence in 1879, when Terence Powderly assumed leadership. Powderly opened the union's doors to almost all workers, and it became, for a brief time, the largest union in the country. In 1884 and 1885, the Knights of Labor entered the national spotlight when its members staged successful strikes against railroad companies in the Southwest. After the railroad strikes, membership in the Knights of Labor exploded; the union had approximately 100,000 members in 1884, and by 1886 its membership rolls had swelled to more than 750,000 workers.

THE FALL OF THE KNIGHTS

As quickly as it had grown, the influence of the Knights of Labor faded away. Ultimately, the Knights simply could not coordinate the activities of its members, who came from a variety of regions, industries, and ethnic backgrounds. Also, although the union owed much of its growth to the success of strikes, Powderly resisted using strikes because he believed, correctly, that they would jeopardize the union's public standing.

THE HAYMARKET RIOT

Powderly's distrust of strikes proved well founded. Regardless of other problems plaguing the Knights of Labor, in the end it was a single event that caused the demise of the union. In spring 1886, workers demanding an eight-hour workday went on strike against the McCormick Harvester Company of Chicago. On May 3, four picketers were killed during a clash with the police. The next day a rally was held in Chicago's Haymarket Square to protest the police's actions. When police tried to break up this second gathering, someone threw a stick of dynamite. The resulting explosion killed seven policemen and wounded dozens of others. Those police who were not injured then fired their guns into the crowd; four more people were killed, and more than a hundred others were trampled and shot at as they fled. The "Haymarket Affair," as it was called in the press, was believed to be the work of anarchists (who believe governments are unnecessary and should be abolished), and the incident created a state of hysteria among middle-class citizens, who mistakenly feared that all laborites were anarchists. Eventually, eight reputed anarchists were arrested for conspiring to kill the policemen, and although none of the men could be tied to the actual bomb, they were convicted, and seven received the death sentence.

North Wind Picture Archives

>> Strikes often turned violent. Here, striking workers during the Homestead Strike of 1892 fired on boats carrying men armed to break the strike.

After the Haymarket bombing, anti-union editorials appeared in newspapers across the country, and the Knights of Labor was a frequent target. One of the convicted men was a union member, and, although Powderly condemned the bombing, his organization became synonymous with anarchist activity. It could not survive the mischaracterization, and by the early 1890s the union was gone, and, for a short time at least, its vision of a coalition of all workers disappeared with it.

17-4d Growth and Frustrations

Despite the setbacks, in the late 1880s and throughout the 1890s, workers continued to organize, although usually on a smaller scale than had the Knights. Particularly after 1893, when the country experienced a severe economic depression, union activity intensified.

But the labor movement was no match for big business. In two important struggles, the Homestead strike of 1892 (which began when the Homestead Steel Factories outside Pittsburgh cut wages and tried to break the local union) and the Pullman strike of 1894 (which began when the railroad developer George Pullman cut wages of his workers by 25 percent, after firing a full third during the previous weeks), business owners successfully called upon the full weight of the U.S. government to crush labor activism. In both cases, industrial leaders destroyed the strikes and the unions supporting them by calling on the state or national guard. It was clear who had the upper hand.

> "The issue is Socialism versus Capitalism. I am for Socialism because I am for humanity. We have been cursed with the reign of gold long enough. Money constitutes no proper basis of civilization. The time has come to regenerate society—we are on the eve of universal change."
>
> —Eugene V. Debs, "Open Letter to the American Railway Union," 1897

17-4e The Rise of the AFL

At the time of these highly publicized strikes, another union, the **American Federation of Labor (AFL)**, became the leading labor organization in America. Founded in 1881, the AFL gained momentum throughout the 1880s by pursuing a different strategy than the Knights of Labor—one that made it more attractive to middle-class Americans. The AFL was a loose federation of roughly one hundred **craft unions** rather than a single national union. It was also avowedly antisocialist and anti-anarchist. Its leader, Samuel Gompers, coordinated the craft unions' actions without making any central decisions for them, and by arbitrating disputes, he ensured they stuck by each other. However, Gompers did not believe in organizing unskilled laborers, who were easily replaced by strikebreakers.

American Federation of Labor (AFL) The leading labor organization in America, founded in 1881 by Samuel Gompers and composed of craft unions rather than a single national union

craft union Union of skilled laborers, the type of union assembled under the American Federation of Labor

American Socialist Party Political party formed in 1901 and led by Eugene V. Debs that advocated replacing the nation's capitalist system

International Workers of the World (IWW) A collection of militant mining unions founded in 1905 in Colorado and Idaho; sought to use labor activism to overthrow the capitalist system

anarcho-syndicalism A radical form of political protest that advocates the use of labor activism to overthrow the capitalist system

The AFL's successes helped offset failures like the Homestead and Pullman strikes. Its most important early achievement took place in 1890, when Gompers's own cigar makers' union established the eight-hour workday. Up until then, the typical workday had been ten hours or longer. In a pattern typical for the AFL, other AFL unions also demanded the shortened workday, and before long, printers, granite cutters, and coal miners were also working fewer hours per day. By the 1890s, the AFL had replaced the Knights of Labor as the most important labor lobby in the nation.

17-4f Labor and Politics

Despite the AFL's victories, by the turn of the century government favoritism toward big business had convinced many labor leaders of the need for political solutions. But the labor movement was far from united in how to do this. The AFL's Samuel Gompers argued that entering the political arena was too costly and that labor's best strategy was to focus on winning individual concessions from owners.

Other laborites chose to enter the political arena by creating new parties. In 1901, socialists formed the **American Socialist Party**, led by Eugene V. Debs. The party fielded candidates in both national and local elections, with some success. It sought to help workers by replacing the nation's capitalist system, but through involvement in the democratic process.

More radical forms of political protest also emerged, among them those employed by the **International Workers of the World (IWW)**. Founded in 1905, the IWW grew out of a collection of militant mining unions in Colorado and Idaho, where workers scorned the AFL's exclusiveness. Under the leadership of "Big Bill" Haywood, most "Wobblies," as IWW members were called, pursued **anarcho-syndicalism**, which sought to use labor activism to overthrow the capitalist system, favoring it instead of anarchism or socialism. They brought in all laboring outcasts, including racial and ethnic minorities and women, and favored strikes and sabotage in order to win fewer working hours or greater pay.

THE MAINSTREAM

Most labor leaders, however, followed the AFL's example and avoided challenging the country's political establishment. Nonetheless, union leaders did begin to see that influencing government officials through the political process could be beneficial to their cause. For example, when President Theodore Roosevelt arbitrated a coal miners' strike in 1902, he forced mine owners to make concessions to the union. During the years following 1902, laborites became active participants in the nation's politics—a role they would continue to play throughout the twentieth century.

Between 1865 and the early 1900s, the American economy was transformed from one run by family shops and small factories to one generally controlled by large corporations. As these corporations consolidated their business practices, they helped improve access to food, material wealth, and new technologies. They also helped expand large urban centers, especially in the North, and pushed their innovations into the West and the South, creating what looked like the first national consumer culture to many Americans, where Nabisco crackers could be found in most American grocery stores and where the Sears catalogue could be found in all regions of the country.

Many of the inventions of the late nineteenth century did not seem particularly transformative to contemporaries. The New York Times reporter covering the 1882 story of Edison's first large-scale light bulb test, in New York City, passively described the test as "in every way satisfactory." He did not recognize the electric light bulb as something all that different from the gas bulbs that had illuminated the city before. But what the reporter missed was that the bulb required a grid of electrical power that could be extended for miles. He missed the fact that electric automation would lead to widespread electrification and spark hundreds of other inventions.

One group that understood the transformative nature of the Industrial Revolution was the working class. They sought to counter the growing size and power of their new corporate bosses by coming together in unions, although beyond the perceived need for solidarity there was little in common between the variety of organizations that emerged in the late nineteenth century. And no matter their particular outlook, unions were often frustrated in their endeavors to improve the lives of the working class, if not by the power of the corporations, then by the actions of the state and federal governments. They did achieve some success, including generally winning the eight-hour workday and the forty-hour workweek, but these were hard fought and it was difficult to see if more was coming.

The inventions of the Industrial Age and the expansion of corporate America affected the entire nation, although they affected each region somewhat differently. In the North, the Industrial Revolution would help transform society by inspiring the arrival of millions of immigrants and creating an urban society, along with reactionary politics, as working-class laborers sought to make the government more responsive to their needs in the budding labor movement. The South would struggle to overcome the disruptions of the Civil War and try to forge what it called a "New South." And the West would utilize the developments of the Industrial Age to establish itself as a vital and increasingly well-developed part of the nation. It is to these transformations that we now must turn.

STUDY TOOLS 17

READY TO STUDY? IN THE BOOK, YOU CAN:

❏ Rip out the Chapter Review Card, which includes key terms and chapter summaries.

ONLINE AT WWW.CENGAGEBRAIN.COM, YOU CAN:

❏ Collect StudyBits while you read and study the chapter.

❏ Quiz yourself on key concepts.

❏ Find videos for further exploration.

❏ Prepare for tests with HIST5 Flash Cards as well as those you create.

❏ Learn more about Tammany Hall.

❏ Read excerpts from William Riordan's *Plunkitt of Tammany Hall.*

❏ Read a contemporary piece chronicling Rockefeller's business tactics.

❏ Read Henry Demarest Lloyd's "Wealth Against the Commonwealth."

❏ Read the original Knights of Labor platform.

❏ Read Terence Powderly's *Thirty Years of Labor.*

❏ Find out more about Andrew Carnegie and the steel business.

❏ Read Samuel Gompers's congressional testimony regarding AFL unions.

❏ Read Eugene Debs's "How I Became a Socialist."

What Else Was Happening

▶ **1860–1890** U.S. Patent Office issues 144,000 licenses, four times more than in 1790.

▶ **1866–1868** In Erie Railroad War, Cornelius Vanderbilt and competitors exemplify new ruthless business practices.

▶ **1867–1872** Crédit Mobilier railroad financing scandal tarnishes Grant administration.

▶ **1868** Congress introduces eight-hour day in federal work projects.

▶ **1869** Completion of transcontinental railroad.

▶ **1872** Montgomery Ward launches mail order business.

▶ **1873** Drastic wage cuts in Panic of 1873 anger and mobilize workers.

▶ **1876** Alexander Graham Bell's telephone speeds up long-distance communication.

1876–1882: The right arm and torch of the Statue of Liberty cross the Atlantic three times.

▶ **1877** National railroad strike kills over 100, brings labor tensions to forefront.

▶ **1878** Refrigerated rail cars permit long-distance transportation of perishable goods.

▶ **1879** John D. Rockefeller's Standard Oil Company controls 90 percent of petroleum market.

Thomas Edison completes experimentation on the incandescent light bulb.
Knights of Labor emerge as nation's largest union.

1883   Congress passes civil service reform with Pendleton Act.

1884: *N. Thompson, founder of Coney Island Luna Park, introduces the roller coaster, calling it Switchback.*

1886: *Explosion at Chicago Haymarket protest kills seven, puts Knights of Labor in disrepute.*

Statue of Liberty is dedicated. The statue, a gift from France intended to commemorate the two nations' founding ideal of liberty, will come to symbolize American freedom to millions of immigrants.

1892   Carnegie steel plant strike in Homestead pits workers against Pinkertons and militia.

1893   Severe economic recession drives further labor organization.

1894   Government intervenes on side of industrialists in Pullman strike.

1895: *Independent Labour Party founded in Britain.*

1896: *The first comic strip character—the "Yellow Kid"—appears in the* New York Journal.

1899: *Felix Hoffmann patents aspirin.*

1902   Theodore Roosevelt mediates miners' strike in favor of workers.

1905   Colorado miners form anarcho-syndicalist International Workers of the World.

1911   Triangle Shirtwaist Company fire.

18 | The Industrial Age: North, South, and West

North Wind Picture Archive

LEARNING OBJECTIVES

After reading this chapter, you should be able to do the following:

18-1 Describe the urbanization and immigration in the North during the second half of the nineteenth century, and how those two factors shaped the region's social relations, including its disparities of wealth.

18-2 Evaluate the accuracy of the term *New South* in describing the post-Civil War South, and discuss ways in which the term was and was not appropriate.

18-3 Describe the development of the American West that took place during the second half of the nineteenth century, addressing both industrialization and the general defeat of Native American nations on the plains.

18-4 Discuss the problems that confronted America's farmers in the North, South, and West during the late 1800s, and describe how their attempts to solve those problems led to the formation of a new political party.

AFTER FINISHING THIS CHAPTER GO TO **PAGE 353** **FOR STUDY TOOLS**

The Industrial Revolution affected all aspects of American life, and it provoked more changes than just those in the factories. But how one experienced the Industrial Revolution depended on where one lived. In the North, the small factories that had emerged in the early nineteenth century took on gigantic proportions. There were also many, many more of them. Jobs in these factories turned northern cities into magnets for people far and wide and created a rambunctious urban life that we still associate with modern living. The jobs created by this industrial growth also made the North a draw for European immigrants searching for economic opportunities and freedom from persecution. Unlike previous waves of immigration, though, the immigrants that came during the last quarter of the nineteenth century mostly came from southern and eastern Europe, speaking foreign tongues, coming from different political backgrounds, and often practicing different religions. These turn-of-the-twentieth-century immigrants made America an even more polyglot nation than it had been and prompted questions about the meaning of America more generally. These two impulses—urbanization and immigration—shaped the Industrial Age in the North.

While the North grew tremendously during the years after the Civil War, it had a foundation on which to grow. Factories were familiar sights in the North starting in the late eighteenth century, and urban life had been part of the landscape since the colonial era. This was not the case in the newly developing South and West.

In the South of the 1870s and 1880s, a collection of regional civic boosters attempted to harness the power of the Industrial Revolution to reshape the image of that region. In the antebellum era, the South was powered by a few crops (especially "King Cotton") and controlled politically and economically by a handful of wealthy families. And of course it was slaves who had done much of the South's laboring. Post-Reconstruction civic boosters in the South, however, made the argument that, after the Civil War, a "New South" had emerged, one based on economic opportunity, rich natural resources, and increased racial equality. While these hopes were sometimes met (some cities did in fact blossom), the promise of the New South was all too often frustrated. This frustrated promise was manifested in perhaps the deepest legacy of the New South: the system of racial segregation known as Jim Crow. Indeed, if the Industrial Age in the North was shaped by urbanization and immigration, in the South it was shaped by slower economic development and hardened racial segregation.

But even the South had more of an industrial foundation upon which to grow than the West. No region of the country was transformed more rapidly by the changes of the Industrial Age than the land west of the Mississippi River. During the final third of the nineteenth century, vast stretches of arable land were rapidly populated by millions of Americans who built great cities, decimated Indian populations, and created industries controlled by industrial magnates. Indeed, even the cowboy, the most memorable image of the late-nineteenth-century West, was often working at the behest of a millionaire industrialist who was sending cattle to a slaughterhouse in one of the West's new great cities. The corporate life of the late nineteenth century knew no boundaries.

But farming would remain central to both the South and the West, and the corporate-friendly politics whose unresponsiveness had sparked the labor movement provoked a rural movement for reform in the South and the West. Collectively called the Populist movement, it was often just as radical in its challenges to industrial capitalism as the labor movement, and it too would encounter more frustration than success. But these rural reformers put forward a platform that would succeed long after the Populists had exited the political stage.

This chapter will examine the social and cultural manifestations of the Industrial Revolution in the North, South, and West, before turning to the second home-grown response to the seemingly unfettered advance of corporate capitalism, the Populist Movement.

 18-1 **THE NORTH**

Most of the massive industries of the Industrial Age emerged in the North. And because these industries created jobs, the cities of the North ballooned into metropolises. As they did, however, the gulf between rich and poor became increasingly pronounced. The corporations of the Industrial Age had generated enormous fortunes for a handful of people in the North, leaving most industrial laborers in poverty.

18-1a Urbanization

By 1900, more than a third of America's people lived in cities, and city populations were growing twice as fast as the population as a whole. Between 1870 and 1920, the number of Americans living in cities increased fivefold,

◀◀◀ **The railroad was vital in opening the western frontier for American settlement. This image shows trains taking hunters to the western plains to shoot bison (note the discarded carcasses). By 1891, the bison population had dropped from 13 million to just 865 on account of over-hunting by both Native and white Americans.**

from 10 million to 54 million. The population of New York City went from 800,000 in 1860 to 2 million in 1900. The population of Boston increased from 180,000 in 1860 to 600,000 in 1900. And Chicago grew from 109,000 in 1860 to 1.7 million in 1900. Cities were booming.

TENEMENT LIFE

Most of the people living in these growing cities were workers employed in the new factories of the Industrial Age. Manufacturers sometimes provided company housing close to factories so the entire work force could walk to work. For most others, independent builders made quick profits by rapidly building inferior houses. They got away with it because few cities at the time had building codes. Developers also carved previously built single-family homes into multiple-unit dwellings called **tenements**, which often had thin walls and frequently lacked windows as well. Quarters were tight, and bathrooms were frequently outside, in the front or backyard, meaning a person renting a room on the sixth or seventh floor had a long haul to use the facilities. These kinds of close quarters led to communal childcare networks, but they also pushed people out into the streets, creating a raucous, lively, and sometimes dangerous street scene. The housing stock of the era was quickly overwhelmed by all the urban growth, leading to creative, often unsafe solutions.

One effect of such rapid building was a dearth of parks in the new cities. More pertinently, adequate plumbing was virtually nonexistent, and few pre-1900 workers' houses had an indoor water supply; most shared pumps and wells in back alleys. City governments began to build sewers after 1860, but these sewers were primitive; most ended at the nearest river or lake, where raw sewage was simply dumped into the water. Typhoid epidemics swept through city populations at a time when the connection between sewage and disease transmission was not widely understood. In 1900, the city of Chicago reversed the direction of the city's main river, diverting it to the Mississippi River in order to send the city's waste products away from Lake Michigan, its primary water source. Of course, dumping the city's waste

Hulton Archive/Getty Images

>> For working-class families in cities, many of whom were recent immigrants, living in cramped quarters was the norm. This photograph shows an immigrant family living and working in the common room of their tenement.

into the Mississippi River had unsanitary effects as well, just not for Chicago. The cities were growing tremendously, but the expansion was haphazard, and those at the bottom of the pay scale were often deprived of basic necessities.

WEALTHY NEIGHBORHOODS

Meanwhile, successful industrialists devoted enormous resources to the building of cultural institutions and wealthy neighborhoods. Many had amassed huge fortunes during the rapid industrial growth. By 1890, for instance, the wealthiest 1 percent of the American population owned as much property as the remaining 99 percent. And in the cities of the North, the leading industrialists ostentatiously displayed their fortunes. Fifth Avenue in New York City, for example, was lined with mansions and townhouses, and on New Year's Day, hostesses drew back their curtains to reveal opulent interiors. The working classes would line the streets in awe and anger. The Newport home of William Vanderbilt, the grandson of Cornelius Vanderbilt, now called "Marble House," cost more than $11 million—a staggering $169.5 million today. "Diamond" Jim Brady, a wealthy New York City financier, was notorious for sitting two inches from his dinner table and continuing to eat until his expanding stomach touched the table. New York socialite Mrs. Stuyvesant Fish threw a party to honor her dog, which arrived wearing a diamond collar worth

tenements Crowded slum houses in urban areas, which housed mostly immigrants

Library of Congress/Getty Images

>> Child labor, like the young miners here, was used extensively during the Industrial Revolution. "One of the sights which this coal side of our civilization has to show is the presence of herds of little children of all ages, from six years upward, at work in the coal breakers, toiling in dirt, and air thick with carbon dust, from dawn to dark, of every day of the week except Sunday. These coal breakers are the only schools they know. A letter from the coal regions in the Philadelphia 'Press' declares that 'there are no schools in the world where more evil is learned or more innocence destroyed than in the breakers. It is shocking to watch the vile practices indulged in by these children, to hear the frightful oaths they use, to see their total disregard for religion and humanity.'"—Henry Demarest Lloyd, "The Lords of Industry," 1884

$15,000 (today, nearly $350,000). The wealthy of this era were extremely wealthy, and not shy about showing it off.

This gross materialism did not go unnoticed. Mark Twain and Charles Dudley Warner published a novel called *The Gilded Age* (providing the era with its most notable label) that satirically described the greed, materialism, and political corruption that accompanied the Industrial Age. To gild something, of course, is to provide a thin coat of gold over a much cheaper metal, suggesting the harsh and debased economics hiding behind the supposed refinement. Economics professor Thorstein Veblen, in his book *The Theory of the Leisure Class* (1899), called the opulent purchasing of the wealthy "conspicuous consumption." He argued that, ultimately, the selfishness of the rich harmed economic growth. Edith Wharton's novels, particularly *The House of Mirth* (1905), mocked the emptiness of the life led by the wealthy and the stifling social conventions that

ruled their lives. Andrew Carnegie, one of the most conscientious of the captains of industry, described the problem of the Gilded Age as that of reconciling the wealthy and the poor in order to maintain a prosperous nation. In the burgeoning cities of the North, the two seemed to be worlds apart.

SUBURBS

Often the growing middle classes would try to flee the polarities of the city, and in the late nineteenth century, suburbs began their initial growth. Street railways made it possible to live 4 or 5 miles from work (or farther), yet still get there fairly quickly each morning. Streetcar companies often built their lines beyond the edge of town in the confident expectation that housing developments would soon follow. They were often right; their lines formed the backbone of new suburban communities inhabited by the middle-class wage-earning bookkeepers, sales people, and managers. Slowly, city populations became increasingly stratified, with upper- and middle-class people living outside the noisy industrial districts, venturing as far away as bona fide suburbs, while the working classes and those enduring discrimination because of their race, religion, or country of origin lived in less desirable areas close to the industrial hubs.

ENTERTAINMENTS

Cities had long been spaces of public entertainment, and in the nineteenth century they teemed with vaudeville houses, dance halls, and saloons. These spaces were often deemed immoral or improper by the upper classes. In the 1890s, however, with the growth of the middle and working classes, entrepreneurs found a more wholesome way to lure the city's masses: large, magnificent amusement parks. In 1895, New York's **Coney Island** opened, featuring roller coasters, water slides, and fun houses. Unlike other public amusements like vaudeville and saloons, amusement parks attracted both men and women because they were considered more respectable. For instance, Coney Island helped spur dating among working-class young men and women.

Coney Island Public amusement park opened in New York in 1895; it featured roller coasters, water slides, and fun houses

>> "The Breakers," the Vanderbilt family's summer home in Newport, Rhode Island, was a seventy-room Renaissance-style palazzo inspired by the sixteenth-century palaces of Genoa and Turin. And, as this photo shows, it was just one of many mansions along the Rhode Island coast.

Attending professional baseball games was another way to relax, and baseball became a source of urban pride during these years. It began in 1876, with the formation of the **National League** by the Cincinnati Red Stockings (America's first professional team) and seven others. The league's success depended on reliable, intercity rail transport to carry the teams to each other's fields, as well as the telegraph lines along which

National League The first professional baseball league, begun in 1876 with eight teams

American League The second professional baseball league, begun in 1901

World Series Baseball competition between the National League and the American League, played for the first time in 1903

rapid news of scores and results could be carried. The National League's success prompted the creation of the rival **American League** in 1901, and the two leagues competed in the first **World Series** in 1903, all due to the transportation and communications revolutions of the late nineteenth century, as well as the creation of a middle class with enough disposable income to enjoy an afternoon at the ballpark. In that first World Series, pitcher Cy Young led the Boston Americans to victory, five games to three, over the Pittsburgh Pirates, whose star pitcher had injured his shoulder while trap shooting just before the start of the Series.

18-1b Immigration

Along with urbanization and the growing disparities of wealth, another important development in the industrializing North was immigration. Between 1880 and 1920, approximately 25 million people came to the United States. Unlike earlier arrivals, these new immigrants did not migrate from the British Isles or northern Europe; instead, they came predominantly from eastern, central, and southern Europe. They were Poles, Greeks, Italians, Bulgarians, Ukrainians, Czechs, Serbs, and Croats; they were Orthodox Jews, Eastern Orthodox Catholics, and Roman Catholics. This new immigration was the result of at least four factors (see "The Reasons Why . . ." box).

>> Crowds at a daytime baseball game in the bleachers of Forbes Field in Pittsburgh, Pennsylvania. Their presence at a daytime baseball game suggests the leisure time allotted to the Industrial Age's new middle class.

There were at least four reasons for the rise in immigration during these years:

European population growth. Europe had experienced tremendous population growth during the nineteenth century, creating gaps between the number of workers and the number of jobs.

Urban crowding in Europe. The Industrial Revolution in Europe drew people away from agricultural industries to cities, where the crush of newcomers made employment even harder to find.

Antisemitism. A rise in antisemitism, especially within the Russian Empire, forced many Jews to flee.

Economic opportunities. America served as a magnet because it promised economic opportunity and personal freedoms. Many who came planned only to acquire enough wealth to make a better life for themselves back in Europe. For example, between 1910 and 1914, more than 400,000 Italian immigrants left the United States to return to Italy. These immigrants were usually men who came to America alone, planning to return home and rejoin their families.

THE IMMIGRANT EXPERIENCE

Most of these new immigrants, who were sometimes called **greenhorns** because of their awkward, uncultivated ways, faced a hard life in America. After successfully passing through well-known gateways like New York's **Ellis Island**, these immigrants struggled against tremendous adversity. America itself provided a tight labor market, and many immigrants came with limited knowledge of English, limited education, and limited work skills. Most stayed close to where they had landed, settling in urban areas like New York City, Philadelphia, Chicago, and Boston. They found themselves on the bottom rung of the industrial hierarchy, working low-paying factory jobs.

Nevertheless, they kept coming, and by the end of the 1800s, immigrants made up a majority of the populations of most major American cities. By 1890, for example, New York's population was 80 percent immigrant. Chicago's population was a remarkable 87 percent immigrant. Most immigrants lived in crowded tenements, and unsurprisingly, poverty and overcrowding precipitated murder and other violent crimes. Some immigrant girls, driven by poverty and desperation, turned to prostitution.

ETHNICITY, ASSIMILATION, AND THE AMERICAN DREAM

Despite the struggle, immigrants also had their share of triumphs. Some even prospered, and many eventually gained a material stake in their new country by owning property. However, there was a fundamental tension at the core of the immigrant success story. Immigrants often sought to maintain a sense of connection to their native countries, but their status in America was inextricably tied to assimilation into American culture. New York and other major cities contained an amazing patchwork of different ethnic communities. These communities developed numerous resources for comforting lonely and homesick immigrants, including foreign-language newspapers and fraternal and religious organizations. These were the years when America's cities evolved into complex mosaics of ethnic neighborhoods.

 THE "NEW SOUTH"

Even before the Civil War, the South lagged behind the North in urbanization and industrialization, mainly because of its dependence on slavery and the domination of plantation owners in the state governments. But after the war, southerners such as Henry Grady, the owner and editor of the *Atlanta Constitution*, argued that the South should improve its cities and provide for the growth of industry. It should partake in the Industrial Revolution and encourage economic relations with the North, including accepting northern loans. Grady's stirring speech, "The New South," argued that the postwar South was a different world from the antebellum South, especially because it was not built on the subjugation of an entire race or the domination of a single industry like cotton. A spirit of enterprise characterized southern life in the late 1870s and 1880s, he argued.

Southern iron, steel, textile, and tobacco industries all emerged during the thirty-five years following

greenhorns European newcomers to America

Ellis Island Immigrant gateway to New York City from 1892 to 1954

the Civil War, too, as did numerous cities. Still, despite Grady's celebration of cooperation between black and white southerners in the New South, black people rarely benefited from any of these changes. Worse still, the era bore witness to the rise of the segregated society that would last until the 1960s and beyond. Thus, there were two components of the New South: (1) the halting and haphazard creation of an industrialized South, and (2) the quick and summary creation of a racial caste system, with white people on top, black on bottom. If many southerners shared the optimism, energy, and inventiveness that characterized the Industrial Revolution in the North, it nonetheless manifested itself far differently.

18-2a Southern Industries

Southern industry grew up around railroads, iron manufacture, textile production, and tobacco. However, the South never developed a strong industrial base, at least not one comparable to what was taking place in the North.

RAILROADS

Railroads led the South's industrial expansion, attracting capital from wealthy northern investors. Railroads also provided much-needed connections between the cities and towns of the South. Before the Civil War and up until about 1880, southern railroad development was very slow. But between 1880 and 1890—just one ten-year period— southern rails grew from 16,605 miles to 39,108 miles, an increase of more than 100 percent. Southern state governments poured resources into supporting rail companies, and northern rail companies began to expand into southern states, seeing an opportunity for profit in the developing southern economy. By 1890, southern railroads had become a model for railroad development worldwide.

IRON PRODUCTION

The expansion of the railroads also helped foster the urbanization of southern cities and the growth of the iron industry. Many New South advocates hoped that iron production would become the central means for the South to compete with the North in industry. Because the demand for iron was high, especially in construction trades and in laying railroad lines, the iron industry seemed an ideal place to invest. As a result, it grew; the southern iron industry expanded seventeenfold in the 1800s.

COTTON AND TEXTILES

The easy transportation provided by new railroads also allowed for the expansion of the southern textile industry. The industry grew fast in the South because of the abundance of cheap labor and the wide availability of cotton. Throughout the 1880s and 1890s, a mill-building craze swept the South. In 1870, about 10,000 people were employed in textile manufacturing. By 1900, nearly 100,000 people worked in the industry. The work was harsh, reflecting the typical labor conditions of the Industrial Age, and it was not uncommon for a mill worker to work a fourteen-hour day.

Library of Congress Prints and Photographs Division Washington, D.C.[LC-USZC4-1584]

>> Vendors of all sorts of goods with their many pushcarts on crowded Mulberry Street, the heart of New York's Little Italy, around 1900.

>> Child labor was common in the southern textile industry. Here, an 8-year-old boy named Leo picked up bobbins for 15 cents a day in a Tennessee mill. He said, "No, I don't help me sister or mother, just myself."

TOBACCO

Tobacco was another growth industry in the New South. In the 1880s, James Buchanan Duke took advantage of the invention of the automatic cigarette-rolling machine to overwhelm the tobacco-producing competition. The new machine, invented in 1881 by James Bonsack, could roll 200 cigarettes per minute, the same as what a skilled worker could produce in an hour. Using this competitive advantage, and aggressively advertising his cigarettes across the nation, Duke bought up more than two hundred of his competitors, ultimately forming the American Tobacco Company, one of the largest companies in the country and one of the original twelve companies included in the Dow Jones Industrial Average. It alone was known as "the Tobacco Trust."

INDUSTRIAL FAILURES

Despite the growth of the southern iron, textile, and tobacco industries, hopes of a new industrial South proved fleeting. The growth of the steel industry in Pennsylvania eventually surpassed southern iron production. Furthermore, although textile growth was impressive, the industry employed only a small percentage of southerners, and wages were as much as 30 percent lower than they were in the North, limiting the development of an expansive marketplace (because there were fewer dollars in circulation). Finally, although men like Grady had touted the contributions of African Americans, most black southerners were still barred from industrial employment. Poor white people were far more likely to be employed in railroads, iron, or textiles than African Americans, and these poor whites often resisted efforts at integration in their workplaces. Despite the industrial developments of the late 1800s, agriculture still led the southern economy.

18-2b Southern Urbanization

For supporters of the New South, Birmingham, Alabama, became the symbol of southern urbanization. The city was ideally suited for growth because the Louisville and Nashville Railroad connected Birmingham with coal-mining towns all over Alabama, making it easy to ship the raw iron ore to the city's production facility. And grow it did. Birmingham became the center of the South's iron production in the late nineteenth century, and visitors from all over the world marveled at Birmingham's promise for future expansion. Many investors, including industrialist Andrew Carnegie, fueled this growth by pouring money into Birmingham's iron production, and Birmingham became the crown jewel of southern urbanization.

Atlanta, Nashville, and Memphis all followed suit, taking precedence over water-centered, "Old South" cities like New Orleans and Charleston. But beyond them, similar cities were slow to develop. There was simply not enough industry to merit continued urban expansion, in part because of southerners' unwillingness to increase wages for the South's black population, which would have expanded markets, encouraged growth, and made southern industry more competitive. Immigrants, who could choose where to settle, almost always chose the cities of the North over those of the South because of the depressed wages throughout the South.

18-2c Segregation in the New South

Worse than low wages, though, was the southern drive to repeal political and social rights for black people. After the North retreated from military rule of the South in 1877, race relations became increasingly rigid and violent, especially in areas where black and white Americans competed for economic opportunities. Southern white Democrats continued to deprive African Americans of their civil and political rights by passing laws that disenfranchised African Americans and separated blacks from whites. These efforts were coupled with an even more violent effort to block black citizens from participating in southern public life. Both efforts would prove only too successful. While the South did not have a monopoly on racism, it was where 95 percent of African Americans lived in 1865. And thus racism's worst manifestations appeared there.

>> Workers from the blast furnace at Ensley, six miles from Birmingham, Alabama, where iron ore was converted into about 200 tons of pig iron per day in each of the three functioning furnaces. Note the racial distinction between worker and manager in the New South. New South, with the foreman in front white, while all the workers in the back row are African American.

RACIAL DISENFRANCHISEMENT

Since the decline of Reconstruction, southern states had sought to disenfranchise African American voters, although it typically had to depend on utilizing violence in order to succeed. Formal, and legal, disenfranchisement began in Mississippi in 1890 with what came to be called the "**Second Mississippi Plan**." The plan established legal barriers preventing African Americans from voting. The plan served as a model for other states, and politicians across the South amended their state constitutions to deny black people the right to vote (South Carolina did so in 1895, Louisiana in 1898, and North Carolina in 1900). They did this through a series of questionable laws, such as the poll tax, which required voters to pay a fee to vote; literacy tests, which required voters to prove various levels of literacy; and property qualifications, which

"Second Mississippi Plan" Plan that established legal barriers (the poll tax, literacy tests, and property qualifications) to prevent African Americans from voting in Mississippi; served as a legislative model for other states

Jim Crow laws State and local laws, usually passed in southern states, that mandated racial segregation in public facilities, including schools, restaurants, and rail cars

Louisiana Separate Car Act 1890 law mandating that black people and white people ride in separate train cars; challenged by Homer Plessy

disqualified most black people, who were often too poor to own property. Eventually black citizens in every southern state effectively lost the right to vote. For example, in Louisiana, 95.6 percent of the state's black population was registered to vote in 1896, and more than half of them voted. In 1904, after the passage of these shady laws, only 1,342 of the state's black people were still registered—more than a 90 percent decline in just eight years.

JIM CROW SEGREGATION

Disenfranchisement occurred simultaneously with the development of other laws between 1890 and 1913 that segregated African Americans from white Americans in every public place in the South. These laws, known as **Jim Crow laws**, prevented African Americans from attending the same schools as white people or sitting in the same areas of restaurants. They couldn't ride in the same train cars, drink from the same drinking fountains, or stay in the same hotels. The name "Jim Crow" has its origins in the 1830s, when the famous white minstrel actor, Thomas D. Rice, did a black-face performance baffooning African Americans. His fictional black character was named "Jim Crow," and because of Rice's popularity the name quickly became a prevailing pejorative for a black person. The press began to use the phrase "Jim Crow laws" in the 1890s, and, citing these Jim Crow laws, one historian has called the 1890s the nadir of American race relations. For more on why southerners created the system known as Jim Crow, see "The Reasons Why . . ." box.

PLESSY V. FERGUSON

Black people, of course, challenged these laws, but they were mostly frustrated in their efforts. The most important case emerged in Louisiana, when Homer Plessy, who claimed to be one-eighth black, challenged segregation on trains by sitting in a white car and announcing he was black. Plessy intentionally violated the 1890 **Louisiana Separate Car Act** in order to support a local protest movement against the law. After his arrest, Plessy hoped the courts would rule that the law violated the equal protection clause of the Fourteenth Amendment.

The case eventually went to the Supreme Court, which, in 1896, issued one of its landmark decisions. In

Hulton Archive/Getty Images

The Reasons Why...

There were at least four reasons why southerners created the racially segregated system known as Jim Crow during the decades after the Civil War:

History of slavery. The South, of course, was where the vast majority of American slaves lived before the Civil War, and the major underlying cause of the war was the perpetuation of slavery. Despite losing the war, many southerners sought to restore the South to what they idealized as its antebellum grandeur. This imperfect vision included, and indeed was predicated upon, creating a racist system as close to slavery as possible. The segregated social vision was, however, historically inaccurate, because slavery relied on relatively close proximal relations between black and white people, whereas segregation introduced social and spatial differences that were entirely new.

Science. The South did not have a monopoly on racism, though, and in most states throughout the nation black people could not vote and were denied many other basic rights. Indeed, the best science at the time openly advocated that the white race was superior and ranked the other races in descending order, with African Americans almost always at the bottom. Measurements of skulls and a variety of aptitude tests seemed to confirm the thesis. Using this **hierarchy of races**, white Americans in the North rebuked southern and eastern European immigrants (who were often not deemed "white"). White Americans in the West confidently lorded over Indians and Chinese. And white Americans in the South found justification for creating a social system that not only denied basic rights to African Americans but also segregated them from the rest of society. A large part of the fear, it must be noted, was that these evolutionary "lesser" beings might try to improve their genetic stock by having sexual relations with white women, and interracial sex became a bogeyman behind much of the South's justification for segregation.

Economics. In 1865, about 95 percent of African Americans lived in the South. When the Industrial Age came south, the availability of black workers often kept wages low. This created tremendous animosity from much of the South's white working class. They argued that if black workers could be denied access to certain jobs, wages for white workers would go up. Indeed, the towns that had the highest number of lynchings in this period were those that had witnessed industrial growth and that had a competitive number of African American and white workers.

Politics. The Democratic Party shamelessly took advantage of all these factors, using its political power in the South to create the legal system of segregation known as Jim Crow. While claiming to be honoring southern history and using science as its justification, the Democratic Party secured votes by calling for racial solidarity within the white working class. When the Populist Party threatened to create an interracial working-class party, the Democrats fought back by calling for racial solidarity and by disenfranchising the "unfit" African American voters. By the 1890s, the legal system of segregation that would last until the 1960s was largely in place.

Plessy v. *Ferguson*, the Court declared that segregation laws were constitutional, claiming that, as long as the accommodations were "separate but equal," it was legal to have separate facilities for black and white America. The nation's highest court had evaluated racial segregation and let it stand.

LYNCHING

Violence was another form of political and social intimidation, and it was especially effective in areas where black and white Americans competed for similar jobs. Much of this violence came in the form of lynching, whereby a mob would gather to murder (usually by hanging, then burning) someone whom they believed to have violated a law or social custom. In the 1880s and 1890s, nearly 2,000 black men were lynched in the South.

hierarchy of races A theory based on the idea that some racial groups are superior to others; in the nineteenth and twentieth centuries, many Americans used purported scientific evidence and social science data to argue that white people from British descent sat atop the hierarchy, while racial minorities and new immigrants were less sophisticated and less capable of self-rule

Plessy v. *Ferguson* 1896 Supreme Court case that declared that segregation laws were constitutional, claiming that, as long as the accommodations were "separate but equal," it was legal to have separate facilities for black and white Americans

>> Lynchings were often communal events, similar to a neighborhood picnic. Here, white onlookers observe the hanging body of Ruben Stacy, who was lynched for "threatening and frightening a white woman."

T. Washington exemplified this accommodationist response. In Atlanta in 1895, he delivered a speech that became known as the **Atlanta Compromise**, encouraging black economic development and assuaging white fears of racial intermingling. Black and white people, Washington said, should remain as separate as the fingers on a hand, but they should work together to reach common economic ground. Economic progress, he believed, could take place without racial integration. Washington believed that self-help within the African American community would stop the violence and allow for the progress of the race. He had enormous influence in the late nineteenth century, and his beliefs won wide support among white and black people into the twentieth century.

The other response from black America exemplified a refusal to compromise. For example, Ida B. Wells-Barnett, a writer and editor, led a crusade against lynching during the late nineteenth century after three of her friends were murdered in Memphis, Tennessee. In 1892, Wells-Barnett authored one of the most powerful anti-lynching pamphlets in the country, *Southern Horrors*. She became internationally famous for her protests.

W. E. B. Du Bois similarly criticized Washington's Atlanta speech. In the **Niagara Movement** (an attempt at political organization among black activists in the early 1900s), Du Bois drafted a "Statement of Principles" declaring that African Americans should fight for their rights rather than accept abuse and separation. Du Bois later played an important role in organizing the National Association for the Advancement of Colored People (NAACP). Formed in 1909, the NAACP led a decades-long assault on lynching and Jim Crow laws, continuously (and, for more than half a century, unsuccessfully) pressuring the government to end segregation and outlaw lynching. Du Bois and Washington openly debated black people's options, with Du Bois offering a stinging critique of Washington in Du Bois's famous book *The Souls of Black Folk* (1903). Both responses, it must be noted, failed to prevent the creation of the Jim Crow South.

AFRICAN AMERICAN RESPONSES

Although every African American had thoughts about the rise of racial segregation in the South, there were two major responses from the African American community. The first called for black Americans to accommodate their situation and not fight for political and civil rights, focusing instead on economic success. Booker

Atlanta Compromise Speech delivered by Booker T. Washington in 1895 encouraging black economic development and assuaging white fears of racial intermingling; black and white people, he said, should remain as separate as the fingers on a hand, but they should work together to reach common economic ground

Niagara Movement An attempt at political organization among black activists in the early 1900s; W. E. B. Du Bois drafted a "Statement of Principles," which declared that African Americans should fight for their rights rather than accept abuse and separation

>> The great anti-lynching reformer Ida B. Wells-Barnett, pictured here with her family in 1909, was brought into the crusade after three of her friends were lynched in Memphis.

18-2d Society and Culture in the Postwar South

The white South's brutal restrictions on the region's African American population gained greater popular acceptance in the late nineteenth century through a cultural revival that centered on the "myth of the lost cause." This myth tried to diminish the importance of slavery as a cause of the Civil War by lionizing the rebels of the Confederacy as avid defenders of "states' rights." Not only were many southerners attempting to reinstitute antebellum social practices, but many were also aiming to glorify the cause and culture of institutionalized slavery.

THE MYTH OF THE LOST CAUSE

If the hierarchies of race science provided an intellectual justification for the creation of Jim Crow laws, the myth of the lost cause provided cultural justification for the return of white political power. Associated with the defeat of the Confederacy, the myth was first presented in Edward Pollard's book *The Lost Cause* (1866). The war, as portrayed by Pollard, was a valiant effort fought against overwhelming odds to protect southern independence. Slavery, he argued, was not a cause of the Civil War; rather, it was northern aggression that disrupted the peaceful relationship between white masters and black slaves.

Many organizations were established in the late-nineteenth-century South to defend this myth. These included the Southern Historical Society, founded in 1869 by a former Confederate general to promote a "proper" interpretation of the Civil War; the United Confederate Veterans Association, founded to establish a "Confederate Memorial Day"; and the United Daughters of the Confederacy, founded in 1895 to celebrate the southern war effort. Many northerners, racists themselves, were all too eager to accept this demotion of the importance of slavery as a cause of the war, and throughout the North historians reconceptualized the history of Reconstruction as a horror, characterized not by the violence of the Ku Klux Klan, but by corrupt black domination.

AFRICAN AMERICAN CULTURAL LIFE

As white southerners variously confronted the impact of the Civil War and the meaning of the region's race relations, African Americans found ways to support their struggle for freedom and independence. For example, in Texas, black Americans celebrated their own holidays to keep the issues

>> Forbidden from learning to read or write by pre-Civil War slave codes, African Americans made literacy and education a central priority after the war. In this photo, African American children and teacher are shown in a classroom studying corn and cotton at Annie Davis School, near Tuskegee, Alabama.

surrounding slavery and the Civil War alive. The celebration of **Juneteenth**, marking the date that slaves were formally freed in Texas (June 19, 1865), was the most popular of these holidays, and it spread to black communities across the South. It is still celebrated in many southern communities today. But two other institutions reveal the central concerns of southern black people in the late nineteenth century: (1) education and (2) the church.

BLACK LITERACY AND EDUCATIONAL INSTITUTIONS

One of the most important goals of African Americans after the Civil War was expanding educational opportunity. Forbidden from learning to read or write by pre-Civil War slave codes, African Americans made literacy and education a central priority after the war. As a result, black literacy rates grew dramatically in the late nineteenth and early twentieth centuries. Schools popped up, and African Americans attended institutions of higher learning, such as Fisk University in Nashville (founded in 1866), Howard University in Washington, D.C. (1867), and Atlanta University in Georgia (1865).

The most prominent institution was Booker T. Washington's **Tuskegee Institute** in Tuskegee, Alabama (1881). Washington pioneered higher learning for African Americans and devoted his life to the growth of black education at all levels. However, he was often chastised for his belief that it would be better for black Americans to learn practical skills that would prepare them for industrial machine work than to seek other kinds of education, such as the arts and sciences, that might be perceived as challenging the white hierarchy. In this, as in so many other areas, Washington and Du Bois would spar over the relevancy of different kinds of education. Regardless, educational opportunities for African Americans in the South expanded, if in a segregated manner.

RELIGIOUS LIFE

The second central institution of black life in the South of the late 1800s was the church. After the war, the role of the black church quickly expanded in African American communities. The largest denominations were the Baptist Church and the African Methodist Episcopal

Juneteenth A celebration marking the date that slaves were formally freed in Texas: June 19, 1865

Tuskegee Institute College established for African Americans in Tuskegee, Alabama, by Booker T. Washington in 1881

>> In the aftermath of the Civil War, churches became central organizing institutions within African American society. In this image of an African American church in Washington, D.C., in the 1870s, the congregation sings songs from the hymnal.

North Wind Picture Archives

Church. Churches became the central arenas of black social life after the Civil War because they were supposedly apolitical and therefore unthreatening to the South's white population. Churches did, however, host political meetings and develop social welfare institutions in an era before large-scale public welfare programs existed.

18-3 THE INDUSTRIALIZING WEST

If the Industrial Age brought urbanization and immigration to the North, and if the South entered the age still burdened by the oppressions of history, including a commitment to racial inequality and the myth of the lost cause, the West confronted the new era in its own way. The main concerns of those in the West during the late nineteenth century were getting soil to produce crops and keeping Indians and immigrants at bay. The federal government aggressively assisted in all these efforts.

But working the land is of course difficult, and many farmers struggled to make a living off their newly acquired property. As they fought to make ends meet, another harbinger of the Industrial Age interceded. Large corporations were often lurking in the background, seeking to buy out failed farms in order to create what were then called bonanza farms and what we would today call agribusinesses. The West of the late nineteenth century inspired the lore of the "Wild West," with its tales of cowboys and

Indians. And indeed, some components of the development of the West were in fact wild. But for the most part, those most interested in the development of the West were corporations, usually with bases in the industrial capitals of the North. Like the South, which often depended on northern wealth to industrialize, the West too is sometimes referred to as a mere colony to the rest of the United States. Nevertheless, the Industrial Age did transform the West in ways that few could have predicted.

18-3a Expansive Farming

American settlers in the West had always been farmers, and before the Civil War most Americans in the region were still involved in agriculture. They might have been grain elevator operators, agricultural commodities brokers, or farmers, but in general, most Americans in the West lived off the land. Chicago and St. Louis were booming towns, but most of their wealth was attributable to processing and distributing natural goods like lumber, corn, cattle, and wheat.

THE HOMESTEAD ACT

This commitment to the land only accelerated during the Civil War, when northern congressmen took advantage of the absence of southerners in Congress and encouraged the expansion of a free-labor West by passing the **Homestead Act** in 1862. The Homestead Act awarded 160 acres to settlers who occupied the land for five years, and between 1862 and 1890 it led to the creation of almost 400,000 farms, on which some 2 million people eventually lived. African Americans seeking land, northerners seeking to avoid the industrialization of their cities, and new immigrants all came west.

INDUSTRIAL FARMING

Despite the promises of the Homestead Act, the first homesteaders faced particularly severe trials. On the northern Great Plains, rainfall dwindled to as few as eight inches a year, and pioneers, or **sodbusters** as they were known, faced the ravages of locust swarms, tornadoes, hailstorms, and extreme temperatures. By the 1870s, however, life for Great Plains farmers had improved, mainly because of the Industrial Revolution. As we've seen, between 1870 and 1910, urbanization and immigration led eastern urban populations to increase by 400 percent, and this growth stimulated demand

>> Despite the benevolent promises of the Homestead Act, the first homesteaders faced particularly severe trials. Sodbusters faced the ravages of locust swarms, tornadoes, hailstorms, and extreme temperatures. Here, a family of sodbusters poses outside their earthen home.

Pioneer family pose outside their sod house, Kansas, c.1860 (b/w photo), American Photographer, (19th century) / Private Collection / Peter Newark American Pictures / The Bridgeman Art Library

for western wheat and other crops. In response to this new demand, the eastern plains from Minnesota and the Dakotas and south to Texas became the nation's wheat belt. Corn and hog production also spread throughout much of the West. In addition, the nation's growing rail network offered more, better, and cheaper connections to the markets of the East. Indeed, moving the western commodities to the East was one of the principal reasons for railroad expansion throughout the nineteenth century.

BONANZA FARMS

As technologies improved and markets grew, more and more speculators began growing wheat, and corporations similarly got interested. Often buying land from frustrated sodbusters, these large industrial interests quickly combined several plots of land in order to build huge **bonanza farms** covering thousands of acres.

> **Homestead Act** Federal act, passed in 1862, that awarded 160 acres to settlers who occupied the land for five years
>
> **sodbusters** American pioneers who settled the northern Great Plains
>
> **bonanza farms** Giant farms on the Great Plains, covering thousands of acres and employing hundreds of workers

Across the Great Plains, these "factories in the fields" operated with an economy of scale heretofore unknown to American agriculture. In the 1880s, a single bonanza farm in North Dakota's Red River Valley covered 13,000 acres and employed a thousand workers. By embracing the newest technologies, recruiting cheap laborers from Chicago and other midwestern cities, and securing lands from railroad companies, bonanza farmers increased farm yields dramatically, making food more plentiful in the cities to the east. But they also put greater economic pressures on the small farms.

18-3b Industry in the West

Besides farming, three major industries shaped the post-Civil War western economy: (1) railroads, (2) cattle, and (3) mining.

THE RAILROADS

During the Civil War, northern congressmen passed many internal improvement bills, including several that assisted the development of railroads in the West. Their efforts were just the beginning: during the 1800s, Congress awarded various railroad companies more than 223 million acres to encourage the construction of lines connecting East and West. The arrival of a railroad depot spurred the creation of towns. If an established town lay far from the newly built railroad lines, that town usually dwindled into nonexistence. As a boy, Thomas Edison and his family were forced to leave Milan, Ohio, after the railroads bypassed the town.

THE CATTLE INDUSTRY

Cattle was one of the industries that railroads developed the most (see Map 18.1). Beginning in the 1860s, cowboys began to lead mass cattle drives from Texas, where most cattle were, to various cities along the railroad lines, especially Abilene, Kansas. Abilene was the nation's first "cow town," or town developed in order to facilitate the movement of cattle from Texas and Oklahoma to other parts of the country. From places like Abilene, the cattle would then be moved via rail to Chicago's slaughterhouses and meatpacking plants, where the animals would be slaughtered and the meat packaged and sent in refrigerated rail cars to eastern markets. The most recognizable image of the era was the cowboy, but cowboys were often actually employees of large corporations working to supply the world's demand for beef, and in fact they largely disappeared by the 1880s. Barbed wire, first patented in 1874 and spread through the West by the late 1880s, closed the open ranges on which the cowboys' long drives depended.

Between 1865 and 1885, the work of being a cowboy attracted some 40,000 young men from a variety of ethnic and class backgrounds. Many were white, but about 30 percent of the West's cowboys were either Mexican or African American; hundreds were Native American.

THE MINING INDUSTRY

The third pillar of western industry was mining (see Map 18.1), mainly for gold, silver, copper, and coal. Mining had fostered much of the original settlement in the West, when the first California gold rush of 1849 established the rollicking, boom-and-bust cycle that defined the region's economy. Yet the nature of mining changed dramatically after the Civil War, when most of the gold and silver deposits within reach of individual prospectors had been exhausted. Large investors, often backed by corporations with access to new technology, displaced the roughshod world of the forty-niners. Unlike earlier rushes, the silver strike at Colorado's Leadville (1877) and the gold strike at Cripple Creek (1891) offered few opportunities for individual prospectors because big companies controlled access to the mines. As in the North and the South, large corporations controlled most of the wealth in the industrializing West.

18-3c Western Cities

Farming, mining, and cattle were the lifeblood of the West, and that blood flowed through towns and cities. Western cities connected the natural resources of the West to urban centers in the East. Thus huge cities emerged rapidly in the West, humming with all the industries necessary to convert raw material into packaged goods ready for shipping. No city grew faster than Chicago. With its busy train station and its avid business promoters, Chicago became the capital of western commerce. It developed meatpacking plants to turn cattle into cash and a stock market where speculators could bet on that year's yield. By 1900, 1.7 million people lived in Chicago. And Chicago was not alone. By 1890, a greater percentage of westerners lived in cities than in any other region in the nation. Within a few short years, cities like Dodge City, Kansas, transitioned from a fur-trading post to a cattle town to a stockyard city.

18-3d Outsiders in the Industrializing West

The two groups that did not mesh with the way of life developing in the West were American Indians and the Chinese, both of whom were persecuted as outsiders.

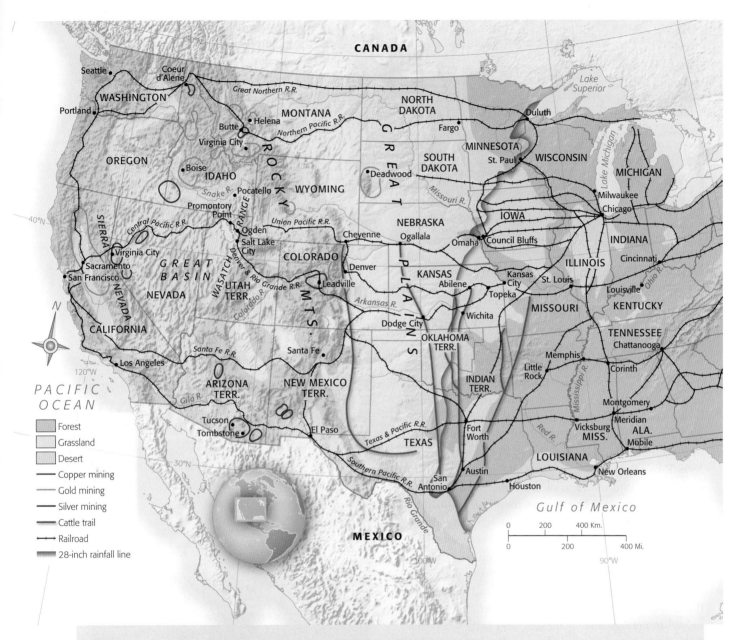

Map 18.1 Use of the Western Lands in the Late Nineteenth Century

>> A map of the western two-thirds of the nation, showing the various uses of the land as well as the cattle trails and railroads.

SUBJUGATING THE PLAINS INDIANS

As always, westward migration entailed conflict with Indians, and it was during the last decades of the nineteenth century that U.S. federal policy became bent on the complete destruction of tribal life. Like immigrants in the northern cities and African Americans in the South, American Indians suffered from the white Americans' racism, paternalism, and belief that the United States had a "manifest destiny" to control all the land between the Atlantic and Pacific Oceans (for more on manifest destiny, see Chapter 13). Although conflict was constant, violence between white Americans and Indians accelerated during the Civil War, as Union troops streamed into the West to put down various Confederate revolts. During those travails, it was often difficult to tell where the Civil War ended and the escalating war against the Indians began.

>> Cowboys push, pull, and persuade cows to get into boxcars that would take them to the slaughterhouses of Chicago.

continuing conflict, U.S. government leaders in Washington, especially President Grant, still declared a desire for peace. In 1869, Grant initiated a so-called Peace Policy that consisted of empowering church leaders to distribute payments and food to the Indians. This "conquest through kindness" aimed to turn the Plains Indians, who had been offered open reservations to continue their traditional lifestyles, to the American ideals of private property, settled farming, and Christianity. Notwithstanding this paternalistic hope, Grant warned the Indians that any Native Americans unprepared to make peace on his terms would be subject to continued military action. In essence, he told them to accept his terms or face eventual destruction.

Unfortunately, many Americans did not follow Grant's Peace Policy, choosing instead to continue to invade lands guaranteed to Indians.

These small "Indian Wars," as the U.S. Army called them, became commonplace throughout the second half of the 1800s. One conflict that epitomizes the violence is the Sand Creek Massacre of 1864. During the early 1860s, the Arapahoe and Cheyenne Indians clashed with white settlers who had been drawn to Colorado by the 1859 Pike's Peak gold rush. As white settlers began to demand the extermination of the Indians, a handful of chiefs sought peace. During one round of negotiation, a Cheyenne delegation near Denver was told it enjoyed army protection until negotiations were complete. The next morning, November 29, 1864, Colorado militiamen attacked the sleeping Indians. By the day's end, more than two hundred Cheyenne lay dead. As news of the massacre spread throughout the Great Plains, anger turned to outrage among Indians, and battles between Indian nations and white settlers escalated.

The increasing violence between Indians and settlers inspired General William T. Sherman, of Civil War fame, to call for the extermination of all the Sioux. But, despite

"Their village consisted of one hundred and thirty Cheyenne and Arapahoe lodges. These, with their contents, were totally destroyed."
—ROCKY MOUNTAIN NEWS, 1864

>> The cowboy boom didn't last long, and cowboys, such as William "Buffalo Bill" Cody, had to be creative to make money, including racing bicycles, as shown here.

One such example is the 1874 military expedition, under General George Armstrong Custer's command, into the Black Hills of present-day South Dakota. When Custer reported to eastern newspapers that there was "gold among the roots of the grass," American prospectors streamed into land not only considered sacred by the Sioux but also promised to them in an 1868 treaty. When the Sioux attacked some prospectors, Custer vowed to protect them. But of course he was unable to do so. On June 25, 1876, his force came upon an encampment of some 2,500 Sioux and Cheyenne warriors, commanded by Chief Sitting Bull and his lieutenant, Crazy Horse. Despite Custer's belief that the Indians would cower to the white army, the two Indian nations annihilated Custer's division of some 200 troops along the Little Bighorn River, in today's southeastern Montana.

The Sioux victory at Little Bighorn was short-lived. The winter of 1876–1877 saw a massive counterattack that caused most of the Indian alliance to surrender. Chief Sitting Bull and some fifty Sioux escaped to Canada. However, cut off from bison, they had a difficult time finding food, and, in 1881, they too surrendered to U.S. forces. Other Indian efforts at resistance also failed. For example, in 1877, Chief Joseph and the Nez Percé nation refused to be moved from their lands in Idaho to a reservation in Washington. Rather than fight, Joseph led a brilliant retreat to Canada with about 250 of his warriors and 450 noncombatants. The army followed Chief Joseph's party through 1,700 miles of mountains before catching up to them and demanding their surrender.

THE DAWES ACT

By the 1870s, many reformers and U.S. policymakers decided that placing American Indians on large reservations might not be the best way to bring order to white–Indian relations. For one thing, reservations obstructed the routes of certain planned railroads. Furthermore, reformers such as Helen Hunt Jackson criticized the U.S. policy on humanitarian grounds. Jackson wrote *A*

>> Chief Joseph.

Library of Congress Prints and Photographs Division[LC-USZ62-1438]

Century of Dishonor (1881), which examined the numerous treaties the United States broke with Indian nations.

Arguments from these reformers led to the passage of the **Dawes General Allotment Act**, which became federal law in 1887. As with Grant's "Peace Plan," the act demonstrated an attempt to alter the tribal nature of Indians. It declared that lands held by Indian nations were to be divided among families and individuals. To prevent speculators from getting title to the lands, the act did not allow Indians to sell them; instead, the government held the land in trust for twenty-five years. At the end of the twenty-five years, individual Indians were to receive title to the land and become U.S. citizens. This was yet another attempt at peace by conversion. In the prevailing American view, Indians were capable of citizenship, but they were not quite ready yet, so they needed to be treated as wards of the state until they learned the ways of American citizens.

As it turned out, the Dawes Act did not help Indians establish farms because the arid land of the northern Plains was unsuited to agriculture. In addition, despite the alleged safeguards, tribal lands were often lost by fraud or coercion, so that, by 1934, white Americans owned two-thirds of lands originally reserved for Indians. Most pointedly, the Dawes Act struck at Indians' greatest strength—their communal ethos—by dividing many of the reservations into individual plots of land.

DIRE CIRCUMSTANCES

In the midst of these efforts, conditions in the Indian nations became desperate. In particular, the loss of the

Dawes General Allotment Act Federal law, passed in 1887, declaring that lands held by Indian nations were to be divided among families, and the Indians were not allowed to sell their lands because the government held these lands in trust for twenty-five years, after which individual Indians were to receive title to the land and become U.S. citizens

> I do not come to fight the white men. If you leave me alone I will harm no one. I have been driven from my home by the white men and am going to the buffalo country to find another.
>
> —CHIEF JOSEPH, ACCORDING TO HIS BIOGRAPHER

bison proved devastating to the way of life that had sustained Indians since they first occupied the Great Plains. In 1865, the number of bison in the United States was some 13 million; by 1891, that number had dwindled to just 865. Railroads and commercial hunters were responsible for most of this decimation, as was over-hunting by the Comache Indians in the Southwest. Without bison to hunt, the Plains Indians had little means of subsistence. Confined to reservations, they obtained only a meager living from farming the barren lands provided by relocation treaties. The poor-quality food supplies from the U.S. government sometimes did not come at all because of the widespread corruption in the government's Bureau of Indian Affairs. Starvation and epidemics pervaded the Indian nations, making it even more difficult for them to defend themselves against further encroachment.

LAST ATTEMPTS AT RESISTANCE

With little hope left, some Indians attempted to participate in a revitalization movement similar to the one preached by Neolin before the Revolutionary War. The central ritual for the Plains Indians became the **"Ghost Dance."** A dance that often lasted five days, the Ghost Dance had different meanings for each Indian nation. One signified a commitment to peace through communicating with one's ancestors and adopting an older way of life. Another interpretation promised that, if done properly and at the right time, the dance would supposedly

"Ghost Dance" The central ritual for the Plains Indians, this was a dance lasting five days that would supposedly raise the Indians above the ground while the land below them was replaced with new land, effectively sandwiching the white men between the two layers of sod, removing them forever

Wounded Knee Massacre 1890 conflict in which the U.S. Army fired on the Sioux, triggering a battle that left 39 U.S. soldiers and 146 Sioux dead

raise the Indians above the ground while the land below them was replaced with new land, effectively sandwiching the white men between the two layers of sod, removing them forever. But, when too many Indians began attending the mass meetings, they attracted the attention of the U.S. government, which sought to arrest several of the leaders. When an attempt to arrest a Sioux Indian who had fired at the army at Pine Ridge Reservation ended in a small battle, killing the Sioux chief Sitting Bull, a group of Sioux seeking to intervene agreed to the U.S. Army's command to encamp near the army at Wounded Knee Creek. On December 29, 1890, an accidental rifle discharge led soldiers from the U.S. Army to fire on the Sioux. After what became known as the **Wounded Knee Massacre**, 39 U.S. soldiers lay dead, while the Sioux suffered 146 deaths, including 44 women and 18 children.

Wounded Knee was the tragic and grisly end of the federal government's century-long war against the Indians. The next forty years witnessed continuing efforts to break up tribal sovereignty—most notably in Indian territories, where the government forced the liquidation of tribal governments. By 1900, the Indian population had reached its lowest point in American history, bottoming out at just 250,000. The "Wild West" of cowboy-and-Indian lore was gone.

THE CHINESE EXCLUSION ACT

In addition to subjugating the Plains Indians, white Americans in the West also targeted another population—the Chinese. In the 1850s, Chinese immigrants began traveling to the American West in search of gold and other lucrative minerals. Most never discovered those riches, but ample work for the railroads provided another impetus for migration, and by 1880, more than 200,000 Chinese immigrants had settled in the United States, mostly in California.

Accounts of their lives suggest that most white Americans initially saw them as hardworking people, but as the number of Chinese immigrants increased, many white Americans challenged their right to be in the United States. In the early 1850s, the California legislature passed a tax on "foreign miners," which led most of the Chinese immigrants to search for work outside of mining. Many found jobs in the railroad industry, which was booming after the Civil War. Indeed, Chinese laborers made up 90 percent of the laborers who worked on the western half of the first transcontinental railroad. Once the American system of railroad tracks was mostly completed, many Chinese immigrants moved to cities, such as San Francisco, and developed an expansive "Chinatown." Most of the urban Chinese worked as laborers and servants, but some rose to prominence and positions

North Wind Picture Archives

Ritu Manoj Jethani/Shutterstock.com

>> San Francisco's Chinese quarter of the 1870s evolved into today's sprawling Chinatown. In the 1870s, Chinese immigrants were forced, by law and practice, to segregate in their own quarters. Today, it's most self-segregation and history that drive the isolation.

of leadership within their communities. These leaders often joined together to handle community disputes, place workers in jobs, and dispense social services.

In the workplace, however, Chinese laborers gained a reputation for working for lower wages than their white counterparts. This situation led to interethnic hostilities, especially among workers. Denis Kearney, an Irish immigrant who created the Workingman's Party of California in 1878, made the issue of Chinese immigration a political one. By the late 1870s, anti-Chinese sentiment extended along the entire Pacific Coast.

In 1882, Congress responded to Californians' demands that something be done to restrict Chinese immigration. At the behest of California's senators, Congress passed the **Chinese Exclusion Act of 1882**, which banned the immigration of Chinese laborers for ten years and prohibited the Chinese who were already in the United States from becoming citizens. The bill was renewed in 1892 and made permanent in 1902. In doing so, it was the first repudiation of the United States's long history of open immigration. While the bill was most certainly racist, it is worth noting that, until 1917, there were few restrictions on wealthy

Chinese immigrants, and in 1898 the U.S. Supreme Court ruled that the children of Chinese immigrants who were born in the United States were still American citizens. Nevertheless, the Chinese Exclusion Act remained law of the land until 1943, when having China as an ally during World War II made the law an embarrassment.

18-4 THE POPULISTS

In the topsy-turvy agricultural worlds of the South and the West, the corporations of the Industrial Age were rapidly turning into transformative players, dominating key industries like railroads and tobacco, and even challenging the sustainability of the self-sufficient farmer. Farmers, both western and southern, felt squeezed by a system that

Chinese Exclusion Act of 1882 Act that banned the immigration of Chinese laborers for ten years and prohibited the Chinese who were already in the United States from becoming citizens

seemed stacked against them. Vulnerable to falling crop prices, often saddled with debt, and unable to meet the forces of corporate capitalism on a level playing field, during the 1860s, 1870s, and 1880s many farmers formed organizations to attempt to protect their rural interests. There were many kinds of farm advocacy groups developed during these years, varying in objective, degree of racial liberalism, and political techniques. But in the 1890s, farmers joined together in the **Populist Party**, which championed the cause of farmers over what it saw as the entrenched powers of banking and credit. Collectively, these agricultural advocates have come to be called the Populists.

18-4a Problems Confronting Farmers

By the late nineteenth century, the business of farming had become a risky endeavor. In addition to the age-old threats of bad weather and poor crops, many farmers were now deeply in debt from loans needed to purchase the large-scale machinery required to increase yields. Thus, while the technological advances of the Industrial Revolution had made farming physically easier, they had also put farmers more in debt. Meanwhile, the great distances between western farms and the markets of the East increased shipping costs, a problem exacerbated by grain elevator owners and railroad companies, who often exploited their monopolies. Similarly, the increase in the amount of goods shipped to market from the expansive and bountiful Great Plains meant that prices plummeted. Farmers who had taken advantage of the Homestead Act were being stretched thin. Sharecroppers in the South owed increasing amounts of money to their landowners. By the late nineteenth century, most farmers were in debt.

DEFLATION

Even worse, they all confronted the basic problem of falling crop prices. While overproduction played a part in pushing down prices, another, more insidious force was at work: deflation. Between 1873 and 1875, the federal government responded to the inflation and rampant speculation that had provoked the Panic of 1873 by putting the nation on a **gold standard**, taking out of

---

Populist Party A political party of the 1890s that championed the "farm" cause of land and crops over the powers of banking and credit

gold standard An economic plan using gold as the primary form of currency while taking paper money and silver coins out of circulation

Munn v. Illinois (1877) A Supreme Court case that declared states could regulate businesses within their borders if those businesses operated in the public interest

---

circulation most paper money ("greenbacks") and silver coins, thus leaving gold as the primary form of currency. But when gold became scarce, the result was deflation, whereby prices fell because there was not enough money circulating in the system. This situation had a ruinous effect on farmers. As deflation pushed down the prices of all goods, including crops, farmers made smaller profits; meanwhile, their debts stayed the same as before. Only now, they had less money with which to pay it off.

18-4b Farmers Unite

Several movements arose in response to farmers' problems of debt and deflation. Two of the most powerful included (1) the Grange Movement and (2) the Farmers' Alliance.

EMERGENCE OF THE GRANGE MOVEMENT

The first movement to protest the farmer's plight emerged shortly after the Civil War. Founded in Washington, D.C., in 1867, the Grange (formally known as the National Grange of the Patrons of Husbandry) began life as a local fraternal organization. But by the early 1870s, as deflation plagued farmers, the Grange became a national movement that expressed farmer discontent. In seeking political solutions to the farmers' problems, it did achieve some limited success. Grangers demanded the regulation of railroad rates, for instance, and succeeded in having rate legislation passed in several states, including Minnesota, Iowa, Illinois, and Wisconsin. They also succeeded in having the Supreme Court declare, in the case of **Munn v. Illinois (1877)**, that states could regulate businesses within their borders if those businesses operated in the public interest. But internal divisions ultimately doomed the Grange, and in the late 1870s its influence waned.

RISE OF THE FARMERS' ALLIANCE

In the late 1880s, another national movement known as the Farmers' Alliance emerged. The Farmers' Alliance was a network of smaller local alliances that first sprang up in the early 1880s in pockets of the South and Midwest and then spread to other farming regions. These alliances acted as cooperatives, meaning that they organized farmers into a unified front to gain bargaining power. Like labor unions, alliances hoped to find strength in numbers, and sometimes they did just that.

THE TURN TO POLITICS

But the alliances failed to be effective in the long term because bankers and commercial interests often simply refused to do business with them. The Farmers' Alliance then sought a political remedy. In 1890, Dr. Charles W. Macune,

>> An idealized view of the National Grange of the Patrons of Husbandry, with each circle representing an aspect of Western life.

the national movement's leader, lobbied members of the U.S. Congress to support his **Subtreasury Plan**. Under this plan, crops would be stored in government-owned warehouses and used as collateral for low-cost government loans to struggling farmers.

In 1890, when legislation to enact the plan was defeated in Congress, desperation among American farmers reached a fever pitch. With deflation running rampant and crop prices continuing to fall, farmers suspected a conspiracy: Eastern bankers and corporations, with the tacit blessing of the government, were deliberately keeping gold out of circulation to lead the farmers to bankruptcy, which would then force the sale of large tracts of agricultural land. The farmers knew they needed to create a stronger, more powerful movement in order to be heard.

18-4c Populism

The farmers thus entered the national political arena in 1892 with a broad and far-reaching movement known as Populism. In 1892, a convention of farmers in Omaha, Nebraska, formed the People's Party (its members were called Populists) to advocate farmers' concerns in local, state, and federal politics. On the one hand, the Populists sought to address such day-to-day issues as high storage and shipping rates. In this vein, Populists also sought to reverse deflation so that crop prices would rise, which would enable them to pay down their debts. In particular, they wanted the government to **remonetize** silver or, in other words, turn silver into an acceptable currency. This would end the economy's reliance on gold, which had made currency hard to find and expensive, and put more currency in the marketplace, boosting prices. On the other hand, they also put forward dramatic and at times radical proposals about ensuring a fairer distribution of wealth, including nationalizing certain industries and creating broad government regulations. Frustrated with what they saw as political inaction, they also advocated increased political transparency, such as the direct election of senators (who had often been chosen by the state legislatures). Like those in the labor movement, the Populists advocated not only improvements in their daily lives but also a dramatic reconsideration of the way the United States was encountering the Industrial Age.

A NATIONAL MOVEMENT

Building from the national network of the Farmers' Alliance, the Populist Movement quickly spread across the country. With their promise of relief for farmers and their far-reaching vision, the Populists overcame existing political and regional loyalties (white southerners were usually Democrats and preoccupied with race, whereas Midwestern farmers, owing their land to Lincoln's Homestead Act, were nearly all Republicans). Tom Watson, a Populist leader from Georgia, argued that white and black sharecroppers alike were in danger of economic ruin, and he spoke to mixed-race audiences that were temporarily united by the Populist message. Some Populists even advocated bringing in industrial workers to fashion a working-class political party. A revolt against the extravagances of the Industrial Age seemed to be brewing.

The Populists rapidly gained ground in the political arena. In 1892, James Weaver, the Populists' presidential candidate, won several western states, and the hard times that followed a financial panic in 1893 sparked

Subtreasury Plan An economic plan advocated by the Farmers' Alliance, in which crops would be stored in government-owned warehouses and used as collateral for low-cost government loans to struggling farmers

remonetize To turn a certain commodity (for instance, silver) back into an acceptable currency

widespread interest in the Populist demands for economic justice. Several Populist candidates won congressional elections in 1894. That same year, Populist supporter Jacob Coxey led an army of roughly four hundred workers on a march from Ohio to Washington to demand government jobs for the unemployed. The year 1894 also saw the publication of *Coin's Financial School*, a national bestseller that made a dramatic appeal for the unlimited government purchase of silver, a plan commonly called "free silver." Populists' demands were on the rise.

THE PRESIDENTIAL ELECTION OF 1896

The mainstream popularity of currency reform, however, proved to be a double-edged sword for the Populists. In the 1896 presidential election (Map 18.2), Democratic nominee William Jennings Bryan was a charismatic thirty-six-year-old Nebraskan whose embrace of the free-silver position left the Populists in a quandary. As a member of one of the two traditional political parties, Bryan stood the best chance of winning the election, but beyond

currency reform, he was not interested in Populist issues such as grain storage and debt relief. Yet a separate Populist candidate would likely split the vote for Bryan, thus handing victory to Republican nominee William McKinley, who favored the gold standard; McKinley's election was the worst possible outcome for the Populists. Faced with this prospect, the Populist Party nominated Bryan for president and Tom Watson for vice president.

The election was one of the most impassioned in American history and ended badly for the Democrats and the Populists. Bryan, whose free-silver "Cross of Gold" speech ("you shall not crucify mankind upon a cross of gold") is one of the most vivid political speeches in American history, never appealed to the largest voting bloc in the Northeast: urban immigrant workers. These workers actually benefited from deflation's low prices because they did not have large debts, and many felt alienated by Bryan's evangelical Protestantism. Thus, by supporting Bryan, the Populists had helped prevent a union of laboring people across the nation.

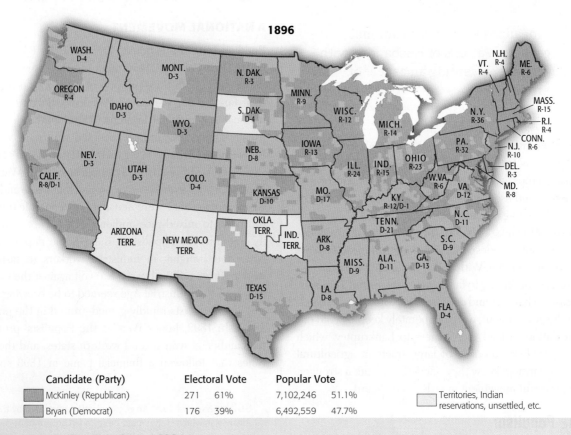

1896

Candidate (Party)	Electoral Vote		Popular Vote	
McKinley (Republican)	271	61%	7,102,246	51.1%
Bryan (Democrat)	176	39%	6,492,559	47.7%

Territories, Indian reservations, unsettled, etc.

Map 18.2 The Election of 1896

>> An electoral map of the 1896 presidential election, showing Bryan's strength in the South and the West, although it wasn't enough to allow him to beat McKinley.

In the end, Bryan carried most of the South and West, but Republican votes in the urban Northeast led to his overwhelming defeat. McKinley gained the presidency, beginning a fourteen-year Republican reign in office and ending the political stalemate that had marked the previous two decades.

THE VANISHING OF THE POPULISTS

After 1896, the Populists' mass movement declined. In the South, southern Democrats beat them back with calls for white solidarity, and indeed, the Democrats' fear of the racial collaboration evidenced by the Populist Movement led to a rapid increase in the speed of African American disenfranchisement, a potent, horrifying response. More importantly to the demise of the Populists, though, was the fact that the long deflationary trend for farmers that had been ongoing since the end of the Civil War finally broke in 1897, allowing many farmers to begin to prosper. When Bryan ran for president again in 1900, he lost even more emphatically than he had in 1896. Nevertheless, despite their political decline, many of the less radical goals of the Populists were achieved in the twentieth century, including the direct election of senators, low-interest government loans for farmers, federal regulation of railroad rates, and regulation of the money supply.

>LOOKING AHEAD...

The Industrial Revolution affected each region of the United States differently. The North became one of the most industrialized regions in the world, confronting the challenges of immigration, urbanization, and the labor movement. Many southerners, meanwhile, attempted to transform their region into a smaller, more humane industrialized hub, but instead fell back into the racial disparities that had long been part of the region's identity. Americans in the West took more and more of that region away from American Indians, as homesteaders and corporate farmers tapped into the soil in order to provide much of the raw materials for the Industrial Age.

All Americans confronted numerous challenges in adapting to the new era. The land did not always prosper. Racism and fear of outsiders provoked reactionary political responses. And northern businessmen lost interest in the regions they exploited once they felt they had tapped their economic potential. Often frustrated by how state and federal governments were not addressing their economic needs, farmers from the West and South combined under the name of the Populists to challenge America's industrial order. Meanwhile, workers came together to fashion the modern labor movement in an effort to protest the most egregious disparities of the new Industrial Age. The Populists and the workers did not achieve most of their goals, but the issues they brought forward—and the radical politics they threatened to usher in—would be central to the third, most successful wave of reformers responding to the Industrial Revolution. It is to those reformers, the Progressives, that we now turn.

STUDY TOOLS 18

READY TO STUDY? IN THE BOOK, YOU CAN:

❑ Rip out the Chapter Review Card, which includes key terms and chapter summaries.

ONLINE AT WWW.CENGAGEBRAIN.COM, YOU CAN:

❑ Collect StudyBits while you read and study the chapter.

❑ Quiz yourself on key concepts.

❑ Find videos for further exploration.

❑ Prepare for tests with HIST5 Flash Cards as well as those you create.

❑ Compare accounts of the Sand Creek Massacre.

❑ Explore the past of Ellis Island.

❑ Read the Dawes Act.

❑ Read Grady's "New South" speech.

❑ Read the "Atlanta Exposition Address."

❑ Read W. E. B. Du Bois's thoughts on Booker T. Washington.

❑ Read Andrew Carnegie's essay "Wealth."

❑ Read the Populists' 1892 election platform.

❑ Read the *Plessy* v. *Ferguson* decision.

❑ Read the Niagara Movement's "Statement of Principles."

What Else Was Happening

1862 Republican Homestead Act grants 160 acres of western lands to farming settlers.

1864 In Sand Creek Massacre, Colorado militia kills over 200 Cheyenne following land disputes with white gold seekers.

1866 Edward Pollard's *The Lost Cause* turns Civil War into Old South mythology.

1869 Completion of transcontinental railroad.

1873–1875 Federal government forces economy back on gold standard at farmers' expense.

1874 Barbed wire closes open range, signaling the decline of cattle drives.

1876: *Sioux and Cheyenne warriors wipe out General Custer's division at Little Big horn.*

Alexander Graham Bell's telephone speeds up long-distance communication.

1877 In *Munn* v. *Illinois,* Supreme Court finds that states can regulate businesses within their borders that operate in the public interest.

1879 John D. Rockefeller's Standard Oil Company controls 90 percent of petroleum market.

Thomas Edison completes experimentation on the incandescent light bulb.

1882 Exclusion Act bans most Chinese immigration and citizenship.

1885: *The first modern hamburger is made in Seymour, Wisconsin.*

1887	With single plots of land, Dawes Act tries to turn Plains Indians into family farmers.	
1890	Second Mississippi Plan models legal black voter disfranchisement for New South.

39 soldiers and 146 Indians die in Wounded Knee Massacre after ritual Ghost Dance. | *Pharmacist Caleb Bradham produces "Brad's Drink" as a digestive aid and energy booster; in 1898 it would be renamed Pepsi-Cola.* |
| 1892 | Carnegie steel plant strike in Homestead pits workers against Pinkertons and militia.

Southern and western farmers form backbone of new People's Party (Populists). | **1893:** *The melody for "Happy Birthday to You" is copyrighted.* |
| 1894 | Populist Jacob Coxey leads unemployed in march on Washington demanding jobs. | |
| 1895 | New York's Coney Island amusement park opens. | |
| 1896 | In *Plessy* v. *Ferguson*, Supreme Court declares racial segregation constitutional.

Democrat-Populist presidential candidate William Jennings Bryan loses to William McKinley. | |
1899	Economist Thorstein Veblen describes "conspicuous consumption" of the rich.	
1903	American and National League teams play first World Series.	
1909	Niagara Movement establishes NAACP.	

19 | The Progressive Era

LEARNING OBJECTIVES

After reading this chapter, you should be able to do the following:

19-1 Discuss the reform efforts of the Progressive era and the groups involved in those efforts.

19-2 Describe the methods used by the various states to bring about reforms in state governments during the Progressive era.

19-3 Compare and contrast the progressivism of Theodore Roosevelt and Woodrow Wilson.

19-4 Discuss the involvement of women's groups in Progressive-era reform movements.

19-5 Describe ways in which American culture was influenced by the Progressive movement.

AFTER FINISHING
THIS CHAPTER
GO TO **PAGE 369**
FOR STUDY TOOLS

If Populism was a rural response to the Industrial Revolution and unionization the working-class response, Progressivism is often seen as the middle- and upper-class response. This is true, in a way. In an attempt to curb the potential radicalism of both the Populists and the working classes, it is often thought that middle-class reformers sought to use ideas of efficiency, sympathy, and a belief in progress to curb the worst abuses of the Industrial Age and ensure a more just social order, one that got rid of abject poverty while still ensuring that their comfortable, middle-class place in American life went undisturbed.

There is some truth to this generalization about Progressivism, but the reality was much more complicated. More than just the middle classes became infatuated with Progressive ideas, and what is today called the Progressive Movement eventually mushroomed to include numerous, sometimes contradicting, projects. Despite the diversity of ideas that fit under the moniker of *Progressivism*, it is true that the ideas at the heart of Progressivism—that benevolent government intervention could rectify the plight of the people, that the economic playing field needed to be regulated to ensure fair access for everyone, that American society could adapt to the advent of the Industrial Age without overthrowing democratic capitalism—became central to much of American social activism no matter what class proposed it. In this way, the ideas central to early-twentieth-century Progressivism have remained a fixture in modern American liberalism, defined most simply as the ideology that lionizes liberty and freedom, but which by the turn of the twentieth century came to mean the idea that the modern Industrial Age requires government to play a role in ensuring a fair distribution of wealth.

The movement that became turn-of-the-twentieth-century Progressivism began with a specific agenda: to clean up the nation's cities. But the social and political endeavors grew from there. Progressivism came to include reforms on state and national levels, including efforts to mitigate poverty, institute labor reform, create greater worker efficiency, and improve the unsatisfactory conditions of urban housing. Borrowing from the Populists, Progressives worked to create a more democratic political process. Borrowing from the labor movement, Progressives also sought greater government regulation of industry. The reforms went on to include the development of conservation efforts like the creation of national parks and the use of experts to help solve persistent social problems. Progressives sought greater efficiency in both government and industry, institutions that would promote and teach middle-class values, and a more codified social order that would teach others the path to middle-class values. Indeed, the Progressives cast their nets so widely that some historians have debated the very utility of the word *progressive*. In general, it is an umbrella term for a host of changes demanded largely by the middle class to rein in the worst abuses of the Industrial Age. Its focus was on the search for stability, efficiency, and kindness within a rapidly changing world. The Progressives' demands propelled them into the political spotlight from the 1890s until the end of the First World War in 1918. Of the three initial waves of reform that emerged in the late nineteenth century, the Progressives were the most influential.

19-1 THE REFORMERS

The Progressives were composed mainly of middle-class men and women, most of whom lived in Chicago, Philadelphia, and New York, although many were from more rural areas like Wisconsin. Most were raised in deeply religious families, and they pursued social reform with the zeal of religious missionaries. As members of the middle class, many Progressives had money, time, and resources to devote to the cause of reform.

19-1a Principal Reform Groups

Two groups were especially important: followers of the Social Gospel movement and women.

THE SOCIAL GOSPEL MOVEMENT

Beginning in the 1880s, Protestant ministers responded to the problems of industrialized society by fighting for social justice and concentrating on ending poverty and prostitution. Ministers like Washington

◄◄◄ **Winning voting rights for women was perhaps the most transformative of the Progressive era reforms, but it was just one of many changes designed to adjust American life to the industrial age. Here, women and their babies march to advocate female suffrage.**

Gladden and Walter Rauschenbusch became nationally known leaders of the **Social Gospel** movement, and their actions prompted many middle-class citizens to fight for Progressive reform. The Social Gospel movement stood in direct contrast with those advocating Social Darwinism, whose focus was not on Jesus-inspired kindness but on the "survival of the fittest."

WOMEN

Progressive reform particularly attracted urban middle-class women. By the late nineteenth century, many women were well educated, and many in this first generation of college graduates ignored traditional social norms and worked outside the home. These women were schoolteachers, nurses, librarians, business clerks, typists, and doctors. However, there were fewer professional jobs for women. Participating in reform organizations was a way to perform a public service and have a job. Furthermore, although since the early nineteenth century women's roles were supposedly confined to indoor domestic spaces (for this, see Chapter 10), with the rise of the Industrial Age it became apparent that the lives of children and families could be affected by government action, such as clean water sanitation, garbage collection, and education for poor children.

Women thus became involved in the public arena as part of their domestic responsibilities. One of the best-known Progressive reformers, Jane Addams, referred to her work as "municipal housekeeping." But Addams was not alone. Women were some of the most active reformers of the Progressive era. For example, nurse Margaret Sanger pushed to increase the availability of contraception. Journalist Ida B. Wells-Barnett led the anti-lynching crusade to stop violence against African Americans. And Alice Paul and others fought for female suffrage on the grounds

Library of Congress Prints and Photographs Division[LC-DIG-ppmsc-04830]

>> By the late nineteenth century, many women were well educated, and many in this first generation of college graduates worked outside the home. Here, a female teacher oversees her classroom full of children.

that women's new role in the public world demanded that they have the right to vote.

19-1b Reforming the Cities

The first target of Progressive reform was the nation's cities. From 1870 to 1900, the urban population of the United States grew from 10 million to more than 30 million. By 1920, the U.S. Census declared for the first time that the United States had more urban than nonurban dwellers. This rapid growth made it difficult for urban governments to provide basic services, such as street cleaning, garbage collection, and schools. Progressive reformers focused on fixing these problems and improving living conditions in the poor areas. If many middle-class people had not noticed the urban poverty of the era, journalist Jacob A. Riis's illustrated book about New York City's tenements, *How the Other Half Lives* (1890), shocked many Americans into "discovering" poverty.

SETTLEMENT HOUSES

One of the most effective Progressive solutions to the problem of poverty was the creation of **settlement houses**, safe residences in poor neighborhoods where reformers could study local conditions. Much like a social

Social Gospel An early-twentieth-century Protestant-inspired movement advocating widespread reforms to curb the worst abuses of the Industrial Revolution; its leaders included Washington Gladden and Walter Rauschenbusch

settlement houses Safe residences in poor neighborhoods where reformers could study local conditions and where residents could hold meetings and receive free health care

>> Urban poverty drove many people to embrace Progressive era changes. Here, immigrant women sell clothes in a crowded marketplace.

PhotoQuest/Getty Images

the moral tone of the Progressive era. Addams emphasized that it was not a matter of *noblesse oblige* that led her into the slums; she wrote that her own life was worthless before she undertook her mission and that the settlement house was as educational and therapeutic for her as its work was beneficial to the poor immigrants around her.

Settlement houses did have their critics, however. Many of the laboring poor who took advantage of the settlement houses were aware that their participation exposed them to "Americanization" efforts that sought to minimize their own cultural heritage and adopt instead middle-class American values. Similarly, many of the reformers disdained the laboring poor's infatuation with popular culture like Coney Island and movies instead of high culture, about which they sought to educate them. Thus, although there was much kindness at the heart of the Social Gospel and the settlement movement, there was a good bit of paternalism involved as well.

THE ANTI-SALOON LEAGUE

Meanwhile, temperance advocates continued to attack the consumption of alcohol, thinking it had a negative effect on the working classes and on the stability of impoverished urban neighborhoods. Reformers saw many women and children plunged into poverty as their husbands and fathers abdicated responsibility by drinking away their paychecks. Temperance workers also feared that the large number of immigrants from southern and eastern Europe, who mostly came from cultures that had long drinking traditions, were increasing America's dependence on alcohol, and thus pushing the nation farther from the middle-class ideal.

To influence legislation, temperance workers started the Anti-Saloon League in 1893, attempting to pass laws at local and state levels. Its interest in politics gave the Anti-Saloon League a higher profile than

scientist's fieldwork, living in the middle of these neighborhoods gave reformers a first-hand look at what needed to be changed. The settlement houses also provided a place for residents to hold meetings and receive free health care. Settlement houses became fixtures in many cities, including Chicago, Boston, and New York.

Hull House was the second but most renowned settlement house in the United States, founded in Chicago in 1889 by Jane Addams (the first, called Neighborhood Guild, was built in New York City in 1886). Hull House exemplified the type of contribution reformers could make. Women made up the majority of its residents, and they lobbied the government to pass

>> Jane Addams of Hull House.

Library of Congress Prints and Photographs Division [LC-USZ62-10598]

better construction and safety laws to improve the conditions in the surrounding tenement houses. The women of Hull House also established a new, more effective process for collecting garbage and fought to eradicate prostitution in the cities by closing red-light districts. Addams's book about her experience, *Twenty Years at Hull House* (1910), became a reform classic and expressed

Hull House The second but most renowned settlement house in the United States, founded in Chicago in 1889 by Jane Addams; its residents lobbied the government to pass better construction and safety laws to improve conditions in the surrounding tenement houses

>> Startling images of urban poverty, such as those created by Jacob Riis and Lewis Hine, helped provoke a middle-class reaction that came to be known as Progressivism. In this image of Lewis Hine's, poor Italian immigrants sit near Chicago's famous settlement house, Jane Addam's Hull House.

the Women's Christian Temperance League (WCTL), which continued to push for local, mandatory temperance education. And, unlike the WCTL, the Anti-Saloon League was composed mostly of men (such as its founder, Howard Hyde Russell, and its most prominent national leader, Wayne Wheeler), who felt the dirty work of politics should be carried out by men. The Anti-Saloon League became the first modern, single-issue lobbying group in the nation. As in the 1830s and 1840s, temperance was one of the major components of the reform impulse.

>> Wayne Wheeler was the chief lobbyist for the Anti-Saloon League, one of the largest Progressive-era organizations. He was said to have controlled six congresses, had the ear of two presidents, and exerted considerable control of innumerable state legislatures.

There were four principal reasons why the Progressive era occurred when it did:

The Industrial Age. The Industrial Age introduced a host of changes to the United States, including the tremendous growth of cities, the increasing plight of the industrial worker, and the close alignment of business interests and government. Toward the end of the nineteenth century, these problems became difficult to ignore, and a large swath of reformers attempted to address them. They sought to end corruption, take politics away from business interests, and create a more caring, if paternalistic, society.

Growth of the middle class. These industries also created an expansive middle class of bureaucrats, marketers, salesmen, and technical workers who possessed the wealth and leisure time to involve themselves in political causes. This was particularly true for middle-class women. The growing recognition that individuals are buffeted by social and economic forces beyond their control led middle-class women to embrace the notion that the outside world was encroaching on domestic space and thus entitled women to push for social and political change. Of course, only women with wealth and leisure were capable of undertaking these tasks, and so it was middle-class women who constituted much of the ground troops of the Progressive movement.

Fears of radicalism. Beyond simply cleaning up cities and making industrial life less dangerous, these reformers were also afraid that, if changes were not instituted, more radical calls for change would gain strength. Thus, while southern and western farmers embraced the potential radicalism of the Populists, and the urban working class formed a potentially radical working-class movement, the middle classes sought to redress the most egregious aspects of the Industrial Age to keep the more radical claims at bay.

Scientific authority. Finally, although the vast majority of Americans claimed to be religious adherents, during the late nineteenth century science rose as an authority with the potential capacity to answer most of society's needs. Thus Progressives embraced a scientific ethos that advanced the notion that, through study and experimentation, people could change the world in which they lived. Scientific knowledge, of course, changes over time, and the Progressives' attempts to harness scientific knowledge led them to embrace dubious positions, such as Frederick Taylor's theory of scientific management and, more damningly, eugenics. But their embrace of scientific rationality also introduced a variety of government regulations and a professional corps of administrators, ensuring that jobs upon which dollars and even lives depended were not in the hands of unskilled political appointees.

19-2 STATE POLITICAL REFORM

Urban reform was just the beginning of the Progressives' battle to rectify the nation's problems. Progressives soon realized that improving conditions for the poor required broader political efforts at both the state and federal levels. They were determined to take the country back from the corrupt and selfish corporate interests that dominated politics without allowing politics to be co-opted by radicals. Many had been influenced by the **Galveston hurricane** of 1900, which utterly destroyed the once-booming island town of Galveston, Texas. Even though previous storms had barraged the city and its population of 42,000, local leaders did not heed the warnings to build a protective storm wall. After the hurricane killed more than 8,000 people, numerous factions began to reform local and state politics, attempting to give the middle class a greater voice in American politics.

19-2a Democratizing Trends

One way Progressive reformers attempted to take greater control of the political process was to change how senators were elected. Hitherto, senators had been chosen by state legislatures. Progressives proposed that senators be elected directly by citizens, enabling citizens to vote for a candidate they trusted. Many senators and businessmen opposed the idea; they distrusted the voters' ability to select candidates and had no desire to campaign before the public. But, in 1913, after several years of agitation, the reform became law as the Seventeenth Amendment to the Constitution.

> **Galveston hurricane** Devastating hurricane that killed more than 8,000 people in Galveston, Texas, in 1900; helped spur demands that local and state governments be more responsive to people's needs

Another democratizing trend was illustrated by the **initiative** and the **referendum**, which together were designed to allow citizens more control over state law. An initiative is a citizen's proposal for a new piece of legislation that can appear on a ballot and be voted on by his or her fellow citizens. A referendum is a citizen-led effort to strike down a law passed by a legislature. Both represented citizen's efforts to take greater control of their state governance. Between 1900 and 1920, initiatives and referendums were adopted in numerous states, and they are still in use today.

Similar democratic reforms were the **primary** election and the **recall**. The primary is a preliminary election designed to let voters choose which political candidates will run for public office, rather than leaving the selection to potentially corrupt politicians plotting in "smoke-filled rooms." The recall is a device by which petitioning citizens can, with a vote, dismiss state officers, governors, and judges deemed to have violated the popular interest.

Despite these democratic impulses, it must be said that most Progressives were not radically democratic, and most did not oppose the spread of the poll tax in the South or, for that matter, other voter elimination tactics that lowered voting numbers dramatically. In general, most Progressives wanted to limit the crony capitalism that shaped Gilded Age politics without allowing radicals to gain control of the political process.

19-2b Professional Administrators

In addition to reshaping the political process in order to ensure that middle-class goals were more easily met, reformers also sought measures to ensure that the right person got the right job. Sometimes this impulse meant that Progressive reformers made certain government positions exempt from voting altogether. One chronic complaint against city political machines was that important administrative posts always went to friends of the "bosses" rather than to experts, and middle-class Progressives wanted to make sure their values were implemented.

To get rid of cronyism, most Progressives supported the creation of a professional corps of administrators. The corps required anyone who wanted a government job to take a competitive exam. Only those who passed could get a job, and only those who excelled could rise to influential, decision-making positions. Ideally, no matter what political party won each new election, jobholders would be allowed to maintain their positions. This system ensured continuity and efficiency rather than a chaotic turnover of personnel each time a new party came into office.

19-2c Progress of Reforms

One by one, states adopted these various reforms, mostly beginning in the West and the Midwest. In Wisconsin, Robert "Battling Bob" La Follette, the first Progressive governor of Wisconsin, created a Legislative Reference Bureau that became known as the "Wisconsin Idea." It consisted of a board of experts (including academics like Richard T. Ely) who ensured sound drafting of Wisconsin's laws for such things as worker's compensation, government regulation of railroad companies, and conservation of natural resources. The keys to reform were appointed commissions of experts working in the name of civil service.

19-3 PROGRESSIVISM IN NATIONAL POLITICS

Progressives had pursued reform at the city and state levels, but the real power of reform lay at the national level. The expansion of Progressivism into the federal arena came after the initial reforms at the state level in the late 1800s and continued under the presidential administrations of Theodore Roosevelt, William H. Taft, and Woodrow Wilson.

19-3a Theodore Roosevelt, Reformer

During his eight years in the White House (1901–1909), President Theodore Roosevelt strongly advocated (from what he called his "bully pulpit" in the White House) Progressive reform and intervened more decisively in national affairs than any president since Abraham

initiative A legislative device designed to allow citizens more control over state law; they could advocate a specific idea and introduce it on the ballot

referendum A legislative device designed to allow citizens more control over state law; citizens could collect a few thousand signatures on a petition in order to advance a specific idea and introduce it on the ballot

primary A preliminary election designed to let voters choose which political candidates will run for public office

recall A device by which petitioning citizens can, with a vote, dismiss state officers, governors, and judges who are deemed to have violated the popular interest

JACK AND THE WALL STREET GIANTS

Everett Collection/Newscom

>> Here, in this political cartoon of the era, a cartoonist compares Teddy Roosevelt to little Jack taking on the giants of Wall Street.

Lincoln. His larger-than-life personality had made him a celebrity. He built on this image during his presidency and developed what he called a "square deal" (a term he borrowed from his poker habit) because he offered an evenhanded approach to the relationship between labor and business.

Roosevelt believed that industrial society was threatened by the immorality of big businessmen, who were more interested in personal gain than in the good of society. Monopolies were the worst offenders, and yet Roosevelt did not believe in hastily breaking up concentrations of wealth and power. Rather, he hoped that large corporations or trusts could benefit the nation by providing more equitable employment and economic expansion. Thus, in 1902, he arbitrated a coal strike in West Virginia by finding a middle ground between the

miners and the owners (recall that earlier most strikes had been broken by the introduction of federal or state troops). Similarly, in 1903, he asked Congress to create a Bureau of Corporations to examine the conduct of businesses in America. As a result of the bureau's findings, Roosevelt prosecuted several companies for breaking the **Sherman Antitrust Act** of 1890, which was the federal government's first attempt to break up monopolies but which was not widely used until Roosevelt took office.

Roosevelt also developed and used the Hepburn Act of 1906, which limited prices that railroads could charge and allowed the federal government to monitor the financial books of the large railroad companies. Roosevelt's actions showed that he was willing to put the force of the federal government behind antitrust laws, garnering him the nickname of **trustbuster**.

And, as a big-game hunter, Roosevelt shared the concern of many Progressives about the loss of the countryside and the conservation of nature. In particular, he was concerned about the nation's dwindling natural preserves. In response, he didn't wait for Congress to act but instead used his executive power to create five new national parks and fifty wildlife refuges designed to protect local animal species. This preserved millions of acres—the greatest amount of land ever protected by a U.S. president. Roosevelt also supervised the creation of the **National Forest Service**.

19-3b William Howard Taft, Reformer?

Roosevelt's successor, William Howard Taft, was a distinguished lawyer and later chief justice of the Supreme Court (1921–1930). He too took on the mantle of being a Progressive. Politically speaking, by the 1910s, it was the only game in town. He busted more trusts than Roosevelt, and he was key in bringing down the Standard Oil Company in 1911. But Taft was never as politically capable as Roosevelt, and in a few instances he overturned some of Roosevelt's own "progressive reforms." Most damningly, Taft broke up U.S. Steel despite the fact that Roosevelt

Sherman Antitrust Act Passed in 1890, the federal government's first attempt to break up monopolies

trustbuster A nickname for those in government advocating antitrust laws

National Forest Service Government agency created by Theodore Roosevelt to preserve land and protect local animal species

> "When i say i believe in a square deal i do not mean to give every man the best hand. If the cards do not come to any man, or if they do come, and he has not got the power to play them, that is his affair. All i mean is that there shall be no crookedness in the dealing."
>
> —THEODORE ROOSEVELT

had previously declared U.S. Steel a "good trust." The various meanings of *progressive* were becoming problematic. Both Republicans and Democrats claimed the term, and it meant different things to different people. Making things even more confusing, in 1912, this dispute between Teddy Roosevelt and Taft led Roosevelt to form a third party, the **Progressive Party**, to win back the presidency from his successor. But in the end, in 1912, Roosevelt and Taft split allegiances and lost to the Democratic candidate, Woodrow Wilson, who advocated parts of the Progressive mission with just as much zeal as Roosevelt.

19-3c Woodrow Wilson, Reformer

When Woodrow Wilson became president in 1913, Progressive ideas were at their most influential. But Wilson did not trust big business as much as Roosevelt. In his platform message, entitled **"The New Freedom,"** Wilson pledged to use government power to destroy big

Progressive Party Political party created by Theodore Roosevelt in 1912 to win back the presidency from Taft

"The New Freedom" Woodrow Wilson's platform message pledging to use government power to destroy big businesses and give smaller ones greater ability to compete

Federal Trade Commission A government agency charged with investigating unfair business practices

businesses and give smaller ones greater ability to compete. He passed a series of laws that increased the size and power of the federal government, and he helped pass the Federal Reserve Act of 1913, which established a regional banking system under the control of the federal government. The act also included a massive tariff reduction, the first since the Civil War, known as the Underwood Tariff. Because Wilson believed that high protectionist tariffs were unfairly enriching America's industrialists, this tariff reduction served as a symbol of his suspicion of big business.

In 1914, Wilson assisted in passing the Clayton Antitrust Act, which put limits on mergers and acquisitions, prevented individuals from being the director of two or more competing companies, and more or less defined what was meant by an illegal monopoly. Also in 1914, Wilson supported the creation of the **Federal Trade Commission**, a government agency that had the right to investigate business practices and issue rulings to prevent businesses from continuing such practices.

Wilson focused on Progressive reforms to regulate businesses, but he never fully supported the social reforms that other Progressives rallied for, such as child labor reform, women's suffrage, and regulation of laborer workdays. Because of the popularity of these ideas, however, Wilson eventually supported the passage of several bills, including the Keating-Owen Child Labor Act, which prevented the employment of children under the age of sixteen (which the U.S. Supreme Court later found unconstitutional), and a bill that mandated a maximum eight-hour workday for American railroad laborers.

By the time he was reelected president in 1916, Wilson had fulfilled many of his Progressive goals, although some were less than benign. For instance, claiming to "clean up" federal government on behalf of the "common good," Wilson allowed the racial segregation of a variety of federal departments within the nation's capital, including the Post Office and the Treasury. Wilson was, of course, a member of the Democratic Party, which, in the South at least, was premised on white supremacy. Thus, as conscientious as they were about the "common good," most Progressives like Wilson were not beyond the common racial perceptions of the time. Reforms of the Progressive era were not always progressive.

 ## 19-4 WOMEN'S PROGRESSIVISM

Although women spearheaded many significant Progressive-era reforms, they were still denied the right to vote. This became increasingly problematic

THE AWAKENING

>> As this political cartoon makes clear (as does Map 19.1), the states in the west were often the first to implement women's suffrage, usually to ensure statehood, and it was from the west that the drive to expand it nationwide emanated. This cartoon depicts a woman from the west reaching out to help the subjugated women in the eastern half of the United States.

Map 19.1 Women's Suffrage Before 1920

WA 1910
OR 1912
ID 1896
MT 1914
ND
MN
WI
ME
VT NH MA
NY 1917
NV 1914
UT 1870
WY 1869
SD 1918
IA
MI 1918
PA
RI
CT
NJ
CA 1911
CO 1893
NE
IL IN OH
DE
MD
KS 1912
MO
KY
WV VA
AZ 1912
NM
OK 1918
AR
TN
NC
SC
MS AL GA
TX
LA
FL
AK 1913
HI

Full voting rights for women with effective date

Women voting in primaries

Women voting in presidential elections

No voting by women

as more and more women understood that individuals in the Industrial Age were buffeted by social and economic forces that were beyond their control and that required the involvement of the federal government. Many women thus sought access to the ballot, and changes began to be implemented, beginning mostly in the western states (see Map 19.1).

Two main groups furthered the cause of women's suffrage: (1) the National American Woman Suffrage Association (NAWSA), founded in 1890, and (2) the National Women's Party (NWP), founded in 1913 and led by Alice Paul. The NAWSA worked state to state (between 1911 and 1914 it achieved the vote for women in California, Oregon, Kansas, Arizona, Montana, and Nevada) to convince opponents that women were valuable assets to society and deserved the franchise. Paul and the NWP, on the other hand, pursued a more aggressive national strategy. On the eve of President Woodrow Wilson's inauguration in 1913, Alice Paul organized a rally of 5,000 women to demand a federal constitutional amendment giving women the right to vote. She also held a six-month vigil outside the White House to protest restrictions of woman suffrage.

Eventually, Paul and several others were arrested on false charges of "obstructing traffic," and, despite receiving wide publicity that embarrassed government officials, were sent to workhouses where they were brutally force-fed after going on a hunger strike and severely beaten by guards. They were eventually released, but their nonviolent efforts increased pressure on the government to give women the right to vote.

The combined efforts of these two groups ultimately led to victory. In 1920, just after the end of World War I, the Nineteenth Amendment was passed, and women won the right to vote.

>> Margaret Sanger.

Library of Congress Prints and Photographs Division [LC-USZ62-29808]

>> Alice Paul.

Hulton Archive/Getty Images

Beyond advocating the right to vote, nonpolitical women's clubs were also vitally important to the Progressive cause. These clubs provided meeting places for African American and southern white women. They also organized social work, invited speakers to discuss topics of the day, and grew networks of women who discussed how issues uniquely affected women. Through these organizations, several women rose to national prominence. Margaret Sanger promoted reproductive rights for women, including advocating birth control. Charlotte Perkins Gilman's extensive writings exposed the inherent paternalism of early-twentieth-century America, especially the organization of its economic life.

muckrakers Investigative writers who exposed bad conditions in American factories, political corruption in city machines, and the financial deceit of corporations

19-5 PROGRESSIVE INFLUENCES ON AMERICAN CULTURE

Progressive reformers did not limit their efforts to improving urban conditions and reforming political systems. Their ideas influenced business and educational practices and attempted to improve the overall quality of life for many Americans. Progressivism was about more than just politics. (To understand why the Progressive era occurred when it did, see "The Reasons Why . . ." box.)

19-5a The Muckrakers

In fact, Progressive ideas spread throughout the nation mainly through the voices of journalists, novelists, professors, and public intellectuals. Among the best remembered are the **muckrakers**, investigative writers who exposed miserable conditions in American factories, political corruption in city machines, and the financial deceits of corporations. Through diverse means, the muckrakers used these exposés to influence city dwellers to be active in flushing out immorality and to understand the positive effects of an urban democracy. Jacob Riis, Lincoln Steffens, Ida Tarbell, and Upton Sinclair were the best-known muckrakers. All wrote classic books in the Progressive tradition, including Riis's *How the Other Half Lives* (1890), Steffens's *The Shame of the Cities* (1904), Tarbell's *The History of the Standard Oil Company* (1904), and, most notable of all, Sinclair's

>> Meat inspectors.

The Jungle (1906), which told the harrowing tale of life in a Chicago meatpacking plant.

The details of Sinclair's factory were real, and middle-class meateaters, including President Roosevelt, were horrified. Sinclair described rats running over piles of rotten meat, embalming fluid mixed into the sausages to disguise the rot, and workers spitting tuberculosis germs into heaps of meat as it baked in the midsummer sun. Roosevelt's staff investigated these tales and found that the writer had not been exaggerating. This prompted Congress to pass, in 1906, the **Pure Food and Drug Act** and the Meat Inspection Act. The first national legislation of their kind, these acts gave the federal government responsibility for ensuring that meat would reach its customers fresh and disease-free.

19-5b Progressivism in Business

In business, Progressives sought not only to improve working conditions and professional standards, but also to improve efficiency. While one of the first measures the Progressives undertook was to improve the relationship between owners and labor, these efforts often

>> Rats running over rotten meat, embalming fluid dripping into sausages, workers spitting into steaks: it's no wonder The *Jungle* prompted the Pure Food and Drug Act. Pictured here is the cover from the book's first edition.

Pure Food and Drug Act Passed in 1906, this act, along with the Meat Inspection Act, gave the federal government responsibility for ensuring that meat would reach its customers fresh and disease-free

> "The task before us, then, narrowed itself down to getting Schmidt to handle 47 tons of pig-iron per day and making him glad to do it."
>
> —FREDERICK W. TAYLOR, *PRINCIPLES OF SCIENTIFIC MANAGEMENT*, 1911

fell flat. For instance, the National Civic Federation, founded in 1900, sought to build a partnership between owners and workers. But the organization never accomplished its goal because there were simply not enough business owners who wanted to help their workers, and many workers did not trust that owners were motivated to help them.

Besides, many Progressives were more interested in improving efficiency, no one more so than the engineer Frederick W. Taylor. Like Progressives who sought to open the political process to more efficient methods, Taylor believed that businesses could also be made more efficient if they changed some of their practices. Taylor's key interests were **scientific management** (the detailed study of the best ways to schedule, organize, and standardize tasks) and time-and-motion studies (the study of exactly how factory jobs functioned). Using minute scrutiny, cameras, and stopwatches, he worked out the most efficient way to wield a shovel full of coal and showed business managers that systematic employment of his methods could boost productivity. He published his results in 1911. However, historians have recently discovered that most of his results were fabricated, leading owners to make what we now know were impossible demands of their workers. Thus Taylor's

scientific management Pioneered by Frederick W. Taylor, the detailed study of the best ways to schedule, organize, and standardize work tasks

Progressive Education Association Formed in 1919, this national association supported and advocated for education reforms that taught children to make good moral and political choices

eugenics An early-twentieth-century movement centered on the belief that it was possible to improve the human species by discouraging or outlawing reproduction by various people thought to have undesirable traits

efforts to improve efficiency made working conditions even more miserable.

19-5c Progressive Education

Progressives also pursued efficiency in the educational system. They argued that, in order for citizens to work better in their jobs and participate in politics, they needed to be well educated. Thus, in cities and towns, Progressives helped build more schools and improved teacher education and salaries.

The most famous Progressive theorist of education was John Dewey, a philosopher at the University of Chicago. Dewey founded the Laboratory School for elementary and middle school children, where he pioneered child-centered education. The idea was to allow students to pursue their own interests rather than force them to memorize a curriculum. Dewey argued that this approach taught children to live in a democracy and to make good moral and political choices for the rest of their lives. Eventually, Progressive educational ideas became so popular that, in 1919, Progressives formed the **Progressive Education Association** to support and advocate for these education reforms.

19-5d The Role of Laws

Above all, the Progressives avowed a stern belief in laws as vital instruments of social change. Instead of using large social movements or force, Progressives sought to change the way Americans lived by crafting laws against what they saw as social wrongs. In addition to the many trustbusting, tariff, and voting laws they advocated, Progressives used the courts to limit the number of hours women and children could work and to end the most brutal forms of racial antagonism. They sometimes succeeded, as in the case of *Muller* v. *Oregon* (1908), which upheld a law limiting the number of hours that women could work in a day. Progressives were, however, unsuccessful in passing lasting child labor laws and in promoting a federal anti-lynching law.

The Progressives' love of laws led in dark directions as well. *Muller* v. *Oregon*, for example, was premised on the argument that women were weaker than men and unable to enter contracts on their own. This idea demonstrated the limitations of Progressivism in a male-dominated society.

More damningly, in the name of improving human genetic qualities on behalf of the common good, some Progressives argued that it would be better to sterilize people with so-called less desirable qualities. This movement, called **eugenics**, was a worldwide phenomenon, led by the Briton Sir Francis Galton, who was Charles Darwin's cousin and who was infatuated with applying his cousin's ideas beyond the forces of biological evolution. In the United States, beginning in 1896, many states began prohibiting anyone who was "epileptic, imbecile, or feeble-minded" from getting married. In 1907, Indiana was the first of more than thirty states to require compulsory sterilization of certain kinds of criminals and the mentally ill. The U.S. Supreme Court upheld the constitutionality of these laws in 1927, and they continued to be the law of the land in certain states until the 1970s. Prominent supporters of eugenics included Teddy Roosevelt, Woodrow Wilson, and Margaret Sanger.

>LOOKING AHEAD . . .

By the 1910s and into the 1920s, three sizeable challenges to the politics and society of the Industrial Age had arisen. All were in some way a reaction to the changes brought about by the Industrial Revolution. The establishment of the first labor unions created a system of industrial labor that existed throughout much of the twentieth century. The agrarian interests associated with the Populists may have failed politically, but some of the principal tenets of their cause eventually came to fruition. Finally, the Progressives, who were the most influential of the three, enacted political, social, and educational reforms that are with us today. Their efforts to fend off the threats to capitalism both from above (corporate interests and trusts) and from below (radicals and socialists) were the most successful, even if the panoply of ideas brought forward under the banner of Progressivism meant that, as a movement, it lost coherence. Still, the number of laws and reforms passed is remarkable, a reflection of the energy of the Industrial Age when that energy is aimed at instituting progressive reform.

By the 1910s, the word *progressive* had become almost synonymous with decency and cleanliness, and politicians of all kinds were careful to depict themselves as Progressives, even if their record showed them to be dyed-in-the-wool conservatives. The fact that such a wide array of political types claimed the Progressive label illustrates how powerful the Progressive impulse had become.

But progressive ideas were not simply an American phenomenon. American reformers borrowed from other nations confronting the Industrial Age, especially those in western Europe. Jane Addams, for example, got the idea for Hull House after visiting a settlement house in England. And the paternalism mixed with kindness that marked American Progressivism would not stay in just the United States either. Many American Progressives sought to spread their ideals throughout the world. Although they often did so with the best of intentions, their actions would generate a host of critics both at home and abroad. And it is to America's renewed interest in world affairs that we turn next.

STUDY TOOLS 19

READY TO STUDY? IN THE BOOK, YOU CAN:

❏ Rip out the Chapter Review Card, which includes key terms and chapter summaries.

ONLINE AT WWW.CENGAGEBRAIN.COM, YOU CAN:

❏ Collect StudyBits while you read and study the chapter.

❏ Quiz yourself on key concepts.

❏ Find videos for further exploration.

❏ Prepare for tests with HIST5 Flash Cards as well as those you create.

❏ Read Jacob A. Riis's *How the Other Half Lives.*

❏ Read Margaret Sanger's speech "The Morality of Birth Control."

❏ Read Taylor's *Principles of Scientific Management.*

❏ Read more from *The Jungle.*

❏ Read "The New Freedom."

CH19 TIMELINE

1882 Electric lights are first used on a Christmas tree.

1883: *Germany institutes the world's first universal health care system.*

1889 Jane Addams founds Hull House in Chicago, the nation's second but most renowned settlement house.

1890 Sherman Antitrust Act is federal government's first effort to curb monopolies.

Founding of National American Woman Suffrage Association (NAWSA).

1893 Temperance activists form Anti-Saloon League to pass laws on state and local level.

1900 National Civic Federation tries to build partnership between workers and owners.

Hurricane kills more than 8,000 in poorly prepared Galveston, Texas, prompting city reform.

1902: *The teddy bear ("Teddy's bear") is created by a Brooklyn shop owner after he sees a newspaper cartoon depicting hunter Theodore Roosevelt with a bear cub.*

1903: *President T. Roosevelt forms Bureau of Corporations to investigate monopolies.*

Crayola crayons go on sale.

1906 Hepburn Act caps railroad prices and introduces federal oversight.

Upton Sinclair publishes novel The Jungle about life in Chicago meatpacking plant.

Congress passes Pure Food and Drug Act and Meat Inspection Act to protect consumers.

1908 Supreme Court upholds maximum-hours law for women in *Muller v. Oregon*.

1911-1914 Women gain suffrage in California, Oregon, Kansas, Arizona, Montana, Nevada.

1911: *Great Britain passes the National Insurance Act, creating a system of social welfare to protect workers against illness and unemployment, as well as providing retirement pensions.*

1912 Disappointed with successor Howard Taft, T. Roosevelt forms Progressive Party.

1913
Seventeenth Amendment replaces senators' election by state legislatures with popular vote.

Founding of National Women's Party led by Alice Paul.

Alice Paul leads march of 5,000 women to White House, demanding suffrage.

Woodrow Wilson signs Federal Reserve Act establishing new banking system.

Wilson signs Underwood Tariff to expose monopolies to competition.

1914
Clayton Antitrust Act defines and outlaws unfair business practices.

Federal Trade Commission investigates and rules on legality of business practices.

1916
Keating-Owen Child Labor Act prohibits employment of children under sixteen.

1920
Nineteenth Amendment grants women the right to vote.

20 | Becoming a World Power

Naval Parade held in honor of Commodore George Dewey, 1877-1917, 1898 (oil on canvas), Fanning, Fred (1850-1917/26) © Museum of the City of New York, USA/Bridgeman Art Library

LEARNING OBJECTIVES

After reading this chapter, you should be able to do the following:

20-1 Explain the major reasons for the growing call in the late 1800s for the United States to develop an empire.

20-2 Describe the first moves the U.S. made toward empire.

20-3 Explain the major reasons for the Spanish-American War of 1898, and discuss the controversy over imperialism that developed after the war.

20-4 Describe the growth of American imperialism during the Progressive era.

20-5 Discuss World War I, including reasons for the war, American experiences during the war, and effects of the treaty ending the war.

AFTER FINISHING
THIS CHAPTER
GO TO **PAGE 391**
FOR STUDY TOOLS

Between 1867 and 1917, the United States became a true world power for the first time. To a large degree, this was a result of the Industrial Revolution. The search for overseas markets and the ideology of manifest destiny (which, as developed in the 1840s, held that Americans were destined by God to possess all the land between the Atlantic and Pacific oceans) spurred the United States to keep pushing outward, building up its navy in the 1880s and beginning to acquire overseas territories in 1890s. During these years, American military might often backed up American commercial interests, creating an "economic imperialism" that sometimes weighed on other countries almost as heavily as outright conquest. Many Americans also felt they had a duty to "civilize" the so-called "lesser" nations of the world, a notion based in no small part on feelings of racial superiority. Victory in the Spanish-American War in 1898 was a turning point, adding to the nation a string of island colonies in the Caribbean Sea and the Pacific Ocean to U.S. territory, and declaring to the world that the United States was an emerging global power.

Many Americans vigorously protested their country's new imperialism, citing the U.S. government's violent atrocities, the racist ideals that propelled America's imperial march, and the moral problem of allowing business interests to drive armed diplomacy. Nevertheless, these imperialist developments led the country into the First World War and then served as the basis for U.S. foreign policy for much of the twentieth century.

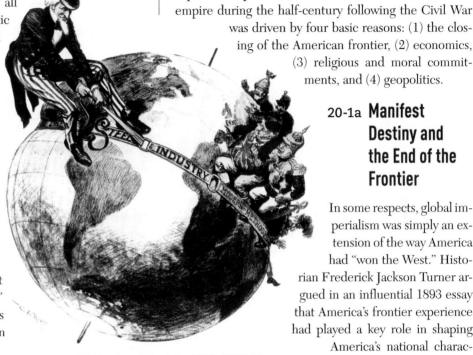

A STEEL CINCH ON THE WORLD

>> This 1901 cartoon, showing Uncle Sam working with American Steel to control the world, demonstrated both the contentious nature of American imperialism, and its rising dominance at the turn of the twentieth century.

North Wind/North Wind Picture Archives

20-1 WHY AN AMERICAN EMPIRE?

While notions of racial superiority justified America's expansionist positions, America's creation of an overseas empire during the half-century following the Civil War was driven by four basic reasons: (1) the closing of the American frontier, (2) economics, (3) religious and moral commitments, and (4) geopolitics.

20-1a Manifest Destiny and the End of the Frontier

In some respects, global imperialism was simply an extension of the way America had "won the West." Historian Frederick Jackson Turner argued in an influential 1893 essay that America's frontier experience had played a key role in shaping America's national character, including its democratic political institutions and its free-spirited capitalism. In "The Significance of the Frontier in American History," Turner even suggested (with some trepidation) that the frontier was so integral to the nation's psyche that Americans might require a new frontier in order to ensure the survival of its democracy. "American energy," the **Turner Thesis** concluded prophetically, "will demand a wider field for its

Turner Thesis Argument put forward by historian Frederick Jackson Turner that the presence of the western frontier had shaped the American character and allowed the development of democracy and capitalism, necessitating in the wake of its 1893 disappearance "a wider field for its exercise"; was used to buttress attempts to propel American interests abroad

◀◀◀ **A national naval parade in honor of Commander George Dewey, celebrating one of his victories—and the might of the U.S. Navy. During the final decades of the nineteenth century and the first decades of the twentieth, the U.S. became a truly global power for the first time.**

exercise." To Turner, the widespread belief in the idea of manifest destiny meant that many Americans might feel it natural to continue to explore and conquer, even if that meant crossing seas and continents.

20-1b Financial Reasons

Another—and in many cases more decisive—reason for the surge in American overseas imperialism was that American business leaders wanted access to overseas markets and materials. Like those who had first explored the American West, these business leaders usually received the assistance and protection of the federal government. They articulated a "glut thesis," which argued that the financial panics of the 1870s and the 1890s were the result of the overproduction of goods, as the industrialized economy endured painful fits and starts. One obvious resolution to overproduction is the creation of new markets, and this led business leaders and politicians to advocate American imperial adventures abroad. In addition to creating new markets, American business leaders worked in close contact with its political leaders in order to use American financial muscle both to allow American businesses greater access to nations around the globe, and also to use American financial strength to bully countries into doing what the U.S. wanted. The use of a country's financial power to extend its diplomatic interests is often called "**dollar diplomacy**." To a great extent, business interests drove American foreign policy very early on.

20-1c Religious and Moral Reasons

Meanwhile, many Christian leaders believed that Christianity had made Western society the evolutionary pinnacle of civilization. American missionaries sought converts, believing they were bringing both progress and salvation to the "uncivilized" peoples of the world. The mood of Protestant imperialism was captured in Reverend Josiah Strong's *Our Country* (1885), which argued that white Christian Americans stood at the top of civilization and therefore had a moral duty to bring less privileged peoples the benefits of progress and the fruit of the Christian Gospel.

The racialist tinge of this argument held that the United States should join the other nations of Europe in spreading the benefits of democracy and white

dollar diplomacy The use of a country's financial power to extend its diplomatic interests, including but not limited to using private capital from the U.S. to further American interests overseas

Treaty of Wanghia Agreement between China and the United States signed in 1844, opening several Chinese ports to American trade

civilization to the world. In his famous 1899 poem, "The White Man's Burden," the British poet Rudyard Kipling urged the United States to embrace what he saw as its imperialist obligations. (For more on "the hierarchy of races," see Chapter 18.)

20-1d Geopolitical Reasons

Finally, beginning in the 1870s, several European powers raced to conquer vulnerable but resource-rich regions of Africa and Asia. Such conquests brought these countries substantial profits and a worldwide network of commercial and military bases. Many Americans feared that the United States, by remaining isolated from the land grabbing, would lose access to world markets and geopolitical power.

20-2 BEGINNINGS

Dollars propelled the initial drive overseas, first throughout the Pacific, then to Latin America.

20-2a Pacific Acquisitions

American businessmen and diplomats had long been attempting to gain access to markets in the Pacific, seeking, first, access to China and Japan, then permanent settlements in various islands in the Pacific. Their goal was to sell American goods to Asia.

ASIA

Ever since the 1840s, the U.S. government had sought to increase commercial ties with China and Japan in hope of selling more U.S. goods. Treaties with China, notably the **Treaty of Wanghia** in 1844, had opened several Chinese ports to American trade. In 1853, the U.S. Navy appeared in Tokyo Bay and ultimately forced Japan to open to the West, too. As the European powers continued to scramble for power in the Pacific, the United States risked losing access to Asian trade unless it created more links to the region, and so it did.

SAMOA

Seeking its first permanent footholds in the Pacific, in 1856 the United States claimed a number of small, uninhabited islands strewn across the Pacific, and the tiny Midway Islands were annexed formally in 1867. In 1872, island chieftains in Samoa granted the United States a naval base at Pago Pago, but instability in the nation during the 1880s prompted Britain, Germany, and the United States to sign a treaty jointly occupying the islands. In 1899, the treaty was revised to grant the

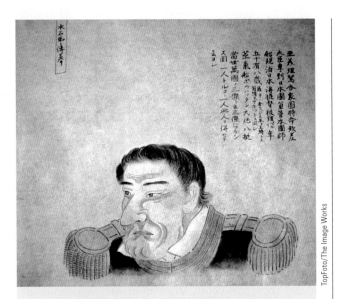

>> A Japanese artist made this rendering of American Commodore Matthew C. Perry at the time of his arrival in Japan, in the 1850s. Its unflattering nature suggests not everyone was happy with the United States expanding its interests beyond its borders.

United States a protectorate over the eastern islands, which became today's territory of American Samoa.

ALASKA

Further Pacific expansion occurred in 1867, when the United States purchased the huge territory of Alaska from Russia. Secretary of State William Seward orchestrated the purchase, claiming that (1) Russia, which had been a Union ally during the American Civil War, needed the money; (2) the United States needed more land for expansion; and (3) Britain, which controlled today's Canada, needed to be warned off the continent; possession of Alaska, he pointed out, would surround Canada from both the north and the south. Alaska was so isolated and barren, though, that the purchase was lambasted in the newspapers and was commonly called "Seward's Folly."

HAWAI'I

But the major object of American expansion in the Pacific was Hawai'i. Since the 1850s the independent kingdom of Hawai'i had looked to the United States for protection against other colonial powers. It signed a trade agreement with the United States in 1875, and in 1887 it granted the United States the right to construct a naval base at Pearl Harbor, on the island of Oahu. By the 1880s, American businessmen had acquired a majority of the island's wealth through heavy investment in Hawaiian sugar plantations.

And in 1887, American settlers staged a nonviolent coup to transfer power from the Hawaiian monarchy to the legislature, which the settlers had elected and thus had some control over.

In 1890, after a change in U.S. tariff policy imposed heavy duties on exports from the islands to the mainland, the same group of settlers urged the United States to annex Hawai'i, thereby granting its products exemption from U.S. tariffs. The Hawaiian leader, Queen Lili'uokalani, rejected this scheme, seeing it as nothing more than the illegal takeover of her country. And so, in 1893, American rebels, with aid from U.S. navy troops in Pearl Harbor, seized the queen and declared a provisional government under Sanford B. Dole, an American lawyer (his cousin was the pineapple magnate James Dole). The rebels applied for annexation to the United States but were rejected by President Grover Cleveland's administration, which considered the coup illegitimate.

>> American business leaders helped orchestrate the dethroning of Hawaii's Queen Lili'uokalani, pictured here.

Using Texas as a model, Dole's rebels remained in control of what they now called the Republic of Hawai'i and continued to agitate for incorporation into the United States. The rebels eventually succeeded in 1898, when America, embroiled in a Pacific war against Spain, rediscovered the strategic importance of Pearl Harbor. Congress approved the annexation of Hawai'i, and, in 1900, the islands' people became U.S. citizens.

20-2b Latin America

Another region of American economic interest was resource-rich Latin America. The European powers had a centuries-old colonial presence there, and under the growing expansionist mood, the United States set about undercutting European control and opening up American business opportunities in Mexico, Colombia, and the Dominican Republic.

An influential showdown came in the Venezuela Crisis of 1895. Independent Venezuela had quarreled with Britain since the 1870s over its eastern border with British Guiana, a region rich in gold and with a river that served as a major commercial route. The British Empire's unrivaled naval power meant that it usually prevailed in conflicts with weaker nations, but in 1895 Venezuela gained the support of the U.S. secretary of state, Richard Olney, who declared that the situation was under the domain of the Monroe Doctrine, meaning that the United States was the controlling power in the Western Hemisphere. Britain backed off, especially when Theodore Roosevelt (the future president) called for war to back up U.S. policy. A British and American team of negotiators then settled the boundary issue peaceably, though scarcely bothering to consult the Venezuelans.

The world's governments took note that Britain had surrendered at least some of its claim rather than antagonize the United States. Thus emboldened, the United States began envisioning an ever-growing role on the world stage.

20-2c The Naval Buildup

Spurred by these kinds of acquisitions in the name of American business interests, in 1883 Congress authorized the construction of powerful all-steel, steam-driven battleships, armed with the latest long-range artillery. The North's decisive use of naval power during the Civil War influenced this buildup. Using ironclad warships, the Union had successfully blockaded several key Confederate ports, all but crippling the South in the process. With its eyes now further afield, the American military began a broad naval buildup.

MAHAN

Another influence on U.S. military leaders was the work of Alfred Thayer Mahan, a former Civil War naval officer. In 1890 Mahan published *The Influence of Sea Power Upon History, 1660–1783*, which argued that, in modern times, national greatness was always based on naval strength. Using eighteenth-century Britain as a model, Mahan argued that America must have warships to protect its merchants and must also maintain overseas colonies for naval supply bases.

BUILDUP

The Civil War experience and Mahan's arguments led the United States to build up its navy. Between 1889 and 1893, the U.S. Navy grew from fifteenth largest in the world to seventh. In addition, Mahan's arguments about the importance of naval warfare led American strategists and policymakers to call for a stronger U.S. territorial presence overseas.

 20-3 # THE SPANISH-AMERICAN WAR

Using this naval might, the next major international dispute—the Spanish-American War of 1898—transformed the United States into a major overseas power. Ironically, the war was not motivated by imperial appetites. Instead, it was fought for a range of humanitarian, geopolitical, and commercial reasons that, once the war was won, prompted the United States to take a larger global role at the turn of the century.

The Spanish-American War was ignited by Spain's harsh treatment of the Cuban independence movement. Cuba was one of Spain's last colonial possessions in the Western Hemisphere, but the Cuban people, resentful of Spain's heavy-handed rule, had struggled for decades to win their independence. In 1895, their resentment burst into violence when Cuban resistance leader José Martí sparked an interracial rebellion that the Spanish government attempted to put down with brutal force. Martí was eventually killed in battle, making him a martyr to the Cuban people. As the war for Cuban independence continued, the political instability devastated Cuba's economy, which was a blow to Americans who had invested in Cuba's sugar plantations. Having an unstable nation so close to U.S. borders concerned American politicians, especially when American business interests might be compromised.

Recognizing a good story when they saw one, newspaper editors (notably Joseph Pulitzer with his

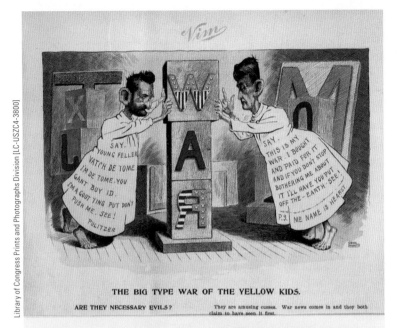

THE BIG TYPE WAR OF THE YELLOW KIDS.

ARE THEY NECESSARY EVILS?   They are amusing cusses. War news comes in and they both claim to have seen it first.

>> Newspapermen Joseph Pulitzer and William Randolph Hearst published provocative, incendiary stories about Spanish atrocities in an effort to push the United States to war—and sell newspapers—a technique known as yellow journalism. This political cartoon shows them in yellow dresses playing with toy blocks that read, "W-A-R."

New York World and William Randolph Hearst with his *New York Journal*) published graphic descriptions of the atrocities committed by the Spanish. These sensationalistic stories fomented anti-Spanish feeling among the American public, who may or may not have known of the substantial American investment in Cuba's sugar and who probably were unaware of the interracial nature of Cuba's fighting forces. During these years, this kind of journalism garnered the name **yellow journalism**, defined as journalism that shows little dependence on fact or research and instead uses sensationalized headlines and storylines to sell newspapers or magazines.

The war between Spain and Cuba had been raging for three years, and Spain was virtually defeated, when two events in February 1898 finally pushed the United States into the fray: (1) American spies intercepted a letter from Spain's U.S. ambassador Enrique Dupuy de Lôme to his superiors back home. Published from coast to coast, the so-called de Lôme letter disparaged U.S. president William McKinley as a petty popularity seeker who was not strong enough to intervene in Cuba and (2) less than a week later, the American battleship USS

Maine (stationed in Havana's harbor, ostensibly to protect American citizens in Cuba from riots) suddenly blew up, killing 266 men. Historians now know that the Maine exploded due to a fire that started in its coal bunkers, but at the time, war provocateurs argued that Spanish saboteurs were responsible.

Cubans did not want Americans to enter the war, considering it an unnecessary and unwelcome imperialistic grab in a war they had nearly already won. However, anti-Spanish animosities in the United States were at a fever pitch, and pro-war agitators such as Theodore Roosevelt and Henry Cabot Lodge insisted on entering the war. The Spanish government, aware of its inferior forces, offered to capitulate to American demands and recognize Cuban autonomy. Nevertheless, President McKinley, fearful of a biracial republic so close to the Florida coast and worried about what a Cuban government might do with American business interests, sought war in order to prevent the Cubans from winning. Two days later he asked Congress for the right to use the military to blockade Cuba.

Spain responded by declaring war on April 24, 1898. McKinley's war message to Congress proclaimed that the United States would fight Spain "[i]n the name of humanity, in the name of civilization, [and] in behalf of endangered American interests." McKinley thus presented the war, not as the beginning of an imperial conquest, but as a necessary humanitarian intervention, although he noted America's economic reasons behind the war as well. Congress tried to hold McKinley to this point by passing the **Teller Amendment**, which barred the United States from annexing Cuba, forcing the U.S. to leave Cuba independent once the war was over.

20-3a **War on Two Fronts**

American military strategists decided to fight Spain on two fronts: in Cuba and the Philippines.

yellow journalism Journalism that shows little dependence on fact or research and instead uses sensationalized headlines and storylines in order to sell more newspapers or magazines; pioneered by Joseph Pulitzer and William Randolph Hearst during the buildup to the Spanish-American War

Teller Amendment Legislation that barred the United States from annexing Cuba, forcing it to leave Cuba independent once the Spanish-American War was over

THE PHILIPPINES

Like Cuba, the Philippines had long been a Spanish colonial possession, and Spain's fleet was stationed in Manila Bay. For months the U.S. fleet in the Pacific had been secretly preparing to invade the Philippines in the event of war, and, when war was finally declared, a squadron of American ships left its port in Hong Kong. In Manila Bay on May 1, the American squadron took advantage of its superior equipment to destroy or damage all Spanish ships, killing nearly four hundred Spanish sailors while suffering no American fatalities. Commodore George Dewey became a hero in America for his leadership.

FILIPINO INDEPENDENCE?

Lacking sufficient ground troops, Dewey was able to beat the Spanish fleet but was unable to occupy the islands. Filipino resistance leader Emilio Aguinaldo, who had been fighting the Spanish for years, declared the Philippines independent in June. In August, American reinforcements arrived, occupying Manila and barring Aguinaldo's forces from the city, a move that would have grave consequences. Filipino independence was not what America had in mind when it decided to fight Spain on the Filipinos' behalf.

CUBA

Meanwhile, back in Cuba, the United States mounted a rapid campaign to shatter the Spanish army and besiege the port city of Santiago, where Spain's Caribbean fleet was anchored. In June 1898, 17,000 U.S. troops invaded Cuba and quickly surrounded Santiago. The most colorful contingent of the American forces was the **Rough Riders**, led by the future president Theodore Roosevelt. An early and energetic supporter of the war, Roosevelt had long argued that American society needed to be more rugged and "manly." It was in this spirit that he resigned his desk-bound naval post in order to lead a regiment of cavalry volunteers. Roosevelt and Leonard Wood, a veteran of the Indian Wars, gathered a mixture of Wall Street businessmen, Ivy League volunteers, western cowboys, and a few Native Americans to fight in Cuba.

SAN JUAN HILL

In early July 1898, the Rough Riders joined other American forces, including an African American squadron, in

Rough Riders The most colorful contingent of the American forces in the Spanish-American War, led by Theodore Roosevelt

>> Roosevelt gathered a mixture of Wall Street businessmen, Ivy League volunteers, western cowboys, and a few Native Americans to fight in Cuba. Here Roosevelt is pictured dressed in Rough Rider garb and striking a "manly" pose.

the attack on Santiago. Roosevelt's group successfully charged the hills overlooking the capital city, Kettle Hill and San Juan Hill (where he met up with the African American squadron, which had already claimed the hill). With these strategic positions now in hand, American forces turned their attention to Santiago's harbor and proceeded to bombard the Spanish fleet, which was almost completely destroyed. The Spanish forces in Cuba surrendered on July 17.

SPANISH SURRENDER

American victories in the Philippines and Cuba prompted a full Spanish surrender. The war had lasted only four months, leading Secretary of State John Milton Hay to refer to it as "a splendid little war." In the peace treaty, signed in Paris, Spain granted independence to Cuba and ceded most of its overseas possessions to the United States, including Puerto Rico, the Philippines, and Guam, in exchange for $20 million. In addition, Congress had annexed Hawai'i during the war.

Within a matter of a few months, then, the United States had amassed an island empire in the Pacific and the Caribbean. It had not created a group of independent nations, but rather developed a string of subordinate countries, beholden to American business and military interests.

20-3b Why Become an Empire? Anti-Imperialism at Home

After the war—and even before—many Americans began to wonder whether the United States should become an imperial power. From the outset of the Spanish-American War, McKinley had assured the American public that the aim of the war was not to create an American empire but to protect the sovereignty of the Cuban people. That was the point of the Teller Amendment. Now that the war was over and Cuba and the Philippines were clearly not independent, McKinley and other political leaders (including Roosevelt and Secretary of State Hay) pushed for annexation of the Philippines by declaring that the Filipinos (as well as inhabitants of Puerto Rico and Guam) were too weak to govern themselves.

ANNEX THE PHILIPPINES?

Many Americans were skeptical about further annexation. In early 1899, during congressional debates over ratification of the Paris treaty with Spain, Democrats and Populists declared that annexation violated America's anti-imperialist principles. William Jennings Bryan argued that the treaty should be accepted, but only as a stage in the liberation of all of Spain's former colonies. In the end, the Senate ratified the treaty with Spain, but just barely. The idea that America should persist in its colonial expansion was meeting rising opposition.

THE ANTI-IMPERIALIST LEAGUE

In 1899, opponents of overseas expansion formed the Anti-Imperialist League, with leaders drawn from a number of disparate groups, including Andrew Carnegie, Samuel Gompers, Mark Twain, and Jane Addams. Labor

> "Is there anything grand or noble in any of these motives of war? Not a bit."
>
> —WILLIAM GRAHAM SUMNER, IN OPPOSITION TO IMPERIALISM, 1881

leader Gompers opposed annexation from a racist and nativist point of view. He feared that Filipino immigrants (he called them "half breeds and semi-barbaric people") would flood the United States with cheap labor. It is important to recognize that, though they were on opposite sides of the debate over imperialism, supporters of expansion and anti-imperialists shared a rhetoric and logic about the superiority of American civilization and the white race.

THE ELECTION OF 1900

The showdown between pro- and anti-imperialist forces came in the election of 1900, a rematch of the 1896 contest that had pitted Bryan against McKinley. This time Bryan based his candidacy not on the idea of free silver but on condemning imperialism and the annexation of the Philippines. Thanks in part to the country's prospering economy, most Americans were uninterested in Bryan's arguments, and McKinley (now with Roosevelt as his running mate) once again emerged victorious. In subsequent years, anti-imperialism ceased to be a major issue in American politics. Detecting its lack of appeal at the ballot box, most American politicians became supporters of America's new imperial role.

20-3c Anti-Americanism Abroad

If most Americans were supportive of a growing American empire, Filipinos and Cubans were not.

> "We cannot retreat from any soil where Providence has unfurled our banner; it is ours to save that soil for liberty and civilization."
>
> —SENATOR ALBERT J. BEVERIDGE, IN FAVOR OF THE WAR, 1898

WHAT THE UNITED STATES HAS FOUGHT FOR

Before the United States intervened in behalf of these oppressed people.

After the United States had rescued them from their oppression.

Wisconsin Historical Society, WHI-3916, Collection 2714

>> American imperialism was often imagined to be a civilizing experience, freeing the darker-skinned people of the world from their various oppressions and turning them into happy Victorian businessmen. This pro-imperialism cartoon shows people from the Philippines, Hawai'i, Puerto Rico, Cuba, and Panama at first under various oppressions only later to be turned into middle-class businessmen after being freed by the US.

Both countries wanted independence, not American overlordship. Americans also frequently relied on violence and threats to preserve control in those countries. These two factors created deep veins of anti-American sentiment. Small nations were fearful that America would never allow them to be independent, and so they fought back in the ways they could.

Platt Amendment Legislation intended to overrule the Teller Amendment and then added to the Cuban constitution, allowing the United States to militarily intervene on the island whenever revolution threatened

FILIPINO RESISTANCE

Enraged at the prospect of a permanent American presence after they had themselves fought so hard to remove Spanish power, Filipino leader Aguinaldo launched the same type of guerrilla war against the Americans that he had waged against the Spanish. In response, a large American force hastened to the islands and, between 1899 and 1902, fought a vicious anti-insurgency war. Both sides tortured and killed their prisoners, treating them as murderers rather than soldiers. American soldiers wrote home questioning the morality of their overseas experiences, citing atrocities like "the water cure," in which American soldiers would hold down a suspect, place a stick between his teeth, and force him to drink tremendous amounts of salt water. If the suspect did not divulge information, an American soldier would stomp on his stomach and begin the "cure" again. In 1901, American forces captured Aguinaldo, and future president William Howard Taft, sent by McKinley to create a government for the Philippines, persuaded Aguinaldo to call for peace.

The fighting subsided the following year: the war had claimed some 4,300 American lives, while more than 200,000 Filipino died, many from disease and starvation brought about by war. This was a major atrocity. Meanwhile, Taft directed the establishment of a new government. The United States designated the Philippines an "unorganized territory" and made Filipinos U.S. citizens. Revolt smoldered there until 1906, and on some islands the fighting did not end until 1935. In 1946, the Philippines, whose people had fought valiantly alongside the United States in World War II, finally gained its independence.

CUBAN RESENTMENT

Resentment of Americans also smoldered in Cuba. Although Cuba was declared independent on January 1, 1899, American occupation of the island continued for two more years while the U.S. installed a Cuban regime that would be friendly to American commercial interests. The new relationship between the two countries was laid out in the **Platt Amendment** of 1901. Written to overrule the Teller

Amendment and then eventually added to the Cuban constitution, the Platt Amendment allowed the United States to militarily intervene on the island whenever revolution threatened. Many Cubans were infuriated when the United States invoked the amendment in 1906, 1912, and 1917. It clearly violated the vision of Cuban independence that the United States had articulated during the buildup to war.

HUMANITARIAN ASSISTANCE

At the same time that their government was guilty of violence and deceit, there were many Americans who genuinely sought to help the peoples of Cuba, the Philippines, Puerto Rico, and Guam. On these islands, American missionaries built churches and orphanages, educators built schools, and doctors built hospitals. One of those doctors, Walter Reed, in collaboration with William Gorgas and Carlos Juan Finlay, solved the mystery of yellow fever transmission. Still, the American-made regimes that had been established in these countries remained a source of anti-American sentiment throughout the twentieth century.

20-4 PROGRESSIVE-ERA IMPERIALISM

After 1900 the United States entered a period of heightened imperialistic activity somewhat similar to that of the 1840s, although this time oceans ceased to serve as boundaries for expansionist activity. Under the energetic Progressive-era presidencies of Roosevelt and Wilson, the United States took a bolder, more aggressive role in international affairs. Toward this end, Roosevelt, whose foreign policy credo was "speak softly and carry a big stick," supported Secretary of War Elihu Root's policy of increasing U.S. armed forces. By 1906, only the navies of Britain and Germany were larger than that of the United States.

The United States used its new power to pursue three major goals: to (1) open trade with China, (2) build the Panama Canal, and (3) police Latin America to protect American interests.

20-4a Trade with China

After winning the Spanish-American War, the United States sought to demonstrate its status as a major international power. American policymakers first turned to China. In 1899, U.S. Secretary of State John Hay called for an "Open Door" policy, which would allow all nations to trade with China on equal terms. This policy also aimed to prevent foreign powers from partitioning China as they had Africa.

FORCING THE OPEN DOOR

The Chinese **Boxer Rebellion** of 1900 helped Hay's plan. Angered by growing outside influence in their country, Chinese nationalists, led by a secret society specially trained in fighting rituals (and thus called "Boxers" by English-speaking foreigners) attacked embassies in Beijing in an attempt to oust foreigners. Supported by the Chinese government, the rebels killed the German ambassador and besieged Christian churches in Beijing. The United States joined a multinational military expedition to put the rebellion down and to rescue businessmen and diplomats who had sought refuge in the American embassy. After the multinational forces successfully suppressed the rebellion, most of the other powers agreed to Hay's Open Door policy in principle (although they did not always honor it in practice). The Chinese government reluctantly agreed. The Boxer Rebellion, instead of ejecting outside influences, actually strengthened America's foothold in the Far East.

20-4b The Panama Canal

The United States next focused on Panama. Ever since the 1840s, American commercial and military planners had eyed Panama's narrow isthmus as a potential site for a canal. Such interest increased after 1898, when America's new empire required easier transit between the Atlantic and Pacific Oceans. Panama, however, belonged to Colombia, whose rights to the isthmus the United States had explicitly guaranteed in an 1848 treaty.

PANAMANIAN REVOLT

In 1901, negotiations with Colombia broke down over the price of renting the right of way for a canal. Undeterred, Roosevelt, the American president, encouraged an independence movement among the Panamanian people. This would free them from Colombia and, presumably, lead them to grant the United States unobstructed access to build its canal. The Panamanian revolt proved successful, thanks in part to an American naval blockade that prevented Colombian soldiers from getting to the rebellion. As a thank-you to the United States

> **Boxer Rebellion** Conflict that erupted in China in 1900; Chinese nationalists attacked embassies in Beijing in an attempt to oust foreigners

>> Building of the Panama Canal.

for its timely intervention, in 1903 the new Republic of Panama leased to it a 10-mile-wide Canal Zone. American companies immediately started construction.

BUILDING THE CANAL

Building the canal was no easy task. French engineer Ferdinand de Lesseps, who had built the Suez Canal in 1869, had already attempted to build a canal in Panama. He went bankrupt in 1887 after most of his work force died of yellow fever. By 1903, however, Walter Reed's work on the disease had made the threat of yellow fever a manageable concern. After cutting through mountains and dense jungle, and then constructing a series of innovative locks, workers completed the canal just before the First World War broke out in 1914. One of the world's modern mechanical marvels, the canal project used tons and tons of concrete and was the largest dam in the world at the time. It cut the sailing distance between America's Atlantic and Pacific Coasts from 15,615 miles to just 5,300.

However, Roosevelt's timely blockade bred a legacy of resentment in Colombia that damaged U.S.–Latin American relations for decades. Moreover, the presence of the Canal Zone eventually caused tensions between Americans and Panamanians until a treaty placed it under Panamanian control in 1999.

20-4c Policing Latin America

Concurrent with the building of the Panama Canal, the United States assumed an interventionist role throughout Latin America. Much of this new activity was prompted by continued rivalry with other imperial powers. In 1902, for example, when the Venezuelan government was unable to pay its foreign creditors, British, German, and Italian naval forces threatened to bombard Venezuelan cities unless payments were resumed. Roosevelt regarded this action as a violation of the Monroe Doctrine; by a combination of threats and promises, he persuaded the European navies to withdraw.

INSTABILITY AS AN AMERICAN PROBLEM

Roosevelt argued that instability in Latin America was likely to be a recurrent problem for American interests. He therefore announced, in 1904, his own amendment to the Monroe Doctrine (called the "Roosevelt Corollary"). The United States, he declared, would not only prevent European colonization of Latin American countries but would also intervene in the domestic affairs of any Latin American nation whose instability threatened the security of the Western Hemisphere. The policy allowed Roosevelt to intervene in the Dominican Republic, Nicaragua, Haiti, and Mexico, routinely resulting in American control of the contested lands for several decades (see Map 20.1).

Nicaragua's experience was typical. In 1909, an American mining company in Nicaragua became dissatisfied with the current regime and provoked a coup. President Taft sent troops in support of the coup and later helped American bankers finance the new regime. When this regime faced its own revolutionary discontent, Taft sent more soldiers to protect it. Thus Taft frequently used American troops to advance the interests of the American business community, which is why his critics derided his policies as little more than "dollar diplomacy."

MEXICO

Taft and Wilson also intervened during the early stages of the Mexican Revolution, which began in 1910. A bewildering succession of soldiers, strongmen, and democratic idealists competed for power after the overthrow of the old dictator, Porfirio Diaz, whose policies had benefited American investors. Both Taft and Wilson tried to find a Mexican candidate who could take care of American businesses. One by one, these candidates proved either too ruthless or too ineffective, provoking political strife that often turned violent. In 1914 and again in 1916, Wilson sent troops to Mexico to restore order, first by capturing the port city of Veracruz, later

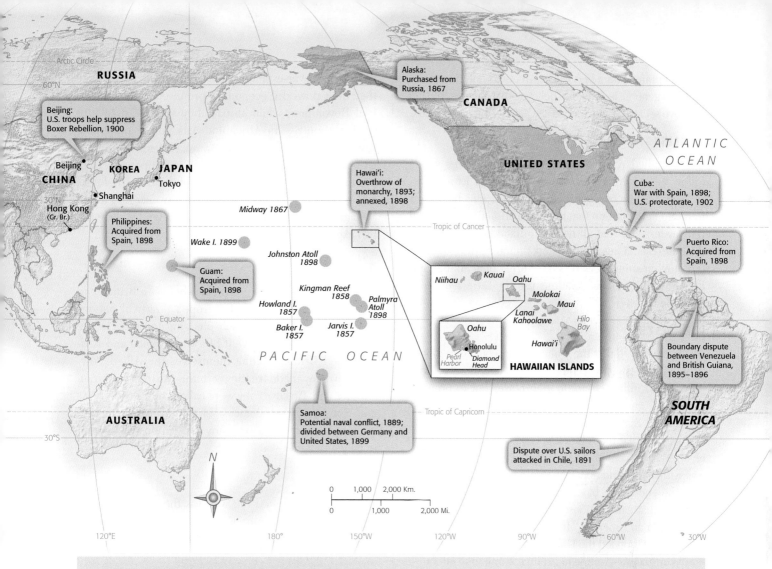

Map 20.1 American Imperialism by 1912

>> This map of most of the world shows the numerous locations of American imperial involvement between 1895 and 1902.

by sending General John Pershing in pursuit of Pancho Villa, a Mexican general and kingmaker who had raided American towns in New Mexico. Neither of these expeditions solved Mexico's instability.

20-4d America as a World Power

By the early twentieth century, the United States was committed to being a major player in Latin America and Asia. The belief that America's interests ended at its oceans had been shattered. Americans could no longer think of themselves as isolated from international affairs. Nor could they smugly see their nation as completely different from the European empires whose navies and armies had conquered much of the globe.

But did American interests end at the nation's borders, at the Western Hemisphere, or never? What

would America's role in the world be now that its commercial interests were worldwide? Should American business interests have a role in the nation's foreign policy? How salient was the notion that the United States should share the "white man's burden" to spread democracy and "white civilization" to the world? Americans fell into three camps when it came to viewing themselves as a world power: (1) isolationists, (2) realists, and (3) idealists.

ISOLATIONISTS

Isolationists believed the United States could return to isolationism and treat the Spanish-American War and its corollaries as an aberration. In the years immediately following the war, many Americans seemed to favor this course of action, especially those who felt that controlling the Philippines was a betrayal of America's anti-imperialist roots. In general, isolationists believed that alliances did not improve security, but simply drew nations into costly wars.

REALISTS

The so-called realists hoped the United States would follow the tradition of the leading states of Europe, assuming the role of a great world power. This belief was founded in the notion that the international environment was lawless and that all nations pursued only their own self-interests. Thus, power and military strength were the only meaningful factors in international affairs. Students of international relations use the term *realism* to describe this viewpoint.

IDEALISTS

Idealists believed that the United States could enter international politics not as a competitor but as a moral reformer, using its influence not to grab power but to promote democracy and free trade around the world. Woodrow Wilson was the most prominent proponent of this view. He believed that the rules of international affairs could be changed to prevent or mitigate conflict between nations. It was within this tradition that President Roosevelt negotiated the end of the bloody Russo-Japanese War in 1905, an event that earned Roosevelt the first-ever Nobel Prize awarded to an American. It was also in this tradition that Woodrow Wilson led the United States into World War I.

While most Americans didn't adopt one of these sensibilities in a hard-nosed way, choosing to alter their perspective depending on the conflict, all of these viewpoints would be represented during the debate over American intervention in World War I.

 # WORLD WAR I

World War I, which lasted from 1914 to 1918, was a conflict of colossal proportions, killing more than 10 million soldiers and civilians, bringing down governments and empires, and pitting armies against each other all around the globe. The United States entered the war in 1917, just in time to try to manipulate the terms of surrender. It was a vital test of America's imperial ambitions.

20-5a The Reasons
ECONOMIC COMPETITION

World War I erupted out of conflicts between rival powers in Europe, largely based on the competition for colonial empires. In the late nineteenth century, European nations were locked in a worldwide competition to establish ever-expanding overseas empires. At home they built powerful economies premised on the Industrial Revolution, while abroad they scrambled to turn weaker countries in Africa and Asia into colonial possessions that would serve as sources of raw materials. Britain and Germany were the two largest powers. Both had embraced the transformations of the Industrial Age, and both were in competition to win raw materials found abroad. To many observers, a confrontation between the two expanding European powers seemed inevitable.

ALLIANCES

Anxiety about the impending clash between Britain and Germany led nearly all of Europe's powerful nations to enter into alliances, each pledging to come to the other's defense in the event of a war. France and Russia joined Britain, calling themselves the Allied Powers. Germany made treaties with the Austro-Hungarian Empire and Turkey. They were called the Central Powers. Forging these alliances set the stage for tragedy, because a conflict between any two nations was bound to trigger a wider war.

THE SPARK

The spark that ignited the war was the assassination of Austria's Archduke Franz Ferdinand, heir to the throne of the Austro-Hungarian Empire. He and his wife Sofia were shot on June 28, 1914, during a visit to Sarajevo, by Gavrilo Princip, a member of the Serbian nationalist group called the Black Hand, which was bent on driving the Austro-Hungarians out of Serbia. This event set off a chain reaction in Europe's military alliances. Austria declared war on Serbia, which prompted Russia to help the Serbians, which led Germany to declare war on Russia and France, which triggered Britain to declare war on Germany. Over the next several weeks, many other nations joined the conflict, and fighting spread to the European colonies in Africa, Asia, and the Middle East (see Map 20.2).

20-5b The European War

Hoping for a quick victory against its enemies to the west, Germany invaded France in August 1914. With British help, the French managed to hold off the German advance. A military stalemate resulted, and both sides dug into the fields of northern France. For the next four years, the Allied and Central Powers battled each other on what became called "the Western Front." Along the Western Front, both the Central and Allied Powers dug deep webs of

Map 20.2 Descent into War

>> A map of Europe showing the various sides of World War I, including a list of the events of the summer of 1914 that led to war.

Map legend:
- Central Powers (Triple Alliance—except Italy—and allies)
- The Allies (Triple Entente and allies)
- Neutral nations

Events list:
1. **June 28** Assassination at Sarajevo
2. **July 28** Austria-Hungary declares war on Serbia
3. **July 30** Russia begins mobilization
4. **August 1** Germany declares war on Russia
5. **August 3** Germany declares war on France and invades Belgium
6. **August 4** Great Britain declares war on Germany
7. **August 6** Russia and Austria-Hungary at war
8. **August 12** Great Britain declares war on Austria-Hungary

trenches just a few hundred feet from one another, spending nights and days fomenting attacks against one another from the depths of their respective trenches. Between the two trenches was "No Man's Land," a bullet-strewn strip of land upon which few men dared tred. Snipers were at the ready, often aiming at the lighted fire at the tip of a cigarette. Searching for ways to win a trench war, the combatants harnessed the power of the Industrial Age, inventing machine guns, poison gases, warplanes, and tanks. The war was more brutal than anyone had anticipated.

And the Western Front wasn't the only front. To the east of Germany, Russia and the Allies battled against the Central Powers in a similarly brutal fashion. All sides were stung by the brutality of a war in which nearly an entire generation of European men would die or fight. The effects of the Industrial Age were felt not only in the factories but in the battlefields as well. Soon everyone knew what a gas mask was, something unheard of before the First World War.

20-5c American Neutrality, 1914–1917

Most Americans were baffled by the rivalries and alliances that had caused the war and horrified at the carnage in France. In the war's first years, Americans called it "the

> "As the car came abreast he stepped forward from the curb, drew his automatic pistol from his coat and fired two shots."
>
> —Borijove Jevtic, who was arrested with Gavrilo Princip

European War," distancing themselves from the conflict. Yet they could not ignore such a massive war for long, and their sympathies were mixed. Following the tremendous immigration that had resulted from the Industrial Revolution, many Americans were recent European emigrants who felt strong ties to their homelands. On the other hand, many of the nation's political and industrial leaders were Anglophiles, who instinctively favored the British.

COMPROMISED NEUTRALITY

Faced with divided loyalties, President Wilson urged his fellow citizens to remain "impartial in thought as well as action." Running for reelection in 1916, he turned the race into a referendum on neutrality. He won easily, campaigning on the slogan "He Kept Us Out of War."

Despite Wilson's best intentions, the United States was slowly being drawn in. With Allied and German armies stalemated in France, both sides realized their best hope for victory was to starve their enemy into submission. They did this all too well, cutting off supply routes and containing each nation as best they could. With their economies in tatters, each side looked to the United States for supplies. By 1915, the economic incentive to trade with them proved irresistible. American farms and factories soon began to work overtime to meet the demands of the war-torn nations of Europe. But could this be done neutrally?

NEUTRAL TRADING?

Both Allied and Central Powers believed it was essential to deprive their enemies of the benefits of trade with

U-boat Primitive but effective submarine invented by the Germans and used extensively in the First World War

ASSASSINAT DE L'ARCHIDUC HÉRITIER D'AUTRICHE ET DE LA DUCHESSE SA FEMME A SARAJEVO

>> This print of an engraving shows the assassination of Franz Ferdinand, which was the domino that began the First World War.

the Americans, and Wilson's call for all sides to respect American trade rights ran directly counter to the military strategies of both the ritich and the Germans. Britain and France, for instance, mined the North Sea, forcing American ships into British ports. There, the British detained supplies headed for Germany. When Wilson protested, the French and British agreed to pay for all materials seized in this way. But they still didn't let the goods get to Germany.

The Germans, meanwhile, concluded that their best hope was to prevent American goods from getting to Britain at all. To do so, they launched a new weapon that profoundly changed the nature of naval warfare and eventually brought the United States into war— the **U-boat**, a primitive but effective submarine. On May 7, 1915, a U-boat sank Britain's *Lusitania*, a famed passenger liner that the Allies had used occasionally

>> The sinking of the *Lusitania* created a rallying cry for the Allies. Pictured here are two posters urging men to enlist.

to transport war material. Knowing of the ship's dual uses, Germany took out advertisements in newspapers warning Americans not to sail on it. Still, many did, and when the *Lusitania* sank, more than 1,000 civilians were killed, including 128 Americans. Provoked by anti-German newspaper editorials, mobs lashed out at innocent German-Americans.

Responding to Wilson's threats that the *Lusitania* disaster would likely force the United States into the war, Germany temporarily halted its use of the U-boat against passenger vessels. By 1917, however, Germany was nearly starved into submission and, in a last-ditch gamble, declared it would wage unrestricted submarine warfare against all shipping in the Atlantic. When Russia negotiated peace after the successful Bolshevik revolution of February 1917, Germany hoped it could handle a one-front war, even if the United States entered the war on the Western Front.

German-named foods were renamed: sauerkraut became "liberty cabbage."

20-5d Declaring War

THE ZIMMERMANN NOTE

After the declaration of unrestricted warfare in the Atlantic, German-American relations deteriorated. Not only had Germany initiated a threatening campaign, but also Americans discovered that Germany was also encouraging Mexico to attack the United States. On January 16, 1917, the German foreign minister, Arthur Zimmermann, sent a note to Mexico in which he promised German support for a Mexican invasion, the goal of which was to reconquer New Mexico, Arizona, and Texas for Mexico. Unluckily for the Germans, the British intercepted the note, and they eagerly turned it over to the United States. The so-called Zimmermann Note proved a powerful tool in rallying American public support for a war against Germany.

DECLARATION OF WAR

By the spring of 1917, the combination of German U-boat attacks and the Zimmermann Note left many Americans feeling the time had come to admit they really were involved in the "European War." On April 2, 1917, Wilson asked Congress for a declaration of war. In his request, Wilson outlined the nation's grievances against the Central Powers and invested the war effort with a moral purpose. American soldiers would go to Europe, he insisted, not to punish Germany, but to help create a new international order. "The world must be made safe for democracy," he declared.

A MIXED REACTION

Americans were not fully united in this decision. Six senators and fifty congressmen voted against the declaration. In addition, a substantial minority of the American public still favored neutrality. Unconvinced by Wilson's idealistic rhetoric, they insisted that sending American troops to settle a distant European war was a misguided departure from traditional American diplomacy.

FORMING PUBLIC OPINION

The government responded to these criticisms by taking unprecedented steps to mobilize public opinion. It formed the Committee on Public Information (CPI), a group led by journalist

George Creel that recruited some of the nation's finest artists to create and distribute millions of pieces of war propaganda. On street corners and in theaters, "Four-Minute Men" delivered stirring pro-war speeches. Newspapers printed government-written stories detailing questionable tales of German war atrocities. Ubiquitous posters urged Americans to buy Liberty Bonds, conserve food and coal, and otherwise do everything possible to "Beat Back the Hun."

HYPHENATED AMERICANS

In addition to worrying about popular support, government officials were particularly anxious about the loyalties of the nation's recent immigrants, many of whom maintained strong ties with their European homelands. These newcomers were branded "hyphenated Americans" (German-Americans, Irish-Americans), the hyphen suggesting that these recent arrivals might not have left their Old World allegiances behind to fully embrace their new American identities. Creel's committee tried to apply its powers of persuasion to turn these newcomers into "100 percent Americans." The CPI included a "Division for Work with the Foreign Born" that encouraged recent immigrants to show their loyalty by purchasing **war bonds** and staging patriotic demonstrations.

WARTIME REPRESSION

The government also took steps to silence critics. In 1917, Congress passed the **Espionage Act**, which meted out large fines and twenty-year jail terms to anyone who protested the draft or said anything that might impede the war effort. A year later the act was broadened, making it illegal to say anything "disloyal" about the American form of government or the armed forces. The U.S. Postmaster General Albert S. Burleson was authorized to seize and destroy any publication he deemed treasonous—a power he exercised freely. School boards banned the teaching of German language and history. Universities fired professors who spoke out against the war.

war bonds Securities bought by ordinary people to fund and support the war effort

Espionage Act Legislation that meted out large fines and twenty-year jail terms to anyone who protested the draft or said anything that might impede the war effort

>> U.S. bonds poster. The U.S. sought not only to raise revenue by selling bonds to its citizens, but also to demonstrate the parameters of good Americanism.

Towns changed street signs to erase German names. German-named foods were renamed: sauerkraut, for example, became "liberty cabbage." "Patriotic" mobs attacked German-language and socialist newspaper offices, beat innocent German immigrants, and, in at least one case, lynched a man wrongly suspected of being a German spy. Government-stimulated war fervor ran hot.

Several prominent Americans spoke out against these forms of repression. Eugene V. Debs was imprisoned for speaking out against the war effort. Hull House's Jane Addams was another outspoken opponent. Watching such dignified opponents be punished or rebuked for their antiwar efforts led many Americans to question what freedom meant, and if it meant the same thing in wartime as in peace.

20-5e American Involvement in the War Effort, 1917–1918

When it came to battle, the United States in 1917 was woefully unprepared. It entered the war with no army and no stockpiles of military supplies, nor any means to recruit, train, equip, or transport a modern army across the Atlantic. And, with the American economy booming, shifting to war production was a slow process. In fact, by the end of the war, the United States managed to mobilize little more than a small fraction of its economy and raised only a modest military force; fewer than 5 million men entered the armed services, and only 2.5 million of them went overseas.

THE AMERICAN ARMY IN BATTLE

In the end, Americans were slow to join the battle. Making matters worse, American political leaders refused to send troops that would fight under the control of French or British Allied commanders. President Wilson sought to maintain American independence, and only when the complete army was ready did American soldiers fight. They fought in two major battles before Germany capitulated and ended the war.

Historians have debated the impact American forces had on the outcome of World War I. Some assert that, even after committing themselves, Americans made only a minimal contribution. Proponents of this view stress that, after such a long delay, American soldiers had little impact in either of the two military battles they fought. Other historians contend that this interpretation downplays the American impact. They argue that the U.S. declaration of war dashed Germany's hope for a quick victory on the Western Front after Russia had sued for peace. Food shortages were widespread on the German home front, and demoralized soldiers threatened mutiny. Plus, not only military might but also field ingenuity helped Americans turn the tide of war. During one large battle on the Western Front, for instance, the U.S. deployed Choctaw Indians to serve as communication agents, thus befuddling any attempt at German espionage. According to this interpretation, the entrance of the resource-rich Americans dealt a powerful psychological and military blow to the Germans and greatly hastened their capitulation.

THE FOURTEEN POINTS

Regardless of how large an impression the American military made on the battling nations, this did not inhibit President Wilson from attempting to determine the conditions for peace. On January 8, 1918, while the war still raged, Wilson issued a proclamation, called the **Fourteen Points**, outlining the principles he believed should shape the postwar peace settlement.

The statement came as a great surprise to the Allies. That an American president, who had brought his country into the war only a few months earlier, was attempting to dictate a sweeping peace program was certainly a shock. But Wilson's independent course was consistent with his actions and statements. To Wilson, the United States could lead the world to a more enlightened way of conducting international affairs. Some of his Fourteen Points involved proposals for resolving specific border disputes, but the rest of Wilson's ideas amounted to a blueprint for what he called "a world made fit and safe to live in." Among the major tenets were free trade, disarmament, and a "general association of nations" that would provide a forum for nations to resolve differences peacefully. Wilson also advocated national self-determination, which would break up empires and allow new national boundaries to be drawn along "clearly recognizable lines of nationality."

20-5f Making Peace

In October 1918, Germany made peace overtures to Wilson, agreeing to end the war on the basis of his declaration that there could be "peace without victory." The Allied Powers wanted to fight on, believing they finally had a decisive advantage on the battlefield. The war had been viciously fought in Europe, especially after the introduction of new technologies such as planes, tanks, and chemical weapons like deadly "mustard gas." The Allied Powers wanted to punish German wartime atrocities. But they yielded when Wilson threatened to pull American troops out of the war if the Allies were unwilling to accept peace. On November 11, 1918, both sides signed an armistice ending the war.

DEBATING PEACE

After the armistice, Wilson made an unusual decision to travel to Europe himself to represent the United

Fourteen Points Declaration by President Wilson that outlined the principles he believed should shape the postwar peace settlement; a blueprint for what he called "a world made fit and safe to live in"

>> Despite the United States' late entry in the war, a buoyant President Woodrow Wilson thought he could dictate the terms of peace. His optimism is contrasted here by the more chastened look of French President Raymond Poincare.

SZ Photo/Scherl/The Image Works

bility for the war and pay heavy fines to the Allies; (2) self-determination for nationalities; and (3) Wilson's "general association of nations," which the treaty called the League of Nations. Each of these provisions would have unforeseen consequences. Forcing Germany to pay steep financial reparations meant that the German economy could not recover from the war, leading to political instability that encouraged the rise of Adolf Hitler. The concept of national self-determination has led to a century of struggle in the Balkan Peninsula and other areas, where groups of people, seeing themselves as distinct nations, resist the rule of others. And the League of Nations would be toothless from the beginning, because the United States, of all countries, refused to participate.

WILSON'S FOLLY

Although Wilson had arrived in Europe as a conquering hero, when he returned to Washington he faced a desperate political fight to save his cherished League of Nations. Many Americans, he discovered, were already disillusioned about the nation's decision to get involved in European affairs. The champion of this brand of isolationism was Republican senator Henry Cabot Lodge of Massachusetts, who worked to block American participation in the new League of Nations because he believed it would draw the United States into future European conflicts. In particular, he objected to Article X of the League's charter, which would have committed the United States to defending the territory of other League members. Wilson considered this "the heart of the League," a provision that would require nations to join together to protect each other from attacks by international aggressors.

Wilson fought hard for the League, touring the country in a direct appeal to the public. But the Senate refused to ratify the Treaty of Versailles, and the United States never joined the League of Nations.

States at the peace talks. Crowds in Paris greeted him as a hero and applauded his vision for a better world. Despite this popular support, however, Wilson ran into difficulties at the bargaining table, as the victorious Allies pursued very different ideas about how to shape the postwar world. After four years of brutal war and suffering, the Allies had little interest in "peace without victory," and they were eager to punish their enemies and divide the spoils of Germany's overseas colonies. Indeed, Germany wasn't even invited to the peace talks. As a result, Wilson had only limited success in incorporating his vision for a new world order into the final peace treaty, which was signed in the French palace at Versailles on June 28, 1919.

THE TREATY OF VERSAILLES

The treaty included three major provisions: (1) reparations that forced Germany to accept full responsi-

The president stubbornly refused to compromise and was crippled by a stroke while waging his campaign. Woodrow Wilson died a broken man in 1924.

A WEAKENED LEAGUE

In 1920, the League of Nations met for the first time, but it was diminished from the start by the absence of the United States. By the mid-1930s, the League was irrelevant, incapable of changing the course of events that would soon draw Europe into World War II. But the idea of a worldwide association of nations had been articulated and would surface again.

>LOOKING AHEAD...

World War I underscored America's role as a significant power in the world. After the war, for instance, America for the first time replaced Great Britain as the world's greatest creditor nation, further enhancing American power.

But Americans' willingness to intervene in world affairs was not a foregone conclusion. After being somewhat grudgingly brought into world affairs by a series of expansionist leaders, Americans continued to debate the importance of playing a role in world affairs. Between 1867 and 1918, the ethos of expansion was strong, and during the four decades following 1880, the United States had flexed its military muscle throughout Latin America, Asia, and Europe. It had done so to (1) support American economic development, (2) establish the United States as a world power worth reckoning with, and (3) show that many Americans believed the United States was destined to share the benefits of democracy and white civilization with the rest of the world. In doing so, it confronted new problems, such as how colonial powers are supposed to manage relations with their subjected peoples. Was the United States to be a great liberating force for democracy in the wider world, or was it to serve the interests of the business classes who advocated dollar diplomacy? These debates would continue throughout the twentieth century.

STUDY TOOLS 20

READY TO STUDY? IN THE BOOK, YOU CAN:

❏ Rip out the Chapter Review Card, which includes key terms and chapter summaries.

ONLINE AT WWW.CENGAGEBRAIN.COM, YOU CAN:

❏ Collect StudyBits while you read and study the chapter.

❏ Quiz yourself on key concepts.

❏ Find videos for further exploration.

❏ Prepare for tests with HIST5 Flash Cards as well as those you create.

❏ Read Frederick Jackson Turner's frontier essay.

❏ Read an excerpt from Josiah Strong's *Our Country*.

❏ Read an excerpt from Mahan's *The Influence of Sea Power on History*.

❏ Read two eyewitness accounts of the American naval attack in Manila Bay.

❏ Read an excerpt from Theodore Roosevelt's *The Rough Riders*.

❏ Read Senator Albert Beveridge's speech in support of the war.

❏ Read more about the Boxer Rebellion from Fei Ch'i-hao, a Chinese Christian.

❏ Read a sample of a war propaganda pamphlet.

❏ Read the Espionage Act.

❏ Read the Fourteen Points.

		What Else Was Happening
▶	**1844** Treaty of Wanghia opens Chinese ports to U.S. trade.	
▶	**1853** U.S. Navy in Tokyo Bay pressures Japan to open to West.	
▶	**1867** United States purchases Alaska from Russia.	
▶	**1895** Cleveland administration invokes Monroe Doctrine in Venezuela Crisis with Britain.	*Cubans rebel against heavy-handed Spanish rule.*
▶	**1898** Spanish-American War transforms United States into major overseas power. **June:** Filipino leader Emilio Aguinaldo declares Philippines' independence from Spain. **July:** Rough Riders' capture of Santiago, Cuba, forces Spain's surrender.	
▶	**1899–1902** Americans fight vicious anti-insurgency war against Filipino nationalists.	*Anti-Imperialist League forms in opposition to annexation of Philippines.* *The Second Boer War in southern Africa between Great Britain and a handful of small African nations leads to the conversion of several small African republics into parts of the British Empire.*
▶	**1899** United States turns former naval base on Samoa into protectorate of American Samoa. U.S. Secretary of State John Hay demands Open Door policy from China.	
▶	**1900** After thirteen years as an American-led republic, Hawai'i becomes part of United States. Republican expansionist McKinley defeats Democrat Bryan in presidential election.	*United States joins multinational military expedition to suppress Boxer Rebellion in China.*
▶	**1901** Platt Amendment to Cuban constitution grants U.S. right to military intervention. Roosevelt encourages Panamanian independence after negotiations with Colombia fail.	

1903	U.S. support for Panama's rebellion leads to U.S. rights to 10-mile-wide Canal Zone.	**1904:** *Russo-Japanese War breaks out because of each nation's imperial ambitions over Manchuria and Korea.*
1905	President Roosevelt negotiates end to Russo-Japanese War, wins Nobel Peace Prize.	
1909	Taft administration supports coup in Nicaragua in the interests of U.S. mining company.	**1912: April 15:** *The Titanic sinks.* *First passenger meal is served on an airplane in flight.*
1914–1916	**June 28:** Assassination of Archduke Franz Ferdinand throws Europe into World War I. **August:** Germany invades France. Wilson administration sends troops into Mexican civil war to restore order. Wilson administration sends more troops into Mexican civil war to restore order.	**1915: May 7:** *German U-boat sinks British Lusitania; 128 U.S. civilians die; protests follow.*
1917	**January:** Zimmerman Note from Berlin to Mexico suggests alliance against United States. **February:** Bolshevik Revolution in Russia prompts talks over separate peace with Germany. **April 2:** Woodrow Wilson asks Congress for declaration of war against Germany. Espionage Acts punish protests and criticisms of draft.	
1918	**January 8:** Wilson proposes conciliatory postwar peace settlement in Fourteen Points. **February:** Both sides sign armistice; World War I ends.	
1919	**June 28:** Treaty of Versailles demands German reparations, adopts few of Wilson's ideas.	
1920	League of Nations meets for first time without U.S. participation.	

21 | Prosperity and Change in the Twenties

Lordprice Collection/Alamy Stock Photo

LEARNING OBJECTIVES

After reading this chapter, you should be able to do the following:

21-1 Describe the consumer economy that developed in the United States during the early twentieth century, especially after World War I.

21-2 Explain the experiences of the nation that effectively put an end to the Progressive movement during the 1920s.

21-3 Describe the various kinds of leisure activities that became popular in the U.S. during the 1920s.

21-4 Discuss the strong reactions among various groups to the changing cultural mores of the 1920s.

AFTER FINISHING THIS CHAPTER GO TO **PAGE 411** **FOR STUDY TOOLS**

During the decade after the First World War, America became the richest society in the history of the world. It had entered what many observers believed was a "new era" of unending prosperity. As always, economic changes prompted social and cultural changes. Exhausted by constant efforts at reform, postwar politicians from both parties largely gave up on the idea of "progressive" change, which had dominated national politics since Teddy Roosevelt. They were tired of moral crusades. Instead, voters elected a series of Republican presidents who promised to facilitate business expansion rather than impose Progressive regulations. Corporations responded by accelerating production and advertising their goods from one end of America to the other, with unbounded boosterism and pep that masked potential troubles within an increasingly unregulated economic system. As a result, the United States witnessed an intensification of the mass consumer culture that had been growing since the start of the Industrial Revolution.

With this backdrop of "good times," new ideas that questioned the established order, such as pluralism, psychoanalysis, and relativity, entered the American lexicon. A series of American writers picked up these themes and made American literature respected throughout the world for the first time, mostly by critiquing America's developing consumer culture. Also in 1920, for the first time, a majority of Americans were living in cities, creating a clash of values between those who lived in cities and those who remained in rural parts of the country. African Americans were attempting to refashion mainstream perceptions of their group, too. Women were looking to establish a new place in society as well. And the culture as a whole seemed to be liberalizing, a development that led to widespread backlashes and America's first culture war between religious conservatives and religious liberals.

In all this turmoil, the 1920s have been depicted by historians as many things: a "new era," a "return to normalcy," the "Roaring Twenties," a period of isolation. This variety of descriptions suggests that the period was characterized by many simultaneous changes. Most of the changes can be described as major shifts inward, toward private consumption, privatized business practices, an inwardly facing foreign policy, a widespread dislike and fear of "outsiders" (variously defined), as well as an end to the calls for broad social justice that had animated the Progressive era. Ultimately, this swirl of cultural newness came to a halt with the 1929 stock market crash and the Great Depression that followed. But, before then, America had begun its transition into what one historian has called "the first years of our time."

21-1 THE CONSUMER ECONOMY

During the 1920s, the United States became the wealthiest nation in the world. It took several years for the American economy to recover from its conversion to wartime production during World War I, when goods like guns and naval ships were produced in lieu of consumer items. But by 1921, the American economy was on an upward surge. American per capita incomes grew by more than 30 percent during the decade, industrial output increased by 60 percent, and unemployment in most

Hulton Archive/Getty Images

>> Car ownership expanded tremendously in the 1920s, serving as a marker of American success. Here, the actor James Hall drives his children around Hollywood, California.

◀◀◀ **Jazz swept through the nation in the 1920s, putting on display the prosperity of the era, as well as the general acceptance of a new role for women and the celebration and abduction of African American cultural forms.**

parts of the country stayed below 5 percent. Immense corporations dominated the economy, and most people enjoyed rising wages and rising standards of living. In 1929, five out of every six privately owned cars in the world belonged to Americans.

The improved economy was both uneven and unstable, however. Some benefited from it far more than others. Many Americans, especially farmers in the South and the West, still lived in poverty, and a recession in 1921 hit farmers particularly hard. Overall, the percentage of national wealth that went to the poorest 60 percent of the population fell by almost 13 percent during the 1920s, meaning that the wealthy were increasing their wealth at the expense of the poor. This poverty particularly affected many of the new immigrants, as well as Native Americans and Latinos living in the American Southwest. The wealth of the "Roaring Twenties" was stratified.

21-1a 1920s Work

GOOD TIMES

Nevertheless, the overall economy was healthy for several reasons. For one, the industrial production of Europe had been destroyed by the war, making American goods the dominant products available in Europe. New techniques of production and pay were another significant factor in the booming American economy. Henry Ford was a leader in developing both. First, he and his team of inventors revolutionized the automobile with his development of the conveyor-belt-based **assembly line**, a mechanized belt that moved a car chassis down a line where each man performed a single small task, over and over again. This innovation dramatically sped up production, reducing the time to produce a single car from more than 12 hours to just 93 minutes. It did come at a cost though, in that mass production of this sort alienated workers from the final product they were producing because they worked on only one small aspect of a larger product.

---

assembly line Mechanized belt that moved a product down a line where each worker performed a single small task, over and over again, until the product was completed

five-dollar day Initiative begun by Henry Ford in 1914 to pay his workers $5 a day, more than three times the normal wage at the time. The initiative made Ford's workers consumers, while also ending any efforts to unionize Ford's plants

welfare capitalism Industry's strategy of improving working conditions and providing health insurance for workers

company unions Organizations of workers from a single company who represent workers' grievances to management

---

Ford had a wonderful solution to this problem: he realized that, in order to keep selling cars by the thousands, he would have to pay his workers enough for them to become *customers*, too. His 1914 innovation, the **five-dollar day** (when a salary of $1.50 per day was standard), shocked other businessmen at first, but by the 1920s, other business owners were coming to understand that they could mass-produce consumer goods only if they also created a supply of consumers. In the 1920s, the economy began to transition from being driven by large industries (such as railroads and steel) to being driven by consumer dollars.

WELFARE CAPITALISM

Along with recognizing the need to pay higher wages, many manufacturers began to think of their factories not just as places of work but also as social settings, where men and women spent a large part of their waking hours. A handful of pioneers in **welfare capitalism**, such as the Heinz Company (producer of soup, ketchup, and baked beans), reasoned that happy workers would be more productive than resentful ones. Heinz and other companies improved lighting and ventilation and also provided company health plans, recreation centers, and even psychologists to tend to their employees. Many companies even shortened the workweek. And in some firms, **company unions** replaced the American Federation of Labor (AFL) in representing workers' grievances to management.

DECLINE OF UNION MEMBERSHIP

The combination of company unions, high wages, and the hunger to own a car and other luxury goods spelled hard times for traditional unions, as did a growing suspicion of communism (described in the section on the Red Scare). The decade witnessed a decline in the number of workers attached to the AFL, from 4 million in 1920 to 2.5 million by 1929.

Employers kept iron fists inside their new velvet gloves, though. They put men who were known union organizers on blacklists, spied on union activities, and pressured employees to sign anti-union pledges. Along similar lines, a group of manufacturers came together in the National Association of Manufacturers to promote what it called the "American Plan," which forced the maintenance of an "open shop" labor environment, meaning that labor unions could not force all employees in a specific company to join their union in order to work there. In addition, pro-business courts in the 1920s struck down a series of Progressive-era laws against child labor. Abusive forms of child labor persisted, particularly

>> Henry Ford's assembly lines, such as the one pictured here, dramatically sped up the production of automobiles and became a sign that consumerism more than industrialization would drive the economy of the 1920s.

in the textile mills of the South. Working conditions in steel mills and coalmines remained atrocious as well.

21-1b 1920s Consumerism

Despite these obstacles, ordinary working-class people enthusiastically entered the consumer society of the 1920s, buying a wide assortment of laborsaving devices. Speeding this process, domestic electrification spread rapidly throughout the United States, giving most urban families electric lighting and power for the first time. People could now aspire to own new inventions like cars, refrigerators, toasters, radios, telephones, washing machines, vacuums, and phonographs, as well as nationally marketed foods, clothes, and cosmetics.

ADVERTISEMENTS

These new consumer products spawned advertisements, which appeared everywhere in the 1920s: on the radio and on billboards, in magazines and newspapers, even painted on rocks and trees. And with nationwide

> By the end of the 1920s, Americans relied on credit to purchase nearly 90 percent of their major durable goods.

marketing came nationwide advertising campaigns by giant companies like Kellogg's, Gillette, Palmolive, and Nabisco. Most of the money consumers spent when they bought goods like toothpaste was used to pay for advertising rather than for the actual product. Supermarkets were another 1920s invention, replacing the old over-the-counter stores. Now the customer, instead of asking a clerk for items one by one, chose items from open shelves, put them into a basket, and paid for them all at once.

Albert Lasker, Alfred Sloan, and Bruce Barton were all pioneers of the field of marketing and advertising, heightening the American public's interest in orange juice (through a 1910s advertising campaign to increase consumption of oranges), tampons (by going into schools to explain to schoolgirls the process of menstruation—and how to manage it by using tampons), and baked goods (by inventing the maternal icon Betty Crocker). Bruce Barton's noteworthy 1925 book, *The Man Nobody Knows*, depicted Jesus Christ as the world's most successful businessman, who formulated a resonating message (as revealed in the New Testament) and an institutional infrastructure (the Apostles) to spread the Gospel. According to Barton, Jesus was the businessman all Americans should emulate.

BUYING ON CREDIT

Equally striking was a decline in the historic American emphasis on thrift. Instead of saving money every month, buying on credit with installment payments became a socially acceptable way to acquire goods. For industrialists, it was necessary to stimulate demand by encouraging people to spend money they hadn't yet earned. Car companies experimented with different forms of financing car purchases. The result was fantastic for car sellers, as more and more Americans bought cars on installment plans.

Issuing credit expanded throughout the 1920s. One leading historian of installment buying estimates that, by the end of the 1920s, Americans relied on credit to purchase nearly 90 percent of their major durable goods. Correspondingly, Americans saved a smaller percentage of their monthly income.

Glasshouse Images/Alamy Stock Photo

Library of Congress/Getty Images

>> During the 1920s, many grocery stores converted from small over-the-counter shops to larger supermarkets, such as the one pictured here, that allowed customers to peruse the aisles on their own. Here, shoppers walk the aisles at one of the first Piggly Wiggly stores.

The Library of Congress Library of Congress, Prints & Photographs Division, LC-USZ62-114699

EARLY CAR CULTURE

In part because of things like installment buying and the five-dollar day, cars became very popular in the 1920s. By the late 1920s, there was one car for every five people in the country. A car was the key object of desire for anyone who could scrape together enough money to purchase one. A group of sociologists studying a small Midwestern town in the late 1920s found dozens of car-owning families still living in houses without bathtubs or indoor plumbing. Young people especially longed for cars; after all, cars bestowed freedom from watchful, restrictive parents. In fact, one preacher in the South called cars "rolling bedrooms."

ADVENTURES IN REAL ESTATE

The economic boom boosted real estate as well as consumer products, and nowhere more so than in Florida. Florida was a remote backwater of the United States until the discovery of effective cures for yellow fever and malaria around 1900. By the 1920s, road and rail connections down to Miami made the area attractive for winter holidays, and between 1920 and 1925, parcels of land, or lots, began to change hands at rapidly escalating prices. In 1926, the weather intervened, as a pair of devastating hurricanes killed four

Lordprice Collection/Alamy Stock Photo

>> The glamour of Wall Street at the end of the decade is captured in this publicity poster for the 1929 movie *Wall Street*, the second of its name. As the poster says, it is about a ruthless "Napoleon of Finance" and a woman with ideals who "regenerates" him.

hundred people, destroyed hundreds of housing projects, threw boats into the streets, and wiped out an entire town. After that, land in Florida appeared less attractive as an investment. Prices began to fall as steeply as they had risen, and thirty-one local banks failed. Much of the area was left a ghostly ruin and did not recover until after World War II.

STOCKS AND SHARES

If speculating on real estate seemed too risky, buying stocks had broader appeal. The managers, lawyers, accountants, advertisers, brokers, and other "white-collar" professional workers whose ranks increased through the 1920s invested in the stock market in great numbers. This meant that they bought shares, or small percentages, of a company, hoping that the value of the company would increase, which would therefore lead to a rise in the price of a share. This would give the owners of these shares a tidy profit when they sold the shares they owned. Throughout most of the 1920s, the price of stocks and shares rose steadily, deceiving growing numbers of investors into thinking that the trend was destined to continue indefinitely.

At the same time, bankers in the 1920s devised the mutual fund, a professionally managed collection of stocks whose shares people could buy. The fund owned several stocks at one time, thus limiting the amount of risk involved for the individual investor. Because of this pretense of security and shared risk, mutual funds were a popular form of investment throughout the 1920s. Tens of millions of dollars poured into Wall Street from all over the world, inflating stock prices far above their realistic value. This would, of course, have dire consequences later on.

21-2 THE END OF THE PROGRESSIVE ERA

21-2a National Politics

These perilous but generally good economic times had a significant effect on politics. After the unprecedented challenges of the Progressive era, when politicians sought to rein in the most egregious effects of the Industrial Revolution, the 1920s witnessed the rise of a dominant Republican Party that embraced a "business-first" philosophy. These Republicans presided over national politics throughout the decade, holding the presidency from 1920 until 1933.

RED SCARE

Before the economic "good times" took hold, however, America confronted a **Red Scare**, or fear that the United States was vulnerable to a communist takeover. Why a Red Scare? In 1917, Vladimir Lenin and his Russian Bolshevik Party (who were called "Reds" during the Russian Civil War) seized power in Russia, declaring the advent of world communism and the end of all private property. According to the plan spelled out by the German philosopher Karl Marx, Lenin believed that his communist revolution would spread to all the major industrial nations, and he called for workers' uprisings everywhere. This development prompted a number of American politicians and businessmen to fear for the safety of the American capitalist system.

On top of this, the pieces of a revolutionary puzzle seemed to be moving into place in the United States. American socialism had been growing alongside the labor movement. The Socialist Party presidential candidate, Eugene V. Debs, won almost 1 million votes in the election of 1920—from his prison cell. (He had been jailed for making speeches against U.S. participation in World War I, which he denounced as a capitalist endeavor.) Many towns elected socialist mayors and council members, especially in the industrialized Northeast and along the northern stretches of the Mississippi River. And during World War I a variety of anarchists had bombed courthouses, police stations, churches, and even people's homes.

Politicians and businessmen reacted to these developments by initiating a hunt for potential revolutionaries. President Wilson's attorney general, A. Mitchell Palmer, set up a federal bureau to seek out communists and anarchists, and the years 1918–1920 witnessed the arrest and deportation of several hundred union members and foreign-born radicals who had usually committed no crimes but were suspected of favoring a Russian-style coup. To be American, the **Palmer raids** suggested, was not to be communist.

SACCO AND VANZETTI

Fears of political radicals surrounded the famous court case of **Sacco and Vanzetti**. Nicola Sacco and Bartolomeo Vanzetti were Italian immigrants living in Massachusetts. They became suspects

Red Scare Fear that the United States was vulnerable to a communist takeover

Palmer raids Anti-communist raids following World War I led by attorney general A. Mitchell Palmer, leading to the arrest and deportation of hundreds of suspected communists

Sacco and Vanzetti Italian immigrant suspects in a 1920 payroll heist, who were arrested, tried, and convicted of robbery and murder despite a flimsy trail of evidence

in a 1920 payroll heist and were arrested, tried, and convicted of robbery and murder of a guard and paymaster despite a flimsy trail of evidence. Under sentence of death, both proclaimed their anarchist beliefs but maintained their innocence in the heist. A long series of appeals followed, with civil libertarians and friends of the political left taking up the convicted men's cause, claiming it was the men's ethnicity and political beliefs that had convicted them, not the evidence in the trial. Nevertheless, a final committee of inquiry concluded that Sacco and Vanzetti were indeed guilty, and both were executed in the electric chair in 1927. Scholars continue to dispute the defendants' guilt (most believe Sacco was guilty while Vanzetti's guilt is less certain), but the case encapsulated the American public's fears about communists and foreigners in the early 1920s. Only in 1977, fifty years after their executions, did the governor of Massachusetts admit the trial was conducted unfairly.

Despite the paranoia of the Red Scare, it is obvious today that a "red" revolution was never a real possibility during these years. The economy was too good. Although some anarchists were willing to use violent methods to achieve their ends, and although a small American Communist Party did follow instructions from Moscow, most American socialists were Christian pacifists rather than atheist revolutionaries. For instance, America's leading socialist Eugene V. Debs had written a biography of Jesus, whom he depicted as a socialist carpenter and a model proponent of a more equitable way of distributing society's wealth.

>> The Tulsa Race Riot of 1921, in which 800 people were injured and 10,000 became homeless after the burning of the African American Greenwood neighborhood (pictured here), was just one of many race riots that followed the First World War, suggesting the deep fears embedded in an uncertain era of social change.

Great Migration The movement of nearly 2 million African Americans out of the southern parts of the United States to the cities of the North between 1910 and 1930; most were rejecting Jim Crow segregation

RACE RIOTS

Fears of change also prompted a series of violent race riots in the years following the First World War. Even before the war was over, in 1917, white workers in East St. Louis, who had kept African Americans out of their unions, were appalled when African Americans agreed to work for lower wages than white workers would accept. Tempers flared when African Americans then agreed to work as strikebreakers. Fears of white women and black men fraternizing together at labor meetings erupted quickly into a full-fledged riot. Three thousand men surrounded the labor meeting, and, in the end, roughly one hundred people died because of the ensuing violence.

The East St. Louis riot was only the beginning. In the summer of 1919 race riots broke out in more than two dozen cities across the United States. Chicago's were perhaps the worst, with dozens dying and hundreds more injured. But riots also broke out in Connecticut, Maryland, Arizona, Texas, Mississippi, and other states, demonstrating that racial tensions affected the nation as a whole, not just the South. They also put on vivid display the fact that many African Americans had begun to leave the South's system of Jim Crow segregation, heading to the supposedly more racially progressive parts of the country in the North, a broad movement called the **Great Migration**.

African Americans were not always welcome in the new locales, and in the heated atmosphere of industrial conflict combined with post-World War I fears of radicalism, they suffered most.

Even after race relations quieted down throughout much of the rest of the 1920s, they always remained potentially violent. In 1921, the most destructive of all the race riots took place in Tulsa, Oklahoma, where the one-day riot led to 800 injuries and 10,000 people becoming homeless as the racially segregated Tulsa neighborhood of Greenwood was essentially burned to the ground. The sentiments of Jim Crow persisted long into the twentieth century.

WARREN G. HARDING

Once the economy settled down after two years of peacetime conversion, politics mellowed as well. Warren G. Harding won the presidential election of 1920 by campaigning largely from the front porch of his house in Marion, Ohio. Harding openly declared his intention to abandon President Wilson's Progressive ideals, including Wilson's idealistic international program, which had transformed American politics during World War I by expanding U.S. involvement in world affairs. Harding also signaled an end to Progressive politics by using the slogan of "a return to normalcy," and by "**normalcy**" (a newly coined word) he meant the pre-Progressive, pro-business politics of the late 1800s.

With the First World War over, Harding dismantled the National War Labor Board and other agencies designed to regulate private industry. Instead, he advocated independent control for corporations. After a two-year recession while the economy transitioned to peacetime production levels, the Republican ascendancy meant that politics in the 1920s would be predictably conservative.

Starting with Harding, three successive Republican administrations pursued limited government via conservative policies on tariffs, taxes, immigration restriction, labor rights, and business administration. For better or worse, these policies created a robust economy—one healthy enough to allow Americans to make light of a major scandal during Harding's administration, the Teapot Dome Scandal of the early 1920s. The scandal implicated Harding's secretary of the interior, Albert B. Fall, and Fall's willingness to lease government land to prominent American oil men in exchange for bribes. The scandal was exposed in the late 1920s, and Teapot Dome came to symbolize the cozy relations between big business and government that characterized the 1920s. Other scandals plagued the Harding administration, including one in which Attorney General Harry M. Daugherty resigned for taking bribes.

"SILENT CAL"

In August 1923, President Harding died of an apparent heart attack in San Francisco during a tour of the West Coast (just before the Teapot Dome Scandal came to light). Harding's flinty vice president, Calvin Coolidge, heard the news in his hometown of Plymouth, Vermont, while visiting his elderly father. A notary public, Coolidge Sr. administered the oath of office to his son late that night, and "Silent Cal," as he was known, became the 30th president of the United States.

Known for his ability to solve political problems with a minimum of words and minimal effort, Coolidge won reelection in 1924, easily beating Democrat John W. Davis (who carried only southern states) and the new Progressive Party's Robert F. La Follette, whose loss signaled the death-knell of the Progressive era in national politics. Coolidge continued Harding's policy of minimizing the federal government's role in American life. He restored his party's reputation for scrupulous honesty and integrity, which had been damaged by Teapot Dome, by creating a bipartisan commission to investigate the improprieties of the Harding administration. Coolidge also avoided using the federal government to crusade for a cause, something that had ultimately damaged Wilson's presidency and reputation. Coolidge's presidency was notable for its paucity of action.

21-2b Prohibition

There was, however, one volatile issue that came to the forefront of American politics in the 1920s: prohibition, or the outlawing of alcohol. After extensive political lobbying extending back before the Civil War, and empowered by the anti-German sentiment of the First World War (Germans being known for their extensive brewing

normalcy A phrase popularized by Warren G. Harding during his 1920 presidential campaign promising a return to the business-friendly, pre-Progressive era politics of the late nineteenth-century tradition), Prohibition became law of the land in 1919. The Eighteenth Amendment to the Constitution prohibited the "manufacture, sale, or transportation of intoxicating liquors" in the United States.

Prohibition was difficult to enforce. Congress passed the **Volstead Act** (1919), which laid down strict punishments for violating the amendment. But from the start there were problems, not the least of which was the fact that enforcement required a high degree of citizen cooperation. This was simply lacking in many parts of the country. Rural Baptists and Methodists were usually strong supporters of Prohibition, and Prohibition was most effective in small towns of the South and Midwest. But even there, farmers with long traditions of taking a surreptitious drink were reluctant to stop doing so. Stills making moonshine whiskey proliferated in mountain and country districts. The most prominent journalist of the day, H. L. Mencken, joked that Prohibition was the work of "ignorant bumpkins of the cow states who resented the fact that they had to swill raw corn liquor while city slickers got good wine and whiskey."

Meanwhile, immigrants from societies with strong drinking traditions, such as Germany, Ireland, and Italy, hated Prohibition. They were demographically strong in cities and formed ethnic gangs (the most notorious of which was the Sicilian Mafia) that made and sold their own supplies of alcohol. Former saloonkeepers, who had been forced by Prohibition to close down, set up clandestine bars known as **speakeasies** and received their supplies from these gangs.

Police, customs officials, and Treasury agents pursued distillers and bootleggers, with little success. Gang leaders like Al Capone in Chicago bribed police and politicians to look the other way when alcohol shipments were coming into town. But bribery didn't always persuade public officials, and those who resisted bribes were often victims of intimidation and even murder.

A large part of the urban middle class found that, despite the problems associated with alcohol, the idea of *never* having a drink was generally unbearable. Novelist Sinclair Lewis described in his satiric novel *Babbitt* (1922) how a generally law-abiding real estate salesman went about preparing for a dinner party at his home. First he enters "a place curiously like the saloons

of ante-prohibition days." Admitted to a back room, he persuades the owner to sell him a quart of gin, then mixes cocktails at home before his guests arrive. They are all longing for a drink and are delighted when he asks, "Well, folks, do you think you could stand breaking the law a little?" After a couple of drinks each, the men declare that they favor Prohibition as "a mighty good thing for the working class" because it "keeps 'em from wasting their money and lowering their productiveness." But they add that Congress has interfered with "the rights—the personal liberty—of fellows like ourselves," for whom a drink could do no harm.

After fifteen contentious and tumultuous years, Prohibition was repealed in 1933, with the Twenty-first Amendment.

21-3 A NEW CULTURE: THE ROARING TWENTIES

With the economy seemingly good, radical politics largely on the run, and national politics not terribly interesting, many Americans turned to a vast array of leisure activities. New technology, including movie-making equipment, phonographic records, and expanded

Photos 12/Alamy Stock Photo

>> In 1927, audiences flocked to see the first "talky" film, *The Jazz Singer*, which told the story of a second-generation Jewish immigrant who wants to become a modern singer, not a Jewish cantor like his father. He succeeds through the use of blackface, as the billboard shows.

Volstead Act Legislation passed in 1919 that laid down strict punishments for violating the Eighteenth Amendment

speakeasy Clandestine bar serving alcohol during Prohibition

commercial radio, enhanced a vibrant social atmosphere, especially in the nation's cities. The "Roaring Twenties," as they were sometimes called, witnessed a dramatic expansion of popular culture. However, this interest in lighter fare led some to political and intellectual disillusionment, based on the sense that Americans were leaving behind the ideals of the Progressive era in favor of less socially engaged interests. Others were more interested in using culture to break stifling bonds of long-standing restrictions. African Americans, women, and leftist intellectuals were some of the groups pushing against the old social limitations.

21-3a 1920s Popular Culture

In the 1920s breakthroughs in several media allowed the public to enjoy new diversions.

MOVIES

Thomas Edison and other inventors had developed moving films at the turn of the century. After a slow couple of years, films caught on in the 1910s, and by 1920 a film industry had developed in Hollywood, California, where there was plenty of open space, three hundred sunny days a year for outdoor filming, and 3,000 miles between it and Edison's patents. Far away in California, ignoring the patents, which had made most of the top-quality moviemaking equipment very expensive, was relatively easy.

Once established in Hollywood, the movie industry made a series of artistic and technical breakthroughs that popularized the art form throughout the nation. Most exciting was the invention of talking pictures, which first appeared in 1927 with *The Jazz Singer*. At the same time, longer feature films with sophisticated plotting, by directors such as Cecil B. DeMille and D. W. Griffith, replaced the melodramas of the 1910s. Urban movie houses were built and decorated like oriental palaces,

far more lavish than they needed to be to show movies. This gave patrons, who regularly arrived in their best clothes, a sense of glamour and enchantment on their night out. Moviegoing was wildly popular, and stars such as Rudolph Valentino, Clara Bow, Mary Pickford, and Douglas Fairbanks Sr. enjoyed worldwide fame.

MUSIC

Along with movies, **jazz** music came into vogue during the 1920s. Originally derived as part of African American culture, jazz followed ragtime music by "crossing over" to white audiences during the 1920s. Most jazz stars of the 1920s were black men such as pianist Duke Ellington and trumpeter Louis Armstrong, some of the first African Americans to have enthusiastic white fans. Before the 1920s, Americans who wanted to listen to jazz (or any other kind of music) had had to create their own sounds or attend a concert. The invention of the **phonograph**, pioneered by Edison in the 1870s and popularized in the first years of the 1900s, birthed the record industry. This enabled fans to listen to their favorite artists on their gramophones as many times as they wanted.

Furthermore, commercial radio began broadcasting in 1922, allowing people everywhere to hear concerts being played hundreds of miles away. That same year, Warren Harding became the first president to make a radio broadcast. Among the earliest groups to make use of the new medium were evangelical preachers. While they insisted on old, established virtues, they had no objection to using new-fangled methods such as radio to help them spread the Gospel.

PROFESSIONAL SPORTS

Radio promoted an interest in professional and college sports in the 1920s, especially baseball, boxing, and college football. Listeners could get real-time play-by-play, hearing the actions of their favorite local team or boxer. The increased popularity of sports during the 1920s made celebrities out of the best players, the biggest of whom was the New York Yankees' slugger Babe Ruth. It was during the 1920s that baseball truly became "America's pastime," and the 1927 New York Yankees are still considered by many to be the best baseball team of all time.

jazz Rhythmic music derived as part of African American culture and popularized by both white and black musicians during the 1920s

phonograph Invention that played recorded music; pioneered by Edison in the 1870s

FADS, TRIUMPHS, AND SEX SCANDALS

Games such as bridge and mah-jongg became popular during these years as well, and a national craze for crossword puzzles began. The nation took pleasure in reading about the first flight over the North Pole by Admiral Byrd in 1926 and the first trans-Atlantic flight by Charles Lindbergh in 1927. Lindbergh became an international celebrity because of his aviation triumphs.

Americans enjoyed a steady stream of celebrity sex scandals too, like the one surrounding the disappearance of radio evangelist Aimee Semple McPherson in 1926. A theatrical preacher who had built up a radio audience and constructed an auditorium called the "Angelus Temple" in Hollywood, she disappeared while bathing in the sea in 1926. Disciples, finding her clothes on the beach, feared that "Sister Aimee" had drowned. She reappeared a few weeks later, claiming that she had been abducted and imprisoned in Mexico, had broken free, crossed the desert on foot, and daringly evaded her kidnappers. Investigators knocked holes in the story almost at once, especially when evidence from Carmel, farther up the California coast, showed she had been enjoying herself in a love nest with an engineer from her own radio station. The widespread interest in this type of gossip-column fare was typical of a carefree, apolitical era.

21-3b The "New Negro"

African American jazz musicians blossomed as the musical facet of a larger ferment among African Americans in the 1920s, known collectively as the **Harlem Renaissance**. Following the First World War and the race riots that followed, many African Americans had grown frustrated with America's entrenched racism and became motivated to challenge the prevailing order. They sought to establish themselves as different from their parents' generation, which they saw as unnecessarily kowtowing to white interests in an effort to advance through accommodation. Instead, the younger generation of African Americans declared it would rather "die fighting" than be further subjugated in American society. This new generation epitomized what one Harlem Renaissance leader, the philosopher Alain Locke, called "the new Negro."

Harlem Renaissance A cultural and political endeavor among African Americans using art and literature to protest the perpetuation of racism in America and in African Americans' historic responses to it; its leaders demanded the rise of a "new Negro" who would stand up and fight American racism; lasted from 1919 to 1929

>> Aaron Douglas was one of the most prominent visual artists of the Harlem Renaissance, creating images full of life and energy that often harked back to Africa, giving pride and a foundation to people often thought to be rootless.

Despite its seemingly political goals, the Harlem Renaissance was mostly a literary celebration, as prominent authors like Langston Hughes and Zora Neale Hurston emerged under its auspices. As African Americans moved north to escape sharecropping and the social segregation of the South, many headed to the large northern cities. No neighborhood grew more than Harlem, which was by real estate code the only large neighborhood in New York City where black people could live as a group.

Several intellectuals, such as W. E. B. Du Bois and James Weldon Johnson, sought to politicize the growing number of urban black people, although few leaders had much luck organizing politically. The NAACP, meanwhile, pursued a legal strategy to end forced segregation in America's cities. Throughout much of the twentieth century, the NAACP brought these challenges to America's courts, forcing the court system to evaluate the segregation that persisted in the United States. Whether the courts were willing to confront and overturn segregation was another matter altogether.

MARCUS GARVEY

The Harlem Renaissance was not a political movement, though, and the legal strategies of the NAACP were unlikely to provoke a social movement. Marcus Garvey occupied this vacuum. The first black nationalist leader to foment a broad movement in the United States, Garvey founded the **Universal Negro Improvement Association** in 1914 and moved its headquarters to Harlem in 1916. Through parades, brightly colored uniforms, and a flamboyant style of leadership, Garvey advocated a celebration of blackness, the creation of black-owned and -operated businesses, and the dream of a return of all black people to Africa. Indeed, he created his own line of steamships, the "Black Star Line," with the intention of tying together black-owned businesses in Africa, the Caribbean, and the United States. His organization eventually counted more than 1 million members worldwide, although most mainstream American politicians ignored him. More damningly, the antipathy he suffered from other African American civil rights workers curtailed his power further. He suffered a harsh decline in the early 1920s, indicted for mail fraud while selling stock in the Black Star Line, and, in 1927, he was deported back to Jamaica, his birthplace.

On a variety of fronts, then, black urbanites, many a part of the Great Migration from south to north, struggled to locate their political and cultural voice. They also became keenly aware that racism did not stop north of the Mason-Dixon line.

21-3c Changing Roles for Women

Women won the right to vote with the Nineteenth Amendment in 1920, one of the final great reforms of the Progressive era. The first election in which they voted put Harding into office. Many people expected the amendment to have dramatic consequences in national politics, but the female vote was actually split evenly between the candidates. Rather than swaying the balance in any one direction, unmarried women generally voted the same as their fathers, and married women generally voted the same as their husbands.

But winning the vote marked the triumphant end of a long and frequently bitter campaign. Suffragists had hoped to transform politics for the better. They imagined national politics as a place where deals were brokered by unscrupulous groups of men in smoke-filled back rooms, and they intended to bring politics into the light of day and bring morality to bear. In light of the corruption scandals of the Harding administration (namely, Teapot Dome), winning the vote had not achieved this, so now what were activists to do?

ERA

Many activists turned their attention to economics and the job market. At the urging of Alice Paul, a former suffragist and now head of the **National Women's Party** (a political lobbying coalition founded in 1913), a group of congressmen proposed an **Equal Rights Amendment** to the Constitution in 1923. It read: "Men and women shall have equal rights throughout the United States and every place subject to its jurisdiction." The amendment's objective was to eliminate all legal distinctions between the sexes, such as those that permitted different pay scales for men and women doing the same job. Some women, especially trade unionists, opposed the amendment because it would have nullified laws that protected mothers and working women from harsh working conditions and excessively long hours. In the end, however, Congress did not approve the amendment until 1972, and even then the necessary three-quarters of the states did not ratify it. In the years since, however, an equal-pay provision has become law, but the ERA never did pass.

THE "NEW" WOMAN

If the political successes largely stopped in 1920, the rest of the 1920s witnessed the development of a distinct youth culture, especially among young single

Universal Negro Improvement Association Marcus Garvey's black nationalist fraternal organization that advocated a celebration of blackness, the creation of black-owned and -operated businesses, and the dream of a return of all black people to Africa

National Women's Party Political lobbying coalition founded in 1913 that promoted women's right to vote and to share political and economic equality

Equal Rights Amendment Proposed amendment to the Constitution meant to eliminate all legal distinctions between the sexes, such as those that permitted different pay scales for men and women doing the same job

Margaret Sanger promoted the liberalizing culture of the 1920s as the leading advocate for birth control (a phrase she coined) and planned parenthood. Sanger became a touchstone for women's rights in the period, lecturing all over the United States and Europe. Putting on display the often contradictory nature of a liberalizing culture, Sanger also favored some aspects of the eugenics movement, including sterilizing people with severe mental disabilities.

There are several reasons why the traditional Protestant morality that had dominated American mores throughout the second half of the nineteenth century came under assault in the early twentieth century (see "The Reasons Why . . ." box).

21-3d Disillusioned Writers, Liberalizing Mores

The 1920s also saw the coming of age of American literature. An influential group of writers, including poets T. S. Eliot and Ezra Pound and novelists John Dos Passos, Ernest Hemingway, and Gertrude Stein, found commercial America vulgar—so distasteful they declined to participate altogether. They went to Europe, usually to London and Paris, where they formed intellectual expatriate communities. But in their self-exile they remained preoccupied by their American roots and wrote some of the most effective American literature of their age. Together, the writers of the 1920s are referred to as "the Lost Generation," mainly because of their disillusionment with the Progressive ideals that had been exposed as fraudulent during the First World War.

Other fine writers felt no desire to flee. Sinclair Lewis produced a long stream of satirical novels about 1920s America that won him a Nobel Prize for literature in 1930, America's first. Literary critic Malcolm Cowley, himself a Paris expatriate in the 1920s, observed that American literature was maturing rapidly and that "by 1930 it had come to be valued for itself and studied like Spanish or German or Russian literature. There were now professors of American literature at the great European universities. American plays, lowbrow and highbrow, were being applauded in the European capitals." It is, of course, ironic that most of the American writers of this formative period made their mark by deriding mainstream America for its conformity, stifling mores, bland commercialism, and empty boosterism. Their own erudition contradicted their claims that America was anti-intellectual.

>> "Flappers" were the decade's outspoken, independent women who openly displayed disregard for the Victorian ethos of the past and suggested one possible avenue for women's roles in the future. This photo of a "modern woman" features a short dress, short hair, and an open sexuality that appalled women of a previous generation.

Burke/Triolo/Brand X Pictures/Getty Images

women. New fashions, notably short "bobbed" hair, knee-length dresses that seemed daringly short, public smoking, and dance crazes such as the Charleston all generated controversy. "Flappers" were the decade's outspoken, independent women, who scorned the "Victorian" inhibitions of their parents' generation. F. Scott Fitzgerald's *This Side of Paradise* (1920) and *The Beautiful and the Damned* (1922) evoked the cosmopolitanism of the era, especially its changing attitudes toward unchaperoned courtship and "petting."

The Reasons Why...

There were at least four reasons why traditional Protestant morality came under assault in the first decades of the twentieth century:

Loss of biblical authority. Charles Darwin's theory of evolution, which questioned the authenticity of the biblical story of creation, and therefore the Bible as a whole, was widely accepted in the second half of the nineteenth century. At the same time, European historians and intellectuals were developing a school of biblical criticism that examined the Bible as a historical artifact worthy of investigation rather than a book of revealed divine truth. The loss of biblical authority unmoored many people's beliefs in Christian morality, and in Christianity in general.

Decline of universal morality. At the same time, anthropologists and sociologists like Franz Boas and Robert Park began arguing that other cultures were not any less valuable or moral than white Protestant culture, just different from it. There were, these thinkers argued, no hierarchies of races or hierarchies of moral authority. If the value of a particular cultural was relative based on one's perception, this meant that any notion of universal morals was highly questionable as well.

Psychology. Meanwhile, psychologists like Sigmund Freud placed sexual desires at the heart of human urges, making sex a legitimate topic of discussion, indeed, a necessary one if someone wanted to learn the various drives that make one human. Sex was no longer an act to be held under wraps, but one worthy of exploration and even trial and error.

Consumerism. Nothing sells better than sex, a fact not missed by the new generation of advertising agents and marketers. At the same time, greater freedoms promoted by inventions like automobiles made it easier to escape the watchful gaze of parents. Meanwhile, movies promoted scintillating images of love and lust as well as valor and honor, at the same time providing a darkened environment for viewers, perhaps hand-in-hand, to enjoy these new images.

21-4 REACTIONS

With all these changes swirling around, many Americans felt uncomfortable with what they saw as the liberal mores of the youth culture and the erosion of community life prompted by the Industrial Revolution. Some of these dissenters found a home in Protestant fundamentalism. Others rejected what they viewed as an increasing acceptance of cosmopolitanism and moral relativity. If the 1920s were an age of social and intellectual liberation, they also gave birth to new forms of reaction that created a clash of values.

21-4a Religious Divisions

Protestants have always been denominationally divided, but in the 1920s, a split between modernists and fundamentalists became readily apparent, leading to a landmark court case.

MODERNISTS

On the one hand, a group of Protestants calling themselves **modernists** consciously sought to adapt their Protestant faith to the findings of scientific theories such as evolution and evidence that called into question the literalness of the Bible, something called biblical criticism. As these twin impulses became increasingly accepted by scholars, some liberal Protestants stopped thinking of the Bible as God's infallible word. Instead, they regarded it as a collection of ancient writings, some of them historical, some prophetic, and some mythological. In the modernists' view, represented in the writings of preacher Harry Emerson Fosdick, God did not *literally* make the world in six days, Adam and Eve weren't *actual* people, and there was no *real* flood covering the whole earth. Men like Fosdick contended that these events were mythic explanations of human origins. Jesus was as central as ever, the divine figure standing at the center of history and transforming it, but Jesus would surely encourage his people to learn modern science and comparative religion, and to focus on other studies that enriched their knowledge of God's world and spread peace and tolerance far and wide. Not to do so was to be intolerant, and this was no way to act in a pluralistic world.

> **modernists** Protestants who consciously sought to adapt their Protestant faith to the findings of scientific theories, such as evolution and evidence that questioned the literalness of the Bible

>> Former baseball player Billy Sunday grew to great fame as a dynamic preacher of what he called the Christian fundamentals.

FUNDAMENTALISTS

On the other hand, the group of Protestants who have come to be known as **fundamentalists** (after the publication in the 1910s of a series of pamphlets labeled "the Fundamentals") insisted that the Bible should be understood as God's revealed word, absolutely true down to the last detail. In their view, the main points of traditional Christian doctrine, including biblical inerrancy, the reality of miracles, and the Virgin birth, must be asserted and upheld. Most fundamentalists were

fundamentalists Protestants who insisted that the Bible should be understood as God's revealed word, absolutely true down to the last detail; they asserted and upheld the main points of traditional Christian doctrine, including biblical inerrancy, the reality of miracles, and the Virgin birth

Scopes Monkey Trial Famous 1925 court case that revolved around a state law prohibiting the teaching of evolution in Tennessee schools; John Scopes, a young teacher, offered to deliberately break the law to test its constitutionality

American Civil Liberties Union (ACLU) Organization founded in 1920 that was dedicated to fighting infringements on civil liberties, including free speech

troubled by evolution, not only because it denied the literal truth of Genesis but also because it implied that humans, evolving from lower species, were the outcome of random mutations, rather than a creation of God in His own image. Traveling evangelists such as Billy Sunday, an ex-major league baseball player, and Aimee Semple McPherson denounced evolution and all other deviations from the Gospel as the Devil's work. They also attacked the ethos of the social gospel (for more on the social gospel, see Chapter 19).

SCOPES MONKEY TRIAL

In 1925, the conflict between modernists and fundamentalists came to a head in Dayton, Tennessee, in the **Scopes Monkey Trial**. The case revolved around a state law that prohibited the teaching of evolution in Tennessee schools. John Scopes, a young teacher, offered to deliberately break the law to test its constitutionality (in order to obtain publicity for this struggling "New South" town) with the understanding that the **American Civil Liberties Union (ACLU)** would pay the costs to defend him. The trial drew journalists from all over America and was one of the first great media circuses of the century.

At the trial, the nation's most prominent defense lawyer, Clarence Darrow, volunteered to help Scopes. William Jennings Bryan, the three-time Democratic presidential candidate and former secretary of state, volunteered to assist the prosecution. Darrow, an agnostic, actually called Bryan as a witness for the defense and questioned him about the origins of the earth. Did not the geological evidence prove the immense age of its rocks? asked Darrow. "I'm not interested in the age of rocks but in the Rock of Ages!" countered Bryan, who believed the earth was about 6,000 years old. Scopes was convicted (the conviction was later overturned on a technicality) and fined $100, and the law against teaching evolution remained in effect. Press coverage by urbane journalists such as H. L. Mencken and Joseph Wood Krutch ridiculed the anti-evolutionists, but fundamentalism continued to dominate rural Protestantism, especially in the South and Midwest.

21-4b Immigration Restriction and Quotas

If modern mores were one cause of fear, another was the transformation provoked by immigration. As we have seen in chapters past, millions of immigrants entered the United States between 1880 and 1920, and in the early 1920s many congressmen and social observers articulated a fear that the "Anglo-Saxon" heritage of the United States was being "mongrelized" by "swarthy" Europeans. These Europeans (Italians, Russians, Greeks, or other people from southern and eastern Europe) would be considered white by today's standards, but they were viewed as "others" during the 1920s because they were Catholics or Jews from countries in eastern and southern Europe, and they spoke foreign languages and cooked odd-smelling foods.

IMMIGRATION RESTRICTIONS

The ideology undergirding the fears of American politicians was the idea of **Americanization**. This was defined as the notion that all American immigrant groups should leave behind their old ways and melt into the Anglo-Saxon mainstream. Some intellectuals challenged this idea with concepts like the **melting pot** (in which all the nation's people contributed their cultural traits to a single mix, creating something altogether new) and **cultural pluralism** (the idea that each cultural group should retain its uniqueness and not be forced to change by a restrictive state or culture).

Despite the power of these countervailing ideas, acts of Congress in 1921 (the Quota Act) and 1924 (the **National Origins Act**) for the first time in the country's history greatly restricted the number of immigrants permitted to enter the United States, creating a series of quotas that mandated how many immigrants could come from each country. These limits were based on immigration figures from the end of the nineteenth century, when most immigrants were from Britain, Ireland, or northern Europe. And they appeased the widespread fear of "the alien" during these years, at a time when antisemitism, anti-Catholicism, nativism, and racism meaningfully influenced the ideas and positions of politicians and public figures. The idea, as one politician of the time put it, was to "shut the door" to immigrants in order to preserve the always-tenuous ideal that what it meant to be American was to be a white, Anglo-Saxon Protestant.

One major result of the new immigration policy was that Italian, Polish, Hungarian, and Jewish communities no longer received a steady flow of "greenhorns" to keep them in touch with the old country. Instead, these communities gradually dissolved as their members learned English in public schools and followed work and housing opportunities into non-ethnically defined

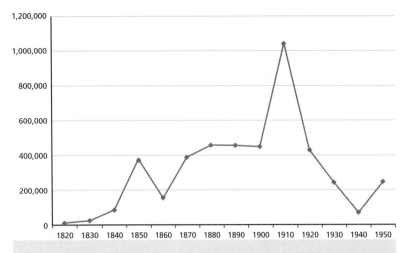

Figure 21.1 Number of Immigrants Entering the United States, 1820–1950

>> After peaking during the first two decades of the twentieth century, the number of immigrants coming to the United States declined precipitously as a result of the immigration restriction laws of the 1920s.

neighborhoods. This process of dissolution was mostly completed by the 1950s.

In addition to greatly limiting the number of immigrants allowed to come to the United States, especially from the predominantly Catholic and Jewish countries of southern and eastern Europe (see Figure 21.1), a second major result of the new immigration policy was to set up widespread institutions for controlling the country's borders, including the U.S. Border Patrol (1924) and the Immigration and Naturalization Service (1933). While the 1920s immigration laws did not restrict the number of immigrants coming from Latin America, the creation of patrols and the mandating of documented paperwork would greatly alter what had been a relatively fluid border between the United States and Mexico.

Americanization Notion that all American immigrant groups should leave behind their old ways and melt into the Anglo-Saxon mainstream

melting pot Concept that all the nation's people contributed their cultural traits to a single mix, creating something altogether new

cultural pluralism Idea that each cultural group should retain its uniqueness and not be forced to change by a restrictive state or culture

National Origins Act Legislation that restricted the number of immigrants permitted to enter the United States, creating a series of quotas in 1924

QUOTAS

Alongside Congress's implementation of immigration quotas, many colleges and universities, especially in the Northeast, began instituting quotas to limit the number of Jews who could attend. Social fraternities and housing developments limited membership by racial and religious restrictions, and most attempts to circumvent these restrictions were met with strong resistance and sometimes violence. The boosterism and "pep" of the 1920s extended only so far. For many Americans, the national narrative only concerned the advancement of white, Anglo-Saxon Protestants.

21-4c Social Intolerance

Perhaps unsurprisingly, alongside immigration restriction, a new nativism emerged in response to all the economic and social changes taking place.

THE RESURGENCE OF THE KLAN

For example, the **Ku Klux Klan**, an organization formed to "redeem" the South after Reconstruction, enjoyed a revival in the 1920s after being reborn in a ceremony on Georgia's Stone Mountain in 1915. Attesting to the power of movies during this era, the Klan's resurgence was in part inspired by the positive portrayal it received in D. W. Griffith's three-hour film *Birth of a Nation*. This movie is often considered the most influential film in American history for its innovative techniques and sweeping dramatic arc—despite the fact that it was overtly racist and lionized the Klan. The Klan of the 1920s saw itself as the embodiment of old Protestant and Southern virtues. In the new era of the 1920s, however, the Klan enlisted members in the North as well, especially in cities, thus reemerging in response to the new urban culture of the time. Hiram Wesley Evans, a Texas dentist, was the Klan's Imperial Wizard during these years. He declared he was pledged to defend decency and Americanism from numerous threats: race-mixing, Jews, Catholics, and the immoralities of urban sophistication.

Ku Klux Klan A quasi-military force formed immediately after the Civil War by former Confederate soldiers in order to resist racial integration and preserve white supremacy; after a temporary decline, the group reformed in 1915 and sporadically returned to prominence throughout the nineteenth and twentieth centuries.

The Klan was mainly anti-Catholic in northern and western states. For instance, Klan members won election to the legislature in Oregon and then outlawed private schools for all children ages eight to sixteen. This was meant to attack the Catholic parochial school system that had been established in response to the overt Protestantism taught in public schools in the 1800s. Oregon's Catholics fought back, eventually battling to the U.S. Supreme Court, which, in the case of *Pierce* v. *Society of Sisters* (1925), upheld the Catholic Church's right to run its own school system.

This wave of Klan activity came to a highly publicized end when one of the organization's leaders, David (D.C.) Stephenson, was convicted of the abduction, rape, and second-degree murder of a woman who ran a literacy program in Indiana. When Indiana governor Ed Jackson refused to commute his sentence in 1927, Stephenson released the names of several politicians who had been on the Klan's payroll, leading to the indictment of many politicians, including the governor, for accepting bribes. Both the Klan and several Indiana politicians were shamed in the debacle.

21-4d The Election of 1928

The multitude of modernizing changes during the 1920s and the variety of reactions against them were symbolized by the candidates in the presidential election of 1928. The election pitted the Democrat Al Smith against Republican Herbert Hoover. Hoover was idealized as a nonpolitical problem solver and an advocate of big business. He represented the freewheeling Republican values of the 1920s and also epitomized America's Anglo-Saxon Protestant heritage. Smith, meanwhile, was the Democratic governor of New York and the first Catholic to be nominated for president by one of the major parties. He represented the surging tide of social change. Although no radical, he was known to be a friend of the immigrant and a supporter of civil liberties and Progressive-era social welfare.

During the election, the major issue dividing the two men was Prohibition. More than anything else, that issue symbolized the clash of values that had surfaced in American life in the 1920s: Hoover represented the rural and Protestant population that advocated and understood the reasons for Prohibition, while Smith represented the ethnic and urban groups who viewed it as restrictive and racist. Although Smith had a surprisingly strong showing in every large city, Hoover won in a landslide (see Map 21.1).

1928

Candidate (Party)	Electoral Vote		Popular Vote	
Hoover (Republican)	444	83.6%	21,392,190	58.0%
Smith (Democrat)	87	16.4%	15,016,443	40.7%

Map 21.1 The Election of 1928

>> The election of 1928, which pitted Herbert Hoover versus Al Smith, the first Catholic presidential nominee from a major political party, was not close. Hoover won 83.6% of the electoral vote.

> LOOKING AHEAD . . .

The Democrats, with their hodgepodge of supporters, were on the rise, but as yet they lacked an issue that would propel them to power. They wouldn't have to wait long. In October 1929, the stock market, rising steadily from 1925 to mid-1929, began a steep drop. On October 29, later known as "Black Tuesday," 16 million shares changed hands and countless stocks lost almost all of their value. During the next three years, the supply of capital flowing into the economy contracted sharply, dozens of businesses went bankrupt, factories with inventory closed down, and growing numbers of men and women lost their jobs. Complex problems in the American and international economy meant that the crash wasn't just one of the periodic "adjustments" the market always experiences, but something much more serious: an economic depression that would affect the entire world for a decade. The Great Depression would cause Democratic political landslides throughout the 1930s, which saw the rise of Franklin D. Roosevelt as president and his New Deal plan of social action. It is to the Great Depression that we turn next.

STUDY TOOLS 21

READY TO STUDY? IN THE BOOK, YOU CAN:

❏ Rip out the Chapter Review Card, which includes key terms and chapter summaries.

ONLINE AT WWW.CENGAGEBRAIN.COM, YOU CAN:

❏ Collect StudyBits while you read and study the chapter.

❏ Quiz yourself on key concepts.

❏ Find videos for further exploration.

❏ Prepare for tests with HIST5 Flash Cards as well as those you create.

❏ Read a 1931 report on the difficulties of enforcing Prohibition.

❏ Read advertisements from the 1920s.

❏ Read a congressman's denunciation of quotas.

❏ Read H. L. Mencken's account of the Scopes trial.

CH21 TIMELINE

What Else Was Happening

1915 Ku Klux Klan resurges in the wake of "rebirth" at Georgia's Stone Mountain.

1916 Marcus Garvey opens Universal Negro Improvement Association in Harlem.

1919 Eighteenth Amendment and Volstead Act impose nationwide prohibition on alcohol.

1920: *Nineteenth Amendment grants women the right to vote.*

Imprisoned socialist presidential candidate Eugene V. Debs gets 1 million votes.

Harry Burt, a Youngstown, Ohio, candy maker, sells first ice cream on a stick, the Good Humor bar.

1922: *Commercial radio begins broadcasting.*

The Union of Soviet Socialist Republics is formed after communists take power in the Russian Revolution of 1917.

1923 Teapot Dome scandal reveals corrupt ties between White House and big business.

Women propose Equal Rights Amendment to Congress, which acts on it in 1972.

1924 National Origins Act creates biased restrictions on immigrants.

1925: *Supreme Court upholds Catholic Church's right to run its own schools.*

Modernists and fundamentalists debate evolution in Scopes Monkey Trial.

Yale students invent the Frisbee while tossing empty pie plates from the Frisbie Baking Company.

1926 Florida hurricane kills 400, crashes speculative land prices and investing banks.

Marcus Garvey deported to Jamaica for mail fraud in sale of Black Star Line shares.

1927: *Charles Lindbergh's cross-Atlantic flight makes him an international celebrity.*

Italian immigrants Sacco and Vanzetti sentenced to death with minimal evidence.

The Jazz Singer is the first major talking motion picture. The first words heard in a motion picture are spoken by actor Al Jolson: "Wait a minute! You ain't heard nothing yet!"

1928 Herbert Hoover defeats Catholic New York Democrat Al Smith in landslide.

Color television pictures are transmitted in New York.

Museum of Modern Art opens in New York City, celebrating the birth of modern art that developed alongside the Industrial Revolution.

1929 **October:** After four years of steady growth, stock market begins worst decline in history.

1933 The Twenty-first Amendment repeals Prohibition.

HIST
ONLINE

ACCESS TEXTBOOK CONTENT ONLINE—INCLUDING ON SMARTPHONES!

Includes Videos & Other Interactive Resources!

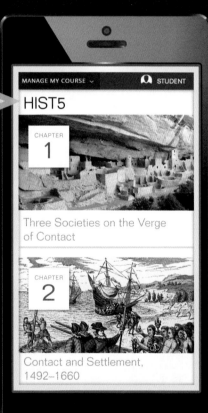

MANAGE MY COURSE ∨   STUDENT

HIST5

CHAPTER
1

Three Societies on the Verge of Contact

CHAPTER
2

Contact and Settlement, 1492–1660

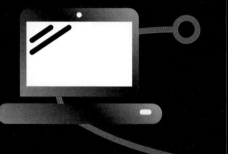

4LTR
PRESS

Access HIST5 ONLINE at www.cengagebrain.com

22 | The Great Depression and the New Deal

LEARNING OBJECTIVES

After reading this chapter, you should be able to do the following:

22-1 Explain the underlying causes of the economic depression, and evaluate President Hoover's attempts to help the economy recover.

22-2 Describe the experiences of both urban and rural Americans during the Great Depression, and explain ways in which the Great Depression affected American politics.

22-3 Evaluate FDR's actions designed to alleviate the effects of the economic decline, and discuss the opposition he faced.

22-4 Discuss the most significant long-term effects of the New Deal.

AFTER FINISHING
THIS CHAPTER
GO TO **PAGE 434**
FOR STUDY TOOLS

In 1928, when Herbert Hoover defeated Al Smith for the presidency, Hoover had every reason to believe the future of the country was bright. In his Inaugural Address, he expressed his belief that the United States was "rich in resources; stimulating in its glorious beauty; filled with millions of happy homes; blessed with comfort and opportunity." He later added, "We in America today are nearer to the final triumph over poverty than ever before in any land in history. The poorhouse is vanishing from among us."

Just eight months after his inauguration, Hoover was facing a very different situation. The stock market had crashed, the bottom had fallen out of an already weakened housing market, markets for agricultural goods stalled, demand for consumer goods fell precipitously leading factories to slow production, and the United States entered into the Great Depression.

The Great Depression caused massive unemployment and declining wages. People lost their homes, their savings, their aspirations, and their dreams. The poorest faced the literal threat of starvation. Breadlines became common. Nearly one in four working Americans was out of work, and in some cities it was nearly every other person.

The Great Depression affected people's everyday lives in ways that are hard to describe. Americans were terrified of succumbing to a disaster they did not understand. In the 1920s, many things seemed possible. You were sure that if you worked hard you would have a job, and maybe even prosper. Now the hurdles seemed insurmountable. Year after year colleges and universities produced graduates with little to no prospects for jobs. The birthrate declined. In an effort to increase prices by limiting the amount of goods that reached markets, farmers in Iowa, Indiana, and elsewhere destroyed livestock and let milk rot, all while many urban dwellers teetered on the edge of starvation. Even Babe Ruth took a significant pay cut, while moderates, not used to having a radical thought cross their minds, began to wonder if democracy and capitalism were somehow fatally flawed. Fear overcame hope.

In the end, hope was revived before the economy was. The election of Franklin D. Roosevelt in 1932 inaugurated a new era of social and economic experimentation. Under Roosevelt's guidance, a "New Deal" of government intervention into the economy and everyday lives of Americans attempted to rein in the economic collapse. This chapter examines the causes and effects of the Great Depression before turning to Franklin D. Roosevelt's attempts to control them.

22-1 THE ECONOMICS AND POLITICS OF DEPRESSION

There was no single cause of the Great Depression. Instead, a series of events combined to cause the economic crisis (see "The Reasons Why . . ." box).

22-1a Statistics

The stock market crash and the collapsing world economy pushed the United States into the deepest economic decline in its history. The simplest statistics explain the disaster: between 1929 and 1933, about 9,000 banks closed. Business investments in industrial construction declined from $23.3 billion in 1929 to $10.1 billion in 1932. The automobile industry's earnings dropped 40 percent between 1929 and 1930. Between 1929 and 1932, the United States gross national product declined from $103.1 billion to $58 billion. The national unemployment rate skyrocketed from 3.2 percent in 1929 to nearly 25 percent in 1933. In some areas, the rate was even higher. In Detroit, for example, unemployment was more than 50 percent in the early 1930s. When people lost money, they could not buy products, forcing industries to slow production and lay off workers, which left even fewer consumers.

22-1b Hoover

Naturally, most Americans looked to the president to solve the national crisis. But Hoover had a difficult time. An orphan as a young man, Hoover had worked his way up from the bottom, becoming a millionaire in the mining industry and eventually becoming one of only two presidents to redistribute his presidential salary (John F. Kennedy was the other, giving it to charity). Hoover believed his success was due to self-reliance, hard work, and the fact that he always had to work his way out of his own problems. He was not anti-government, but he felt that government assistance would make people dependent on handouts and defeat the self-reliance he deemed sacrosanct. Instead, he, like most Republicans of the era, believed that citizens, businesses, and the government should work together voluntarily to overcome the economic depression, instead of being rescued through government-mandated programs. He thus formulated policies based on his idea of voluntary cooperation, which held that business leaders would make sacrifices for the benefit of the nation,

◀◀◀ **Dorothea Lange's famous photo of a 32-year-old mother of seven captured the pain and hopelessness of the Great Depression.**

The Reasons Why...

Three events were of paramount importance in causing the Great Depression:

The stock market crash. Throughout the 1920s, the stock market seemed to reflect the strength of the U.S. economy, and stock investments increased dramatically. In part, this growth reflected the expansion of business profits during the 1920s. In addition, the federal government reduced taxes during the 1920s (especially for the wealthy), putting more money in the pockets of investors. But the most important factor affecting the rise of the stock market was credit. The most common form of credit for stock purchases was the **call loan**, which allowed a stock buyer to put down anywhere from 10 to 50 percent of a stock's price and borrow the rest of the money in order to make the full payment. The lender could then "call back" the loan and demand repayment when a stock fell below a certain price. By the end of 1928, there was nearly $8 billion in outstanding call loans.

When, in September 1929, the Federal Reserve Board raised interest rates, a move they hoped would prevent over-speculation in the stock market, banks cut back on lending because costs had increased. With less money available for loans, fewer people were buying stock, so stock prices began to fall. Once they fell slightly, some banks began to call in their call loans, leading to more selling and further drops in the market, creating a cycle of selling and more selling. After a slight recovery of prices in late September, the market eventually collapsed. Journalists and social watchers had begun to spread word that the economic bubble was about to burst, prompting a selling frenzy. By early November, stock values had decreased an unimaginable $26 billion, more than a third of what the stock market's value had been in August. It would only get worse during the next two years. When the stock market finally stabilized in 1932, stocks had lost nearly 90 percent of their value.

>> In this photo, groups of depositors congregate in front of the closed American Union Bank, New York City on April 26, 1932.

The National Archives and Records Administration

Internal weaknesses in the American economy. The stock market crash compounded existing problems within the American economy. The agricultural sector had been in a severe depression since the early 1920s. The industrial sector, including the vital home construction and automobile industries, was beginning to slow down from its amazing growth in the previous decade. If these markets had been strong, the nation's economy would not have been as vulnerable to the decline of the stock market. Instead, because so much of the 1920s boom was attributable to consumption, when people stopped buying goods the economy ground to a halt.

The European economy. The third reason had to do with problems in Europe. The economies of Britain, France, and Germany experienced problems similar to the American economy in the late 1920s: (1) declining industrial production, (2) low prices in agriculture, and (3) over-speculation in the stock market. But the biggest problem stemmed from the end of World War I, when the Treaty of Versailles forced Germany to pay back the costs of the war. These reparations were difficult for Germany to pay back because the war had destroyed its industrial infrastructure.

The solution came from U.S. banks. In order to pay the reparations, Germany borrowed from American banks. Britain and France, in turn, used that money to repay the debts they had incurred during the war, most often to the U.S. government. The United States was sending money to Germany, which was giving it to France and Britain, which were sending it back to the United States. This cycle of debt, though very unstable, was supported by U.S. businesses because the borrowed funds also allowed European countries to buy U.S. products.

When the stock market crashed, this system fell apart. U.S. businesses that had lost money in the crash cut back on production and stopped buying products from European countries. In addition, after the crash U.S. banks wanted their debts repaid. This was impossible. When European countries couldn't pay back those loans and U.S. banks began to fail, the economic decline of both the United States and other countries worsened.

just as workers would too. But in both farming and banking, the idea of **voluntary cooperation** failed to stabilize the troubled industries. Simply asking industry leaders and laborers to sacrifice for the good of the country was not going to be enough.

While he understood that he would have to do more than simply ask business leaders to help, one of Hoover's first efforts to help the American economy proved to be the most ruinous. In June 1930, Hoover signed the **Hawley-Smoot Tariff** (named for the congressmen who helped write the legislation). The bill raised American tariffs on foreign agricultural and manufactured goods by as much as 50 percent.

Hoover believed that raising prices on foreign products would protect American products from competition. But the effect was disastrous. European governments, already saddled with debts, were further damaged because the bill hurt their ability to earn money to pay back World War I debts. Furthermore, these nations retaliated with very high tariffs of their own, making it difficult for American businesses to sell their products overseas.

Hoover had better luck providing relief to the unemployed, but again, he relied most heavily on voluntary organizations rather than the federal government. Unemployed workers, the Red Cross, and church groups came together to offer surplus food to those in need. The Unemployed Citizen's League in Seattle, for instance, created a system whereby people could exchange work for food, clothing, and other goods.

Eventually responding to perpetual public pressure, Hoover pledged some federal funds to assist the worsening economic situation. By the end of his presidency, he nearly doubled the budget for public works expenditures, which funded the Hoover Dam, one of the largest government construction projects ever undertaken. He also established the President's Organization on Unemployment Relief (POUR), which persuaded local organizations across the country to raise money and form voluntary groups that would sponsor soup kitchens and clothing exchanges.

But Hoover's belief that the federal government should not come to the aid of its citizens because it would damage their capacity for self-reliance and hard work elicited a stern rebuke from the population. In the depths of the Great Depression, relying on volunteerism was not enough.

While running for reelection in 1932, Hoover realized he needed to do still more to ease people's financial

The Granger Collection, NYC

>> No matter what he tried, Hoover seemed ill-equipped to deal with the Great Depression, leading to much public scorn. In this political cartoon, a variety of American interests, from labor to business, all point the finger at Hoover.

woes. In January 1932, he established the Reconstruction Finance Corporation (RFC), a federally funded agency that loaned money to businesses with the hope they

call loan Most common form of credit for stock purchases; allowed a stock buyer to put down from 10 to 50 percent of a stock's price and borrow the rest of the money in order to make the full payment; the lender could then "call back" the loan and demand repayment when a stock fell below a certain price

voluntary cooperation Name for Herbert Hoover's belief that the American economy could rebound from the Great Depression if people willingly worked together and made sacrifices in order to benefit the whole society, including asking business leaders to pay more and laborers to accept less

Hawley-Smoot Tariff Bill passed in 1930 that raised American tariffs on foreign agricultural and manufactured goods by as much as 50 percent; triggered European retaliation

>> The Hoover Dam, begun in 1928, was the single largest public works project in American history up to that point. In the historical image, workers are constructing the retaining wall that gives support to the road leading over the top of Hoover Dam.

would hire more workers. The RFC also provided loans to states to undertake public projects such as buildings and roads.

But Hoover's plan, ambitious as it was, still didn't help the average American quickly enough. The RFC's cautious, business-centered approach defeated its purpose of helping as many Americans as possible. No matter what Hoover did, the Great Depression seemed hopeless to most Americans.

22-2 THE DEPRESSION EXPERIENCE IN AMERICA

Numbers tell only part of the story. The experiences of millions of Americans suffering in terrible conditions between the late 1920s and the early 1930s tell the rest. As hundreds of thousands of people in the nation's urban areas grappled with homelessness, rural America was pounded by a series of environmental catastrophes that made the situation even worse and created the image that the government was powerless.

Hooverville   Popular name for a shantytown built by homeless Americans during the Great Depression

22-2a Urban America

City life during the Great Depression was a stark contrast to the carefree 1920s. In many places, homeless Americans built makeshift towns on the outskirts of cities and in abandoned lots and parks. They derisively nicknamed these towns **Hoovervilles** after the president. These people built homes from abandoned cardboard boxes, scrap lumber and metal, and anything else they could find to devise shelter. In some places, Hoovervilles grew enormous. For many it was the only alternative to living on the street.

Hoovervilles existed in virtually all of the nation's cities, but homelessness was a problem much larger than these shantytowns. By 1932, there were an estimated 250,000 homeless children in the country. But the homeless problem was far greater than even these numbers indicate, because people living in Hoovervilles were usually not counted as "homeless."

AFRICAN AMERICAN NEIGHBORHOODS

In these hard times, African Americans generally suffered more than urban white people. African American neighborhoods were often already in a depressed state before the stock market crash, as business slowdowns and other signs of a weak economy in the 1920s hurt black communities first. In most places, African Americans were routinely the "last hired and first fired" for jobs. Thus, even before the depression hit Chicago's South Side, home to 236,000 African Americans, all the banks and businesses in the neighborhood had already closed.

Many African American communities turned to self-help. In Harlem, the African American spiritual leader Father Divine led his Divine Peace Mission and created a network of businesses, church groups, and self-help organizations, enabling him to serve more than 3,000 meals a day to the destitute and homeless in the neighborhood. Community members in Harlem began a campaign against white shop owners and landlords who charged too much for consumer goods and rent. The agitation led to the establishment of the Consolidated Tenants League (which organized strikes against landlords who charged too much) and the Harlem Boycott of 1934 (which discouraged consumers from purchasing products at white-owned stores).

HUNGER

In the cities, many people, white and black, suffered from hunger. Although the country's farms produced plenty of food, the lack of funds to support commercial transportation prevented most food from reaching urban marketplaces. **Breadlines** formed in all of America's cities. Hunger triggered a number of problems in the nation's cities, ranging from malnourishment to riots and looting.

The problem of hunger triggered major political activity, especially among women, who actively partici-

>> Hoovervilles like this one in Seattle appeared in all major cities of the country.

pated in a number of riots all over the country. In 1930, women in Minneapolis, Minnesota, marched on a local food store and raided its shelves. Food riots expanded to other parts of the country in 1931 and 1932; nearly every city in the country had some kind of protest movement driven by the lack of food.

22-2b Rural America

Americans in rural areas suffered as well. For the most part, the Great Depression simply exacerbated a decade-long problem of overproduction, which led to already low prices. Then, in the 1930s, rural poverty was intensified by a massive drought and a series of severe dust storms in the South and Midwest. Southern states like Arkansas, Alabama, and Mississippi received less than half their normal rainfall during the early 1930s. Crop failures became commonplace and reliance on one or two crops led to weakened root systems, which loosened the soil. From the early 1930s to the early 1940s, parts of Kansas, Oklahoma, Nebraska, and Texas were called the "**Dust Bowl**" because the dust storms and drought were so punishing.

Crop losses plunged farmers even deeper into the debts they had acquired early in the Industrial Revolution. Foreclosures on farms became commonplace, and the dust storms and drought prompted an exodus from the rural regions of the country to the Far West. John Steinbeck's novel *The Grapes of Wrath* (1939) traced the story of Dust Bowl migrants making their way to California, where they hoped for a better life. The Okies (as the Midwest migrants were called) were not always welcome in California, however, and

breadline A line of people waiting to receive free food handed out by a charitable organization or public agency

Dust Bowl Parts of Kansas, Oklahoma, Nebraska, and Texas that suffered punishing dust storms and drought from the early 1930s to the early 1940s

>> Huge dust storms like the one in this photo conspired with the economy against many farmers, forcing refugees to flee with all their belongings to places like California in search of a new life.

many suffered discrimination, just as African Americans, Chinese, and Japanese did.

MEXICAN REPATRIATION

One group that perhaps suffered more than any other, though, was the large number of Mexicans and Mexican Americans living in the American Southwest, stretching from Los Angeles to San Antonio. As the American economy worsened in the 1920s and 1930s, local and federal officials, including labor leaders and relief workers, threatened and publicly abused widespread numbers of Mexican Americans, hoping they would return to their countries of origin and preserve what jobs there were for white Americans. Because the southern border of the United States had previously been porous and largely unregulated, many Mexican Americans had no documentation attesting to their status. Many in fact were in the United States legally, and indeed many were American citizens. Nevertheless, the federal government greatly increased the number of U.S. Border Patrol agents in the late 1920s and early 1930s. The result of the heightened fear of immigrants and the development of an enhanced enforcement team was a series of public raids in predominantly Mexican American communities during which large numbers of Mexicans and Mexican Americans were arrested and given a choice: return to their nation of origin or face expensive legal proceedings. Most simply chose to repatriate.

In the midst of this threatening environment, many localities simply provided free transportation to those willing to leave the United States of their own accord. They were thus not technically deported, but were under threat to repatriate. In total, during the 1920s and 1930s, between 500,000 and 2 million Mexicans and Mexican Americans left the United States and repatriated to Mexico, at least half of whom were U.S. citizens who left without access to due process of law. In 2006, the state of California became the first (and only) state to apologize formally for its actions.

22-2c Cultural Politics

While many businesses dried up during the Depression, people still found time for leisure activities like attending movies, reading fiction, or flipping through widely

>> During the Great Depression local, state, and federal government made concerted efforts to get Mexicans and Mexican Americans to go to Mexico, which, they felt, would open up jobs to non-Mexican Americans. Somewhere between 500,000 and 2 million Mexicans and Mexican Americans, including this mother and son, left the US and repatriated to Mexico, at least half of whom were U.S. citizens.

popular comic books. These cultural products responded to the psychological needs of the people by offering either dreamy escapism or a leftist political message that criticized the current capitalist order. Cultural outlets grew so popular during the Depression that one historian has argued that this "Cultural Front" helped move American politics as a whole to the left during the 1930s.

MOVIES

During the Great Depression, nearly 60 percent of the nation attended at least one film a week. Hollywood studios responded by churning out more than 5,000 movies during the 1930s. This prodigious output came courtesy of the "studio system." Just as Henry Ford had pioneered the assembly line to mass-produce his automobiles, studios learned to streamline their production process to make many more movies. Both sound and color techniques were mastered in this era; they were employed with increasing frequency throughout the 1930s.

Responding to the psychological needs of Depression-era audiences, Hollywood films served up seductive dreamscapes, most notably with stories of wealthy and carefree people. The "rags-to-riches" theme was immensely popular, as were musicals and gangster films. Hollywood films many times took gentle jabs at the upper classes, while reassuring the audience that the old rags-to-riches dream was still alive.

The films of Frank Capra are the most renowned of the era, and they often dramatized the fight to rise from poverty to success. At a time when many individuals felt powerless, Capra's films, such as perennial favorites *Mr. Deeds Goes to Town* (1936) and *Mr. Smith Goes to Washington* (1939), called for a return to the virtues of small-town communities, placing hope in the power of one man to stand up against the iniquities of big business, corrupt government, and a cynical media.

The struggle to realize the American dream was a popular theme in slapstick comedian Charlie Chaplin's films as well, most notably in his *Modern Times* (1936). Chaplin's character in the film, the Little Tramp, is rendered helpless in the face of daunting machines as the gears of business literally swallow him up. The Tramp is then thrown out of work and mistakenly jailed for being a dangerous radical. *Modern Times* captured the plight of American workers who were buffeted by the impersonal forces of modern industrial society.

Another performer who buoyed everyone's spirits with her carefree antics and her attempts to always remain on the sunny side of the street was Shirley Temple. Like many other performers, her work provided an escape from the harsh realities of the Great Depression,

>> Charlie Chaplin's iconic 1936 film *Modern Times* (publicity poster shown here) told the story of a likeable man besieged by the huge anonymous forces of the industrial era.

but she also came to symbolize the fact that Hollywood was not accurately portraying the real woes that most Americans faced in the 1930s. People often enjoyed the films of Shirley Temple, but it was obvious to many that she was too much a part of the Hollywood dreamscape to represent real problems.

WRITERS

In the 1930s a growing number of writers shared Chaplin's critique. During the prosperous 1920s, writers felt ignored in a society dominated by business concerns. When the stock market crashed and the Great Depression hit, many intellectuals felt energized. "One couldn't help being exhilarated at the sudden collapse of that stupid gigantic fraud," said the leftist social critic Edmund Wilson.

Intellectuals basically agreed on the cause of the economic depression: for too long, they said, the United States had been devoted to unbridled competition, sacrificing social good for individual wealth. Many intellectuals subsequently called for government control and greater centralized planning. This position was most skillfully articulated by philosopher John Dewey in many articles and his books *A Common Faith* (1934) and *Liberalism and Social Action* (1935), and by writer Alfred Bingham in his journal *Common Sense*.

More radical critics were drawn to the Communist Party. During the 1930s, communism seemed an

>> What better time than the Great Depression for a superhero to come and save the day? Superman first appeared in 1938. Pictured here is one of the covers from the comic book.

Hulton Archive/Getty Images

attractive and plausible alternative to capitalism, mainly because the Soviet Union seemed to be thriving. There were certainly problems with this contention—namely, that the Soviet Union was not doing as well as it seemed (its successes were mostly a product of its international propaganda) and that what advances it did have were coming at a brutal human cost under the harsh regime of Josef Stalin. Nevertheless, many intellectuals drifted dramatically leftward during these years.

Fiction writers moved left as well. Chief among them was John Steinbeck, who aimed to create a proletarian literature that sympathetically portrayed the struggles of the working classes. African American authors such as Richard Wright used their writing to examine the political activities of the Communist Party and the struggles for African American civil rights. The Southern Agrarians, notably John Crowe Ransom and Allan Tate, wrote of their hopes for the nation to return

to its rural roots in order to address the problems caused by modern industrial society.

RADIO

Radio was wildly popular during the 1930s, too. By 1926, the National Broadcasting Company (NBC) had hooked up stations around the country, creating the first nationwide radio network. The Columbia Broadcasting System (CBS) followed a year later.

The same songs were now popular nationwide, and a handful of them dealt with Depression-era themes (most notably, Bing Crosby's rendition of "Brother, Can You Spare a Dime?"). The songs of Woody Guthrie were generally about farmers affected by the Depression. His song "This Land Is Your Land," although today regarded as a celebration of the country, is actually about the nation's suffering during the 1930s. The most popular music of the day, however, usually avoided economics and advised listeners to, as songwriters Dorothy Fields and Jimmy McHugh put it, stay "on the sunny side of the street." The upbeat grandeur of large swing orchestras dominated popular music, led by such masters as Duke Ellington, Count Basie, Glenn Miller, and Tommy Dorsey.

Radio also featured sitcoms, the most popular of which was *Amos 'n' Andy*, which captured an amazing 60 percent of the American radio audience. Beginning in 1929, millions of Americans listened to the comical misadventures of two black friends (played by two white actors who mocked black speech) trying to make their way in Harlem. Most episodes focused on "getting ahead," a topic on the minds of Depression-era audiences. Amos was hardworking and hopeful, while his friend Andy was a lazy schemer, always looking to make a quick buck. Their elaborate plans inevitably failed for a variety of humorous reasons, but by the end of the show, offering a note of reassurance to their listeners, they always managed to salvage some self-respect.

In addition to its entertainment value, the radio also served as a key source of news. Over the course of the decade, a growing number of Americans, who had previously relied on newspapers to learn of daily events, preferred to get their news from radio commentators. Colorful personalities like Walter Winchell attracted listeners by freely combining the daily headlines with personal editorial opinions.

In total, American popular culture in the 1930s was deeply influenced by the Great Depression. All forms of popular culture, from movies to fiction to radio, helped Americans deal with the nation's economic crisis. They also helped push American politics leftward, something made evident by the radicalizing politics of the era.

22-2d Radicalizing Politics

Predictably, political events were especially contentious during the Great Depression. The political climate of the early 1930s created the impression of a nation out of control.

COMMUNIST PARTY

In the United States, the party leading most of the organized protest was the Communist Party of the United States, which, under the direction of Earl Browder and William Z. Foster, sought to eliminate all private property and make the state responsible for the good of the people. With capitalism experiencing violent turbulence, communism seemed a plausible alternative. The party had led hunger marches in the early 1930s and continued its activities into the presidential election year of 1932. Its actions gained it considerable attention from the American public, making communism a greater force in American politics than ever before.

The Communist Party intended to use its strength during the Great Depression to highlight racist dimensions of American society (which would show the worldwide communist effort to be the true egalitarian force in the world). Notably, the party funded the legal defense of nine African American boys accused of raping a white woman in Scottsboro, Alabama, in 1931. The convictions of the **Scottsboro Boys**, as the nine came to be called, served notice to the world that the United States retained its racist ways despite its efforts to promote an egalitarian rhetoric. The boys were tried separately, and four were released in 1937, after six years in jail. The other five languished in prison, their guilt never established conclusively, and remained imprisoned until the 1940s.

THE BONUS ARMY

But it was the gathering of the **Bonus Army** that became one of the most influential protests in American history. The Bonus Army consisted of World War I veterans who demanded the immediate payment of their military bonuses (which were scheduled to be paid in the 1940s). In the spring and summer of 1932, about 15,000 veterans converged on Washington, D.C., to push Congress and

>> *Amos 'n' Andy*, the most popular radio program of the 1930s, portrayed two black friends humorously trying to improve their lot in life. The actors, shown here, were actually white men who used blackface for their photo shoots.

Bettmann/Getty Images

the president to pass a bill authorizing early payment of the bonuses. Some illegally hopped on trains, and some came from as far away as California. When police attempted to evict the marchers, violence broke out and one police officer was killed. President Hoover then

>> Along with a wide range of programs and initiatives, FDR brought a smiling optimism and hope to the American people.

Everett Collection/AGE Fotostock

Scottsboro Boys Nine African American boys accused of raping a white woman in Scottsboro, Alabama, in 1931; they were imprisoned, although their guilt was never established conclusively

Bonus Army Group of 15,000 World War I veterans who staged a protest in Washington, D.C., in 1932, demanding immediate payment of their military bonuses

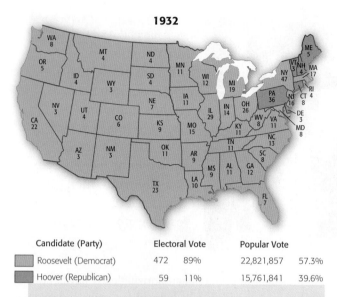

1932

Candidate (Party)	Electoral Vote		Popular Vote	
Roosevelt (Democrat)	472	89%	22,821,857	57.3%
Hoover (Republican)	59	11%	15,761,841	39.6%

Map 22.1 **The Election of 1932**

ordered the removal of all the protesters. On the night of July 28, troops burned the veterans' encampment to the ground. Two protesters were killed and hundreds were injured. Hoover became a vilified figure, increasingly unlikely to win reelection.

22-2e **The Election of 1932**

Lose he did. Franklin D. Roosevelt, governor of New York and a protégé of Al Smith, won the Democratic nomination in July 1932. Little known outside New York, Roosevelt had served under President Wilson and had been influenced by his cousin Theodore Roosevelt. After an unsuccessful run for vice president in 1920, Roosevelt was stricken by poliomyelitis, a disease that at times confined him to a wheelchair, which Roosevelt loathed and carefully concealed from the public.

Despite his polio, Roosevelt responded to the Great Depression with vibrancy and cheer. His demeanor—jovial, flexible, perhaps unprincipled—sparked divergent opinions: was he a humanitarian pragmatist or an arrogant politician? His demeanor was sometimes softened by the presence of his wife, Eleanor, a dynamic figure in her own right who would promise to reshape the role of the First Lady. Regardless of one's perception of the man, Roosevelt's charm contrasted starkly with the

bank holiday Business day when banks are closed; used strategically by Roosevelt immediately after assuming the presidency

Brain Trust Group of leading intellectuals charged with formulating policy with Roosevelt

somber Hoover, and Roosevelt's victory was assured. He received 22.8 million votes to Hoover's 15.7 million. The Electoral College was even more lopsided, as Roosevelt took 472 electoral votes to Hoover's 59 (Map 22.1).

In the months between Roosevelt's election in November and his inauguration on March 4, 1933, the Great Depression worsened. The Republicans blamed Roosevelt for the downturn because the president-elect would not comment on what he would do once in office. Hoover, meanwhile, was a lame duck president with little power. In February 1933, banks closed across the nation. Vagrants wandered the streets, and vigilantes had begun to incite riots.

22-3 **THE NEW DEAL**

In his inaugural speech, in which he eloquently declared, "The only thing we have to fear is fear itself," Roosevelt tried to reassure the country about its future. Should the crisis continue, he said, he would ask for power "to wage a war against the emergency, as great as the power that would be given to me if we were in fact invaded by a foreign foe." The very next day, March 5, 1933, Roosevelt declared a four-day national **bank holiday** and summoned Congress into special session to deal with the worsening situation.

These two actions signaled the beginning of a series of laws and programs intended to end the Great Depression. Collectively called the "New Deal," these measures were designed to regulate the economy, provide for national recovery, and create a social safety net for all Americans. The New Deal was a collection of initiatives, each aiming to address political, economic, and social demands all at once. Once enacted, the programs of the New Deal expanded the role of the federal government into the economic lives of ordinary Americans to an unprecedented degree.

22-3a **The First New Deal**

Over the course of his first hundred days in office, Roosevelt dramatically boosted the nation's mood. With the help of what he called his **Brain Trust** (a group of leading intellectuals charged with formulating policy), Roosevelt proposed a series of dramatic measures meant to reorganize the country's financial system and raise the living standards of all Americans, especially working people. He offered, he said, "relief, recovery, and reform," and that is the best way to characterize what historians call the First New Deal.

RELIEF

First, FDR tried to provide relief to suffering people and the industries whose weaknesses compounded that suffering. Congress's first act was to address the banking crisis. Many Americans, afraid that banks would collapse, refused to place their money in them. The Emergency Banking Relief Act, passed on March 9, 1933, established federal control over banks and, if necessary, rescued them from disaster with government loans. Roosevelt then took the United States off the gold standard, meaning that the government would no longer redeem paper money in gold. With the end of the gold standard, the price of silver, stocks, and commodities rose, encouraging investment in these areas and putting money back into the economy.

Roosevelt next turned to helping people directly. Congress increased the federal contribution to city and state relief agencies by creating the **Federal Emergency Relief Administration (FERA)**, with funding of $500 million. FERA's chief administrator, Harry Hopkins, preferred public works projects to direct payments to people, believing that the former were more considerate of the recipients' pride. Thus FERA set about creating economic programs that would directly employ the unemployed.

Reflecting this belief, one of FERA's most successful programs was the **Civilian Conservation Corps (CCC)**, established in March 1933. The CCC enlisted unemployed young men ages eighteen to twenty-five in building and repairing highways, forest service sites, flood control projects, and national park buildings. By 1941, 2.5 million young men had worked in military-style CCC camps. Enlistees received $30 a month, part of which they had to send home. Other projects started in 1933 included the Public Works Administration (PWA), which built roads and buildings, and the Civil Works Administration (CWA), which provided seasonal employment.

In addition to financial relief, Roosevelt supported a proposal he felt would bring psychological relief to millions of Americans: the end of Prohibition. In February 1933, the Democratic majority in Congress submitted a constitutional amendment to the states that repealed Prohibition, and in December it was ratified as the Twenty-first Amendment.

RECOVERY

FDR then turned to recovery. His signature recovery act (and arguably the First New Deal's most meaningful piece of legislation) was the **National Industrial Recovery Act (NIRA)**. Under the stewardship of Secretary of Labor Frances Perkins (the first-ever

>> The Civilian Conservation Corps, or CCC, put young men to work, like these pictured here excavating.

Library of Congress, Prints & Photographs Division, Reproduction number LC-USF33-T01-000067-M3 (b&w film dup. neg.) LC-USZ62-130370 (b&w film copy neg. from file print) LC-DIG-fsa-8a00075 (digital file from original neg.)

female cabinet member), the NIRA instituted programs to regulate industry, establish labor rights, and improve working conditions. **Section 7a** of the NIRA guaranteed the right of labor unions to organize. As a result, labor representatives sat down with business and government officials in committees to set working standards and wage levels. The codes drawn up by these committees in every American industry established a forty-hour workweek, banned child labor, and implemented a minimum weekly wage.

The NIRA's most important creation was the **National Recovery Administration (NRA)**. Led by

Federal Emergency Relief Administration (FERA) Federally funded department creating economic programs to employ the unemployed

Civilian Conservation Corps (CCC) New Deal program that enlisted unemployed young men ages eighteen to twenty-five in building and repairing highways, forest service sites, flood control projects, and national park buildings

National Industrial Recovery Act (NIRA) New Deal act that instituted programs to regulate industry, establish labor rights, and improve working conditions

Section 7a A component of the NIRA that legalized and granted rights to labor unions, leading to the dramatic expansion of labor unions across the nation

National Recovery Administration (NRA) Department that enforced fair-trade rules set by industry associations during the 1920s, encouraged companies and workers to meet and agree on prices and wages, and established a public relations campaign to mobilize support of the New Deal

General Hugh Johnson, the NRA focused on the issue of "cutthroat" competition. In the early years of the Depression, companies and small businesses had fought for survival by slashing prices, thus destroying profit margins, lowering workers' wages, and preventing national economic recovery. The NRA responded by enforcing fair-trade rules set by industry associations during the 1920s. More importantly, it encouraged companies and workers to meet and agree on prices and wages. Additionally, the NRA launched a public relations campaign in mid-1933, encouraging participants to stamp their products with a blue eagle and the NRA's slogan, "We do our part." The blue eagle became a symbol of the progressive optimism spurred by Roosevelt and his New Deal.

REFORM

In addition to providing relief and prompting recovery, many of FDR's most dramatic gestures came through several reforms intended to prevent an economic depression from happening again. In hindsight, we can see that these reforms changed the nature of American government for the rest of the twentieth century. They inserted the federal government into the American economy more forcefully than ever before by managing, directing, or controlling parts of it outright.

The first big program FDR passed was a farm reform proposal called the **Agricultural Adjustment Act (AAA)**. The AAA attempted to address the great problem of agriculture, which was excess supply. The Agricultural Adjustment Administration offered farmers cash subsidies to *not* grow crops or even to plow up crops already planted. With the drop in supply, the theory went, the cost of farm products would rise.

> Despite his enormous popularity, Roosevelt never lacked for critics, many of whom looked on the New Deal with horror.

The AAA quickly became one of the most important New Deal agencies in the South and West, although reducing the amount of output hurt sharecroppers and tenant farmers more than more stable large landowners. Congress also created the Emergency Farm Mortgage Act, which helped refinance farm loans and prevented a number of farms from being repossessed.

Second, an emphasis on cooperative planning found its broadest expression in the **Tennessee Valley Authority (TVA)**, created by Congress in May 1933. The TVA gave the federal government the power to build a series of dams on the Tennessee River in order to improve river navigation and, significantly, create electricity for the area's rural residents, the achievement for which the TVA is best remembered. The TVA brought electricity to poor and isolated populations in seven states.

A third group of reforms governed banking. In May 1933, Congress passed the Federal Securities Act, which regulated the stock market and prosecuted individuals who took advantage of "insider" knowledge to enrich themselves in stocks and bonds. In June 1933, Congress passed the **Glass-Steagall Banking Act**, which regulated the size of banks and created the Federal Deposit Insurance Corporation (FDIC), a program that guaranteed individual deposits of up to $5,000. These steps reassured millions of Americans that it was safe to put their money in banks again.

THE HUNDRED DAYS

Congress adjourned on June 16, 1933. Although it would enact many laws during the subsequent years, few would have the dramatic impact of these acts, all of which were passed within Roosevelt's first hundred days in office.

22-3b Critics of the First New Deal

Despite his enormous popularity, Roosevelt never lacked for critics, many of whom looked on the New Deal with horror.

CRITICISM FROM THE REPUBLICANS

Republicans argued that periodic downturns were an inevitable part of the business cycle. In their view, the best cure for economic depression was to let market forces take their course, knowing that, in time, there would be growth and recovery.

Agricultural Adjustment Act (AAA) A transformative act of the New Deal that established an agency that, among other things, paid farmers not to grow crops in order to curb supply; was one of the most influential federal agencies in the South and West

Tennessee Valley Authority (TVA) Department created in May 1933 to build a series of dams on the Tennessee River in order to improve river navigation and create electricity for the area's rural residents

Glass-Steagall Banking Act A law regulating the banking industry, including its loans, and creating the FDIC to guarantee individual deposits

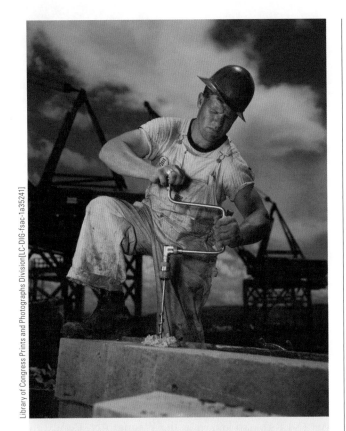

>> Carpenter at work on Douglas Dam, Tennessee, under the auspices of the Tennessee Valley Authority.

CRITICISM FROM CONSERVATIVE DEMOCRATS

Equally dismayed were conservative Democrats, who deplored Roosevelt's tampering with the gold standard and feared his programs were increasing the power of the federal government at the states' expense. In 1934, Al Smith, the unsuccessful Democratic presidential candidate of 1928, and John W. Davis, the unsuccessful Democratic presidential candidate of 1924, joined a group of conservative politicians and business leaders in the Liberty League, an anti-New Deal organization. The League argued that many of Roosevelt's measures were leading the United States toward socialism. Citizens' lives, those in the League believed, ought not to be too much in the hands of the federal government. They saw it as immoral that farm products and livestock were being stored away or killed while a great number of Americans were suffering from hunger.

Southern Democrats also had their complaints. They were concerned that the new federal mandates might threaten Jim Crow segregation in the South. Because of their seniority in Congress, they were successful in exempting farm workers and domestic servants (who in the South likely would have been black) from receiving certain New Deal benefits.

CRITICISM FROM THE LEFT

If conservative Democrats saw the New Deal as an overextension of federal power, other voices on the Left saw it as a timid set of reforms that merely reinforced the American status quo. America's small Socialist Party, led by Norman Thomas, believed that the Depression was evidence that capitalism was a failure. The New Deal, in the Socialists' view, had made the mistake of shoring up capitalism rather than getting rid of it once and for all.

The even smaller Communist Party, which favored the abolition of all forms of private property, used the Soviet Union as an example of an economic system that (in theory) had no unemployment at all. During these years, the Communist Party attracted support from numerous sources, including from African American sharecroppers in the South, mainly because of the party's opposition to racial segregation. Nevertheless, at its peak in 1938, Communist Party membership numbered just 75,000.

Another plan to redistribute wealth was proposed by novelist and Progressive crusader Upton Sinclair in his 1934 bid for governor of California. A former socialist, Sinclair championed a program called End Poverty in California (EPIC), which aimed to turn over idle factories and farms to workers' cooperatives. A powerful coalition of conservative business interests banded together to defeat Sinclair in the November election.

Another dramatic plan for reform emerged in 1934, when Senator Huey Long of Louisiana announced his "Share Our Wealth" plan. A former governor, Long proposed punitive taxation of the rich and a guaranteed yearly payment of $5,000 to every American family. He wanted to go even further than the New Deal in making the national government every citizen's guardian. The colorful Long had a history of flamboyance and corruption, and his national stature was on the rise when he was assassinated in September 1935.

A more extreme rival of the New Deal was Charles Coughlin, a Catholic priest from Detroit. Coughlin was a spellbinding speaker, as talented a public performer as Roosevelt, and his weekly radio show had a largely Catholic audience of more than 30 million. Coughlin went from being an early supporter of the New Deal to being one of its harshest critics, accusing Roosevelt of being in league with communists and Jewish bankers. In 1934, Coughlin founded the Union for Social Justice, which argued for radical redistribution of incomes and a nation free of bankers. Coughlin's conspiratorial antisemitism eventually prompted his censure by the Catholic Church.

CRITICISM FROM THE COURTS

Amid these voices of dissent, Roosevelt faced his largest challenge from the Supreme Court. In its May 1935 decision in *Schechter Poultry Corp.* v. *U.S.*, the Court invalidated the NIRA on the grounds that it gave unconstitutionally broad powers to the federal government. The logic of the Court's decision, written by conservative Chief Justice Charles Evans Hughes, suggested that the other parts of the New Deal's legislation would be overturned when they came up for review. Of all the critiques Roosevelt faced, the Supreme Court's promised to be the most threatening.

22-3c The Second New Deal

Despite the Supreme Court's challenge, Roosevelt believed that, without a national plan for economic reform, the country would succumb to demagogues like Long and Coughlin. Emboldened by Democratic victories in the 1934 mid-term elections, Roosevelt laid out a new set of proposals in January 1935 that would push the New Deal even further in assisting the working and lower classes. Ultimately enacted by Congress in July and August of 1935, these new reform measures are known collectively as the "Second New Deal."

The Second New Deal can best be understood as Roosevelt's attempt to gain support from the working and lower-middle classes. Even if it cost him the support of the wealthy (whom he called "economic royalists"), Roosevelt decided to co-opt the ideas of some of his leftist critics by: (1) pressing for more jobs, (2) strengthening the position of labor, and (3) providing a greater social safety net.

MORE JOBS

One of the most notable programs of the Second New Deal was the **Works Progress Administration (WPA)**, which employed more than 8.5 million Americans before it closed in 1943. WPA workers built roads, dams, schools, subways, housing projects, and other federal projects. The WPA also sponsored cultural programs for

Works Progress Administration (WPA) New Deal agency whose workers built roads, dams, schools, subways, housing projects, and other federal projects; it also sponsored cultural programs for unemployed artists and writers

Wagner Act Legislation passed in July 1935, also known as the National Labor Relations Act (NLRA); strengthened the legal position of trade unions

Social Security Act Most far-reaching element of all 1930s legislation, passed in August 1935; intended to provide a "safety net" for citizens who could not financially support themselves

unemployed artists and writers, who worked on original plays and artworks, compiled historical records, wrote a series of guidebooks for tourists, and gave classes and performances to the public. In one of the most far-reaching WPA projects, the federal government hired historians and folklorists to interview former slaves about their journeys from slavery to freedom.

At the same time, Roosevelt established other agencies designed to help Americans cope with the continuing economic depression. In May 1935, the administration created the Resettlement Administration (RA), which provided assistance in relocating workers away from economically weak areas and funded flood control and reforestation projects. The National Youth Administration (NYA), founded in June 1935, provided work relief programs, job training, and part-time work for men and women ages sixteen to twenty-five, including high school and college students.

LABOR SUPPORT

Perhaps more significant than the creation of these jobs was Congress's strengthening, in July 1935, the legal position of trade unions with the National Labor Relations Act (NLRA), also known as the **Wagner Act**. Even with the guarantees established under the NRA, unions had been vulnerable to court injunctions that prevented strikes. Plus, management had often refused to negotiate with them. The Wagner Act established a National Labor Relations Board to oversee industrial compliance and resolve employee grievances against management. In subsequent years, union membership grew dramatically (despite the unemployment rate), even among unskilled workers in the mining, steel, and automobile industries.

THE SOCIAL SAFETY NET

Along with creating jobs and supporting unionization efforts, a third aspect of the Second New Deal was the **Social Security Act**, passed in August 1935. This was probably the most far-reaching element of all 1930s legislation. Social Security was intended to provide a "safety net" for citizens who could not financially support themselves.

Different elements of the Social Security plan served different social needs. Social Security provided pensions to Americans age sixty-five and over. Unemployed people received assistance through a fund created by a payroll tax. Federal grants provided help for the disabled. Children of unwed mothers were covered under the Aid to Dependent Children Act (ADC), or "welfare." A federal program for national health insurance would have widened the social safety net even more, but Congress shelved the idea after complaints from the medical profession.

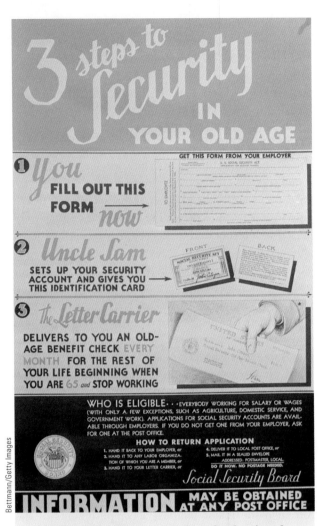

Bettmann/Getty Images

>> Although retirement plans had existed in the industrialized countries of Europe for decades, they were new to the United States in the mid-1930s. This poster encourages the use of the new public benefit.

As a plan for social welfare, Social Security was cautious and limited in comparison to models in other nations. Germany, for example, had been putting many social safety net programs in place since the 1880s. But despite its limitations, in the United States, Social Security, particularly its old-age pension elements, proved to be the most popular and enduring of New Deal measures. Roosevelt himself said many times that the Social Security Act was the greatest legacy of his presidency.

ATTACKS ON THE WEALTHY AND LARGE CORPORATIONS

How did he pay for these increased programs and benefits? As he pushed these programs through Congress,

Roosevelt had observed the popularity of Huey Long's denunciations of big business and the rich. Hence, Roosevelt usurped Long's rhetoric and created a "soak the rich" tax reform plan (passed as the Revenue Act of 1935), which imposed steep income taxes (up to nearly 80 percent) on wealthy Americans and large corporations. The Public Utility Holding Company Act, passed the same year, placed rigorous political controls on utility companies and warned that if they did not offer good service at low cost to customers, they would be broken up.

THE NEW DEAL'S PEAK: 1935–1936

Congress passed a number of other New Deal measures as well, regulating specific industries, providing for further rural electrification, and carrying out additional farm reforms. This burst of political activity consolidated Roosevelt's reputation as a friend of the workingman and opponent of special privilege. All together, the passage of so many transformative laws was a testament to the growing expectation that the government would take responsibility for the social welfare of its citizens. This was a far cry from Hoover's volunteerism.

By mid-1936, Roosevelt's political successes had bestowed him with tremendous popularity with the public, even though the American economy had yet to substantially revive and some 80 percent of American newspapers (generally owned by Republicans) went on record as opposing his reelection. During that fall's presidential campaign, the Republicans nominated Alfred Landon of Kansas, who was considerably more liberal than his party. Meanwhile, Charles Coughlin attempted to get his followers to join up with Huey Long's and coalesce behind the new Union Party and its nominee, William Lemke.

In a landslide, Roosevelt won the election by 11 million votes, carrying every state except Maine and Vermont, which went to Landon. Lemke won fewer than a million votes, while the Socialist candidate, Norman Thomas, and the Communist candidate, Earl Browder, attracted barely a quarter of a million votes between them. Farmers and workers, who were pleased with the relief acts and the union protection, joined middle-class homeowners, who were bailed out by the mortgage protection laws, to support Roosevelt. The Democratic Party had more than three-quarters of the seats in both houses of Congress. In 1936, the New Deal appeared invincible.

22-3d Decline and Consolidation

After the election, the New Deal appeared to be at its height. But Roosevelt soon committed a series of political and economic errors that threatened some of the most far-reaching elements of the New Deal. Thus, after 1936 the New Deal entered a period of consolidation, when its changes in culture, labor relations, and politics took firm root in American life.

COURT PACKING

In his second inaugural speech, Roosevelt declared an attack on standards of living that left "one-third of a nation . . . ill-housed, ill-clad, [and] ill-nourished." Soon after, in February 1937, Roosevelt made what was for him an unusual blunder. Vexed by the Supreme Court's decision against the NRA in the *Schechter* case, its overturning of the AAA in 1936, and its unfavorable decision in five of seven other cases testing New Deal laws, Roosevelt resolved to change the Court's ideological makeup. The Constitution does not specify how many justices can sit on the Court, but by long-standing convention the number had been nine. Roosevelt now proposed laws that would allow him to appoint up to six new justices and would force judges to retire at age seventy. Given that the Court's opinions reflected the Republican attitudes of the 1920s, Roosevelt felt the Court's actions threatened American democracy in the 1930s. He felt he needed to fill the Court with supporters of the New Deal.

Congressional Democrats, arguing that Roosevelt had overreached, delayed considering this plan to "pack the Court." Yet the need for the legislation seemed to diminish after March of 1937, when Justice Owen Roberts changed from his previous position and unexpectedly began voting to uphold New Deal laws, creating a 5-to-4 pro-New Deal majority on the Court. Some observers speculated that Roberts had changed his mind to protect the principle of a nine-judge Court. In any event, during the next four years, Roosevelt had the chance to appoint seven new justices, allowing him to change the political tilt of the Court.

But the Court-packing episode cost Roosevelt some popular support from Americans who were cautiously monitoring the rise of authoritarian dictators in Europe. New economic problems compounded the damage. In early 1937, satisfied that the nation was well on its way to recovery, Roosevelt cut enrollment in the WPA, and the Federal Reserve Bank raised interest rates in order to fight inflation. As a result, production slowed, unemployment increased, and critics declared a "Roosevelt recession."

Keynesianism The belief that governments should engage in deficit spending in order to stimulate a depressed economy, premised on the economic thought of British economist John Maynard Keynes, upon which FDR in particular based his actions

That fall, when Roosevelt called Congress into special session to pass emergency relief legislation, Congress failed to act on his proposals. The Democratic Party suffered losses in the 1938 election, and congressional conservatives of both parties joined together in order to block future New Deal measures.

CONSOLIDATION

But all was not lost for FDR. The Supreme Court's new-found support of New Deal programs actually strengthened the New Deal and ensured that its reforms would last several decades. Also, the expenditures that were passed in reaction to the "Roosevelt recession" of 1937, although not as dramatic as Roosevelt had hoped, greatly eased the economic decline. They also lent new legitimacy to the idea that government spending could help induce economic recovery. This demonstrated a growing acceptance of the ideas of the British economist John Maynard Keynes, who had long advocated that governments should engage in deficit spending in order to stimulate a depressed economy. His ideas have collectively come to be called **Keynesianism**.

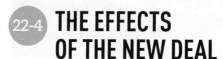

22-4 THE EFFECTS OF THE NEW DEAL

Although the major political accomplishments of the New Deal had ended by the late 1930s, the programs that had already become law continued to influence Americanpolitics, society, and culture for the remainder of the twentieth century. The New Deal thus effected changes in the American landscape more far-reaching than just economics or legislation. Most especially, theyaffected culture, crime, labor, politics, race relations, and minorities.

CULTURE

The New Deal included a number of programs that examined social realities that Hollywood and other cultural outlets often ignored. Problems such as poverty, crime, prostitution, and suicide had always existed in America, but New Deal cultural programs focused on their effects and placed them in the center of American social consciousness. For example, the Resettlement Administration hired photographers such as Dorothea Lange and Ben Shahn (Lange's photographs are represented in this chapter) to record the lives of Americans struggling through the Great Depression. By documenting the breadlines, migrant camps, and withered farms of the era, these photographers made a powerful indictment of economic inequality. At the same time, the WPA hired artists to create murals, sculptures, and other art-works in post offices, air-ports, and schools. The best known of these works depicted American farmers and workers and celebrated the working classes. The federal government also pro-vided funds for actors in the Federal Theatre Project, mu-sicians in the Federal Music Project, and writers in the Fed-eral Writers' Project.

Other writers contributed to the aesthetic of these gov-ernment cultural programs. Magazines ran stories about Great Depression refugees. For instance, *Fortune* sent the jour-nalist James Agee to the rural Deep South to write about pov-erty there. From his researches, he wrote a book that quickly became a classic: *Let Us Now Praise Famous Men* (1941), a dramatic tale of poverty that was made even more powerful by the stark photographs of Walker Evans. Rural poverty became a way to symbolize the experience of the Great Depression as a whole, as in John Steinbeck's *The Grapes of Wrath*. This novel showed a newly responsive federal government sheltering migrants in a work camp and providing the poorest of Americans with decent living conditions.

CRIME

The New Deal also initiated a war on crime in an effort to snuff out the gangster-ridden crime syndicates of the 1920s. Spearheaded by U.S. Attorney General Homer Cummings and Director of the Federal Bureau of Inves-tigation (FBI) J. Edgar Hoover, this initiative strength-ened the FBI and led to the arrest and/or execution of notable American criminals Bonnie and Clyde (in 1934, for armed robbery), Charles Arthur "Pretty Boy" Floyd (in 1934, for armed robbery and murder), and John Dill-inger (in 1934, alleged leader of the violent Dillinger gang). These criminals had become something like folk heroes in the 1930s, both for their seeming invincibil-ity and for their rebuke of the establishment. Removing

Library of Congress Prints and Photographs Division[LC-USZC2-5684]

>> The New Deal extended into the arts as well, including this production of the Federal Theatre Project.

them from the scene assured Americans that the law would dictate right and wrong in America.

LABOR

The New Deal proved a huge boon for the American labor movement as well. Previ-ous economic downturns had usually increased union rolls, but they had also made union members vulnerable to layoffs and replace-ment by strikebreakers. But after the New Deal, the NLRA guaranteed unions the right to organize and negotiate with their employers. In 1935, a new, broadly based trade union, eventually to be called the **Congress of Industrial Organizations (CIO)**, began recruiting unskilled men and women on a large scale, particularly in the mining and clothing industries. Under the able leadership of John L. Lewis and advocating a "culture of unity" to bring workers together despite racial or ethnic differences, the CIO rapidly became the nation's most powerful labor union.

Greater size engendered greater militancy. On December 31, 1936, for example, workers at General Motors (GM), led by Walter Reuther, went on strike in Flint, Michigan, demanding better pay, better working conditions, and recognition of their union, the United Auto Workers (UAW). Rather than simply not show up to work, as previous generations of strikers had done, GM workers staged a **sit-down strike**, locking themselves in the factory so that strikebreakers could not take their places. Although Roosevelt was openly critical of the

Congress of Industrial Organizations (CIO) Broadly based trade union that recruited unskilled men and women on a large scale, particularly in the mining and clothing industries

sit-down strike Action in which workers stop working and lock themselves in the factory so that strikebreakers cannot take their places

>> Public support for American bank robbers Clyde Barrow and Bonnie Parker, popularly known as Bonnie and Clyde, pictured here, demonstrated how the economic crisis prompted many people to root for and romanticize criminals.

strike, he refused to use federal troops to stop it. Roosevelt believed that industrial peace could be achieved only by integrating unions into the economy. Ultimately, GM gave in and negotiated.

Not all strikes concluded so peacefully. For example, on Memorial Day 1937, strikebreaking police fired on a line of picketers in front of the Republic Steel plant in Chicago, killing ten workers. Roosevelt stepped in and helped convince the steel factory and mine owners to come to terms with unions. Such successes led to a rapid rise in unionization. By the 1950s, more than 20 percent of all American workers belonged to unions.

POLITICS

The New Deal also dramatically altered American politics. Many workers revered Roosevelt, and his

Black Cabinet Informal group of black officials appointed to government posts who discussed African American issues with FDR

photograph became an ubiquitous fixture in urban households and small businesses.

The result was a fundamental realignment of American politics. "New immigrant" Catholic and Jewish voters, many of whom had in the past been alienated by the Democratic Party's tilt toward Southern conservatives, now flocked to the party. Democratic Southern whites, who would never countenance joining the Republican Party, which, after all, was the party of Lincoln, joined them. So did a large majority of African Americans, whose gratitude for New Deal relief programs led them to abandon the Republican Party in favor of the Democrats. The Democrats thus made a national majority by fashioning the alliance of the "producing" classes (farmers and laborers) they had dreamed of since the Populist movement.

CONTINUED SEGREGATION

The successes of this New Deal coalition set in motion fundamental changes in the Democratic Party itself. The support of African Americans reflected the fact that some New Deal programs seemed to combat discrimination. The CCC, for example, briefly housed both black and white workers together. In addition, a number of black officials appointed to government posts assembled as an informal **Black Cabinet** to discuss African American issues, although FDR did not appoint a single black person to a cabinet position. Roosevelt relied especially heavily on his powerful wife, Eleanor Roosevelt, to serve as a conduit to the African American community.

Nevertheless, opposition to ending desegregation came from many quarters: labor unions, for example, consistently excluded African Americans from their ranks and prevented the inclusion of nondiscrimination clauses in the Wagner Act. At the same time, the Roosevelt administration often gave in to segregationist demands in the 1930s, meaning that many of the key benefits of the New Deal were denied to America's black population. The doling out of benefits primarily to America's white population has led one historian to label the New Deal as a time "when affirmative action was white."

THE INDIAN NEW DEAL

At the same time, Roosevelt sought to address the concerns of other minorities. Shortly after his election in 1932, Roosevelt appointed John Collier as commissioner of the Bureau of Indian Affairs. In 1924, Congress granted American citizenship to all Indians, an event that was thought to be the culmination in the perpetual attempt to incorporate Indians into American society.

>> Although Roosevelt had an aristocratic background, the warmth of his conversational radio addresses, or "fireside chats," made many Americans feel they had a personal connection with the man.

Collier took a different perspective. He sought to restore Indian culture and heritage and to regenerate tribal autonomy. He used a variety of New Deal agencies to create an Indian Civil Conservation Corps and Works Progress Administration. He also lobbied for the Indian Reorganization Act of 1934, which authorized the acquisition of land for reservations and provided special federal appropriations for schools and other forms of Indian self-government. Collier faced stern critics, including assimilated Indians who tried to discredit his ideas as communist plots against America. But for the most part, his ideas began a new chapter in American Indian history, redirecting the federal government's efforts from forcing assimilation to respecting self-reliance.

WOMEN

Women were also of course greatly affected by the New Deal. During the Great Depression, increasing numbers of women went to work. While economically valuable, these efforts to support their families provoked hostility from many Americans who thought women workers were taking jobs away from men. Indeed, some scholars have seen within the Great Depression a "crisis of manhood," where men were unable to feed and clothe their families and where women had to come in to shoulder these responsibilities. In this critical mold, many New Deal policies addressed women as mothers rather than as workers, creating jobs programs for men, for instance, while providing support for women primarily in their domestic roles. In the Aid to Families with Dependent Children program, for instance, single mothers were eligible for aid only after they endured means and morals testing, testifying that they were not engaging in and benefiting from immoral behavior (such as premarital promiscuity). Similarly, many of the programs targeting women became derided as temporary relief efforts (such as welfare) rather than full-scale entitlements earned by workers (such as Social Security and unemployment insurance). In the words of one historian, women were "pitied but not entitled" to New Deal benefits.

>> FDR often used his wife Eleanor to reach out to the African American community. Here Eleanor Roosevelt awards the NAACP Spingarn Medal to singer Marian Anderson.

The New Deal did not end the Great Depression. Throughout the 1930s, nearly 10 million men remained unemployed. What the New Deal did was bring the federal government closer to the lives of ordinary citizens than ever before, reshaping national politics and culture with a host of relief, recovery, and reform initiatives. In so doing, it transformed the way Americans thought about their government, leading them to assume that the government was there to prevent them from going without food or shelter, to assure them that they would not be helpless during times of unemployment, and to provide financial security when they got old. This change also inspired a movement to oppose the New Deal initiatives, although this "small-government" coalition would not mature until later in the twentieth century.

Emboldened by his successes, in 1940 Roosevelt decided to run for an unprecedented third term as president. Just as he had been willing to override tradition in his Supreme Court packing plan, so now he overrode the tradition established by George Washington of holding the presidency for no more than two terms. Running against Republican nominee Wendell Willkie, FDR urged voters not to "switch horses in mid-stream." Americans overwhelmingly responded, voting him to a third term as president. With the 1940 election, the nation left the problems of the 1930s behind and attempted to gain strength to meet the challenges posed by a world at war. And it is to that world conflict that we now turn.

STUDY TOOLS 22

READY TO STUDY? IN THE BOOK, YOU CAN:

❏ Rip out the Chapter Review Card, which includes key terms and chapter summaries.

ONLINE AT WWW.CENGAGEBRAIN.COM, YOU CAN:

❏ Collect StudyBits while you read and study the chapter.

❏ Quiz yourself on key concepts.

❏ Find videos for further exploration.

❏ Prepare for tests with HIST5 Flash Cards as well as those you create.

❏ Read more on the Scottsboro Trial, including several primary sources.

❏ Read Roosevelt's inaugural speech.

CH22 TIMELINE

			What Else Was Happening
▶	1929–1933	National GDP declines from $103.1 to $58 billion; 9,000 banks go bankrupt.	
▶	1930	Hawley-Smoot Tariff raises prices on imports, deepens international depression.	*Vannevar Bush at MIT invents the "differential analyzer," or analog computer.*
▶	1931	Nine African American boys convicted on rape charges in Scottsboro, Alabama.	*Japan, seeking raw materials for its own industrial growth, invades Manchuria, bringing Japan and China into conflict that would erupt into war in 1937.*

1932

January: Reconstruction Finance Corporation makes business loans but has little impact.

July: Veterans march on capital to demand their bonus and are dispersed violently.

November: Franklin D. Roosevelt defeats Hoover in nation's largest landslide election.

1933

Roosevelt declares four-day bank holiday to disperse run on banks.

Emergency Banking Relief Act establishes federal control over banks.

Federal Emergency Relief contributes $500 million to state and local government.

Civilian Conservation Corps employs 2.5 million in conservation work.

Public and Civil Works Administrations ease unemployment.

National Recovery Act enforces industry and wage standards to stabilize prices.

Agricultural Adjustment Act restricts output to stabilize commodity prices.

Tennessee Valley Authority builds dams and regional economy in seven-state region.

Federal Securities Act creates oversight of stock exchange to curb insider trading.

Glass-Steagall Banking Act creates federal deposit insurance and ends bank panics.

Ruth Wakefield bakes the first chocolate chip cookie.

1934

"Share Our Wealth" plan of Louisiana senator Huey Long challenges New Deal.

African American consumers protest white price gouging in Harlem Boycott.

General strike in support of longshoremen brings San Francisco to standstill.

The first laundromat, the "washeteria," opens in Texas.

Amid Germany's own economic depression, Adolf Hitler becomes dictator.

1935

Works Progress Administration employs millions in public works, arts, humanities.

Congress of Industrial Organization organizes unskilled men and women.

U.S. Supreme Court invalidates NRA in *Schechter Poultry Corp.* v. *U.S.*

Resettlement Administration aids flood control, reforestation; relocates workers.

Social Security Act provides safety net against old age, disability, unemployment.

"Soak-the-rich" Revenue Act increases tax rates for very rich.

United Auto Workers gain contract from GM after sit-down strike in Flint, Michigan.

1937: *FDR's court-packing plan tries to tilt Supreme Court in president's favor but fails.*

WPA cuts and interest rate hikes trigger "Roosevelt recession."

Chicago police kill ten protesters in front of steel plant; FDR intervenes.

Hormel introduces its canned pink mystery meat, Spam.

23 | World War II

LEARNING OBJECTIVES

After reading this chapter, you should be able to do the following:

23-1 Explain the causes of World War II.

23-2 Explain U.S. foreign policy as it developed after World War I, called isolationism, and describe how that policy changed as World War II progressed.

23-3 Describe the major events of World War II, both in Europe and the Pacific, and explain why the United States acted as it did throughout the conflict.

23-4 Describe and discuss the American home front during World War II, paying special attention to long-term societal changes.

23-5 Explain how World War II ended, both in Europe and in the Pacific, and discuss the aftermath of the war both in the United States and around the world.

AFTER FINISHING THIS CHAPTER GO TO **PAGE 458** **FOR STUDY TOOLS**

If the New Deal could not end the Great Depression, a world war would. Beginning in the early 1930s, tensions grew fierce between China and Japan as each tried to claim authority over much of Asia, eventually leading to full-scale war by 1937. By the late 1930s, talk of war was becoming more urgent throughout Europe as well. The uncertainty created by the worldwide economic depression created political vulnerabilities that assisted the rise of militant, expansion-minded dictators in Japan, Italy, and Germany. Americans watched all these situations nervously, uncertain how Asian and European affairs might affect them. Little did they know that, in the end, the Second World War would transform America even more than the New Deal.

The war prompted a mobilization of American resources at a level unseen since the Civil War. Long-quiet industries were revitalized, the agricultural sector started to grow again, and the American economy ramped up to become the most powerful economy in the world. The demands of war created opportunities for women, who filled jobs left open by the men who enlisted in the service, and for African Americans and other minorities, who did not hesitate to use the facts of Hitler's racism and antisemitism to demonstrate the flaws of the American promise. The ethnic enclaves formed during the massive immigration between 1880 and 1924 lost some of their unique character as well, dwindling due to 1920s immigration restrictions and calls for unity put forward by the federal government. Sometimes the concept of American unity excluded racial minorities, as it did in the internment of thousands of Japanese Americans, whose sole supposedly un-American characteristic was their country of descent. For the most part, however, Americans embraced the call for greater tolerance, a tolerance that prompted the civil rights movement and other liberation movements that were to come.

In the end, the war created a world dominated and heavily influenced by two major powers, the Soviet Union and the United States. Their attempts to remake the world torn apart by the Second World War are the subject of the next chapter. But first, to the war and the dramatic transformations it set in motion.

23-1 CAUSES OF WAR

There were multiple causes of the Second World War, but the Great Depression was perhaps the most significant.

23-1a Provocations for War

The stock market collapse between 1929 and 1932 ended American investment in Europe and caused economic slowdowns there. Without American dollars, European countries faced industrial decline, unemployment, and widespread homelessness.

These problems increased political tensions. In France and Spain, for example, fighting broke out between Communists and Nationalists over which group had the best plan to manage the disrupted economy. But the crash had a devastating effect on Germany, whose reparation payments for World War I were largely financed by American lenders. When American businesses withdrew investments in Germany, German production fell by half between 1929 and 1933. In 1933, with the economy in a shambles and chaos raging throughout German politics and in German streets, Adolf Hitler's National Socialist (Nazi) Party ascended to power and ruthlessly consolidated its control of the state. Hitler then began a massive armament campaign that put millions of Germans to work on public works projects and in factories. In some ways, it was a militant and extreme version of the New Deal. And in a sense it worked. The economic depression there was over by 1936, providing dramatic proof that the deficit spending advocated by John Maynard Keynes would work. A similar program for reform emerged in Italy under the dictatorship of Benito Mussolini.

But Hitler and Mussolini did not stop at economic reform. Driven by delusions of grandeur and by racist and antisemitic ideologies, and seeking to remake Europe (and, after that, the world) to match his nationalistic vision, Hitler defied World War I's Treaty of Versailles by occupying the industrialized Rhineland in 1936 and annexing German-speaking Austria in 1938. He was intent on expanding further, too. He roused the German public with promises of German power and antisemitic screeds that blamed Germany's plight on the Jews. Encouraged by Germany's example, Mussolini invaded and conquered Ethiopia in 1935 and Albania in 1939.

Meanwhile, on the other side of the globe, Emperor Hirohito of Japan was attempting to bring all of Asia under Japanese control. In 1931, Japanese forces, fearful that Japanese investments in the contested terrain of Manchuria were threatened by Chinese nationalist aspirations, occupied the Chinese territory of Manchuria. The Japanese used an explosion of a railroad track near the city of Mukden as an excuse to occupy the entire

◀◀◀ **During the war, 12 million men joined the Armed Services, creating plentiful opportunities for American women. Here, three women assemble a B-17 bomber in Long Beach, California.**

>> Benito Mussolini (left) and Adolf Hitler (right) both came to power promising to end the ravages of the worldwide economic depression.

region. The occupation clearly violated Japan's pledges as a member of the League of Nations, but neither the League nor the United States was immediately eager to respond. Instead, the United States warned Japan against further territorial aggression. Japan ignored the warning, attacking and briefly occupying China's famous port city of Shanghai in 1932.

Four years of quiet tensions simmered in Asia, until 1937, when Japan launched a full-scale invasion of China, occupying most of the large cities along the Chinese coast. Emperor Hirohito sought to create a region entirely dominated by Japan and Japanese business interests, and he saw China as his main competitor. By 1940, the two nations were stuck in a military stalemate: Japan was unable to defeat its much larger neighbor, while China's military suffered from internal political divisions. Japan had the upper hand, but it had not yet finished the military takeover, becoming bogged down in China's vast interior. To America's east, then, the European continent was on the verge of full-scale war as aggressors placed their pawns in position to attack. To America's west, the two major powers in Asia were locked

Munich Agreement 1938 treaty in which the leading powers of western Europe allowed Hitler to annex strategic areas of Czechoslovakia in order to satisfy his territorial aspirations (strategy of appeasement)

in a bloody military stalemate. The United States was an island of peace in the midst of tremors all around.

23-1b Reactions

Many Americans hoped the United States would avoid armed conflict in both Asia and Europe. Congress passed a series of neutrality acts between 1935 and 1937 that placed arms embargoes on all belligerent powers. Roosevelt signed these measures, but, leery of the offensive actions of Germany, Italy, and Japan, in 1937 he called for the world community to "quarantine" these states. Eventually, he would come to regret signing the neutrality acts at all.

France and Britain also seemed reluctant to oppose these aggressive nations. Both countries had suffered greatly during the First World War and wanted to avoid further bloodshed. Their leaders hoped to appease Mussolini and especially Hitler by giving them some of what they wanted so as not to enrage them. In what has come to be called the **Munich Agreement** (1938), for example, the leading powers of western Europe allowed Hitler to annex strategic areas of Czechoslovakia in order to satisfy his territorial aspirations, hoping he would go no further. They assumed that if they allowed him to unify all the German-speaking people in Europe under one flag, Hitler would abide by historic German territorial demands. They were, of course, wrong in this assumption.

Beyond his territorial ambitions, Hitler also began denouncing and terrorizing Jews, communists, gays, and other groups he deemed undesirable and un-German. This was the beginning of what came to be called the Holocaust. Many in France, Britain, and the United States did not agree with or condone Hitler's brutal actions (although some did), but they all failed to confront him.

The British cautiously claimed that appeasement with German's historic territorial ambitions might bring "peace for our time" (although they were arming themselves while they said it), but it was not to be so. Hitler continued his relentless expansion into neighboring countries. In March 1939, Hitler broke his various promises and moved his armies into Czechoslovakia. He also demanded control over the German-speaking areas of Poland. British and French diplomats urgently solicited an alliance with Soviet leader Joseph Stalin. But Stalin distrusted the West, which was, after all, the capitalist rival of his communist nation.

Heritage Images/Getty Images

>> Joseph Stalin, seen here in a propaganda poster, led the Soviet Union beginning in 1924.

In a bold and ultimately wrongheaded move in August 1939, Stalin agreed to a secret **nonaggression pact** with Hitler that divided Poland between Germany and the Soviet Union. Unafraid of how France and Britain might respond, Hitler invaded Poland on September 1, 1939. Now finally understanding that Hitler was after something more than just bringing together all of Europe's German-speaking people, Britain and France declared war on Germany. Europe was once again at war, just as Asia was across the Pacific.

23-2 AMERICAN FOREIGN POLICY BEFORE THE WAR

Americans at first tried to stay out of the war, but this became less feasible as Hitler's aggression continued.

> **nonaggression pact** 1939 agreement between Stalin and Hitler that divided Poland between Germany and the Soviet Union and said the two nations would not attack each other

AFP/Getty Images

>> The attempts of Emperor Hirohito, pictured here, to consolidate all of Asia under Japanese rule led to war with China in 1937.

23-2a 1930s Isolation

In the United States, the Great Depression had provoked a strong drift toward isolationism. The trend was already manifested in the American rejection of the League of Nations following World War I, but during the Great Depression many Americans remained preoccupied by domestic affairs. (For more on the reasons why many Americans resisted involvement in European affairs, see "The Reasons Why . . ." box.)

LATIN AMERICA

Concerning foreign policy, FDR was initially of the same mindset as his predecessor, Herbert Hoover. He was not a strict isolationist, but he was not eager to engage too deeply in foreign affairs. Indeed, rather than help the troubled European economy in the 1930s, American policymakers focused their efforts on improving relations with nations closer to home, particularly in Central and South America. At his 1933 inauguration, FDR announced that the United States would pursue a **"good neighbor" policy** toward Latin America, thus

> **"good neighbor" policy** American strategy of renouncing military intervention in Latin American affairs

renouncing military intervention in Latin American affairs, and during the next few years he signed treaties with various Central and South American nations. Their goal was to maintain political stability without using military means.

THE WORLD'S ARSENAL

Despite this diplomatic activity in Latin America, isolationism remained the key feature of American foreign policy. Polls showed that more than 90 percent of the American public did not want to go to war. But with the unrest in Asia and Europe, the United States, as a major world power, could not look away for long. The economic prospect of a military buildup was too alluring. For one thing, the warring nations needed American guns and armor, and from 1937 to 1941, Britain, France, China, and the Soviet Union all began rapid armament, boosting the American economy. In 1939, for example, American outrage over the invasion of Poland translated into a new neutrality act that allowed belligerent powers, particularly Britain and France, to buy arms aggressively from the United States. Roosevelt believed that France and Britain could win a European war on their own if the United States provided material assistance and served as the world's arsenal. At the same time, Roosevelt requested and

·The Reasons Why...

There were several reasons why so many Americans favored isolationism before the Second World War:

World War I. Their memories of the First World War made many Americans leery of getting involved in European affairs. In 1914, Americans watched as a dizzying series of alliances led one nation into battle with another, without any apparent justification. The brutality of the First World War also made Americans shy away from any involvement in European affairs. Why risk American lives to protect European freedoms?

The Great Depression. The Great Depression deepened this isolationism. Most Americans were simply too focused on improving life in the United States to advocate getting involved in diplomatic disputes abroad.

Respect for Hitler. At the same time, some Americans had profound respect for Adolf Hitler, who had, after all, plucked Germany from its own economic depression in record time. By the late 1930s, American icons like the aviator Charles Lindbergh argued that the Nazis were unstoppable under the leadership of Hitler and that the United States should negotiate with rather than fight against them.

Antisemitism. Lindbergh, like Hitler, was also an antisemite. Although the worst abuses of the Holocaust would only begin to occur in 1941, by the late 1930s many American Jews were asking President Roosevelt to take a stronger stance against Hitler. Roosevelt, aware that a large majority of Americans would not want to get involved in war in order to save Europe's Jews, opted to wait until he could rally greater public opinion. That only occurred in December of 1941, with the bombing of Pearl Harbor.

received congressional authorization to build 50,000 warplanes per year, just in case. America was beginning to build its own defenses. This also helped boost the American economy, although the nation was still officially neutral.

BLITZKRIEG AND DOUBT

The belief that Britain and France could effectively fight Germany was summarily negated when, in the spring of 1940, Germany launched a series of *blitzkrieg* (or "lightning wars") that utilized surprise, speed, and unrelentingly concentrated attacks to defeat most of its neighbors. In April and May 1940, the Germans ripped through Denmark and Norway. Other German forces swept through Belgium and the Netherlands. On June 5, German armies attacked France and captured Paris after only six weeks of battle. Germany forced the French to sign a treaty creating a pro-German French regime, headquartered in **Vichy** and known by the name "Vichy France." By the summer of 1940, Germany controlled most of western Europe, and had conquered it with astonishing ease.

In the process, Hitler now imprisoned the continent's (not just Germany's) Jews, gypsies, and other societal scapegoats in a web of concentration camps. By now, it was apparent that these efforts to intimidate, isolate, and concentrate European Jewry were more than just political stunts but methodological attempts to rid Europe of its so-called "undesireables." Hitler had trod on the ground of early-twentieth-century social Darwinism and eugenics and was, by his own account, putting those ideas into frightful practice.

By late 1940, soldiers guarding these concentration camps began killing the Jews inside. By 1941, Hitler began using death squads to kill entire villages of Jews in eastern Europe. And by 1942, he had set up his infamous death camps, where gas chambers were built to speed up the process of mass killing and where disgusting scientific experiments were conducted on unwilling captives. These horrific events would later become known as the **Holocaust**. Until 1940, however, few outside Europe knew about Hitler's processes of intimidation and murder (and when they learned of them, even fewer were spurred into action until much later in the war).

In Europe, only the British stood against the Germans. In the summer and autumn of 1940, the two nations fought in the **Battle of Britain**, in which

>> During the 1940 Battle of Britain, German planes bombed London incessantly, destroying much of the city. This photo shows some of the devastation around St. Paul's Cathedral.

Keystone Archives/HIP/The Image Works

Hitler attempted to break Britain's air power by heavily bombarding British cities and by deliberately targeting British civilians, hoping to sap their will to fight. Many Americans sympathized with the British people suffering through the bomb attacks, the horrors of which were relayed nightly from London by radio correspondents.

PARTIAL INVOLVEMENT

The devastation of Britain set the stage for American involvement. In May 1940, Roosevelt asked Congress to increase spending on American national defense and to authorize sending surplus arms to Britain.

blitzkrieg "Lightning war"; fast and brutal attacks staged by Germany on its neighbors starting in 1940

Vichy City in central France, headquarters of the pro-German French regime installed in 1940

Holocaust Systematic killing of 11 million Jews, gypsies, and other societal scapegoats in Nazi concentration camps all over Europe

Battle of Britain Fierce battle fought in the summer and autumn of 1940; Hitler attempted to break Britain's air power through heavy bombardment of British cities

Globe Photos/ZUMAPRESS.com/Alamy Stock Photo

>> During the buildup to war, a strong bond grew between President Franklin D. Roosevelt and British Prime Minister Winston Churchill, pictured here, and between the United States and Britain in general.

That same month, Winston Churchill was appointed Britain's prime minister. An inspiring speaker who had long warned of Hitler's growing power, Churchill pledged to fight the Germans in the streets of Britain, if necessary. Churchill also believed that an alliance with the United States was the key to Britain's survival. Determined to win Roosevelt's friendship and support, Churchill frequently wrote Roosevelt and later visited the White House for long stays.

23-2b From Isolation to Intervention

American public sentiment still fell considerably short of favoring direct intervention, but the idea that the United States should grant some form of aid had been

America First Committee Organization created to oppose U.S. involvement in the Second World War; committee leaders argued that the Nazis were unstoppable and that the United States should negotiate with them

Four Freedoms Basic human rights articulated by FDR to ensure that America's involvement in World War II was seen as ideologically sound: freedom of speech, freedom of worship, freedom from want, freedom from fear

growing since Germany's invasion of Poland in 1939. Many Americans foresaw dangers for the United States should Germany conquer Britain. With control of all of Europe, Germany might become unbeatable. American Jews were especially active in advocating a more aggressive stance against Hitler, but in an America controlled by a white, Anglo-Saxon elite, and with American antisemitism still socially acceptable and in fact growing, the urgings of American Jews did not carry enough weight to power a full-scale intervention.

In late 1940, Roosevelt approved the first peacetime draft in U.S. history. He also announced that the United States was giving the British fifty renovated naval destroyers, referring to the United States as "the arsenal of democracy."

Roosevelt's moves prompted criticism from the left and the right, but it was conservatives like William Randolph Hearst and Montana senator Burton Wheeler who formed an opposing organization, called the **America First Committee**. Aviator Charles Lindbergh became the group's notable spokesman (for more on Lindbergh, refer back to "The Reasons Why . . ." box).

Opinion polls found that most Americans supported providing aid to Britain. American politicians responded. In the fall of 1940, Roosevelt, running for an unprecedented third term of office, repeatedly declared that the United States would not enter the war, but he warned that dangerous waters lay ahead. What he proposed instead was "aid short of war."

23-2c Aid Short of War

Roosevelt handily won the election of 1940 and soon began articulating a plan for American involvement in the war.

THE FOUR FREEDOMS

America had to take a stand, Roosevelt declared, in order to create a world based on what he dubbed the **Four Freedoms**: freedom of speech, freedom of worship, freedom from want, and freedom from fear. This was Roosevelt's clearest statement yet that the United States would take a powerful role in creating a new order in world affairs. In almost every way, these four freedoms were directly opposed to what the Nazis were doing in conquering Europe. If Roosevelt had his way, the war would be fought on ideological grounds.

Roosevelt then pressured Congress, in March 1941, to pass the **Lend-Lease Act**, empowering the president to lend weapons and supplies to nations fighting the Germans or the Japanese. These measures became even more urgent with a series of German, Italian, and Japanese victories in late 1940 and early 1941. In fact, Germany, planning an attack on Russia and searching for a Pacific partner, had begun to make overtures to Japan to form an alliance. Japan, still stalemated with China, thought the resources won from the toppling of the British Empire (if Germany won) would help Japan control the Pacific. Along with Italy, the nations came together in the Tripartite Pact; they were known as "the Axis Powers."

> By the middle of 1941, the United States was in an undeclared shooting war with Germany.

In August 1941, Roosevelt met with Churchill in a secret conference off the coast of Newfoundland. Roosevelt told Churchill he would give assistance but not declare war. The two leaders issued a set of aims known as the **Atlantic Charter**, which stated that the war was being waged in the name of national self-determination and was not a war of conquest. With the charter, the United States had committed itself to the defeat of Germany and the victory of Britain. But it was not yet at war.

Roosevelt ordered his navy to escort ships across the Atlantic, which was being heavily patrolled by German U-boats. The Germans sank U.S. ships in the fall of 1941, after which Roosevelt ordered the navy to fire on German and Italian submarines. By the middle of 1941, the United States was in an undeclared shooting war with Germany.

23-2d Conflict in the Pacific

Events in Asia would tilt the nation toward formally declaring war. Japanese attempts to conquer China violated the American belief that China should be kept free from foreign domination and thus open to American trade, which had been called the "open door policy." But Japan did not stop in China. In July 1941, Japanese forces occupied the French colony of Indochina, which included Cambodia, Laos, and Vietnam. Alarmed by the aggressive nature of these invasions, the United States perceived a Japanese plan to control all of Asia. It retaliated by cutting off all trade with Japan.

This was a grave threat to the Japanese. Without raw materials from the United States, the Japanese economy would slow down. The United States had therefore given Japan a difficult choice: either withdraw from Indochina and China or seek resources elsewhere. Japanese planners chose to look elsewhere. They invaded British and Dutch possessions in the East Indies. But despite these acquisitions, the Japanese felt that the U.S. presence in the Far East was limiting Japan's capacity to expand into other territories. In their view, the United States had to be forcibly expelled from Asia.

In September 1941, the Japanese imperial command decided to stage an attack on the main U.S. fleet in the Pacific, anchored at Pearl Harbor, Hawai'i. If they succeeded in handicapping the American fleet, they might be able to finish their desired conquests before the United States could rebuild. American intelligence officials had cracked Japanese codes in 1940 but were unable to discern where or when an attack might come.

On the morning of December 7, 1941, Japanese bombers appeared in the skies above Pearl Harbor. The bombers sank or damaged eight U.S. battleships and killed 2,403 Americans before returning to aircraft carriers, some 220 miles away. At the same time, Japan launched offensives against American positions in the Philippines, Guam, and Midway Island, as well as British-held Hong Kong and Malaysia. Crucially, American aircraft carriers were at sea during the attack and therefore survived. Otherwise, the vast majority of the American Pacific arsenal was destroyed.

Shocked and furious, Roosevelt announced that December 7 would become "a date which will live in infamy." He then asked Congress for a declaration of war. On December 8, both houses of Congress declared war with only one dissenting vote (Congresswoman Jeanette Rankin of Montana, a pacifist). Honoring his alliance with Japan, Hitler declared war on the United States on December 11, making the war a world war.

Lend-Lease Act Legislation passed in March 1941 empowering the president to lend weapons and supplies to nations fighting the Germans or the Japanese

Atlantic Charter Set of aims issued by Roosevelt and Churchill stating that the war was being waged in the name of national self-determination and was not a war of conquest

>> "AIR RAID PEARL HARBOR . . . This is no drill."—Navy Lieutenant Commander Logan Ramsey's first broadcast alert on December 7, 1941. Pictured here are burning vessels. Much of the U.S. Pacific Naval fleet was destroyed.

National Archives/MCT/Newscom

23-3 THE WAR

In December 1941, the German-Japanese Axis seemed all-powerful. On all fronts, the Allies were losing. In the Pacific, the Japanese had mauled the Americans at Pearl Harbor and scored rapid victories in the Dutch East Indies and the Philippines. By mid-1942, Japan's quest for control of a unified Asia was almost complete. Meanwhile, German and Italian forces occupied much of North Africa and most of Europe except Britain. Despite his nonaggression pact with the Soviet Union, Hitler's armies were nearing Moscow as well. They had also begun the process of murdering all of Europe's Jews and political radicals in an effort to remake Europe in Germany's Aryan image; the Holocaust was under way.

These frightening developments brought the United States, Britain, and the Soviet Union together in a **Grand Alliance** that would eventually turn the tide of the war.

Grand Alliance Group of three countries allied to fight Hitler: the United States, Britain, and the Soviet Union

four policemen Four major allies: the United States, the Soviet Union, Britain, and China; Roosevelt suggested that after the war, these countries exert their military power to ensure international peace

But it was a long journey from those initial defeats to eventual victory.

23-3a The Alliance

Although most Americans viewed Japan as the main aggressor, Roosevelt and Churchill agreed that Germany posed the greater threat. For the time being, however, neither the United States nor Britain was strong enough to mount an attack. For many months, the Soviet Union was the only force battling the Axis on the European continent.

To help the Soviets, the United States and Britain sent $11 billion in trucks, food, and other supplies. The Soviets were grateful, but Stalin wanted a permanent alliance. The question was, on what terms? Stalin would not accept the Atlantic Charter because of its insistence on democratic elections, which might threaten his creation of a communist empire. Stalin also wanted to reclaim Poland from Germany, which was forbidden by the charter's commitment to national determination. Stalin had decided he would never agree to any European settlement that would let armies sweep eastward, unimpeded, toward Moscow. He wanted to ensure Soviet security from western Europe, and that meant control over Poland.

In May 1942, the Soviet Red Army struggled alone against Germany. Roosevelt, fearing the Soviets might make a separate peace with Germany, suggested that, after the war, the four major allies (the United States, the Soviet Union, Britain, and China) exert their military power to ensure international peace. Stalin enthusiastically agreed to this **four policemen** approach, believing it was Roosevelt's way of promising that governments friendly to Soviet interests would be installed in central Europe. Roosevelt probably envisioned only a general Soviet role in guaranteeing security. Thus, even as the United States entered the war, Roosevelt's vision of the postwar world was on a collision course with that of the Soviet leader, a course that would lead to the Cold War. For the time being, though, a remarkable alliance had been forged, one that brought together the largest capitalist nation in the world (the United States), the largest communist nation, which was still committed to the goal of world revolution (the Soviet

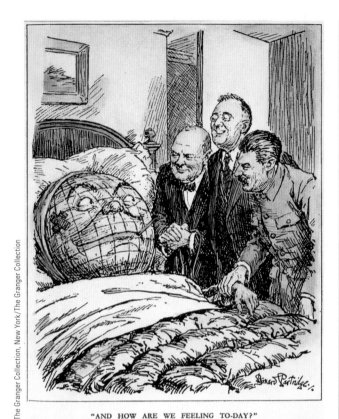

"AND HOW ARE WE FEELING TO-DAY?"

>> Britain's Winston Churchill, the U.S.'s Franklin Roosevelt, and the Soviet Union's Joseph Stalin imagined themselves, and were imagined as this cartoon illustrates with them asking the ailing world, "And how are we feeling today?"

Union), and the largest colonial power actively struggling to keep its vast global empire closed to American trade (Great Britain).

23-3b The Pacific Theater, 1941–1942

Although the Allies recognized that Germany was a larger threat than Japan, the United States had a larger presence in the Pacific than in Europe. Thus, American troops fought their first battles in the Pacific. Japan's strategy was to keep the United States at bay long enough to take control over much of the Pacific, which would limit American involvement in Asian affairs. American forces suffered many defeats in those early months. In the Philippines, the Wake Islands, and near Australia, Allied troops lost repeatedly. In mid-1942, the Japanese even took several of the Aleutian Islands (off the coast of Alaska), which, although no one knew it then, was destined to be the only

American land occupied by the Japanese throughout the course of the war. Still, sensing an opportunity to eject the American presence from the Pacific once and for all, the Japanese actively sought possession of Hawai'i. By taking Hawai'i, they hoped to end the American threat in thePacific before the United States had fully mobilized for war.

Good news came in May 1942, when Americans finally slowed the Japanese advance in the Pacific at the Battle of the Coral Sea. Then in June, a Japanese plan to deal a knockout punch to American forces backfired at Midway Island, when the Japanese suffered a decisive defeat. After the **Battle of Midway**, Japan had reached the limit of its expansion in the Pacific, about halfway across the ocean. It was no longer an offensive threat pushing toward the American West Coast. It had reached the limits of its expansionary capacities. But what would it take to beat Japan back entirely? As it turned out, quite a lot.

23-3c The European Theater, 1942–1943

In the early months of 1942, the Axis Powers reached the limit of their expansion in Europe too. In the west, German U-boats had sunk more than four hundred American ships in the Atlantic and were handily in control of almost all of western Europe. In the south, German troops moved from Libya to Egypt, African land they sought in order to shut down the Allies' last unfettered supply routes and win sole access to Middle Eastern oil. In the east, the Germans launched a summer counteroffensive in southern Russia and the Caucasus Mountains, taking Stalingrad on September 13. By the middle of 1942, the Germans had buttressed their hold on western Europe on all sides. Only Britain remained unoccupied. The German goal of reconquering all the European lands through to be "German" and providing a buffer around them to ensure Germany's safety seemed to be coming to fruition.

For the Allies, better news came in late 1942, four months after Japan had been slowed in the Pacific. In October, British troops checked the Axis advance in Africa at the second battle of El Alamein in Egypt. Shortly thereafter, American troops arrived in North Africa, bottling up the Germans in Tunisia. The south was increasingly secure; Axis advances were repelled, and an avenue appeared through which the Allies could

Battle of Midway Turning point of the Pacific battle when, in 1942, the Allies finally stopped the expansion of Japan

AP Images/British Official

>> Italian women applaud as Allied troops take over the islands of southern Italy. It was the first step in conquering the whole of Europe.

began a strategy of "island-hopping," in which it flew over heavily defended outer islands and attacked less defended islands, isolating Japanese strongholds. In Africa, by May 1943, all German and Italian forces had been defeated. The grip was loosening. American war power and materiel (equipment), together with the British and the other Allied forces, seemed to be strong enough to mount a successful battle.

THE TEHRAN CONFERENCE

The first meeting between Churchill, Roosevelt, and Stalin took place in November 1943, in Tehran, Iran. Their main topic was the opening of the second front against Vichy France, which would bolster the Soviet forces fighting on the eastern front. By opening a second front in France, the Allies hoped to divide the German forces and ensure the defeat of Hitler. At the meeting, the three powers set a launch date in mid-1944. In exchange for this attempt to surround Germany in Europe, Stalin agreed to open a front against Japan once Germany had been defeated.

23-3d 1944: Victory in View

In early 1944, with the spirit of cooperation between the major Allies stronger than ever, Allied forces attacked German and Japanese troops on a number of fronts. But all eyes were on the planned Allied landing in northern France, which Hitler was anticipating. If Hitler could stop the Allies from securing a foothold in France, he would be able to rush troops back to Russia and possibly hold off the advancing Soviets, perhaps securing his empire.

NORMANDY

Hitler didn't know where the attack was going to come, though. And on June 6, 1944, an amphibious American, Canadian, and British assault on a 60-mile stretch of Normandy, France, supervised by American general Dwight Eisenhower, established a landing zone. After D-Day (a military euphemism for "designation day," also in this case known as Operation Overlord), 1 million Allied troops poured into France and struck eastward, taking Caen and St. Lô en route to securing Paris on August 25.

enter Europe. In the east, meanwhile, the Soviets stopped the German advance in the titanic **Battle of Stalingrad**. The Soviet Union slowly began to reconquer lands it had just lost. After years of deadly brutal war, by late 1942 Axis advances were blocked on all fronts. Millions had died already.

TURNING POINTS: 1943

In 1943, Allied leaders faced the question of how to translate these initial successes into a strategy for winning the war. Roosevelt and Churchill, avoiding a direct assault on Axis strongholds like France or Germany, agreed to invade Sicily and Italy, which the Allies succeeded in doing rather quickly. They were making progress on other fronts, too. The United States had launched its first offensive in the Pacific at **Guadalcanal**, finally winning a foothold there. It also

Battle of Stalingrad Five-month-long battle in southwestern Russia that halted the advance of Germany into the Soviet Union in 1942. With somewhere near 1.5 million casualties, it is often considered one of the bloodiest battles in the history of warfare

Guadalcanal One of the Solomon Islands in the Pacific, the location of a 1943 battle that gave the United States and its allies a foothold in the Pacific

Moving swiftly, more than 2 million American, British, and other Allied troops entered France by September 5, and German defenses crumbled. By September 11, 1944, all of France, Belgium, and Luxembourg had been liberated, and the next day Allied troops entered Germany (see Map 23.1). On the eastern front, Soviet troops invaded the Baltic states and East Prussia in the north and the Balkans and Hungary in the south. In the Pacific, American troops landed on Mindoro Island in the Philippines on December 15, and in a series of naval battles, destroyed most of Japan's remaining sea power (see Map 23.2). By late 1944, with Allied troops moving on all fronts toward Berlin and Tokyo, the defeat of the Axis was assured.

Map 23.1 Allied Advances and Collapse of German Power

>> This map of Europe during the Second World War shows the dramatic expansion of Hitler's Axis powers before the series of battles from 1943 that turned the tide of war.

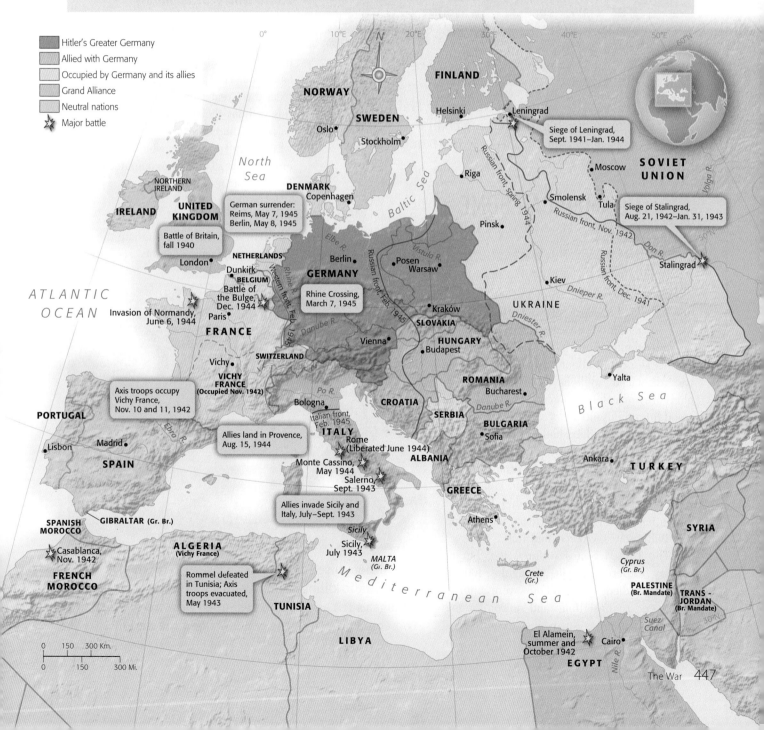

Legend:
- Hitler's Greater Germany
- Allied with Germany
- Occupied by Germany and its allies
- Grand Alliance
- Neutral nations
- ★ Major battle

Siege of Leningrad, Sept. 1941–Jan. 1944

German surrender: Reims, May 7, 1945; Berlin, May 8, 1945

Battle of Britain, fall 1940

Rhine Crossing, March 7, 1945

Battle of the Bulge, Dec. 1944

Invasion of Normandy, June 6, 1944

Siege of Stalingrad, Aug. 21, 1942–Jan. 31, 1943

Axis troops occupy Vichy France, Nov. 10 and 11, 1942

VICHY FRANCE (Occupied Nov. 1942)

Allies land in Provence, Aug. 15, 1944

Monte Cassino, May 1944

Salerno, Sept. 1943

Allies invade Sicily and Italy, July–Sept. 1943

Sicily, July 1943

Casablanca, Nov. 1942

Rommel defeated in Tunisia; Axis troops evacuated, May 1943

El Alamein, summer and October 1942

>> The 1944 D-Day landing at Normandy, France, pictured here, was a major turning point in the European theater, allowing Allied troops to enter Europe easily.

23-4 THE AMERICAN HOME FRONT

World War II was a remarkably destructive war, laying waste to much of Europe. Indeed, one would be hard pressed to overstate its destruction. The war killed off almost an entire generation—more than 23 million Soviets alone and about 62 million total. The war displaced millions more. Buildings—churches, castles, monasteries—that had stood for a thousand years or more were obliterated. Hitler's soldiers had annihilated nearly all of European Jewry—roughly 6 million Jews died in Nazi concentration camps. About half of the Jews killed were from Poland; the rest came from almost every other European nation, including France, Germany, the Ukraine, the Baltic states, Greece, and Italy.

The United States suffered too, but on a very different scale. Roughly 400,000 Americans died, and millions were injured. However, as unsettling and uncomfortable as it might seem to do so, the Second World War can be seen as an energizing event in American history rather than a destructive one. Very little American land or property was destroyed; the economy recovered from the Great Depression; and groups that were long excluded from full participation in American life slowly gained a measure of inclusion. This is not to say that World War II was a "good war": soldiers died, many suffered, and discrimination persisted. But it is true that the war had a transformative effect on the American home front.

23-4a The War Economy

The economy showed the most remarkable improvement. Wartime mobilization boosted production, increased demand for labor, and rescued the national economy from the Great Depression. And it did all this without the extreme measures advocated by some experts. For instance, there was no draft for labor, which would have ensured that all industries operated at maximum capacity.

MANUFACTURING FOR WAR

Despite this, World War II did in fact initiate the most significant federal management of the economy in

>> Although some Americans knew about the systematic killing of European Jewry as early as 1942, images such as this one of starved prisoners, which emerged only after the war, horrified the nation.

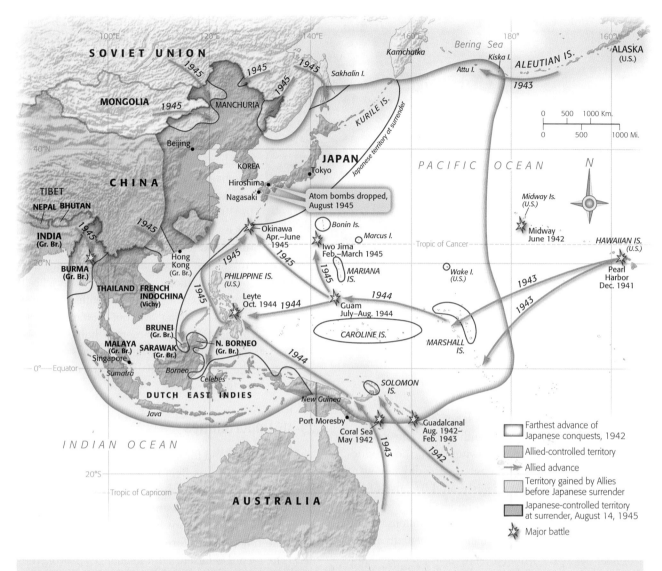

Map 23.2 The Final Assault Against Japan

>> This map shows the war in Asia, including Japan's rapid expansion into the Pacific until 1943, when the tide of war shifted.

American history. When the war began, President Roosevelt implemented the War Production Board (WPB) to steer the economy into manufacturing weapons rather than consumer goods. Under WPB contracts, Ford, Chrysler, and General Motors shifted from making cars to producing tanks and airplanes. Firestone, Goodyear, and B.F. Goodrich ceased production of civilian car tires and made tires for jeeps, trucks, and airplanes.

In 1943, Roosevelt instituted the Office of War Mobilization (OWM) to oversee the distribution of essential materials such as steel, rubber, and aluminum. Meanwhile, to conserve resources, the WPB banned production of nonessential items and prioritized war-related industries. Farmers produced crops in record amounts as well. Through careful direction, the government worked with industry to handle the explosion in war-related manufacturing.

LABOR

The expansion of the economy increased the size of the labor force. On one hand, 12 million Americans joined the armed forces, subtracting them from the domestic labor pool. On the other hand, formerly depressed industries were now replete with contracts, hiring men and women at unprecedented levels. Roosevelt established the National War Labor Board

>> Rationing notices such as this one adorned American stores, ensuring that all Americans felt they were a part of the war effort.

particularly attractive to Americans because government rationing had already limited consumer spending. With nowhere else to spend their bigger paychecks, many people bought bonds. Finally, the federal government rationed goods. For example, in order to redirect food to soldiers, the government sponsored the "Victory Garden" movement, which encouraged people to grow their own vegetables. More extensive rationing and price controls were also instituted. Early in 1942, Congress opened the Office of Price Administration (OPA), which had the authority to impose rationing and control wages, prices, and rents. Among their many sacrifices, Americans sporadically lived without sugar, butter, coffee, meat, or gasoline. Doing without certain luxuries brought the war closer to home, creating an environment where civilians far from the battlefields felt they were contributing to the war effort.

(NWLB) in 1942 to minimize labor disputes and set wages, working conditions, and hours. The government did not want strikes slowing down the production of war-related goods, but it also did not want workers to be squeezed or mistreated because of the more intense wartime production levels.

This need for workers was a boon to unions. Union membership grew from 9 million in 1940 to nearly 15 million in 1945. Although some strikes did break out during the war, most laborers felt it unpatriotic to leave work while their compatriots were fighting. They were aided in this pledge by the Smith-Connally Act of 1943, which formally prohibited strikes. In return for working longer hours, workers received heftier paychecks.

PAYING FOR WAR

It was expensive to pay for all these war supplies. In total, the government spent $321 billion on the war effort. To pay for the war, Roosevelt did three things. First, he pushed for increased taxation, particularly on the wealthy and big business. Inheritance and corporate taxes were also assessed. As a result, taxes paid for 45 percent of the war's cost. Second, the government issued U.S. Savings Bonds, which people bought in expectation of repayment, with interest, later. These bonds increased the national debt from $40 billion in 1940 to $260 billion in 1945, but they provided a lot of money up front to the government. Savings bonds were

23-4b Opportunities

The sudden demand for labor, fueled by the notion that the United States was fighting a cadre of brutal racist dictators, led to increased opportunities for women and minorities. These groups were now offered high-paying jobs that had never before been available to them. At the same time, certain forms of discrimination continued. The record is mixed, but the changes provoked by the war prompted social changes that resonated long after 1945.

WOMEN

As millions of men enlisted in the armed services, U.S. industries needed more workers to replace them. American women filled this vacuum. By 1945, female employment outside the home had increased by more than 50 percent, to 20 million. In the process, women entered into fields that were not typically thought of as "women's work," including industrial jobs in defense factories.

To promote American women's involvement in the effort, a government campaign featured the character of Rosie the Riveter, a robust, cheerful woman in overalls who labored on the assembly lines. This campaign, coupled with the acute labor shortage, helped change employers' attitudes. Though they sometimes had to cope with the hostility of their male coworkers,

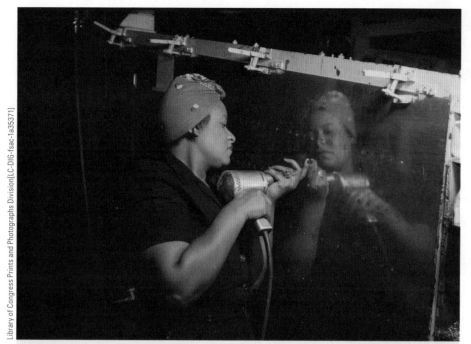

>> By 1945, female employment outside the home had increased by more than 50 percent, to 20 million. Meanwhile, annual wages for African Americans went from $457 before the war to $1,976 after. This photo shows an African American woman drilling rivets, a conspicuous look-alike of the famous image of Rosie the Riveter.

measures in the industries that had lucrative defense contracts and (2) to end segregation in the military. President Roosevelt feared that Randolph's threat to bring more than 100,000 African Americans to march on the capital might provoke a race war. In response, the president issued Executive Order 8802, which gave Randolph half of what he demanded. Executive Order 8802 established the **Fair Employment Practices Committee (FEPC)**, which required companies with federal contracts to make jobs available without regard to "race, creed, color, or national origin." Coupled with the demand for labor, the FEPC had some effect. In total, the percentage of African Americans in war production work rose from 3 percent to 9 percent during the war. Between 1942 and 1945, the number of African Americans in labor unions (traditionally the province of higher-skilled workers) doubled to more than 1 million. The average annual wage for African Americans quadrupled in the war years, from $457 to $1,976. Randolph's second demand, to integrate the armed services, would have to wait until after the war.

Despite the formal segregation enforced in the military, about 1 million African Americans served in the armed forces. Most served in segregated units commanded by white officers. African Americans nevertheless took pride in notable achievements during their service. A black Air Force squadron known as the Tuskegee Airmen, for example, won eighty Distinguished Flying Crosses for successful combat missions flown against the Germans.

Their commitment and service during the war encouraged many African Americans to believe that fighting for a victory over oppression and race hatred abroad should have a corresponding effect on ending

women workers demonstrated diligence and skill. Women comprised more than a third of workers at shipyards and aircraft plants.

Women also served in military units during the Second World War. In 1942, the U.S. Army created the Women's Army Corps (WACs), and a few months later, the U.S. Navy created the WAVES (Women Accepted for Voluntary Emergency Service). During the course of the war, more than 86,000 women volunteered for the WAVES, serving in hospitals, defense jobs, wartime communications, and intelligence operations. These organizations anticipated the Women's Armed Services Integration Act in 1948, which formally allowed women to serve in the military during both peacetime and war.

AFRICAN AMERICANS

Just as wartime demands for labor created opportunities for women, it opened doors for African Americans. The movement to challenge racial bias in employment began in the early 1940s. Months before Pearl Harbor, A. Philip Randolph, leader of the Brotherhood of Sleeping Car Porters (an African American union), started the March on Washington Movement. Its goal was twofold: (1) to pressure the government to develop and enforce antidiscrimination

Fair Employment Practices Committee (FEPC) Agency that required companies with federal contracts to make jobs available without regard to "race, creed, color, or national origin"

> "It is my belief that some Los Angeles policeman or group of policemen suggested to some sailor or group of sailors that they get together and sap up on the zoot suiters. Everyone knows that it has been a long and bitter complaint of Los Angeles policemen that they were not allowed to beat up the zoot suiters themselves."
>
> —CHESTER B. HIMES, "ZOOT RIOTS ARE RACE RIOTS"

discrimination at home. This movement, demanding "democracy at home and abroad," became known as the **Double V** campaign. The *Pittsburgh Courier,* a black-owned newspaper, launched the public relations campaign, asking readers to endorse the slogan and to wear pins with the Double V symbol.

But gains were not easy to win. African Americans continued to battle discrimination in the workplace. They also contended with violent responses from white workers resistant to working with black people. Racial violence flared intensely in the summer of 1943, when more than 250 riots raged in fifty cities across the country. One 1943 riot in Detroit left twenty-five African Americans and nine white people dead.

For African Americans, the war created opportunities and spotlighted continuing discrimination. It epitomized what sociologist Gunnar Myrdal called, in his popular 1944 book of the same name, "an American dilemma"—the difference between the open-minded American ideology and the true nature of American race relations. As Myrdal might have predicted, leaders emerged from the war who would pave the way for the civil rights movement.

Double V Campaign championed by African Americans during World War II, demanding "democracy at home and abroad"

bracero program Wartime arrangement in which the U.S. government brought several hundred thousand Mexican migrants to work on California farms

HISPANICS

Hispanics also found new opportunities during the war. Many went to work in agriculture and the booming defense industry of southern California. The government's *bracero* **program** brought several hundred thousand Mexican migrants to work on farms in the American Southwest, which were experiencing an acute labor shortage due to war demands. Similarly, in 1942, as a result of labor shortages and antidiscrimination guidelines, 17,000 Mexican Americans were hired for shipyard jobs that had previously been barred to them. Hispanics also contributed to the war effort in the services: more than 300,000 Mexican Americans served in the armed forces.

But Mexican Americans also faced hostility as they advanced. In 1943, a series of clashes between whites and Hispanics in Los Angeles became known as the Zoot Suit Riots. A subculture of Hispanic young men wore "zoot suits" (long suit coats over baggy, pleated pants), a fashion connected to the culture of swing music (and worn by

Everett Collection/Newscom

>> The Zoot Suit Riots, 1943. In LA in 1943, a number of young Latino men were beaten for wearing a Zoot Suit, a fashion of the time, but one that went against the government's allocation of material.

some African Americans and whites as well). But because the voluminous suits violated wartime fabric-conservation guidelines, many white people perceived the zoot suit as a brazen, unpatriotic refusal to make sacrifices for the war. White outrage turned into an excuse for violence when groups of white sailors stationed near Los Angeles attacked young Mexican American men, some wearing zoot suits and some not. The men were beaten and their clothing was torn off them and burned. Police failed to protect the Mexican American youths. Instead, authorities dealt with the problem by barring military personnel from certain parts of the city and making it a crime to wear a zoot suit.

JAPANESE AMERICANS

Of all American minority groups, Japanese Americans experienced the most egregious mistreatment during the war. Soon after Japan's bombing of Pearl Harbor, the U.S. government ordered the internment of "aliens of enemy nationalities." It was President Roosevelt, with Executive Order 9066, who ordered the internment of people thought to be possible spies. Though some Italian and German nationals were targeted, Japanese Americans were the only ethnic group forced into internment camps. The Japanese had long suffered discrimination throughout the West Coast, where most Japanese Americans lived. The internment camps were simply the culmination of that distrust. Fearing disloyalty or the presence of enemy spies, the military forcibly removed 112,000 people of Japanese descent from California, Oregon, and Washington. Many of them were American citizens, having been in the United States for several generations. Nevertheless, although entirely innocent of treason, the entire ethnic Japanese population was forced to leave their homes and property behind and move to ten War Relocation Authority internment camps in the deserts of California and the American Southwest and Southeast. For the duration of the war, interned Japanese Americans lived in bleak barracks surrounded by barbed wire, with few amenities beyond the possessions they carried with them. The Supreme Court upheld the constitutionality of Japanese internment in the 1944 case of *Korematsu* v. *United States*. The camps closed months after the war ended, in 1945 and 1946.

>> "We saw the picture in the newspaper shortly after and the caption underneath it read, 'Japs good-natured about evacuation.'"—Monica Sone, *Nisei Daughter*. This picture shows more of the reality: the desolate internment camps where Japanese Americans, many of them US citizens, were forced to live for much of the war.

In 1988, more than three decades later, the United States formally apologized to those it interned, saying Japanese internment was premised on "race prejudice, war hysteria, and a failure of political leadership." It granted each survivor $20,000 in reparations.

THE GI BILL

The war created unprecedented opportunities for another group—returning soldiers. Near the end of the war, Congress passed a number of influential social programs directed to ease the soldiers' reentry to civilian life after the war. The most significant of these was the Servicemen's Readjustment Act of 1944, better known as the GI Bill of Rights (or the **GI Bill**). It promised unemployment benefits, educational opportunities, low-interest housing loans, and medical care to millions of soldiers. One of the bill's most consequential effects was to provide returning veterans with financial aid for college, which had long been the exclusive domain of the upper-middle class and the wealthy. More than 2 million ex-servicemen enrolled

GI Bill Servicemen's Readjustment Act of 1944, which promised unemployment benefits, educational opportunities, low-interest housing loans, and medical care to millions of soldiers in colleges in the decade following the war. It also provided affordable home loans that prompted soldiers to buy homes in the rapidly developing suburbs.

The GI Bill typified the ways that government action could dramatically change American society and set the stage for further welfare-state legislation in later years. But the bill failed to acknowledge racial disparities, and it allowed local control of home loans and university admissions, which often perpetuated ingrained forms of discrimination. Thus, the GI Bill tacitly endorsed some aspects of racial discrimination in the United States and created opportunities for white Americans that their African American counterparts did not enjoy.

23-4c Demographic Shifts

Perhaps as important as the new opportunities for women, minorities, and returning soldiers, the upheavals of the war included dramatic shifts in the nation's population. About 15 million Americans moved during the war, mainly for jobs in the new centers of the defense industry. This was one of the largest internal migrations in the nation's history.

THE WEST

Almost 8 million people relocated to states west of the Mississippi during the 1940s. Most of this migration was directly tied to defense industry jobs, because the West Coast was the staging area for the war in the Pacific. With 10 percent of all defense contracts in California, the state became an employment magnet; the population increased by 2 million during the war. With so many people moving, cities suffered housing shortages and overcrowding. To deal with the problem, Roosevelt established the Federal Housing Agency to facilitate new building. Nearly 2 million new housing units were built during the war. Thus, the war's job opportunities included not only defense work but also home and road construction to accommodate all the newcomers.

THE SOUTH

Though the largest boom took place in the West, the South also benefited from industrial investment, although its demographic transition was more complicated than the West's. Black and rural white southerners left the region in tremendous numbers. All told, about 1.3 million southerners moved to cities in the North or Midwest during the war, and 600,000 more moved to the West. The majority of southern migrants were African Americans fleeing the South, continuing the Great Migration that had peaked from 1910 to the 1930s. In the California cities of Richmond, Oakland, Los Angeles, and San Diego, black migrants carved out new communities for themselves, usually in close proximity to factories producing goods for the war. The migration of African Americans from the South dispersed their population more widely, making race relations more of a national issue, not just confined to a single region.

Northerners also moved south. Because Southern legislators were able to secure nearly $6 billion in defense contracts during the war, nearly 1 million northerners migrated into the South during the 1940s. The South consequentially became more industrial and more urban, even in some parts softening its traditional stance to racial segregation.

THE MIDWEST

While the population in the Midwest did not increase dramatically during the war, the region did experience other upheavals. In Detroit, the nation's largest manufacturing center, war mobilization led to racial discord even as it virtually ended the problems of unemployment, which had been as high as 50 percent during the Great Depression. The migration of more than 200,000 African Americans to Detroit changed the racial composition of the city. Riots there in 1942 and 1943 stemmed in part from white hostility to black people moving into historically white neighborhoods.

23-4d Leisure in Wartime

The war also affected the way Americans had fun. The period's limitations (long work hours, few men present, rationing of goods) generated a new kind of resourcefulness. After the departure of many male athletes for the armed services, for example, women's baseball leagues filled the void. The Rockford Peaches, Kenosha Comets, Racine Belles, and South Bend Blue Sox drew hundreds of thousands of fans to women's baseball games across the Midwest. In 1948, the All-American Girls Professional Baseball League reached a peak of ten teams and nearly 1 million in attendance, impressive in light of the small size of the cities that hosted the teams.

In music, jazz captured the energy of the era and embodied the push toward racial integration. Jazz, especially the styles practiced by the big swing bands, was America's favorite music in the 1940s. Millions of Americans found respite from the war while listening to the radio and dancing in nightclubs. Swing music popularized jazz for white audiences, encouraging

Wallace Kirkland/Time & Life Pictures/Getty Images

>> The 1992 film *A League of Their Own* was inspired by the Rockford Peaches, a team in the All-American Girls Professional Baseball League, shown here in 1945. The Peaches won the championship four of the League's eleven years.

greater racial integration and symbolizing the promise of a more democratic society.

23-5 A WORLD REMADE, 1945

Meanwhile, the war continued on its many fronts. By late 1944, the war was nearing its end.

23-5a Germany's Last Stand

Realizing the tides of battle had turned against them, on December 16, 1944, German forces launched a desperate counteroffensive in Belgium, forcing thinly spread Allied troops to retreat for 50 miles. The **Battle of the Bulge**, the largest battle of the western front, ended when the Germans failed to capture the Allied stronghold of Bastogne, Belgium. Although the battle stymied Allied progress in the west in January 1945, it diverted badly needed resources from the rest of Germany, leaving the country virtually undefended from other sides. Thus, in January, the Soviets made rapid progress toward Berlin from the east.

YALTA

Yet, just at the point of their imminent success, relations among the Allies grew strained. Roosevelt, Churchill, and Stalin, meeting at the Crimean town of Yalta in early February 1945, faced the question of what the world should look like after the war. Although the Allies had been issuing joint statements for years, serious problems emerged over how to put these principles into practice. The most intense disagreements between the western Allies and the Soviet Union concerned Poland, now occupied by Soviet forces. Stalin reiterated his desire for a defensive buffer between the Soviet Union and the rest of Europe, while Britain and the United States wanted an independent Poland.

In the end, the **Yalta agreement**, though vague and contradictory, yielded to Soviet demands on many points. It promised independent regimes in Poland and eastern Europe, yet conceded that pro-Soviet parties would have a large role in creating and sustaining these regimes. In subsequent years, as disagreements between the West and the Soviets escalated into the Cold War, critics charged that Roosevelt, who did not share Churchill's keen mistrust of Stalin, sold out eastern Europe at Yalta and emboldened Soviet aggression.

23-5b Final Moves

Before the postwar world could be arranged, however, the Axis had to be defeated. Beginning their final offensive on February 8, 1945, Allied troops crossed the Rhine River and rapidly dominated the German heartland. Throughout mid-February, the British and American air forces conducted an intense firebombing campaign over the beautiful German city of Dresden, creating a cocktail of bombs that blew roofs off

Battle of the Bulge Largest battle of the western front; ended when the Germans failed to capture the Allied stronghold of Bastogne, Belgium, and allowed Soviet forces to advance on Germany from the east

Yalta agreement Statement issued by Roosevelt, Churchill, and Stalin in February 1945 that promised independent regimes in Poland and eastern Europe, yet conceded that pro-Soviet parties would have a large role in creating and sustaining these regimes

Everett Collection/Newscom

>> Jazz, and especially big band swing music, was wildly popular during the war years, a hint of the promise of greater harmony between black and white Americans after the war. Pictured here is the Count Basie Orchestra at the Savoy Ballroom in Chicago, Illinois.

the Pacific—and about 21,000 of the 22,000 Japanese who had been on the island. American troops encountered the same fierce resistance on the island of Okinawa, where it took American troops three months to claim victory, at the cost of 140,000 civilians, 66,000 Japanese soldiers, and 12,000 American soldiers. American forces learned in these two battles that attaining Japan's unconditional surrender would be a long, exhausting ordeal.

THE POTSDAM CONFERENCE

The Potsdam conference, held from late July to early August 1945, brought the leaders of Britain, the United States, and the Soviet Union together for the last time during the war. But the faces had changed: President Harry Truman now represented the United States, having taken office after President Roosevelt's death in April. Then Churchill left mid-conference after being voted out of office. The turnover in leaders brought a new sense of uncertainty and mistrust to the proceedings.

Much of the tension could be attributed to the suspicion felt by American and British officials for what they saw as aggressive moves by the Soviets. Stalin demanded that Germany never be permitted to wage war again, proposing to take $20 billion in reparations from any future German state. The western Allies resisted this demand, recalling the effects that high reparations had on Germany after World War I. A compromise emerged, allowing the Soviets to gain some reparations in the form of industrial machinery and equipment from the western occupation zones. At the same time, Stalin was also adamant that pro-Soviet governments be established in Soviet-conquered areas of eastern Europe. His blunt message and hostile tone discouraged Western leaders, particularly Truman, from making concessions.

Matters became even more complicated when Truman learned from his advisors that the United States had successfully tested a nuclear weapon. He did not share the specifics of the atomic bomb with Stalin, but he did reveal that the United States had a new weapon of unimaginable proportions. Stalin, who had been aware of the American project to build the bomb (the **Manhattan Project**) even before Truman was, knew that the United States had succeeded in harnessing the power of the atom.

buildings. In a typical campaign, the Allies then dropped "matchstick bombs" to ignite building frames and followed these with high explosives onto main avenues into town, which prevented rescue missions. Within days, the city was destroyed and approximately 30,000 Germans were killed. The controversial goal of the mission was to sap the German will to fight and to ensure that German troops could not move east to fight the Soviet Union. The Soviets, meanwhile, entered Berlin on April 24. Knowing the end was near, Hitler committed suicide on April 30 and all German forces surrendered on May 8, known as "Victory in Europe Day," or V-E Day.

In the Pacific, Japan did not capitulate when the Germans did. The naval war had largely ended by late 1944 with a resounding Allied victory, but the prospect of a drawn-out invasion of Japan in order to get the Japanese to surrender loomed. Japanese forces, given orders to fight to the death, hoped to hold off the Allied demand for unconditional surrender. It took a month for American forces to eliminate Japanese resistance on the island of Iwo Jima. Victory at Iwo Jima came at a cost of 6,800 American lives—more Marines than in any other battle in

Manhattan Project American project during World War II designed to harness the power of the atom and create an atom bomb

Eventually the Allies found broad agreement in several punitive steps against Germany. In the Potsdam Declaration, the Allies divided Germany and Austria into four occupied zones, and German-speaking people in Czechoslovakia, Hungary, and Poland were forcibly moved to Germany. The Potsdam conference ended on August 2, with the Allies demanding Japan's unconditional surrender.

23-5c Defeat of Japan

In 1945, Japan was only lightly defended against American attack; huge firebombings of Japanese cities went unanswered. But American planners estimated that an invasion of the Japanese home islands, scheduled for November 1945 and March 1946, would cost 50,000 American casualties in its first phases alone. The battles at Iwo Jima and Okinawa demonstrated the extent to which Japanese soldiers would fight to avoid full capitulation. At the same moment, Truman was slowly coming to accept that he had the power to use the atomic bomb to end the war. Truman chose to use the massive new bomb on the city of Hiroshima after the Japanese government failed to respond to an Allied ultimatum to surrender or face "utter devastation." On August 6, 1945, a B-29 bomber named *Enola Gay* dropped the bomb, destroying Hiroshima and ultimately causing death or injury to 160,000 people. After a second bomb destroyed Nagasaki on August 9 (killing between 60,000 and 80,000 people), the Japanese government surrendered on the

>> Pictured here is what little remained of Hiroshima after the atomic bomb was dropped on August 6th, 1945.

Topfoto/The Image Works

> "One of my classmates . . . muttered something and pointed outside the window, saying 'A B-29 is coming.' . . . Looking in the direction he was pointing . . . all I can remember was a pale lightning flash for two or three seconds."
>
> —YOSHITAKA KAWAMOTO, THIRTEEN YEARS OLD ON AUGUST 6, 1945, AND HALF A MILE AWAY FROM THE HIROSHIMA BOMB SITE

condition that the Japanese emperor be allowed to keep his throne. The Allies accepted. The hostilities of World War II were over, but at a tremendous cost, both human and moral.

Truman himself said he never lost sleep over the decision to use nuclear bombs, but others were more conflicted. Perhaps most disturbed by the moral dimensions of nuclear weaponry was Robert Oppenheimer, the scientist in charge of the Manhattan Project. Upon seeing the first nuclear bomb test in the deserts of the American Southwest, Oppenheimer was appalled at the magnitude of the blast. Aware that the bomb had the capacity to kill thousands in an instant, Oppenheimer simply said, "I am become death." Others argue that the Second World War had already ushered in mass death and, indeed, a changed morality. Not only had the Holocaust killed 6 million Jews, but also the conventional bombing of Dresden had already extended well beyond military targets to civilian ones, killing 30,000 Germans in a matter of days. In the Pacific, the battle over the island of Okinawa had killed 140,000 civilians, 66,000 Japanese soldiers, and 12,000 American soldiers. In light of these numbers, some argue that dropping a nuclear bomb simply expedited an end to a tragic war.

>LOOKING AHEAD...

World War II ravaged huge parts of the world, leaving more than 60 million people dead, 38 million of them civilians. Germany had lost more than 7 million lives, and its major cities were in ruins; the Soviet Union had lost about 23 million people; and Japan had also suffered massive losses, including more than 2 million deaths. The cities of one of the victors, Britain, lay in ruins. Furthermore, as American and Soviet troops liberated Nazi work and death camps, the world saw for the first time the extent of Hitler's Holocaust, which had killed nearly 11 million people in total, including nearly all of European Jewry. American losses in the war were comparatively small. By the end of the war, the United States had suffered 400,000 military deaths and 11,000 civilian deaths. In addition, the United States had escaped major destruction of its economic infrastructure.

Just as World War II transformed the world, it also transformed the United States' role in world affairs. Between 1939 and 1945, the United States moved from being a neutral party to being a world superpower. Diplomatic successes played as important a role as military triumphs in this development: Roosevelt's ability to take the lead role in the Grand Alliance ensured that American power would endure. But these same forces propelled the Soviet Union to superpower status as well, and as the last shots of World War II were fired, the Cold War between the world's two superpowers was just beginning, with each power soon to have nuclear weapons to fight it. It is to that battle that we now turn.

STUDY TOOLS 23

READY TO STUDY? IN THE BOOK, YOU CAN:

❑ Rip out the Chapter Review Card, which includes key terms and chapter summaries.

ONLINE AT WWW.CENGAGEBRAIN.COM, YOU CAN:

❑ Collect StudyBits while you read and study the chapter.

❑ Quiz yourself on key concepts.

❑ Find videos for further exploration.

❑ Prepare for tests with HIST5 Flash Cards as well as those you create.

❑ Read a 1941 Lindbergh address to the America First Committee.

❑ Listen to the "Four Freedoms" speech.

❑ Hear Roosevelt's war message to Congress, December 8, 1941.

❑ View a series of images of the restored Topaz Internment Camp.

❑ Read about eight women who came to the front.

❑ See a video of news coverage of D-Day.

❑ View a series of images of Hiroshima and Nagasaki.

CH23 TIMELINE

What Else Was Happening

1931 Japan invades Chinese territory Manchuria.

1933 Hitler's National Socialist Party ascends to power in Germany.
Italian dictator Benito Mussolini invades and conquers Ethiopia.
FDR's "good neighbor" policy renounces past invasions.

1936 Hitler defies Treaty of Versailles and rearms demilitarized zone west of Rhine.

1937 Japan launches full invasion of Chinese mainland.

1938
Germany annexes Austria.

France and Britain consent to German annexation of western Czechoslovakia.

1939
March: Hitler breaks Munich Agreement and marches into Czechoslovakia.

August: Hitler and Stalin make secret nonaggression pact, plan division of Poland.

September 1: Hitler declares war against Poland and launches invasion.

1940: *Germany occupies Denmark, Norway, Belgium, Netherlands.*

June 5: *Germany invades France, captures Paris within six weeks.*

German air force targets civilians with city bombing raids in Battle of Britain.

1941
Lend-Lease Act provides military aid to nations attacked by Germany and Japan.

Japan occupies French Indochina; United States cuts off all trade with Japan.

Roosevelt and Churchill state aim of national self-determination in Atlantic Charter.

December 7: Japan bombs U.S. naval station at Pearl Harbor, Hawai'i.

1942
February 19: Roosevelt orders internment of 112,000 Japanese Americans.

June: Victory in Battle of Midway turns tide in Pacific war against Japan.

October British check Axis advance in North Africa in battle of El Alamein.

1943
November: Stalin, Roosevelt, Churchill agree on second front against Germany in 1944.

Supreme Court finds internment of Japanese Americans constitutional in *Korematsu*.

1944: *GI Bill aids veterans in housing, employment, health care, education.*

June 6: *Allies launch largest amphibian assault in history in French Normandy.*

Capture of Iwo Jima costs lives of 6,800 Americans and 21,000 Japanese.

September 11: *Allied troops enter Germany after reclaiming France, Belgium, Netherlands.*

December: *American victory in Battle of the Bulge.*

1945
February: Roosevelt, Churchill, Stalin discuss post-war Europe at Yalta.

May 8: Germany surrenders, Americans celebrate V-E Day.

July/August: Potsdam Conference reveals tensions between Britain, United States, and Soviet Union.

August 6: U.S. drops atomic bomb on Hiroshima, killing 160,000.

August 9: Second atomic bomb on Nagasaki kills 60,000 to 80,000 people.

24 | Cold War America

THE ADVERTISING ARCHIVES LTD.

LEARNING OBJECTIVES

After reading this chapter, you should be able to do the following:

24-1 Explain the causes of the Cold War between the United States and the Soviet Union, and discuss some of the more serious incidents between the two superpowers.

24-2 Describe American life as it developed during the 1950s, including social, economic, and political issues, and evaluate the significance of the Cold War in these changes.

24-3 Explain the rise and effects of McCarthyism.

24-4 Describe breakthroughs forged by African Americans in the 1950s and the retaliatory movement that came to be called "massive resistance."

AFTER FINISHING
THIS CHAPTER
GO TO **PAGE 481**
FOR STUDY TOOLS

Two impulses ran through the America that emerged from the Second World War. The first was the distrust, suspicion, and hostility engendered by the Cold War. The Cold War began when the United States, without question the most powerful country in the world following World War II, tried to use its power to proclaim a new global order based on democracy and capitalism. Meanwhile, the Soviet Union, which undeniably bore the brunt of the fighting during the war, with an astounding 23 million dead, rejected the American world order, favoring instead communism and a world revolution in the name of the worker. It also more simply wanted to create a buffer of countries friendly to its communist system. After all, Germany had invaded the Soviet Union twice in thirty years, and used Poland and other countries of eastern Europe to do so. But where the Soviets saw a protective barrier of friendly states, the United States saw communism on a revolutionary march to dethrone capitalism. The result was an ideological, economic, and military contest known as the **Cold War** that shaped American politics, economic life, and even its cultural and social developments throughout the 1940s, 1950s, and 1960s.

The second impulse running through postwar America was a far-reaching optimism that the world could be made a better, safer place and that the quality of life for most people in the world could fulfill Roosevelt's Four Freedoms, which had promised material and spiritual freedom after a decade and a half of struggle. In this optimistic spirit, the United States and its Allied Powers created the **United Nations (UN)** in 1945, an international organization that would foster discussions among the world's nations and monitor the well-being of almost all individuals in the world. The first meeting of the UN took place in San Francisco on April 25, 1945. In 1948, the UN adopted its Universal Declaration of Human Rights, which still today outlines the UN's view of inalienable rights reserved for all people, including life, liberty, security of person, and equal protection of the law. It also outlaws slavery, servitude, and torture. The UN was Franklin D. Roosevelt's vision for extending the Four Freedoms throughout the world, and, after he died in office in 1945, his wife Eleanor helped shepherd through the Universal Declaration of Human Rights.

On the home front, such optimism appeared less ideological and more material. Stoked by the rapid conversion to a peacetime economy and American consumers' eagerness to devour more and more goods after fifteen years of depression and war, the American economy grew stronger in the 1950s. Affluence and consumerism promoted a new style of life in America, as people moved to the suburbs, drove automobiles in massive numbers, and stayed home to watch television. The seeming conformity of this culture fueled a host of critics, including intellectuals, the youth, women, and numerous minorities. This chapter describes, first, the contours of the international Cold War, then how the Cold War influenced American life from 1945 to 1960.

THE COLD WAR

24-1a Decade of Build-Up

The Cold War was decades in the making. American politicians had long been suspicious of a communist ideology that called for the destruction of international capitalism via worldwide revolution. They rued and feared the work of the primary theorist of communism, the German intellectual Karl Marx (1818–1883), who not only diagnosed many of the inherent problems of capitalism but also predicted that workers would not put up with economic inequalities forever; they would revolt, taking power from the wealthy and the powerful and putting themselves in charge. And once the revolution started, so Marx's prediction went, it would spread to other nations, taking down one capitalist country after the next. The workers of the world would unite.

Most Americans feared this development, and the American commitment to capitalism makes some sense. The United States had, after all, emerged in the early twentieth century as the wealthiest nation in the world because of its commitment to industrialized

Cold War The postwar ideological, economic, and military contest between the United States and the Soviet Union

United Nations (UN) International organization that fosters discussions among the world's nations and monitors the well-being of almost all individuals in the world

◀◀◀ **The decade-and-a-half after the Second World War witnessed a dramatic expansion of America's car culture, highlighted by the creation of the Interstate Highway System, which is still in existence today. This advertisement also demonstrates the hope of a brighter future, another hallmark of Cold War America.**

capitalism. So throughout the twentieth century the United States pushed back against the growth of communism not only within its own borders but abroad as well. In 1918, for instance, in the notable Polar Bear Expedition, the United States landed 5,000 troops in Russia in an unsuccessful bid to aid anticommunist forces during the Russian Revolution that first led the communists to power. Throughout the twentieth century, then, many Americans were perpetually leery that Karl Marx's prediction might come true.

After World War II, two issues mushroomed this long-standing distrust into a hostile Cold War: (1) atomic power and (2) the Soviet Union's attempt to create buf-

containment U.S. strategy for dealing with the Soviet Union as outlined by George F. Kennan, with the intent of containing communism and not letting it advance any further than it already had

fer states between it and western Europe (see "The Reasons Why . . ." box).

24-1b The Policy of Containment

Was communism advancing or was the Soviet premier Joseph Stalin just trying to protect his nation from European invasion? Despite Stalin's declarations, the United States saw communism on the march. In a "long telegram" drafted in 1946 by George F. Kennan, the senior American diplomat stationed in Moscow, the Americans developed a response to communist expansion that came to be called **containment**, which declared that the United States would not allow communism to advance any further than it already had. As the policy of containment went into effect, it was clear the United States was not only in an ideological war with communism and the Soviet Union, but was also willing to back it up with military might and economic support.

The Reasons Why...

In addition to historic fears about the threat of communism, there were at least two issues that pushed a basic mistrust into a volatile Cold War:

Atomic fears. Less than three months after Hiroshima, President Truman called for international arrangements to stop "the use and development of the atomic bomb." To do this, the United States called for international controls over the technology, saying it would give up its atomic weapons after the controls were in place. The Soviets, however, did not believe Truman's promise that the United States would disarm. They insisted the Americans disarm first or the Soviets would be forced to create a bomb of their own. The Americans, in turn, feared that the Soviets needed to be forced to accept the nuclear controls by the threat of U.S. attack. A stalemate was in the works, and, in he months immediately following the Second World War, negotiations ground to a halt. It seemed clear that the international wartime alliance between

iStock.com/perqsista

Russia and the United States would not segue gracefully into a peaceful postwar order.

Communism "on the march." As talks over atomic disarmament collapsed in a cloud of mistrust and suspicion, a more vital debate about what to do with dilapidated central Europe led to even more stringent disagreements. The enormous Soviet losses in World War II (more than 23 million Russians had died) convinced Stalin that the security of the Soviet Union depended on developing a buffer of friendly neighboring states. Most of all, he wanted to eliminate the possibility that Germany would once again invade Russia unimpeded, as it had done twice in the previous thirty years. In early 1945, the Soviets imposed communist-dominated regimes in several central European states. But where the Soviets saw a protective buffer, the United States saw aggressive invasions of sovereign countries and communism "on the march" per the prediction of Karl Marx. Another showdown loomed. Neither side responded to the overtures of the other to discuss the growing suspicions. In March 1946, Winston Churchill publicly declared, "From Stettin in the Baltic to Trieste in the Adriatic, an iron curtain has descended across the continent." East of the "curtain" lay a Soviet-controlled sphere; west of it lay an American- and British-controlled one.

THE POLICY

In his "long telegram," Kennan suggested that communism was on a collision course with capitalism and that the Soviets would do four things in order to win: (1) perpetually seek to expand their territory unless checked by economic, political, and military pressure; (2) undermine Western colonial development in Africa and the Middle East; (3) develop their own economic bloc closed off to the rest of the world; and (4) attempt to penetrate Western civil society to promote Soviet interests.

Kennan proposed that Western governments fight back. They should educate their publics about the Soviet threat, promote democracy abroad, and work to solve their own social problems in order to prevent exploitation by communists. What the West needed to do was contain communism and not let it advance any farther than it already had. Many Americans understood the policy of containment in terms of the **Domino Theory**, which held that the United States was obligated to prevent the communist "dominoes" from falling for fear that they would tip off the next domino and begin a process of communist world domination. The idea of containing communism to prevent the dominoes from falling propelled American foreign policy for the next five decades.

> If the Soviets were creating a union of like-minded states, Truman felt the need to organize one, too.

INSTITUTIONS OF CONTAINMENT

After Kennan had formulated the intellectual rationale for the Cold War, Congress passed the National Security Act of 1947, which created a unified Department of Defense, the U.S. Air Force, the Central Intelligence Agency (CIA), and the National Security Council (NSC). The passage of this act showed that, in the two years since the war, American leaders had given up on guaranteeing peace through the United Nations and were preparing for a long confrontation with the Soviet Union.

THE TRUMAN DOCTRINE AND THE MARSHALL PLAN

In addition to the stick of military containment as expounded in the National Security Act of 1947, Americans offered a carrot to the contested states of Europe who might choose one side over the other. In 1947, Truman appealed to Congress to aid nations that might be susceptible to communist infiltration. He first developed this idea with the **Truman Doctrine**, an offer to support Greece and Turkey with money and arms if they would forego Russian assistance. The plan was most broadly promoted by General George Marshall, and the specifics of his plan came to be called the **Marshall Plan**. The Marshall Plan sent $13 billion to governments that promised to become or remain democracies, primarily Britain, France, and the Western occupied zones of Germany. There were some contingencies on how this money was spent, but the primary one was allegiance to the United States.

24-1c Hardened Lines

Shortly after the Marshall Plan was unveiled, Moscow declared that Soviet-occupied countries would not be permitted to take American funds. Stalin was afraid that capitalism and democracy might stimulate anti-Soviet governments to form along its border, threatening Soviet security. In 1948, Stalin consolidated his control of Eastern Europe by ousting the last Eastern European government not dominated by communists in Czechoslovakia. In 1955, the members of this union formalized their organization with the Warsaw Pact. The sides were beginning to harden (see Map 24.1). Disagreement and suspicion were turning into an armed standoff.

24-1d The Berlin Crisis

The first significant confrontation of the Cold War developed in Germany. The Allies from World War II had agreed to divide postwar Germany into four occupation zones (one for the United States, one for the Soviet Union, one for Great Britain, and one for France). The capital city of Berlin (which sat directly in the center of the Soviet zone) was similarly divided into four zones, one for each member. In February 1948, the Americans, British, and French met in London to plan the economic reconstruction of

---

Domino Theory Metaphor referring to unstable nations as dominoes, with the United States obligated to prevent the dominoes from "falling," which would begin a process of communist world domination

Truman Doctrine U.S. strategy of offering aid to nations that might be susceptible to communist infiltration

Marshall Plan Truman Doctrine as it was administered in Europe by General George Marshall, in order to diminish the allure of communism; under the auspices of the plan, the U.S. sent $13 billion to governments that promised to become or remain democracies

Map 24.1 Europe in the Cold War

>> This map of Europe during the Cold War shows the famous metaphorical "Iron Curtain" between eastern Europe and western, as well as a detailed map of Berlin and the various sparks that occurred between East and West.

their zones, and, on June 23, 1948, they announced the extension of the West German currency, the *Deutschmark*, into West Berlin in an effort to sew together the nation in the name of Western democracy and capitalism. Fearing too much Western influence, Stalin was not prepared to allow this currency into the heart of the Soviet zone, so on June 24, the Soviets blockaded West Berlin, preventing food and supplies from entering the non-Soviet sections of the city. This was the first "battle" of the Cold War.

BREAKING THE BLOCKADE

The two sides were now directly opposed. But Truman had no desire to initiate actual fighting. He opted instead for a massive, peaceful air operation, authorizing an airlift

in order to counter the growing power of the Soviets. They did so through a pact called the **North Atlantic Treaty Organization** (NATO) in 1949. Its key provision, Article V, declared that an attack against one or more treaty partners "shall be considered an attack against them all." NATO cemented an alliance of Western nations, a project that grew more urgent after Truman announced that the Soviet Union had successfully tested an atomic bomb of its own in 1949. Churchill's "iron curtain" had fallen into place, and both sides were armed with nuclear weapons.

Historians still debate which side bears the most responsibility for the advent of the Cold War. Some see Stalin's aggressive stances in central Europe and Berlin as indications that Kennan's predictions might have been correct and that the Soviet Union was on a long-standing aggressive march to defeat capitalism. Others see Stalin's attempts to control central Europe as understandable considering the events of the first half of the twentieth century. They instead see American actions as misguided and overly reactionary. A subtler approach than armed containment, they say, might have led to more amicable relations, without both nations having to see the other as enemies.

24-1e Conflicts in Asia

Despite the continued debate, by 1949, the two sides had consolidated their positions on either side of the iron curtain. But after the Berlin Crisis, the Cold War stalled in Europe; the iron curtain was largely in place, and neither side was ready for a nuclear confrontation. Instead, the focus of the Cold War shifted elsewhere.

Asia was the first stop. Britain and France had huge colonial possessions in Asia and Africa, but after World War II they no longer had the money to maintain those empires. Countries like Vietnam and Laos were in open revolt against their former colonial overlords. Moreover, the Atlantic Charter had plotted the Allied Powers at least rhetorically against colonialism. This fact allowed an opening for Soviet-backed revolutionary movements. Would these colonial holdings in Asia become communist? Would the United States allow them to?

"LOSING" CHINA

As nationalist battles in Vietnam, Laos, and Cambodia threatened Western colonial power (and would later lead to the Vietnam War), more immediate issues loomed in China. Although China had been on the winning side in

> **North Atlantic Treaty Organization** Pact that cemented an alliance of Western nations; prompted by the Berlin Crisis

Iain Masterton/Alamy Stock Photo

>> This mural on the wall of Tempelhof Airport in Berlin depicts a German girl handing flowers of gratitude to an American soldier, in commemoration of the Berlin airlift, the first "battle" of the Cold War.

of food and supplies for eleven months. In the end, the United States and its allies flew more than 200,000 flights over Berlin, dropping 4,700 tons of daily necessities. It was a major endeavor. It was also filled with tension. Truman knew that the Soviet Union would have a massive military advantage in any European conflict (the United States had largely demobilized its army after the Second World War). On the other hand, at the time of the blockade, the United States was still the only nation with the atomic bomb. Meanwhile, an embargo placed on Eastern European goods by Western nations convinced the Soviets to back down. The Soviet Union ended the blockade of West Berlin in May 1949. Truman's Berlin airlift had worked.

NATO

The events of the Berlin Crisis pushed American allies to formalize their commitment to one another

World War II, the war had damaged its stability, and immediately after the war the country fell into civil war between Chinese Communists (under Mao Zedong) and Chinese Nationalists (under Chiang Kai-shek). The United States funneled billions of dollars to the Nationalists even though America's diplomats warned that a communist takeover was inevitable. In October 1949, Mao completed his conquest; China was now controlled by a communist ruler. Mao soon signed a treaty with Stalin, while the Chinese Nationalists were forced to withdraw to the island of Taiwan.

The situation in China sent shock waves through the United States. Truman was accused of having "lost" China to communism, and some people even hinted that there were communist agents within the State Department. Mao's victory raised the stakes of containment. Not only was communism potentially on the march, but also it had taken over the largest Asian nation in the world. It looked like the United States was losing the Cold War.

24-1f American Rearmament

American leaders were determined to prevent other states from "falling." In a classified paper known as **NSC-68**, American diplomats portrayed an uncontrollably aggressive Soviet Union whose program for "world domination" required the "ultimate elimination" of any opposition. NSC-68's sweeping recommendations to stop the threat included a massive military buildup, the creation of hydrogen bombs, and the rooting out of all communists on American soil.

To critics, NSC-68 seemed out of proportion to the threat. But on June 25, 1950, communist powers in North Korea invaded South Korea, thus beginning the Korean War. Afraid of what this meant for the march of communism, the National Security Council adopted NSC-68 as official policy. To prepare to impede communist progress, it embarked on a vast rearmament plan, increasing the 1951 defense budget from $13.5 billion to $48.2 billion. The Korean invasion had made the incredible—a worldwide communist takeover—suddenly seem plausible.

24-1g The Korean War

Korea seemed an unlikely place for World War III to break out. It was remote, and it did not possess vital natural resources. But "losing" China had taken its psychological toll

NSC-68 Classified paper written by American diplomats that portrayed an uncontrollably aggressive Soviet Union and recommended stopping the threat through a massive military buildup, the creation of hydrogen bombs, and the rooting out of all communists on American soil

on American leaders. Plus, just as with Berlin, Korea, which had been controlled by Japan during the war, was divided between the Allies after the war, with the Soviets controlling the northern half and the United States controlling the southern half. The country was supposed to be reunified in 1948, but the deadline passed without the nation coming together. Tensions between the north and the south simmered, and when North Korean forces (aided by Soviet planners) attacked and easily took the South Korean capital of Seoul, Americans felt the need to respond (see Map 24.2).

Map 24.2 The Korean War

>> This map of the Korean peninsula shows the divide between North Korea and South Korea, and the various ebbs and flows of the battle between 1950 and 1953.

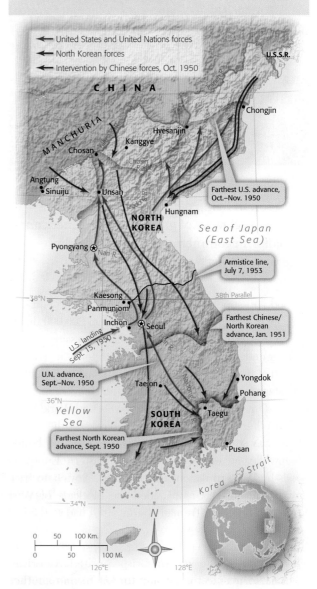

THE AMERICAN RESPONSE

Truman immediately ordered troops into Asia. He also ordered the development of the hydrogen bomb and secretly dispersed atomic bombs and short-range missiles to American air and naval bases all over the world. At home, leaders drew up plans of what to do in case of nuclear war. With the Soviet Union now armed with a bomb of its own, the threat seemed imminently plausible.

Despite these preparations, by late September 1950, things looked bad for the South Korean and American forces (who were led by the United Nations). Then a surprise attack led by the American general and UN commander-in-chief for Korea, Douglas MacArthur, at Inchon, a port near Seoul, helped turn the tide. Taking the North Koreans by surprise, UN troops cut their supply lines. The North Korean war machine collapsed, and UN forces recaptured Seoul. UN troops pursued the North Korean remnants all the way up the Korean peninsula, and by November they were positioned close to theChinese border, along the Yalu River. Would they now invade China, almost certainly sparking World War III?

CHINA INTERVENES

As the UN troops approached the Chinese frontier, Mao grew concerned. Truman had decided against invading China, but Mao did not know this. On November 27, 1950, a huge number of Chinese forces, totaling at least 200,000 troops and officially called "volunteers" for the North Korean cause, crossed the Korean border and attacked UN forces. Caught by surprise, UN forces reeled southward, and on January 4, 1951, communist troops recaptured Seoul, keeping several thousand American prisoners of war. As the situation worsened, Truman wondered aloud about using the atomic bomb. But as winter gave way to spring, the UN troops again took the offensive, retaking Seoul in March 1951.

STALEMATE

Once UN forces reached the original dividing line between North and South (the 38th parallel), Truman halted the offensive. He was intent on avoiding an open conflict with China and the Soviet Union. General MacArthur, however, determined to carry the fight to China for a final showdown, publicly raged against the president, writing to congressional Republicans, "There is no substitute for victory." In April 1951, Truman relieved MacArthur of command for his insubordination.

Addressing the American people, Truman said, "We are trying to prevent a third world war." A long stalemate settled along the 38th parallel, and many frustrated Americans treated MacArthur as a hero.

ARMISTICE

In late July 1953, North Korea, exhausted by the high casualties associated with the stalemate, agreed to an armistice. The armistice brought the Korean War to an end almost exactly where it had begun—but only after 35,000 American deaths, 114,000 Chinese deaths, and roughly 300,000 Korean fatalities (including both North Korean and South Korean casualties).

24-1h A Cold War, Not a Hot One

In the wake of the Korean War, many Americans concluded that the United States could not afford another land war against the Soviet Union and its allies. While still committed to containment, starting in the mid-1950s the United States relied less on open warfare and instead emphasized (1) covert operations, (2) formal alliances, and (3) nuclear weapons.

COVERT OPERATIONS

In this environment, one approach that maximized the effectiveness of American foreign policy was overthrowing

>> The Korean War Memorial, in Washington, D.C. includes a depiction of a platoon on dawn patrol in Korea. The platoon consists of 19 figures, representing each branch of the US military. The general sense of fighting proxy wars against the Soviet Union—in far-flung places many Americans had never heard of, like Korea— ensured the battle with the Soviet Union would be a cold war, not a hot one.

uncooperative foreign governments through agencies like the CIA. The pattern was set in 1953, in Iran, and in 1954, in Guatemala. In both countries, the CIA and its functionaries acted on the U.S. federal government's belief that left-wing governments might be susceptible to communist influence, even if these governments had been democratically elected. The governments of Iran and Guatemala were both overturned covertly, and the United States repeatedly resisted getting involved in situations that would have to be made public. The American government was hoping it could fight the Cold War quietly, keeping unfriendly governments from ever gaining power by covertly influencing elections and economic development.

There was a negative side to these covert operations, however. For instance, the political instability that the CIA forced on these countries led to a forty-year civil war in Guatemala and a twenty-five-year dictatorship in Iran that was so authoritarian during the period of American sponsorship that it generated the conditions of its own downfall. In 1979 these conditions in Iran would lead to a civil war that empowered the Islamic revolutionary Ayatollah Ruhollah Khomeini.

ALLIANCES

Another approach the American government employed was the use of treaties and generous economic arrangements. In Indochina, where the decline of European colonialism had led to tremendous political instability, the United States at first gave millions of dollars to the French colonial government in Vietnam. In effect, U.S. dollars were being used to fight against a revolutionary insurrection to keep the French in power. Once the French decided the effort wasn't worth it, the U.S. then gave substantial military aid to the new anticommunist state of South Vietnam, a state it had in fact done a great deal to help create. In Vietnam at least, the United States was willing to do whatever it could to keep communism at bay, first by supporting the French, then by propping up a puppet government that opposed the communist revolutionaries. The U.S. also helped create the Southeast Asia Treaty Organization (SEATO). In this way, the U.S. government hoped to prevent a chain of "falling dominoes," or neighboring countries inexorably succumbing to communism one at a time.

NUCLEAR WEAPONRY

The third approach was more frightening: hydrogen bombs. In January 1954 the United States articulated a strategy of "massive retaliation," by which it meant a substantial buildup of hydrogen bombs, each a thousand times more powerful than an atomic bomb. This strategy had its strengths. For instance, when the Chinese Communists in mainland China threatened the Chinese Nationalists on Taiwan in 1954 and 1958, American threats of massive retaliation helped hold the Communists at bay. But this experience also prompted the Chinese to seek Soviet aid in developing their own nuclear arsenal, something it would successfully begin in 1964.

THE ARMS RACE BEGINS

Because of the fear of being outgunned and because of the occasional usefulness of the idea of "massive retaliation," an arms race began between the United States and the Soviet Union. America's first hydrogen bomb

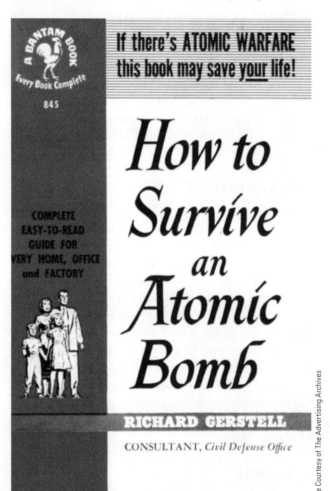

>> During the unsettling arms race, the American public turned to booklets like this one, offering such unlikely cure-alls as covering one's head or ducking under furniture in the event of an atomic bomb blast.

was tested on November 1, 1952. Within a year, the Soviet Union matched this achievement with a test of its own. American decision makers concluded that, if the United States was to continue to derive some advantage from the hydrogen bomb, it must stay ahead of the Soviets in numbers of bombs, destructive power, and the ability to deliver them swiftly. The Soviets responded in kind, with each side forcing the other to go higher and higher, accelerating the potential for an ever more devastating conflict. Eventually this policy came to be called "mutually assured destruction," or MAD, because the policy behind the arms race suggested that an attack by one side would almost necessarily mean a destruction of both sides in the conflict. Some Americans, notably the scientists who worked on the first nuclear bombs, protested the arms race. But the escalation continued.

FROM ARMS RACE TO SPACE RACE

With time, hydrogen bombs were getting smaller and less complicated, meaning that smaller nations without bomber technology, such as Britain, France, and Israel, could develop atomic weapons systems. In August 1957, the Soviets tested the first intercontinental ballistic missile (ICBM), which could travel from one continent to another. Two months later, they launched the world's first artificial satellite, *Sputnik I*, into orbit.

These events inspired a wave of dread across America. The idea that the enemy had actually placed a device in space that was passing over the United States frightened the American public and eroded confidence in American technological superiority. American war planners were alarmed as well, because the launch implied the Soviets could now deliver nuclear warheads to U.S. territory in about half an hour. The United States matched the feat of *Sputnik* three months later, in January 1958, by placing *Explorer I* into orbit. Over the course of the following year, the United States made major investments in science initiatives and established the National Aeronautics and Space Administration (NASA) as a central body for space research. The Soviet challenge inspired American government leaders to attain a new level of technological mastery, one that would ultimately lead to a moon landing in 1969. But in the short term, it merely heightened the mistrust that characterized the Cold War.

>> When the USSR launched the world's first two artificial satellites in 1957, many Americans were petrified that the Soviet Union was now literally hovering over the United States and that the state of American science was inferior to that of its Cold War adversary. Pictured here is a stamp printed in North Korea for the 30th anniversary of the first flight satellite, Sputnik-1, shown on the stamp.

THE COLD WAR HOME FRONT

The Cold War shaped American domestic life in many ways. For one thing, it helped keep the economy hot despite the demobilization after World War II. Fear of nuclear war also inspired both a second Red Scare (usually called McCarthyism, as explained later in this chapter) and a religious revival. The Cold War contributed to a tide of conservatism, too, as many politicians warned that communists had gained a foothold in American political and cultural life and any left-leaning initiative might be the secret work of covert communists. This conservatism diminished some of the momentum of postwar liberals, who believed the rhetoric of World War II had given them leverage to pass their pro-union, antidiscrimination agenda.

Amid these uncertainties, many Americans adjusted somewhat comfortably to life in a Cold War, taking advantage of good wages and the new luxury items that appeared by the truckload. These values were unaffected by the anxieties provoked by the Cold War, and in fact many Americans exerted their democratic freedoms through consumerism. Historians have for good reason called the period from 1945 to 1960 the Age of Affluence, even if that affluence was tempered by knowledge that, at any given moment, the Cold War might flash hot, and nuclear war might begin.

24-2a Truman and the Postwar Economy

THE FAIR DEAL

At the end of World War II, President Truman saw all the returning soldiers and feared that job shortages were imminent. With this in mind, in late 1945 he submitted a twenty-one-point plan, later called the **Fair Deal**, that sought to expand the welfare state initiated during the New Deal. The Fair Deal included increases to the minimum wage, federal assistance in building homes, federal support for education and health care, and an attempt to reach full employment through public works. Showing Truman's commitment to civil rights, the Fair Deal also renewed the Fair Employment Practices Commission (FEPC), which

Fair Deal Truman's twenty-one-point postwar plan that provided increases in the minimum wage, federal assistance in building homes, federal support for education and health care, and jobs in public works; represented a renewal of the Fair Employment Practices Commission

Roosevelt had established to end racial job discrimination in federal jobs.

Despite the Fair Deal's breadth, Truman faced many obstacles. For one, he was not terribly popular as president. His reserved demeanor made him seem small compared to the charismatic Roosevelt. Moreover, Truman faced a hostile Congress: although controlled by Democrats, Congress was led by an informal coalition of conservatives from both parties. Southern Democrats and northern Republicans often found common cause in checking the growth of the federal government, if for different reasons (southern Democrats didn't want the federal government to intervene with their segregated society, while northern Republicans wanted to ensure low taxes and fewer government restraints on business growth). As a result, Truman had few domestic successes.

THE CONVERSION ECONOMY AND LABOR UNREST

Truman's problems were compounded by the truly tempestuous postwar economy. In the months after the war, the return of GIs pushed wages down, while inflation rose 25 percent during the first year. Labor organizers demanded increased wages to compensate, but because there were more workers available than ever before, employers felt little pressure to capitulate. The result of this impasse was a remarkable series of strikes. By the end of 1946, about 5 million workers had walked off the job in more than 5,000 strikes across the country. Workers were shifting jobs rapidly, and security seemed a faraway promise.

Truman, generally a friend of labor but worried about the economy, soon grew intolerant of the strikes. When two railroad unions went on strike in May 1946, Truman requested that Congress draft the strikers into the military, which would then force them to work. Although the strike was soon settled and the authority to draft strikers was never made law, union workers were angry at Truman for his threats. Meanwhile, conservatives complained that Truman had not taken stronger anti-union steps. That fall, a Republican slogan asked Americans if they had "Had Enough?" In November 1946, the public answered by sending a Republican majority to both houses of Congress for the first time since 1928.

TAFT-HARTLEY

With their new power, pro-business Republicans attempted to scale back the role of the federal government, particularly with regard to labor disputes. Led by Senator Robert Taft, Congress passed the Labor Management Relations Act (better known as the

>> Rather than attend social forms of entertainment like movies or sporting events, with TV, people could be entertained while staying home. This constituted a transformation in the way Americans lived, as they became increasingly private and joined fewer clubs and organizations. Here, a family relaxes and snacks in front of the TV, something that never happened before the 1950s.

Taft-Hartley Act) in June 1947. Taft-Hartley banned the closed shop, meaning that jobs could not be exclusively limited to union members only. It also outlawed collective bargaining within industries and authorized the president to delay strikes by declaring a "cooling-off" period. Predictably, Truman vetoed Taft-Hartley, but Congress overrode his veto. Truman's presidency seemed destined for oblivion. More importantly, the rights of labor, which unions had fought for so ardently since the 1930s, were dramatically curbed—and would remain so for the rest of the century.

24-2b Economic Growth

After these initial flurries of uncertainty, however (and indeed the lasting restrictions of the Taft-Hartley Act), the postwar economy picked up. Indeed, it grew red hot. From 1947 to 1960, the gross national product doubled. Wages went up, inflation stayed low, and leisure activities became accessible to more and more Americans. So did comforts like electricity, air conditioning, and indoor plumbing. Well more than half of all Americans were now considered "middle class." Fears about a distressed economic picture melted away as the American nation successfully converted to a peacetime economy.

CONSUMERISM

How did this happen so quickly? The change occurred because Americans were spending more due to higher wages, veterans' benefits, and demand that had been restrained during wartime. American industries were meeting people's desires by producing new products. Things like dishwashers, washing machines, and televisions rapidly moved from luxuries to necessities. *Automation* became a key word in the vocabulary of the American consumer. Fewer concerns about carrying debt helped as well, as credit cards became more popular in the 1950s. And the commitment to the Cold War meant that government dollars were continuously pouring into a variety of defense-related industries.

> **Taft-Hartley Act** Labor Management Relations Act of 1947 that banned the closed shop, outlawed collective bargaining within industries, and authorized the president to delay strikes by declaring a "cooling-off" period

Out of the emerging strong economy, business leaders greatly curbed the postwar wave of strikes by offering benefits like health insurance and pensions to workers. Labor leaders like Walter Reuther were only marginally pleased with these offers. Certainly they liked the fatter paychecks, but Reuther and others felt that the burdens of health care and retirement should not be borne by an individual company because that made retirement plans dependent on the health of that particular company. Nevertheless, because they could not make much headway in crafting national health or retirement plans, Reuther and other labor leaders accepted the system whereby a single company provides a worker with health care and retirement—the system on which most Americans depend today.

TELEVISION AND THE AUTOMOBILE

Out of this expanded economy, two products transformed American life more than any others: (1) television and (2) the automobile. In the 1950s, the technology behind the television was perfected, and it immediately became immensely popular. Nine out of ten American families owned at least one set by the end of the decade. Television changed the way Americans relaxed and recreated. Rather than attend social forms of entertainment like movies or sporting events, people could be entertained while staying home. Initially, neighborhood social and political clubs emerged to replace more casual social gatherings, but by the end of the 1950s, memberships in social clubs were beginning to decline as well. Furthermore, television produced strong, indelible images that were disseminated widely, cutting through regional differences and creating a genuine national experience.

The automobile also transformed American life, and the 1950s were the years when cars were made accessible to many in the middle and lower classes. Not only were more Americans wealthier in the 1950s, but also in 1956, the federal government passed the **National Interstate and Defense Highways Act**, which authorized $25 billion to build 41,000 miles of interstate highways over the following ten years. The largest public works project in American history to that time, the act greatly eased suburbanization and car transportation. By the end of the decade, eight in ten Americans owned at least one car. Motels, drive-ins, and fast-food restaurants sprang up

National Interstate and Defense Highways Act The largest public works project in American history when it was passed; authorized $25 billion to build 41,000 miles of roads, greatly assisting the burgeoning car culture of the 1950s

throughout the country, reflecting the dominance of this form of transportation. The suburbs expanded as well, in no small part because now nearly everyone could afford to drive to a job in the city. But Americans' love of cars came at a cost: plans for extensive public transportation systems were put on hold. Rather than build train tracks or subway systems, the federal and state governments expanded the roads.

24-2c Suburban Nation

The new interest in cars combined with a quirk in the GI Bill led to another change in American life: the dramatic growth of the suburbs. The GI Bill made loans available for new homes, but it did not finance the renovation of old homes. For this and other reasons, more and more Americans moved out of the cities to the green ring around them.

Suburbs had been growing since the 1890s and especially since the 1920s, but they expanded even farther in the 1950s. By 1960, suburbs claimed a larger portion of the nation's population than did the city, small town, or countryside. Most of this expansion was due to the work of developers like William Levitt, who transformed orange groves and empty fields on the outskirts of cities into large towns made of prefabricated homes. The rapid growth of the suburbs and the conformity that seemed to set in there had at least five important results: (1) the sudden end to the transformed gender roles created by World War II; (2) an increase in racial segregation; (3) a postwar religious revival; (4) a chorus of critics of conformity; and (5) a lasting environmental footprint outside America's major metropolises.

GENDERED SPHERES

While millions of women entered industrial and white-collar jobs during the war, the return of soldiers sparked the massive firing of most women workers. One result of this transition was the creation of an ethos whereby women became guardians of domestic life once again, who should stay home to ensure the raising of good, democracy-loving children. Besides enforcing age-old stereotypes, there was a social reason too: following the war, the twenty-somethings who had fought for the Four Freedoms wanted to begin families. A baby boom resulted. After World War II, 76 million children were born in less than twenty years. In 1940, women were having, on average, 2.1 children; in 1960, they were having 3.5 children.

In the 1950s, the domestic ideal of the nuclear family became a dominant cultural image. Childcare experts, television, magazines, and politicians all propagated the notion that women should leave the work world and return home. For instance, according to many psychiatrists, caring for children was not simply a task, but was meant to be the central focus of women's lives. The concept of the child-centered family was popularized by Dr. Benjamin Spock, a pediatrician and expert on child development whose enormously popular manual, *Baby and Child Care* (1946), sold more than 50 million copies. Meanwhile, *Ebony*, a magazine for African Americans, celebrated the prosperity that allowed some black women to become primarily wives and mothers and no longer domestic servants. Black or white, domesticity was the presumed feminine ideal.

>> Childcare experts, television, magazines, and politicians all propagated the notion that women should leave the work force and return home. Here a happy, aproned housewife vacuums a den.

George Marks/Getty Images

American politicians promoted women's roles as mothers and homemakers as well. In 1959, Vice President Richard Nixon proudly told Soviet premier Nikita Khrushchev that American women prided themselves on stocking their kitchens with the latest appliances. Debating the relative merits of capitalism versus communism, Nixon reasoned that American women were fueling the economy by spending, rather than by marching off to industrial jobs as Soviet women did. The exchange between the two leaders became known as the **Kitchen Debate**.

Though suburban domesticity was promoted throughout American life as a desirable ideal, the reality was somewhat harsher. Because many mothers had two or three children, their days were demanding. New suburban homes required a great deal of upkeep as well. Even with new household inventions, many of which were advertised as "time-saving," the amount of time women spent on housework actually increased during the 1950s. If women did have free time, they were encouraged to channel it into caring for their families.

For the women who did remain in the employment sector, there was an increase in occupational segregation between the sexes. With men returning from military service, working women were forced into an employment niche in the service sector. For the most part, they worked as secretaries, teachers, nurses, and waitresses. Most women's jobs offered few possibilities for career advancement.

During the 1950s, African American women made some gains, moving out of primarily domestic service and agricultural work and into clerical work, nursing, and teaching. In 1960, 58 percent of all African American women worked outside the home. Many Japanese American and Hispanic women also worked outside the home to support their families.

RACIAL SEGREGATION

The physical distance of suburbia hardened racial segregation. As millions of white Americans left the cities for the suburbs, millions of black Americans were moving from the South to the cities of the North or West. In New York City, about half a million Puerto Ricans moved into what had been the Italian American neighborhoods of East Harlem. As a symbol of what was happening elsewhere, during the 1950s, a majority of Italian Americans moved out of East Harlem, favoring New York's suburbs instead. These types of migrations created many racially defined urban ghettos. White realtors and politicians frequently made matters worse by excluding black people from certain neighborhoods or making home loans impossible for African Americans to obtain. Even when they could afford it, black people were routinely barred by covenant or custom from many neighborhoods. The federal government refused to insert protections against such practices in federal housing bills. As a result, the new suburbs were overwhelmingly white, and the cities housed higher populations of racial minorities.

RELIGIOUS REVIVAL

If segregation was the rule concerning racial minorities, religious minorities—Catholics and Jews—developed a new kind of pluralism in these years. Previously denied access to many social arenas in American life, these minority groups

Kitchen Debate Discussion between Soviet premier Nikita Khrushchev and Vice President Richard Nixon in 1959 debating the relative merits of capitalism and communism

took advantage of a 1950s consumerism to move more fully into the mainstream. More importantly, fears awakened during the Cold War, the baby boom, and the move to the suburbs all led to a dramatic religious revival in the 1950s. This was when "Under God" was added to the U.S. Pledge of Allegiance and "In God We Trust" was added to U.S. currency. What distinguished this religious revival from all previous ones was that Catholics and Jews were included; it was not solely a Protestant revival. As Catholics and Jews earned allowances for their public displays of religion, they expanded the scope of American religious life, moving it beyond simply Protestantism. This transition to acceptable pluralism led to many debates about the place of religion in American life, especially when Catholics sought federal funds for parochial schools and Jews sought to ensure protection by emphasizing the separation of church and state.

CRITICS OF CONFORMITY

Life in the suburbs, with its stereotype of two cars, husband at work, wife at home, and children in the yard, seemed to many to be both refreshing after the uncertain depression years and boring because of its homogeneity. Focusing on this conformity, critics derided what they saw as *The Lonely Crowd* (1950), to use sociologist David Reisman's title, which described a society in which people determined their self-worth by the opinions of others, as the inner-directed life of previous eras faded away. Films such as *Invasion of the Body Snatchers* (1956) and *Rebel Without a Cause* (1955), novels like J. D. Salinger's *The Catcher in the Rye* (1951), the poetry of a youthful group of poets called the Beats, and sociological tracts like *The Lonely Crowd* and William H. Whyte's *The Organization Man* (1956) all focused on the supposed blandness of American suburban life at mid-century. Historians have noted how these critics understated the continued diversity of American life and the very real psychological problems of living in a world shrinking because of mass communications and unimpeded transportation. Furthermore, these critics overlooked other, perhaps more serious problems such as poverty, environmental destruction, and persistent racism. But they tapped into a psychological sentiment that was shared by many Americans who, supposedly living the American Dream, found themselves bored by it or excluded from it.

THE LARGE ENVIRONMENTAL FOOTPRINT

Postwar suburban living, with its large detached houses, unwieldy yards, dependence on the automobile, and incursion into wild lands and wetlands, greatly enlarged the size of the average American's environmental footprint. As Americans left dense cities behind, they encroached on lands that had lain undisturbed for years. In doing so, they were also relying on goods and services that were not easily reclaimable by the earth, like petroleum for automobiles. There was, therefore, a large environmental cost to the growth of suburbia, too.

24-2d Postwar Domestic Politics

As American social life changed in the 1950s, so did national politics, drifting toward conservatism and propelled by persistent fears of Soviet influence in the United States.

TRUMAN'S DECLINE

Viewing Truman as a spent force after his labor troubles in 1947, the Republicans eagerly anticipated the presidential election of 1948. Their chances seemed improved by internal dissension among Democrats. First, Truman's support for civil rights (for example, his 1948 order to end segregation in the armed forces) antagonized southerners, who had been vital members of Roosevelt's New Deal coalition and loyal Democrats for nearly eighty years. Truman also put a civil rights plank in the 1948 party platform. In protest, southern delegates literally walked out of the Democratic National Convention and formed their own party, the States' Rights Democratic Party, and then selected their own candidate for president. These so-called Dixiecrats threatened to disrupt the Democratic hold on the South that dated back to Reconstruction, all over the cause of civil rights.

Second, Truman had alienated many liberals when he fired Henry Wallace from his cabinet. Former vice president Wallace had openly criticized Truman's Cold War policies and advocated greater cooperation with the Soviets. Wallace's followers formed the Progressive Party and nominated Wallace as their candidate. Truman was therefore under assault from the right and the left, and this was just within his own party.

TRUMAN'S RESURGENCE

For their part, Republicans nominated Thomas E. Dewey, indicating that they had made peace with some elements of the New Deal legacy. Dewey advocated several liberal policies, hoping to appeal to the middle of the political spectrum. In July 1948, however, Truman cleverly called Congress back into session and demanded that the Republicans pass an agenda based on their own party platform. When congressional

>> Dewey defeats Truman in one of the most notorious journalistic mistakes in American history, a fact attested to by Truman's giant grin while waving the newspaper with the headline, "Dewey Defeats Truman."

increasingly unpopular, Truman decided not to seek reelection in 1952. The country, he felt, was moving to the right.

REPUBLICANS RETURN

And indeed it was. In the fall of 1952, World War II hero Dwight D. Eisenhower became the Republican candidate and easily won the presidential election, outdistancing by a wide margin the Democratic nominee, Illinois governor Adlai Stevenson. Republicans gained majorities in the House and Senate as well. The New Deal, the Fair Deal, and twenty years of Democratic power in Washington seemed to have run its course. But, like Dewey, Eisenhower, while rhetorically favoring smaller government, did not fundamentally oppose the New Deal. And Cold War concerns would, in the long run, provide a new impetus for expanding the government, which in fact grew during Eisenhower's presidency. Eisenhower was a folksy conservative who was friendly to big business, but he was not averse to pouring money into the economy, especially for national defense. He defined national defense broadly, employing it as a pretext to fund the giant interstate project that built most of the nation's highways, as well as several housing projects. He also oversaw the development of the Cold War strategy of crafting covert operations, forming alliances, and building up the nation's nuclear weapon supply. And the economy was good during his presidency, in no small part because of the tremendous amount of federal spending Eisenhower poured into it. Lots of people had good reason to "Like Ike."

By the end of his presidency, Eisenhower began to express reservations about these expenses. In his 1961 farewell address, he himself sounded the alarm against the "military-industrial complex" that tied the military too closely to the economy and jeopardized American democracy. But during his presidency, Eisenhower had not been shy about expanding the federal government, and indeed much of his success had depended on it.

Republicans refused to act, Truman attacked the "do-nothing Republican Congress." This made it appear as if they were making election-year promises that they did not intend to keep. Many union workers also returned to the Democratic fold, encouraged by Truman's veto of Taft-Hartley and by his calls for the nation to strengthen the New Deal (although he still lost union-heavy Michigan, New York, and Pennsylvania). Farmers came out particularly strong for Truman as well, giving him all but six states west of the Mississippi. In November 1948, Truman pulled off a stunning upset, defeating Dewey and helping recapture both houses of Congress for the Democratic Party.

DEMOCRATIC ECLIPSE

Truman triumphantly viewed his election as a mandate for the Fair Deal. But he was wrong. Upon starting his second term, Truman resubmitted the proposals in his platform, but, once again, a watertight coalition of conservative southern Democrats and northern Republicans meant that few of Truman's proposals became law. Southern Democrats continued to reject civil rights laws, and, in 1950, interest in Truman's domestic agenda was overshadowed by the Korean War. Frustrated and becoming

AP Images/Bill Allen

>> The World War II hero Gen. Dwight Eisenhower served as president from 1953 to 1961, overseeing both an economic boom and the growth and expansion of the Cold War. While many Americans "liked Ike," many others thought he represented a bland, conformist culture. Here President Eisenhower swings around in his White House office chair in Washington, January 17, 1961, before starting his farewell television/radio address to the nation.

24-3 THE SECOND RED SCARE

All this politicking took place with dramatic background music: the second Red Scare. For those caught in its sweep, it was more than just background music. The Red Scare was little short of a crusade against communist influence within the United States. Its scope was wide and deep, curtailing civil liberties and quelling political dissent from the top levels of national politics to the lowest neighborhood school board meeting. All the developments of postwar American life must be understood to have occurred within the confines of a restrictive fear that communism was on the march and might one day influence what was coming to be called "the American way of life."

24-3a Loyalty Oaths

The second Red Scare began almost as soon as World War II ended; its prominence paralleled the progress of the Cold War. Fearful of allegations that there were communists working in his government, in 1947 Truman established the Federal Loyalty-Security Program, which investigated the backgrounds of all federal employees and barred hiring anyone who was deemed a security risk. Meanwhile, Truman's attorney general, Tom C. Clark, compiled a list of hundreds of organizations considered potentially subversive. The organizations were then subjected to investigations. Many state and city governments and private companies emulated the loyalty program and required employees to sign loyalty oaths. Between 1947 and 1965, roughly 20 percent of all working people in the United States were required to take an oath.

24-3b Nixon, Hoover, and McCarthy

With fingers pointing everywhere, many powerful Americans grew worried about an insidious conspiracy to overthrow the government. Congressman Richard

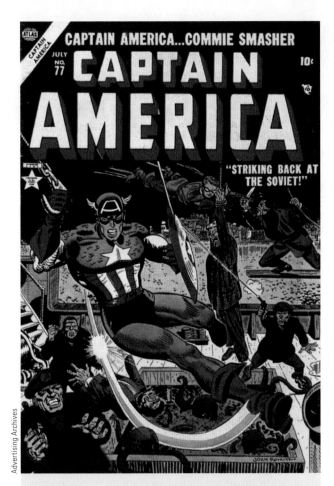

Advertising Archives

>> Even Marvel Comics' Captain America, now billed as "Captain America . . . Commie Smasher!" on the cover pictured here, became a crusader against communism.

Nixon, FBI director J. Edgar Hoover, and Senator Joseph McCarthy of Wisconsin were at the center of this storm. For his part, Nixon propelled himself to fame in 1948 by charging former State Department official Alger Hiss with espionage. Although the evidence of his association with communists at first appeared shaky, Hiss was convicted of lying about his Soviet contacts in 1950. Decades later, his guilt is still debated by historians, although most now conclude that Hiss was in fact a spy. Meanwhile, Hoover insisted that communists were everywhere, "even at your front door," and he instructed the FBI to keep tabs on people who might be associated with communism. In general, his investigations extended to any group that challenged conformity, including liberals, labor activists, civil rights workers, and especially homosexuals.

But it was Senator Joseph McCarthy who best leveraged the supposed threat of communism to launch himself into prominence. His speeches were shrill and bombastic as he publicized his communist purges. In an infamous 1950 speech, the senator declared that the State Department was "thoroughly infested with communists." He claimed to have a list of more than two hundred communists, but he did not allow the press to confirm his evidence. In the end, McCarthy's demagoguery, which destroyed lives and led to many a ruined career, was based on false accusations. His influence reached deeply into American culture, though, so much so that the aggressive tactics of the Red Scare became known as "McCarthyism."

With Truman, Hoover, and McCarthy all asserting the presence of communists in the United States, Americans began pointing fingers at each other. Regardless of the evidence against them, once someone was labeled a subversive, his or her life was often dramatically altered. These individuals found it difficult to find work, became socially isolated, and had a hard time recovering their reputation. This was most dramatically illustrated by accusations against Hollywood actors. The congressional House Un-American Activities Committee (HUAC) focused on Hollywood beginning in 1947. HUAC members believed that the movie industry was teeming with communists; they also knew that a formal investigation of Hollywood would generate considerable publicity. As part of the anticommunist purge, writers, directors, actors, and film executives were called to testify about their political beliefs and also those of their family, friends, and colleagues. The question HUAC most famously asked was: "Are you now or have you ever been a member of the Communist Party of the United States?"

In 1947, a group of screenwriters and directors known as the **Hollywood Ten** appeared before HUAC and refused to answer any questions, citing their right to freedom of speech. The Supreme Court, however, denied them protection under the First Amendment. The members of the group, many of whom were or had been members of the Communist Party in the 1930s, were each charged with contempt, fined $1,000, and sentenced to a year in jail. More damningly, they were also put on a **blacklist**, which contained names of people deemed "subversive" and whom Hollywood executives agreed not to hire. The blacklist expanded to include hundreds of Hollywood professionals between 1947 and 1965.

Hollywood Ten Group of screenwriters and directors accused of being members of the Communist Party

blacklist Collection of names of hundreds of people deemed "subversive" whom Hollywood executives agreed not to hire

COMMUNIST PARTY ORGANIZATION U.S.A-FEB. 9, 1950

Hulton Archive/Getty Images

>> Sen. Joseph McCarthy, pictured here, used bombast and smear tactics to fight what he saw as homegrown communism.

McCarthy himself confronted the extent of his powers when, in 1954, he accused the U.S. Army of hiding coercive elements in its realm. The U.S. Army counsel, Joseph Welch, demanded that McCarthy produce the names of the purported communists, and, unable to do so, McCarthy instead attacked a junior associate working with Welch. When McCarthy wouldn't drop the lengthy, sidestepping attack on Welch's young associate, Welch yelled, "Have you no sense of decency, sir? At long last, have you no sense of decency?" It was clear McCarthy couldn't back up his claims, and the U.S. Senate shortly thereafter voted to censure McCarthy for his unfounded accusations. His attacks in Congress at least stopped. But the atmosphere of accusation and guilt by innuendo continued long after McCarthy's own personal decline.

24-4 CIVIL RIGHTS BREAKTHROUGHS

Despite the tendency toward McCarthy-inspired conservatism during these years, minorities achieved significant breakthroughs in the 1950s. Indeed, many minorities used the language of freedom inspired by the Cold War to push for their own increased rights. European immigrant groups, which had faced discrimination

before the war, were generally assimilated into American culture during the war. They became accepted in social groups and the workplace in ways that would have been unthinkable just two decades prior. And African Americans began to mobilize their forces for what would become the civil rights movement.

24-4a Desegregation in the Military

President Truman displayed an early example of this new consideration for minorities. Truman was the first president to address the NAACP at its national convention. More importantly, in 1946, Truman formed the first Committee on Civil Rights to assess the state of citizenship rights across the country. The committee issued a report, *To Secure These Rights*, that recommended "the elimination of segregation, based on race, color, creed, or national origin, from American life." Based on these recommendations, Truman ordered the desegregation of the U.S. armed forces in 1948. The process was slow and laborious, and not complete until 1954. But it was a monumental accomplishment that brought black and white Americans together in the close confines of the U.S. military.

Desegregating the armed forces also sent a clear signal that the federal government was willing to challenge segregation in its own ranks. The armed forces became a model example that interracial desegregation could work, something not generally accepted before the 1940s (and, for many Americans, not until much later than that). That same year, Truman endorsed a plank in his party's platform at the Democratic National Convention that supported civil rights for all Americans, regardless of race, creed, or color. Though many Democrats expressed outrage, civil rights had entered the national dialogue.

24-4b Desegregation in Sports

Professional baseball featured another popular example of civil rights liberalism. In April 1947, Jackie Robinson, a World War II veteran, made his major league baseball debut with the Brooklyn Dodgers. Aware that his presence would generate hostility, Robinson vowed not to retaliate against racist taunts. As expected, fans threw debris at him, rival players attacked him, and he was often barred from eating with his teammates on the road. Despite these stressful hardships, Robinson flourished. He won the National League Rookie of the Year award in 1947 and the league's Most Valuable Player award in 1949, and later he became the first African American inducted into the Baseball Hall of Fame. Within a few years, a number of other stars of the Negro Leagues entered the historically white major leagues, successfully integrating "America's pastime," a highly visible aspect of the nation's cultural life.

BROWN V. BOARD

Legal challenges to segregation were meeting with some success as well, especially those led by the NAACP's legal team. One landmark case was *Shelley v. Kraemer* (1948), in which the U.S. Supreme Court outlawed neighborhoods from inserting legal clauses (called "restrictive covenants") that forbade the sale of a home in that area to a racial minority. Another landmark

> "Mob rule cannot be allowed to override the decisions of our courts."
> —PRESIDENT DWIGHT D. EISENHOWER,
> SEPTEMBER 24, 1957

case was *Brown* v. *Board of Education* (1954), in which the Supreme Court ruled that separate educational facilities for black and white people were "inherently unequal." This was a major breakthrough, overturning nearly sixty years of legal segregation that began with *Plessy* v. *Ferguson* (1896). But it was slow to trigger changes. For one thing, President Eisenhower believed that states rather than the federal government should deal with civil rights, and he refused to endorse the *Brown* decision. For another, the Court decreed in 1955 that desegregation of southern schools should proceed "with all deliberate speed," which was vague enough to allow southern states leniency in enforcing the new law.

Another near breakthrough came with Eisenhower's assistance. In September 1957, nine black

Bettmann/Getty Images

>> Elizabeth Eckford endures the taunts of classmates as troops ensure African Americans' entry into Little Rock's Central High School. When the federal troops left a month later, the taunts and jeers reappeared, and Gov. Orval Faubus closed Little Rock's public schools the following year in order to prevent integration.

students were selected to integrate Central High School in Little Rock, Arkansas. When classes began, the students were met by angry, racist mobs threatening violence, as well as by the Arkansas National Guard, which had been ordered by Arkansas Governor Orval Faubus to prevent integration. Believing he had little choice but to uphold the Supreme Court's order in *Brown*, Eisenhower sent a thousand troops from the U.S. Army's 101st Airborne Division to Little Rock to protect the black students. They stayed for a month before being replaced by the Arkansas National Guard, which looked on as white students taunted and tortured the African American students for the remainder of the school year. The following year, Faubus chose to close all of Little Rock's public schools in order to prevent further integration. When Arkansas public schools reopened, it was only after white residents had funded the creation of numerous private schools, thus maintaining a semblance of segregation that operated outside the law.

24-4c Massive Resistance and the Black Response

Faubus was not alone in fighting against civil rights advances. In the South, black advances were almost always met by **massive resistance** from the dominant white population. Certainly some white southerners supported racial integration, but the loudest and most agitated did not. African American activists and their white sympathizers were beaten, picketed, and generally maltreated, sometimes even killed. The *Brown* decision itself had led to the creation of several **White Citizens' Councils**, which were organized to defend segregation. The Ku Klux Klan also experienced a revival in the middle 1950s, especially in the South. And parts of the South, such as Prince Edward County, Virginia, chose to close their public school system and their public pools rather than be forced to integrate.

massive resistance A campaign and policy begun by politicians in Virginia to craft laws and do whatever possible to resist racial integration; spread throughout the South

White Citizens' Councils Committees organized in the 1950s and 1960s to defend segregation in the South

bus boycott A campaign to boycott an area's buses until change is instituted; used frequently during the civil rights movement

EMMETT TILL

One of the most-discussed acts of racist violence occurred in 1955, when a fourteen-year-old Chicago-born African American boy named Emmett Till was beaten and murdered for supposedly whistling at a white woman who worked at a grocery store in Money, Mississippi. The woman's husband and his half-brother were arrested for kidnapping and murder, and the American public closely followed their trial in newspapers and on television, especially after Till's mother allowed reporters to photograph Till's badly beaten body. Although several African Americans testified that they had seen and heard the beating, the jury found the two men innocent. The world press also followed the story closely, leading one German newspaper to report, "The Life of a Negro Isn't Worth a Whistle." The communist presses also picked up the Till case and other civil rights abuses in order to make a statement about the hypocrisy of the United States' claims to be fighting for freedom in the Cold War. Although lynching was still, evidently, permissible in the Deep South, the case of Emmett Till provoked outrage, leading many northerners who had been cool on civil rights to see the depth of segregation still extant in the South and making white southerners aware that the world was watching their actions; the two men acquitted of Till's murder were later ostracized by their local white society. Many later civil rights activists saw the murder of Till as a turning point in their lives, demonstrating that the legal system in the South was not going to protect them and that they needed activism to create change. Few were surprised when, more than fifty years later, Till's accuser admitted to fabricating the most salacious parts of her story.

MONTGOMERY BUS BOYCOTT AND SCLC

Indeed, white resistance did not prevent African Americans from continuing to push for equal treatment and access to public services. In fact, despite the continued violence, civil rights activism increased in the late 1950s. Following a successful 1953 **bus boycott** in Baton Rouge and the public outcry over Emmett Till's murder, in 1955 Rosa Parks refused to give up her seat in the "whites only" section of a Montgomery, Alabama, bus. After her arrest, the African American community in Montgomery, which had been planning for such an event for more than a year, boycotted the city's bus system. Despite significant loss of revenue, the white owners of the bus lines initially refused to integrate their seating policy. They held out until 1956, when the Supreme Court declared that segregation in public transportation was unconstitutional.

The Montgomery Bus Boycott, a remarkable success that mobilized the black community and demonstrated the possibilities of a widespread social movement, led directly to the formation of the Southern Christian Leadership Conference (SCLC), founded in January 1957 to challenge Jim Crow laws in a direct way. Several veteran civil rights activists were present at the inception, including Bayard Rustin, Ella Baker, Stanley Levison, Ralph Abernathy, and Martin Luther King, Jr. King was selected as the group's leader. The SCLC initiated and organized massive revolts in the Deep South against racial oppression, and it embraced a philosophy of peaceful integration and **nonviolence**. But it would take increased grassroots protests to push the movement forward, protests that would start in 1960.

>LOOKING AHEAD...

The conflicts over race in 1950s America would turn out to be dress rehearsals for the massive social changes that would come in the 1960s. But more than just civil rights were affected by the changes in postwar America. The political spectrum was colored by the Cold War for the next half-century. Americans were to have access to greater luxuries than in any other society in the history of the world. Jobs were mostly plentiful, and churches were generally full. But these changes came with costs. The fear of unpredictable nuclear holocaust loomed over everything. Women were socially prescribed to remain in the home if the family could afford it. Racial disparities were made worse by restrictions in suburban housing. And the consumerist impulse of American life led many Americans to critique their society as hollow and bland. Whatever else it might be, the coming decade, when these complaints would have ramifications, would not be described as bland, conformist, or dull. It is to that subject, "the sixties," that we now must turn.

nonviolence Strategy for social changes that rejects the use of violence

STUDY TOOLS 24

READY TO STUDY? IN THE BOOK, YOU CAN:

❑ Rip out the Chapter Review Card, which includes key terms and chapter summaries.

ONLINE AT WWW.CENGAGEBRAIN.COM, YOU CAN:

❑ Collect StudyBits while you read and study the chapter.

❑ Quiz yourself on key concepts.

❑ Find videos for further exploration.

❑ Prepare for tests with HIST5 Flash Cards as well as those you create.

❑ Read excerpts from Truman's message to Congress.

❑ Read Churchill's iron curtain speech.

❑ Read George F. Kennan's "long telegram."

❑ Read the Truman Doctrine.

❑ Read Truman's 1947 loyalty oath.

❑ Read Mao Zedong's account of the Chinese Communist Party.

❑ Read excerpts from NSC-68.

❑ Read McCarthy's speech warning of the communist threat.

❑ Read the National Security Administration's briefing book on the Iranian coup.

❑ Read John Foster Dulles's "Massive Retaliation" speech.

❑ Read Eisenhower's response to the Little Rock crisis.

❑ Read the decision in *Brown v. Board of Education.*

❑ Read a transcript of the Kitchen Debate.

1945

April 25: United Nations holds first meeting in San Francisco.

Soviets impose communist regimes on several eastern European states.

September 6, 1945: Truman delivers his reconversion speech, a special message to Congress presenting a 21-point program for the reconversion period.

1946

March: Churchill describes division between East and West as "iron curtain."

U.S. George F. Kennan's "long telegram" from Moscow advocates containment.

1947

Truman Doctrine commits United States to aid nations in fight against communism.

Marshall Plan aids European recovery in return for allegiance against communism.

Taft-Hartley Act bans closed shop, introduces "cooling off"; Truman's veto fails.

National Security Act creates CIA, Air Force, Department of Defense, Security Council.

Truman establishes loyalty security program; states, cities, and companies follow.

Hollywood Ten refuse to testify at House Un-American Activities Committee.

AT&T invents the cellular phone, which becomes commercially available only in 1983.

1948

United Nations adopts Universal Declaration of Human Rights.

Truman desegregates armed forces.

NSC-68 proposes military buildup, hydrogen bombs, eliminating U.S. communists.

Southern Democrats split as Dixiecrats, protest Truman's civil rights support.

Western Allies' introduction of Deutschmark triggers one-year Soviet Berlin blockade.

1949

Soviet Union successfully tests own atomic bomb.

United States and western European nations form NATO.

1950: *State Department official Alger Hiss convicted for lying about Soviet contacts.*

June 25: *Communist North Korea invades South Korea.*

Danish doctor Christian Hamburger performs the first sex change operation on New Yorker George Jorgensen, who becomes Christine Jorgensen.

1951   **April:** President Truman relieves MacArthur of command in Korea for insubordination.

1952   **November 1:** United States successfully tests first hydrogen bomb.

1953   CIA covert operations overthrow government in Iran.

July: Armistice between North and South Korea along prewar borders.

1954: *CIA covert operations overthrow democratic government in Guatemala.*

Supreme Court rules segregation unconstitutional in Brown v. Board of Education.

United States articulates strategy of "massive retaliation."

Ray Kroc buys the small-scale franchise McDonald's Restaurant and begins to turn it into the most successful fast-food chain in the world.

1955   Soviet-dominated eastern Europe consolidates under Warsaw Pact.

White men lynch teenager Emmett Till in Mississippi for whistling at a white woman.

Rosa Parks's refusal to give up bus seat triggers Montgomery Bus Boycott.

1957   **August:** Soviet Union tests first intercontinental ballistic missile (ICBM).

September: Federal troops enforce desegregation of high school in Little Rock, Arkansas.

October: Soviet Union launches first satellite, Sputnik.

1958   President Eisenhower establishes National Aeronautics and Space Administration (NASA).

1959: *Kitchen Debate between Vice President Nixon and Soviet premier Khrushchev.*

The Beatles form.

1961   Eisenhower warns of the military-industrial complex in farewell address.

25 | The Sixties

LEARNING OBJECTIVES

After reading this chapter, you should be able to do the following:

25-1 Describe the experiences John F. Kennedy had while president that led some to label him the "ultimate cold warrior."

25-2 Discuss attempts made both by African Americans and by the legal system to provide voting and other rights to black citizens.

25-3 Discuss Lyndon Johnson's desire to build a "Great Society" and evaluate the relative success of his programs.

25-4 Explain the Cold War origins of the Vietnam War, and evaluate the decisions Johnson made that pushed the war into the forefront of Americans' minds.

25-5 Discuss the growth of the "counterculture" in U.S. society during the 1960s, the coming together of protesters against American culture and protesters challenging the war, and describe the various movements that began to gather strength as Americans sought to have their voices heard.

AFTER FINISHING THIS CHAPTER GO TO **PAGE 507** **FOR STUDY TOOLS**

From today's perspective, the years 1960, 1961, and 1962 look a lot more like the fifties than what we have come to think of as "the sixties." The economy remained strong, those advocating for dramatic social change remained largely on the margins, and the child-focused world of the postwar years retained its grip in the ever-expanding suburbs.

The transition to the excitement and disenchantments that we today associate with "the sixties" took place slowly, beginning about 1963 or 1964. It culminated in 1968, as **liberalism** seemed under attack from all sides. Liberalism was America's dominant political system at the time, which stressed democracy, corporate capitalism, a generous system of social entitlements, and an ordered social system premised on obedience to the prevailing culture. Some felt postwar liberalism was too generous, creating a class of entitled loafers unwilling to do their fair share. Others felt postwar liberalism wasn't generous enough, sacrificing equality for the sake of freedom, and placing a priority on appearances and consumerism rather than authenticity and generosity. By the end of the decade, nonviolent political stances—against racial discrimination and the Vietnam War—so infuriated those who opposed them that the opposition sometimes turned to violence, which was sometimes met in return by further violence. By the late 1960s, this violence included even the assassinations of leaders like John F. Kennedy, Malcolm X, Martin Luther King, Jr., and Robert Kennedy. Furthermore, sexual and social mores seemed to be changing too, as a widespread drug culture emerged and as women pushed against society's long-held restrictions against them. African Americans and other repressed minorities also began to demand greater access to power. In the end, "freedom" won the 1960s, but it surprised almost everyone that freedom could mean free speech and free love, and also free markets. It was almost as if the containment policy of the early Cold War somehow extended beyond foreign policy and into the realm of American society, and in the 1960s everyone wanted to bust free from being contained.

25-1 KENNEDY AND THE COLD WAR

The 1960s started conventionally enough. After eight years in the White House, Eisenhower was still beloved by much of America. But the Twenty-second Amendment, ratified in 1951 in reaction to FDR's four terms as president, did not permit Eisenhower, or anyone else, to run for more than two terms in office. Eisenhower tepidly endorsed his vice president, Richard Nixon, who had risen to fame through the anticommunist witch hunts of the 1950s Red Scare.

For their part, the Democrats nominated a young (forty-three-year-old) Massachusetts senator named John F. Kennedy. The scion of a prosperous Boston Irish family, Kennedy was a World War II hero with an easy demeanor and a good sense of humor. He had been a middle-of-the-road congressman and senator, removing himself from debates about the tactics of the McCarthy supporters, although both he and Nixon promised to execute the Cold War more aggressively than had Eisenhower. Kennedy was also Catholic, and at a time when Catholics and Jews were just beginning to feel part of the national mainstream, many Americans still believed he would be unable to lead the country without consulting the pope.

In a masterful performance in front of a group of Protestant ministers in Houston, Kennedy claimed that he felt it was inappropriate for any church to demand specific actions from a government leader. He hoped that both Catholics and Protestants would not vote for a candidate based on the candidate's religion alone. His Catholicism may have helped develop his character, but it did not dictate his moral life. Masterfully given, the speech helped transform the political landscape for religious minorities. In one stroke he made the anti-Catholic diatribes of his detractors irrelevant. More importantly, Kennedy rightly viewed his election as a generational transition and surrounded himself with young advisors, few of whom were older than fifty. In the first-ever televised presidential debate, Kennedy came off as cool and demure, while Nixon appeared clammy and untrustworthy. In the end, Kennedy won an extremely narrow victory over Nixon, and though his Catholicism may have cost him some votes, he

liberalism A political philosophy founded on the ideas of liberty and equality but which, in the aftermath of the Industrial Revolution, came to signify the federal government's role in providing a counter-balance to free-market capitalism

◄◄◄ Of all the divisive events of the 1960s, perhaps none was more divisive than the Vietnam War. The first war to be fought with integrated troops, the war provoked questions about the nation's racial and class divides, as well as the proper place of the American empire. And it was just one of many transformative events of the decade. This photograph shows an integrated squadron marching through the forests of Vietnam, with a helicopter flying away in the background.

>> The first-ever televised presidential debate took place in 1960 between Richard M. Nixon (left) and John F. Kennedy. Kennedy used the new medium to showcase his youthful vigor, while Nixon's shifting eyes and moving hands made viewers uncertain he was ready to be president. Many radio listeners, though, thought Nixon won the debate.

prevailed to become the first Catholic president in American history (see Map 25.1).

25-1a President Kennedy

During the 1960 campaign, Kennedy often spoke of a "new frontier," although once he was in office, his agenda rarely diverged from that of standard-issue Democrats like Truman. Like Truman, he lacked a congressional majority to enact major new programs. As a result, Kennedy's calls for increased federal aid for education,

> **nation building** Facilitating the economic and political maturation of developing nations; political strategy employed by President Kennedy in order to prevent developing nations from adopting communism

medical care, mass transit, the unemployed, and a cabinet-level urban affairs department generally went nowhere.

25-1b Kennedy the Cold Warrior

But Kennedy did become an avid Cold Warrior. During the election, he vowed to take a more aggressive approach to the Cold War than Eisenhower had, by challenging communism all over the world.

NATION BUILDING

To do this, Kennedy sought the support of developing nations around the world, which he intended to win by facilitating their economic and political maturation—a process known as **nation building**. Kennedy believed

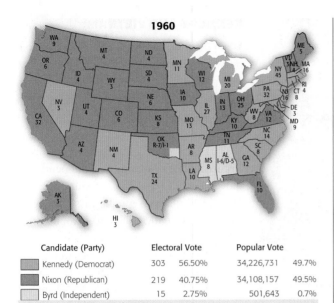

1960

Candidate (Party)	Electoral Vote		Popular Vote	
Kennedy (Democrat)	303	56.50%	34,226,731	49.7%
Nixon (Republican)	219	40.75%	34,108,157	49.5%
Byrd (Independent)	15	2.75%	501,643	0.7%

Map 25.1 The Election of 1960

wholeheartedly in the doctrine of containment and announced his willingness to wage preemptive strikes to prevent the march of communism. The Kennedy administration pursued this policy all over the globe, specifically with his Alliance of Progress program, which provided $25 billion in aid to countries in Latin America.

One response to the United States' promoting wealth for its allies was the construction, in 1961, of the **Berlin Wall**, built by the communist government to separate impoverished, Soviet-controlled East Berlin from the more prosperous West Berlin.

KENNEDY AND CUBA

After the election, however, Cuba and Vietnam rapidly developed as the president's two biggest areas of concern, and nowhere did Kennedy's hard-line approach to the Cold War manifest itself more dramatically than in dealing with Cuba. Located 90 miles off the coast of Florida, Cuba had been a main concern of U.S. foreign policy since the Spanish-American War for two reasons: (1) the United States feared any political turmoil so close to its border, and (2) many Americans had invested in the country. These long-standing concerns were compounded when Fidel Castro took power in 1959 and established a communist regime. This new regime distressed Kennedy not only because it meant one more communist country in the world, but also because the Soviet Union now had an ally just 90 miles from U.S. shores. Kennedy soon dedicated himself to removing Castro and the communists from power.

BAY OF PIGS INVASION

Under Eisenhower, the CIA had designed a plan to overthrow Castro. Kennedy implemented the plan in April 1961, when the CIA sent American-trained Cuban exiles back to their homeland to spark a rebellion. This seemingly simple scheme quickly went awry. Inadequate air cover, treacherous reefs, and swampy terrain meant that the 1,400 commandos had a tough landing. In addition, the plan was hardly a secret to Castro; there had been a lot of talk about the invasion in the Cuban immigrant community in the United States, and the news got back to him. When the commandos arrived on Cuban shores, Castro's forces were waiting to capture them as they landed.

Kennedy, wanting to conceal U.S. aims to overthrow or even assassinate another nation's leader, waffled as to how to salvage the operation. His options were to do nothing and allow the operation to fail, or send U.S. military forces into Cuba, escalating the conflict. He chose to do nothing, meaning that more than 1,200 exiles were captured and went on trial; some were executed, and most were sentenced to thirty years' imprisonment. Those imprisoned were released in twenty months, in exchange for $53 million in food and medicine. It was Kennedy's greatest humiliation as president.

CUBAN MISSILE CRISIS

After the Bay of Pigs incident, the president launched a multifaceted assault on the Castro regime, including radio broadcasts, assassination plots, and sabotage raids. Castro knew that another invasion of Cuba was imminent. Determined to protect his communist revolution, in April 1962 Castro agreed to allow the Soviet Union to base a few of its nuclear missiles in Cuba. These missiles would be easily capable of reaching U.S. targets and therefore of triggering a nuclear war between the United States and the Soviet Union. The Soviet premier, Nikita Khrushchev, also knew the United States had missiles close to the Soviet Union, in American ally Turkey, and he wanted to have at least some semblance of balance in the arms race. A nuclear conflict was on the horizon.

In October 1962, a U.S. reconnaissance plane photographed the storage site of the missiles. This shocking discovery set off a thirteen-day confrontation

> **Berlin Wall** Barrier built in 1961 by the communist government to separate impoverished, Soviet-controlled East Berlin from the more prosperous West Berlin

KENNEDY AND VIETNAM

>> The fear and dread provoked by the Cuban Missile Crisis made Americans confront the possibility of nuclear annihilation. Here, Americans in an appliance store watch a broadcast of President Kennedy during the Crisis.

While Kennedy was dealing with Cuba, he was also supporting an anticommunist government in South Vietnam. Throughout the first half of the twentieth century, the southeast Asian country of Vietnam had been a French colony, and after World War II, it sought its independence from France. The Vietnamese independence movement was led by communist leader Ho Chi Minh, who sought assistance from China and the Soviet Union. In an effort to prevent another domino from falling in the Cold War, the United States began funding the French fighters, a situation that lasted until 1954, when the Vietnamese effectively defeated the French in the Battle of Dien Bien Phu. Minh sought to unify the north of the country, which he controlled, with the south, which had been the French stronghold. But before he could do so, the United States intervened. It propped up another leader, a noncommunist named Ngo Dinh Diem, to rule in the south, and, under the terms of the Geneva Convention which ended the French-Vietnam War, proposed that elections be held in 1956 so that the Vietnamese people could choose its leader. When it became apparent that the communist Minh was going to win the election, the U.S. engineered the election's cancellation. Then it devoted resources to propping up the South Vietnamese government. By 1961, the U.S. was spending more than $40 million on improving the South Vietnamese police system and on establishing a number of programs to help the South Vietnamese battle communist-backed guerrilla forces in the south, called the Viet Cong. The Viet Cong often fought with the assistance of the North Vietnamese military but were an independent unit. To prevent the Viet Cong from becoming too powerful in the south, Kennedy increased the U.S. military presence in South Vietnam from 5,000 to 16,700. The United States was slowly drawing itself in, all in an attempt to prevent another domino from falling.

known as the **Cuban Missile Crisis**. Kennedy hastily convened a committee of top advisors to discuss how to handle the situation. Options ranged from invading Cuba to negotiating with the Soviets, although most of Kennedy's advisors favored some form of direct standoff. Kennedy ultimately decided to establish a naval "quarantine," or blockade, of Cuba to prevent Soviet weapons from reaching port. The tension heightened on October 27 when a U.S. pilot flying over Cuba was shot down and killed. The frightening standoff subsided only when the Soviets agreed to remove their missiles from Cuba in exchange for a promise that the United States would not invade Cuba. The Kennedy administration also privately pledged to dismantle U.S. nuclear missiles in Turkey. Successful negotiations meant that both sides had averted nuclear war, and the secrecy of the agreement about removing missiles in Turkey made it appear that Kennedy had won the standoff. The two sides also took steps to avoid getting that close to a nuclear standoff again, including putting a direct telephone line between the White House and the Kremlin. For thirteen days, the world had gotten perilously close to nuclear war.

But when an internal battle in South Vietnam between Catholic leaders like Ngo Dinh Diem and the Buddhist majority led to protests (several Buddhists publicly burned themselves to death to protest the repression of the Buddhist majority), the United States felt it was necessary to intervene in order to maintain stability. Diem, who was a ruthless leader in his own right, was not doing an effective job ruling South Vietnam and was making the region susceptible to a communist takeover. In August 1963 the U.S. ambassador

Cuban Missile Crisis Thirteen-day confrontation between the Kennedy administration and the Cuban communist regime in October 1962; Castro had agreed to allow the Soviet Union to base a few of its nuclear missiles in Cuba, thus potentially triggering a nuclear war between the United States and the Soviet Union

>> In one of the most horrific images of the decade, a Buddhist monk in Saigon makes the ultimate protest against the repression of the Buddhist majority by setting himself on fire.

THE SIT-INS AND SNCC

In one of the most influential protests in American history, on February 1, 1960, four black college freshmen from the North Carolina Agricultural and Technical College began a sit-in at a local Woolworth's lunch counter in Greensboro. The young men would not leave until they were served a cup of coffee, a practice regularly refused in a segregated society. The students sat quietly until the store closed. The next day, twenty-seven students sat in. Within a few days there were more students than seats at Woolworth's, which prompted the students to spread their protest to other white-only restaurants in the city. Within three days, there were more than three hundred students participating in the sit-in.

By the end of February, students in other southern cities began similar protests, and by late spring, almost seventy thousand students had participated in sit-ins all over the country. The students staged the sit-ins almost entirely in the Upper South, while the hardened system of Jim Crow intimidation prevented civil rights protests in the Deep South states of Mississippi, Alabama, South Carolina, and Georgia. And even in the Upper South, the students confronted humiliations and violence: food was thrown at them, cigarettes were put out on their arms, and many were forcibly removed from their seats. But the students

to Vietnam, Henry Cabot Lodge, gave U.S. support (and $40,000) to a group of South Vietnamese generals who launched a coup against Diem. Within a few days, the U.S.-backed officers executed the old leaders and took charge. Nevertheless, political instability persisted, only increasing the apparent need for U.S. intervention. By 1963, Vietnam was a small but volatile front in the Cold War.

25-2 THE FREEDOM MOVEMENT

As Kennedy navigated the difficult terrain of a multifaceted worldwide Cold War, a movement at home was emerging just as dramatically. After the civil rights victories of the 1950s, African Americans stepped up their activism in the early 1960s, using Cold War rhetoric to demonstrate that America itself was not living up to its claim of being a beacon of freedom.

25-2a Expanded Nonviolence

Civil rights protests had been ongoing since the Second World War, but they increased in intensity and number in the early 1960s, beginning with the actions of a collection of university students.

"Some way through, an old white lady, who must have been seventy-five or eighty-five, came over and put her hands on my shoulders and said, 'Boys I am so proud of you. You should have done this ten years ago.'"

—FRANKLIN MCCAIN, ONE OF THE ORIGINAL FOUR SIT-IN PROTESTERS AT GREENSBORO

stayed true to nonviolent principles and refused to retaliate. In many cities (including Greensboro), southern business owners agreed to desegregate because sales had dipped so low.

In May 1960, students organized the Student Nonviolent Coordinating Committee (SNCC, pronounced "snick") and selected Marion Barry, a student activist from Fisk University in Nashville, as chairman. SNCC had the youngest and most energetic membership of the major civil rights organizations, spreading the student-led sit-in movement throughout the Upper South. A group mostly made up of college students, they practiced nonviolence and put forward a vision of a racially integrated America, which they called "the Beloved Community." Young people were particularly active in the growing civil rights movement because they didn't face the same kind of economic retaliation adults faced, like losing their job or having loans called in.

FREEDOM RIDES

Rejuvenated by the sit-ins, civil rights organizations grew increasingly active. In 1961, the Congress of Racial Equality (CORE), which had been founded during the Second World War, renewed its efforts to test segregation in interstate transportation facilities by organizing Freedom Rides into the South. After notifying President Kennedy, the FBI, and the Justice Department, CORE volunteers of many races began their journey through the South.

On May 14, 1961, a Greyhound bus carrying Freedom Riders arrived in Anniston, Alabama. It was met by white supremacists who attacked the bus, slashed its tires, and threw a bomb on board. The terrified passengers exited the bus through flames and smoke. Once outside the bus they were beaten with bats, iron bars, iron chains, and bricks. The local hospital refused to help the wounded. Alabama governor John Patterson and Birmingham public safety commissioner Eugene "Bull" Connor did not prosecute the perpetrators.

CORE was forced to abandon its efforts. A week later, however, SNCC continued the Freedom Rides, and a bus left from Birmingham to Montgomery on a two-hour ride. At the bus station in Montgomery, the passengers were savagely attacked by hundreds of racist southerners.

RESULTS

The Freedom Rides generated national and international publicity. Predictably, communist propaganda eagerly reported stories of American repression, and newly independent African and Asian countries paid close attention to white supremacy struggles in the United States. On September 22, 1962, the Interstate Commerce Commission issued a new policy that required all interstate carriers and terminals to display signs indicating that seating "is without regard to race, color, creed or national origin." The efforts of the Freedom Rides were a legal success. They demonstrated the power of interracial activism, the philosophy of nonviolence, and the skillful use of the media, all of which would become standards in the civil rights movement that was then bubbling into the national consciousness.

25-2b National Successes

While SNCC and CORE were orchestrating the Freedom Rides, other groups were attempting to dismantle social aspects of segregation.

>> The leaders of the civil rights movement made sure the media was present when southern racism was on full display, as in this 1963 demonstration in Birmingham, Alabama. President Kennedy said images like this one of a young black being mauled by a police dog while a white police officer holds the man in place, made Kennedy "sick."

AP Images /Bill Hudson

JAMES MEREDITH, PROJECT C, AND THE CHILDREN'S CRUSADE

In 1962, James Meredith sought to enroll as the first African American student in the history of the University of Mississippi. His attempt was met with strong resistance, prompting Kennedy to go on live television arguing against the inhumanity of persistent segregation. Kennedy also sent in federal troops to quell riots and ensure that Meredith be allowed to attend the university.

Building on the successes of nonviolent protest, in 1963 the Southern Christian Leadership Conference (SCLC) under Martin Luther King, Jr., launched a campaign in what was called "the most segregated city in America," Birmingham, Alabama. They called their campaign Project C, which stood for "confrontation." King and others organized marches—often bringing along children dressed in their Sunday best—protesting segregation even after Birmingham's mayor outlawed such protests. More than 20,000 black people were arrested, including thousands of children. The notoriously brutal Bull Connor directed his men to attack the protesters with police dogs, electric cattle prods, and high-powered water hoses. National media captured the action, sending images across the globe of children being arrested and women being beaten.

The campaign ended in bitter victory for the civil rights protesters, but only after white supremacists bombed the 16th Street Baptist Church in Birmingham during a church service, injuring several people and killing four African American girls. Millions of Americans were outraged by the violence and demanded federal action. As pressure mounted, the Kennedy administration implored local white leaders to end the violence. Birmingham's white leaders agreed to meet with black leadership and adopted a desegregation plan. As a result, not only were parks and various public spaces desegregated, but black people also had access to city jobs previously denied them. But it had come at a momentous cost.

MARCH ON WASHINGTON

In 1963, in an effort to push for federal civil rights laws, SCLC cosponsored the historic March on Washington for Jobs and Freedom. At the August 28 gathering, leaders from every major civil rights organization spoke. No other orator was as powerful as Martin Luther King, Jr., who delivered his "I Have a Dream" speech from the steps of the Lincoln Memorial. King's ability to tap into both Christian and American symbolism was tremendously effective. He extolled the belief "that my

AP Images/Anonymous

>> Martin Luther King, Jr., waves to supporters from the steps of the Lincoln Memorial during the 1963 March on Washington for Jobs and Freedom. The event still stands as the high point of the civil rights movement.

four little children will one day live in a nation where they will not be judged by the color of their skin but by the content of their character." The simple, forceful demand that America live up to its national creed was difficult to reject or dismiss.

A RIFT APPEARS

SNCC workers also helped organize the March. John Lewis, the new chairman of SNCC, had written a militant speech that demanded an immediate end to civil rights violations. Organizers, however, edited his speech, deleting Lewis's desire to march through the South "the way [Civil War General] Sherman did." They found it too militant. SNCC activists became increasingly disaffected with what they considered the more cautious politics of other organizations. They found the continual requests for new laws to be infuriatingly slow and unlikely to change the country, and sought instead a more

> "I remember the very first time that my dad, when they went to the courthouse, and they stood in the line so long, and, you know, they said the white people just looked at them, and asked them, 'Well, niggers, what are you doing here? You know you have no business here.' And they didn't even allow them to even register that very first day."
>
> —ESTELL HARVEY, RECALLING HER FATHER'S ATTEMPT TO REGISTER TO VOTE IN THE SUMMER OF 1964

aggressive civil rights movement. This disaffection and frustration would lead to dissent later on.

FREEDOM SUMMER

After these early, hard-won successes, civil rights organizers led an effort to dismantle the discriminatory southern voting system, which denied most black people the right to vote. The work was tough: as volunteers went into the rural South and tried to convince black people to register to vote, they were under constant watch by white southerners and nearly always under threat. The most concerted effort emerged in the summer of 1964, when thousands of black and white volunteers headed south to establish "Freedom Schools" and register southern black people to vote in the upcoming election. The Freedom Summer was not without its share of violence. In Mississippi, Ku Klux Klan members, who were being supplied information by the state government, killed three young CORE members who were trying to register southern black voters. Of the three, two were white middle-class Jewish men from New York, whose deaths created images of an interracial struggle against southern barbarity.

Civil Rights Act of 1964 Legislation outlawing all discrimination in public facilities based on color, religion, sex, and national origin, and establishing the Equal Employment Opportunity Commission to investigate violations of the law in employment

25-2c Laws and Rifts

In the atmosphere of the popular March on Washington, activists pushed for new civil rights laws (indeed, support of these kinds of laws was one purpose of the march). Kennedy agreed, announcing his intention in the summer of 1963 to put forward a bill. The anticipation ended when the president was assassinated in Dallas, Texas, on November 22, 1963, in one of the iconic moments of the twentieth century (discussed further in Section 25-3 The Great Society).

THE TWENTY-FOURTH AMENDMENT AND THE CIVIL RIGHTS ACT

Within days of being sworn in, Kennedy's successor, Lyndon Baines Johnson, a tall Texan with a southern drawl, surprised everyone when he insisted he would fight on behalf of Kennedy's legislative plan for civil rights. Johnson worked with several civil rights organizations and appealed to the public in press conferences. With his shepherding, in January 1964 the states ratified the Twenty-fourth Amendment to the United States Constitution, which outlawed the use of the poll tax in federal elections (it was extended to cover state elections in 1966).

Then, a major civil rights bill passed the House on February 10, 1964. After a failed filibuster by South Carolina senator Strom Thurmond, it won Senate approval late in June. On July 2, 1964, Johnson signed into law the **Civil Rights Act of 1964**. The act outlawed all discrimination in public facilities based on color, religion, sex, and national origin and established the Equal Employment Opportunity Commission to investigate violations of the law in employment— something that had never been done before. Discrimination remained permissible in some aspects of the private sphere, but the Civil Rights Act was of paramount importance in outlawing discrimination within the mechanisms of the state.

VIOLENCE CONTINUES

Despite the victories, or perhaps because of them, violence against civil rights activists continued, especially for the Freedom Summer workers who were in the South to get southern black people registered to vote. Even after dozens of their homes and churches had been bombed, FBI director J. Edgar Hoover refused to extend protection to civil rights activists. Fearing for their lives, some activists began carrying guns, and by the end of 1964, some organizations acknowledged their members' right to arm themselves, moving away from the nonviolent creed of Dr. King. Frustration was simmering. Successes were coming, but actually changing the nature of American life was a slow-moving process. It appeared as though there were two civil rights movements: one to end legal segregation in the South, another to generate true economic, political, and social equality for African Americans. Civil rights activists were successful in addressing the first, but less successful when it came to the second.

MISSISSIPPI FREEDOM DEMOCRATIC PARTY (MFDP)

To address the persistent racism in the South's major institutions, in 1964 Fannie Lou Hamer and a collection of civil rights workers founded the Mississippi Freedom Democratic Party (MFDP). The MFDP was open to all citizens, regardless of race, unlike the Democratic Party for the state of Mississippi, which was restricted to white people. MFDP members traveled to the 1964 Democratic National Convention in Atlantic City in an attempt to be seated as the genuine Mississippi representatives of the national party. White southern delegates threatened to splinter the Democratic Party if the MFDP was seated. In order to avoid a complete collapse of the party, on the one hand, or appearing as a bigot on the other, President Johnson (the party's nominee for the 1964 election) convinced the delegates to allow the MFDP to be seated at the convention "at large," while still allowing the all-white Mississippi delegation to be seated. Some civil rights leaders felt betrayed. Some became disaffected with traditional, incremental civil rights activism. And southern segregationists were growing increasingly aware that their time at the helm of the Democratic Party might be nearing its end.

By 1964 and 1965, many SNCC workers were eagerly listening to the fiery Black Nationalist rhetoric of Malcolm X, who advocated armed self-defense, a celebration and perpetuation of African American life, and a rejection of white assistance in the civil

>> Fannie Lou Hammer, demanding an integrated Democratic Party.

Library of Congress Prints and Photographs Division[LC-DIG-ppmsc-01267]

rights movement. The rift in the movement was growing.

VOTING RIGHTS ACT

But legal victories were continuing. Although the Twenty-fourth Amendment had outlawed the use of the poll tax, other laws prohibiting black people from voting remained in place. But, through boycotts, marches, and sit-ins, SCLC and SNCC had galvanized many poor southern black people to participate in the movement. Through these organizations, a tremendous groundswell of activism had emerged. From January through March 1965, SCLC and SNCC led large marches in Selma, Alabama, to advocate dismantling laws that prevented black suffrage. State troopers met the Selma march with a bloody attack. On March 25, 1965, Klansmen murdered Viola Liuzzo, a white mother of five from Detroit who had volunteered for the voting registration effort.

On March 15, 1965, in a televised speech, the president introduced a comprehensive voting rights bill to Congress. "Their cause must be our cause, too," Johnson said. The president ended his speech with the words of the movement's anthem: "And we *shall* overcome." Over the objections of southern senators like Jesse Helms and Strom Thurmond, Congress overwhelmingly passed the **Voting Rights Act of 1965**. The new law outlawed attempts to deny suffrage to African Americans through literacy tests, poll taxes, or any other attempt to disfranchise citizens. From 1964 to 1968, the number of registered black people in Alabama jumped from 22 to 57 percent. In Mississippi the percentage of black registered voters leapt from a mere 7 percent to 59 percent.

Voting Rights Act of 1965 Legislation outlawing attempts to deny suffrage to African Americans through literacy tests, poll taxes, or any other attempt to disfranchise citizens

SUCCESS AND RIFTS

By the mid-1960s, the civil rights movement had achieved substantial success. The Twenty-fourth Amendment, the Civil Rights Act, and the Voting Rights Act, as well as the local protests against segregation, were major milestones. Perhaps more important, the progress these activists made produced a major shift in the national consciousness regarding race, equality, and the meaning of democracy. The challenge to the idea that there was a hierarchy of races, a challenge that began in earnest during the Second World War, had come to predominate American thinking in the 1960s.

But there was much discontent within the movement over tactics and goals, and many black Americans thought civil rights workers had ignored the poverty of America's black people, north and south. Furthermore, as Vietnam began to escalate, many young black men were being recruited into the armed forces and away from the civil rights movement. In the late 1960s, these issues—and the rift they created—would grow more apparent, and more violent.

 25-3 ## THE GREAT SOCIETY

While John Kennedy came into office promising a "new frontier" of liberal policies, his day-to-day agenda was made up largely of issues related to the Cold War and the civil rights movement. Tragedy struck before he could move beyond those objectives.

25-3a The Kennedy Assassination

On November 22, 1963, Kennedy was gunned down while riding in an open limousine in Dallas. The assassin, Lee Harvey Oswald, left few reasons for his murder, and Oswald himself was gunned down two days later while being transported from police headquarters to jail, an event aired on live television. For four days, the nation collectively mourned its fallen leader. In death, the image of the brash Cold Warrior and the tepid civil rights supporter underwent a transformation to that of a liberal legend, the king of Camelot.

25-3b Lyndon Johnson

Kennedy's replacement was Lyndon Johnson, who did not have Kennedy's charisma but did possess ample political skill, and it was through him that the nation made its most significant attempt to expand the American welfare state.

Having grown up in poverty in Texas, and having cut his political teeth as a fervent New Dealer, President Johnson viewed poverty as more divisive than race, and he thus sought to transform American liberalism through a series of programs intended to end poverty and expand education. In 1964, Johnson called for America to become a "Great Society," where "no child will go unfed and no youngster will go unschooled; where every child has a good teacher and every teacher has good pay, and both have good classrooms; where every human being has dignity and every worker has a job." Running on this platform, Johnson won a mandate for change in a resounding landslide election victory over Barry Goldwater in November 1964.

25-3c Johnson's Great Society

With a much stronger base in Congress, Johnson laid out a series of ambitious goals during his second term. In addition to the war on poverty, Johnson sought new funding and programs for (1) education, (2) health care, (3) social welfare programs, (4) immigration reform, and (5) civil rights bills.

DECLARING WAR ON POVERTY

In his State of the Union address of January 1964, Johnson called for the nation to undertake a comprehensive "war on poverty." Interest in the issue had been growing since the publication of Michael Harrington's *The Other America* (1962), a sweeping survey of the 40 to 50 million Americans who remained mired in poverty despite the fact that America in the 1960s continued to enjoy the post-World War II economic boom. Harrington argued that a poor "underclass," trapped in central cities and rural areas, was hidden from the consciences of affluent Americans. A report of the Council of Economic Advisers in January 1964 estimated that 22 percent of the nation's population lived in poverty, lacking adequate food, shelter, and clothing. Johnson wanted to defeat this scourge in the wealthiest nation in the world.

In August 1964, Johnson persuaded Congress to pass the Economic Opportunity Act (EOA), designed to attack poverty. The EOA comprised a number of agencies and programs, including (1) Head Start (a child-development program for disadvantaged preschoolers), (2) Volunteers in Service to America (or VISTA, to recruit volunteers for antipoverty programs), (3) work-training programs, (4) Job Corps (for inner-city youth), and more. Congress provided $3 billion for these programs in 1965 and 1966.

George Tames/Krt/Newscom

>> Lyndon Johnson, the big Texan who assumed the presidency after Kennedy's assassination, was a master of political persuasion, often literally throwing his weight around in order to win votes. The technique was called "the Johnson Treatment."

EDUCATION

The first "Great Society" measure, passed into law in April 1965, was the Elementary and Secondary School Act, which granted $1.3 billion to be divided between individual school districts according to their number of students who lived in poverty; the money went to educational equipment, textbooks, and learning programs, and the goal was to uplift and provide for the nation's neediest. In October 1965, Congress enacted the Higher Education Act, creating new funding for college education and enhancing existing programs. The Educational Opportunity Act of 1968 granted young people from impoverished backgrounds new access to higher education, particularly through the Upward Bound program and various scholarships.

HEALTH CARE

In the early 1960s, millions of elderly and poor Americans lacked adequate health care. Johnson insisted that the government remedy this situation. Congress responded by creating Medicare (1965), which provided medical insurance for the elderly, and Medicaid (1965), which helped finance medical treatment for the poor. To combat other deficiencies of the nation's health care system, Congress signed into law the Child Health and Improvement Act (1968), which provided prenatal and postnatal care for pregnant women and new mothers.

SOCIAL WELFARE AND OTHER PROGRAMS

Johnson also undertook measures to address social welfare issues. He increased funding to programs such as Aid to Families with Dependent Children (popularly called **welfare**), while also increasing public eligibility for such programs. Congress continued to raise the minimum wage and to extend it to workers in sectors such as retail, restaurants, hotels, and agriculture. Another $1.1 billion went to economic programs in remote rural regions, in the Appalachian Regional Development Act of 1966. A large housing bill passed in 1965 to fund low- and middle-income housing. To direct federal housing policy, Congress approved the creation of a new cabinet position, Secretary of Housing and Urban Development (HUD), in 1966. Robert Weaver, the former president of the NAACP, was appointed the first head of HUD. Weaver was also the first African American member of any presidential cabinet.

welfare Umbrella term referring to many government assistance programs, especially Aid to Families with Dependent Children

Other Great Society acts similarly expanded the purview of the federal government in the areas of health, safety, and culture, including the Water and Air Quality Acts, the National Foundation of the Arts and Humanities, the Public Broadcasting Corporation (PBS), and several consumer safety standards.

RACE AND IMMIGRATION

Johnson also bolstered his liberal credentials by appointing civil rights attorney Thurgood Marshall to be solicitor general in 1965 and then, in 1967, to serve as the first African American Supreme Court justice. Johnson's commitment to civil rights also prompted him to call for a liberalization of immigration laws; in 1965 he signed the **Hart-Cellar Act**, curtailing the quota system of the 1920s and permitting larger numbers of non-Europeans to settle in the United States. The unintended consequence was a dramatic rise in the number of Asian and Latin American immigrants. Of all the laws passed in the 1960s, the Hart-Cellar Act was one of the most influential in changing the nature, and appearance, of American society.

CONCLUSION

The Great Society undeniably expanded the power and reach of the federal government during the 1960s. It helped reduce poverty levels and created a vast social welfare system that has, more or less, lasted ever since. It was not without its failures, however. Public housing and racial segregation remained persistent problems, and many argue that the solutions proposed by Johnson's Great Society have made these problems worse, not better.

The pendulum, however, was about to swing the other way. Portended by Barry Goldwater's conservative 1964 candidacy for the presidency, and fueled in part by the perception that the federal government had grown too large, a conservative backlash was on the horizon. One issue that would spur this reaction along was the Vietnam War.

 25-4 JOHNSON'S VIETNAM

Johnson inherited the same Cold War problems that Truman, Eisenhower, and Kennedy had faced. But over time, Vietnam was the Cold War flashpoint

that flared most persistently. By 1964, U.S. troops stationed in South Vietnam had become mired in a complex civil war that would keep them there for nearly a decade. And how Johnson handled or mishandled the war would shadow the remainder of his presidency.

25-4a Initial Decisions

When Johnson took office in November 1963, he agonized over whether the United States should make a significant commitment to prevent South Vietnam from becoming a communist nation. He knew the United States might become embroiled in a lengthy war that would drain resources from his envisioned Great Society. But he also knew the United States had to retain credibility as a fighter of communism. Johnson's policy advisors were equally conflicted, offering a variety of recommendations about what to do, ranging from air strikes against the communist Viet Cong to complete withdrawal because victory seemed so unlikely. (Most, however, favored escalating the amount of American involvement in order to ensure communist defeat.) In the end, Johnson decided that fighting communism outweighed the risks involved. He sent more troops.

TONKIN GULF INCIDENT

On August 2, 1964, the U.S. destroyer *Maddox,* a spy ship, was cruising in Vietnam's Tonkin Gulf to support South Vietnamese coastal raids on the north. The weather was poor, and in the fog, North Vietnamese patrol boats fired torpedoes at the *Maddox.* The *Maddox* destroyed the torpedoes and suffered no damage. The spy ship returned two days later to continue collecting intelligence. That night, sonar readings aboard the *Maddox* and a second U.S. ship, the *Turner Joy,* again indicated that North Vietnamese torpedoes were being launched at them. The U.S. warships opened fire and called for air support. This second "attack" proved unfounded—neither of the ships had been attacked. The indications that they were under fire were either the actions of an overeager sonar man or the deliberate misreading of information by those higher up the chain of command (see Map 25.2).

Despite the sketchy evidence of a second attack, President Johnson argued that this encounter was a blatant act of aggression by the North Vietnamese. By a vote of 416 to 0 in the House and 88 to 2 in the Senate,

Hart-Cellar Act Legislation passed in 1965 curtailing the quota system of the 1920s and permitting larger numbers of non-Europeans to settle in the United States

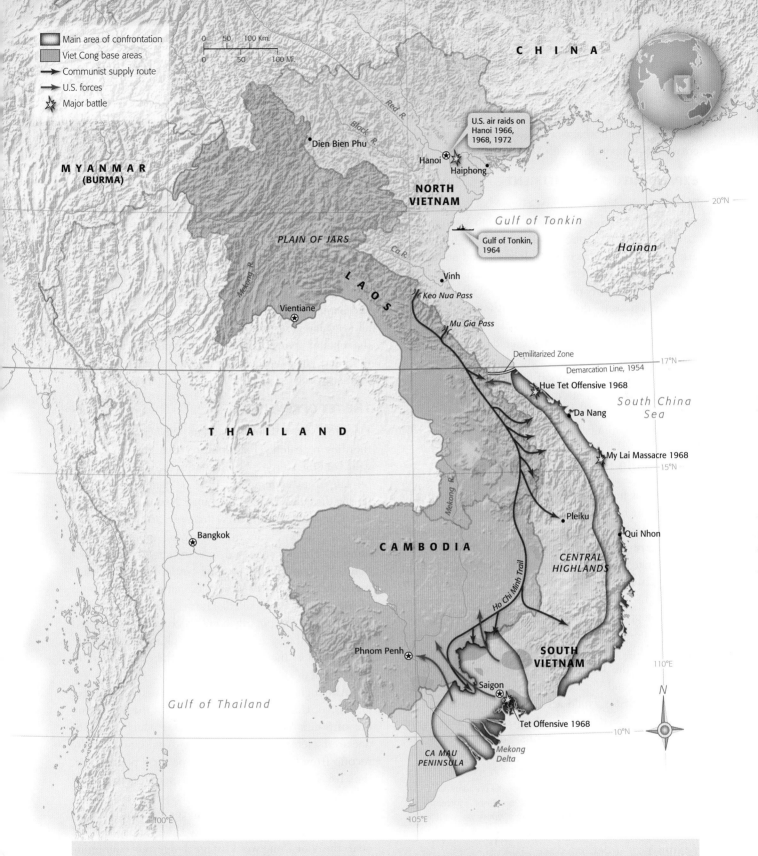

Map 25.2 Vietnam

>> This map of Southeast Asia shows the contested terrain of North and South Vietnam, including some of the major battles and the Ho Chi Minh Trail through Laos and Cambodia, a central supply line for the North Vietnamese.

Congress passed the **Tonkin Gulf Resolution**, which allowed the president to "take all necessary measures to repel armed attack against the forces of the United States and to prevent further aggression." This legislation supplied Johnson with what was called a "blank check" to increase U.S. support for South Vietnam.

EXPANDING U.S. COMMITMENT

The blank check provided by Congress allowed Johnson to expand the U.S. commitment to South Vietnam and to attack the Viet Cong full force without technically declaring war. By March 1965, Johnson had authorized heavy bombing and a U.S. troop commitment of 80,000.

The U.S. military pursued a variety of war strategies, all of which were designed to crush the Viet Cong and North Vietnamese forces but cause minimum aggravation to China, which shared a border with Vietnam, and to the Soviet Union, which provided North Vietnam with military support. As in Korea and Cuba, Vietnam began as an attempt by the Cold War powers to attack each other through proxies—an attempt to stop a domino from falling.

25-4b Battle

The war was instead mostly a war of attrition, trying to inflict as much pain to the opposing forces as they were willing to take. Progress was determined by body count, not by territory gained. Beginning in March 1965, the United States began bombing North Vietnam, targeting the **Ho Chi Minh Trail**, a winding path through North Vietnam, Laos, and Cambodia that the North Vietnamese used to supply the Viet Cong in the south. American bombers never completely blocked the path; supplies kept coming. And indeed targeting these supply lines forced the United States into pursuing battle in countries beyond Vietnam. Over the course of the war, the United States would actually drop more bombs on Laos than on Vietnam. The United States also began **search-and-destroy operations**, during which the U.S. Army would locate enemy forces, retreat, and call in airpower. Because Johnson did not want to provoke the Soviet Union or China, he never called for a full-scale ground war. Critics complained that this "war from afar" was simply pointless meandering through the jungle.

THE SOLDIERS

From the ground soldier's perspective, it was a difficult war to fight. Vietnam lacked any discernible front line, so one might just as easily die from a Viet Cong explosive left in a city bar as on patrol in the jungle. U.S. soldiers seldom met their enemy face to face, experiencing battle instead through unexpected snipers, land mines, and booby traps. Because the Viet Cong recruited from all ages and sexes, any man, woman, or child could be the enemy. Army morale and discipline eroded over time, and, given the increased availability of illicit drugs in Vietnam, drug use among U.S. servicemen skyrocketed.

THE TET OFFENSIVE

Despite these difficulties, by late 1967 many U.S. authorities repeatedly told Johnson that the Viet Cong were on the verge of defeat: South Vietnam would be safe from communism. But on January 30, 1968, during the celebration of the Lunar New Year of Tet, the Viet Cong and the North Vietnamese army launched a surprise attack southward, occupying more than one hundred communities and military targets throughout South Vietnam. In the ensuing battle, terrible damage was inflicted on South Vietnamese cities, and hundreds of Vietnamese were killed. During the offensive, Viet Cong soldiers temporarily bombarded and even entered the U.S. embassy in Saigon, the ultimate symbol of U.S. power in the region. However, after six hours of fighting, all the insurgents were dead.

Although stunned by the boldness of the Tet Offensive, U.S. forces eventually drove the Viet Cong out of South Vietnamese cities, after which the U.S. declared victory. The Viet Cong would never fully recoup from the loss. But from a political perspective, the Tet Offensive constituted a major setback for Johnson, because the belief only deepened back home that the United States could never win the war, no matter how long it fought. Every time victory seemed near, the Viet Cong would stage a vigorous counterattack. The Tet Offensive demonstrated not only that the war in Vietnam was not nearly won, but also that the U.S. government was either unclear about American prospects for victory or deliberately deceiving the American public. Neither prospect was reassuring.

Tonkin Gulf Resolution Legislation allowing the president to "take all necessary measures to repel armed attack against the forces of the United States and to prevent further aggression," which was used to justify U.S. involvement in Vietnam

Ho Chi Minh Trail Winding path through North Vietnam, Laos, and Cambodia that the North Vietnamese used to supply the Viet Cong

search-and-destroy operations Strategy used during wartime in which the U.S. Army would locate enemy forces, retreat, and call in airpower

As the Vietnam War went on, criticism came from both domestic leaders and soldiers on the front. Here, American soldiers carry a wounded warrior through Vietnamese swamps in 1969.

25-4c Domestic Criticism

The Tet Offensive, dispiriting reports from the front, and reports from questioning journalists all prompted many Americans to criticize the war. The media initially had been generally supportive of the war effort, but as the army got bogged down, as the sunny reports from the administration were countered by gloomier reports from the front, the media became some of the war's harshest critics. Television coverage grew increasingly negative, and most reporters said the war could not be won on terms acceptable to the United States.

With domestic criticism of the war increasing and the U.S. government spending enormous amounts of money to manage the conflict, President Johnson reached his breaking point. On March 31, 1968, the president addressed the nation with a call for peace negotiations—which began in Paris later that year—and a dramatic reduction in bombing runs over North Vietnam. Johnson also astonishingly withdrew from the presidential campaign to punctuate his desire to conclude the war. He would not succeed, and American involvement in Vietnam would last until 1975. But Johnson's decision not to seek a second term as

president demonstrated the war's divisiveness in American life and Johnson's inability to repair that divide. By 1968, it was unclear if anyone could.

 LIBERALISM ADRIFT

By the middle of the 1960s, significant changes had taken place in American life. The civil rights movement had questioned America's commitment to equality and brought the issue of social justice more forthrightly into public consideration. The Great Society had expanded the welfare state and redefined the role of government in American life. Meanwhile, the Vietnam War had provoked large-scale protests about what critics saw as a meaningless war. These protests swirled together, sometimes in concert, sometimes in conflict. The result was to make the late 1960s and early 1970s a contentious time, one in which most forms of authority were brought under scrutiny.

25-5a Protests on Campus

Besides the civil rights movement, the first large-scale protests emerged from the college-aged youth of the 1950s.

THE NEW LEFT

Inspired by the civil rights movement, student activism began to spread across America's college campuses in the early 1960s. The seminal group on the left was **Students for a Democratic Society (SDS)**, founded in 1959. SDS garnered public notice for declaring that young people were tired of older political movements, even older radical ones. The members of SDS formed the core of a self-conscious "New Left" movement, which

Students for a Democratic Society (SDS) Organization founded in 1959 declaring that young people were tired of older political movements, even older radical ones; formed the core of a self-conscious "New Left" movement, which rejected the Old Left's ideologies of economic justice in favor of an ideology of social justice

rejected the Old Left's ideologies of economic justice in favor of an ideology of social justice.

The SDS manifesto was the "Port Huron Statement" of 1962. It argued that the American idealism bred by the Cold War had been contradicted by the reality of segregation and the threat of nuclear war. The statement advocated "participatory democracy," which meant reconnecting average Americans with their communities and with society at large. While vague as a plan of action, the Port Huron Statement's language signaled that tempers were flaring and that protests were coming from the youth on the left.

FREE SPEECH MOVEMENT

SDS fostered an atmosphere of restlessness on college campuses, as students nationwide challenged the limits of expression. In fall 1964, the University of California at Berkeley enforced a ban on public protests and on the distribution of political reading materials in an effort to rein in student political activity. When a member of CORE, Jack Weinberg, was arrested for passing out political literature, graduate student Mario Savio led a spontaneous demonstration to protest. The demonstrators surrounded a police car and prevented the police from taking Weinberg to jail. The standoff between students and the police lasted thirty-two hours; police eventually arrested the protesters. Savio and others argued that colleges should be domains of free political discussion and not arenas where discussion was curtailed, even if it threatened to overturn the current social order.

News of the Berkeley event was reported nationally, and the Free Speech Movement, as it became known, spread to campuses such as Columbia, the University of Michigan, and Yale. Student activists across the country ultimately demanded further changes to academia, including student representation in university decisions and the modification of college curricula to include Black Studies, Chicano or Puerto Rican Studies, and Women's Studies programs. The university protests smoothly transformed into political rallies in support of the civil rights movement and in opposition to the Vietnam War, the two movements that sparked the most protest and outrage in the 1960s. But because of the questioning nature of many college students, the radicalism of their protests often was difficult to gauge or limit, especially when they confronted the Vietnam War and the

escalation of the draft, which enrolled college-aged men with increasing intensity in the latter 1960s. In practice, going to college was an allowed deferment from the draft, and thus it was typically working-class and minorities—those with disproportionate numbers enrolled inhigher education—who often went to war. Nevertheless, college students' awareness of their precarious situation amplified their rebelliousness.

25-5b Black Power, Chicano Power

At about the same time—the middle years of the 1960s—a new militancy was brewing in the African American community.

MALCOLM X AND THE NATION OF ISLAM

As the civil rights movement fought its major battles in the South during the early 1960s, a new Black Nationalist movement was rising in the North. The **Nation of Islam** and its charismatic spokesman, Malcolm X, attained prominence for criticizing the timidity of mainstream civil rights protesters. The Nation of Islam's leaders rejected the integrationist perspective of these leaders, calling instead for an independent black nation-state. They demanded that black Americans patronize only black-owned stores. They declared that nonviolence was fruitless. As some white people ratcheted up their rejection of the civil rights movement, the Nation of Islam seemed for many black people to be a more realistic solution than nonviolent resistance.

URBAN RIOTS, SNCC, AND BLACK POWER

Despite the political gains of the 1960s for African Americans, Black Nationalist militancy continued to gather strength, mainly because social and economic discrimination persisted. Beginning in the summer of 1965, following riots in the Watts section of Los Angeles, urban unrest became endemic to many northern black communities. The Watts riot exploded when a seemingly routine traffic stop erupted intoviolence. The riot lasted six days and left thirty-four dead and more than one thousand injured. Persistent racism was certainly one cause of the riots, but so was the civil rights movement's strategic decision not to address urban poverty outside the South.

SNCC hoped to tap into the urban rage by establishing chapters in the North and developing programs to channel energy into constructive activities. Yet the increasing anger soon changed SNCC itself. In 1966, after being attacked by police during a peaceful march in Mississippi, SNCC chairman Stokely Carmichael rallied a crowd by calling for "black power," and the crowd began chanting the phrase. White people were

Nation of Islam Black Nationalist organization whose leaders rejected the integrationist perspective of mainstream civil rights protesters, calling instead for an independent black nation-state

soon purged from SNCC and instructed to go fight racism in white communities. This development alarmed many of both races: Roy Wilkins, the head of the NAACP, called it "a reverse Ku Klux Klan."

By the late 1960s, **Black Power** emerged as a movement bridging the gap between Black Nationalism and the civil rights struggle. Leaders in the Black Power movement argued that black people should have control over the social, educational, and religious institutions in their communities. Black Power advocated black pride at a time when blackness was stigmatized.

BLACK PANTHER PARTY

Perhaps no Black Power organization captured the attention of America more than the Black Panther Party, founded in 1966 in Oakland, California. The Black Panthers believed that providing goods and services to the most downtrodden people of the black community would be essential to a black revolution, and they developed free clothing and medical programs, as well as a free breakfast program that fed thousands of poor children each week. They also began patrolling the streets in armed groups in an attempt to end police brutality.

WHITE REACTION

The racial violence of these years, as well as the angry separatism of Black Power leaders, prompted many white Americans to fear and condemn the Black Power movement, and the civil rights movement in general. Referred to as the "white backlash," this sentiment gave a wider audience to conservative political leaders, such as Richard Nixon, who emphasized the restoration of "law and order" in the nation's cities. Angry white Americans began efforts to reclaim their past "outsider" ethnicities, prompting an ethnic revival that lasted into the 1970s. They also asserted that, with the civil rights laws, the country had already done all that it needed to do to dismantle the legal apparatus of segregation.

Perhaps the most significant white reaction to the successes of the civil rights movement and its

Black Power Movement bridging the gap between Black Nationalism and the civil rights struggle; its leaders argued that black people should have control over the social, educational, and religious institutions in their communities and advocated black pride

>> A dramatic and emphatic speaker, Malcolm X (shown here in 1964) sought a form of black nationalism, promoting a vision of America starkly different than that of the more integration-minded Martin Luther King, Jr.

persistent and increasingly aggressive demands was the assassination of Martin Luther King, Jr., on April 4, 1968. King had flown to Memphis to lead the city's African American sanitation workers in a strike protesting their pay and work conditions, both of which were worse than white workers who performed the same work. While on the balcony of the Lorraine Motel, King was shot by James Earl Ray, an escaped convict from the Missouri State Penitentiary and a professed segregationist. Ray fled the country only to be found in London two months later and eventually sentenced to 99 years in prison (he plead guilty so he wouldn't be eligible for the death penalty). More immediately, however, angry riots flared in more than 100 cities across the country.

THE CHICANO MOVEMENT

Following in the wake of the Black Power movement came several other movements to earn respect for their particular group. Hispanics powered one influentialmovement. Throughout the 1960s, most Mexican Americans were farm laborers in California and the Southwest. Many lived in dire poverty and faced discrimination. Between 1965 and 1970, labor leaders César Chávez and Dolores Huerta organized many farm laborers in a series of strikes. Their initial targets were grape growers, who were known for treating their employees badly. Chávez and Huerta drewnational attention when they called for a national boycott of grapes. In the highly charged atmosphere of the decade's social activism, the boycott was successful, and Chávez and Huerta won their demands for higher wages and better living conditions.

Maintaining their successes would be difficult, though, and throughout the early 1970s, Chavez and Huerta fought not only for further advances but also even to retain the ones they had already achieved. Nevertheless, their movement awoke a sense of solidarity among many Hispanics, who would follow the lead of African Americans already struggling against the persistent prejudices they encountered in 1960s America.

25-5c The Women's Movement

As before, a movement to increase the voice of women in American life grew alongside activism for African Americans. The inception of the revived women's movement is usually identified as Betty Friedan's 1963 book, *The Feminine Mystique.* Friedan described "the problem that has no name," which she defined as the pervasive dissatisfaction of middle- and upper-class women who hadconfined their lives to raising children and keeping a home. Friedan's book sparked a long consideration of the social norms that defined a woman's role in American society.

In addition to the critique of middle-class gender roles, Friedan and a group of politically engaged women had grown frustrated by the federal government's refusal to enforce a provision in the Civil Rights Act that outlawed discrimination against women. To fight against this, these women created an organization modeled on the NAACP that would fight for equality for women. In 1966, they created the National Organization for Women (NOW), a still-potent organization fighting for women's rights.

A second strand of the women's movement emerged more directly from the civil rights and student movements. These women were less interested in pursuing fulfilling jobs and in critiquing middle-class domesticity. Instead, they sought a broader cultural change to the way in which women were valued and viewed in society. They rejected the gendered aspects of standard social norms, more pointedly discussed the

>>Betty Friedan, pictured here, sparked to life the women's movement with her 1963 book *The Feminine Mystique.* The book discussed society's expectations for middle-class women, and how it limited their capacities to achieve. Friedan followed up the book by starting in 1966 the National Organization for Women (NOW).

deeply entrenched social oppression faced by American women, and sought to revolutionize things such as the conception of female beauty and the legitimacy of marriage. Many members of this second strand were racial minorities, many of whom were already in the workplace and did not desire to fight for access to the workplace. Sometimes called radical feminists, what they sought to challenge instead was woman's assumed status as second-class citizens in American culture and life.

25-5d The Vietnam War at Home

In the late 1960s, all of these contentious issues—the frustration of youth searching for a more authentic status quo, the rise of Black Power, women seeking to change American society's perceptions of gender roles—fused together with protests against the war in Vietnam to create a swirling, acrimonious time filled with change, hope, and frustration. From 1965 to 1970, opposition to the war increased in proportion to the American military commitment and the increased implementation of the military draft that had begun in 1965. By 1968 there were more than half a million American troops in Vietnam. Opposition grew from a small-scale protest movement in the middle 1960s to a mainstream force by 1967 and 1968. By the early 1970s, it had had a major impact on American society.

TEACH-INS

Opposition to the war crystallized on college campuses. There, the Free Speech Movement had politicized students, who were also of draft age (although, as students, they could defer). In March 1965, faculty and students at the University of Michigan held special night lectures and classes to speak out against the war. Such "teach-ins" spread to other universities in the following months.

ESCALATING ANTIWAR PROTEST

In 1967, protests calling for an end to the war dramatically increased, and the antiwar movement became a mainstream phenomenon, as a number of leading politicians grew critical of the war. In 1966, Senator J. William Fulbright of Arkansas, the powerful chairman of the Senate Foreign Relations Committee, openly criticized the war. In 1967, Martin Luther King, Jr., publicly

>> The counterculture, shown here at the Woodstock Music Festival in 1969, tried to ignore social and cultural norms, proposing instead a new moral foundation for American life.

criticized the war too. Many other religious leaders joined King in protesting what seemed to be an unjust war.

These streams of dissent converged by mid-1967 in massive protests. Campuses grew increasingly restive. In October 1967, the National Mobilization Committee to End the War in Vietnam (the MOBE) led a march of more than 100,000 people from the Mall in Washington, D.C., to the Pentagon. In addition, throughout the conflict more than half a million men committed draft violations, sometimes burning their draft cards. Thousands moved to other countries, primarily Canada and Mexico, to avoid the conflict.

COUNTERCULTURE

The radical antiwar protesters' attacks implied broader challenges to American culture. As a result, 1966 and 1967 saw the dramatic growth of a **counterculture** of young people consciously rejecting traditional politics, social values, and corporate consumerism. Counterculture adherents, sometimes called **hippies**, who rejected attempts to change American society and chose instead to "check out" of society, formed

counterculture Social movement of the sixties that consciously rejected traditional politics, social values, and corporate consumerism

hippies Counterculture adherents who embraced new attitudes toward drugs, sex, popular culture, and politics

communities throughout the United States, most famously in the Haight-Ashbury section of San Francisco. Some formed communes, relying less on consumerism and more on sharing their possessions and responsibilities. Members of the counterculture often demonstrated their change in lifestyle by embracing new attitudes toward drugs, sex, popular culture, and politics.

Drugs and popular music often came together in the counterculture to reflect the political currents at large. Bob Dylan and other folk singers wrote songs about civil rights and social justice and spoke out against the Vietnam War. The Beatles, the most popular musical group of the decade, transitioned from singing about paltry childhood romances in the early 1960s to singing about revolution and drugs by the end of the decade. This musical output culminated in the Woodstock Music Festival, held in the summer of 1969 in upstate New York. Woodstock attracted 400,000 people to celebrate "peace, love, and freedom," symbolizing the ability of popular culture to be explicitly political and successfully promote an agenda of social justice.

25-5e Social Divisions and Popular Unrest

THE ANTI-ANTIWAR MOVEMENT

A considerable number of Americans were shocked by the antiwar protests and by the rise of the counterculture, which seemed to solidify by 1967. Although one poll in 1967 showed that 46 percent of the public thought the war was a "mistake," most Americans believed that the United States should attempt to win now that it was involved. As the antiwar movement spread, it provoked anger from conservatives, who saw protests against the war as treasonous. In 1970, construction workers (known as "hard hats") violently attacked antiwar demonstrators in New York City. The hard hats viewed their attacks as their patriotic duty against treasonous kids. It was true, however, that many of the war's protesters were students who had deferrals from the military, while most of the soldiers were from working-class families who did not have the money to go to college and thus had no way of avoiding the draft.

1968

In 1968, such tensions began to split the Democratic Party, which had succeeded in the past as a coalition of union workers, Southern segregationists, and racial and religious minorities. In the aftermath of the Tet Offensive of January, an increasing number of Americans came to believe that the war could not be won. In March, President

Johnson suffered a humiliating near-defeat in the New Hampshire Democratic primary against peace candidate Senator Eugene McCarthy. Johnson subsequently withdrew from the race and backed his vice president, Hubert Humphrey. Robert Kennedy, the brother of John F. Kennedy and also a peace candidate, entered the race and attracted substantial public support. But, like his brother, he too was shockingly killed by an assassin. With strong support among "establishment" Democrats, Humphrey won the party nomination, committing the Democrats to a continuation of Johnson's Vietnam policies.

Before he won the nomination, though, members of the New Left organized a protest against the war in August 1968 at the Democratic National Convention in Chicago. While Humphrey supporters defeated antiwar planks to the party platform inside the convention, between 10,000 and 15,000 demonstrators protested outside. Chicago police and the protesters had been battling throughout the convention, but on the third night, a near riot broke out, and hundreds were injured as police

"There's Money Enough To Support Both Of You — Now, Doesn't That Make You Feel Better?"

---from The Herblock Gallery (Simon & Schuster, 1968)

A 1967 Herblock Cartoon, copyright © by The Herb Block Foundation

>> LBJ's dreams of using the federal government to create a Great Society bottomed out as the cost of the Vietnam War soared.

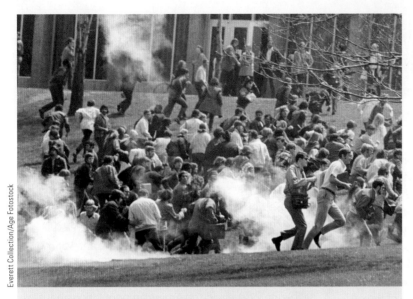

Everett Collection/Age Fotostock

>> When Nixon reneged on his promise to wind down the Vietnam War, protests erupted on college campuses across the United States. Pictured here, tear gas disperses a crowd on Kent State University Commons. Shortly afterward, National Guardsmen fired 67 rounds in 13 seconds into a crowd of 500 anti-war protesters, killing four students.

and as such, it was becoming a polemical voice in American politics, rather than the unifying one it had hoped to become in the early 1960s.

NIXON

Amid the turbulence, the Republican presidential nominee Richard Nixon argued for a restoration of "law and order" and "traditional values." He claimed there was a "silent majority" of Americans who still supported the Vietnam War and who hadn't joined the counterculture. Nixon also vaguely promised to end the war in Vietnam by achieving "peace with honor." Paralleling the New Left's SDS, the 1960s also witnessed the creation of the **Young Americans for Freedom (YAF)**, a student movement fashioned to advocate conservatism. At the same time, as challenges arose from African Americans, Hispanics, and women, a growing coalition of conservatives became increasingly eager to defend conservative values and retain some aspects of the traditional social order. The fall election featured three pro-war candidates (Nixon, Humphrey, and segregationist George Wallace, a Democrat who rejected the Democrats' civil rights plank) and ended in a Nixon victory.

25-5f Nixon and Vietnam

After Richard Nixon took office in 1969, he began to withdraw American troops from Vietnam. This decreased the strength of antiwar protests. Nixon's solution (known as **Vietnamization**) attempted to replace U.S. troops with South Vietnamese forces and keep Vietnam from falling to the communists. While Vietnamization proceeded, Nixon continued bombing raids on Vietnam's neighbors, Cambodia and Laos, in an attempt to destroy communist posts. And in April 1970, American forces invaded Cambodia to wipe out North Vietnamese staging areas. Nixon was trying to have it both ways: remain in the war, yet look as if he was pulling out.

attacked demonstrators and passersby who were caught in the melee. Some protesters responded violently. Police then waded into the crowd to beat the protesters who refused to follow their orders to disband. The violence, which played out on national television, was later described as a "police riot" in an official inquiry. Many people were appalled by the level of violence used against the demonstrators. Others viewed the police action as appropriate against the actions of the defiant youth. Nevertheless, the violence and abuse symbolized the loss of control many of America's established organizations once possessed.

With the entire political system seeming to be teetering, some members of the New Left became even more militant. By 1969, SDS had dissolved because its members could not agree on tactics. One of SDS's offshoots, the "Weathermen" (or the "Weather Underground"), committed bombings and arson on various college campuses where technical aid for the Vietnam War was being developed. In 1970, three members of the Weather Underground died when a bomb they were preparing exploded in a Greenwich Village brownstone in New York. In the following years, much of the New Left movement dissipated as its former organizations collapsed while debating the issue of violence in political protest. The New Left was becoming more violent,

·The Reasons Why...

There are several reasons why the Vietnam War was so divisive in the United States:

A questionable rationale. After the Cuban Missile Crisis of 1962, many Americans were skeptical about the very rationale of the Cold War. Was communism really a threat to American well-being? Was fighting the Cold War worth potentially destroying all of humankind? Stanley Kubrick's 1964 film *Dr. Strangelove, or: How I Learned to Stop Worrying and Love the Bomb* made exactly this critique. Thus, while most Americans initially approved of American involvement in Vietnam (especially after the articulation of the Domino Theory and the Gulf of Tonkin incident), many Americans by the mid-1960s did not think fighting the Cold War was worth the potential costs. Plus, many Americans realized that the Vietnamese people simply wanted independence after centuries of colonial rule. Antiwar protests based on these critiques began in 1964 and gathered strength when President Johnson committed ground troops in 1965, which greatly increased the number of men drafted. At the same time, and despite the protests, many Americans still firmly believed the United States had to fight communism wherever it might be budding. To the war's supporters, the protesters seemed to be cowards unwilling to fight a dangerous enemy. From the beginning, it was a contentious war.

Class conflicts. These divisions developed class distinctions throughout the 1960s. The initial protests against the Vietnam War swirled together with the other protests of the era, particularly the civil rights movement and the student protests. These other movements were, at root, questioning the United States' commitment to extending liberty to all and, indeed, its very integrity as a nation. To those fighting the war, or to their families, this seemed unpatriotic or even treasonous. Furthermore, most of the initial protesters were university students with student deferrals from the draft, while many working-class young men did not have access to such

deferrals. Thus, many of those protesting the war did so in front of parents whose children were fighting in it.

Economic costs. These arguments took a political turn when it became evident that the financial cost of the war was infringing on the benefits proposed by Johnson's Great Society. In the end, the war cost $140 billion. To those who felt their tax dollars were better spent on improving education, eliminating poverty, and other social services, the Vietnam War seemed like a misappropriation of funds. For those who felt that fighting communism was the most important issue of the day, this money was well spent.

Government deceit. From these roots, the antiwar movement picked up steam once it became clear, well before the end of the conflict, that the federal government had deliberately deceived the American population about what was happening in Vietnam. This deception was confirmed with the 1971 publication of the Pentagon Papers, a secret history of the Vietnam War leaked to the *New York Times*. The study revealed that four presidents, from Truman to Johnson, had deceived Americans about American involvement in Southeast Asia; that the conflict would have been avoided had the United States honored the 1954 Geneva Convention, which mandated democratic elections in Vietnam; that Nixon had ordered carpet-bombing of large swaths of Vietnam, Cambodia, and Laos; and that the most important reason the federal government maintained troops in Vietnam was to avoid a humiliating defeat, not to improve the lives of the South Vietnamese or win a strategic battle in the Cold War. War protesters argued that the leaders of a democratic nation should not deliberately lie to their constituents in order to wage war. Many of the war's supporters argued that it was acceptable for the federal government to maintain secrets in the name of national defense.

Anger. These divisive reasons created anger and resentment on both sides. Some Americans spit on and harassed returning American soldiers, even though many of these veterans were simply eighteen-year-old kids who had been drafted into the army. Others declared that all protesters were spineless weaklings. These kinds of actions further polarized the sides, and the nation as well.

The invasion of Cambodia reinvigorated antiwar protests, which erupted on a massive scale in 1970. The protests shut down more than four hundred college campuses, and more than 100,000 demonstrators converged on Washington, D.C., surrounding the White House.

On May 4, 1970, Ohio National Guardsmen shot and killed four Kent State University students during antiwar demonstrations on campus. Days later, police killed two more students at Jackson State University in Mississippi during demonstrations. In both episodes, the use of deadly force by government troops against unarmed protesters shocked the country.

VIETNAM AS A MISTAKE

The campus unrest eventually dissipated, and protests declined in 1970 and 1971. Nixon was, after all, also actively reducing the American troop presence in Vietnam from its 1969 peak of 540,000 to only 60,000 in 1972. But the widespread conviction that Vietnam had been a mistake deepened in American society and originated a trend of public suspicion of and cynicism about its political leaders. News of American troops' abuses of Vietnamese civilians shocked the public, too, most notably after reports surfaced in 1970 of a massacre of more than three hundred women, children, and old men in the village of My Lai. The June 1971 publication of a secret Defense Department study known as the **Pentagon Papers** was another disillusionment. It revealed that the government had lied to the American public over major events in the Vietnam War in an attempt to manipulate public opinion. More basically, many Americans questioned whether the threat of communism existing in Southeast Asia was really a threat worth spilling American blood for. This was just one of the reasons why the Vietnam War was so divisive in American society in the late 1960s and early 1970s. For more, see "The Reasons Why . . ." box on the next page.

>LOOKING AHEAD...

In January 1973, the United States signed a treaty with North Vietnam to end the war, and by March 1975, the United States removed its final troops and support staff, including many Vietnamese who had aided their effort. Shortly after the U.S. departed, the Viet Cong unified Vietnam under communist control. Yet the announcement did little to heal the wounds raised by years of internal argument over the war's merits. The war had led to the death of more than 58,000 American soldiers and some 3 million Vietnamese. But it also exposed deep rifts in American society. Perhaps the second tragedy of Vietnam, beyond the death toll, was that it drained resources from programs that attempted to rectify social wrongs, such as poverty, hunger, and unequal education. It was the Vietnam War as much as anything else that derailed Johnson's Great Society.

The Vietnam War also provoked a shift in American culture, both to the left, in the form of expanded women's rights and multicultural education, and to the right, in prompting a resurgence of social conservatism in the political sphere and a white ethnic revival that often scorned the advances African Americans had won. It is to these transitions that we will turn next.

Pentagon Papers Secret Defense Department study, published in 1971, that revealed that the government had lied and purposely deceived the American public over major events in the Vietnam War in an attempt to manipulate public opinion

STUDY TOOLS 25

READY TO STUDY? IN THE BOOK, YOU CAN:

❑ Rip out the Chapter Review Card, which includes key terms and chapter summaries.

ONLINE AT WWW.CENGAGEBRAIN.COM, YOU CAN:

❑ Collect StudyBits while you read and study the chapter.

❑ Quiz yourself on key concepts.

❑ Find videos for further exploration.

❑ Prepare for tests with HIST5 Flash Cards as well as those you create.

❑ Read the Port Huron Statement.

❑ Explore documents related to the Bay of Pigs invasion.

❑ Read oral histories and see pictures from the Freedom Riders' campaign.

❑ Hear Martin Luther King's "I Have a Dream" speech.

❑ Hear Fannie Lou Hamer's address to the rules committee of the DNC.

❑ Read an oral history from Estell Harvey, who experienced Freedom Summer firsthand.

❑ Hear Dr. Martin Luther King, Jr. discuss Vietnam.

❑ Hear LBJ's "We Shall Overcome" speech.

❑ Read a speech given by César Chávez during one of his protests.

❑ Hear Malcolm X speak on Black Nationalist demands.

❑ Read an account of the Tel Offensive.

❑ Read a denunciation of antiwar protesters by Vice President Spiro Agnew.

What Else Was Happening

1959 Fidel Castro leads successful revolution against Cuba's Batista regime.

Students for a Democratic Society (SDS) define social justice as goal of New Left.

1960 **February:** Students defy segregation with sit-in at Greensboro Woolworth lunch counter.

November: John F. Kennedy becomes first Catholic president over Republican Richard Nixon.

May: Student Nonviolent Coordinating Committee (SNCC) begins civil rights activism.

Two hackers from MIT create the first computer video game, Spacewar.

1961 **April:** CIA-orchestrated Bay of Pigs invasion fails.

May: Congress of Racial Equality (CORE) challenges segregation in Freedom Rides.

August: Soviets and East Germany erect Berlin Wall to prevent further defections.

1962 **October:** Cuban Missile Crisis brings world to brink of nuclear war.

1963 Media coverage of Birmingham police beating civil rights marchers stirs nation.

August: White supremacists bomb black Birmingham church, killing four girls.

August: United States supports generals' coup and killing of South Vietnam leader Ngo Dinh Diem.

August 28: Martin Luther King, Jr., gives "I Have a Dream" speech at March on Washington for Jobs and Freedom.

November 22: John F. Kennedy assassinated in Dallas.

Betty Friedan's The Feminine Mystique *defines "the problem that has no name."*

Harvey Ball, a Worcester, Massachusetts, commercial artist, devises the yellow smiley face for an insurance firm that wants to improve employee morale after a bitter corporate takeover.

1964 **January** President Johnson seeks expansion of welfare state and "war on poverty."

July 3: Civil Rights Act ends public segregation and discrimination in employment.

Summer: Volunteers travel south to build "Freedom Schools" and register black voters.

August: Economic Opportunity Act creates Head Start, VISTA, Job Corps, other agencies.

August: Gulf of Tonkin Resolution gives full support for South Vietnam.

The G.I. Joe doll—dubbed "America's movable fighting man" by Hasbro—makes his debut.

1965

March: Johnson authorizes heavy bombing of North Vietnam and 80,000 troops for South Vietnam.

Congress passes Voting Rights Act.

Hart-Cellar Act enables growing immigration from Asia and Latin America.

August: Deadly L.A.-Watts riots begin urban unrest across nation.

Biggest power failure in history causes nine-hour blackout in eastern Canada and the United States, leading to a surge in the national birthrate nine months later.

1966

Black Panther Party forms in Oakland, California.

October: 100,000 people march in Washington to protest Vietnam War.

1968

January 30: Communist Tet Offensive undermines president's claims of success in Vietnam.

March: Johnson calls for peace negotiations, vows not to seek reelection.

April 4: White supremacist kills Martin Luther King, Jr.; riots rock cities.

August: Police quell protesters at Democratic National Convention in Chicago.

November: Republican Richard M. Nixon wins presidency over Democrat Hubert Humphrey.

1969: *Summer: Woodstock Music Festival.*

1970

May 4: Ohio National Guardsmen kill four students protesting invasion of Cambodia.

November: News of U.S. massacre of more than 300 civilians in My Lai.

1971

June: Publication of secret Pentagon Papers on Vietnam policy.

1973

January: United States and North Vietnam sign treaty; U.S. troops withdraw.

1975: *Communists unify Vietnam.*

26 | The Age of Fracture: The 1970s

National Archives and Records Administration

LEARNING OBJECTIVES

After reading this chapter, you should be able to do the following:

26-1 Evaluate Richard Nixon as president, focusing on his policies in the United States and abroad.

26-2 Describe the events of Watergate and its ramifications for the country.

26-3 Describe the economic conditions of the 1970s, including stagflation and the end of the post-World War II economic boom, and describe how Presidents Ford and Carter attempted to confront the problem.

26-4 Describe the perpetuation of 1960s-style activism and how it transformed into a politics of identity in the 1970s.

26-5 Evaluate the reaction to 1960s social movements and describe the rise of the New Right.

AFTER FINISHING THIS CHAPTER GO TO **PAGE 524** **FOR STUDY TOOLS**

The social activism of the late 1960s continued into the 1970s, as Americans continued to seek to bust free from the culture of postwar liberalism, but during the 1970s that activism ran into roadblocks. A variety of minority movements seemed poised to fracture any national unity leftover from the 1960s, as increasing numbers of people went from thinking they were working for the good of the country to working on behalf of their own particular group, or even just themselves. At roughly the same time, the postwar economic boom came to a startling end in 1973, raising poverty and unemployment as contentious and serious issues. American politicians learned the limits of politics' ability to create change, and they simultaneously learned that they could not publicly discuss these limits and expect to be reelected.

This widespread awareness of American limits had many sources. The war in Vietnam ended in 1975, but only after it had increased friction and schisms between Americans and diminished American expectations of imperial power. After Vietnam, it was difficult for anyone to think the United States could willfully dictate events around the world. In addition, the countless fabrications that Johnson and Nixon had fed the public about the progress of the war made many Americans suspicious of their country's leaders. Meanwhile, the civil rights movement had succeeded in winning political rights for African Americans, but it then faced social and economic limits that tested the reality of America's commitment to racial equality. And a series of new social movements—by women, Chicanos, American Indians, and others—that followed in the wake of the civil rights movement seemed to cast African Americans as just another minority group vying for institutional recognition rather than one that has been historically and uniquely wronged. Interest in other causes, such as environmentalism, also exploded during the 1970s.

All this turmoil and diverse social action provoked a backlash from voters, who, by 1980, were willing to overlook one Republican president's shady dealings in order to elect another conservative to the nation's highest office. Many Americans had tired of calls for social justice, and this sheer exhaustion led many to turn inward, contributing to what one writer called the "me generation." The civil rights anthem "We Shall Overcome" seemed to lose its collective meaning in the 1970s. Few knew who "we" were.

At the same time, while the economy had remained healthy during the 1960s, it soured badly during the 1970s, officially ending the long post-World War II boom. The economic decline lasted the entire decade, casting a pall over the other events of the era. While the causes of the downturn are complex, a significant part was played by the demise of American manufacturing. Companies moved out of the Northeast and Midwest, heading to the South or the West in order to find better weather, cheaper labor, and fewer unions. This demographic and economic shift created "the Sunbelt," a region stretching from Florida to California. As more companies moved to the Sunbelt, American politics and culture took on the traditionally southern cast of anti-elitism and antigovernment individualism. "Get government off our backs" became a staple slogan of the late 1970s—one that epitomized a tax revolt that opened the door for a rightward shift in American politics that Americans still live with today.

 ## 26-1 PRESIDENT NIXON

Richard Nixon, who had made his political name as a ruthless anticommunist during the McCarthy years, who had served dutifully as Eisenhower's vice president throughout most of the 1950s, and who had nearly beaten Kennedy in the presidential race of 1960, finally won the office he so ardently sought in 1968. Some historians cite that year as the beginning of "the seventies."

As president, Nixon capitalized on divisions within the Democratic Party over the Vietnam War to beat the Democratic nominee, Hubert Humphrey. Nixon, a son of a California grocer, is considered one of our most complex presidents, reviled by liberals but not necessarily beloved by conservatives either. He was brilliant but unprincipled. Nixon responded to problems with a creativity and drive that stemmed not from concern for social justice, but from a persistent fear of how history would judge him. He was driven by a long-smoldering resentment against what he saw as "the Eastern Establishment," which he defined as the bankers, politicians, and businessmen who had controlled American social, cultural, and political life for years. More than anything though, Nixon hated the Democratic establishment, which he thought was perpetually out to get him. His mistrust and suspicion would

◄◄◄ **One of the first visible signs that the post-World War II economic boom was over was long lines during the gasoline shortage of 1973. Suggesting that Americans were going to have to live with limits to what was possible, motorists in this picture line up at a gas station in Oregon, hoping to fill their tanks.**

>> In efforts to redirect the Cold War, Nixon became the first president to visit China, meeting with Mao Zedong and Zhou Enlai in 1972. With regard to Chinese–Soviet relations, Nixon confided to Zhou that if Moscow marched either east or west, he was ready to "turn like a cobra on the Russians."

AFP/Getty Images

PING-PONG DIPLOMACY

As Vietnam simmered down as a national issue, Nixon saw that relations between China and the Soviet Union were beginning to break down. The two communist superpowers were at odds about how expansionary the communists should be in Asia, and in an attempt to push the two further apart, Nixon began talks with China. His first step was to accept an invitation to send the American table tennis team to compete in a friendly international event in China. This gave his foreign policy toward China its name: Ping-Pong Diplomacy. The players were the first Americans invited into China since its founding as a communist country in 1949. In 1972, Nixon himself went to China, and the two nations increased trade and cultural exchanges. They also agreed that the Soviet Union should not be allowed to expand farther into Asia. Beginning friendly relations with one of the powerful communist countries in the world was a remarkable step for someone who rose to fame for attacking communism.

SALT AND THE COLD WAR

Increasingly worried about the cost of the arms race, Nixon also made overtures to the Soviet Union. Just months after going to China, Nixon went to Moscow to meet with Soviet premier Leonid Brezhnev. During the meeting, Nixon agreed to sell excess American wheat to the Soviets. The fact that their country needed wheat was an early sign that Soviet-style communism was not performing well economically, even though the Soviets attempted to hide this fact. Under the auspices of the **Strategic Arms Limitation Talks (SALT)**, the two leaders also agreed to freeze the number of long-range missile launchers and build certain new missiles only after they had destroyed the same number of older missiles. This did not signify an end to the Cold War, but it did demonstrate that the nations' leaders were beginning to recognize the problems inherent in an unchecked arms race.

Thus, within four years, Nixon, perceived as a hard-nosed anticommunist Republican, had removed the American presence in Vietnam, ceding it to communists,

score him significant political gains in matters of foreign policy and the environment. But it would also lead to his historic downfall.

26-1a Nixon's Foreign Policy

Nixon's greatest triumphs as president were in foreign policy. As explained in the previous chapter, his Vietnamization plan simultaneously pulled American troops out of Vietnam and increased the American military presence in other nations of Southeast Asia. Nevertheless, by 1972, Vietnamization was in fact removing American troops from the entire region. The last American troops left Vietnam in 1973. Most Americans were relieved to be removed from a situation that was perceived as a stalemated "quagmire," where American soldiers were dying while fighting a war that could not be won.

Strategic Arms Limitation Talks (SALT) Sessions held between President Nixon and Soviet premier Leonid Brezhnev, in which the two leaders agreed to freeze the number of long-range missile launchers and build certain new missiles only after they had destroyed the same number of older missiles and made overtures to both China and the Soviet Union. This softened approach toward America's supposed enemies was orchestrated largely by Nixon's assistant for national security affairs and, later, his secretary of state, Henry Kissinger. These more relaxed relations are labeled *détente* (a French term meaning "a relaxing" or "an easing").

LATIN AMERICA AND AFRICA

While the Cold War cooled with China and the Soviet Union, it heated up in Latin America and Africa. Each time a nation in one of these regions elected a leftist—potentially communist—regime, the United States actively supported coups and the installation of new governments that would support U.S. interests. These new right-wing regimes routinely punished political opponents. For instance, the United States supported the ousting of Chile's Salvador Allende in 1973, opting instead to provide assistance to the authoritarian regime of General Augusto Pinochet. In Africa, the United States tolerated the racist regime of South Africa and sided with anticommunists in the Angolan civil war. But, taking a lesson from Vietnam, Nixon was leery of using American troops in these situations, preferring instead more covert operations.

26-1b Nixon the Accidental Liberal

While Nixon's foreign policies often represented significant breakthroughs, his domestic policies were even more transformative, although not always in the way Nixon's supporters had hoped. Upon entering office, Nixon claimed to be a typical small-government Republican. But in reality, Nixon's relentless preoccupation with and fear of being defeated for reelection led him to advocate many goals of the left and of the Democratic Party. Cagily, however, while Nixon sought to increase budgets for liberal causes, he made these increases contingent upon greater local control. This put Democrats in a tough political position, because they could not reject funds for causes they had long advocated, but they could not control how those funds were spent locally. In this way, Nixon became an advocate of many liberal causes, but he did so while weakening the supposed Eastern Establishment he despised.

INCREASING THE SIZE OF GOVERNMENT

For instance, in 1970 Nixon signed into law the National Environmental Policy Act, which paved the way for him to establish the Environmental Protection Agency (EPA) later that year. He endorsed the Occupational Safety and Health Administration (OSHA), which sought to make workplaces safer. He doubled the budgets of the National Endowment for the Humanities (NEH) and the National Endowment for the Arts (NEA). Nixon also became the first president to embrace affirmative action, as discussed later in the chapter.

But each of these progressive developments came at a cost to the liberals who had long advocated them. For instance, Nixon's increases to the National Endowment for the Humanities were earmarked for popular artists in Middle America or for local museums, instead of the large museums in New York and Boston, which championed abstract art that was appreciated mostly by the well educated and affluent. Politically, Democrats could not reject his proposal to increase funding for the arts. It was a stroke of political genius: Nixon got credit for being an advocate of the arts, at the same time draining support from his nemesis, the eastern liberal elite.

26-2 WATERGATE

Before Nixon could do more, though, he became mired in scandal. During his successful reelection bid in 1972, five men were arrested breaking into the Democratic National Committee offices at the Watergate Hotel in Washington, D.C. One of the burglars worked directly for Nixon's Committee to Re-Elect the President (CREEP), a fact that did not impede Nixon's landslide victory in the election. But print journalists, spurred by the investigative reporting of the *Washington Post*'s Bob Woodward and Carl Bernstein, continued to follow the story and discovered that orders for the break-in had been issued from high up in the Nixon White House. The Senate convened hearings, which were televised nationally. It seemed to many Americans that Nixon had possibly ordered a break-in of his opponent's Washington offices. If proven, this would be a tremendous breach of public trust and a dangerous attempt to use the power of the federal government to illegally stifle his political opposition. It was potentially a threat to the very nature of democracy.

The televised testimony captivated millions, and, although the testimony never revealed whether or

> *détente* French term meaning "a relaxing" or "an easing"; refers to more relaxed relations with America's supposed enemies, China and the Soviet Union

not Nixon himself had ordered the break-in, what did become clear were Nixon's suspicious nature and his other attempts to spy illegally on Americans. Watergate became an investigation about much more than a simple break-in; it became a portentous glimpse inside the mind of the president. The Senate learned that the president had traded favors, spoken offensively about many of the nation's minority groups, and, most damningly, taped nearly every conversation that had happened in the White House. When the Senate demanded to see the tapes, Nixon fired the special prosecutor leading the Senate's investigation, prompting a series of sympathy resignations from members of his own administration.

As the scandal mushroomed, Nixon's vice president, Spiro Agnew, admitted to tax evasion and bribery. He resigned and President Nixon, following the advice of Congressional leaders, chose the Republican leader of the House, Gerald Ford, to replace him. The credibility of the entire administration was under attack.

Americans watched the scandal with alarm. It seemed to confirm many people's beliefs that American leaders were untrustworthy. After the Supreme Court ordered Nixon to turn over the White House tapes, it was evident he was going to be impeached. Nixon instead chose to resign from office, which he did after a dramatic televised speech to the nation on August 9, 1974. His new vice president, Gerald Ford, became president. To understand the reasons why Watergate was so pivotal to the 1970s political culture, see "The Reasons Why . . ." box.

26-3 THE TROUBLED ECONOMY AND POLITICS ADRIFT

The backdrop for all this political commotion was an economic recession that officially ended the great post-World War II economic boom. The conditions that had made the American economy the most powerful in the world after World War II vanished quickly in the 1970s. The two presidents that succeeded Nixon, Gerald Ford and Jimmy Carter, had little success in solving this large structural problem.

>> Americans were understandably transfixed at the prospect of a president calling it quits. But that's exactly what Richard Nixon did, after a scandal surrounding a 1972 break-in at the Democratic Party headquarters in the Watergate Hotel led to numerous revelations of presidential abuse.

Everett Collection/Newscom

There were at least four reasons why the Watergate scandal was so pivotal in American life:

The death of political idealism. The disclosures of Watergate put the nail in the coffin of the political idealism of the early 1960s. During that earlier period, social movements like the civil rights movement turned to the federal government and the American system of law to advocate change. After the frustrations of the civil rights movements and a decade of lies about the Vietnam War, the Watergate scandal validated many Americans' darkest suspicions that a politician's first priority was not to serve the public, but simply to get reelected.

Americans turn inward. These suspicions led many Americans to turn away from politics, often choosing to search for answers to large social problems through the individual groups that gave them their identity. This, in turn, helped lead to the rise of identity politics, an effort to ensure benefits for one's own group rather than ponder what might be best for the nation as a whole. American national politics seemed corrupt.

The irony. One major irony of the Watergate scandal was that it served Republican ends. Since at least the New Deal, Republicans had been advocating a smaller role for government. The disaffection toward politics inspired by Nixon, a Republican, was a long-term boon to the Republican Party. After Watergate, many people began to see government as part of the problem rather than part of the solution, and thus they too began advocating for smaller government.

New political scrutiny. Meanwhile, before Watergate, presidents were usually given a wide berth by the media and forgiven their personal flaws, which frequently went unreported. After Watergate, every dimension of a politician's life was deemed newsworthy. President Ford, who became president after Nixon resigned, was a talented athlete and former college football star at the University of Michigan, but he was widely portrayed as a goof and a bumbling klutz because every stumble he made was televised and reported on. Where there once had been deference and respect, now there was cynicism and ire.

26-3a Economic Woes

In the late 1960s, Vietnam, the Great Society, and the costs of the arms race had diverted a lot of money from federal coffers, and Johnson had refused to raise taxes to pay for these expensive ventures. Furthermore, by the early 1970s, America's industrial sector was weakening due to foreign competition and decreasing demand for American goods. The economy was cooling off after its long period of post-World War II growth. With the United States having to maintain its tremendous expenditures during a time of declining tax receipts, it had to borrow tremendous amounts of money to balance its budget. This led the value of the dollar to decrease, meaning it took more dollars to pay for the same goods. This condition is called inflation.

Nixon did not really know what to do to control the problem. First, he made it more difficult to borrow money, which, he hoped, would lower the amount of investments and keep dollars spare. However, all this did was constrict the economy even more, leading to an economic recession.

In 1971, facing reelection, Nixon initiated the first-ever peacetime wage and price freeze. He also accepted large federal deficits. These initiatives reversed the direction of the economy long enough for him to win reelection in 1972, but his economic plan was erratic and short term, confidence remained low, and the American industrial sector was beginning to decline in the face of cheaper prices on imported foreign goods.

OIL EMBARGO

The whole problem was compounded by matters in the Middle East. The establishment of Israel in 1948 as a haven for the world's Jews after the atrocities of the Holocaust was perpetually contested by many of the Islamic nations of the Middle East, whose religious differences with the Jews were compounded by the imposition of a political state on land they claimed as their own. Egypt, Syria, and other nations of the Middle East fought numerous battles against Israel in the 1950s and 1960s, and Israel won each of them with the help of the United States and several countries of Europe. After yet another confrontation, the Yom Kippur War of 1973, the oil-rich nations of the Middle East sought to punish the United States for supporting Israel by placing an embargo on oil sold to the United States.

The result was that oil prices in the United States quadrupled. Gas became hard to find, and long lines of drivers were seen waiting at filling stations. Other sources of energy were not immediately available. Beyond the daily frustrations of expensive gas at the pump, the oil embargo raised the cost of making goods and moving them from one place to another. Prices of all consumer goods went up. Thus, the American economy entered a complicated cycle in which prices kept going up (inflation) but the economy began losing jobs (or stagnating). Economists called this unique condition **stagflation**.

Stagflation is notoriously difficult to fight, because most of the tools the government has to control the economy—such as regulating the interest it charges banks to borrow money from the Federal Reserve banks—are primarily designed to either slow growth and end inflation, or increase growth and boost inflation. Tools to lower inflation while growing the economy do not exist. The economy would continue to perform badly throughout the 1970s, bringing to an abrupt halt the almost consistent economic growth the country had enjoyed since 1946.

THE DECLINE OF CITIES

Another force compounded these economic pressures. Since the Second World War, Americans had been leaving cities at alarming rates, heading to the suburbs, where good schools, bigger homes, and larger spaces beckoned. Stagflation slowed the American economy down, especially the manufacturing sector that was overwhelmingly based in large Northeastern and Midwestern cities like Chicago and Philadelphia. As these sectors declined in productivity, many Americans lost their jobs and left the industrial cities of the North in search of work in the South or Southwest. As businesses left, the tax base left with them, making the 1970s the roughest time in the history of most American cities. For instance, during the 1970s, more than 1 million residents left New York City and the city tottered on the brink of bankruptcy; it took the city nearly two decades

stagflation Economic cycle in which prices keep going up (inflation) while the economy is losing jobs (or stagnating)

to make up that population loss. American cities, which had once symbolized America's embrace of modern life, now gained a reputation for being dangerous places one should avoid if they could afford to.

26-3b President Ford

After Watergate and the Vietnam War had discredited the role that government might play in solving deep social problems, the two presidents who followed Nixon appeared rudderless and without confidence that the American people would listen to, much less enact, their attempts to solve the country's problems. For his part, President Ford was the first president to have never been elected president or vice president, having assumed the vice presidency when Spiro Agnew resigned, and risen to the presidency after Nixon's decline. A good-natured, well-liked man who self-effacingly admitted he was "a Ford, not a Lincoln," Gerald Ford weathered the wrath of the American public in the aftermath of Watergate. And one of his first acts as president did not generate widespread goodwill: Ford offered Nixon a full presidential pardon. This action ended the possibility of criminal proceedings and, perhaps, of finding out whether or not Nixon had ordered the Watergate break-in. But the pardon did allow the nation to move beyond political scandal in order to focus on the dire problems of the economy and the Cold War. Unfortunately, Ford was unable to take complete control of either.

DOMESTIC POLICY

Ford's chief domestic problem was stagflation, but, like Nixon, Ford had little luck tackling it. At first, he encouraged Americans to save rather than spend their money. Then he offered a large tax cut. Neither measure worked to improve the sagging economy. With little national support, Ford regularly vetoed congressional bills, only to have his vetoes overridden.

FOREIGN POLICY

Ford had better luck overseas. He laid the basis of another arms agreement with the Soviets, which was finalized as SALT II a few years later, under President Carter. Ford's secretary of state Henry Kissinger negotiated between Israel and Egypt, leading to a short-term break in hostilities in the Middle East.

26-3c President Carter

In 1976, Ford stood little chance of reelection. Affable and open as he was, even within his party he faced a strong challenge from California's former governor, Ronald Reagan, a symbol of the new Sunbelt conservatism that would dominate the 1980s and 1990s.

THE ELECTION OF 1976

The Democrats, for their part, took a chance and won. They nominated a little-known, one-term Georgia governor named Jimmy Carter. Carter struck a note with the electorate because he appeared to be honest, was a "born again" Christian, was progressive on issues of poverty and treatment of minorities, and was a southerner capable of talking to the demographically growing southern half of the nation (Map 26.1). Carter won the election, in which he competed against the ghost of Nixon as much as against Ford.

DOMESTIC POLICY

Domestically, Carter faced the same economic conditions that Nixon and Ford had: stagflation. Carter could not manage it either, and when he proposed to increase government spending to create jobs (à la the New Deal), inflation skyrocketed. He then made the ultimate political blunder when he asked the nation to sacrifice on behalf of the "common purpose" and offered a list of small and specific proposals as to how that might be done. These modest proposals did not capture the public's imagination, and his political inexperience in Washington, D.C., contributed to his making several gaffes, which repeatedly made him look weak and ineffectual.

Carter was further burdened by the nationwide energy crisis, which had surged after the Yom Kippur War of 1973 and had not subsided since. By 1977, elementary and high schools were forced to close because there was not enough energy to heat them. Carter's ambitious plan to remedy the crisis combined higher taxes and a vigorous search for alternative fuels. This plan was met with general disapproval by Congress and did not pass. Making matters worse, the meltdown of a nuclear reactor at **Three Mile Island**, Pennsylvania, in 1979 discredited nuclear power, a potentially viable alternative to oil. With an economy this troubled, Carter could not advocate any of the plans he had for expanding American social justice.

Map 26.1 Election of 1976

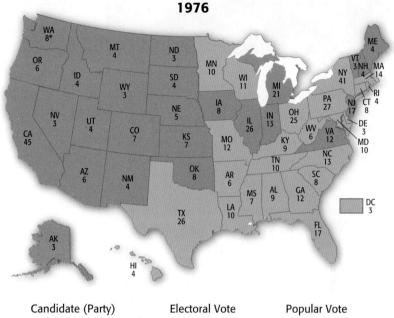

1976

Candidate (Party)	Electoral Vote		Popular Vote	
Carter (Democrat)	297	55.2%	40,830,763	50.1%
Ford (Republican)	240*	44.6%	39,147,793	48.0%

*One Ford elector in Washington voted for Republican Ronald Reagan of California.

FOREIGN POLICY

Carter made more progress abroad. His longest-lasting achievement in foreign policy was in establishing human rights as an element of American policy. Doing so energized him to (1) call for the end of apartheid in South Africa, (2) give up control of the Panama Canal, and (3) cite human rights considerations as a factor in the granting of American aid. In the Middle East, Carter oversaw a peace agreement between Israel and Egypt, called the **Camp David Accords**, in late 1978.

But this accomplishment was overshadowed just six months later when Islamic militants took fifty-two hostages from the American Embassy in Tehran, the capital of Iran. The militants were part of a coup in

Three Mile Island Nuclear reactor in Pennsylvania that suffered a meltdown in 1979

Camp David Accords 1978 peace agreement between Israel and Egypt, brokered by President Carter

Dirck Halstead/The Life Images Collection/Getty Images

>> President Jimmy Carter, wearing the kind of sweater he urged all Americans to wear in order to reduce their consumption of energy.

which fundamentalist Islamists seized power from the American-supported dictatorship, in place since 1953. The terrorists held the American hostages for more than a year. Each day that went by, Carter seemed more and more unable to handle the problem. But the inability to bring together the nation was not Carter's doing alone.

identity politics A view of politics premised on how one identifies oneself within a nation, usually based on some sense of belonging to a minority group eager to win greater parity with the national majority

26-4 THE RISE OF IDENTITY POLITICS

One historian has described the social movements of the 1960s as a "coming together" of sorts, when large gestures—the civil rights movement, the War on Poverty—were intended to create a more unified and inclusive nation. The 1970s, however, served as a spin cycle, scattering the social energy of the sixties in a thousand different directions. Without a magnetic social vision to unify the populace, the 1970s came to be characterized as a time of turning inward or, to use a term from the era, a celebration of the culture of narcissism. People's interest in pet causes flourished, as did a variety of new faiths, most of which prioritized personal renewal or an individual relationship with God. If the latter 1960s represented a busting free from the culture created in postwar America, the 1970s might best be interpreted as a time when liberal demands for increased freedom battled against conservative demands for freedom.

26-4a Identifying with a Group

One of the most contentious and transformative sociopolitical events of the decade was the codification and resurgence of identity politics. **Identity politics** can be defined as a politics premised on how one identifies oneself within a nation, usually based on some sense that one belongs to a minority group eager to win greater parity with the national majority. Identity politics had been made both politically potent and divisive by African Americans, Mexican Americans, Native Americans, and others following the civil rights movement, especially in the militancy that emerged in the late 1960s.

AFRICAN AMERICAN ACTIVISM

America's black population was the first to embrace this brand of politics, which intended to change the culture as well as public policy. Despite the federal laws passed in the 1960s, racism against America's black people persisted. For the most part, though, racism was no longer legally codified or socially acceptable at the broad institutional level, but it remained entrenched in the personal-level institutions of society and culture. Thus, many African American activists broadened their focus from just politics to politics *and culture*, hoping to change the way Americans thought about their nation. Cultural acceptance was different from political acceptance. Political acceptance concerned the enforcement of color-blind laws, while social acceptance depended on an awareness of differences and a conscious decision to ignore them.

In response to this heightened awareness, "Black is beautiful" became a widespread call in the black community. Africa became a destination for many Americans seeking to understand their cultural past, a sentiment epitomized in and popularized by Alex Haley's 1976 bestseller, *Roots*. Attending historically black colleges acquired cultural cachet. Black Studies writers and professors established this field as an accepted academic discipline within America's colleges. The cultural politics of the Black Freedom Movement surpassed attempts to create protective legal structures to ensure equal access. Social and economic acceptance required different methods.

AFFIRMATIVE ACTION AND BUSING

Amid this transition toward greater interest in changing American culture, federal and state governments attempted to rectify the continuing effects of racism. Because many white Americans were afraid of dropping property values if their neighborhoods became racially integrated, and because of deeply entrenched fears of interracial mingling, schools generally remained segregated. To remedy this persistent problem, cities such as Boston and Los Angeles began busing students from one school district to another in order to desegregate schools. This action provoked much ire from parents, black and white, who had their children bused far from home. Riots erupted in Boston, and the level of suspicion increased between the groups on either side of the color line.

Meanwhile, the federal government developed programs of **affirmative action**, in which employers were supposed to ensure that a certain percentage of employees were minorities, or that a certain percentage of government contracts were given to minority-owned businesses. In another example of Nixon's ruthless politics, affirmative action's federal origins can be traced to his proclaimed free-market administration. He did this to cause political rifts between white and black laborers, which would, and did, break up a Democratic political coalition that was first formed by President Roosevelt in the 1930s.

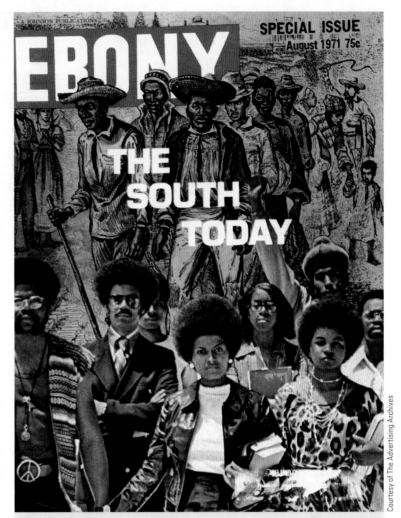

Courtesy of The Advertising Archives

>> *Ebony*, a monthly magazine targeting African American readers since 1945, used this 1971 cover to demonstrate the long road African Americans had traveled since slavery, now celebrating natural hairstyles like the Afro and the Black Power symbol of the raised fist.

Affirmative action also became policy in many of the nation's universities. In 1978, the Supreme Court upheld the legality of some elements of affirmative action, but disallowed the use of exact quotas, in a case that emerged when a white student claimed he was denied entrance to medical school because of the color of his skin. The case, *Regents of*

affirmative action Program meant to ensure that a certain percentage of a company's employees are minorities or that a certain percentage of government contracts are given to minority-owned businesses

Bob Kreisel/Alamy Stock Photo

>> In 1969, a group of activists called "Indians of All Tribes" occupied Alcatraz Island in California, demanding the land be returned to the tribes that had once occupied it. The occupation lasted 19 months.

the University of California v. *Bakke*, not only codified affirmative action in American education but also dramatically displayed the overwhelming backlash against affirmative action brought forward by many white Americans. Some members of this furious group were children of turn-of-the-century immigrants who, ignoring the centuries of racism and favoritism inherent in America's institutions, claimed to have never wronged America's racial minority groups during the time of slavery and conquest. They claimed that they were not responsible for paying the debt for America's offenses during the pre-colonial and colonial eras.

THE CHICANO MOVEMENT

After the variety of successes won by labor leaders César Chávez and Dolores Huerta in the late 1960s, in 1970 a more radical aspect of the Chicano movement emerged and was embodied by the organization *La Raza*. This term literally means "the Race," although colloquially it is synonymous with "the People." *La Raza* explicitly focused on electing Mexican American politicians to office in the West and Southwest. Demonstrating their frustration with the persistent racism that they had confronted throughout their history, members of *La Raza* rejected the name "Mexican American" in favor of the more particular "Chicano," a term derived from barrio slang.

RED POWER

Heartened by African American and Chicano efforts toward social, cultural, and economic equality, many American Indians sought political redress as well. Many Indians

lived at the poverty level, and most Indian reservations had no industry of any kind. The crushing poverty inspired protests. Holding several sit-ins of their own, in 1969 a group of activists called "Indians of All Tribes" occupied Alcatraz Island in San Francisco Bay. Demanding the land be returned to the tribes that had once occupied it, they intended to make an Indian cultural center out of the former prison. The occupation lasted nineteen months; the protesters were finally removed by the federal government, but only after sparking numerous copycat occupations and bringing the plight of AmericanIndians to the attention of the nation.

The protest recalled the pan-Indian resistance of the early 1800s, although in 1970s language. Indeed, the activists boldly declared "Red Power!" echoing Stokely Carmichael's Black Power campaign of the late 1960s. In 1968, a group of Native Americans coordinated the American Indian Movement and began a series of audacious political protests, including occupying the federal Bureau of Indian Affairs building, Mount Rushmore, and Wounded Knee, South Dakota. As with the occupation of Alcatraz, these protests provoked headlines and benefited several moderate groups helping to craft laws in Washington, D.C. They wrote a dozen new laws and steered more than $100 million to educational and health programs on Indian reservations. Furthermore, the number of Americans who identified as Indians more than doubled between 1970 and 1990.

26-4b The Women's Movement

The politics of identity moved beyond racial groups too. Throughout the 1970s, American women continued to press for increased political and economic rights.

ERA AND EQUAL RIGHTS

Throughout the 1970s, women fought against sexual harassment in the workplace and for greater awareness of women's health issues. They also secured congressional approval of the Equal Rights Amendment (ERA) to the U.S. Constitution, which would have made it illegal to discriminate based on sex. Once the Amendment passed Congress, though, it suffered defeat at the state level after grassroots campaigners organized potent protests (as described later in the chapter). The ERA never passed. Nevertheless, in 1972, Congress passed Title IX of the Higher Education Act, which obligated universities to spend the same amount of money on women's athletics that they spent on men's athletics.

ROE V. WADE

The most controversial milestone of the women's movement was a landmark legal case. In 1973, the Supreme Court handed down a decision in **Roe v. Wade** that struck down laws in forty-six states that limited a woman's access to a safe, legal abortion. The decision, which referenced a woman's right to privacy, extending that right to her reproductive system, stunned the opposition, who generally felt abortion was morally equivalent to murder. The debate about abortion has increased the polarization between the left and the right ever since.

SOCIAL AND ECONOMIC PARTICIPATION

In a change perhaps more profound than the debates about laws that delineated women's place in American society, in the 1970s women began to play a more active role in the economy and in forming the parameters of American social life. Like other minority groups, they fomented a social movement that existed outside of normal politics. For instance, consistently struggling against a "glass ceiling" that limited their ability to rise beyond a certain corporate level, in the 1970s women fought for and sometimes won the right to earn pay equal to that of men. Some companies opened day-care centers and job-training programs specifically for working mothers. Beyond economics, the 1970s saw a rise in the use of gender-neutral terms (for instance, using the terms *firefighter* and *flight attendant* in place of *fireman* and *stewardess*).

THE SEXUAL REVOLUTION

Some women also embraced their own sexuality in what was called the sexual revolution. There was a new cultural atmosphere in which women more openly discussed their sexual needs and desires, while sometimes flouting conventional arrangements, such as maintaining a single partner in a traditionally identifiable relationship. Divorce became more common. Breaking such long-standing taboos began a fundamental transformation in American gender relations. The image of the ideal man transitioned from the masculine if inarticulate swashbuckler of the 1940s to the man who was more "in touch with his feelings." Women forthrightly demanded equality in their private as well as their public lives, although in the 1970s, women were not always in agreement as to what exactly that meant.

Courtesy of The Advertising Archives

>> The image of the ideal man transitioned from the masculine if inarticulate swashbuckler of the 1940s to the man who was more "in touch with his feelings."

26-4c The Gay Liberation Movement

Also in the 1970s, gay men and lesbians began to demand equality as people living outside what had been perceived as the heterosexual norm. As barriers against racial and religious minorities collapsed, as women advocated and sometimes won equality, gay men and women still faced considerable legal discrimination. For example, consensual sex between two people of the same sex was illegal in nearly every state.

In 1969, a police raid on the bar at the **Stonewall Inn** in New York City sparked the Gay Liberation Movement. Gay men fought back against the police

Roe v. Wade Supreme Court decision of 1973 that struck down laws in forty-six states that limited a woman's access to a safe, legal abortion

Stonewall Inn Site in New York City of the riots that ignited the Gay Liberation movement in the late 1960s and 1970s; at the time of the riots, all fifty states had antisodomy laws, and police busts of gay bars were routine

New York Daily News Archive/Getty Images

>> A crowd of young men, shown here, attempt to stop a police raid of the popular New York City gay bar, the Stonewall Inn. The police continued their push, leading to a riot in the streets of New York. The Stonewall riot gave spark to the gay rights movement in America, which would become increasingly prominent throughout the remainder of the twentieth century.

raid, proclaiming "Gay Power." The riot propelled many gay men and lesbians into politics and political activism, advocating for legal equality such as marriage rights. In 1977, Harvey Milk, on being elected to the Board of Supervisors in San Francisco, became the first openly gay person to win a major political campaign. He was assassinated shortly thereafter and continues to be an iconic martyr of the gay rights movement.

26-4d High Tide of Environmentalism

Demanding respect for the environment was another facet of 1970s social activism. Launched in 1962 by Rachel Carson's book *Silent Spring*, the environmental movement grew through the 1960s. In 1970, the United States celebrated the first "Earth Day," which stimulated greater awareness of humans' treatment of the land, sea, and air. Vital to 1970s environmentalism was advocacy of preserving unspoiled lands and promoting ecologically sound practices in industry, manufacturing, and automobile use.

Beyond creating valuable awareness, the political record of the environmental movement is mixed. Environmentalists cheered when Richard Nixon

established the Environmental Protection Agency in 1970 and when Congress passed eighteen environmental laws throughout the decade. They rued the construction of the Trans-Alaska Pipeline in 1973, however. Most damning was the sense that, in an era when Americans were searching for belonging, the cause of environmentalism asserted a species-wide identity, something too diffuse and broad to command much allegiance.

26-4e Popular Culture

American popular culture also reflected the broader, inward-focused trend of the 1970s, often in increasingly flashy ways that demonstrated a more complicated morality, where one might feel like cheering for the traditional bad guy. The music of the 1960s icons Sly and the Family Stone, for example, transitioned from celebrating American unity and possibility in the 1960s to being more introspective and aware of the limits of broad social change in the 1970s. In one poignant instance, Sly changed the lyrics of one of his most popular 1960s songs from "Thank You (Falettinme Be Mice Elf Agin)" to, in 1971, "Thank You for Talkin' to Me Africa." In addition to demonstrating the decline of hope for broad social change, the changed lyrics also capture the rise of identity politics, with Sly looking for his roots in Africa rather than the United States.

In the later 1970s, disco music throbbed in America's cities. The 1977 film *Saturday Night Fever* enshrined disco music as a typical "seventies" cultural form, but the film also displayed as its depressing backdrop the decline and plight of American cities of the Northeast. Recently, historians have begun to debate the meaning of disco. Some see it as a reflection of the narcissistic and individualized culture of the 1970s, as people danced largely by themselves and for their own glorification. Others, meanwhile, see disco as a last gasp of the "coming together" attitude of the 1960s, as African American music propelled a Latino dance culture that was open to homosexuals and white ethnics, all in an arena of respect and fulfillment. If the meaning of disco remains open to interpretation, similarly conflicted emotions were reflected in the landmark films of the era, such as *The Godfather*, *The Godfather, Part II*, and *Bonnie and Clyde*, in which viewers were compelled to root for the success and freedom of violent criminals who defy traditional American morals. Thus the moral complexity

>> In *Saturday Night Fever* (1977), John Travolta, shown here, did most of his dancing by himself.

of the period, with its dramatically changing social and economic background, inspired many vibrant contributions to the popular culture that also reflected the era's malaise.

26-5 THE RISE OF THE NEW RIGHT

Perhaps predictably, all of these calls for liberal change led to a combative conservative reaction. This movement, collectively dubbed the "New Right" by the press, utilized the elite intellectual conservatism symbolized by William F. Buckley's *National Review* magazine, which was founded in 1955, and took conservatism to the grassroots. The New Right was largely composed of two groups, social conservatives and economic conservatives. Social conservatives opposed abortion and what they saw as the moral decline of society, while economic conservatives urged tax cuts to limit the size and reach of government. Both types of conservatives continued to urge an aggressive stance against the Soviet Union. Both also strove to diminish government intervention in people's lives. The expansion of the federal state during the Great Society of the 1960s and what conservatives saw as the loosening of laws regarding morality spurred this new coalition to work together, and it would continue to do so for the remainder of the century.

26-5a Economic and Political Conservatism

A key dimension of 1970s conservatism arose in opposition to what were viewed as excessive tax policies in an era of

inflation. If government was deemed corrupt, went the refrain, why should a significant percentage of our income go to taxes? This sentiment was most evident in California, where skyrocketing house prices meant dramatic increases in property taxes. When homeowners could not pay these higher property taxes, they revolted and passed Proposition 13, which limited all further increases on property taxes to 2 percent a year. Within months, nearly three-quarters of other states passed similar laws. The Republican Party capitalized on this populist anger, positioning itself as the antigovernment party.

The state of California had a large economic surplus, so the decline in property taxes there did not immediately limit services. In many other places, however, states could not afford to pay for public schools, road maintenance, or effective fire and police departments. In a familiar theme of the 1970s and 1980s, Americans would have to turn inward—to their communities—to solve these institutional problems. Those cities and towns that could afford a good level of local control thrived; those that could not faced dire straits.

26-5b The Religious Right

Some of the shock troops of the New Right were evangelical Christians, a growing force in the 1970s. These Protestant evangelicals poured their efforts into three things: (1) forming an intense personal relationship with Jesus; (2) gathering converts, usually former mainline or liberal Protestants; and (3) advancing a political agenda that stressed traditional "family values" that countered the women's rights movement and the Gay Liberation movement. This new crop of evangelicals especially targeted feminism and was visibly enraged by the Supreme Court's *Roe* v. *Wade* decision, which has since served as a rallying cry for the entrance of the fundamentalist movement into American politics.

In 1979, conservative Christians led by Rev. Jerry Falwell founded the **Moral Majority** political lobbying group, which, alongside tax-revolting economic conservatives, formed the other arm of the Republican Party. Evangelicals became increasingly visible in popular music and fiction. Seemingly diminished were what had been in the 1950s the

Moral Majority Conservative political organization begun by Rev. Jerry Falwell in 1979 and consisting of evangelical Christians who overwhelmingly supported the Republican Party

paramount religious divisions between mainline Protestants, Catholics, and Jews, surging were new divisions between conservatives and liberals of all faiths, but especially Protestants. Not only did the appearance of a more public aspect of faith reflect the "southernization" of American culture, but it also demonstrated the inward turn that took place in the 1970s, as religion became a realm of division and exclusion rather than one of inclusion and community building.

"FAMILY VALUES"

Predictably, the women's movement served as a touchstone for strong opposition. While many women sought to take advantage of the new opportunities open to them in the 1970s, a substantial percentage wanted to preserve the traditional roles of American womanhood. If securing the right to low-wage work was what the women's movement was about, some of these women thought the cost of equality too high. Others cited biblical passages about a woman's obligation to submit to her husband. Still others saw the women's movement and the sexual revolution as putting traditional families in jeopardy, by encouraging women to focus on themselves rather than their children. Phyllis Schlafly, a conservative activist, headed the opposition by founding STOP ERA to block the Equal Rights Amendment, claiming that the women in NOW were using politics to remedy their personal problems. She also asserted that the women in the women's movement were all lesbians, a mischaracterization intended to capitalize on America's homophobia. But Schlafly's tactics were effective. When she began STOP ERA in 1972, thirty of the necessary thirty-eight states had approved the amendment. After she began her organization, the amendment languished, finally expiring without passage in 1982.

>LOOKING AHEAD . . .

At the end of the 1970s, the dominant news story seemed to come from nowhere, even if it was a perfect symbol of the weaknesses felt by much of the American population. During the final year of Carter's presidency, Islamic militants took control of the American Embassy in Tehran, taking 52 hostages and starting what came to be called the Iranian hostage crisis. The crisis, which lasted 444 days and sparked numerous poorly executed rescue missions, would help propel into office a president who projected a more positive image of the United States and who promised to return America to a perceived greatness of old. But rather than serving as a definitive transition, the election of Ronald Reagan solidified many of the changes that had taken place during the 1970s.

Perhaps most importantly, Reagan symbolized the political conservatism that had gathered strength in the 1970s, and also its anti-government ethos. While projecting the Sunbelt image of a tough individual leader, he argued that government was more of a problem than a solution to society's problems. He paid homage (if usually only that) to minorities whose concerns had come to the forefront of 1970s identity politics, by, for instance, appointing Sandra Day O'Connor as the first female associate justice to the U.S. Supreme Court. Thus, despite Reagan's rhetoric of a new America, the legacy of the 1970s influenced developments for the remainder of the twentieth century. And it is to those decades that we turn next.

STUDY TOOLS 26

READY TO STUDY? IN THE BOOK, YOU CAN:

❑ Rip out the Chapter Review Card, which includes key terms and chapter summaries.

ONLINE AT WWW.CENGAGEBRAIN.COM, YOU CAN:

❑ Collect StudyBits while you read and study the chapter.

❑ Quiz yourself on key concepts.

❑ Find videos for further exploration.

❑ Prepare for tests with HIST5 Flash Cards as well as those you create.

❑ View a collection of Bob Woodward and Carl Bernstein's papers.

❑ Read the text of *Roe* v. *Wade*.

❑ Read a State Department briefing on the status of Chile, 1970.

❑ Hear Nixon's resignation speech.

❑ Learn more about Watergate.

❑ Read a *Saturday Night Live* transcript of Chevy Chase's impression of Gerald Ford.

❑ Read the *Bakke* decision.

❑ See a slide show about the award-winning photo from the Boston busing crisis.

❑ Watch Carter's "crisis of confidence" speech.

1969 Police raid of New York's gay bar Stonewall Inn triggers gay rights movement.

"Indians of All Tribes" occupy Alcatraz as demonstration of Red Power.

1970: *In Southwest, La Raza works to get Chicanos elected to office.*

The Beatles split up.

1971 Nixon stabilizes economy with first ever peacetime wage and price freezes.

Invitation of American table tennis players to China begins "Ping-Pong Diplomacy."

1972 Title IX of Higher Education Act requires equal spending on male and female sports.

Burglars at Democratic headquarters in Watergate Hotel linked to CREEP.

1973 *Roe* v. *Wade* legalizes abortion on grounds of women's right to privacy.

Soviet Union and United States slow arms race with first SALT agreement.

U.S. assistance to Israel in Yom Kippur war triggers oil embargo from Arab nations.

Nixon establishes Environmental Protection Agency.

United States aids in ousting Chile's Salvador Allende and installing General Pinochet.

Trans-Alaska pipeline built.

1974 **August 9:** Threatened with impeachment, President Nixon resigns over Watergate scandal.

Art Fry invents Post-it®-Notes by using a colleague's "failed" adhesive while working at 3M.

1975: Popular Electronics *announces Altair, the first "personal computer."*

1976 Born-again Christian Jimmy Carter defeats Gerald Ford in presidential election.

1977 San Francisco's Harvey Milk, first openly gay man in higher office, is assassinated.

1978 *Regents of the University of California* v. *Bakke* disallows quotas in affirmative-action programs.

Carter negotiates peace between Egypt and Israel in Camp David Accords.

Fiscal conservatives celebrate property tax limits in California's Proposition 13.

1979 Islamic revolutionaries take 52 U.S. embassy staff members hostage.

Meltdown of Pennsylvania's Three-Mile Island reactor discredits nuclear power.

Shortly after signing, SALT II agreement ends with Soviet invasion of Afghanistan.

1980 Moral Majority political action group helps Ronald Reagan win presidency.

27 | Reagan's America

David Paul Morris/Getty Images

LEARNING OBJECTIVES

After reading this chapter, you should be able to do the following:

27-1 Evaluate the domestic policies of Ronald Reagan as president.

27-2 Describe the "culture wars" that plagued the nation during the 1980s.

27-3 Discuss the problems Reagan's successor faced in paying for the "Reagan Revolution."

27-4 Describe the conditions for, and aftermath of, the end of the Cold War.

AFTER FINISHING
THIS CHAPTER
GO TO **PAGE 540**
FOR STUDY TOOLS

The growing conservative movement and its prioritization on the freedoms most valued by conservatives, including opposing New Deal and Great Society fiscal policies and the restoration of what it defined as traditional family values, was given an optimistic face by the actor-turned-politician Ronald Reagan. Born in 1911, Reagan had been a New Deal Democrat and supporter of FDR, but his staunch anticommunism and his sense that the government was growing too large pushed him in a conservative direction beginning in the 1950s and 1960s. A former actor, Reagan never claimed to be a deep thinker, but he was an astute judge of the public mood and an incredibly personable man, with endless anecdotes and a mannerism that made even his political enemies often smile. Thus, Reagan combined his conservative beliefs with the ability to bring those ideas to the public in a nonthreatening way. By advocating tax and budget cuts, he wooed economic conservatives, while his Supreme Court appointees usually made decisions that favored social conservatives. In foreign policy, he adopted strong anticommunist rhetoric and dramatically increased the military budget, even as changes in the Soviet Union diminished the communist threat. He also sought to reinstitute school prayer in public schools and to ban abortions, smilingly harkening America back to what he saw as its more innocent days. More than anybody else, Reagan defined the confident, conservative America of the 1980s.

This was a stark contrast to the uneasy malaise of 1970s America and to Carter's moralistic quests for American austerity. As opposed to Carter requesting Americans to remember to be thrifty and live within their means, Reagan promised it was "morning in America" again, and the way to maintain American greatness was to boost the institutions of capitalism and invest heavily in the nation's defense. In some ways, Reagan symbolized the end of the communal spirit of the 1960s by emphasizing the power and talent of American individuals.

But Reagan's policies came with a cost: his insistence on defending traditional "family values" allowed him to ignore the growing AIDS crisis that emerged in the 1980s, seeing it as disease that affected only the gay community. Equally damningly, he ignored growing disparities in wealth throughout the decade, as the rich got richer and the poor got poorer. Turning a blind eye to these kinds of problems led to a growing and contentious divide between America's social conservatives and its social liberals. During the 1980s, the Democrats aligned more with social liberalism, while the Republicans established themselves as advocates for social conservatism, and the debates between the two parties became increasingly polarized, spurring what many scholars now label a culture war.

This chapter examines Reagan's presidency both at home and abroad and then turns to the internal American social divisions whose political head butting would lead to the contentious political arena that existed during the remainder of the twentieth century and into the twenty-first.

27-1 REAGAN'S DOMESTIC POLITICS

Toward the end of his presidency, Jimmy Carter was beleaguered by the stagnating economy and the Iranian hostage crisis. As an advocate of several of the identity politics movements, Carter also suffered from the mounting white backlash against them. In the 1980 election, Carter struggled to secure his party's nomination, and he emerged from the Democratic Convention severely weakened. He was no match for the charismatic personality of the Republicans' nominee, Ronald Reagan.

Reagan, previously a movie actor and two-term governor of California, not only took advantage of his personal charisma during the election but also took notes from previous presidential elections, which saw the South become increasingly aligned with the Republican Party. The South had been staunchly Democratic since the Civil War (recall that Abraham Lincoln had been the first Republican president), but after a hundred years, starting in the 1960s, the South's political allegiance began to noticeably shift. Partly this emerged in reaction to the civil rights movement, when Democratic Presidents Kennedy and Johnson advocated civil rights laws, angering many white southerners. Partly the South's transition to the Republicans emerged from the fact that the region was becoming increasingly wealthy as more and more corporations moved south to avoid paying the higher taxes of the northern states and skip out on having to work with entrenched labor unions. In what Republicans called the Southern Strategy, Reagan took advantage of the South's political realignment, actively courting southern leaders and making many references to the similarities between his home state of California

◀◀◀ **Throughout the 1980s, Ronald Reagan, depicted here in a piece of art made of his favorite candy, jelly beans, came to symbolize a newly confident America. However, that confidence masked a rise in economic inequality and political polarization, as the freedoms prized most by conservatives battled against those valued most by liberals.**

>> Reagan handled the tasks of the presidency with smiling ease, leading some to see confidence and others to see aloofness.

Second, Reagan made significant cuts in social programs, particularly welfare, food stamps, and unemployment compensation. Strategically, the administration avoided cutting such politically popular programs as Social Security and Medicare.

And third, the administration proposed a massive increase in military spending, equaling $1.2 trillion over a five-year period. Despite using the rhetoric of shrinking the size of the government, Reagan's investment in defense actually caused a tremendous growth in government spending. This, combined with a cut in taxes, led to a dramatic rise in the nation's already growing debt.

The Reagan Revolution sent the economy on a variable course. In 1982, Reagan's cuts initially produced an economic recession; the supposed trickle-down of wealth did not trickle down and the cuts to welfare programs limited the amount of consumer dollars entering the market. By 1984, however, some of the policies, especially the large defense expenditures, sparked an economic recovery, allowing Reagan to coast to an easy reelection in 1984 against Democrats Walter Mondale and his running mate Geraldine Ferraro, the first woman to run on a major party's ticket (and another symbol of the success of the women's movement).

By the late 1980s, however, Reagan's policies had produced the largest peacetime budget deficit in American history, which even conservatives agreed was bad for the economy. The annual deficits had created a ballooning national debt, and it became clear that the supply-side economics of the 1980s did not yield higher tax revenues, but did help shift a greater percentage of wealth to the top of the economic pyramid. In addition, it also assisted a transition that prioritized the interests of finance and real estate over that of industry.

and the South, combining the two in what has come to be called the Sunbelt. Reagan handily won the election, and Republican candidates riding his coattails established a Republican majority in the Senate as well.

27-1a Comfortably Conservative

Reagan synthesized the central themes of the conservative movement. These were defined as (1) an almost religious belief in the power of the free market and (2) a commitment to "traditional values," all under (3) the umbrella of staunch anticommunism. As president, Reagan proposed and had passed three key economic policies, comprising the so-called Reagan Revolution.

First, he cut taxes by 25 percent over a three-year period. Reagan argued that tax cuts would produce new investment, which would, in turn, generate an increase in federal revenues. Rather than have taxpayers send money to support the federal government, he argued, revenues would eventually "trickle down" to the lower classes in the form of more jobs. This argument is known as **supply-side economics**.

supply-side economics Theory that tax cuts would produce new investment, which would, in turn, generate an increase in federal revenues; these revenues would eventually "trickle down" to the lower classes in the form of more jobs

27-1b Deregulation

Reagan also advocated limiting government involvement in business. Following this policy, he deregulated several industries from government control, including airlines and savings and loan institutions (which led to

>> The supposed trickle down of wealth did not trickle down.

iStock.com/Andyd

a mammoth scandal, discussed later in this chapter). He also loosened regulations on air pollution and motor vehicles, actions that allowed corporations to continue polluting and delay installing air bags in cars for several years. He was worried that such regulation would slow economic development.

27-1c Judicial and Administrative Appointments

While Reagan's fiscal policies reflected free-market conservatism, his judicial and administrative appointments appealed to social conservatives. He encouraged conservative positions on issues like abortion, school busing, affirmative action, and prayer in schools. Reagan appointed three conservatives to the Supreme Court, Sandra Day O'Connor (1981), Antonin Scalia (1986), and Anthony Kennedy (1988); he also named William Rehnquist (a Nixon appointee) as chief justice. These appointments did not ensure a conservative victory in every case, as some justices supported more liberal positions than others (especially, it turned out, O'Connor), but they were valuable bricks in the conservative fortress.

27-2 AMERICA IN THE 1980s: POLARIZATION OF THE AMERICAN PUBLIC

The American public has always been divided by wealth, politics, and religion. But in the 1980s these divisions grew more prominently in American society and in American politics. There were logical reasons for this. Throughout the decade the wealthier amassed increased wealth, and the poor slipped further into trouble. Also during the decade, and perhaps more importantly, the New Right emerged as an organized right-wing lobbying group. Their stress on "family values," moral issues, and popular culture challenged those who had supported the new direction of social justice advocated in the 1960s and 1970s.

27-2a Divisions in Wealth

Reagan's tax cuts and his cuts to social welfare programs affected different groups of Americans differently. The policies clearly favored the wealthy. Their taxes dropped, and they benefited the most from Reagan's business-friendly policies, including deregulation of big industries. The number of American billionaires grew from just one in 1978 to forty-nine in 1987. The number of Americans earning more than $500,000 increased by a factor of ten. On the other side of the scale, the poor were becoming poorer. The percentage of Americans living below the poverty line increased dramatically during Reagan's first term.

More transformative, however, were the effects on the middle class, which during the 1980s began to capture an increasingly smaller percentage of the nation's wealth. During Reagan's years in office, the wealthiest 1 percent of Americans earned more than 40 percent of the nation's wealth, a threefold increase over the previous two decades. The bottom 90 percent of earners, meanwhile, earned slightly more than 20 percent of the nation's wealth in the 1980s, nearly a threefold decrease from the 1960s. Reagan's social welfare cuts and the decline of middle-class industrial jobs had taken their toll (see Figure 27.1).

It became increasingly apparent that this inequality was afflicting various racial groups differently. While the black middle class was in fact growing, and while the majority of impoverished Americans were white, the proportion of poor people *as a percentage of their race* indicated that people of color were vastly overrepresented below the poverty line. The African Americans, Puerto Ricans, and Latinos who had moved to the northern cities after World War II had been hurt by the departure of large manufacturers. These manufacturers had moved either to the South or the West, where labor unions were less powerful or, increasingly during the 1980s, abroad, where businesses could find cheap labor and pay fewer taxes. While 1950s America was characterized by a robust and growing population of middle-class Americans, the 1980s highlighted a reemergence of economic disparities that had been absent since the 1920s.

THE RISE OF JAPAN AND THE AMERICAN TRADE DEFICIT

These economic problems were compounded by the rise of Japan as an economic power. Partly as a result of a deliberate American policy to build up a major East

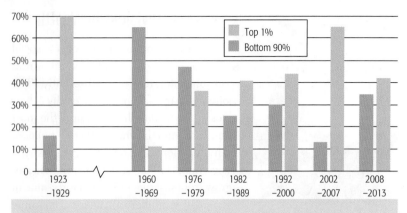

Figure 27.1 Decline of the Middle Class, Share of Income Gains

>> Deregulation, new tax policies, and deindustrialization have all contributed to the decline of the middle class since the 1960s.

Source: CBPP calculations based on data from Piketty and Saez

Asian ally after China became a communist country in 1949, Japan became the world's first fully modernized non-Western country during the second half of the twentieth century. Japan's economic "arrival" became

>> The economic rise of Japan in the 1980s led many Americans to wonder if their nation's days as a superpower were numbered. Hollywood picked up this theme in the 1986 film *Gung Ho*, which portrayed the Japanese takeover of a failed American auto plant.

trade deficit Inequality in trade whereby one country's exports to another outweigh the second country's exports to the first country

plainly evident during a time when the American economy was showing signs of weakness following the end of the postwar boom. The United States developed a growing **trade deficit** with Japan, which meant that Japan was now successfully exporting products such as cars, steel, and consumer electronics to the United States, while the Japanese were buying fewer and fewer American goods. As a result, American congressmen began to press for an increase in import tariffs on Japanese goods. But these efforts hardly stemmed the flood. Just as the economic muscle of oil-exporting countries had humbled the United States in the 1970s, the rise of Japan led many Americans to wonder if their nation's days as an economic superpower were numbered.

27-2b Continued Crisis in the Cities

These economic crises, combined with the demise of many social welfare programs, led to the continued breakdown of many American cities. While cities had always been portrayed as dangerous places, by the 1980s the growth of the suburbs, the departure of social organizations and industries, and the subsequent decline in tax revenues had solidified that image. Many major cities became symbols of decay, poverty, and racial disparity. Accelerating the decay, a cheaper form of cocaine called "crack" appeared in the mid-1980s. This drug was highly addictive, and its use spread rapidly throughout many inner cities. Meanwhile, inner-city youth seeking identity and security increasingly turned to gangs. Gang violence escalated throughout the decade, leading in some cities to an average of one gang murder per day.

Perhaps due to racism, perhaps due to fear, lawmakers instituted harsh penalties for crimes committed in the inner cities. Possession of small amounts of crack cocaine, for instance, merited a punishment equal to that for owning much larger amounts of cocaine, the more expensive version of the same drug. As these penalties increased, so did the American prison system, which was disproportionately populated by racial minorities from cities. In addition to building prisons, the Reagan administration addressed the growing drug problem with a public relations campaign entitled "Just Say No." Nancy Reagan, the First Lady, spearheaded the campaign, and she got many celebrities to join in. Critics claimed that the campaign was nothing more than hollow rhetoric that missed the underlying provocations that drove drug use. The causes of the urban crisis are complex and were decades in the making, but politicians seemed both uneager and unable to rectify the most central problems.

27-2c Culture Wars

While a transformation in the distribution of wealth led to one significant division in American life, another emerged in the realm of culture. On the one hand, beginning in the 1980s, inner-city youth fully embraced a new style of music called hip hop or rap. Often featuring poetic rhymes and beatbox music, rap musicians told stories of inner-city plight, of often violent searches for manhood, and of casual escapism that sometimes scandalized mainstream culture. Artists like Grandmaster Flash, Run-D.M.C., Slick Rick, and LL Cool J honed the music into a formative player in the American music scene, and by the later 1980s, the music was receiving both accolades and scorn. And just as jazz had done in the 1920s, rap music's tone of protest and sexualized masculinity drew adherents from well beyond the sources from which it derived, most readily white suburbanites with the purchasing power to sustain rap's growth. Hip hop culture spread well beyond its inner-city origins, and it articulated a vision of America that was racially and ethnically diverse, as well as unkind and ungenerous to the have-nots.

In an almost polar opposite fashion, white conservatives sought to reshape the image of the nation in another direction. With leaders like Pat Robertson, James Dobson, and Jerry Falwell, evangelical Christians made up the bulk of the proponents of the New Right, while conservative radio personalities like Rush Limbaugh fueled the movement and stoked the belief that the United States had become unmoored from its Christian principles. With some success, they protested what they saw as the sexual licentiousness on television, the general permissiveness of American secular society, the emphasis on relativism and pluralism in America's educational system, and the liberties with which the courts had interpreted the privacy clause of the Constitution, especially regarding a woman's right to have an abortion.

Although Reagan only tacitly endorsed the New Right, he did make appearances with its leaders, giving the movement mainstream leverage. They made headlines when they fought to have textbooks remove evolutionary theory from their pages, arguing that evolution contradicted a biblical explanation for the origins of the world. They similarly struggled to remove sex education from public schools, as well as works of literature that they perceived to be overly sexual in nature. Because many of these battles were fought at the level of local school boards, the so-called culture wars were felt deeply in the heart of America.

The rise of the New Right stimulated the formation of a left-wing opposition. Political liberals founded organizations like People for the American Way (1981) and older groups like the American Civil Liberties Union revamped and actively lobbied against the policies of the New Right. They presented a full agenda based on separation of church and state, individual privacy laws, and expanded systems of social welfare.

>> "I was making close to $2,000 a week selling weed when I decided to join the Unknown Vice Lords. Doing so allowed me to expand my drug-selling territory. Life seemed great."—Jeremiah, teen gang member. "Or so said Jeremiah," explaining the appeal of joining a gang when almost all other options in America's cities seemed foreclosed.

27-2d AIDS

Along with increasing divisions in wealth and the culture wars, a third social crisis emerged in the 1980s,

I HOPE HE DOESN'T HAVE AIDS!

I HOPE SHE DOESN'T HAVE AIDS!

YOU CAN'T LIVE ON HOPE.

Image courtesy of The Advertising Archives

REPRINTED WITH PERMISSION OF SAATCHI & SAATCHI COMPTON, INC.

>> During the eighties, state departments of public health wielded the power of advertising in a massive effort to educate the public and prevent the spread of AIDS. The federal government opted not to, with Reagan himself ordering his surgeon general to refrain from discussing the disease publicly.

this one deadly. Acquired immune deficiency syndrome (AIDS) is a deadly disease that attacks a person's immune system, the system that powers a person's body to fight other diseases. AIDS is spread through transmission of bodily fluids, most especially by blood or semen. Because it compromises the immune system, it leaves the body vulnerable to other diseases. When undiagnosed or untreated, AIDS is deadly.

AIDS was first detected in the United States in 1981, and by 1988 more than 57,000 cases had been diagnosed. But throughout the 1980s, no one knew quite what it was; its etiology remained a mystery. More troubling, because in America the disease was initially detected in homosexual men, many Americans were leery to respond, thinking it was simply a disease contained

"Read my lips: no new taxes."

—George H. W. Bush, 1988 Republican National Convention, uttering a sentence that would come back to haunt him during his 1992 bid for reelection

within one American community. Demonstrating the levels of homophobia that existed in the 1980s, politicians were incredibly slow to respond to the epidemic because it affected people they felt they could safely ignore without political ramifications. Reagan himself ordered his surgeon general, the leading spokesperson of matters of public health in the federal government, to refrain from discussing the AIDS crisis publicly, dismissing it as only a gay disease and thereby limiting federal funds for research on the disease and aid to those who suffered from it. But it quickly became apparent that, in places like Haiti and Africa, AIDS had spread beyond the gay community and was a disease that had little to do with one's sexual preference. When basketball star Earvin "Magic" Johnson announced in 1991 that he had contracted AIDS despite being heterosexual, he helped transform the perception of the disease beyond one that simply impacts the gay community. Safe-sex education and heightened awareness of the disease have curbed the runaway epidemic of AIDS in the United States, but it is still a key concern of American society, and it certainly roiled the veneer of confidence and prosperity in Reagan's America, while at the same time putting on dramatic display the nation's continued homophobia.

27-3 PAYING FOR THE REAGAN REVOLUTION

Despite Reagan's upbeat image, his "revolution" and the cultural and economic divides that it seemed to exacerbate had immense costs that were borne by his successors.

27-3a The 1988 Election

Reagan's vice president, George H. W. Bush, emphasized Reagan-style conservatism as he campaigned for president in 1988. In the campaign, he portrayed Democratic candidate Massachusetts Governor Michael Dukakis as a big-government liberal who supported high taxes and who was too soft on crime. Bush ran ads describing an African American Massachusetts prison inmate named Willie Horton who, released by Dukakis on a temporary furlough, kidnapped a Maryland couple and raped the woman. Whereas liberals in the 1960s had been able to scare the public with ads playing on fears of nuclear war, Bush turned *liberal* into a derogatory term that implied a connection between Democratic policies and social disorder.

>> George H.W. Bush, pictured here, won the 1988 election by a comfortable margin, but was left to pay for the Reagan Revolution, including by raising taxes.

the weaker companies to make them profitable or eliminating them altogether. In the business world, this forced companies to streamline production and remain competitive.

Some S&L investors, however, were less successful in their investments, leading to waves of layoffs, companies burdened with huge debt, and overly consolidated industries. When several of these high-risk deals went sour, millions of Americans lost their savings. President Bush orchestrated a program to allow depositors to recoup their lost savings, but this plan came with a price tag of nearly $500 million for Americans. American taxpayers were paying the price of bank deregulation.

Elected by a comfortable margin, Bush continued many of Reagan's social and economic policies. In appointing a very conservative justice, Clarence Thomas, to the Supreme Court, Bush increased the conservative majority on the Court. But his economic policies were not as successful. Indeed, in both domestic and international affairs, Bush struggled to manage several of the long-term problems that Reagan's policies had created. He was stuck paying for the Reagan Revolution.

27-3b Bush's Domestic Policies

Bush's first hurdle was cleaning up a savings and loan scandal produced by Reagan's attempt to deregulate that industry.

THE S&L CRISIS

Unbridled from government oversight, large numbers of savings and loans (S&Ls) emerged to compete with banks as depositories of people's money. But instead of securing that money, S&Ls invested people's deposits in shady real estate deals, bonds of dubious reliability, and other high-risk investments. Some of these high-risk investments were successful: large companies used the money to buy up weaker competitors, using their debt as a tax write-off and downsizing

NO NEW TAXES?

The combination of Reagan's increased military spending, his tax cuts, and the payouts to rectify his deregulation created a huge national debt. During his election campaign, Bush tried to maintain Reagan's optimistic demeanor and promised the American people that he would not raise taxes. It was, he argued, still morning in America. This promise became untenable by 1990. That year, Bush proposed and passed a budget that raised taxes and cut defense spending, because maintaining high outlays without recouping money via taxes was deemed dangerous federal policy. Politically, however, the move was a disaster for Bush. Reneging on his word about raising taxes would, in 1992, cost him his bid for reelection. Even worse, raising taxes and cutting defense spending did little to forestall a serious recession. It was too little, too late.

RECESSION

By 1990, unemployment had risen to 7 percent, and companies were regularly downsizing. The number of impoverished Americans rose by 2 million, and the cost of operating with a huge national debt was becoming apparent. Incredibly, Bush failed to respond immediately. He eventually proposed tax credits and a middle-class tax cut, but these proposals came much too late to stem a recession.

27-4 FOREIGN RELATIONS UNDER REAGAN-BUSH

During their time in office, both Reagan and Bush supported an active, interventionist foreign policy. This was disastrous for balancing America's budget, but it did help end the Cold War, albeit in ways that even Reagan himself didn't predict.

27-4a The End of the Cold War Era

When he first entered office, Reagan took a hard line with the Soviet Union, provocatively portraying it as an "evil empire." He also began various new weapons programs that, in an effort to keep up in the so-called arms race, helped lead to the economic collapse of the Soviet Union.

STAR WARS

Among the many ways Reagan expanded the Cold War to, the bluntest was to increase the number of American weapons, reigniting the arms race that had slowed through the 1970s. Reagan revived military programs Carter had cut. He dismissed overtures from the Soviet leader, Yuri Andropov, to cut back certain missiles if the United States would refrain from deploying intermediate-range missiles of its own in Europe. Reagan also proposed building new defensive weapons capable of "rendering . . . nuclear weapons impotent" by zapping them from space. This "Strategic Defense Initiative" or

SDI (denigrated by critics as "star wars") violated the 1972 ABM Treaty, which forbade defensive systems capable of covering either the entire United States or the Soviet Union. Andropov and other Soviet leaders saw SDI as a rejection of arms control overtures in favor of a new quest for global supremacy.

Reagan may have been betting that the Soviet Union could not afford to keep up. After all, in August 1980, shipworkers in Poland staged a series of strikes that led to the formation of Solidarity, the first independent labor union in a communist-controlled country. The union's launch sparked a wave of sympathy strikes and indicated that the Soviet Union was having problems maintaining its empire.

PERESTROIKA

Relations between Reagan and the Soviets softened during Reagan's second term. The chief impetus for change was the arrival of a new Soviet premier, Mikhail Gorbachev. Gorbachev was a reformer eager to restructure the Soviet economy (the Russian word for "restructuring" is *perestroika*, a catchphrase of the 1980s and 1990s). He was also in favor of softening the opposition between the West and the East (the Russian word for "openness" is *glasnost*, another catchphrase of the era). Gorbachev was keenly aware of the exceptional costs of Reagan's burgeoning arms race, and he sought to rectify the Soviet Union's financial problems by slowing the nuclear buildup. In 1987, the two leaders—Reagan and Gorbachev—agreed to eliminate thousands of intermediate-range missiles in the Intermediate Nuclear

Courtesy Ronald Reagan Presidential Library

>> President Reagan developed a solid partnership with the Soviet Premier Mikhail Gorbachev, leading to several breakthrough summits and the opening of the Soviet nations to some Western goods. It wasn't all good will, though: the Soviet Union was in fact going broke. Here they are pictured at a plenary meeting at the Soviet Mission during the Geneva Summit.

>> The end of the Cold War shifted the focus of American diplomatic interests, with no area deemed more important than the Middle East. Here, the American flag flies next to a sign for Kuwait City, which American troops had just liberated from Iraq.

Forces (INF) Treaty. Gorbachev then removed troops from Afghanistan, signaling Russia's willingness (and financial need) to stop actively promoting the spread of communism around the world, one of the key fears coloring the American understanding of the Cold War. With the Soviet Union's removal from Afghanistan, the American-supported Mujahideen took control, and the Mujahideen's inability to control the war-ravaged nation led to the rise of the Taliban, something that would have deadly ramifications for the United States in 2001. But by the late 1980s, it was clear the United States had the upper hand in the Cold War.

THE MIDDLE EAST

In addition to the delicate relations with the Soviet Union, the United States experienced several complicated new foreign policy problems throughout the 1980s. Its most complex international relations involved the Middle East. There, an attack in Lebanon, the country immediately north of Israel, was the initial flashpoint. Lebanon had been torn apart since 1975 by a civil war between Muslims and Christians, and the small country had been turned into a battlefield by the foreign armies of Syria, the Palestine Liberation Organization, and Israel. Fearing the presence of troops from Soviet-friendly Syria so close to Israel, the United States sent peacekeeping forces to Lebanon in August 1982. The

Hezbollah terrorist organization viewed U.S. peacekeepers as targets and kidnapped a number of American educators and missionaries. The worst blow came in October 1983, when Hezbollah terrorists attacked the barracks of U.S. peacekeepers in Beirut; a single suicide bomber driving a truck filled with explosives killed 241 servicepeople.

Of course, much of the U.S. interest in the Middle East centered on oil. Americans had become increasingly dependent on the energy source during the second half of the twentieth century. When America's oil supplies were repeatedly threatened throughout the 1970s and 1980s, the United States took military or diplomatic action. In 1980, for instance, Iraq, a militarily powerful oil-producing Arab state at the head of the Persian Gulf, attacked its neighbor Iran in an attempt to secure control of local waterways. The United States, the Soviet Union, and other Arab states in the region supported Iraqi dictator Saddam Hussein in his fight against Iran's militant Islamic republic. When Iran struck back against Iraq and its allies by firing missiles at their oil tankers, the United States responded by reflagging Kuwaiti tankers with American colors, bringing them under the defensive umbrella of the U.S. Navy. The threat of direct American military force reinforced the idea that the free passage of oil traffic was a key national interest. It also signaled deeper American involvement in the Middle East. Whereas from the 1950s to the 1970s, American involvement in the Middle East was mostly covert, from the 1980s onward, this was less and less the case.

THE IRAN-CONTRA AFFAIR

America's Cold War focus on keeping left-wing governments out of Latin America and Reagan's desire to guard American interests in the Middle East converged in the Iran-Contra affair. In 1985, at the urging of Israel, the United States sold weapons to Iran for use in its war with Iraq, which Israel viewed as its most dangerous enemy in the region. Reagan did this despite an embargo against Iran (imposed after the 1979 hostage crisis) and the fact that Iran was an avowed enemy; indeed, the United States was at the same time offering support to Iran's enemy, Iraq. It sold weapons to Iran because top officials in the Reagan

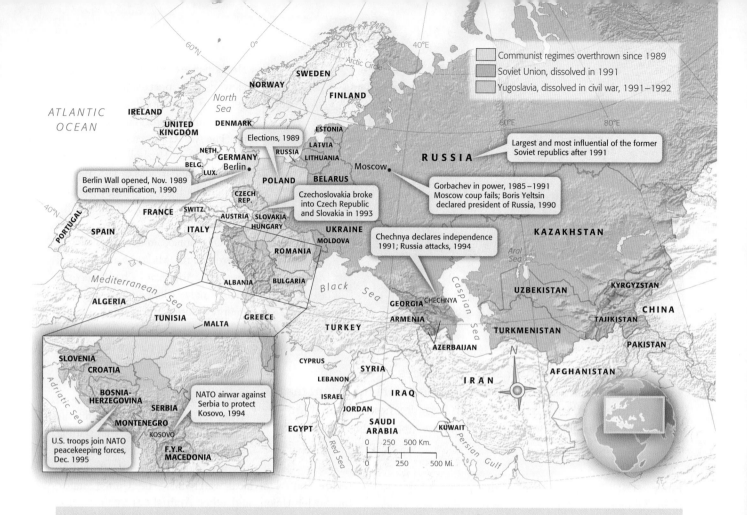

Communist regimes overthrown since 1989
Soviet Union, dissolved in 1991
Yugoslavia, dissolved in civil war, 1991–1992

Berlin Wall opened, Nov. 1989
German reunification, 1990

Elections, 1989

Czechoslovakia broke into Czech Republic and Slovakia in 1993

Largest and most influential of the former Soviet republics after 1991

Gorbachev in power, 1985–1991
Moscow coup fails; Boris Yeltsin declared president of Russia, 1990

Chechnya declares independence 1991; Russia attacks, 1994

NATO airwar against Serbia to protect Kosovo, 1994

U.S. troops join NATO peacekeeping forces, Dec. 1995

Map 27.1 The End of the Cold War

>> As this map shows, beginning in 1989, several Soviet-controlled countries became free of the Soviet Union, ultimately leading to the end of the Soviet Union altogether.

administration hoped that doing so would ease relations between the United States and that oil-rich nation.

More damning, however, was the discovery that members of Reagan's administration took profits from the sale of arms to Iran and sent the money to a right-wing guerrilla group in Nicaragua called the **contras**, who were battling the left-wing government. It was never proven that Reagan was aware that the Iran arms sale funds had been diverted to the *contras*, but the nationally televised testimony of Lieutenant Colonel Oliver North demonstrated that Reagan had not sufficiently controlled members of his own administration. Cold War imperatives were, and had been since 1946, causing rifts in American diplomatic circles, and Reagan's

contras Right-wing Nicaraguan guerrilla group during the 1980s

administration was not above the law when it came to executing American foreign policy.

THE COLLAPSE OF THE SOVIET UNION

By the late 1980s, the *perestroika* and *glasnost* initiated by Soviet premier Gorbachev had begun to blossom. Inspired by their exposure to capitalism, Western popular culture, and the loosened Soviet controls allowed by Gorbachev, in 1989, Poland, Hungary, and Czechoslovakia, then Bulgaria and Romania, all overthrew their communist regimes. In November 1989, the Berlin Wall came down. In 1990, Latvia, Lithuania, and Estonia all declared their independence. In 1991, the once-mighty Soviet Union petered out, collapsing into a number of independent states—Russia, Ukraine, and many others (see Map 27.1). The USSR was no longer.

This meant that the United States had won the Cold War. Or, more realistically, that the Soviet Union had lost it. In the early 1990s, it quickly became apparent that Gorbachev's motives for *perestroika* were financial: the Soviet Union simply could not afford to maintain the huge military presence needed to keep its buffer states under control. Historians still debate the role of the United States in the demise of the USSR, with some saying America's sometime hardline approach actually prolonged the Cold War by giving political cover to Soviet leaders who would rather talk about the evils of the United States than poverty and hunger at home. Others argue that the policy of containment, first articulated in 1946 and lasting through the presidency of George H. W. Bush, had succeeded in keeping communism from conquering and dominating the world and that capitalism had clearly triumphed over Soviet-style communism. Regardless, the end of the Cold War led to a reduction of nuclear weapons by both the United States and the former Soviet Union, although many weapons still exist. It also allowed the United States to station fewer troops in Europe. To understand why the Soviet Union collapsed, see "The Reasons Why . . ." box.

27-4b Other Foreign Affairs

With the dissolution of the Soviet Union, several small, brutal wars emerged as people fought for control of their now-independent nations. Nowhere was this more troubling than in Bosnia-Herzegovina, a part of the former Yugoslavia. There the various factions engaged in

The Reasons Why...

There were several reasons why the Soviet Union dissolved in 1991:

Containment and the arms race. Since 1946, the policy of the United States had been to contain communism where it was and fight any efforts to spread it beyond the Soviet Union. This policy had been incredibly divisive in the United States, leading to several wars (both declared and undeclared), violent protests, and vast expenditures on military supplies and nuclear weapons. But it had succeeded in checking the expansion of communism in various parts of the world, including Latin America. More importantly, it also had forced the Soviet Union to spend vast amounts of money fighting wars around the world and maintaining a huge nuclear arsenal.

Widespread poverty. By the 1970s and 1980s, the draconian leadership of the Soviet Union and its overly centralized economic planning had led the countries of the Eastern bloc to lag behind the countries of the West, some of which had enjoyed technological advances absent in Soviet-controlled nations. In Poland, for instance, more than 60 percent of the population lived in poverty throughout the 1980s, while the people of Western Germany were faring significantly better. This led to protests in many of the countries of the Soviet Union, protests that were expensive to contain and defeat.

Gorbachev's policies. By the middle 1980s, it became clear to many in the Soviet Union that it was nearing bankruptcy and could not afford to keep fighting the Cold War or to maintain strict controls over its subordinate nations. In 1985, the Soviet premier Mikhail Gorbachev began a series of initiatives, called "glasnost" (openness) and "perestroika" (restructuring), aimed at softening relations with the United States, and perhaps ending the Cold War. This, of course, would also keep down the cost of the arms race. He also later tacitly invited the nations of the Eastern bloc to secede, suggesting the Soviet Union would not punish them for doing so.

The defections of 1989. In 1989, several Eastern bloc nations simply declared their independence from the Soviet Union. Poland, Hungary, and Czechoslovakia departed first, then Bulgaria and Romania. Only in Romania was there any resistance. In the other countries, the Soviet-backed communists simply stepped down. The most dramatic moment occurred in November 1989, when the Berlin Wall was destroyed in a public protest against Soviet rule and the Cold War more generally. By 1991, there were only a handful of nations left in the Soviet Union, and the union formally dissolved. Not all communist countries fell, however. Protests in 1989 in China were rebuffed, and the communist government there still retains control.

>> In November 1989, the Berlin Wall came down. The event became a key symbol of the fall of communism and, ever since, has continued to be a touchstone in the struggle for increased freedoms around the world.

to the demise of the Soviet empire and the rise of several brutal nationalist wars, but in China, the Communist Party still exerted considerable control.

THE PERSIAN GULF WAR

The Middle East was another foreign policy crisis point. In 1988, the war between Iran and Iraq ended without a clear victor. The United States had actively supported the Iraqi dictator Saddam Hussein throughout the struggle, despite selling arms to Iran in the Iran-Contra affair of 1985. In 1990, Hussein attempted to reestablish Iraq's control of the Middle East and ease some of his war debt by taking over the tiny oil-rich neighboring country of Kuwait. Bush feared that Hussein might use this as a base to threaten American oil supplies, and he responded by condemning the action and organizing a broad coalition of nations (including several Middle Eastern nations) in an embargo against Iraq. He set a deadline for Iraq to remove its troops from Kuwait and threatened to use the coalition to fight him if necessary.

In this game of brinksmanship, Hussein did not blink, and in January 1991, the Persian Gulf War began

ethnic cleansing, defined as the complete expulsion of an entire ethnic population from a particular area. With the Soviet Union no longer serving as watchful overlord, several nationalist movements clashed in civil wars throughout central and eastern Europe.

TIANANMEN SQUARE

Meanwhile, in June 1989, several spontaneous prodemocracy rallies in China coalesced in Beijing's Tiananmen Square. The Communist Chinese government used force to end the rallies, killing at least several hundred of the student activists. This action strained U.S.–China relations and demonstrated that even as some governments were willing to liberalize their policies in certain arenas, such as economics, they would obstinately oppose any movement toward ceding political power. Communism as practiced in the USSR may have failed, leading

ethnic cleansing Complete expulsion of an entire ethnic population from a particular area

>> Vietnam was the first televised war, but the Gulf War was the first to be televised live.

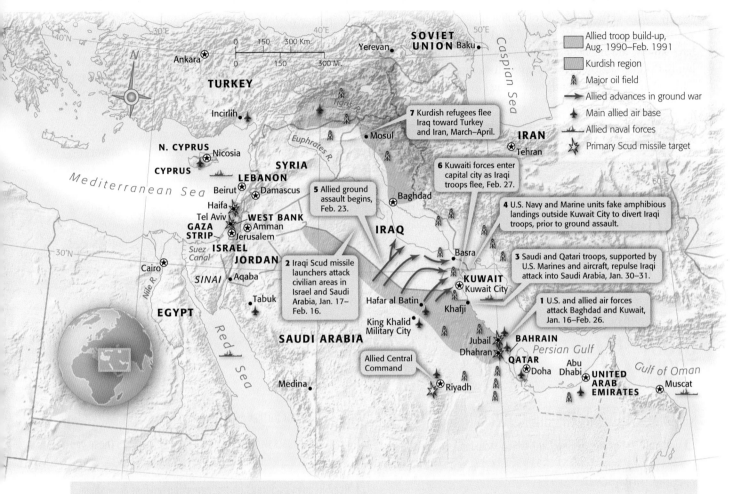

Map 27.2 **The Persian Gulf War**

>> A map of the Middle East, showing the stages of war in the Persian Gulf in 1991.

Legend:
- Allied troop build-up, Aug. 1990–Feb. 1991
- Kurdish region
- Major oil field
- Allied advances in ground war
- Main allied air base
- Allied naval forces
- Primary Scud missile target

7 Kurdish refugees flee Iraq toward Turkey and Iran, March–April.

6 Kuwaiti forces enter capital city as Iraqi troops flee, Feb. 27.

5 Allied ground assault begins, Feb. 23.

4 U.S. Navy and Marine units fake amphibious landings outside Kuwait City to divert Iraqi troops, prior to ground assault.

3 Saudi and Qatari troops, supported by U.S. Marines and aircraft, repulse Iraqi attack into Saudi Arabia, Jan. 30–31.

2 Iraqi Scud missile launchers attack civilian areas in Israel and Saudi Arabia, Jan. 17–Feb. 16.

1 U.S. and allied air forces attack Baghdad and Kuwait, Jan. 16–Feb. 26.

Allied Central Command

(see Map 27.2). It was more of a rout than a war: 40,000 Iraqis were killed, compared to 240 coalition troops. Hussein's attempt to attack Israel and break up the coalition aligned against him failed after U.S. antiballistic missiles destroyed the bombs headed for Israel. Hussein had played his last card, and once the ground war began in earnest, in late February 1991, the war was over within days. Covered by satellite television and twenty-four-hour television news networks—both relatively new developments—Americans and the world watched from cameras in Baghdad hotels as missiles dropped and ground troops advanced. Vietnam was the first televised war, but the Gulf War was the first to be televised live.

In the end, Iraq quickly gave up Kuwait. Bush decided not to invade Iraq and remove Hussein because such an action would have destroyed the coalition he had amassed and also because he did not know who would succeed Hussein. This decision left certain factions in Iraq vulnerable to Hussein's harsh regime, including the ethnic Kurdish minority in northern Iraq and the **Shia Muslims** in the south, both of whom were hated by Hussein's **Sunni Muslim** base. The Sunni–Shia split within Islam dates back to the death of Islam's founder, the Prophet Mohammad, and concerns not only a battle

Sunni Muslims A branch of Islam containing the vast majority of the world's Muslims, who follow closely the teachings of the Prophet Mohammed and who have codified his teachings in Islamic law

Shia Muslims A branch of Islam containing a minority of the world's Muslims, who believe clerics have offered ongoing interpretations of Islamic texts

over who was the rightful heir to Mohammad but also certain religious principles. Historically, Sunnis have more strictly followed the teachings of Mohammad, while Shias see their leaders as reflections of God on earth. Sunnis have almost always been in the overwhelming majority, but both sides see the other as apostates sullying the true faith, which has led to continued conflict in the region.

>LOOKING AHEAD...

When the war in the Persian Gulf ended in 1991, President Bush enjoyed strong support. His approval rating soared to a record-breaking 91 percent. But the weak American economy kept plaguing him.

Nevertheless, two historic transitions marked the years between 1980 and 1992. First was the increasing division between the country's haves and have-nots. Appeased by the friendly face of Ronald Reagan, large numbers of Americans lost interest in supporting the broad social welfare programs of the New Deal and the Great Society, favoring smaller government instead. One result of the decline of the social safety net was an increase in disparities of wealth.

The second historic transition of the era was the end of the Cold War, which terminated the fifty-year struggle between the United States and the Soviet Union. With the conclusion of the Cold War, the world became a more open, accessible place, and this development, sometimes called globalization, would be a key part of the world economy that would shape the 1990s.

STUDY TOOLS 27

READY TO STUDY? IN THE BOOK, YOU CAN:

❏ Rip out the Chapter Review Card, which includes key terms and chapter summaries.

ONLINE AT WWW.CENGAGEBRAIN.COM, YOU CAN:

❏ Collect StudyBits while you read and study the chapter.

❏ Quiz yourself on key concepts.

❏ Find videos for further exploration.

❏ Prepare for tests with HIST5 Flash Cards as well as those you create.

❏ Read Reagan's address on the campaign against drug abuse.

❏ Read an article discussing income disparities.

❏ Hear Reagan's "Evil Empire" speech.

❏ See a timeline of events about the S&L crisis.

CH27 TIMELINE

What Else Was Happening

▶ 1980	Ronald Reagan defeats Democrat Jimmy Carter in presidential election.	*Polish "Solidarity" becomes first independent labor union in Communist bloc.* *Iraq attacks Iran.*

1981 Reagan appoints Sandra Day O'Connor to U.S. Supreme Court.

1982: Reagan's spending cuts trigger recession.

August: *United States sends peacekeeping forces to Lebanon.*

PacMan is named Time *magazine's Man of the Year.*

1983 Reagan's Strategic Defense Initiative (SDI) violates treaty with Soviet Union.

October: Hezbollah suicide bomber attacks U.S. barracks in Beirut, killing 241 servicepeople.

1984 Democrat Geraldine Ferraro is first female vice-presidential candidate in U.S. history.

Military spending boosts economy, aiding Reagan's reelection.

1985 Deregulation leads to high-risk deals and failures of savings and loans.

Arms sales to Iran finance right-wing guerrillas in Nicaragua in Iran-Contra affair.

1986 Reagan appoints Antonin Scalia to U.S. Supreme Court.

Mikhail Gorbachev and Reagan reduce arms in INF Treaty.

Tom Cruise stars in Top Gun.

1988 George H. W. Bush defeats Michael Dukakis in presidential election.

1989: June: *Chinese forces quell prodemocracy protests in Beijing's Tiananmen Square.*

November: *East Germans bring down Berlin Wall, leading to German reunification in 1991.*

1990 National debt forces Bush to raise taxes, despite promise of "no new taxes."

Latvia, Lithuania, and Estonia declare independence from Soviet Union.

Former U.S. ally Saddam Hussein invades Kuwait.

Children's classic My Friend Flicka *is pulled from the optional reading lists for fifth- and sixth-graders in Clay County, Florida, because the book reportedly uses objectionable language.*

1991 Persian Gulf War for liberation of Kuwait kills 40,000 Iraqis and 240 allied troops.

December: End of Soviet Union.

28 | America in the Information Age

Carlos Amarillo/Shutterstock.com

LEARNING OBJECTIVES

After reading this chapter, you should be able to do the following:

28-1 Evaluate the presidency of Bill Clinton, discussing how he tried to cultivate a middle ground between affirming globalization and assuaging the needs of the disaffected.

28-2 Discuss the technological revolution that took place in the 1990s, and describe the social and economic changes that took place as a result of this revolution.

28-3 Discuss the new focus on multiculturalism during the latter part of the twentieth century.

28-4 Explain the kinds of homegrown terrorism that shocked many Americans in the 1990s.

28-5 Describe how the political, cultural, and economic polarization of the nation came to a head in the presidential election of 2000.

AFTER FINISHING THIS CHAPTER GO TO **PAGE 556** **FOR STUDY TOOLS**

America since 1992 has been shaped by three forces: (1) the rise of new information technologies, such as personal computers and the Internet, which have powered increased and inexpensive communications throughout America and the world; (2) a commitment to reducing trade restrictions between nations, which, aided by the rise of new information technologies, has made national boundaries seem less significant, a phenomenon labeled "globalization"; and (3) the perpetuation of the political divide between the right and the left, as battles over affirmative action, multiculturalism, abortion, homosexuality, and gender roles have continued into the new century.

All these developments have had their share of critics from both the right and the left. Globalization has been criticized for limiting the capacity of American industry to recover since its decline in the 1970s and for exporting Western values to non-Western nations. Multiculturalism has been contested because of increased immigration from Latin America, especially Mexico, which has considerably changed the ethnic makeup of the United States. And the culture wars have provoked critics to complain that debates about cultural issues have gotten in the way of concern about important economic issues. And yet, these three changes, in various ways, helped transform the American economy throughout the 1990s, as it changed from an economy mostly premised on industrial and manufacturing output to one based on service and information technology.

In addition to reducing trade barriers, America's international agenda during the 1990s focused on confronting and handling the end of the Cold War, as several states emerged to contest the extraordinary political and cultural influence of the United States, making the world a more complex, sometimes more dangerous, place. By the advent of the twenty-first century, global affairs had become central to Americans' conception of themselves and their nation. Both internally and externally, then, Americans from the 1990s to today have tried to respond to the forces of global capital and the fact that the nation is a multicultural place. In the 1990s, the first American leader to try to locate a new political center was William Jefferson (Bill) Clinton.

28-1 THE NEW POLITICAL CENTER

The 1992 presidential election illustrated many of the themes that would dominate American politics during the 1990s. Notably, the campaign saw the rise of Bill Clinton, a leader who combined rhetorical appeal with a political **centrism** that eclectically blended liberal and conservative philosophies and policies, sometimes called "the Third Way." The Third Way consciously sought to avoid the liberal politics of the New Left and the conservatism of the New Right.

The 1992 contest also highlighted outsider candidates, such as Patrick Buchanan and H. Ross Perot, each of whom mobilized voters disaffected with the major parties and disaffected with American life as it seemed to be heading.

28-1a The Fall of Bush

But the initial frontrunner was the then-current president, George H. W. Bush. Saddled with a worsening economy, Bush's poll numbers declined throughout 1991. Compounding his problems was a sense of despair that took hold of the nation during 1991 and 1992. Stories of the poor economy and episodes illustrating deep divisions in America dominated the news media, including (1) the Clarence Thomas confirmation hearings, (2) the culture wars, and (3) the Los Angeles riots.

CLARENCE THOMAS

One such division emerged in October 1991, when law professor Anita Hill accused Bush's Supreme Court nominee Clarence Thomas of sexual harassment. Hill's testimony at Thomas's confirmation hearings split the country and the Senate. Those on the political right, who supported Thomas, considered Hill a symbol of aggressive feminism gone awry. Those on the left accused

centrism Political ideology that eclectically blended liberal and conservative philosophies and policies, sometimes called "the Third Way," during Bill Clinton's presidency; components included conservative economic principles and liberal social principles

◀◀◀ **The 1990s have rightly been called the Information Age, when personal computers and the Internet became omnipresent in American life. Not only did the "1s" and "0s" of coding, represented here, spark to life the American economy, but also the Internet made communication and commerce over long distances easier and quicker, speeding up a process called globalization.**

the right of ignoring women's claim to equal and civil treatment in the workplace. The controversy also invoked questions of race, because both Thomas and Hill were black, and both had worked at the Equal Employment Opportunity Commission. At one point, Thomas claimed that the Supreme Court confirmation hearings were nothing more than a "high tech lynching for uppity blacks." The Senate eventually confirmed Thomas by the narrow margin of 52 to 48. But the debate showed once again that divisions between left and right in America were more than just political divisions, but positions on how one viewed American pluralism, women's rights, and more.

THE "CULTURE WARS," CONT.

At the same time, several books appeared alleging that multiculturalism on college campuses was undermining students' awareness of the Western intellectual tradition, which conservatives said contained the core of American values. Multiculturalism can be defined as the view that nearly every culture deserves respect and a hearing, even those long denied mainstream acceptability. In the 1980s and 1990s, multiculturalism came to signify the inclusion of more than "dead white males" in literary and history curriculums and the growing prevalence of affirmative action regulations in schools and in the workplace. As conservatives and liberals debated the rightful role of minorities in the country, many saw conservatives as xenophobic; others saw liberals as disrespectful of core American principles, although these were rarely defined. Issues like abortion, gay rights, and religion in the public sphere also seemed to play into this growing divide.

L.A. RIOTS

Most troubling of all, however, was a deadly multiethnic riot that erupted in South Central Los Angeles in April 1992. An all-white jury acquitted four white police officers who had been videotaped beating a black man named Rodney King after King fled their pursuit, driving at speeds of more than 110 miles per hour to escape. King had been drinking alcohol at a friend's house before driving home and sped away when officers tried to pull him over. When they finally did stop him after an eight-mile chase, he acted bizarrely, leading the officers to gang tackle him and beat him with their batons, an event that was videotaped and publicized widely. After the acquittal, the city erupted in riots, which were broadcast live to viewers around the nation, dramatizing long-standing tensions among many of the nation's

>> Video image of L.A. police beating black motorist Rodney King as he lies on the ground, taken by camcorder enthusiast George Holliday from a window overlooking the street. The video and subsequent trial of police officers led to the 1992 Los Angeles riots.

ethnicities. South Central's problems had begun decades earlier, when in the 1950s white people abandoned the cities for suburbs and then again in the 1970s and 1980s, when companies moved out of the area, leaving many in the predominantly African American neighborhood without jobs. At the same time, new immigrants from Latin America and Asia moved into the area as a result of the Immigration Act of 1965. The newcomers competed for the few jobs that remained. Korean Americans and African Americans were especially at odds in South Central. When the L.A. riots began, it was unclear who was on which side, or how many sides there were. In all, fifty-three people died, and nearly a billion dollars' worth of property was destroyed.

This level of violence, against the backdrop of the declining economy and other divisive political events, made Bush's America look like it was reeling out of control.

28-1b The Rise of Bill Clinton

Despite these problems, Bush seemed a formidable enough candidate that few Democrats wanted to challenge him, especially after his popularity had risen so high in the aftermath of the 1991 Gulf War. The field of Democrats had few nationally known figures, but, from the beginning, Arkansas governor Bill Clinton emerged as a party favorite. Reflecting a challenge to the Republicans' Southern Strategy, Clinton was

>> A rioter in downtown Los Angeles breaks the glass door of the Criminal Courts building in April 1992, protesting the acquittal of four white police officers who had been videotaped beating a black man who lay seemingly helpless on the ground. The riots lasted six days and 53 people died.

Another political outsider played a pivotal role in impeding Bush's chances. In spring 1992, Texas billionaire H. Ross Perot launched an independent presidential campaign, calling for balancing the federal budget and attacking both parties as beholden to special interests. A critic of globalization and hard-line free-market principles, Perot's plainspoken style and outsider stance energized alienated voters, and, for a brief time in the summer of 1992, he topped the list of candidates in public opinion polls. Perot drew supporters almost equally from Democrats and Republicans, but his attacks on establishment politicians, particularly in later campaign debates, were perceived as disproportionately harmful for Bush.

At the Democratic National Convention, Clinton chose as his running mate another youthful southerner, Senator Al Gore, and made the revival of America's moribund economy the centerpiece of his campaign. Taking as their campaign song Fleetwood Mac's "Don't Stop (Thinking About Tomorrow)," Clinton and Gore were the first presidential candidates to come from the post-World War II baby boomer generation, and they presented themselves as the vanguard of a new style of leadership.

a southerner and polled well in the South, a region Democrats had lost since 1976. He also defined himself as a political moderate; he was in favor of the death penalty and welfare reform, which were typically Republican positions. And he proved remarkably able to weather political scandal. During the New Hampshire primary, he admitted to marital problems and apologized for his actions. The gamble worked, as voters seemed impressed by his honesty, and Clinton went on to win most Democratic primaries.

> The culture wars had gone prime time.

OUTSIDE CHALLENGERS

Meanwhile, Bush was hampered by a challenge within his own party. Former Nixon, Ford, and Reagan advisor Patrick Buchanan launched a fierce right-wing campaign against Bush, capturing media attention and some primary votes. Later, Buchanan was given a prime speaking slot at the Republican National Convention, an opportunity he used to describe the nation as caught in a "religious war . . . a culture war . . . for the soul of America" between liberals and conservatives. The culture wars had gone prime time, and the speech struck many moderates as an indication that ideological extremists on the right had taken control of the Republican Party.

A DIVIDED ELECTORATE

Clinton's charisma and encyclopedic knowledge of the issues carried him to victory, although the electorate was clearly divided. Clinton won a plurality of the popular vote, taking 43 percent to Bush's 38 percent, while 19 percent of voters backed Perot; many Americans (45 percent of eligible voters) simply stayed home (Map 28.1). This fractured electorate gave Clinton a scant mandate for his programs.

28-1c Bill Clinton, Free Trader

One of Clinton's chief messages, as candidate and president, was that America and the world were rapidly changing, making old ideological divisions obsolete.

CLINTON'S "THIRD WAY"

The key to Clinton's promise of innovation was what he called the "Third Way," a centrist and eclectic blend of

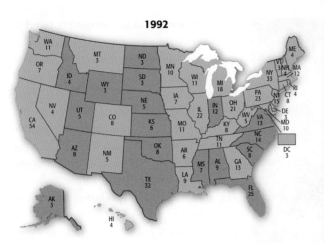

1992

Candidate (Party)	Electoral Vote		Popular Vote	
Clinton (Democrat)	370	68.8%	44,908,233	43.0%
Bush (Republican)	168	31.2%	39,102,282	37.4%
Perot (Independent)	0	0.0%	19,741,048	18.9%

Map 28.1 The Election of 1992

policy ideas taken from both liberal and conservative perspectives. He supported programs that were popular with a majority of the voters regardless of who had first proposed the plan. He was a strong advocate of liberal proposals like Head Start, air and water quality regulation, and moderate gun control. But he also supported conservative programs, such as tough anticrime measures, welfare reform, and reducing the federal deficit.

FREE TRADE

In the most substantial break with traditional Democratic policies, Clinton energetically advocated free-trade agreements that would open foreign markets to American companies and foreign companies to American markets. Many workers and the traditionally Democratic labor unions opposed trade deals, fearing that American companies would move their manufacturing jobs overseas, which is exactly what happened. But Clinton argued that, by lowering costs to consumers, such agreements would aid technological change and result in a net economic plus for the United States. And in a way, this is also exactly what happened, as the GDP went up and unemployment went

North American Free Trade Agreement (NAFTA)
Legislation signed in 1993 that removed tariff barriers between the United States, Mexico, and Canada

World Trade Organization (WTO) International agency designed to resolve disputes between trading partners and advocate free trade

Wally McNamee/Getty Images

>> One of Bill Clinton's chief legacies was the expansion of free trade. Here, he touts the benefits of the North American Free Trade Agreement (NAFTA) by demonstrating how American apples will be able to reach a broader market.

down. To be sure, though, most of the new jobs were located in the service and information technology sectors, which were typically not unionized and thus helped exasperate already growing divisions in wealth.

In 1993, Clinton worked hard to pass the **North American Free Trade Agreement (NAFTA)**, which removed tariff barriers between the United States, Mexico, and Canada. George H. W. Bush had begun negotiating the deal in the early 1990s, and Clinton supported and signed it in 1993. Two years later, Clinton secured American membership in the newly formed **World Trade Organization (WTO)**, an international agency designed to resolve disputes between trading partners and to advocate free trade. These were not uncontroversial issues in American life, but Clinton was convinced that the United States needed to work through the problems presented by modern information technologies and not fight against them.

DEFICIT REDUCTION

Clinton also made America's deficit reduction a priority, hoping to correct the imbalance created by Reagan's huge defense spending and sputtering economy of the late 1970s. Against bitter Republican opposition, Clinton passed a deficit reduction package that raised taxes on the wealthy and curtailed government spending. By 1998, the federal budget had gone from running a yearly deficit to showing an annual surplus, although there was still a tremendous debt to pay off.

28-1d Post-Cold War Foreign Policy

In the post-Cold War world, international diplomacy was trickier than it might have at first appeared. While the demise of the Soviet Union had made the United States the only superpower in the world, it was unclear how Clinton would use American force. Would he walk softly and allow the nations of the world to work out their political problems themselves? If they engaged in civil wars, should he intervene? Or would he just use American power to force the nations of the world to adhere to American demands?

He seemed to support UN peacekeeping missions, especially when they were acting on behalf of humanitarian efforts. But when in 1993 U.S. Marines in the East African nation of Somalia came under attack, Clinton withdrew American troops from the UN mission of which they were a part. In the wake of the Vietnam War, he was afraid to commit American troops to other nations' civil wars. This hesitancy prevented Clinton from intervening in Rwanda, where in 1994 the ethnic Hutu majority butchered 800,000 ethnic Tutsis.

Clinton was similarly hesitant to use American troops to create peace in the areas once controlled by the Soviet Union, especially in the Balkans, which had erupted in a series of ethnic wars between Bosnian Muslims, Serbs, and Croats. Through diplomacy, Clinton helped create the fragile state of Bosnia-Herzegovina. But the Serbian leader Slobodan Milosevic did not stop the ethnic violence, finally prompting Clinton, in 1999, to support a NATO aerial assault against the Serbs. He also committed the United States to support UN peacekeeping troops there. For every foreign policy success, Clinton seemed to tally a failure as well. And just as the Cold War had flung American foreign policy far and wide, the post-Cold War situation did the same, only without the United States having a preordained and fixed opposition.

28-1e The Republican Surge

Clinton ran into further trouble when he tried to push for certain social policies that brought out the rancorous partisanship of the cultural wars.

DON'T ASK, DON'T TELL

Upon taking office, Clinton fulfilled a campaign promise to end the U.S. government's ban on homosexuals' serving in the military. Civil rights groups applauded, but the measure was unpopular with military leaders and some members of Congress. Clinton quickly backtracked and offered a "Don't Ask, Don't Tell" policy preventing the

mark peterson/Getty Images

>> Among the many compromises Bill Clinton stumbled into during the first years of his presidency, the "Don't Ask, Don't Tell" policy provoked perpetual opposition from both the political right and the political left. Shown here is a demonstration advocating gay rights, protesting Clinton's "Don't Ask, Don't Tell" policy.

armed forces from inquiring about the sexual orientation of their members, while restoring their right to remove known homosexuals from service. The strained compromise satisfied neither side.

COMPREHENSIVE HEALTH CARE

Clinton suffered his most serious political defeat of the first years of his presidency with his ambitious proposals to change the nation's health care system. Clinton had made health care a central element of his campaign, responding to the fact that 37 million Americans lacked health insurance and that the policy that developed in post-World War II America, where Americans received the bulk of their health care from policies subsidized by their employer, had developed when the American economy was strong. Soon after taking office, the administration charged a task force, headed by First Lady Hillary Rodham Clinton, to develop a comprehensive health care plan.

As details of the proposals emerged (including a mandate that all employers offer insurance), small businesses and doctors began denouncing the plan as big government run amok. In September 1993, opponents of the plan began running TV ads featuring "Harry and Louise," a fictitious couple appalled that the Clinton plan would prevent them from choosing their doctor. Republicans, who until this point had been unsure of how to treat the Clinton plan, launched an all-out opposition. By late August 1994, the Democratic leadership in Congress, divided by internal arguments over the plan, decided to abandon it. Genuine health care reform would have to wait.

THE "CONTRACT WITH AMERICA"

The defeat of his health care plan and his waffling attitude about gays in the military eroded Clinton's popularity heading into the 1994 congressional elections. Conservatives were enraged by several of Clinton's social policies, while local issues (such as the nationwide push for **term limits** and a California ballot initiative to cut off illegal immigrants from social services) mobilized grassroots Republican voters and demonstrated a generalized mistrust of politicians.

term limits Legal restriction that limits the number of terms a person may serve in political office

Contract with America Document released by the Republican Party during the 1994 congressional elections promising to reform government, impose term limits, reduce taxes, increase military spending, and loosen regulations on businesses

The Republicans were remarkably united at this moment to take advantage of Clinton's weakness: House minority leader Newt Gingrich of Georgia pledged a "**Contract with America**," calling for significant tax and budget cuts, the return of many governmental responsibilities to the states, more defense spending, and a loosening of environmental regulations. The conservative coalition that was born in the 1950s and that matured in the 1970s and 1980s was coming of age in the 1990s.

The November 1994 congressional election results delivered a devastating blow to the Clinton presidency. Republicans gained a net total of fifty-two seats in the House of Representatives, recapturing control of the chamber for the first time since 1955. They also gained ten seats in the Senate. Clinton would have to govern with a hostile Congress for the remainder of his presidency.

28-1f Clinton's Recovery

Gingrich began 1995 as Speaker of the House, championing his ambitious Contract with America. As promised, he did usher most of the proposals in the Contract with America through the House. But the Senate rejected many of the proposals, and others passed the Senate only to be vetoed by the president. Clinton opposed the tax and spending cuts that were central to the conservative agenda, and he cleverly used his power to undercut popular support for Republicans. Notably, Clinton declared in his 1995 State of the Union address that "the era of big government is over." He thus seemed to agree with Republicans' antigovernment philosophy, while vetoing the biggest cuts, declaring certain government functions too vital to shut down.

CLOSING DOWN THE GOVERNMENT

As Clinton's popularity rose again, Gingrich overreached. In 1995, the president refused to approve the Republicans' budget, which would have forced cutbacks in federal spending on the environment, workplace safety, and consumer protection. In retaliation, Gingrich tried to pressure the president by refusing to pass any budget at all, forcing a shutdown of many federal offices around the country. National parks, museums, and federal agencies were closed, and many government employees were laid off. The shutdown proved to be a tremendous miscalculation on Gingrich's part: a majority of Americans agreed with the president that Gingrich had attempted to blackmail him. After three weeks, Republicans gave in and approved the funds needed to reopen the government. But the damage was done. Clinton enjoyed a resurgence of popularity, while the legislative initiatives of Gingrich's coalition slowed down.

THE 1996 ELECTION

During 1996, an election year, Clinton again positioned himself as a centrist. Strategically, he agreed to sign a Republican-sponsored welfare act setting limits on the number of years that a person can receive welfare and giving the states more power to draft their own regulations. Although liberals denounced Clinton's approval of the bill, it deprived Republicans of a major campaign issue and solidified Clinton's high ratings.

And as in 1992, Clinton benefited from chaos affecting his rivals. Ross Perot mounted another third-party campaign, while the eventual Republican nominee, Kansas Senator Bob Dole, had to spend campaign funds battling other candidates. In contrast, Clinton ran unopposed. Furthermore, Dole, a World War II veteran, had amassed an impressive record of public service, but voters saw his age (seventy-three) as a liability. Tapping into these concerns, Clinton declared at the Democratic Convention that his policies would better prepare Americans for the new challenges of the information age, building "a bridge to the twenty-first century." He coasted to an easy reelection, taking 49 percent of the vote to Dole's 41 percent. Clinton became the first Democrat since Franklin D. Roosevelt to be elected to two terms as president.

 ## 28-2 THE INFORMATION REVOLUTION

Throughout his two terms in office, Clinton was aided by a solid economic rebound, largely caused by a revolution in information technology.

28-2a Economic Rebound

The American economy began to recover from its post-Reagan recession in 1992 and had shot upward by the late 1990s. In 1993, the United States' real annual growth rate in GDP was a healthy 2.7 percent; it ran more than 4 percent per year between 1997 and 1999, a level economists usually associate with high-growth economies in developing countries. Millions of new jobs were created during the 1990s, and the country enjoyed low rates of unemployment and slight inflation. The average price of stocks more than tripled during the decade, too; the composite index of the NASDAQ stock exchange, which listed many new technology company stocks, grew by almost 800 percent.

Clinton received some credit for this development, with many commentators pointing to his administration's deficit reduction plan as important groundwork for economic growth. A more common view, however, was that having a Democratic president and a Republican-controlled Congress prevented either from making new policies that might interfere with the economy's success. The news media saw Alan Greenspan, chairman of the Federal Reserve Board (the central bank of the United States, which tries to regulate the economy's ups and downs), as the wizard behind the economic growth. Greenspan succeeded in setting healthy interest rates and controlling the money supply to avoid both recession and inflation. The widespread praise for Greenspan subtly demonstrated a continuing public cynicism about the abilities of elected political leaders, a cynicism prevalent since Watergate.

28-2b The Digital Age

To explain this growth, many economists argued that an "information revolution" had taken place.

THE INTERNET AND INFORMATION TECHNOLOGIES

The rapid development of new information technologies (IT) such as cellular phones and personal computers led many analysts to explain the sudden economic rise as a

>> During the 1990s, the Internet rapidly transformed into an electronic public square, becoming in the process a key component of American education. Here a group of young students use the Internet in their classroom.

result of the unforeseen savings brought on by expedited communications. Central to these gains was the Internet, a vast network of linked computers that allows information to be shared easily and instantly. Although universities and the federal government had developed much of the infrastructure behind the Internet in the 1970s and 1980s, it only emerged as a commercial tool in the mid-1990s, after inexpensive desktop computers became common fixtures in American homes and offices. As millions of Americans started going online, the Internet rapidly transformed into an electronic public square, a place to exchange ideas and sell wares, as well as to be educated and entertained. It helped to democratize the marketplace, as the widespread awareness of one product might lead someone else to invent a complementary product.

OTHER COMMUNICATIONS

Digital technology fueled rapid economic growth in other areas of the economy, as computers streamlined manufacturing processes, helped American companies reach overseas markets, and revolutionized new areas of medical research, particularly in biotechnology. Underpinning the information revolution was the work of hundreds of new companies laying fiber-optic cable, building cell-phone towers, networking offices, digitizing libraries, streamlining computer chips, and designing websites. Expanding the lines of digital communication also helped usher in a broader network of cable television networks, including a number of 24-hour cable news channels, which were constantly on the lookout for up-to-the-minute news stories and which fractured the unity perceived when there were only a handful of national news outlets. It also ushered in a trend in which fewer Americans read newspapers.

COSTS

Even as productivity remained high and unemployment dropped, some saw a downside to this revved-up American prosperity. Many economists warned that the growth in the price of stocks was driven not by sound investment but by what Greenspan termed "irrational exuberance." Others warned of the widening disparity between rich and poor. Similarly, after NAFTA and other free-trade agreements lowered tariffs between the United States and other countries, it became more profitable for American companies to move their factories overseas to take advantage of lower labor costs. This left many American industrial workers unemployed and continued the decline of the American manufacturing sector. Ross Perot presciently won significant political points in 1992 by referring to NAFTA as "that giant sucking sound" of jobs leaving the United States and heading elsewhere in the world. Many Americans simply felt as though the economy had left them behind, and politicians were unwilling or unable to help.

BENEFITS

Nevertheless, the economy of the late 1990s brought benefits as well. Earning power improved dramatically for the wealthiest Americans, work was plentiful, and unemployment was generally low. The healthy economy helped federal and state governments balance their budgets, while police across the nation reported a steady decline in the crime rate, a trend usually attributed to the "trickle down" of American prosperity.

28-2c Consolidation and Globalization

The growth of the Internet and the information revolution had two other consequences beyond improving the economy: (1) corporate mergers and (2) increased globalization.

CORPORATE CONSOLIDATION

First, the information revolution stimulated a round of large corporate mergers because business leaders were convinced they should try to integrate media content with its transmission. Thus, companies that produced television, films, or music made efforts to provide their material to consumers through all available media: phone, cable, or

Janine Wiedel Photolibrary/Alamy Stock Photo

>> Critics complained that 1990s "globalization" merely meant imposing Western ideals and products on everyone without regard for native customs. Demonstrators here are protesting against Nike and its policy of using "sweatshop slavery."

fiber-optic lines, over the airwaves, or on movie screens. This view was encouraged by Congress, which deregulated the industry in the Telecommunications Act of 1996.

Nowhere was this process more obvious than in the area of mass communication, as giant companies merged to create even bigger corporations, hoping to dominate aspects of the new information economy. The Disney Company bought the American Broadcasting Company; Time Warner bought Turner Broadcasting, only to then be taken over by Internet provider America Online. Each of these mega-corporations acquired a variety of media outlets, including television networks, cable channels, publishing houses, movie studios, home video stores, and Internet sites. This allowed them to both produce and distribute their news and entertainment programs.

The result has been that much of the information received by most Americans now comes from a small number of multinational corporations. Ironically, in an age of choice symbolized by countless cable channels and infinite websites, Americans receive their news and entertainment from an ever-shrinking number of corporate sources. The market consolidations of the 1990s resemble those of the Industrial Revolution of the previous century, when the process of industrialization led to the development of hundreds of new businesses, many of which were eventually consolidated within large corporations.

GLOBALIZATION

The other dramatic result of the information revolution has been the speeding up of a process called globalization. Globalization is easiest to understand in the business world, where companies from different nations have little difficulty working together because of the ease with which they can communicate and transport goods. National parochialisms seemed to be dying off.

Viewing globalization as a positive force, the Clinton administration advocated it energetically. It was the reason Clinton cited when signing the NAFTA agreement. It was the source of Clinton's drive to expand fiber-optic cable lines throughout the globe. And it was the reason Clinton endorsed the founding of the WTO in 1995. Indeed, Clinton did not fight the creation of multinational corporations, defined as companies that have offices and production centers in more than one nation. Throughout the 1990s, these companies expanded busily, moving production centers to where the cheapest labor could be hired.

CRITICS OF GLOBALIZATION

Not everyone was enamored with globalization. For their reasons why, see "The Reasons Why . . ." box.

In 1999, protesters against globalization staged a large rally outside a WTO meeting in Seattle, effectively halting the meeting. In 2001, an equally large protest descended on Genoa, Italy, to protest a meeting of the World Bank and the International Monetary Fund.

·The Reasons Why...

There were several reasons why many people were disenchanted with the new globalization:

Cultural imperialism. Critics complained that globalization simply meant imposing Western ideals and products on everyone throughout the world with little regard for native or local customs. For every McDonald's that critics saw on the streets of some non-American nation, they thought of the local restaurateurs who could not compete with its streamlined operations and low wages.

Job departures. Labor unions argued that globalization was depriving working-class Americans of jobs, as reduced trading borders made it easier for companies to build their products in one place and sell them in

another. Many American companies began operations in Indonesia and China, taking advantage of the fact that foreign labor was so inexpensive that it did not matter that the goods would have to be transported halfway across the world. Corporations also realized they could easily move their headquarters overseas to avoid paying American taxes.

Environmental critiques. Environmentalists argued that globalization was creating industries and pollution in countries that were not equipped to handle them. These countries often countered that it was unfair for the United States to engage in its Industrial Revolution before the advent of environmental laws while these latecomers now had to abide by a stricter set of rules. Despite the arguments, the number of overseas factories powered by American corporations has increased dramatically during the past quarter-century.

Individual activists targeted specific companies for unsavory business practices and for maintaining sweatshops. One popular T-shirt used the Nike shoe company's trademark swoosh as the *v* in the word *slavery*.

More daunting were militant critics of globalization who were furious about Western ideals encroaching on their lands and cultures. The most prominent of these violent protesters was Osama bin Laden and his al Qaeda network in the Middle East. Throughout the late 1990s, bin Laden and his associates used pinpointed assaults on American installations in the Middle East to challenge, disrupt, and discourage the Western presence there. In 1998, bin Laden, the wealthy scion of a successful Westernized businessman, escaped an assassination attempt approved by President Clinton.

28-3 MULTICULTURALISM

By the 1980s, the transformations brought about by the Immigration Act of 1965 had become increasingly visible in American life, and the number of immigrants from Latin American and Asian nations mushroomed. There were only about half a million immigrants coming to the country each decade in the 1920s and 1930s. By the 1990s there were more than a million immigrants coming to the country *each year*. The census of 2000 revealed that, for the first time, Hispanics had become the country's largest minority group (at 13 percent of the total population), displacing African Americans (at about 11 percent), who had composed the largest racial minority group since the nation's founding. These immigrants also brought with them their many and various religions, such as Islam and Hinduism. By the 2020 census, it is projected that Protestants will, for the first time in American history, constitute less than 50 percent of the American population.

Combined with calls for political and social recognition from African Americans, Chicanos, and American Indians during the 1960s and 1970s, this widespread immigration made most attempts to prioritize the British origins of the American nation seem untenable and xenophobic. Even Nathan Glazer, a Harvard sociologist who had been a staunch critic of Black Nationalism and other forms of early multiculturalism, wrote a book in 1997 called *We Are All Multiculturalists Now*. Throughout the 1990s, corporations attempted to demonstrate their friendliness to minority groups (even if the realities of their hiring and promotion priorities did not always live up to the images they were trying to foster). And as this happened, many but not all Americans began to accept racial and ethnic diversity as a positive good, something to be celebrated as a unique American achievement.

The heavily Hispanic and Asian post-1965 immigration was buttressed by huge numbers of illegal immigrants coming from Latin America, usually from Mexico. In search of better opportunities or searching for their families, illegal immigrants often came across the southern border of the United States, facing a treacherous crossing from Mexico. Although the number of illegal immigrants in the United States is unknown, the best estimates suggest that about 10 million illegal immigrants were living in the United States during the first years of the twenty-first century. Many of these immigrants come from Mexico and other Latin American countries, but thousands more come from Europe and other parts of the world.

Critics complained that illegal immigrants were burdening America's social services, such as hospitals and schools, and were doing so without paying proper taxes. Illegal immigration became a political issue, especially in states that border Mexico, like California, Arizona, and Texas. Democrats often showed concern for the wellbeing of illegal immigrants, suggesting that amnesty for those already in the United States combined with an immigration policy more aligned with reality might be the best solution. Republicans seemed more concerned about the work that illegal immigrants were doing, arguing that those jobs would be better suited for those born in the United States or those who had come here legally. Both parties agreed that the current immigration laws were ineffective, and the stalemate continues.

HOMEFRONT TERRORISM

Although the economy remained good throughout the 1990s, several violent events made Americans question the moral integrity of their nation. Was it really on the right track? How might Americans respond to globalization and multiculturalism?

28-4a Discontent

With the economy humming along, few would have predicted that extreme instances of violence would flare up. But that is exactly what happened.

OKLAHOMA CITY

In 1995, Gulf War veteran Timothy McVeigh protested the federal government's fiery intervention into violent antigovernment sects (those at Ruby Ridge, Idaho, and the Branch Davidians at Waco, Texas), where the government had attacked and destroyed armed encampments of Americans angered by the growing size and reach of federal government. Using some of the skills he had learned as a soldier, McVeigh blew up a federal building in Oklahoma City. Unlike most Americans, McVeigh chose to vent his frustration through an act of homegrown terrorism. The blast killed 168 people, most of whom were children attending day care in the building. Authorities immediately captured McVeigh, and his actions provided a window into a widespread network of antigovernment militias scattered throughout the nation. These groups thought the federal government had become too big and was infringing too much on Americans' lives. They would only continue to grow throughout the 1990s and 2000s.

JAMES BYRD, JR.

Three years later, in 1998, three white supremacists from Jasper, Texas, murdered a forty-nine-year-old black man named James Byrd, Jr. They then dragged him from the back of their truck for miles. Such a savage maiming had not been perpetrated for decades and was met with widespread horror by a nation that thought this kind of racial hatred was a thing of the past.

MATTHEW SHEPARD

Later in 1998, two men attacked Matthew Shepard, a young gay man, for allegedly approaching them in a Laramie, Wyoming, bar. The men beat and robbed him, then tied him to a fence in rural Wyoming. Shepard died of brain damage shortly thereafter. Many Americans pointed to Byrd's and Shepard's deaths as a signal that, despite the general acceptance of multiculturalism and America's pluralism, brutal racism and homophobia still existed in the United States, and was becoming increasingly brazen.

COLUMBINE

But perhaps most shocking of all, in 1999 two high school students in Columbine, Colorado, went on a shooting rampage at their school. In a highly orchestrated attack, the two students brought weapons to campus and killed thirteen classmates and one teacher before killing

Kevin Moloney/Getty Images News/Getty Images

>> One of the most chilling moments of the 1990s took place on April 20, 1999, when two angry and heavily armed students engaged in a seemingly random massacre of their peers at Columbine High School, near Denver, Colorado. Thirteen students lay dead before the two gunmen turned the weapons on themselves.

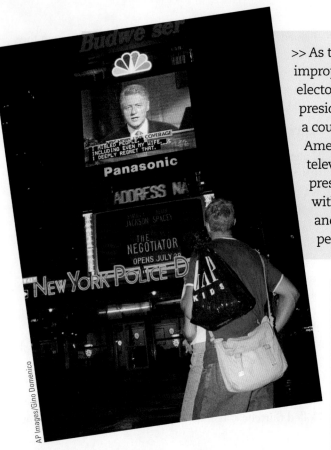

AP Images/Gino Domenico

themselves. No one has ever established a firm motive for their actions, but their violent actions and the number of copycats they inspired demonstrated discontent with some aspects of American society.

28-5 POLITICAL POLARIZATION AND THE 2000 ELECTION

Americans viewed these tragedies with nearly universal disgust, and some interpreted this disgust as a sign that Americans were ready for strong hate-crime legislation. Others saw these events as the result of an overly permissive society that provoked, encouraged, and even glorified violence. These polarized explanations gained further expression in a scandal concerning Bill Clinton's sexual liaisons.

28-5a The Lewinsky Episode

In 1998, a House of Representatives special investigator named Kenneth Starr determined that Clinton had inappropriate sexual contact with a White House intern named Monica Lewinsky. Clinton denied the claim, but when Starr found out that one of Lewinsky's friends had taped telephone conversations in which Lewinsky described the sexual conduct, Starr called Clinton's bluff. Starr then

demanded that the House of Representatives impeach the president for committing perjury (Clinton had said under oath that he had not had "sexual relations" with Lewinsky). Clinton's critics argued that his unethical behavior had degraded and sullied the office of the president. Others, without defending the president's actions, claimed that he was the victim of a new kind of information age political warfare, his private life exposed to public scrutiny in a way that few public figures could survive.

28-5b Rebuking the Republicans

Polls showed that, although voters disapproved of Clinton's actions, they were also fed up with the partisan bickering associated with the Lewinsky case. Perhaps as a result, the congressional elections of 1998 delivered an unexpected rebuke to the Republicans. They lost six seats in the House of Representatives and held on to only a slim majority in the Senate. The unexpected losses prodded Newt Gingrich to resign.

Despite the election results, Republicans pressed ahead with the impeachment of the president. In the Constitution, impeachment is defined as a formal accusation of "high crimes and misdemeanors." And on December 19, 1998, on votes of 228 to 206 and then 221 to 212, the House approved two articles of impeachment and sent the case for trial to the Senate. The vote in the House was divided almost entirely along party lines, with most Democrats opposing impeachment and virtually all Republicans favoring it. These results foreshadowed the failure of the measure in the Senate, where Democrats had more than the 34 votes needed to block Clinton's removal from office. On February 12, 1999, the best prosecutors could secure was a 50-to-50 tie in the Senate over the issue of whether or not Clinton had obstructed justice and should therefore be removed from office. Clinton completed his term.

28-5c The 2000 Election

While Clinton certainly bears responsibility for his actions, the assault against him was prosecuted with particular energy and vigor. As such, it was a symbol of a larger political divide, as Republicans attempted to position themselves as moralistic defenders of pre-1960s order and Democrats sought to portray themselves as capable of maintaining order while acknowledging the social liberalism of the 1960s and 1970s. Clinton's scandal did not bolster the Democrats' image, but Kenneth Starr's investigation, which much of the public considered trite and juvenile, hurt Republicans.

THE CANDIDATES

At first, the 2000 campaign promised to be dull, as most commentators regarded the respective party nominees as foregone conclusions. For Republicans, George W. Bush, governor of Texas and son of the former president, appealed to party regulars; a conservative, he had also compiled a record of working with Democrats to pass legislation. On the Democratic side, the favored candidate was Vice President Al Gore, who promised to continue the Clinton policies that had brought eight years of "peace and prosperity." Gore chose as his running mate Senator Joseph Lieberman of Connecticut, the first Jewish vice-presidential nominee from one of the major parties. Gore faced a challenge from the political left, as the Green Party put forward the longtime consumer advocate Ralph Nader as its candidate. Nader argued that both Bush and Gore were beholden to big business and thus were not putting forward suitably different platforms, including ending corporate donations to political campaigns. Although Nader failed to win a single electoral vote, his candidacy reflected growing anger from the left at Clinton's centrism, in a similar fashion to what Perot and Robertson had done to Republicans in 1992

THE VOTE

Neither major party candidate generated much enthusiasm. Gore was criticized as being stiff and wonkish; Bush was more affable, but many worried that he lacked experience and intellect. Uninspired and disillusioned with politics after eight years of scandal and partisanship, only 50 percent of eligible voters cast their ballots on Election Day. The lack of passion for either candidate was manifested in the extremely slim vote margins between the two. As millions of Americans tuned in to the major TV news networks to learn who their next president would be, they saw normally confident news anchors reduced to stuttering confusion. Projections switched back and forth on election night; neither candidate had captured the 270 votes necessary to win a majority of the Electoral College.

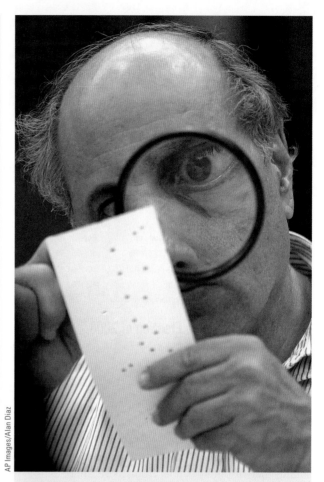

AP Images/Alan Diaz

>> In the confusing aftermath of the 2000 election, millions of Americans learned what a "hanging chad" was, although knowing what it was didn't make the election's outcome any easier to discern. Here a Broward County canvassing board member uses a magnifying glass to examine a disputed ballot at the Broward County Courthouse in Fort Lauderdale, Florida.

The results illuminated a peculiarity of the American electoral system not seen since 1888: a candidate with a minority of the popular vote was poised to win a majority of the votes in the Electoral College. Gore actually won the popular vote by more than half a million votes. Yet Bush emerged with a razor-thin lead of 537 votes in Florida, a tiny fraction of the 6 million cast in that state, but enough to gain the state's 25 electoral votes, which gave him a total of 271 electoral votes overall—the bare minimum needed to become president (Map 28.2).

2000

Candidate (Party)	Electoral Vote		Popular Vote	
Bush (Republican)	271	50.4%	50,465,169	47.79%
Gore (Democrat)	266	49.4%	50,996,062	48.29%
Nader (Green)	0	0.0%	2,529,871	2.40%

* One elector from the District of Columbia abstained.

Map 28.2 The Election of 2000

THE CONTROVERSY

With this narrow margin, Florida law called for an automatic recount, a process made complicated by claims of voting irregularities around the state. Gore's team pushed for recounts in counties carried by Gore, reasoning that disputed ballots from these areas might help their candidate if they were counted. Bush's staff resisted holding any recount in the hope of hanging on to their lead. In some locations, such as Miami-Dade County, recounts were abandoned after crowds of Bush supporters disrupted the proceedings. Many were suspicious that Florida's governor, who happened to be George W. Bush's brother, might intervene and use his power to determine Florida's vote. Others grew concerned when stories emerged alleging that many African Americans had been denied access to the polls. Gore went to court to ask for a recount of "undervotes," the thousands of ballots that the vote-counting machine could not read, and, on December 8, the Florida Supreme Court granted Gore's request.

Four days later, in the case of *Bush* v. *Gore* (2000), the U.S. Supreme Court voted 5 to 4 to halt the recount, allowing Florida governor Jeb Bush to certify George W. Bush's 537-vote margin in Florida, thus making George W. Bush president. The conservative majority on the Court argued that Florida law made no provision for recounting undervotes and that the state had no fair way to evaluate partially marked ballots. Four justices dissented, insisting that the federal government had no right to interfere with Florida's attempt to determine the winner of its own electoral votes.

The confusing outcome provided more drama than had the year of political campaigning that preceded the election. It also revealed a sharply divided electorate.

>LOOKING AHEAD...

The United States in the 1990s had entered a new era of free trade, the economy had rebounded from recession due to the growth and expansion of new information technologies, and most Americans generally accepted America's increasing racial, ethnic, and religious diversity. Still, there were widening divides between various factions of Americans, and these divides seemed to be provoking increasingly violent responses. The gap between the left and the right seemed to be widening, and toeing the line of Clintonian centrism appeared to be an increasingly difficult act.

STUDY TOOLS 28

READY TO STUDY? IN THE BOOK, YOU CAN:

❏ Rip out the Chapter Review Card, which includes key terms and chapter summaries.

ONLINE AT WWW.CENGAGEBRAIN.COM, YOU CAN:

❏ Collect StudyBits while you read and study the chapter.

❏ Quiz yourself on key concepts.

❏ Find videos for further exploration.

❏ Prepare for tests with HIST5 Flash Cards as well as those you create.

❏ Read Clinton's speech to the 1996 Democratic National Convention.

❏ Read excerpts from the Starr Report.

1991 Clarence Thomas appointed to Supreme Court.

1992 **April:** South Central L.A. riots after exoneration of police captured on video tape beating Rodney King.
November: Bill Clinton defeats incumbent Bush, and independent Ross Perot in presidential election.

1993 Clinton signs North American Free Trade Agreement (NAFTA).

1994 **November:** Republicans capture congressional majority.
Telecommunications Act deregulates media and mass communications.
Congress defeats health care plan championed by Hillary Clinton.
Republican minority leader Newt Gingrich pledges "Contract with America."

1995 United States becomes part of World Trade Organization.
Antigovernment activist bombs Oklahoma City federal building, killing 168.

1996 **November:** Bill Clinton defeats Bob Dole, becomes first Democrat reelected to presidency since FDR.

1997: *Nevada becomes the first state to pass legislation categorizing Y2K data disasters as "acts of God," protecting the state from lawsuits that might be brought against it by residents in the year 2000.*

Scientists at Roslin Institute in Scotland clone a sheep, Dolly.

Princess Diana killed in a car crash in Paris.

1998 Clinton turns federal budget deficit into surplus.

Osama bin Laden escapes U.S.-orchestrated assassination attempt.

1999 Clinton's impeachment for hiding Monica Lewinsky affair ends in Senate with Clinton's exoneration.

Two students kill thirteen classmates and teacher in Columbine, Colorado.

2000 U.S. Supreme Court decides deadlocked election in *Bush* v. *Gore*.

2001 Activists disturb World Bank and International Monetary Fund meetings in Genoa.

29 | Globalization and Its Discontents

AP Images/Mark Lennihan

LEARNING OBJECTIVES

After reading this chapter, you should be able to do the following:

29-1 Describe the initial events of what came to be called "the War on Terror."

29-2 Describe George W. Bush's plans for democracy in the Middle East, including his declaration of a "War on Terror," and assess the degree of his success.

29-3 Discuss the domestic problems that America faced during George W. Bush's second term.

29-4 Explain some of the hopes and frustrations of Barack Obama's two terms in office, and some of the persistent divisions within the United States.

29-5 Explain the rise of Donald J. Trump and the increased political polarization within the U.S.

AFTER FINISHING THIS CHAPTER GO TO **PAGE 574** **FOR STUDY TOOLS**

The advent of the information age spawned challenges as well as opportunities. Cyber-thieves capable of stealing information over the Internet used that information to apply for credit cards to make a quick profit. International markets became more challenging to predict and manage. Most deadly of all, many people in the world began to view America's predominant place in the global economy as a threat to their way of life. Several nebulous multinational groups, inspired by religious fanaticism and anti-Americanism, and tied together by easy access to information and global communication, rose to challenge the United States, drawing the nation into what was called a global war on terror.

President Bush initiated the policies and legislation in the war on terror, although this was never his intended goal. He had emerged from the troubled presidential election of 2000 somewhat weakened, but he nonetheless governed from the right, passing tax cuts and expanding America's military profile. Before his first year in office was over, though, vital Republicans had defected, and the humming economy of the 1990s seemed to be fading into a recession. Then, in September 2001, the focus of his presidency changed. Critics of America's international power struck a terrible blow against the United States by hijacking four airplanes and flying three of them into iconic American buildings, symbolizing an attack on America's trading prowess and military reach. The September 11 attacks propelled the nation into a global war on terror, which influenced not only America's international policies but its domestic ones as well.

Bush's successor, Barack Obama, confronted many of the same problems Bush did: a faltering economy, a complex morass of diplomatic issues, and a divided and deeply partisan electorate. With two terms of Democratic Party leadership under Obama, the country remained evenly divided between right and left, although the gulf between the two sides seemed to widen, as issues like immigration, American economic interests, and the battle between security and freedom polarized the two political sides. The results of this division bore fruit in the 2016 election, when populist leaders on the right and left arose to challenge middle-of-the-road liberalism, embodied in the 2016 election by Hillary Rodham Clinton, President Bill Clinton's wife. During the Democratic primary, she successfully fended off a challenge from the left, in the form of Senator Bernie Sanders. But she eventually lost the presidency to a populist voice on the right, Donald J. Trump, who became the forty-fifth president of the United States in 2017. As in much of the rest of the world, widespread disaffection with the political center has led to populists on the right and left being the loudest voices heard. But first, a deeper look into the presidency of George W. Bush.

29-1 THE WAR ON TERROR

Winning only a minority of the popular vote, Bush came to office with no mandate. But he pressed ahead with his conservative agenda nonetheless. The centerpiece of this agenda was a large tax cut for wealthy Americans. And, despite critics' claims that the tax cut would wipe out the budget surplus created during the Clinton years, the Republican Congress passed Bush's $1.3 trillion tax cut. Some argued that Bush was simply continuing the Reagan Revolution of "starving the beast" of government regulations and entitlements that had developed since the rise of the Industrial Age at the end of the nineteenth century and was carried through the Progressive era, the New Deal, and the Great Society. Bush similarly followed conservative strategy when it came to the environment, promising to search for oil reserves in the Arctic National Wildlife Refuge, which critics called America's last wilderness. He also pulled out of missile treaty agreements with Russia and refused to participate in an international agreement to control global warming.

But Bush faced a strong rebuke on May 24, 2001, when Senator Jim Jeffords, a Republican from Vermont, declared himself unhappy with the president's rightward approach to governing, and announced that he would caucus as an independent, which shifted control of the Senate to the Democrats. Bush's policies now seemed unlikely to pass. His right-wing rhetoric had cost him necessary votes. In early September 2001 he was a president adrift.

29-1a September 11

Bush's presidency was revived on September 11, 2001, when nineteen of Osama bin Laden's associates hijacked four U.S. airliners and attempted to fly them into various buildings across the country. Three of the four planes hit their targets. Two flew into each of New York City's World Trade Center towers, causing both of the 110-story towers to collapse. Another plane crashed into the side

◄◄◄ **The National September 11 Memorial & Museum, on the site of the World Trade Center attacks in New York City, opened in 2011, exactly a decade after the attacks. The 9/11 terrorist attacks challenged the nation to think anew about its role in the world and how the Information Age presented both challenges and opportunities to Americans everywhere.**

>> September 11, 2001. On September 11, 2001, 19 associates of Osama bin Laden hijacked four American airplanes and targeted four iconic American sites. Three of them reached their targets, including two that hit the twin towers of New York City's World Trade Center.

Sean Adair/Landov/Reuters

of the Pentagon, the government's central military office. On the fourth jet, passengers, aware of the unfolding tragedy through the use of cellular phones, overtook the hijackers, and the jet crashed into a field in Pennsylvania. In total, more than 3,000 people died in the attacks.

The country was stunned by the tragedies, which were totally unanticipated by the public and which emerged from a source that was completely unknown to most Americans. Within hours of the attack, the Bush administration determined that bin Laden's **al Qaeda** network had masterminded the plan and that al Qaeda operated out of Afghanistan with the blessing of that country's ruling party, the Taliban, which had risen to power after it quelled an Afghan civil war in 1996. The Taliban's ideology of Islamic fundamentalism was combined with a severely repressive rule and also made it sympathetic to militant fundamentalist groups such as

al Qaeda A global militant Islamic organization founded in 1988 or 1989 by Osama bin Laden to advocate through publicity and violence a strict interpretation of Islamic law and to prohibit the penetration of the Middle East by Western and other outside influences

Bush doctrine Political principle articulated by President George W. Bush in which he declared America's right to fight a "preemptive war" against any nation that, one day, might threaten the United States

al Qaeda, who were willing to use violence to protest American involvement in the Middle East.

Throughout the 1990s, Osama bin Laden, the son of a wealthy Saudi developer whose allowance from his parents totaled $7 million a year, tried to rid the Middle East of any Western influence in order to return it to what he saw as its purer Islamic roots. To understand more about why al Qaeda was so angry at the United States, see "The Reasons Why . . ." box.

Bush, with the country's overwhelming blessing, decided to forge an international coalition and go to war against Afghanistan in order to oust al Qaeda.

29-1b War in Afghanistan and War on Terror

The war in Afghanistan started in October 2001, and the Taliban were driven from power two months later. Unfortunately, U.S. and coalition troops at first found neither bin Laden nor many of his leading associates, who fled to the mountains of Pakistan. Coalition forces and Afghanis, meanwhile, had a difficult time establishing a stable government capable of holding the nation together, and the American military began a lengthy presence in Afghanistan, perhaps a major irony of Osama bin Laden's attacks on 9/11, which of course sought to oust the U.S. from the Middle East. Instead, the continued American presence in Afghanistan has made it the United States' longest war.

The seemingly easy initial victory in Afghanistan and the stinging memory of the September 11 attacks prompted Bush to call for an expanded, broader war, which he called a "war on terror." While many said that a war on a tactic, could not be easily fought because there was no definable end, no specific battleground, and no specific enemy, most Americans went along with the president. He established military bases in Central Asia and the Philippines to combat militant Islamic insurgencies. He also sought to renew friendships with India and Pakistan in order to have well-positioned allies within the Middle East. He developed a new doctrine, called the **Bush doctrine**, which declared America's right to fight a "preemptive war" against any nation that, one day, might threaten the United States.

Bush also used the war on terror to reorganize the U.S. intelligence community. Shortly after September 11, he created the Department of Homeland Security as a cabinet-level position. In 2005, Bush established the director of National Intelligence, which supplanted the CIA director as the principal intelligence officer in the nation, coordinating the efforts of the entire intelligence community.

The Reasons Why...

There were several reasons why Osama bin Laden and his al Qaeda network were so angry at the United States:

Cold War blowback. Throughout the 1980s, Afghanistan was the location of yet another Cold War proxy battle, with the Soviet Union attempting to exert control over Afghanistan and the United States supporting Afghan resistance fighters. (One American-supported organization was Osama bin Laden's Maktab al-Khadamat, which funneled weapons and guns to Afghan fighters.) The war ended in 1988 when the Soviets departed, unable to control the country. Like the Soviet Union, the United States pulled its support in 1988, long before the country was politically stable. The subsequent instability led to several years of civil war and the rise of a radical Islamic government, the Taliban, which would later allow al Qaeda to use Afghanistan as its base of operations. The American and Soviet departure also allowed bin Laden to claim the role of the savior of the Middle East who had helped bring down the mighty Soviet Union.

American involvement in the Middle East. Osama bin Laden was radicalized during the Afghan civil war. Sensing that the Middle East had departed from its historic and godly ways, he laid the blame on outside influences, including American cultural and military involvement in the area. He was alarmed that, after the Gulf War of 1991, the American military had remained in the Middle East, and in 1996 he issued his first call for the United States to leave. Bin Laden and many others argued that the American military presence existed only to preserve American access to Middle Eastern oil. They did not want to be part of an American Empire.

Bin Laden also did not want the Middle East to be exposed to what he perceived as Western values, which to him included sexual licentiousness, tolerance of outsider faiths, and a revision of traditional gender roles.

Israel. Another flashpoint was American support for Israel. Since Israel's founding in 1948, the United States has supplied Israel with weapons and military support. Many, though certainly not all, Muslims believe Israel has no right to exist as a nation in the Middle East, on land that was largely populated by Muslim Palestinians before Israel came into existence. (Israel sits on land that is holy to Muslims, Christians, and Jews.) Several Middle Eastern nations came together in 1967 and 1973 to try to push Israel out of the Middle East, but the Israelis, with American support, resisted the attacks. American support for Israel has been a persistently contentious issue between the United States and many Middle Eastern nations. In a 1998 religious statement called, in Islam, a fatwa, bin Laden formally objected to American foreign policy toward Israel and to the continued American military presence in Saudi Arabia. Seeing these as threats to the creation of the pure Islamic Middle East he envisioned, bin Laden also urged the use of violence against the United States until his demands were met.

Islamic justifications. While many people might criticize American involvement in the Middle East or its support for Israel, the vast majority do not resort to violence. To justify his violent diatribes, bin Laden embraced an Islamic schismatic movement that believed things could only be set right in the Middle East by restoring Islamic Sharia law (or, God's law) throughout the land. Bin Laden used Islam to justify the killing of innocent bystanders, arguing that, if they are right with God, they will enter Paradise for their sacrifice. The combination of legitimate complaint, wrong-headed scapegoating, advocacy of violence, and the promise of holy reward proved a deadly concoction.

29-1c USA PATRIOT Act

September 11 also allowed Bush to push his conservative social agenda domestically. Claiming his policies were useful in the war on terror, Bush (1) passed another round of tax cuts, aimed especially at the wealthy; (2) increased the size of the military; and (3) cut back spending on social welfare programs, the same three agenda items begun during the Reagan Revolution.

The war in Afghanistan gave Bush the political capital to push for greater intrusions into privacy as well. In an effort to root out terrorism, the **USA PATRIOT Act** allowed the federal government to monitor—without

> **USA PATRIOT Act** Act passed in October 2001 allowing the federal government greater latitude in surveillance of its citizens in order to monitor for potential acts of terrorism

judicial warrants—libraries, bookstores, banks, and even people's homes, although notable abuses of these policies have yet to emerge.

29-2 REMAKING THE MIDDLE EAST?

With justifiable fears of another 9/11 attack keeping him, in his words, "up at night," Bush decided to use his recently declared right to "preemptive action" in the war on terror.

29-2a Regime Change in Iraq

First on Bush's list was Iraq, the country his father had battled a decade before in the 1991 Gulf War, but which had been friendly toward the United States during the Cold War. Some of Bush's key advisors had been his father's advisors as well, and many of them were troubled by his father's 1991 decision not to invade Iraq in order to remove dictator Saddam Hussein. One of these was Bush's powerful vice president, Richard "Dick" Cheney.

To justify an invasion, the second Bush administration argued that Iraq had a variety of weapons of mass destruction (WMDs), including nuclear weapons, that it could use against the United States. (This claim has since proved to be false, and CIA director George Tenet resigned for this failure of intelligence.) The administration also argued that there were traceable connections between bin Laden and Iraq (also never proven). And the Bush administration argued that Iraq had committed horrific and sustained human rights abuses against its political enemies since the U.S. departed in 1991, a claim no one rejected.

Critics and proponents alike disregarded most of this rhetoric and instead viewed the potential invasion as an attempt to remake the Middle East, which had been the breeding ground of much anti-American terrorism for three decades and which continued to be a crucially important region for the United States because of its large oil reserves. After several months of struggling for authorization, first from the U.S. Senate, then from the United Nations, Bush decided that their lukewarm approval was enough to merit an invasion. On March 19, 2003, 250,000 American and 45,000 British troops invaded Iraq, overtaking it and marching on the capital of Baghdad less than three weeks later. Nine months later, in December 2003, U.S. forces rooted Hussein out of a dirt hole and handed him over to his Iraqi enemies, who hanged him after a speedy trial (Map 29.1).

29-2b A Democratic Middle East?

After the fall of Baghdad and the death of Saddam Hussein, the American military attempted for eight years to create a democracy in Iraq. Violent attacks from insurgents continued throughout the attempt, and nearly ten times more Americans died in Iraq after President Bush declared victory in 2003, but some progress has been made. A hateful and hated dictator, Saddam Hussein, was ejected. In early 2005, Iraqis voted for members of a constitutional convention, and in May 2005, the convention elected its first prime minister and cabinet. By December 2011, the nation was deemed stable enough for the American operation to end formally, but the violent insurgency continues to kill Iraqis and destabilize the

>> An Iraqi boy cheers as a statue of Iraqi leader Saddam Hussein topples in Baghdad's al-Fardous (Paradise) Square on April 9, 2003.

Scott Nelson/Getty Images News/Getty Images

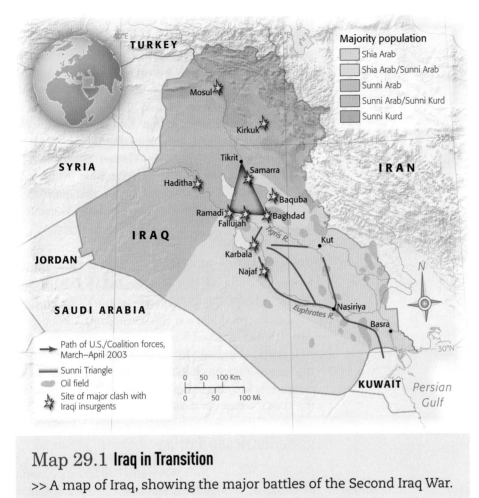

Map 29.1 **Iraq in Transition**

>> A map of Iraq, showing the major battles of the Second Iraq War.

This debate carried over into the U.S. government's decision to bring some of the war's prisoners to a military detention camp in Guantanamo Bay, Cuba, where the United States secures a naval base opened by President Bush in 2002. The U.S. government quickly determined that the detention camp resided outside international law and thus could be used to bring alleged criminals and not grant them the benefit of a trial. Even worse, news reports emerged claiming that many of the alleged criminals had been tortured during their tenure in the prison. The United Nations and other international bodies have requested the camp be closed, but the U.S. government has yet to do so. As of early 2017, there were 41 prisoners there, once again calling into question the U.S. government's commitment to many tenets of democracy.

nation, leading many commentators, including some American military leaders, to suggest that creating a democratic state in Iraq might be impossible, with the more likely short- and perhaps long-term result being an enduring civil war between rival religious and ethnic factions.

29-2c Abu Ghraib and Guantanamo Bay

In April 2004, at the same time U.S. forces were attempting to rebuild Iraq into what many hoped would be a stable democratic republic in the mold of the United States, America's claims to be fighting to expand freedoms in the Middle East were undermined by reports from Iraq. These news reports revealed that U.S. Army prison guards had tortured suspected terrorists in the Iraqi prison of Abu Ghraib. When pictures surfaced showing inmates strapped to electrical charges and stripped naked while being exposed to growling dogs, many Americans wondered how the U.S. government could claim to be advancing democracy while engaging in such behavior.

29-3 DOMESTIC WOES

As expenses for the fight against terrorism mounted, the economy slowed considerably from the frenetic pace of the 1990s. One reason was that the information technology companies that had sustained much of the 1990s growth began to consolidate. The broad expansion associated with creating an entirely new industry began to slow down.

29-3a Corporate Scandals

Concurrent with this slowdown, a number of corporate scandals erupted. The most shocking of these concerned the Enron Corporation, a large Houston energy company, which filed for bankruptcy in December 2001. Badly overextending itself in its quest to consolidate different kinds of businesses and led by unscrupulous cheats, the company could not pay its bills, leading to a spiral of other business

Anna Bryukhanova/iStock.com

>> The prison at Guantanamo Bay, where "enhanced interrogation techniques" were used to glean information from prisoners, has called into question America's commitment to many tenets of democracy.

failures. Twenty thousand employees lost much of their pensions, while corrupt and mercenary executives, who saw the crash coming, cashed out before the company's decline and were well provided for. The scandal prompted a congressional investigation, especially because President Bush was a close friend of several of Enron's leaders, including its chairman, Kenneth Lay. Several other companies, including Arthur Andersen and Halliburton, also came under scrutiny, and many similarly fell into disrepute.

29-3b The Election of 2004

Bush came up for reelection with the newspapers filled with corporate scandals, continued insurgencies in Iraq, and a slowing economy. But his approval rating remained high, and many Americans praised his leadership following the September 11 attacks. In addition, the extreme partisanship that had emerged during the Clinton years ensured that Bush would have a strong base of conservative supporters, no matter what his current political status.

THE CANDIDATES

For their part, the Democrats nominated Massachusetts senator John Kerry, a Vietnam War hero who in

the 1970s had alarmed many veterans when he came home from Vietnam and began publicly calling the war a mistake. During the 2004 election, Kerry argued that Bush had lost touch with middle-class Americans. He pointed to Bush's tax cuts for the wealthy and his eagerness to intervene in Iraq despite the American population's tepid support. But Kerry was hurt by his lack of charisma and his uncertainty about what he would do in Iraq if he were elected president. His image was also tarnished by an expensive media blitz from conservative shadow organizations that questioned his heretofore untarnished military record in Vietnam.

THE ELECTION

Polls revealed that the election would be close. It was. But in the end, Americans decided that Bush had done an acceptable job defending America's interests abroad. The president was also boosted by the continued development of Republican grassroots support in states vital to the election. In 2004, Florida was clearly a Bush state after the Republicans had spent millions of dollars there to develop and encourage voter turnout. In the 2004 election, no recount was necessary.

29-3c Hurricane Katrina

Seven months after Bush was sworn into his second term as president, a huge hurricane swept across the Caribbean, pummeling the Gulf Coast. Katrina had been a mild, Category 1 hurricane as it crossed Florida from the Atlantic, but it picked up strength in the Gulf of Mexico, wreaking havoc on Gulf Coast cities in Florida, Mississippi, and Alabama. Then the storm took an unexpected northward turn, slamming into New Orleans. While many locals had fled the city, most of those who remained witnessed a harsh storm but, they thought, not one strong enough to destroy the city. They were wrong. After the hurricane passed, it became clear that the storm had fatally weakened several already defective levees that protected the city from nearby waterways. Because much of the city sits below sea level, once the levees failed, the city filled with water. Entire districts drowned. People were told to go to the Louisiana Superdome for shelter, only to find the Superdome overcrowded, leaking, and generally unprepared to handle the crisis.

The federal government was slow to respond to the Katrina disaster, waiting several days to send in relief workers. The Federal Emergency Management Agency (FEMA), which was supposed to assist in these kinds of tragedies, was slow to coordinate efforts and, in numerous instances, stopped or impeded state or

STR/Reuters

>> The destruction caused by Hurricane Katrina showcased the persistence of racialized poverty in America. Many of the poor neighborhoods destroyed when New Orleans's levees broke were overwhelmingly populated by black Americans. Here, some of those stranded spell out H-E-L-P.

local efforts to provide relief because of its insistence on being the principal relief coordinator. Meanwhile, news cameras televised the destruction for the world to see. People were stranded on roofs for days, holding signs that read, "Help us, please." The most badly affected were African Americans, who made up a disproportionate number of the city's poor people. In total, around 1,900 people lost their lives during the hurricane, and the catastrophe showcased the continued racial imbalance in America's impoverished class.

29-3d The Financial Crisis of 2008

Domestic woes continued throughout 2008, culminating toward the end of that year with the announcement that several of the nation's largest banks had overextended themselves and were filing for bankruptcy protection from the federal government. Many smaller banks had consolidated into a handful of large ones, taking advantage of the 1999 repeal of the Glass-Steagall Act, the act that had been passed during the Great Depression to prevent rampant speculation by banks. Most of these large banks either had offered housing loans to unqualified buyers by enticing them through low, "teaser"

rates or had purchased large numbers of these risky loans from other banks. When buyers began defaulting on their loans, often once the three-or five-year "teaser" rates expired, banks stopped receiving payments and went into a cash crisis. Unwilling to part with their remaining cash reserves, they made it more difficult for borrowers to obtain loans and less money entered the American economy. Businesses stopped expanding, and people became increasingly unable to borrow money to buy homes and goods. With the consumer market slowing down, the rest of the economy slowed down as well, and by late 2008 the American economy settled into what economists have called "the Great Recession."

Making matters worse, the economic crunch was not simply an American phenomenon. European banks had made similar gambles, badly overextending investments and often defaulting. Many nations took these banks into receivership, taking on the burden of their debts, and many nations whose economies were not as large as the United States (including Iceland, Greece, and Spain) are still badly in debt, barely managing to stave off national bankruptcy.

To address the growing urgency of the crisis, the American federal government passed a financial bailout of its own banks in October 2008, offering as much as $750 billion of taxpayers' money to ease the credit crunch. The bank bailout prevented many of the nation's largest banks from declaring bankruptcy, but nonetheless, with less money in the markets, that money harder to access, and countries around the world falling into similar travails, a deep recession took hold in 2008, and world markets reacted erratically and unhelpfully. Throughout 2008, for example, the Dow Jones Industrial Average, the benchmark average of stock prices, declined by nearly 40 percent.

During 2008 and 2009, the U.S. unemployment rate remained just under 10 percent, significantly less than the 25 percent mark reached during the Great Depression, although changes in the way the number of unemployed are tallied make direct comparisons difficult. The housing market stalled as well, and many consumer industries had a difficult time convincing Americans to part with their money.

>> Traders were despondent watching the events of October 9, 2008. The Dow Jones Industrial Average dropped 678.91 points that day, to finish at 8579.19, closing below 9000 for the first time since 2003 and representing a crushing 40 percent loss in value for the year.

New York Daily News Archive/Getty Images

29-4 PRESIDENT OBAMA

As Bush concluded his second term in office, the nation was divided by culture wars, frightening foreign events continued to preoccupy Americans, and, most importantly, the economy seemed on the verge of collapse. In the atmosphere of Republican failure, Democrats sensed they could win back the White House and, perhaps, stop the conservative ascendancy that had been mounting since the 1970s. Democrats vowed to expand some social programs, including nationalizing America's health care system. They promised to take a less militant stance in world affairs,

hoping to reach out diplomatically to potentially hostile countries. And they promised to rein in the war on terror.

29-4a The Election of 2008

Within these debates, the Democratic Party witnessed the emergence of two historic candidates, Hillary Clinton, senator from New York State and former First Lady, and Barack Obama, a mixed-race senator from Illinois. After a grueling primary battle, Obama became the first African American to win the nomination of a major political party, a dramatic demonstration of the transformation of American life since the civil rights movement. Promising a change from the cultural wars ascendant since the 1980s, Obama squared off against Vietnam War veteran John McCain, who, at seventy-two, would have become the oldest person to win the presidency. But McCain's candidacy was plagued by his ties to the increasingly unpopular George W. Bush and by a generally disorganized campaign. In addition, his vice-presidential candidate, Sarah Palin, the governor of Alaska, polarized the population with her folksy antigovernment rhetoric and her seeming lack of preparedness for the job, something especially troubling because of McCain's age. Meanwhile, Obama's message of practical centrism and an end to the politics of division was greatly boosted by the economic turmoil taking place in the midst of the campaign (and on the watch of a Republican president). On Election Day, the race was not close, with Obama handily winning the Electoral College and emerging with 52 percent of the popular vote to McCain's 46 percent—a difference of more than 7 million voters (see Map 29.2).

2008

Candidate (Party)	Electoral Vote		Popular Vote	
Obama (Democrat)	365	68%	69,498,459	52.9%
McCain (Republican)	173	32%	59,948,283	45.6%

Map 29.2 The Election of 2008

29-4b Obama's Presidency

As president, Obama confronted a host of challenges, but three issues occupied him most: (1) drawing down the war on terror; (2) passing the nation's first comprehensive health care bill; and (3) handling the Great Recession and the collection of protestors surrounding it.

DRAWING DOWN THE WAR ON TERROR

The expenses of waging a nebulous war on terror continued to mount throughout Obama's first term, although he did develop several benchmarks by which U.S. troops would be removed from both Iraq and Afghanistan. Some of these were quickly met, and in December 2011, the United States officially withdrew its troops from Iraq, the last troops departing on December 18.

Sectarian violence has continued to plague the Middle Eastern nation, though, especially between Sunni and Shia Arabs competing for political control of Iraq. In 2013 and 2014, several extremist militant Sunni groups from Iraq merged with various militant groups in Syria and created a new organization, called the Islamic State of Iraq and the Levant (**ISIL**). Demanding a return to a caliphate ruling over all Muslims in the world, and governed by a stern interpretation of Islamic law, ISIL has gained converts in both the Middle East and several Western nations. It currently controls land occupied by more than ten million people in the region. The State Department has declared ISIL to be among the world's most dangerous groups, and almost every mainstream Muslim group has disavowed it.

Creating a stable Afghanistan has been equally tricky. On December 28, 2014, NATO officially ended combat operations with a ceremony in Kabul, although the U.S. continued to have a significant military presence throughout the country. The goal of the more than 10,000 American troops is to prevent political instability and curtail the continued use of violence by radical Islamic groups. It is unclear when a complete withdrawal will happen. The United States' broad departure from Afghanistan, though, was due in large part to the death of Osama bin Laden, who was finally located and assassinated on May 2, 2011. For a few days thereafter, the United States briefly overcame its increasing

>> President Obama greeting troops during his surprise visit to Afghanistan on May 1, 2012.

White House Photo/Pete Souza

political divisions to celebrate the death of the mastermind of 9/11. Shortly thereafter, President Obama announced an end to the "war on terror," favoring instead more targeted attacks against specific groups.

Obama was, however, less willing to draw down other instruments in the name of national security. The detention camps at Guantanamo Bay continue to exist despite Obama's campaign promises to close them, and Obama did renew George W. Bush's PATRIOT Act. He also revealed that, as American troops left the Middle East, the military has increasingly relied on unmanned drones that, guided by on-the-ground-intelligence, have targeted and sometimes killed key enemy personnel (as well as many innocents) in an effort to prevent American enemies from rising to power.

In addition, President Obama did little to dismantle the various spying programs developed by the National Security Agency (NSA). This led to some embarrassing diplomatic situations, as when it was discovered that the NSA had been spying on a close American ally, the German Chancellor Angela Merkel, by tapping her cellular phone.

This culture of surveillance has led to many criticisms, including several occurrences of citizens leaking huge amounts of classified information on the Internet. The most dramatic of these leaks occurred in

ISIL a jihadist militant group that follows a fundamentalist doctrine of Sunni Islam and uses violence and terrorism in its attempts to return an Islamic caliphate

>> In 2009, Sonia Sotomayor became the U.S. Supreme Court's 111th justice, its third woman, and its first Hispanic. With Sotomayor's confirmation, the Court also for the first time did not have a single Protestant member, but six Catholics and three Jews. It was a measure of Catholic and Jewish acceptance in modern America that hardly anyone noticed.

2010, when the hacking organization wikileaks posted more than 250,000 classified documents relating to all sorts of government activity. Wikileaks was not alone however, and the sheer amount of leaks has led to vigorous debates about what a government is entitled to keep from its citizens.

THE HEALTH CARE ACT

While having marginal success in drawing down the war on terror, Obama did have better luck passing the nation's first comprehensive health care bill. It came after a difficult, year-long debate, concluding in March 2010. The bill's aim was to ensure that all Americans had some form of health insurance, including the 40 million who at the time of the bill's signing did not have any. The law allowed parents to extend coverage to their children until they turn twenty-six years old. It also made it illegal for health insurance companies to deny insurance to people with

Affordable Care Act A federal statute signed into law by President Barack Obama on March 23, 2010, designed to increase health insurance quality and affordability, and increase the number of Americans covered by health insurance. Opponents derisively called it "Obamacare," a name President Obama eventually adopted himself

preexisting conditions, a common occurrence before the bill passed. It gave small businesses tax breaks for offering health care for their employees. And it set a deadline to create a marketplace for affordable care. The U.S. Supreme Court upheld challenges to the **Affordable Care Act** in 2012 and 2015, and the Act was completely rolled out in 2014. Republican attempts to overturn it failed in fall of 2017, and the law was one of the major liberal accomplishments of the first decades of the twenty-first century, expanding, however slightly, the social safety net first proposed during the Progressive Era more than one hundred years prior.

CONTINUED DIVISIONS OF WEALTH

If Obama had success in passing a comprehensive health care bill and concluding certain aspects of the war on terror, the economy continued to plague him. In 2010, Obama modestly increased banking regulations, attempting to prevent further financial crises in an industry that has quickly sped ahead of outdated laws and been hampered by thirty years of deregulation. He also passed a large stimulus bill that initiated more than 75,000 projects across the nation. And indeed, the economy began to grow again, beginning in 2010 and picking up pace ever since.

This growth, however, has been uneven. The growing sectors of the economy have largely favored the well educated. Manufacturing, on the other hand, has continued to decline, leaving less educated Americans with few job options beyond working in the service industry. The result has been an increase in the division of wealth that re-appeared in the late 1970s and has grown ever since.

29-4c Backlash from the Right and the Left

Given that Reagan, then Bill Clinton, then George W. Bush all used the language of advocating small government (even if their actions did not live up to the rhetoric), it was predictable that a conservative backlash would emerge to Obama's efforts to institute things like mandatory health care and to bail out several failing industries. Calling themselves the Tea Party and embracing the folksy language of Sarah Palin, in early 2009 many conservative Americans began protesting what they saw as Obama's expansion of the federal government, a complaint made against Democrats since the New Deal. With Tea Party support, in 2010 Republicans won back control of the House of Representatives, although it wasn't entirely clear whether the results reflected a genuine sentiment against Obama's expansion of the welfare state or a broader discomfort with the stalled economy. Furthermore, in 2010 Republicans took advantage of the U.S. Supreme Court's decision in the case of *Citizens United* v. *Federal Election Commission*, which prohibited the federal government from limiting the amount of money corporations could spend on elections. The combination of increased corporate expenditures and free-market libertarianism espoused by the Tea Party has captured increasing amounts of the Republican Party since its inception.

If the Tea Party flanked Obama from the right and took hold of the Republican Party, another movement emerged from the left. Calling themselves Occupy Wall Street, in September 2011, a group of disaffected Americans began to camp out in Zuccotti Park, adjacent to Wall Street in lower Manhattan, New York. Using the slogan "We are the 99 percent," the protestors raged against the growing gap in wealth distribution in the United States, especially between the top 1 percent of wealth capturers and the rest of the population. The protestors rejected more typical political protests, seeing politics as overly infected by corporate wealth and useless in advocating real social change. The protest sparked a wave of sympathy movements across the nation, movements that demonstrated large-scale frustrations with the widening gap between America's haves and have-nots, and the perceived inability of either party to advocate for real progressive change.

29-4d Obama's Second Term

Despite the challenges from the right and the left, in 2012, Obama was easily re-elected, although the excitement he generated in 2008, when he promised "hope" and "change" from the divisive politics of the 1980s and 1990s,

seemed to have vanished, as his promise to introduce a new kind of responsive politics appeared largely unfulfilled. Nevertheless, Obama handily defeated his opponent, Willard "Mitt" Romney, who, when nominated by the Republican Party, became the first Mormon put forward as a presidential candidate from a major political party.

The election was less notable for its presidential election than for other results. Perhaps most telling was how the changes of the previous fifty years had transformed the electorate, especially the transformations brought about by the 1965 Immigration Act and the increasing recognition of the diversity of the United States. For instance, overwhelming numbers of ethnic and racial minorities voted for Obama (making up 45 percent of his total popular vote—a record), while white Americans supported Romney, 59 percent to 39 percent. Meanwhile, more than 55 percent of women voted for Obama, while only 47 percent of men did.

Reflecting similar trends, in Wisconsin, Tammy Baldwin became the first openly gay person elected to the U.S. Senate. Ballot initiatives allowing same-sex marriage passed in Maine, Maryland, and Washington, while Minnesota voters rejected a constitutional ban on the practice. Twenty women were elected to the Senate, a record, while a state like New Hampshire sent all women to Congress, elected a female governor, and chose a female-controlled state legislature.

GAY MARRIAGE

Another major transition has occurred in the years following Obama's re-election: the widespread acceptance of gay marriage, which, in June 2015, became the law of the land. Since 2004, when Massachusetts legalized same-sex marriage, several states passed laws making similar allowances. An opposition arose, with opponents of same-sex marriage pushing for state laws, and sometimes even state constitutional amendments, assuring

>> In 2011, protestors in New York City began a movement to challenge increased income disparity in American life. Using the slogan, "We are the 99%," the protest quickly spread nationwide.

Spencer Platt/Getty Images

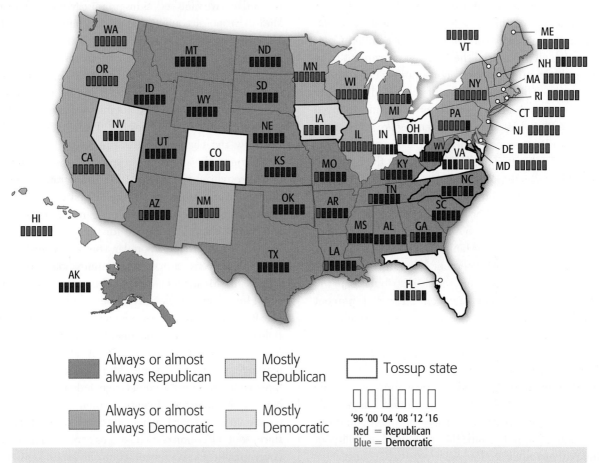

Always or almost always Republican	Mostly Republican		Tossup state
Always or almost always Democratic	Mostly Democratic		'96 '00 '04 '08 '12 '16 Red = Republican Blue = Democratic

Map 29.3 How States Have Voted Since 1996

>> Since 1996, most states have consistently voted Democratic or Republican, with only a very small number of states vacillating between the two parties.

that legal marriage only be between a man and a woman. When gay-rights activists challenged the legality of those laws, however, courts almost universally overturned them, paving the way for same-sex marriage in unlikely conservative states such as Utah. By early 2015, 37 states and 22 Native American tribal jurisdictions allowed gay marriage, paving the way for an historic U.S. Supreme Court decision. On June 26, 2015, in the case of *Obergefell v. Hodges*, the U.S. Supreme Court found that the denial of marriage licenses to same-sex couples violated both the Due Process and the Equal Protection clauses of the Fourteenth Amendment. Many commentators suggested the decision did for the gay rights movement what the historic *Brown v. Board* decision did for the civil rights movement–give it judicial support to make greater claims for equality. Meanwhile, popular support for same-sex marriage has increased from 25% in 1996 to somewhere around 60% in 2015.

The United States was the twenty-first and most populous country in the world to allow same-sex marriage.

29-5 POLITICAL POLARIZATION AND THE 2016 ELECTION

Each of Obama's political victories, however, sparked fierce opposition. Sometimes this came from the populist left, who, for instance, thought Obamacare fell far short of government-financed health care, and who felt that despite the color of his skin, his successes simply masked continued racism in the country. But most came from the populist right, who variously interpreted Obama as the abandonment of the country's racial heritage or as yet another political elitist out of touch with the lives most Americans lived. Various protest movements in the latter

>> The movement to increase the rights of gay Americans started a major uptick in the 1990s, beginning with the movement to allow openly gay people to serve in the military (shown here) and continuing to the legalization of same-sex marriage in 2015.

by police, of Micheal Brown in Ferguson, Missouri, Walter Scott in South Carolina, John Crawford III in Ohio, and Eric Garner in New York City. Large numbers of Americans of all races began to protest the seemingly wanton violence targeted at African American men. That many of these murders were filmed by passers-by using mobile phones prompted many Americans to wonder how widespread the practice was and how many instances went unrecorded. Rather than serve as a harbinger of a postracial America, where ethnic and racial identities didn't matter as much as they had in previous years, it seemed the Obama presidency was just as markedly amping up age-old racial hatreds.

To call attention to the violence, a protest campaign, under the banner "Black Lives Matter," held marches across the country. Alas, it wasn't marches but more violence that led to perhaps the most substantive change. On June 17, 2015, a 21-year-old white man named Dylann Roof allegedly entered Emanuel African Methodist Episcopal Church in downtown Charleston, South Carolina, killing nine people including the senior pastor, state senator Clementa C. Pinckney. The church's history as one of the nation's oldest black churches, and Roof's apparent engagement with several racist organizations (including numerous photographs of him with a Confederate flag) suggested it was a racist hate crime. In response, several Southern leaders, Republican and Democrat, demanded the removal of Confederate flags from public buildings throughout their states. Many quoted President Obama's eulogy for Pinckney, where he said, "history can't be a sword to justify injustice or a shield against progress. It must be a manual for how to avoid repeating the mistakes of the past, how to break the cycle, a roadway toward a better world."

half of his presidency paved the way for populism on the right and left to help shape the 2016 election.

29-5a Black Lives Matter

If Obama could celebrate the legalization of same-sex marriage, he, and many other Americans, were troubled by a seeming increase in racialized violence in 2014 and 2015. It began with the 2013 killing of an unarmed black Florida teenager named Trayvon Martin by George Zimmerman, a member of the local neighborhood watch. Zimmerman was later acquitted of second-degree murder, leading to bouts of protest across the nation. Unrest continued through the 2014 killings, all

29-5b The Rise of Hate Groups

The shooting in Charleston may have been the work of a lone gunman, but groups embodying this type of hate almost doubled in the United States during the first decades of the twentieth century. Hate groups are those perpetuating beliefs or practices that attack an entire class of people, usually for characteristics those people can't change. The spike could be attributed to increased immigration and the inability of the federal government to curb it, President Obama's skin color, and negative media images (and actions) of Muslims and other groups committing acts of terrorism. Since 2015, anti-Muslim groups increased by almost 200%. In 2016, there were at least 130 Ku Klux Klan groups operating, and the number of "patriot" groups, threatened by the perceived

>> A 2014 march in New York City protesting the continued harassment and violence perpetrated against African Americans. Under the banner "Black Lives Matter," the protesters brought national attention to an issue that has plagued the African American community for decades.

a katz/Shutterstock.com

decline in power of white Protestant Americans, grew to more than 660. These groups would come to play an outsized role in the 2016 presidential election.

29-5c The 2016 Presidential Campaign

In 2016, the economy remained strong but gains were increasingly tilted to the wealthiest Americans. Obama had shored up American banks and corporations with bailouts and other government incentives. But he had done little to promote jobs programs for the middle class or rebuild the sagging American infrastructure. Wages for most of his two terms stagnated. He had tread softly in shaping environmental policy, shepherding the United States through various international agreements without becoming an environmental leader. And he had done little to solve longstanding issues such as immigration or increased corporate involvement in American politics. In short, his socially moderate, internationally minded, business-friendly policies resembled "the third way" pioneered by Bill Clinton in the 1990s. Even his most far-reaching expansion of the social safety net, the Affordable Care Act, had its origins in Republican think tanks and was moderate compared to proposals coming from the political left.

Both the major parties, in turn, were beset by outsider candidates, populist politicians from the left and the right. From the left, Vermont Senator Bernard "Bernie" Sanders voiced a sustained critique of Obama's mainstream liberalism. Sanders advocated a stronger social safety net developed by the government, higher taxes on the wealthy, regulations on corporations, and a rebuilding of the nation's infrastructure through a broadening of middle-class jobs. Many on the left saw his rebuke of both mainstream Democrats and Republicans as a breath of fresh air; the Clintonian

third way, in their view, seemed only to enhance the fortunes of the wealthiest Americans.

In the Democratic primary, Sanders gained traction in states in the American northeast, where factories had been hollowed out after the great post-World War II economic boom. But it was another candidate who eventually secured the nomination. Hillary Clinton, who had narrowly lost the 2008 nomination to Barack Obama, eventually defeated Sanders after a long primary season, and served as the embodiment of continuing the policies of mainstream American liberalism. The populist left had been defeated, but only narrowly.

There would be no such defeat on the right. A large number of seasoned politicians entered the Republican primary, but it was a true outsider who, from the beginning, stole the limelight. Donald J. Trump was not taken very seriously as a candidate at first. The scion of a millionaire real estate mogul from New York City, Trump continued his father's legacy and made a name for himself as America's businessman *par excellence* in the 1980s and 1990s. He parlayed that success into becoming a reality television star, using the signature line, "you're fired," in his show "The Apprentice." He then became increasingly political during the Obama presidency, firing off tweets and Facebook messages that constantly criticized the president, even going so far as to question the president's birth place, claiming Obama wasn't born in the United States and was thus ineligible to be president. On the campaign trail, Trump spoke his mind, made numerous gaffes and false accusations, but his rambunctious sensibility resonated with a certain part of the electorate that was disaffected by mainstream liberalism and tired of constant reminders that the United States was a multicultural nation committed

>> The 2016 election was full of raucous name-calling and dismissiveness, on both sides. Here, supporters of Donald Trump lambast Hillary Clinton for her supposed corruptness.

JASON REDMOND/Getty Images

to diversity and multiculturalism. Trump's most insistent campaign promises included building a thousand-mile long wall along the border between the United States and Mexico in order to keep Mexicans from illegally crossing into the U.S.; repealing the Affordable Care Act, which he derisively called "Obamacare"; having a stronger hand in international affairs; and passing a vague series of economic reforms. All told, he vowed to "Make America Great Again," although he never specified to what past it was he was referring.

Up until the night of the election, pollsters anticipated a Clinton triumph, a seeming reassurance of the continued success of mainstream liberalism. It quickly became apparent, however, that several of the states in the American Rust Belt were increasingly leaning toward Trump. In addition, in the large cities of those states, which Obama had carried overwhelmingly, Clinton was not winning by as wide a margin, or drawing as large of a turnout. By the end of the night, it was clear Clinton was going to win the popular vote by as many as three million votes, but that Trump would take the electoral college and become the next president. And that is exactly what happened. Clinton won overwhelming majorities in reliably Democratic states like California and New York, but Trump had narrowly carried many more mid-sized and smaller states, like Wisconsin, Michigan, and Pennsylvania, giving him the win in the Electoral College. For the fifth time in American history, and the second time since 2000, the winner of the popular vote would not become president (and in both recent occurrences, it was a Democrat who won the popular vote but lost the electoral college).

29-5d President Trump

Since becoming president, Trump has forged ahead tumultuously. During his first hundred days, he tried to halt travel from several Middle Eastern nations, attempts that were eventually barred by the courts. He tried to repeal the Affordable Care Act, but could not get enough votes in Congress to pass a full repeal, despite Congress being controlled by Republicans. And he continues to be hounded by his close ties to leading members of the right-wing media and by his relationship with Vladimir Putin, the president of the Russian Federation. He even took flack for firing the Director of the FBI, James Comey, who was in charge of investigating Trump's connections to the role Russian hackers played in the 2016 election. Trump did succeed in getting Neil Gorsuch appointed to the US Supreme Court, assuring that body's conservative tilt for the foreseeable future.

But Trump's presidency has also revitalized activists on the left. Immediately following his election, protestors around the U.S. staged simultaneous protests in what was called "the Women's March." Its list of demands included women's rights, immigration reform, healthcare reform, LGBTQ rights, racial equality, and workers' rights. Between the 408 simultaneous marches around the country, it was the largest one-day protest in U.S. history.

Trump's presidency seems to have exacerbated political divides in the country, as increasing numbers of Americans leave behind mainstream liberalism in favor of something more responsive to their needs. In this, the U.S. is following the trend of other nation's around the world, including Britain, France, and the Netherlands.

>LOOKING AHEAD...

As the United States delves deeper into the twenty-first century, it proceeds with its unique blend of belief and fear: belief that the country will inevitably and always improve, and fear that any change will unmoor the country from the traditions of the past. Issues such as environmental degradation, political gridlock, and increased income inequality continue to plague the country, as does a broader sense that the nation is unified in any significant way. What does it mean to fulfill the American dream? Who decides what that dream is, anyway? Regardless of how the debate turns out, it is the debate itself that is the most American of traits, a debate about the shape of the future that continues to create the American present.

STUDY TOOLS 29

READY TO STUDY? IN THE BOOK, YOU CAN:

❏ Rip out the Chapter Review Card, which includes key terms and chapter summaries.

LOCATED AT WWW.CENGAGE.COM/LOGIN:

❏ Collect StudyBits while you read and study the chapter.

❏ Quiz yourself on key concepts.

❏ Find videos for further exploration.

❏ Prepare for tests with HIST5 Flash Cards as well as those you create.

❏ Read a revealing biography of Osama bin Laden published by *The Observer* of London.

❏ Read the BBC's examination of the Enron scandal.

❏ Read Secretary of State Colin Powell's speech to the UN advocating war with Iraq.

CH29 TIMELINE

		What Else Was Happening
▶ 2000	Reality TV shows experience an explosion of popularity, beginning with *Big Brother* and *Survivor*.	
▶ 2001	Republican Congress passes Bush's $1.3 trillion tax cut.	*Apple launches the iPod, revolutionizing the music industry.*
	September 11: Terrorists fly hijacked planes into World Trade Center, Pentagon; over 3,000 die.	
	October: United States invades Taliban-controlled Afghanistan to hunt down al Qaeda and bin Laden.	
	Bush forms fifteenth cabinet position for Department of Homeland Security.	
▶ 2002	Enron bankruptcy begins series of corporate scandals of fraud and corruption.	

2003

March 19: United States preemptively invades Iraq for harboring weapons of mass destruction.

April: United States armed forces march into Baghdad.

Saddam Hussein captured

August: Hurricane Katrina devastates Mississippi Gulf Coast and parts of New Orleans, kills 1,900, reveals poor disaster response and the prevalence of race-based poverty.

2004: April: *News about torture in U.S.-run Abu Ghraib prison shocks Americans and world.*

November: *George W. Bush prevails over Democratic challenger John Kerry in presidential race.*

A partially eaten, ten-year-old grilled cheese sandwich said to bear the image of the Virgin Mary sells on eBay for $28,000.

2005: *Iraqis elect members of constitutional convention.*

Video-sharing website YouTube is launched by three former PayPal employees.

2006: *Saddam Hussein is found guilty of crimes against humanity in Iraqi court and executed.*

2008

Barack Obama becomes the first black presidential nominee for a major political party.

Crisis in global financial markets prompts governmental "bailout."

November: Barack Obama defeats John McCain in presidential election.

Democratic primaries led by first woman and African American candidates.

Dramatic increases in oil and food prices.

2010

Using support from the emerging Tea Party Movement, Republicans win control of the House of Representatives.

2011

The Occupy Wall Street movement takes over Zucotti Park, adjacent to Wall Street, in New York City. The Occupy Movement, under the banner of "We Are the 99%," spreads nationwide.

2012

February: George Zimmerman's killing of an unarmed African American teenager named Trayvon Martin sparks nationwide protests against violence perpetrated against the African American community.

November: Barack Obama is elected to his second term as president, defeating Republican opponent Mitt Romney.

2015

In the case of *Obergefell v. Hodges*, the U.S. Supreme Court legalized same-sex marriage throughout the nation.

2016

November: Election of Donald J. Trump as 45th president of the United States of America.

INDEX

In this index *i* indicates images, *m* indicates maps, and *t* indicates table. Defined terms are in **bold**.

A

Abernathy, Ralph, 481
Abilene, Kansas, 344
abortion
  culture wars and, 531
  Roe v. *Wade* and, 521, 523
Abu Ghraib prison, U. S. Army
    torture and, 563
Acquired immune deficiency
    syndrome (AIDS), 532
activism. *See also* protest(s)
  of African Americans,
    518–519
  Chicano movement, 520
  environmental, 522
  Gay Liberation Movement,
    521–522
  Native American, Red Power,
    520
  women's movement, 520–521.
    See also women's movement
Adams, Charles Francis, Jr., 319
Addams, Jane
  as anti-imperialist, 380
  Hull House and, 359, 359*i*,
    369, 388
  as progressive reformer, 358
advertisements, 397
advertising
  in 1920s, 397
  consumer demand and, 315
affirmative action
  African American activism
    and, 519–520
  Nixon and, 513
Affordable Care Act, 568, 572,
    573
Afghanistan
  al Qaeda and, 560
  bin Laden and, 561
  civil war, 560
  political instability in, 567
  Soviet troops removed from
    535, 561
  U. S. troops withdraw from,
    567
  war in, 560
Africa
  as African American destina-
    tion, 519
  AIDS in, 532
  defeat of German/Italian
    forces in, 446
  Germany, in World War II,
    445
  Italy in north, World War II
    and, 444
  Nixon foreign policy and, 513
African Americans, 309, 318.
    See also civil rights; Col-
    ored Americans; race; racial

discrimination; racism;
    segregation; slave society;
    slavery
"40-acres-and-a-mule",
    292, 294
activism, 518–519
affirmative action, 519–520
anti-lynching crusade, 358.
    See also Wells–Barnett,
    Ida B.
black codes, 294–295
Black Freedom Movement,
    519
Black Lives Matter protest,
    police violence and, 571
black officeholders, 299
Black Studies, 519
Communist Party and, 427
Congressional/Senatorial
    representatives, 305
crack cocaine and, 530–531
cultural acceptance, 518–519
cultural life, 341–342, 341*i*
desegregation, civil rights and,
    478–480
election of 1868 and, 297
Emmett Till lynching and, 480
Fair Employment Practices
    Committee (FEPC) and,
    451
Fifteenth Amendment and,
    298–299
as freedmen and freedwom-
    en, 291–292
Freedom Summer, voting
    rights and, 492
Great Migration and, 400–401
Harlem Renaissance, 404–405
Hoovervilles, the Great
    Depression and, 418–419
Horton, Willie, 532
hunger, 419
Hurricane Katrina and,
    564–565
immigration and, 552–553
industrial employment, 337
integration into the work-
    place, 337
jazz music and, 404
Jim Crow laws, 338
King, Rodney, Los Angeles
    riots and, 544, 544*i*
literacy, educational institu-
    tions and, 342
lynching, responses to, 339,
    340*i*
murder of James Byrd, white
    supremacists and, 553
neighborhoods, 418–419
New Deal, segregation and,
    432–433
opportunities for, 451–452

Populist Movement and, 353
race riots and, 401
racial discrimination and, 302
racial segregation, Cold War
    era, 473
rap/hip hop music, 531
religious life of, in industrial
    South, 342
responses, 340–341
segregation, in industrial
    South, 337–340. *See also*
    segregation *entries*
sexual crimes, post Civil War,
    303
sharecropping and, 300–301,
    302*i*
Social Darwinism and, 319
Tuskegee Airmen, 451
unions, exclusion from, 432
violence against, 306. *See also*
    Ku Klux Klan
voting restrictions on, 303
White League and, 303*i*
women's clubs, suffrage and,
    365–366
women's roles, Cold War era,
    473
World War II, opportunities
    and, 451
writers, Great Depression
    and, 422
**African Methodist Episcopal
    Church (AME Church)**, 342
Afro, 519*i*
Agee, James, 431
Age of Affluence, 470
age of fracture
  Carter, 516–518
  identity politics, 518–523
  New Right, 523–524
  Richard Nixon, 511–513
  troubled economy and politics
    adrift, 514–518
  Watergate scandal, 513–514
Agitator, The, suffrage journal,
    299
Agnew, Spiro, corruption of, 514
**Agricultural Adjustment Act
    (AAA)**, 426
agriculture
  American, in World War II,
    449
  crop failures, dust bowl,
    depression and, 419
  farm reform, depression era,
    426
  sharecropping and. *See* share-
    cropping
  slavery and. *See* slavery
  tobacco. *See* tobacco
  wheat sales to USSR, 512–513
Aguinaldo, Emilio, 378, 380

AIDS epidemic, 531–532
Aid to Dependent Children Act
    (ADC), 428
Aid to Families with Dependent
    Children program, 433, 495
airlines, 9/11 attacks and,
    559–560
al-Fardous Square, Baghdad,
    Iraq, 562*i*
Alabama
  dust storms in, 419
  Freedom Riders in, 490
  Hurricane Katrina and,
    564–565
  iron production in, 337
  Jim Crow protests in, 489
  registered black voters, 494
  Scottsboro Boys, 423
  Tuskegee Institute in, 342
  Union, readmittance to, 297
Alaska
  acquisition of, 375
Alcatraz Island, California, 520*i*
Alger, Horatio Jr., 319
All-American Girls Professional
    Baseball League, 455*i*
Allende, Salvador, 513
alliance, 444–445
Allied Powers, World War I,
    384–385, 389
al Qaeda, 560, 561. *See also* ter-
    rorist/terrorism
America First Committee, 442
American Broadcasting Com-
    pany, merger of, 551
**American Civil Liberties Union
    (ACLU)**, 408, 531
American Civil War, 293
American Dilemma, An
    (Myrdal), 452
American Embassy, Tehran,
    Iran, hostage crisis and, 517
American empire
  by 1912, map, 383
  anti-American sentiment, 380
  army in battle, 389
  Bill Clinton, 544–549
  Bush, George H. W., 543–544
  Cold War, 543
  dream, 335
  economy, 416
  financial reasons for, 374
  frontier, end of, 373–374
  geopolitical reasons, 374
  globalization, 543
  homefront terrorism, 553–554
  in information age, 543–556
  information revolution, 549–552
  isolationists and, 383–384
  Latin America and, 376
  manifest destiny and end of
    frontier, 373–374

Connecticut
  race riots in, 401
Connor, Eugene, 490
conservatism
  Bush, George H. W. and,
    532–533. *See also* Bush,
    George H. W.
  "New Right," 523–524. *See
    also* "New Right"
  Reagan and. *See* Reagan, Ronald
Conservative Democrats, First
    New Deal criticism from,
    427
Consolidated Tenants League,
    419
consolidation, New Deal, 430
constitution. *See* state constitu-
    tions; U. S. Constitution
constitutional convention, 293
consumer demand, 315–317
  advertising, 315
  harmful business practices,
    316–317
  national brands, 315
  stores and mail order,
    315–316
  working conditions, 317
consumer economy, 395–399
  consumerism, in 1920s,
    396–399
  union membership, decline
    of, 396–397
  welfare capitalism, 396
consumerism, 471–472
  in 1920s, 396–399
  adventures in real estate,
    398–399
  advertisements, 397
  buying on credit, 397
  car culture, 398
  stocks and shares, 399
containment, 462
  institutions of, 463
  policy of, 462–463
contraception Margaret Sanger
    and, 358, 366
Contract Labor Law, 324
Contract with America, Clinton
    and, 548
contras (Nicaragua), 536
convict leasing, reconstruction
    and, 301
Coolidge, Calvin (Silent Cal),
    presidencies of, 401
corporate consolidation,
    550–551
Corporate Scandals, 563–564
corporation(s), 551. *See also*
    business
  consolidation, mergers and,
    550–551
  deregulation and, 529
  Enron scandal, 564
  globalization and, 551
  growth of, Industrial Revolu-
    tion and, 314
  mega, mergers and, 551
  outsourcing, 550
  Second New Deal and, 429
corruption
  Agnew, Spiro, 514
  Industrial Revolution, political,
    319–320

Nixon, Watergate and,
    513–514
  political divisions and,
    321–322
  post Civil war, 301–302, 304
cotton
  "King Cotton," 331
  sharecroppers picking, 302*i*
  in South, 1880–1900, 336
  and textiles, 336, 337*i*
Coughlin, Charles
  New Deal, Union for Social
    Justice and, 427
  Union Party and, 429
Count Basie, 422
counterculture, 503–504
court packing, New Deal,
    430
covert operations, of U. S.
    government, 467–468, 475
cowboys, 345
Cowley, Malcolm, 407
cow town, 344
Coxey, Jacob, 352
"crack" cocaine, 530
craft unions, 326
Crawford, John, III, 571
credit
  in 1950s, 472
  buying on, 397
  Great Recession of 2008 crisis
    and, 565
Crédit Mobilier Company, 320
Crédit Mobilier Scandal, 320
Creel, George, 388
  Clinton, anti-crime measures,
    546
  crime economy, decrease in
    and, 550
  hate-crime, 571
  hate-crime legislation, 554
  immigrants and, 335
  inner city, 530
  liberals soft on, 532
  New Deal and, 431
  sex, racial hierarchy and, 303
  zoot suits and, 453
Crimea, Yalta, World War II
    and, 455
Cripple Creek silver mind, 345
Crocker, Charles, 310
Crosby, Bing, 422
Crow, Jim, 331, 339
Cuba
  Bay of Pigs invasion, 487
  Castro, Fidel, 487–488
  Cuban Missile Crisis and,
    487–488
  Guantanamo Bay prison,
    563, 567
  humanitarian aid in, 381
  independence of, 379, 381
  Kennedy and, 487
  resentment of Americans
    and, 381
  Rough Riders and, 378
  San Juan Hill, 378
  Spanish-American War and,
    377–379
Cuban Missile Crisis, 487–488,
    506
Cuban resentment, 380–381
cultural imperialism, 551

cultural pluralism, 409
cultural politics, Great Depres-
    sion and, 420–422
  movies, 421
  radio, 422
  writers, 421–422
culture. *See also* architecture;
    art(s); entertainment; fam-
    ily; leisure time; literature;
    music; religion; society
  New Deal effects on, 431
  popular, identity politics and,
    522–523
  in postwar South, 341–342
  of unity, 431
culture wars
  abortion and, 531
  economic issues and, 543
  Middle East and, 561
  multiculturalism and, 544
  of Reagan years and, 531
Cummings, Homer, 431
currency. *See* money
Custer, George Armstrong, 347
cyber-thieves, 559
Czechoslovakia, communist
    regime overthrown,
    536, 537

D

D-Day, Normandy, 446, 448*i*
Dallas, Texas, Kennedy assas-
    sination in, 494
dance, Latino culture of, 523
Darrow, Clarence, 408
Darwin, Charles, 319, 369, 407
Daugherty, Harry M., 401
Davis, John W., 402, 427
Dawes Act, 347
Dawes General Allotment Act,
    347
Dayton, Tennessee, Scopes
    Monkey Trial, 409
"dead white males," 544
deaths. *See* casualties
debating peace, 389–390
Debs, Eugene V., 326, 388,
    399–400
debts
  federal deficits, 515
  national, deficits, Reagan
    and, 528
declaring war
  declaration of war, 387
  forming public opinion,
    387–388
  hyphenated Americans, 388
  mixed reaction, 387
  wartime repression, 388
  Zimmermann note, 387
decline of cities, 516
deficit
  American, Japan and, 530
  Clinton and, 546, 547
deflation, Populist Party
    and, 350
deindustrialization, 530*i*
de Lesseps, Ferdinand, 382
de Lôme, Enrique Dupuy, 377
DeMille, Cecil B., 403
democracy

Democratic National Conven-
    tion, 474, 493, 504
  election of 1992, Bill Clinton
    and, 545
  election of 1996 and, 549
democratic eclipse, 475
Democratic establishment,
    511–512
Democratic Party
  in 1968, 504–505
  civil rights and, 478
  Clinton, Bill and, 545
  Compromise of 1877
    and, 304
  Confederate Flag and, 571
  congressional elections, of
    1998, 554
  election of 1876 and, 304, 517
  election of 1988 and, 532–533
  election of 2004 and, 564
  election of 2008 and, 566
  election of 2012 and, 569–570
  First New Deal, criticism, 427
  Gore as candidate and, 555
  health care reform and, 548
  illegal immigration and,
    552–553
  impeachment of Clinton and,
    554
  KKK, crime and, 303
  New Deal effects on, 432
  Nixon liberalism and, 513
  political divisions and,
    321–322
  racism and, 302–304
  Reagan and, 527–528
  Truman and, 474–475
  white superiority and, 305
  Wilson, Woodrow, and, 364
democratic political organiza-
    tion, 320
demographic shifts, post WWII
    in U. S., 454–455
Denmark, 441
  Descent into War, 385*m*
  German invasion, 441
depression-era themes, 422
depression, economics and
    politics of, 415–418
  Hoover, 415–418
  statistics, 415
depression experience in
    America, 418–424
  cultural politics, 420–422
  election of 1932, 424
  radicalizing politics, 423–424
  rural, 419–420
  urban, 418–419
deregulation
  Reagan and, 528–529, 530*i*,
    533
  Telecommunications Act of
    1996, 551
desegregation
  Brown v. *Board of Education*,
    479–480
  massive resistance to, 480
  of military, 478
  in schools, 479–480
  in sports, 478–479
détente, 513
Detroit, Michigan
  Deutschmark, 464

progressive-era imperialism, 381
  America as World Power,
    383–384
  forcing open door, 381
  Panama Canal, 381–382
  policing Latin America,
    382–383
  trade with China, 381
Progressive-era reforms, 364–365
"progressive" change, 395
Progressive Education Associa-tion, 368
progressive era, end of, 399–402
  immigration restriction, quo-
    tas and, 408–410
  Ku Klux Klan, 410–411
  national politics, 399–401.
    See also national politics,
    in 1920s
  prohibition, 401–402
  religious divisions, 407–408.
    See also religious divisions,
    of 1920s
Progressive Party, 364
progressives, 357 *See also*
    reformers
  in business, 368
  in education, 368
  influences on American cul-
    ture, 366–369
  laws role, 368–369
  in national politics, 362–364.
    See also politics, progres-
    sives in
  in national politics, 362–364
  state political reform,
    361–362
  women's progressivism,
    364–366
Progressivism, 357, 360i
  in national politics, 362–364
  women, 364–366
prohibition, 401–402
Project C, Birmingham, Alabama,
    491
Prophet Mohammad, 539
protest(s)
  antiwar, 503
  "Black Lives Matter",
    571–572
  Bonus Army, 423
  Buddhist monk burning and,
    488
  campus, 499–500
  civil rights, 489–490
  Democratic National Conven-
    tion, Chicago, 1968, 504
  ERA protests, 521
  Freedom Rides, 490
  Genoa, Italy, World Bank,
    IMF, 552
  globalization, 551–552
  grape boycott, Chicano Power
    and, 502
  Kent State University, 505
  Occupy Wall Street, 569
  sit-ins, 489–490
  Student Nonviolent Coordi-
    nating Committee (SNCC),
    490
  teach-ins, Vietnam War, 502
  Tiananmen Square, China,
    538

World Bank/IMF, 2001Genoa,
    Italy, 552
Protestant(s). *See also* religion
  evangelicals, conservatism
    and, 523–524
  fundamentalists, 408–409
  imperialism of, 374
  modernists, 408
  morality and, 318, 407
  Social Gospel movement, 358
Public Broadcasting Corpora-
    tion (PBS), 496
Public Utility Holding Company
    Act, 429
Public Works Administration
    (PWA), 425
Puerto Rican Studies, 500
Puerto Rico
  humanitarian aid in, 381
  Reaganomics and, 529–530
Pulitzer, Joseph, 377i
Pullman George, 325
Pullman strike of 1894, 325
Pure Food and Drug Act, 367

Q

Quota Act of 1921, 409
quota system, Hart-Cellar Act
    and, 496

R

race
  crack cocaine and, 530–531
  Hart-Cellar Act and, 496
  identity and. *See* identity
    politics
  illegal/legal immigration and,
    552–553
  and immigration, 496
  King, Rodney, Los Angeles
    riots and, 544, 545i
  Reagan economic policies
    and, 529
  Thomas/Hill scandal and, 544
race riots
  in 1920s, 401
  in 1940s, 452
racial discrimination. *See also*
    discrimination; segregation
  Civil Rights Act and, 301–302
  Jim Crow laws. *See* Jim Crow
    laws
  Ku Klux Klan and. *See* Ku
    Klux Klan
  segregation, 301, 337–340.
    See also segregation *entries*
  voting and, 491–492
racial disenfranchisement,
    338
racial minorities, Obama
    and, 569
Racine Belles, 454
racism
  affirmative action and,
    519–520
  annexations and, 380
  black activism and, 519
  Democratic Party and,
    302–304

imperialism and, 374, 380
  Mexican Americans and, 453
  murder of James Byrd, Jr.,
    and, 553
  in north, 301
  Plains Indians and, 346
  Scottsboro Boys, 423
  Social Darwinism and, 319
  Watts riots, 500
radicalism, fears of, 361
radicalizing politics, 423–424
Radical Republicans, 295
  Andrew Johnson and,
    295–296, 298
  Congressional Reconstruction
    and, 296–297
  reconstruction and, 295
radio
  in 1920s, 404
  in Great Depression, 422
  sports and, 404
Ragged Dick (Alger), 319
"rags-to-riches" theme, 421
railroad
  expansion, 1870–1920, 312m
  Industrial Revolution and,
    310
  in industrial South, 336
  in industrial West, 343
  migration and, 348
  oil shipments and, 316
  price gouging and, 316
  strike of 1877, 322–323, 322i
  strikes of 1946, 470
Randolph, A. Philip, 451
Rankin, Jeanette, 444
Ransom, John Crowe, 422
rap music, 531
rationing, World War II and,
    450
Rauschenbusch, Walter, 358
Ray, James Earl, 502
Reagan-Bush, foreign relations
    under, 534
  Cold War, 534–537
Reagan, Nancy, 531
Reagan Revolution, 528, 532
  1988 Election, 532–533
  Bush's domestic policies,
    533
Reagan, Ronald, 527
  AIDS epidemic and, 531–532
  America in 1980s, 529–532
  charisma of, 528i
  collapse of Soviet Union and,
    536
  conservative movement, 528
  crisis in cities, 530–531
  culture wars, 531
  decline of middle class, 530i
  deregulation, 528–529
  divisions in wealth, 529–530
  domestic politics, 527–529
  early life, 527
  economic conservatism of,
    528–529
  election of 1980 and, 527
  election of 1984, 528
  election of 1988, 532–533
  end of Cold War and,
    534–537
  foreign relations under
    Reagan-Bush, 534–540

Iran-Contra Affair and,
    535–536
  Japan, American deficit and,
    530
  judicial and administrative
    appointments, 529
  partnership with Mikhail
    Gorbachev, 534i
  perestroika/glasnost, Gor-
    bachev and, 534–535
  Star Wars program and, 534
real annual growth rate (GDP),
    549
real estate, adventures in,
    398–399
real estate, in 1920s, 398
realism, 384
realists, international relations
    and, 384
Reasons Why features
  al Qaeda, bin Laden, 9/11
    and, 561
  communism, 462
  globalization, 551
  Great Depression, 416
  Industrial Revolution, 311
  isolationism, 440
  Jim Crow laws, 339
  progressive era, 361
  Protestant morality, 407
  reconstruction, equality and,
    305
  reconstruction failure, 305
  Soviet Union, collapse of, 537
  Vietnam War, divisive at
    home, 506
  Watergate scandal, 515
Rebel Without a Cause (movie),
    474
recall device, 362
recession
  Bush's domestic policies, 533
  Great Recession of 2008, 565
  post growth, Clinton and, 549
Reconstruction era, 291
  black codes, 294–295
  Civil Rights Act of 1875 and,
    301
  collapse in North, 301–302
  collapse in South, 303–305
  collapse of reconstruction,
    301
  congressional, 295–297
  Fifteenth Amendment,
    297–298
  freedmen, freedwomen,
    291–293
  grassroots, 299–301. *See also*
    grassroots reconstruction
  grassroots reconstruction,
    299–301
  Johnson's impeachment,
    297–298
  Military Reconstruction Act,
    296–297
  National political ambiva-
    lence, 305
  Northern indifference, 305
  political plans for reconstruc-
    tion, 293–299
  presidential 1865–1867,
    294–295
  racism in, 301

S

Sacco and Vanzetti, 399–400
Sacco, Nicola, 400
safe-sex education, 532
Saigon
  attack on U. S. embassy in, 498
  burning of Buddhist monk in, 489i
Salinger, J. D., 474
SALT II, 516
Salt Lake City, Utah, 238
same-sex marriage, 569–570
Samoa, Pacific acquisitions, 374–375
Sand Creek Massacre of 1864, 346
San Francisco Bay, 520
San Francisco, California
  Chinatown in, 348–349
  Milk, Harvey, 522
  United Nations and, 461
Sanger, Margaret
  contraception and, 358, 366
  eugenics and, 369
  image, 365i
  liberalizing culture, of 1920s and, 406–407
Sanger, Margaret, 366
San Juan Hill, Cuba, 378
Sarajevo, assassination of Archduke Ferdinand and, 385
satellites, Cold War and, 469
Saturday Evening Post, 403
Saturday Night Fever (film), 522, 523i
Saudi Arabia, Islamic terrorism and, 561
savings and loans (S&Ls), 533
savings, in 1920s, 398
Savio, Mario, 500
scalawags, 300
Scalia, Antonin (Justice, SCOTUS), 529
Schechter Poultry Corp. v. U. S., 428
Schlafly, Phyllis, 524
school(s). See also education; universities
  busing, affirmative action and, 519
  Columbine, Colorado, shooting, 553
  desegregation in, 479–480
  energy crisis and, 517
  evolution in, 531
  segregation, in public, 301
  sex education in, 531
Science, 339
scientific authority, 361
scientific management, 368
Scopes, John, 408
Scopes Monkey Trial, 408
Scottsboro Boys, 423
Scott, Walter, 571
search-and-destroy operations, 498
Sears, Richard W., 316
Sears Roebuck catalogue, 316i
Seattle, Washington, 417, 551–552

Second Mississippi Plan, 338
Second New Deal, 428–429
  attacks on wealthy and large corporations, 429
  jobs, 428
  labor support, 428
  peak, 1935–1936, 429
  social safety net, 428–429
  wealthy/large corporations, attacks on, 429
Second Reconstruction Act, 296–297
Second Red Scare, 476–478
Second World War, 489
Section 7a of NIRA, 425
segregation
  African American responses, 340–341
  Cold War era, 473
  in industrial South, 337–341
  Jim Crow laws, 338
  lynching, 339–340, 340i
  lynching/responses to, 338–340
  New Deal, 432
  Plessy v. Ferguson, 338–339
  in public schools, 301
  racial disenfranchisement, 338
  in representation, 305
  separate but equal, 338
  in U. S. military, 451–452, 478
Selma, Alabama, civil rights marches in, 493
Senate, 398
  apportionment and, 293
  black Americans serving in, 305
  Civil Rights Act of 1964 and, 492
  Compromise of 1877 and, 304
  confirmation of Clarence Thomas, 544
  Federal Elections Bill and, 302
  invasion of Iraq and, 562
  McCarthy censure and, 478
  racial makeup, 305
  Tenure of Office Act and, 298
  Tonkin Gulf Resolution, 498
  Treaty of Versailles and, 391
  treaty with Spain, ratification of, 379
  Watergate hearings, 514
Senate Foreign Relations Committee, 503
Senate Tickets, 298i
senators, election of, 361
"separate but equal", 339
September 11, 2001, terrorist attacks, 559–560, 560i
Serbia
  assassination of Archduke Ferdinand, 384
  ethnic war, with Bosnia, 547
Servicemen's Readjustment Act of 1944 (GI Bill), 453–454
settlement houses, 358–359
Seventeenth Amendment, 361
Seward's Folly, 375
Seward, William H., 375
sewer systems, 332

sex scandals
  in 1920s, 404
  of Bill Clinton, 554
sexual crimes, race and, 303
sexual harassment, Thomas/Hill scandal, 543
sexual orientation, "Don't Ask, Don't Tell" policy, U. S. Military, 547–548. See also gay rights
sexual revolution, women's movement and, 521
Seymour, Horatio, 298
Shahn, Ben, 430
Shame of the Cities, The (Steffens) (1904), 367
shantytowns, depression and, 418–419
sharecroppers, 350
sharecropping system, 300–301, 302i
  labor battle, 301
  sharecropping system, 301
  system of, 301
Sharia law, Islam and, 561
Shelley v. Kraemer, 479
Shepard, Matthew, 553
Sherman Antitrust Act of 1890, 363
Sherman, William T., 346
Shia Muslims, 539
Sicilian Mafia, 402
Sierra Club, 317
Significance of the Frontier in American History, The (Turner), 373
Silent Spring (Carson), 522
Silliman, Benjamin, 312–313
Sinclair, Upton, 367, 427
sit-down strike, 431
sit-ins protests, 489–490
sitcoms, 422
Sitting Bull (Sioux Chief), 348
16th Street Baptist Church, bombing, 491
sixties, 485
  battle, 498
  civil rights movement, 490i
  domestic criticism, 499
  freedom movement, 489
  Great Society, 494–496
  Johnson's Vietnam, 496–499
  Kennedy and Cold War, 485–489
  laws and rifts, 492–494
  liberalism, 499–507
  national successes, 490–492
  nonviolence, 489–490
slavery, 79
  "40-acres-and-a-mule," 292, 294
  Jim Crow laws and, 339
Slick Rick, 531
Sloan, Alfred, 397
Sly and the Family Stone, 522
Smith-Connally Act of 1943, 450
Smith, Al, 424, 427
Smith, Hyrum, 237
social and economic participation, 521
Social Darwinism, 319

Social Darwinism theory, 323
Social Gospel movement, 357–358
social intolerance, Ku Klux Klan, 410
socialism
  American Socialist Party, Eugene Debs and, 326
  Eugene Debs and, 326
Socialist Party, 399
  New Deal and, 427
social life
  in commercial North, 213–221
  in cotton south, 221–228
  in postwar South, 340–342
social revolution, 294
social safety net, 428–429
Social Security, 528
Social Security Act, 428–429
Social similarities of native North Americans, 8
social welfare and programs
  acts to create, 496
  Medicaid, 495
  Medicare, 495, 598
  Reagan cuts to, 529
  Social Security Act, 428–429, 528
  welfare, 429, 495, 552–553, 568
society, 14–15, 16
  information technology, Internet, effect on, 549–550
  in postwar South, 341–342
society, New Deal effects on, 430–434
  crime, 431
  culture, 431
  labor, 431–432
  politics, 432
  segregation continues, 432–433
  women, 433–434
sodbusters, 343, 343i
Somalia, U. S. Marines in, 547
Sotomayor, Sonia, 568i
Souls of Black Folk, The (Du Bois), 340
South, "New," in Industrial Age, 335–342
  African American cultural life in, 341
  black literacy/educational institutions in, 341–342
  cotton/textiles, 336
  industrial failures, 336–337
  iron production in, 336
  myth of lost cause, 341
  railroads in, 336
  religious life, of African Americans in, 342
  segregation in, 337–341. See also segregation, in industrial South
  society/culture in postwar, 341–342
  tobacco in, 337
  urbanization, 337
South Africa
  apartheid, Carter and, 517
  racist regime of, 513

What Else Was Happening

1863   Abraham Lincoln proposes the lenient Ten-Percent Plan.

1864   Lincoln pocket-vetoes the stricter Wade-Davis Bill for Reconstruction.

1865: *John Wilkes Booth assassinates Abraham Lincoln.*

1865–1867   Johnson's presidential Reconstruction demands loyalty oath from Confederates.
Congress establishes Freedmen's Bureau.
Congress passes Civil Rights Bill.

1866   The Ku Klux Klan forms in Tennessee.

1867: *Congress enacts Military and Second Reconstruction Act. Benjamin Disraeli helps pass the 1867 Reform Bill in Britain, which extends the franchise to all male householders, including, for the first time, members of the working class.*

1867–1877   During Congressional Reconstruction Congress enforces its rules for readmission.

1868   Fourteenth Amendment grants full citizenship to all persons born in United States.
North Carolina, South Carolina, Georgia, Florida, Alabama, Arkansas, Louisiana return to Union.

1869: *Opening of the Suez Canal in Egypt connecting the Mediterranean Sea and the Red Sea, allowing water travel between Asia and Europe without having to navigate around Africa.*
1873: *Marketing of Remington typewriter opens clerical positions for women.*
Financial panic causes severe recession and mass unemployment. Mark Twain patents the scrapbook.

1870   Fifteenth Amendment bans state disfranchisement based on race but not gender.
Virginia, Mississippi, Texas return to Union.

First New York City subway line opens.

1871   Force Act of 1870 and Ku Klux Klan Act permit federal government to respond to Klan violence.

Euphemia Allen, age sixteen, composes simple piano tune "Chopsticks."

1875   Mississippi Plan calls for use of violence to restore Democratic control.
Civil Rights Act forbids racial discrimination in public places.

1877   To overcome election stalemate, Republicans grant Democrats home rule in return for presidency.

1883   In Civil Rights Cases, U.S. Supreme Court declares Civil Rights Act unconstitutional.

16-1   **Describe the changed world of ex-slaves after the Civil War.** In Reconstruction South, African American were legally no longer any one else's property, but black codes and "Jim Crow" laws held freed slaves still in a state of servitude. Ex-slaves could move, buy dogs, learn to read, attend schools, and more, and the Freedmen's Bureau provided assistance to black people, and also poor white people, in the South. The Bureau opened thousands of schools and improved medical care across the South. But it would confront challenges everywhere, as many white southerners sought to return the South to its antebellum days.

Reconstruction The federal government's attempts to resolve the issues resulting from the end of the Civil War in order to reconstitute the nation (p. 291)

Ku Klux Klan A quasi-military force formed immediately after the Civil War by former Confederate soldiers in order to resist racial integration and preserve white supremacy; after a temporary decline, the group reformed in 1915 and sporadically returned to prominence throughout the nineteenth and twentieth centuries (p. 292)

Freedmen's Bureau Government agency designed to create a new social order by government mandate; this bureau provided freedmen with education, food, medical care, and access to the justice system (p. 292)

16-2 **Outline the different phases of Reconstruction, beginning with Lincoln's plan and moving through presidential Reconstruction to Congressional Reconstruction.** During the war, Lincoln wanted to allow southern states to return to the Union if 10 percent of voters signed a loyalty oath. The Wade-Davis bill wanted 50 percent to take the oath. Lincoln's assassination meant that neither became law. President Johnson pardoned most who took the oath—even military leaders and the wealthy, thus ending any hope for a property realignment after the war. Southern states, uncowed, returned the same people to office and enacted restrictive black codes. To counter this, Radical Republicans expanded the Freedmen's Bureau and passed a Civil Rights Bill. Their Military Reconstruction Act laid out strict guidelines for southern states: organizing state conventions, writing new constitutions, protecting black voting rights, and passing the 14th Amendment. After only 12 years, the North abandoned Reconstruction. There was to be no land redistribution, education guarantee for freedmen, or racial equality. Southern whites were freed to push segregation.

Ten-Percent Plan Plan issued by Lincoln in 1863 that offered amnesty to any southerner who proclaimed loyalty to the Union and support of the emancipation of slaves; once 10 percent of a state's voters in the election of 1860 signed the oath, it could create a new state government and reenter the Union (p. 293)

Wade-Davis Bill Bill that would have allowed a southern state back into the Union only after 50 percent of the population had taken the loyalty oath (p. 293)

iron-clad oath Oath to be taken by southerners to testify that they had never voluntarily aided or abetted the rebellion (p. 293)

black codes Post–Civil War laws specifically written to govern the behavior of African Americans; modeled on the slave codes that existed before the Civil War (p. 294)

Radical Republicans Wing of the Republican Party most hostile to slavery (p. 295)

Civil Rights Act Bill that granted all citizens mandatory rights, regardless of racial considerations; designed to counteract the South's new black codes (p. 295)

Congressional Reconstruction Phase of Reconstruction during which Radical Republicans wielded more power than the president, allowing for the passage of the Fourteenth and Fifteenth Amendments and the Military Reconstruction Act (p. 296)

Fourteenth Amendment Amendment to the U.S. Constitution passed in 1868 that extended the guarantees of the Constitution and Bill of Rights to all persons born in the United States, including African Americans and former slaves; it promised that all citizens would receive the "due process of law" before having any of their constitutional rights breached (p. 296)

Military Reconstruction Act Act that divided the former rebel states, with the exception of Tennessee, into five military districts; a military commander took control of the state governments and federal soldiers enforced the law and kept order (p. 296)

Fifteenth Amendment Amendment that extended voting rights to all male citizens regardless of race, color, or previous condition of servitude (p. 299)

16-3 **Explain how Reconstruction evolved at the individual states' level.** During Reconstruction, about 2,000 southern African Americans gained state and local political office. Some Northerners traveled to help; some Southerners became Republican to aid Southern recovery. Gains were short-lived in the turbulent political climate, which was still ruled by wealthy whites. White landowners devised a new "sharecropping" agricultural system to ensure sufficient field hands. Sharecropping oppressed black & poor white southerners (most of the population) until World War II.

carpetbagger Northern-born white who moved south after the Confederacy's defeat (p. 300)

scalawag Southern-born white Republican; many had been nonslaveholding poor farmers (p. 300)

sharecropping System in which a family farmed a plot of land owned by someone else and shared the crop yield with the owner (p. 301)

16-4 **Evaluate and understand the relative success and failures of Reconstruction.** During Reconstruction, protections were added to the Constitution, but most existed on paper only. Clinging to the Democratic Party, white voters reasserted control of elections. Society became controlled via harassment, intimidation, and murder, helped by the new Ku Klux Klan. Industrialized Northerners tired of trying to change Southerners, especially after the Panic of 1873. Many also feared an exodus of ex-slaves into the North, and long-held racist tendencies emerged. After the Compromise of 1877, federal troops left the South, leaving Reconstruction mostly a failure. In the "solid South," for decades African Americans existed as neither slave nor free. Only after WWII, and the modern civil rights movement, would Reconstruction-era laws be enforced.

Civil Rights Act of 1875 Act that forbade racial discrimination in all public facilities, transportation lines, places of amusement, and juries; it proved largely ineffective (p. 302)

Civil Rights Cases Cases in which, in 1883, the Supreme Court declared all of the provisions of the Civil Rights Act of 1875 unconstitutional, except for the prohibition of discrimination on juries (p. 302)

Panic of 1873 Financial crisis provoked when overspeculation, high postwar inflation, and disruptions from Europe emptied the financial reserves in America's banks; many banks simply closed their doors; this emergency focused northern attention on the economy rather than on civil rights (p. 302)

Mississippi Plan 1875 Democratic plan that called for using as much violence as necessary to put Mississippi back under Democratic control (p. 304)

Redeemers A collection of southern Democrats and their supporters who used violence, intimidation, and the law to win political and social control away from those promoting greater racial equality in the region (p. 304)

Compromise of 1877 Compromise in which Republicans promised not to dispute the Democratic gubernatorial victories in the South and to withdraw federal troops from the region, if southern Democrats accepted Hayes's presidential victory and respected the rights of black citizens (p. 304)

		What Else Was Happening
1860–1890	U.S. Patent Office issues 144,000 licenses, four times more than in 1790.	
1866–1868	In Erie Railroad War, Cornelius Vanderbilt and competitors exemplify new ruthless business practices.	
1867–1872	Crédit Mobilier railroad financing scandal tarnishes Grant administration.	
1868	Congress introduces eight-hour day in federal work projects.	
1869	Completion of transcontinental railroad.	
1872	Montgomery Ward launches mail order business.	
1873	Drastic wage cuts in Panic of 1873 anger and mobilize workers.	
1876	Alexander Graham Bell's telephone speeds up long-distance communication.	**1876–1882:** The right arm and torch of the Statue of Liberty cross the Atlantic three times.
1877	National railroad strike kills over 100, brings labor tensions to forefront.	
1878	Refrigerated rail cars permit long-distance transportation of perishable goods.	
1879	John D. Rockefeller's Standard Oil Company controls 90 percent of petroleum market.	Thomas Edison completes experimentation on the incandescent light bulb. Knights of Labor emerge as nation's largest union.
1883	Congress passes civil service reform with Pendleton Act.	**1884:** N. Thompson, founder of Coney Island Luna Park, introduces the roller coaster, calling it Switchback. **1886:** Explosion at Chicago Haymarket protest kills seven, puts Knights of Labor in disrepute. Statue of Liberty is dedicated. The statue, a gift from France intended to commemorate the two nations' founding ideal of liberty, will come to symbolize American freedom to millions of immigrants.
1892	Carnegie steel plant strike in Homestead pits workers against Pinkertons and militia.	
1893	Severe economic recession drives further labor organization.	
1894	Government intervenes on side of industrialists in Pullman strike.	**1895:** Independent Labour Party founded in Britain. **1896:** The first comic strip character—the "Yellow Kid"—appears in the New York Journal. **1899:** Felix Hoffmann patents aspirin.
1902	Theodore Roosevelt mediates miners' strike in favor of workers.	
1905	Colorado miners form anarcho-syndicalist International Workers of the World.	
1911	Triangle Shirtwaist Company fire.	

17-1 Describe and discuss the development of the Industrial Revolution in America after the Civil War, concentrating on the major industries and their leaders. Post-Civil War industrialization accelerated thanks to federal support and technological breakthroughs. In 1869 the new transcontinental railroad fed this growth, connecting cities and growing companies. Andrew Carnegie's steel industry included new business practices such as "vertical integration"—the ability to control all aspects of the industry, from the extraction of iron to shipping it to customers. The growth of petroleum promoted development of other, sometimes harmful,

business practices. John D. Rockefeller perfected "horizontal integration," monopolizing the oil industry to control prices. Innovators and risk takers introduced the light bulb, telephone, steel skyscrapers, elevators. New business practices brought more wealth and product diversity. Entrepreneurs streamlined operations, improved bookkeeping, merged and grew their companies, and made use of corporations to gain more investors and decrease the likelihood of losing entire fortunes. Greater wealth flowed to many members of management, helping grow a much larger middle class. Stock manipulation, higher prices, and environmental damage were byproducts of this rapid growth.

Industrial Revolution Transformation in the way goods were made and sold, as American businessmen between 1865 and 1915 used continuing technological breakthroughs and creative financing to bring greater efficiency to their businesses, dramatically increasing the nation's industrial output (p. 310)

vertical integration The system by which a business controls all aspects of its industry, from raw materials to finished product, and is able to avoid working or sharing profits with any other companies (p. 312)

horizontal integration The system by which a business takes over its competitors in order to limit competition, lower costs, and maximize profits (p. 313)

17-2 **Describe how the United States' regional and local markets merged into one national market and how this influenced consumer demand for products and services, as well as some of the costs associated with the transition.** Railroads could bring goods to customers, but businessmen now needed to advertise their availability. They created roadway billboards, placards on city streets, large newspaper ads, and ad agencies. By improving packaging, companies could ship farther, and brand-names became known nationwide. Celebrities wore specific brands, causing the general public to want the same thing. Chain stores grew national markets, as did mail order catalogues (such as Montgomery Ward, Sears, and Roebuck). The ability to order anything through the mail tied rural families into the country as nothing had before. To cut costs, workers were exploited by jobs that were grueling, monotonous, and dangerous. It took years for protective laws to be passed and even longer for employers to obey them.

Triangle Shirtwaist Company New York City garment factory; scene of a horrific fire in 1911 (p. 317)

sweatshop Crowded factory in an urban setting, often one where workers are exploited (p. 317)

17-3 **Discuss the functioning of national, state, and local politics during the late 1800s.** "Corruption" is the best descriptor of American politics during the late 1800s. Urban growth and overpopulation overpowered local governments, which sought political "machines" with "bosses" to manage neighborhoods in return for government contracts and a sense of power. Reform was slow, thanks to Social Darwinism's "survival of the fittest" outlook. The successful often embraced novelist Horatio Alger's belief that if a man were willing to work, he would succeed. The working poor, who knew better, had no one to turn to when in need except the political bosses. The Crédit Mobilier scandal, involving railroad executives and even the vice president, spurred reform. New York's "Boss" Tweed had a hand in virtually every aspect of building the city's infrastructure. Political machines could have done good, but without checks, power bred corruption.

Social Darwinism The theory that "survival of the fittest" extended to the business realm; tycoons believed they were justified in their overbearing behavior because they had shown themselves to be the most successful competitors in an open market (p. 319)

Crédit Mobilier Company A construction company set up by the directors of the Union Pacific in 1867 in order to build part of their transcontinental railroad—in essence, they were their own subcontractors and awarded themselves generous contracts (p. 320)

Tweed Ring Friends and cronies of New York's corrupt "Boss" William M. Tweed (p. 320)

Tammany Hall A political organization known as a "machine," whose members regarded politics as an opportunity to get rich while providing favors to the urban underclass (p. 320)

mugwumps The machine's mischievous nickname for Republicans who supported Democrat Grover Cleveland in the 1884 election only because Republican candidate James Blaine was considered a product of machine politics (p. 322)

17-4 **Describe the formation of the early labor unions in the United States, including their goals, activities, and confrontations at the end of the nineteenth century.** While entrepreneurs and owners got rich, the working poor lived and worked in pitiful, unsafe places. Assembly lines took their toll, with tens of thousands of workers (kids and adults) killed each year. Employers disliked unions because of "strength in numbers"; they wanted employees under control. Over time, several unions gathered strength, including the International Ladies' Garment Workers' Union, the Knights of Labor, the American Railway Union, and the American Federation of Labor. All pushed for better, safer working conditions, decent wages, and a shorter workweek. Early successes gave way to frustration and failure during the economic depression of 1893. Strikes at Carnegie's Homestead Steel and McCormick Harvester Company led to violence, as did the nationwide Pullman Strike. The violence frightened people, and union numbers plunged. Union organizers began working with rather than against the political system, which proved helpful.

yellow dog contract Contract stipulating that an employee would not join a union (p. 323)

blacklist A compilation of known union activists in a particular area; employers refused to hire anyone whose name appeared on one (p. 323)

strikebreakers Workers who agreed to work while union workers were on strike (p. 323)

International Ladies' Garment Workers' Union (ILGWU) Major New York City union that often conducted its union meetings in five different languages simultaneously (p. 324)

Contract Labor Law Passed in 1885, this prohibited employers from forcing immigrants to work to pay off the costs of their passage to America (p. 324)

American Federation of Labor (AFL) The leading labor organization in America, founded in 1881 by Samuel Gompers and composed of craft unions rather than a single national union (p. 326)

craft union Union of skilled laborers, the type of union assembled under the American Federation of Labor (p. 326)

American Socialist Party Political party formed in 1901 and led by Eugene V. Debs that advocated replacing the nation's capitalist system (p. 326)

International Workers of the World (IWW) A collection of militant mining unions founded in 1905 in Colorado and Idaho; sought to use labor activism to overthrow the capitalist system (p. 326)

anarcho-syndicalism A radical form of political protest that advocates the use of labor activism to overthrow the capitalist system (p. 326)

What Else Was Happening

1862	Republican Homestead Act grants 160 acres of western lands to farming settlers.
1864	In Sand Creek Massacre, Colorado militia kills over 200 Cheyenne following land disputes with white gold seekers.
1866	Edward Pollard's *The Lost Cause* turns Civil War into Old South mythology.
1869	Completion of transcontinental railroad.
1873–1875	Federal government forces economy back on gold standard at farmers' expense.
1874	Barbed wire closes open range, signaling the decline of cattle drives.
1877	In *Munn* v. *Illinois*, Supreme Court finds that states can regulate businesses within their borders that operate in the public interest.
1879	John D. Rockefeller's Standard Oil Company controls 90 percent of petroleum market. Thomas Edison completes experimentation on the incandescent light bulb.
1882	Exclusion Act bans most Chinese immigration and citizenship.
1887	With single plots of land, Dawes Act tries to turn Plains Indians into family farmers.
1890	Second Mississippi Plan models legal black voter disfranchisement for New South. 39 soldiers and 146 Indians die in Wounded Knee Massacre after ritual Ghost Dance.
1892	Carnegie steel plant strike in Homestead pits workers against Pinkertons and militia. Southern and western farmers form backbone of new People's Party (Populists).
1894	Populist Jacob Coxey leads unemployed in march on Washington demanding jobs.
1895	New York's Coney Island amusement park opens.
1896	In *Plessy* v. *Ferguson*, Supreme Court declares racial segregation constitutional. Democrat-Populist presidential candidate William Jennings Bryan loses to William McKinley.
1899	Economist Thorstein Veblen describes "conspicuous consumption" of the rich.
1903	American and National League teams play first World Series.
1909	Niagara Movement establishes NAACP.

1876: *Sioux and Cheyenne warriors wipe out General Custer's division at Little Big horn.*

Alexander Graham Bell's telephone speeds up long-distance communication.

1885: *The first modern hamburger is made in Seymour, Wisconsin.*

Pharmacist Caleb Bradham produces "Brad's Drink" as a digestive aid and energy booster; in 1898 it would be renamed Pepsi-Cola.

1893: *The melody for "Happy Birthday to You" is copyrighted.*

18-1 **Describe the urbanization and immigration in the North during the second half of the nineteenth century, and how those two factors shaped the region's social relations, including its disparities of wealth.** Urban population grew 500 percent, and 25 million immigrants arrived, most settling in Eastern cities. Cheap housing for workers resulted in densely populated, disease-ridden, polluted living conditions. Those who could flee slums did so, and the wealthy lived in ostentatious mansions meant to impress. The excesses of the rich led Mark Twain to coin the term "The Gilded Age." Earlier immigrants to America came from western and northern Europe. As economic conditions there improved, they were replaced with Europe's poor, often uneducated and discriminated against at home. New immigrants sought people like themselves to find jobs, learn English, and "become American." Jobs were usually low-paying, and management often exploited their ignorance of American ways. Urban entertainment was diverse, with large amusement parks geared toward families, the widely popular sport of professional baseball, and the more salubrious dance halls and saloons.

tenements Crowded slum houses in urban areas, which housed mostly immigrants (p. 332)

Coney Island Public amusement park opened in New York in 1895; it featured roller coasters, water slides, and fun houses (p. 333)

National League The first professional baseball league, begun in 1876 with eight teams (p. 334)

American League The second professional baseball league, begun in 1901 (p. 334)

World Series Baseball competition between the National League and the American League, played for the first time in 1903 (p. 334)

greenhorns European newcomers to America (p. 335)

Ellis Island Immigrant gateway to New York City from 1892 to 1954 (p. 335)

18-2 **Evaluate the accuracy of the term *New South* in describing the post-Civil War South, and discuss ways in which the term was and was not appropriate.** After the Civil War, cotton remained "king," but some industrialization spread into parts of the South. Textile mills developed, selling much more expensive finished products, rather than just raw cotton. Urbanization was slow, with Birmingham, Alabama, the standout. Slavery was replaced with a mix of laws and codes that held blacks to barely second-class citizenship. After Reconstruction, black people were systematically disfranchised, often illegally, sometimes by law. When a case did reach the Supreme Court (*Plessy* v. *Ferguson*), the court upheld segregation. Booker T. Washington and W. E. B. Du Bois brought hope, but also demonstrated the lack of consensus from the African American community.

"Second Mississippi Plan" Plan that established legal barriers (the poll tax, literacy tests, and property qualifications) to prevent African Americans from voting in Mississippi; served as a legislative model for other states (p. 338)

Jim Crow laws State and local laws, usually passed in southern states, that mandated racial segregation in public facilities, including schools, restaurants, and rail cars (p. 338)

Louisiana Separate Car Act 1890 law mandating that black people and white people ride in separate train cars; challenged by Homer Plessy (p. 338)

hierarchy of races A theory based on the idea that some racial groups are superior to others; in the nineteenth and twentieth centuries, many Americans used purported scientific evidence and social science data to argue that white people from British descent sat atop the hierarchy, while racial minorities and new immigrants were less sophisticated and less capable of self-rule (p. 339)

Plessy v. Ferguson 1896 Supreme Court case that declared that segregation laws were constitutional, claiming that, as long as the accommodations were "separate but equal," it was legal to have separate facilities for black and white Americans (p. 339)

Atlanta Compromise Speech delivered by Booker T. Washington in 1895 encouraging black economic development and assuaging white fears of racial intermingling; black and white people, he said, should remain as separate as the fingers on a hand, but they should work together to reach common economic ground (p. 340)

Niagara Movement An attempt at political organization among black activists in the early 1900s; W. E. B. Du Bois drafted a "Statement of Principles," which declared that African Americans should fight for their rights rather than accept abuse and separation (p. 340)

Juneteenth A celebration marking the date that slaves were formally freed in Texas: June 19, 1865 (p. 342)

Tuskegee Institute College established for African Americans in Tuskegee, Alabama, by Booker T. Washington in 1881 (p. 342)

18-3 **Describe the development of the American West that took place during the second half of the nineteenth century, addressing both industrialization and the general defeat of Native American nations on the plains.** With the population growing rapidly, Americans began to flood westward toward the receding frontier. The 1862 Homestead Act lured families to the Plains, but acreage limitations hampered its success. When small plots consolidated and grew, Plains farmers began to provide the food needed by cities. Mechanization provided by new industry made it possible to move these crops in sufficient quantities. Railroads contributed to a short-lived cattle industry (killed by the 1874's invention of barbed wire, which carved up the formerly open plains). Westward growth meant uprooting the Plains Indians, who were herded onto numerous reservations.

Homestead Act Federal act, passed in 1862, that awarded 160 acres to settlers who occupied the land for five years (p. 343)

sodbusters American pioneers who settled the northern Great Plains (p. 343)

bonanza farms Giant farms on the Great Plains, covering thousands of acres and employing hundreds of workers (p. 343)

Dawes General Allotment Act Federal law, passed in 1887, declaring that lands held by Indian nations were to be divided among families, and the Indians were not allowed to sell their lands because the government held these lands in trust for twenty-five years, after which individual Indians were to receive title to the land and become U.S. citizens (p. 347)

"Ghost Dance" The central ritual for the Plains Indians, this was a dance lasting five days that would supposedly raise the Indians above the ground while the land below them was replaced with new land, effectively sandwiching the white men between the two layers of sod, removing them forever (p. 348)

Wounded Knee Massacre 1890 conflict in which the U.S. Army fired on the Sioux, triggering a battle that left 39 U.S. soldiers and 146 Sioux dead (p. 348)

Chinese Exclusion Act of 1882 Act that banned the immigration of Chinese laborers for ten years and prohibited the Chinese who were already in the United States from becoming citizens (p. 349)

18-4 **Discuss the problems that confronted America's farmers in the North, South, and West during the late 1800s, and describe how their attempts to solve those problems led to the formation of a new political party.** Purchases of machinery led to debt; distances led to isolation and higher shipping costs for products. Railroads favored large farmers; sharecropping took its toll; and lack of specie made repayment hard. As the price of purchased goods rose, the price of sold goods dropped. Farmers began to unify, from the Grange to the national Farmers' Alliance and the People's Party. These "Populists" developed a platform based on reforms, which were then taken up by major parties.

Populist Party A political party of the 1890s that championed the "farm" cause of land and crops over the powers of banking and credit (p. 350)

gold standard An economic plan using gold as the primary form of currency while taking paper money and silver coins out of circulation (p. 350)

***Munn v. Illinois* (1877)** A Supreme Court case that declared states could regulate businesses within their borders if those businesses operated in the public interest (p. 350)

Subtreasury Plan An economic plan advocated by the Farmers' Alliance, in which crops would be stored in government-owned warehouses and used as collateral for low-cost government loans to struggling farmers (p. 351)

remonetize To turn a certain commodity (for instance, silver) back into an acceptable currency (p. 351)

What Else Was Happening

1883: *Germany institutes the world's first universal health care system.*

1882	Electric lights are first used on a Christmas tree.
1889	Jane Addams founds Hull House in Chicago, the nation's second but most renowned settlement house.
1890	Sherman Antitrust Act is federal government's first effort to curb monopolies.
	Founding of National American Woman Suffrage Association (NAWSA).
1893	Temperance activists form Anti-Saloon League to pass laws on state and local level.
1900	National Civic Federation tries to build partnership between workers and owners.
	Hurricane kills more than 8,000 in poorly prepared Galveston, Texas, prompting city reform.

1902: *The teddy bear ("Teddy's bear") is created by a Brooklyn shop owner after he sees a newspaper cartoon depicting hunter Theodore Roosevelt with a bear cub.*

1903: *President T. Roosevelt forms Bureau of Corporations to investigate monopolies. Crayola crayons go on sale.*

1906	Hepburn Act caps railroad prices and introduces federal oversight.
	Upton Sinclair publishes novel *The Jungle* about life in Chicago meatpacking plant.
	Congress passes Pure Food and Drug Act and Meat Inspection Act to protect consumers.
1908	Supreme Court upholds maximum-hours law for women in *Muller* v. *Oregon*.
1911–1914	Women gain suffrage in California, Oregon, Kansas, Arizona, Montana, Nevada.

1911: *Great Britain passes the National Insurance Act, creating a system of social welfare to protect workers against illness and unemployment, as well as providing retirement pensions.*

1912	Disappointed with successor Howard Taft, T. Roosevelt forms Progressive Party.
1913	Seventeenth Amendment replaces senators' election by state legislatures with popular vote.
	Founding of National Women's Party led by Alice Paul.
	Alice Paul leads march of 5,000 women to White House, demanding suffrage.
	Woodrow Wilson signs Federal Reserve Act establishing new banking system.
	Wilson signs Underwood Tariff to expose monopolies to competition.
1914	Clayton Antitrust Act defines and outlaws unfair business practices.
	Federal Trade Commission investigates and rules on legality of business practices.
1916	Keating-Owen Child Labor Act prohibits employment of children under sixteen.
1920	Nineteenth Amendment grants women the right to vote.

19-1 **Discuss the reform efforts of the Progressive era and the groups involved in those efforts.** Political and social causes occupied the reformers of the Progressive era. Middle-class women spearheaded the Women's Christian Temperance Union. Settlement houses did a great deal to help individuals and families mired in poverty.

Social Gospel An early-twentieth-century Protestant-inspired movement advocating widespread reforms to curb the worst abuses of the Industrial Revolution; its leaders included Washington Gladden and Walter Rauschenbusch (p. 358)

settlement houses Safe residences in poor neighborhoods where reformers could study local conditions and where residents could hold meetings and receive free health care (p. 358)

Hull House The second but most renowned settlement house in the United States, founded in Chicago in 1889 by Jane Addams; its residents lobbied the government to pass better construction and safety laws to improve conditions in the surrounding tenement houses (p. 359)

19-2 Describe the methods used by the various states to bring about reforms in state governments during the Progressive era. Progressives sought to bring openness and democracy to politics, most successfully at the state level. Reformers pushed for and won a constitutional amendment in 1913 for direct election of senators. Implementation empowered citizens to petition their state governments to place specific issues on the general ballot, whether state legislatures supported the issue or not. Primaries and recalls gave citizens a greater voice in candidate selection and oversight of officials. States adopted rules for hiring government workers, including civil service exams to replace cronyism.

Galveston hurricane Devastating hurricane that killed more than 8,000 people in Galveston, Texas, in 1900; helped spur demands that local and state governments be more responsive to people's needs (p. 361)

initiative A legislative device designed to allow citizens more control over state law; they could advocate a specific idea and introduce it on the ballot (p. 362)

referendum A legislative device designed to allow citizens more control over state law; citizens could collect a few thousand signatures on a petition in order to advance a specific idea and introduce it on the ballot (p. 362)

primary A preliminary election designed to let voters choose which political candidates will run for public office (p. 362)

recall A device by which petitioning citizens can, with a vote, dismiss state officers, governors, and judges who are deemed to have violated the popular interest (p. 362)

19-3 Compare and contrast the progressivism of Theodore Roosevelt and Woodrow Wilson. As "activists," both believed in encouraging Congress to enact laws to improve the lives of citizens. Roosevelt involved himself with environmental causes, including creating the National Forest Service. He also disliked trusts, and the "trustbuster" set out to break ones he considered the worst. Wilson supported legislation designed to make the entire society work more effectively and equitably. His efforts helped create the Federal Reserve, Clayton Antitrust Act, and Federal Trade Commission. Roosevelt is known as quite Progressive; Wilson's Progressivism was overshadowed by World War I.

Sherman Antitrust Act Passed in 1890, the federal government's first attempt to break up monopolies (p. 363)

trustbuster A nickname for those in government advocating antitrust laws (p. 363)

National Forest Service Government agency created by Theodore Roosevelt to preserve land and protect local animal species (p. 363)

Progressive Party Political party created by Theodore Roosevelt in 1912 to win back the presidency from Taft (p. 364)

"The New Freedom" Woodrow Wilson's platform message pledging to use government power to destroy big businesses and give smaller ones greater ability to compete (p. 364)

Federal Trade Commission A government agency charged with investigating unfair business practices (p. 364)

19-4 Discuss the involvement of women's groups in Progressive-era reform movements. Women were at the core of most reform movements. Many pushed for suffrage for all women, helping usher in the Nineteenth Amendment in 1920. National suffrage culminated decades of perseverance by women for a right long denied them. Women supported each other in social work, and their organizations evolved into groups dedicated to improving life in specific communities as well as across the country.

19-5 Describe ways in which American culture was influenced by the Progressive movement. Reform-minded people found creative ways to raise awareness of important problems. Literature was one way; Upton Sinclair and Jacob Riis shined light on the state of the working poor. Partly because of their works, the Pure Food and Drug Act and Meat Inspection Act passed in 1906. Ida Tarbell and Lincoln Steffens contributed; Tarbell targeted Standard Oil for ill treatment of workers. Frederick W. Taylor developed the business practice of "scientific management." It increased production efficiency and gave Americans better and cheaper consumer goods, improving many lives. In general, reformers sought practical and needed reforms in almost all areas of American life.

muckrakers Investigative writers who exposed bad conditions in American factories, political corruption in city machines, and the financial deceit of corporations (p. 366)

Pure Food and Drug Act Passed in 1906, this act, along with the Meat Inspection Act, gave the federal government responsibility for ensuring that meat would reach its customers fresh and disease-free (p. 367)

scientific management Pioneered by Frederick W. Taylor, the detailed study of the best ways to schedule, organize, and standardize work tasks (p. 368)

Progressive Education Association Formed in 1919, this national association supported and advocated for education reforms that taught children to make good moral and political choices (p. 368)

eugenics An early-twentieth-century movement centered on the belief that it was possible to improve the human species by discouraging or outlawing reproduction by various people thought to have undesirable traits (p. 368)

What Else Was Happening

1844 Treaty of Wanghia opens Chinese ports to U.S. trade.

1853 U.S. Navy in Tokyo Bay pressures Japan to open to West.

1867 United States purchases Alaska from Russia.

1895 Cleveland administration invokes Monroe Doctrine in Venezuela Crisis with Britain.

Cubans rebel against heavy-handed Spanish rule.

1898 Spanish-American War transforms United States into major overseas power.
June: Filipino leader Emilio Aguinaldo declares Philippines' independence from Spain.
July: Rough Riders' capture of Santiago, Cuba, forces Spain's surrender.

1899–1902 Americans fight vicious anti-insurgency war against Filipino nationalists.

Anti-Imperialist League forms in opposition to annexation of Philippines.
The Second Boer War in southern Africa between Great Britain and a handful of small African nations leads to the conversion of several small African republics into parts of the British Empire.

1899 United States turns former naval base on Samoa into protectorate of American Samoa.
U.S. Secretary of State John Hay demands Open Door policy from China.

1900 After thirteen years as an American-led republic, Hawai'i becomes part of United States.
Republican expansionist McKinley defeats Democrat Bryan in presidential election.

United States joins multinational military expedition to suppress Boxer Rebellion in China.

1901 Platt Amendment to Cuban constitution grants U.S. right to military intervention.
Roosevelt encourages Panamanian independence after negotiations with Colombia fail.

1903 U.S. support for Panama's rebellion leads to U.S. rights to 10-mile-wide Canal Zone.

1904: *Russo-Japanese War breaks out because of each nation's imperial ambitions over Manchuria and Korea.*

1905 President Roosevelt negotiates end to Russo-Japanese War, wins Nobel Peace Prize.

1909 Taft administration supports coup in Nicaragua in the interests of U.S. mining company.

1912: April 15: *The Titanic sinks.*
First passenger meal is served on an airplane in flight.

1914–1916 **June 28:** Assassination of Archduke Franz Ferdinand throws Europe into World War I.
August: Germany invades France.
Wilson administration sends troops into Mexican civil war to restore order.
Wilson administration sends more troops into Mexican civil war to restore order.

1915: May 7: *German U-boat sinks British Lusitania; 128 U.S. civilians die; protests follow.*

1917 **January:** Zimmerman Note from Berlin to Mexico suggests alliance against United States.
February: Bolshevik Revolution in Russia prompts talks over separate peace with Germany.
April 2: Woodrow Wilson asks Congress for declaration of war against Germany.
Espionage Acts punish protests and criticisms of draft.

1918 **January 8:** Wilson proposes conciliatory postwar peace settlement in Fourteen Points.
February: Both sides sign armistice; World War I ends.

1919 **June 28:** Treaty of Versailles demands German reparations, adopts few of Wilson's ideas.

1920 League of Nations meets for first time without U.S. participation.

20-1

Explain the major reasons for the growing call in the late 1800s for the United States to develop an empire. "Manifest destiny" and an expanding frontier gave generations a chance to improve their lives. Historian Frederick Jackson Turner claimed the frontier made Americans what they were. As more lands became settled, many talked of a need for a "new" frontier; business leaders sought new colonial materials and markets; religious leaders wanted to take Christianity around the world. The race for colonies by European countries brought them great rewards Americans wanted.

Turner Thesis Argument put forward by historian Frederick Jackson Turner that the presence of the western frontier had shaped the American character and allowed the development of democracy and capitalism, necessitating in the wake of its 1893 disappearance "a wider field for its exercise"; was used to buttress attempts to propel American interests abroad (p. 373)

dollar diplomacy The use of a country's financial power to extend its diplomatic interests, including but not limited to using private capital from the U.S. to further American interests overseas (p. 374)

20-2

Describe the first moves the U.S. made toward empire. After the Civil War, the U.S. determined to show other countries that it deserved respect. Alfred Thayer Mahan advocated warships, merchant ships, and colonies for supplies: imperialism. America purchased Alaska in 1867; next, Samoa and Hawaii came under American influence. The U.S. then became involved with Mexico and Venezuela because of natural resources.

Treaty of Wanghia Agreement between China and the United States signed in 1844, opening several Chinese ports to American trade (p. 374)

20-3

Explain the major reasons for the Spanish-American War of 1898, and discuss the controversy over imperialism that developed after the war. With U.S. business interests menaced by Spanish expansion, the U.S. fought Spain in 1898 over Cuba. The sinking of an American warship in Havana Harbor and an intercepted telegram led to the war. Though refusing to take over Cuba, victory did give the U.S. Guam, Puerto Rico, and the Philippines. The Filipinos warred with the U.S. for four years. Dealings with Cuba also remained strained.

yellow journalism Journalism that shows little dependence on fact or research and instead uses sensationalized headlines and storylines in order to sell more newspapers or magazines; pioneered by Joseph Pulitzer and William Randolph Hearst during the buildup to the Spanish-American War (p. 377)

Teller Amendment Legislation that barred the United States from annexing Cuba, forcing it to leave Cuba independent once the Spanish-American War was over (p. 377)

Rough Riders The most colorful contingent of the American forces in the Spanish-American War, led by Theodore Roosevelt (p. 378)

Platt Amendment Legislation intended to overrule the Teller Amendment and then added to the Cuban constitution, allowing the United States to militarily intervene on the island whenever revolution threatened (p. 380)

20-4

Describe the growth of American imperialism during the Progressive era. Under Roosevelt and Wilson, America became involved in China (with the "Open Door" policy), Central America (with the Panama Canal), and many Western Hemisphere areas under the Roosevelt Corollary. Americans remained divided over imperialism, but it was clearer the U.S. would play a vital role in world affairs. Isolationists wanted no part of such a role.

Boxer Rebellion Conflict that erupted in China in 1900; Chinese nationalists attacked embassies in Beijing in an attempt to oust foreigners (p. 381)

20-5

Discuss World War I, including reasons for the war, American experiences during the war, and effects of the treaty ending the war. World War I's prelude involved alliances, distrust among European states, and economic competition. The assassination of Austria-Hungary's archduke by a Serbian nationalist set the war in motion. At first neutral, Americans leaned toward Britain and France, as German subs sank U.S. merchant ships. Germany's declaration of unrestricted submarine warfare, following the Zimmermann Note, in which Germany attempted to goad Mexico into war against the U.S., brought America into the war in 1917. The significance of American participation is disputed, but U.S. troops clearly impacted later battles. The war ended in November 1918, with Germany suing for peace under Wilson's Fourteen Points plan. The Versailles Treaty punished Germany. The Allies pushed aside Wilson's ideas on self-determination. Germany had to pay reparations with money it lacked. Its bitterness would lead to the rise of Hitler.

U-boat Primitive but effective submarine invented by the Germans and used extensively in the First World War (p. 386)

war bonds Securities bought by ordinary people to fund and support the war effort (p. 388)

Espionage Act Legislation that meted out large fines and twenty-year jail terms to anyone who protested the draft or said anything that might impede the war effort (p. 388)

Fourteen Points Declaration by President Wilson that outlined the principles he believed should shape the postwar peace settlement; a blueprint for what he called "a world made fit and safe to live in" (p. 389)

What Else Was Happening

1915 Ku Klux Klan resurges in the wake of "rebirth" at Georgia's Stone Mountain.	
1916 Marcus Garvey opens Universal Negro Improvement Association in Harlem.	
1919 Eighteenth Amendment and Volstead Act impose nationwide prohibition on alcohol.	**1920:** *Nineteenth Amendment grants women the right to vote.* *Imprisoned socialist presidential candidate Eugene V. Debs gets 1 million votes.* *Harry Burt, a Youngstown, Ohio, candy maker, sells first ice cream on a stick, the Good Humor bar.* **1922:** *Commercial radio begins broadcasting.* *The Union of Soviet Socialist Republics is formed after communists take power in the Russian Revolution of 1917.*
1923 Teapot Dome scandal reveals corrupt ties between White House and big business. Women propose Equal Rights Amendment to Congress, which acts on it in 1972.	
1924 National Origins Act creates biased restrictions on immigrants.	**1925:** *Supreme Court upholds Catholic Church's right to run its own schools.* *Modernists and fundamentalists debate evolution in Scopes Monkey Trial.* *Yale students invent the Frisbee while tossing empty pie plates from the Frisbie Baking Company.*
1926 Florida hurricane kills 400, crashes speculative land prices and investing banks. Marcus Garvey deported to Jamaica for mail fraud in sale of Black Star Line shares.	**1927:** *Charles Lindbergh's cross-Atlantic flight makes him an international celebrity.* *Italian immigrants Sacco and Vanzetti sentenced to death with minimal evidence.* *The Jazz Singer is the first major talking motion picture. The first words heard in a motion picture are spoken by actor Al Jolson: "Wait a minute! You ain't heard nothing yet!"*
1928 Herbert Hoover defeats Catholic New York Democrat Al Smith in landslide.	*Color television pictures are transmitted in New York.* *Museum of Modern Art opens in New York City, celebrating the birth of modern art that developed alongside the Industrial Revolution.*
1929 **October:** After four years of steady growth, stock market begins worst decline in history.	
1933 The Twenty-first Amendment repeals Prohibition.	

21-1 **Describe the consumer economy that developed in America during the early twentieth century, especially after World War I.** By the early 1920s, America's economy appeared robust and healthy, and consumerism grew rapidly. The assembly line pioneered by Henry Ford made goods cheaper to produce. Unions complained, but Ford's "$5 day" turned workers into consumers; companies following his example had happier workers. Methods for selling to ordinary Americans evolved, with radio and billboards reaching the masses. Buying on credit replaced saving for purchases, especially for large items such as cars and appliances. Ominously, new business practices began luring ordinary Americans into investing in the stock market.

assembly line Mechanized belt that moved a product down a line where each worker performed a single small task, over and over again, until the product was completed (p. 396)

five-dollar day Initiative begun by Henry Ford in 1914 to pay his workers $5 a day, more than three times the normal wage at the time. The initiative made Ford's workers consumers, while also ending any efforts to unionize Ford's plants (p. 396)

welfare capitalism Industry's strategy of improving working conditions and providing health insurance for workers (p. 396)

company unions Organizations of workers from a single company who represent workers' grievances to management (p. 396)

21-2 Explain the experiences of the nation that effectively put an end to the Progressive movement during the 1920s. In the aftermath of World War I and Russia's revolution, many Americans grew to fear communism. The "Red Scare" limited the possibility of the kinds of social changes advocated by some Progressives. Also, new conservative economic policies seemed to be improving economic and working conditions. Prohibition of alcohol production, transport, sale, and consumption did pass (if largely unenforceable). The focus of reforms shifted from the national to the local level and individual communities.

Red Scare Fear that the United States was vulnerable to a communist takeover (p. 399)

Palmer raids Anti-communist raids following World War I led by attorney general A. Mitchell Palmer, leading to the arrest and deportation of hundreds of suspected communists (p. 399)

Sacco and Vanzetti Italian immigrant suspects in a 1920 payroll heist, who were arrested, tried, and convicted of robbery and murder despite a flimsy trail of evidence (p. 399)

Great Migration The movement of nearly 2 million African Americans out of the southern parts of the United States to the cities of the North between 1910 and 1930; most were rejecting Jim Crow segregation (p. 400)

normalcy A phrase popularized by Warren G. Harding during his 1920 presidential campaign promising a return to the business-friendly, pre-Progressive era politics of the late nineteenth-century (p. 401)

Volstead Act Legislation passed in 1919 that laid down strict punishments for violating the Eighteenth Amendment (p. 402)

speakeasy Clandestine bar serving alcohol during Prohibition (p. 402)

21-3 Describe the various kinds of leisure activities that became popular in America during the 1920s. Movies exploded in popularity. In 1927 came the first talking movie, *The Jazz Singer*. The phonograph and radio brought music and entertainment home to millions of Americans. Sports, participatory and spectator, became widely popular, especially baseball, boxing, and football. People began to enjoy mass-culture fads, gossip, and sex scandals similar to what we see today. The Harlem Renaissance brought together black writers, dancers, artists, actors, singers. Many white people came, to experience the perceived freedom and sensuality of African American culture.

jazz Rhythmic music derived as part of African American culture and popularized by both white and black musicians during the 1920s (p. 403)

phonograph Invention that played recorded music; pioneered by Edison in the 1870s (p. 403)

Harlem Renaissance A cultural and political endeavor among African Americans using art and literature to protest the perpetuation of racism in America and in African Americans' historic responses to it; its leaders demanded the rise of a "new Negro" who would stand up and fight American racism; lasted from 1919 to 1929 (p. 404)

Universal Negro Improvement Association Marcus Garvey's black nationalist fraternal organization that advocated a celebration of blackness, the creation of black-owned and -operated businesses, and the dream of a return of all black people to Africa (p. 405)

National Women's Party Political lobbying coalition founded in 1913 that promoted women's right to vote and to share political and economic equality (p. 405)

Equal Rights Amendment Proposed amendment to the Constitution meant to eliminate all legal distinctions between the sexes, such as those that permitted different pay scales for men and women doing the same job (p. 405)

21-4 Discuss the strong reactions among various groups in America to the changing cultural mores of the 1920s. Rapid change caused much confusion and consternation among certain groups of Americans. Religious fundamentalists attacked many new social practices, especially the teaching of evolution in public schools. The most famous example of this was the Scopes Monkey Trial in Tennessee. Concerns about the "wrong" kinds of immigrant resulted in increasingly strict immigration quotas. A briefly resurgent Ku Klux Klan drew middle-class support targeting many of the newly arrived immigrants, especially Jews and Catholics, in addition to their customary enemies, black Americans.

modernists Protestants who consciously sought to adapt their Protestant faith to the findings of scientific theories, such as evolution and evidence that questioned the literalness of the Bible (p. 407)

fundamentalists Protestants who insisted that the Bible should be understood as God's revealed word, absolutely true down to the last detail; they asserted and upheld the main points of traditional Christian doctrine, including biblical inerrancy, the reality of miracles, and the Virgin birth (p. 408)

Scopes Monkey Trial Famous 1925 court case that revolved around a state law prohibiting the teaching of evolution in Tennessee schools; John Scopes, a young teacher, offered to deliberately break the law to test its constitutionality (p. 408)

American Civil Liberties Union (ACLU) Organization founded in 1920 that was dedicated to fighting infringements on civil liberties, including free speech (p. 408)

Americanization Notion that all American immigrant groups should leave behind their old ways and melt into the Anglo-Saxon mainstream (p. 409)

melting pot Concept that all the nation's people contributed their cultural traits to a single mix, creating something altogether new (p. 409)

cultural pluralism Idea that each cultural group should retain its uniqueness and not be forced to change by a restrictive state or culture (p. 409)

National Origins Act Legislation that restricted the number of immigrants permitted to enter the United States, creating a series of quotas in 1924 (p. 409)

Ku Klux Klan A quasi-military force formed immediately after the Civil War by former Confederate soldiers in order to resist racial integration and preserve white supremacy; after a temporary decline, the group reformed in 1915 and sporadically returned to prominence throughout the nineteenth and twentieth centuries. (p. 410)

Timeline		*What Else Was Happening*
1929–1933	National GDP declines from $103.1 to $58 billion; 9,000 banks go bankrupt.	
1930	Hawley-Smoot Tariff raises prices on imports, deepens international depression.	*Vannevar Bush at MIT invents the "differential analyzer," or analog computer.*
1931	Nine African American boys convicted on rape charges in Scottsboro, Alabama.	*Japan, seeking raw materials for its own industrial growth, invades Manchuria, bringing Japan and China into conflict that would erupt into war in 1937.*
1932	**January:** Reconstruction Finance Corporation makes business loans but has little impact. **July:** Veterans march on capital to demand their bonus and are dispersed violently. **November:** Franklin D. Roosevelt defeats Hoover in nation's largest land-slide election.	
1933	Roosevelt declares four-day bank holiday to disperse run on banks. Emergency Banking Relief Act establishes federal control over banks. Federal Emergency Relief contributes $500 million to state and local government. Civilian Conservation Corps employs 2.5 million in conservation work. Public and Civil Works Administrations ease unemployment. National Recovery Act enforces industry and wage standards to stabilize prices. Agricultural Adjustment Act restricts output to stabilize commodity prices. Tennessee Valley Authority builds dams and regional economy in seven-state region. Federal Securities Act creates oversight of stock exchange to curb insider trading. Glass-Steagall Banking Act creates federal deposit insurance and ends bank panics.	*Ruth Wakefield bakes the first chocolate chip cookie.*
1934	"Share Our Wealth" plan of Louisiana senator Huey Long challenges New Deal.	*African American consumers protest white price gouging in Harlem Boycott.* *General strike in support of longshoremen brings San Francisco to standstill.* *The first laundromat, the "washeteria," opens in Texas.* *Amid Germany's own economic depression, Adolf Hitler becomes dictator.*
1935	Works Progress Administration employs millions in public works, arts, humanities. Congress of Industrial Organization organizes unskilled men and women. U.S. Supreme Court invalidates NRA in *Schechter Poultry Corp.* v. *U.S.* Resettlement Administration aids flood control, reforestation; relocates workers. Social Security Act provides safety net against old age, disability, unemployment. "Soak-the-rich" Revenue Act increases tax rates for very rich. United Auto Workers gain contract from GM after sit-down strike in Flint, Michigan.	**1937:** *FDR's court-packing plan tries to tilt Supreme Court in president's favor but fails.* *WPA cuts and interest rate hikes trigger "Roosevelt recession."* *Chicago police kill ten protesters in front of steel plant; FDR intervenes.* *Hormel introduces its canned pink mystery meat, Spam.*

22-1 Explain the underlying causes of the economic depression, and evaluate President Hoover's attempts to help the economy recover. After World War I, struggling European countries received U.S. loans, intertwining their economies. America saw great disparity in wealth. Some business sectors thrived, but farmers were hurting. When Americans began to overspeculate in the stock market and European countries could not repay loans, banks began to falter, and the stock market crashed in October 1929. The crisis became global.

call loan Most common form of credit for stock purchases; allowed a stock buyer to put down from 10 to 50 percent of a stock's price and borrow the rest of the money in order to make the full payment; the lender could then "call back" the loan and demand repayment when a stock fell below a certain price (p. 417)

voluntary cooperation Name for Herbert Hoover's belief that the American economy could rebound from the Great Depression if people willingly worked together and made sacrifices in order to benefit the whole society, including asking business leaders to pay more and laborers to accept less (p. 417)

Hawley-Smoot Tariff Bill passed in 1930 that raised American tariffs on foreign agricultural and manufactured goods by as much as 50 percent; triggered European retaliation (p. 417)

22-2 **Describe the experiences of both urban and rural Americans during the Great Depression, and explain ways in which the Great Depression affected American politics.** Urban Americans lost jobs in all sectors. The newly homeless congregated in "Hoovervilles." By 1932, a quarter of a million American children were homeless. Hunger led to food riots in cities. African Americans were hurt most, losing their jobs before white Americans did. They formed associations, helped each other, and boycotted white businesses and white landlords when charged unfairly. Rural residents, already hit by low farm prices, faced drought, dust storms, and a "Dust Bowl." Many fled West; those who remained experienced crop losses, loan defaults, and foreclosures. The Communist Party of the United States strengthened, as faith in capitalism ebbed. The violent, heavy-handed eviction of the Bonus Army, who had marched on Washington seeking early payment of a promised war bonus, helped ensure Hoover's loss to Democrat Franklin Roosevelt in 1932.

Hooverville Popular name for a shantytown built by homeless Americans during the Great Depression (p. 418)

breadline A line of people waiting to receive free food handed out by a charitable organization or public agency (p. 419)

Dust Bowl Parts of Kansas, Oklahoma, Nebraska, and Texas that suffered punishing dust storms and drought from the early 1930s to the early 1940s (p. 419)

Scottsboro Boys Nine African American boys accused of raping a white woman in Scottsboro, Alabama, in 1931; they were imprisoned, although their guilt was never established conclusively (p. 423)

Bonus Army Group of 15,000 World War I veterans who staged a protest in Washington, D.C., in 1932, demanding immediate payment of their military bonuses (p. 423)

22-3 **Evaluate FDR's actions designed to alleviate the effects of the economic decline, and discuss the opposition he faced.** Franklin D. Roosevelt came into office with the promise of an honest effort, the truth, and a New Deal. He attacked the banking crisis, created the Civilian Conservation Corps, and offered financial assistance and jobs through various agencies. Some thought he went too far, some not far enough. Many conservatives felt the economy would right itself; others feared abandoning the gold standard. Those on the left felt he was too timid and that the government should do more. The Supreme Court entered the fray, declaring several New Deal programs unconstitutional.

bank holiday Business day when banks are closed; used strategically by Roosevelt immediately after assuming the presidency (p. 424)

Brain Trust Group of leading intellectuals charged with formulating policy with Roosevelt (p. 424)

Federal Emergency Relief Administration (FERA) Federally funded department creating economic programs to employ the unemployed (p. 425)

Civilian Conservation Corps (CCC) New Deal program that enlisted unemployed young men ages eighteen to twenty-five in building and repairing highways, forest service sites, flood control projects, and national park buildings (p. 425)

National Industrial Recovery Act (NIRA) New Deal act that instituted programs to regulate industry, establish labor rights, and improve working conditions (p. 425)

Section 7a A component of the NIRA that legalized and granted rights to labor unions, leading to the dramatic expansion of labor unions across the nation (p. 425)

National Recovery Administration (NRA) Department that enforced fair-trade rules set by industry associations during the 1920s, encouraged companies and workers to meet and agree on prices and wages, and established a public relations campaign to mobilize support of the New Deal (p. 425)

Agricultural Adjustment Act (AAA) A transformative act of the New Deal that established an agency that, among other things, paid farmers not to grow crops in order to curb supply; was one of the most influential federal agencies in the South and West (p. 426)

Tennessee Valley Authority (TVA) Department created in May 1933 to build a series of dams on the Tennessee River in order to improve river navigation and create electricity for the area's rural residents (p. 426)

Glass-Steagall Banking Act A law regulating the banking industry, including its loans, and creating the FDIC to guarantee individual deposits (p. 426)

Works Progress Administration (WPA) New Deal agency whose workers built roads, dams, schools, subways, housing projects, and other federal projects; it also sponsored cultural programs for unemployed artists and writers (p. 428)

Wagner Act Legislation passed in July 1935, also known as the National Labor Relations Act (NLRA); strengthened the legal position of trade unions (p. 428)

Social Security Act Most far-reaching element of all 1930s legislation, passed in August 1935; intended to provide a "safety net" for citizens who could not financially support themselves (p. 428)

Keynesianism The belief that governments should engage in deficit spending in order to stimulate a depressed economy, premised on the economic thought of British economist John Maynard Keynes, upon which FDR in particular based his actions (p. 430)

22-4 **Discuss the most significant long-term effects of the New Deal.** Though the New Deal did not end the Depression, its effects still remain integral to American life. The Depression's chroniclers explored the social problems that plagued America as never before. The New Deal helped labor, with union protections and legislation designed to aid negotiations. In politics, a much stronger Democratic Party emerged. Both immigrants and African Americans flocked to the Democratic ticket, because New Deal programs helped even them. Significantly, Americans proved willing to accept more government intervention in their daily lives.

Congress of Industrial Organizations (CIO) Broadly based trade union that recruited unskilled men and women on a large scale, particularly in the mining and clothing industries (p. 431)

sit-down strike Action in which workers stop working and lock themselves in the factory so that strikebreakers cannot take their places (p. 431)

Black Cabinet Informal group of black officials appointed to government posts who discussed African American issues with FDR (p. 432)

World War II 23

CHAPTER 23 TIMELINE

CHAPTER REVIEW

		What Else Was Happening
1931	Japan invades Chinese territory Manchuria.	
1933	Hitler's National Socialist Party ascends to power in Germany.	
	Italian dictator Benito Mussolini invades and conquers Ethiopia.	
	FDR's "good neighbor" policy renounces past invasions.	
1936	Hitler defies Treaty of Versailles and rearms demilitarized zone west of Rhine.	
1937	Japan launches full invasion of Chinese mainland.	
1938	Germany annexes Austria.	
	France and Britain consent to German annexation of western Czechoslovakia.	
1939	**March:** Hitler breaks Munich Agreement and marches into Czechoslovakia.	**1940:** *Germany occupies Denmark, Norway, Belgium, Netherlands.*
	August: Hitler and Stalin make secret nonaggression pact, plan division of Poland.	**June 5:** *Germany invades France, captures Paris within six weeks.*
	September 1: Hitler declares war against Poland and launches invasion.	*German air force targets civilians with city bombing raids in Battle of Britain.*
1941	Lend-Lease Act provides military aid to nations attacked by Germany and Japan.	
	Japan occupies French Indochina; United States cuts off all trade with Japan.	
	Roosevelt and Churchill state aim of national self-determination in Atlantic Charter.	
	December 7: Japan bombs U.S. naval station at Pearl Harbor, Hawai'i.	
1942	**February 19:** Roosevelt orders internment of 112,000 Japanese Americans.	
	June: Victory in Battle of Midway turns tide in Pacific war against Japan.	
	October: British check Axis advance in North Africa in battle of El Alamein.	
1943	**November:** Stalin, Roosevelt, Churchill agree on second front against Germany in 1944.	**1944:** *GI Bill aids veterans in housing, employment, health care, education.*
	Supreme Court finds internment of Japanese Americans constitutional in *Korematsu.*	**June 6:** *Allies launch largest amphibian assault in history in French Normandy.*
		Capture of Iwo Jima costs lives of 6,800 Americans and 21,000 Japanese.
		September 11: *Allied troops enter Germany after reclaiming France, Belgium, Netherlands.*
		December: *American victory in Battle of the Bulge.*
1945	**February:** Roosevelt, Churchill, Stalin discuss postwar Europe at Yalta.	
	May 8: Germany surrenders, Americans celebrate V-E Day.	
	July/August: Potsdam Conference reveals tensions between Britain, United States, and Soviet Union.	
	August 6: U.S. drops atomic bomb on Hiroshima, killing 160,000.	
	August 9: Second atomic bomb on Nagasaki kills 60,000 to 80,000 people.	

23-1 **Explain the causes of World War II.** The Treaty of Versailles that ended World War I placed blame on Germany for having started the war. European Allies demanded heavy reparations that ruined Germany's economy. A worldwide depression, spawned by U.S. loans to European countries and American overspeculation in the stock market, led the German people to accept Hitler's promises. Taking power in 1933, Hitler and the Nazi Party remilitarized Germany and began retaking lost lands. European leaders, eager to avoid war, let Hitler get away with taking over Czechoslovakia. In 1939 Hitler invaded Poland, driving Europe finally into war.

Munich Agreement 1938 treaty in which the leading powers of western Europe allowed Hitler to annex strategic areas of Czechoslovakia in order to satisfy his territorial aspirations (strategy of appeasement) (p. 438)

nonaggression pact 1939 agreement between Stalin and Hitler that divided Poland between Germany and the Soviet Union and said the two nations would not attack each other (p. 439)

WWW.CENGAGEBRAIN.COM

23-2 **Explain American foreign policy as it developed after World War I, called isolationism, and describe how that policy changed as World War II progressed.** Roosevelt pledged neutrality, but as war spread, he turned America into an "arsenal for democracy." In 1940 Congress agreed to arm Britain, FDR prepared America for war, and defense spending rose. Japan's actions against its neighbors in the Pacific led America to cut off all trade with Japan. Instead of bowing to economic pressure, Japan bombed the U.S. naval station at Pearl Harbor, Hawai'i. The next day, December 8, 1941, Congress declared war on Japan. In return, Hitler declared war on the United States.

"good neighbor" policy American strategy of renouncing military intervention in Latin American affairs (p. 440)

blitzkrieg "Lightning war"; fast and brutal attacks staged by Germany on its neighbors starting in 1940 (p. 441)

Vichy City in central France, headquarters of the pro-German French regime installed in 1940 (p. 441)

Holocaust Systematic killing of 11 million Jews, gypsies, and other societal scapegoats in Nazi concentration camps all over Europe (p. 441)

Battle of Britain Fierce battle fought in the summer and autumn of 1940; Hitler attempted to break Britain's air power through heavy bombardment of British cities (p. 441)

America First Committee Organization created to oppose U.S. involvement in the Second World War; committee leaders argued that the Nazis were unstoppable and that the United States should negotiate with them (p. 442)

Four Freedoms Basic human rights articulated by FDR to ensure that America's involvement in World War II was seen as ideologically sound: freedom of speech, freedom of worship, freedom from want, freedom from fear (p. 442)

Lend-Lease Act Legislation passed in March 1941 empowering the president to lend weapons and supplies to nations fighting the Germans or the Japanese (p. 443)

Atlantic Charter Set of aims issued by Roosevelt and Churchill stating that the war was being waged in the name of national self-determination and was not a war of conquest (p. 443)

23-3 **Describe the major events of World War II, both in Europe and the Pacific, and explain why the United States acted as it did throughout the conflict.** Hitler accomplished in World War II what Germany had not done in the First World War: Germany captured France and kept Stalin out of the war for a while through a nonaggression pact. After Pearl Harbor, Germany invaded the USSR, tying FDR, Churchill, and Stalin into an uneasy alliance. America's first priority was to counter Japanese aggression, while the allies remained in Europe. The U.S. turned the tide in 1942's Battle of Midway; however, the Japanese would not give in easily. 1943 brought significant changes, as the Allies invaded Italy and the U.S. won control of Guadalcanal. In June 1944, the D-Day invasion liberated France, and by September Allied troops entered Germany.

Grand Alliance Group of three countries allied to fight Hitler: the United States, Britain, and the Soviet Union (p. 444)

four policemen Four major allies: the United States, the Soviet Union, Britain, and China; Roosevelt suggested that after the war, these countries exert their military power to ensure international peace (p. 444)

Battle of Midway Turning point of the Pacific battle when, in 1942, the Allies finally stopped the expansion of Japan (p. 445)

Battle of Stalingrad Five-month-long battle in southwestern Russia that halted the advance of Germany into the Soviet Union in 1942. With somewhere near 1.5 million casualties, it is often considered one of the bloodiest battles in the history of warfare (p. 446)

Guadalcanal One of the Solomon Islands in the Pacific, the location of a 1943 battle that gave the United States and its allies a foothold in the Pacific (p. 446)

23-4 **Describe and discuss the American home front during World War II, paying special attention to long-term societal changes.** The war brought Americans together and also brought to light discrimination. Sale of war bonds and taxes financed the war; goods were rationed and price controls were enacted. The worst treatment was reserved for Japanese Americans, who were sent to internment camps. The West and the South grew economically.

Fair Employment Practices Committee (FEPC) Agency that required companies with federal contracts to make jobs available without regard to "race, creed, color, or national origin" (p. 451)

Double V Campaign championed by African Americans during World War II, demanding "democracy at home and abroad" (p. 452)

bracero program Wartime arrangement in which the U.S. government brought several hundred thousand Mexican migrants to work on California farms (p. 452)

GI Bill Servicemen's Readjustment Act of 1944, which promised unemployment benefits, educational opportunities, low-interest housing loans, and medical care to millions of soldiers (p. 453)

23-5 **Explain how World War II ended, both in Europe and in the Pacific, and discuss the aftermath of the war both in the United States and around the world.** Germany's last attempt to break through the Allied lines in Belgium, the Battle of the Bulge, failed. In the east, Stalin's armies pushed the Germans back toward Berlin. As the Allies reached the German capital at the end of April, Hitler committed suicide. Germany's final surrender came on May 8. FDR's death in April 1945 left the defeat of Japan to the new president, Harry Truman, who authorized the use of the new atom bomb on Hiroshima and Nagasaki in August. Japan surrendered soon after.

Battle of the Bulge Largest battle of the western front; ended when the Germans failed to capture the Allied stronghold of Bastogne, Belgium, and allowed Soviet forces to advance on Germany from the east (p. 455)

Yalta agreement Statement issued by Roosevelt, Churchill, and Stalin in February 1945 that promised independent regimes in Poland and eastern Europe, yet conceded that pro-Soviet parties would have a large role in creating and sustaining these regimes (p. 455)

Manhattan Project American project during World War II designed to harness the power of the atom and create an atom bomb (p. 456)

What Else Was Happening

1945
April 25: United Nations holds first meeting in San Francisco.
Soviets impose communist regimes on several eastern European states.
September 6, 1945: Truman delivers his reconversion speech, a special message to Congress presenting a 21-point program for the reconversion period.

1946
March: Churchill describes division between East and West as "iron curtain."
U.S. George F. Kennan's "long telegram" from Moscow advocates containment.

1947
Truman Doctrine commits United States to aid nations in fight against communism.
Marshall Plan aids European recovery in return for allegiance against communism.
Taft-Hartley Act bans closed shop, introduces "cooling off"; Truman's veto fails.
National Security Act creates CIA, Air Force, Department of Defense, Security Council.

Truman establishes loyalty security program; states, cities, and companies follow.

Hollywood Ten refuse to testify at House Un-American Activities Committee.

AT&T invents the cellular phone, which becomes commercially available only in 1983.

1948
United Nations adopts Universal Declaration of Human Rights.
Truman desegregates armed forces.
NSC-68 proposes military buildup, hydrogen bombs, eliminating U.S. communists.
Southern Democrats split as Dixiecrats, protest Truman's civil rights support.
Western Allies' introduction of Deutschmark triggers one-year Soviet Berlin blockade.

1949
Soviet Union successfully tests own atomic bomb.
United States and western European nations form NATO.

1950: *State Department official Alger Hiss convicted for lying about Soviet contacts.*
June 25: *Communist North Korea invades South Korea.*
Danish doctor Christian Hamburger performs the first sex change operation on New Yorker George Jorgensen, who becomes Christine Jorgensen.

1951
April: President Truman relieves MacArthur of command in Korea for insubordination.

1952
November 1: United States successfully tests first hydrogen bomb.

1953
CIA covert operations overthrow government in Iran.
July: Armistice between North and South Korea along prewar borders.

1954: *CIA covert operations overthrow democratic government in Guatemala.*
Supreme Court rules segregation unconstitutional in Brown v. Board of Education.
United States articulates strategy of "massive retaliation."
Ray Kroc buys the small-scale franchise McDonald's Restaurant and begins to turn it into the most successful fast-food chain in the world.

1955
Soviet-dominated eastern Europe consolidates under Warsaw Pact.
White men lynch teenager Emmett Till in Mississippi for whistling at a white woman.
Rosa Parks's refusal to give up bus seat triggers Montgomery Bus Boycott.

1957
August: Soviet Union tests first intercontinental ballistic missile (ICBM).
September: Federal troops enforce desegregation of high school in Little Rock, Arkansas.
October: Soviet Union launches first satellite, Sputnik.

1958
President Eisenhower establishes National Aeronautics and Space Administration (NASA).

1959: *Kitchen Debate between Vice President Nixon and Soviet premier Khrushchev.*
The Beatles form.

1961
Eisenhower warns of the military-industrial complex in farewell address.

24-1 **Explain the causes of the Cold War between the United States and the Soviet Union, and discuss some of the more serious incidents between the two superpowers.** The United States and Soviet Union distrusted each other ever since the USSR came into existence. After World War II, the hard-hit Soviet Union wanted a protective barrier between it and Germany. Meanwhile the United States wanted to stop the expansion of communism. After the Soviets achieved atomic power, the tensions heightened to become a true "Cold War." The first major conflict between the U.S. and the Soviet Union occurred in occupied Germany. Having failed to blockade West Berlin in 1948, the USSR built the Berlin Wall in 1961. Churchill's phrase, "iron curtain," well-described the ideological partitioning of Europe. China's shift to communism in 1949 and organizations like NATO and SEATO kept tensions high. The aim of the Cold War was to not go to war—and in that, at least, the two superpowers succeeded. Open conflicts emerged in Korea and Vietnam, as the U.S. government tried to "contain" communism. Thanks to the Truman Doctrine and the Marshall Plan, western Europe never adopted communism.

Cold War The postwar ideological, economic, and military contest between the United States and the Soviet Union (p. 461)

United Nations (UN) International organization that fosters discussions among the world's nations and monitors the well-being of almost all individuals in the world (p. 461)

containment U.S. strategy for dealing with the Soviet Union as outlined by George F. Kennan, with the intent of containing communism and not letting it advance any further than it already had (p. 462)

Domino Theory Metaphor referring to unstable nations as dominoes, with the United States obligated to prevent the dominoes from "falling," which would begin a process of communist world domination (p. 463)

Truman Doctrine U.S. strategy of offering aid to nations that might be susceptible to communist infiltration (p. 463)

Marshall Plan Truman Doctrine as it was administered in Europe by General George Marshall, in order to diminish the allure of communism; under the auspices of the plan, the U.S. sent $13 billion to governments that promised to become or remain democracies (p. 463)

North Atlantic Treaty Organization Pact that cemented an alliance of Western nations; prompted by the Berlin Crisis (p. 465)

NSC-68 Classified paper written by American diplomats that portrayed an uncontrollably aggressive Soviet Union and recommended stopping the threat through a massive military buildup, the creation of hydrogen bombs, and the rooting out of all communists on American soil (p. 466)

24-2 **Describe American life as it developed during the 1950s, including social, economic, and political issues, and evaluate the significance of the Cold War in these changes.** After World War II, the U.S. successfully transitioned from a war economy to a consumer-based one. Women returned to the home, men to good jobs, and life became comfortable for white Americans. After many strikes across industries, in 1946 labor rights were curtailed under the Taft-Hartley Act. The GI Bill sent veterans to college and helped them purchase homes, a dream come true for millions. William Levitt pioneered the suburb, with nearly identical houses built close together. Inhabited exclusively by white families, the new suburbia increased racial segregation.

Fair Deal Truman's twenty-one-point postwar plan that provided increases in the minimum wage, federal assistance in building homes, federal support for education and health care, and jobs in public works; represented a renewal of the Fair Employment Practices Commission (p. 470)

Taft-Hartley Act Labor Management Relations Act of 1947 that banned the closed shop, outlawed collective bargaining within industries, and authorized the president to delay strikes by declaring a "cooling-off" period (p. 471)

National Interstate and Defense Highways Act The largest public works project in American history when it was passed; authorized $25 billion to build 41,000 miles of roads, greatly assisting the burgeoning car culture of the 1950s (p. 472)

Kitchen Debate Discussion between Soviet premier Nikita Khrushchev and Vice President Richard Nixon in 1959 debating the relative merits of capitalism and communism (p. 473)

24-3 **Explain the rise and effects of McCarthyism.** During the 1950s, Senator Joseph McCarthy shaped public culture by insisting that the federal government had been infiltrated by communists bent on tearing the country apart from within. The Red Scare's scope was wide and deep, curtailing civil liberties and quashing political dissent. The fears of the Cold War were always in the background.

Hollywood Ten Group of screenwriters and directors accused of being members of the Communist Party (p. 477)

blacklist Collection of names of hundreds of people deemed "subversive" whom Hollywood executives agreed not to hire (p. 477)

24-4 **Describe breakthroughs forged by African Americans in the 1950s and the retaliatory movement that came to be called "massive resistance."** Despite McCarthy-inspired conservatism, minorities achieved significant breakthroughs in these years. African Americans worked for civil rights, inspired by Martin Luther King, Jr., and Ralph Abernathy. *Brown* v. *Board of Education* ended segregation, but southerners fought change, reactivating the Klan. Arkansas Governor Faubus was finally forced to admit nine black students to Little Rock's Central High School. African Americans continued to push for equal treatment and access to public services.

massive resistance A campaign and policy begun by politicians in Virginia to craft laws and do whatever possible to resist racial integration; spread throughout the South (p. 480)

White Citizens' Councils Committees organized in the 1950s and 1960s to defend segregation in the South (p. 480)

bus boycott A campaign to boycott an area's buses until change is instituted; used frequently during the civil rights movement (p. 480)

nonviolence Strategy for social changes that rejects the use of violence (p. 481)

What Else Was Happening

1959 Fidel Castro leads successful revolution against Cuba's Batista regime.
Students for a Democratic Society (SDS) define social justice as goal of New Left.

1960 **February:** Students defy segregation with sit-in at Greensboro Woolworth lunch counter.
November: John F. Kennedy becomes first Catholic president over Republican Richard Nixon.

May: Student Nonviolent Coordinating Committee (SNCC) begins civil rights activism.
Two hackers from MIT create the first computer video game, Spacewar.

1961 **April:** CIA-orchestrated Bay of Pigs invasion fails.
May: Congress of Racial Equality (CORE) challenges segregation in Freedom Rides.
August: Soviets and East Germany erect Berlin Wall to prevent further defections.

1962 **October:** Cuban Missile Crisis brings world to brink of nuclear war.

1963 Media coverage of Birmingham police beating civil rights marchers stirs nation.
August: White supremacists bomb black Birmingham church, killing four girls.
August: United States supports generals' coup and killing of South Vietnam leader Ngo Dinh Diem.
August 28: Martin Luther King, Jr., gives "I Have a Dream" speech at March on Washington for Jobs and Freedom.
November 22: John F. Kennedy assassinated in Dallas.

Betty Friedan's The Feminine Mystique defines "the problem that has no name."
Harvey Ball, a Worcester, Massachusetts, commercial artist, devises the yellow smiley face for an insurance firm that wants to improve employee morale after a bitter corporate takeover.

1964 **January:** President Johnson seeks expansion of welfare state and "war on poverty".
July 3: Civil Rights Act ends public segregation and discrimination in employment.
Summer: Volunteers travel south to build "Freedom Schools" and register black voters.
August: Economic Opportunity Act creates Head Start, VISTA, Job Corps, other agencies.
August: Gulf of Tonkin Resolution gives full support for South Vietnam.

The G.I. Joe doll—dubbed "America's movable fighting man" by Hasbro—makes his debut.

1965 **March:** Johnson authorizes heavy bombing of North Vietnam and 80,000 troops for South Vietnam.
Congress passes Voting Rights Act.
Hart-Cellar Act enables growing immigration from Asia and Latin America.
August: Deadly L.A.-Watts riots begin urban unrest across nation.

Biggest power failure in history causes nine-hour blackout in eastern Canada and the United States, leading to a surge in the national birthrate nine months later.

1966 Black Panther Party forms in Oakland, California.
October: 100,000 people march in Washington to protest Vietnam War.

1968 **January 30:** Communist Tet Offensive undermines president's claims of success in Vietnam.
March: Johnson calls for peace negotiations, vows not to seek reelection.
April 4: White supremacist kills Martin Luther King, Jr.; riots rock cities.
August: Police quell protesters at Democratic National Convention in Chicago.
November: Republican Richard M. Nixon wins presidency over Democrat Hubert Humphrey.

1969: Summer: Woodstock Music Festival.

1970 **May 4:** Ohio National Guardsmen kill four students protesting invasion of Cambodia.
November: News of U.S. massacre of more than 300 civilians in My Lai.

1971 **June:** Publication of secret Pentagon Papers on Vietnam policy.

1973 **January:** United States and North Vietnam sign treaty; U.S. troops withdraw.

1975: Communists unify Vietnam.

25-1 **Describe the experiences John F. Kennedy had while president that led some to label him the "ultimate cold warrior."** In Kennedy's first year in office, the Berlin Wall and Bay of Pigs proved America was not all-powerful. In fall 1962 Soviet missile silos appeared in reconnaissance photos of Cuba, a serious threat to the U.S. After 13 extremely tense days, diplomats compromised and the Soviets removed the missiles. Kennedy continued the U.S.'s involvement in Vietnam, since Communists were trying to seize power. It is unknown whether he would have become as involved as would his successor, Lyndon Johnson.

liberalism A political philosophy founded on the ideas of liberty and equality but which, in the aftermath of the Industrial Revolution, came to signify the federal government's role in providing a counterbalance to free-market capitalism (p. 485)

nation building Facilitating the economic and political maturation of developing nations; political strategy employed by President Kennedy in order to prevent developing nations from adopting communism (p. 486)

Berlin Wall Barrier built in 1961 by the communist government to separate impoverished, Soviet-controlled East Berlin from the more prosperous West Berlin (p. 487)

Cuban Missile Crisis Thirteen-day confrontation between the Kennedy administration and the Cuban communist regime in October 1962; Castro had agreed to allow the Soviet Union to base a few of its nuclear missiles in Cuba, thus potentially triggering a nuclear war between the United States and the Soviet Union (p. 488)

25-2 Discuss attempts made both by African Americans and by the legal system to provide voting and other rights to black citizens. In the early 1960s, African Americans stepped up their activism for civil rights. Sit-ins, Freedom Rides, boycotts, and activism by leaders like Martin Luther King, Jr., all played a part. The Twenty-fourth Amendment, passed in 1964, outlawed the racially discriminatory poll taxes for voting. President Johnson then pushed through Congress a national Civil Rights Act and a Voting Rights Act. Rifts within the civil rights movement grew, as militant activists like Malcolm X sought swifter change. Amid social unrest, it became clear that society had to change if America were to be for all citizens.

Civil Rights Act of 1964 Legislation outlawing all discrimination in public facilities based on color, religion, sex, and national origin, and establishing the Equal Employment Opportunity Commission to investigate violations of the law in employment (p. 492)

Voting Rights Act of 1965 Legislation outlawing attempts to deny suffrage to African Americans through literacy tests, poll taxes, or any other attempt to disfranchise citizens (p. 493)

25-3 Discuss Lyndon Johnson's desire to build a "Great Society" and evaluate the relative success of his programs. The idea of the "Great Society" was that the U.S. was capable of caring for all, not just a privileged few. LBJ hoped to eliminate poverty, and improve education, health care, social welfare, and the arts. Johnson has received credit for trying to improve America, and blame for expanding the "welfare state." Conservatives and liberals still argue about the merits of Johnson-era programs.

welfare Umbrella term referring to many government assistance programs, especially Aid to Families with Dependent Children (p. 495)

Hart-Cellar Act Legislation passed in 1965 curtailing the quota system of the 1920s and permitting larger numbers of non-Europeans to settle in the United States (p. 496)

25-4 Explain the Cold War origins of the Vietnam War, and evaluate the decisions Johnson made that pushed the war into the forefront of Americans' minds. Johnson believed America had a duty to do what it could to save South Vietnam from Communism. After an overblown incident in the Tonkin Gulf, Congress authorized LBJ to settle the issue. He saw this as a mandate to escalate the war, and American troops were on the ground in Vietnam by mid-1965. Troop strength and casualty counts continually mounted, as did opposition to the war at home. North Vietnam's surprising Tet Offensive of 1968 turned many Americans against the war. Johnson chose not to run for reelection in 1968. But years of fighting in Southeast Asia still lay ahead.

Tonkin Gulf Resolution Legislation allowing the president to "take all necessary measures to repel armed attack against the forces of the United States and to prevent further aggression," which was used to justify U.S. involvement in Vietnam (p. 498)

Ho Chi Minh Trail Winding path through North Vietnam, Laos, and Cambodia that the North Vietnamese used to supply the Viet Cong (p. 498)

search-and-destroy operations Strategy used during wartime in which the U.S. Army would locate enemy forces, retreat, and call in airpower (p. 498)

25-5 Discuss the growth of the "counterculture" in American society during the 1960s, the coming together of protesters against American culture and protesters challenging the war, and describe the various movements that began to gather strength as Americans sought to have their voices heard. The civil rights movement and Vietnam fueled protests questioning the bedrock of American society. Malcolm X and the Nation of Islam chastised blacks willing to "settle" for what whites would give. The Black Panthers provided for the poor, but were condemned by many for their part in urban riots. Chicanos, with leaders such as César Chávez, united and gained better wages and living conditions. The women's movement divided into two camps, both arguing for change. Young people, turned off by their elders' mistakes, used drugs, sex, and music to "find their own way."

Students for a Democratic Society (SDS) Organization founded in 1959 declaring that young people were tired of older political movements, even older radical ones; formed the core of a self-conscious "New Left" movement, which rejected the Old Left's ideologies of economic justice in favor of an ideology of social justice (p. 499)

Nation of Islam Black Nationalist organization whose leaders rejected the integrationist perspective of mainstream civil rights protesters, calling instead for an independent black nation-state (p. 500)

Black Power Movement bridging the gap between Black Nationalism and the civil rights struggle; its leaders argued that black people should have control over the social, educational, and religious institutions in their communities and advocated black pride (p. 501)

counterculture Social movement of the sixties that consciously rejected traditional politics, social values, and corporate consumerism (p. 503)

hippies Counterculture adherents who embraced new attitudes toward drugs, sex, popular culture, and politics (p. 503)

Young Americans for Freedom (YAF) A conservative student organization begun in 1960 and paralleling the left's SDS. Always larger than SDS, YAF advocated conservative principles including free markets and a smaller government (p. 505)

Vietnamization Nixon's plan to reduce American troops in Vietnam by encouraging South Vietnamese troops to take more responsibility for fighting (p. 505)

Pentagon Papers Secret Defense Department study, published in 1971, that revealed that the government had lied and purposely deceived the American public over major events in the Vietnam War in an attempt to manipulate public opinion (p. 507)

What Else Was Happening

1969
Police raid of New York's gay bar Stonewall Inn triggers gay rights movement.

"Indians of All Tribes" occupy Alcatraz as demonstration of Red Power.

1970: *In Southwest, La Raza works to get Chicanos elected to office.*

The Beatles split up.

1971
Nixon stabilizes economy with first ever peacetime wage and price freezes.

Invitation of American table tennis players to China begins "Ping-Pong Diplomacy."

1972
Title IX of Higher Education Act requires equal spending on male and female sports.

Burglars at Democratic headquarters in Watergate Hotel linked to CREEP.

1973
Roe v. *Wade* legalizes abortion on grounds of women's right to privacy.

Soviet Union and United States slow arms race with first SALT agreement.

U.S. assistance to Israel in Yom Kippur war triggers oil embargo from Arab nations.

Nixon establishes Environmental Protection Agency.

United States aids in ousting Chile's Salvador Allende and installing General Pinochet.

Trans-Alaska pipeline built.

1974
August 9: Threatened with impeachment, President Nixon resigns over Watergate scandal.

Art Fry invents Post-it®-Notes by using a colleague's "failed" adhesive while working at 3M.

1975: Popular Electronics *announces Altair, the first "personal computer."*

1976
Born-again Christian Jimmy Carter defeats Gerald Ford in presidential election.

1977
San Francisco's Harvey Milk, first openly gay man in higher office, is assassinated.

1978
Regents of the University of California v. Bakke disallows quotas in affirmative-action programs.

Carter negotiates peace between Egypt and Israel in Camp David Accords.

Fiscal conservatives celebrate property tax limits in California's Proposition 13.

1979
Islamic revolutionaries take 52 U.S. embassy staff members hostage.

Meltdown of Pennsylvania's Three-Mile Island reactor discredits nuclear power.

Shortly after signing, SALT II agreement ends with Soviet invasion of Afghanistan.

1980
Moral Majority political action group helps Ronald Reagan win presidency.

26-1 **Evaluate Richard Nixon as president, focusing on his policies in the United States and abroad.** President Nixon was driven, creative, complex, suspicious, and *always* politically motivated. His 1972 visit to Communist China helped drive a wedge between China and the Soviet Union. He also negotiated the treaty that brought most American troops back from Vietnam in 1973. He visited the Soviet Union, reaching some agreements on arms limitations. His failures usually came from involving the U.S. in internal affairs within Latin America and Africa. Domestically, he took up many liberal causes like federal arts programs, affirmative action, and OSHA. Meanwhile, he championed conservative causes like turning more control over to local governments.

Strategic Arms Limitation Talks (SALT) Sessions held between President Nixon and Soviet premier Leonid Brezhnev, in which the two leaders agreed to freeze the number of long-range missile launchers and build certain new missiles only after they had destroyed the same number of older missiles (p. 512)

détente French term meaning "a relaxing" or "an easing"; refers to more relaxed relations with America's supposed enemies, China and the Soviet Union (p. 513)

26-2 **Describe the events of Watergate and its ramifications for the country.** Nixon's paranoia over what his political enemies were up to was his undoing. The Watergate scandal, in which five men broke into the offices of the Democratic National Committee on orders issued from high in the Nixon White House, led to his resignation in 1974. Watergate fueled Americans' lack of faith in government, and many disengaged from national politics.

26-3 **Describe the economic conditions of the 1970s, including stagflation and the end of the post-World War II economic boom, and describe how Presidents Ford and Carter attempted to confront the problem.** An economic recession in the 1970s officially ended the great post-World War II economic boom. A Middle East oil embargo led to stagflation—rising inflation and declining employment. The economy slowed, many lost jobs, and neither Presidents Ford nor Carter overcame the problems. Ford encouraged Americans to save money and offered a large tax cut. Neither helped the economy. Carter, burdened by the energy crisis, also saw inflation skyrocket from his attempts at job-creation.

stagflation Economic cycle in which prices keep going up (inflation) while the economy is losing jobs (or stagnating) (p. 516)

Three Mile Island Nuclear reactor in Pennsylvania that suffered a meltdown in 1979 (p. 517)

Camp David Accords 1978 peace agreement between Israel and Egypt, brokered by President Carter (p. 517)

26-4 **Describe the perpetuation of 1960s-style activism and how it transformed into a politics of identity in the 1970s.** "Individual rights" was a catch phrase in the 1970s, and everyone, it seemed, had a cause. 1960s-style activism gave way to a turning inward, as individuals sought satisfaction with their lives. Politically, there was a return to people's voting in blocs based on shared belief systems. African Americans sought cultural as well as legal acceptance, embracing and sharing their heritage. Affirmative-action programs tried to undo the injustices in the workforce caused by racism. Chicanos, women, Native Americans, gays, environmentalists—these and many other groups pushed specific agendas. For women, 1973's *Roe* v. *Wade* legalized abortion, but an Equal Rights Amendment remained elusive.

identity politics A view of politics premised on how one identifies oneself within a nation, usually based on some sense of belonging to a minority group eager to win greater parity with the national majority (p. 518)

affirmative action Program meant to ensure that a certain percentage of a company's employees are minorities or that a certain percentage of government contracts are given to minority-owned businesses (p. 519)

Roe v. Wade Supreme Court decision of 1973 that struck down laws in forty-six states that limited a woman's access to a safe, legal abortion (p. 521)

Stonewall Inn Site in New York City of the riots that ignited the Gay Liberation movement in the late 1960s and 1970s; at the time of the riots, all fifty states had antisodomy laws, and police busts of gay bars were routine (p. 521)

26-5 **Evaluate the reaction to 1960s social movements and describe the rise of the** New Right. Conservative "family values" activists fought the women's movement, gay rights, and sexual openness. A conservative and religious Right coalesced, involving itself in politics as never before, and the country experienced a major shift in what was culturally acceptable.

Moral Majority Conservative political organization begun by Rev. Jerry Falwell in 1979 and consisting of evangelical Christians who overwhelmingly supported the Republican Party (p. 523)

What Else Was Happening

Polish "Solidarity" becomes first independent labor union in Communist bloc.

Iraq attacks Iran.

1982: *Reagan's spending cuts trigger recession.*

August: *United States sends peacekeeping forces to Lebanon.*

PacMan is named Time magazine's Man of the Year.

1980 Ronald Reagan defeats Democrat Jimmy Carter in presidential election.

1981 Reagan appoints Sandra Day O'Connor to U.S. Supreme Court.

1983 Reagan's Strategic Defense Initiative (SDI) violates treaty with Soviet Union.

October: Hezbollah suicide bomber attacks U.S. barracks in Beirut, killing 241 servicepeople.

1984 Democrat Geraldine Ferraro is first female vice-presidential candidate in U.S. history.

Military spending boosts economy, aiding Reagan's reelection.

1985 Deregulation leads to high-risk deals and failures of savings and loans.

Arms sales to Iran finance right-wing guerrillas in Nicaragua in Iran-Contra affair.

Mikhail Gorbachev and Reagan reduce arms in INF Treaty.

Tom Cruise stars in Top Gun.

1986 Reagan appoints Antonin Scalia to U.S. Supreme Court.

1988 George H. W. Bush defeats Michael Dukakis in presidential election.

1989: June: *Chinese forces quell prodemocracy protests in Beijing's Tiananmen Square.*

November: *East Germans bring down Berlin Wall, leading to German reunification in 1991.*

Latvia, Lithuania, and Estonia declare independence from Soviet Union.

1990 National debt forces Bush to raise taxes, despite promise of "no new taxes."

Former U.S. ally Saddam Hussein invades Kuwait.

Children's classic My Friend Flicka is pulled from the optional reading lists for fifth- and sixth-graders in Clay County, Florida, because the book reportedly uses objectionable language.

December: *End of Soviet Union.*

1991 Persian Gulf War for liberation of Kuwait kills 40,000 Iraqis and 240 allied troops.

27-1 **Evaluate the domestic policies of Ronald Reagan as president, including the economic challenges the country faced in the 1980s.** Reagan espoused supply-side economics, cutting taxes and cutting welfare and unemployment funds. In the long run, however, there was little "trickle-down" effect, as he had suggested. The large increase in military spending was the primary reason for an improving economy. With his affable and honest demeanor, people largely forgave Reagan's rather laissez-faire presidency.

supply-side economics Theory that tax cuts would produce new investment, which would, in turn, generate an increase in federal revenues; these revenues would eventually "trickle down" to the lower classes in the form of more jobs (p. 528)

27-2 **Describe the "culture wars" that plagued the nation during the 1980s.** In the 1980s long-existent disparities between rich and poor became even more evident. Reagan's economic policies helped the wealthy, but caused more pain for the poorest. The strengthening conservative Right contributed to the widening gaps separating Americans, not just in terms of wealth, but also in defining what America was all about. Whites in general gained economically, while African Americans and other ethnic groups lost ground. Liberals and conservatives differed vastly as to how government should function, what its purpose should be, and how to define America; on both sides, rhetoric became increasingly hostile.

trade deficit Inequality in trade whereby one country's exports to another outweigh the second country's exports to the first country (p. 530)

27-3 **Discuss the problems Reagan's successor faced in paying for the "Reagan Revolution."** The fall of European communism took place under George H. W. Bush, Reagan's former vice president. The U.S. led a coalition to liberate Kuwait from Saddam Hussein in 1991, and Bush's ratings soared. However, shortly after, a recession fueled by a savings and loan crisis hurt the country badly. Bush was forced to break his pledge of "no new taxes," and Americans were not in a forgiving mood.

27-4 **Describe the conditions for, and aftermath of, the end of the Cold War.** On entering office, Reagan pushed for a Cold War arms buildup to defeat the Soviet "evil empire." However, Reagan later worked with Soviet premier Mikhail Gorbachev in helping topple Communism. Many historians suggest U.S. defense spending bankrupted the USSR and led to Communism's demise. By the late 1980s, the Gorbachev "perestroika" had blossomed; by 1991, the USSR was no longer. The fifty-year Cold War was over. With its conclusion, the world became a more accessible place, ushering in an era of globalization.

contras Right-wing Nicaraguan guerrilla group during the 1980s (p. 536)

ethnic cleansing Complete expulsion of an entire ethnic population from a particular area (p. 538)

Shia Muslims A branch of Islam containing a minority of the world's Muslims, who believe clerics have offered ongoing interpretations of Islamic texts (p. 539)

Sunni Muslims A branch of Islam containing the vast majority of the world's Muslims, who follow closely the teachings of the Prophet Mohammed and who have codified his teachings in Islamic law (p. 539)

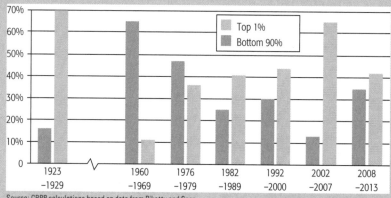

Source: CBPP calculations based on data from Piketty and Saez

What Else Was Happening

1991 Clarence Thomas appointed to Supreme Court.

1992 **April:** South Central L.A. riots after exoneration of police captured on video tape beating Rodney King.
November: Bill Clinton defeats incumbent Bush, and independent Ross Perot in presidential election.

1993 Clinton signs North American Free Trade Agreement (NAFTA).

1994 **November:** Republicans capture congressional majority.
Telecommunications Act deregulates media and mass communications.
Congress defeats health care plan championed by Hillary Clinton.
Republican minority leader Newt Gingrich pledges "Contract with America."

1995 United States becomes part of World Trade Organization.
Antigovernment activist bombs Oklahoma City federal building, killing 168.

1996 **November:** Bill Clinton defeats Bob Dole, becomes first Democrat reelected to presidency since FDR.

1997: Nevada becomes the first state to pass legislation categorizing Y2K data disasters as "acts of God," protecting the state from lawsuits that might be brought against it by residents in the year 2000.

Scientists at Roslin Institute in Scotland clone a sheep, Dolly.

Princess Diana killed in a car crash in Paris.

1998 Clinton turns federal budget deficit into surplus.

Osama bin Laden escapes U.S.-orchestrated assassination attempt.

1999 Clinton's impeachment for hiding Monica Lewinsky affair ends in Senate with Clinton's exoneration.

Two students kill thirteen classmates and teacher in Columbine, Colorado.

2000 U.S. Supreme Court decides deadlocked election in *Bush v. Gore.*

2001 Activists disturb World Bank and International Monetary Fund meetings in Genoa.

28-1 **Evaluate the presidency of Bill Clinton, discussing how he tried to cultivate a middle ground between affirming globalization and assuaging the needs of the disaffected.** Candidate Clinton benefited from the economic recession and his dynamic personality, seemingly more caring than Bush. His early presidency was marked by defeat of his health care plan and indecision on gay rights. A big success was turning the nation's budget deficit into a surplus before he left office. In 1994 Republicans gained full control of Congress, and under House Speaker Newt Gingrich shut down the government over a budget battle with Clinton. Clinton fared best in the court of public opinion. Clinton signed NAFTA into law in 1993, and in 1995 brought the U.S. into the World Trade Organization. Despite a scandal dealing with property sales, the Monica Lewinsky affair, and his near-impeachment, Bill Clinton is best remembered for advocating free trade and his stewardship of the information age.

centrism Political ideology that eclectically blended liberal and conservative philosophies and policies, sometimes called "the Third Way," during Bill Clinton's presidency; components included conservative economic principles and liberal social principles (p. 543)

North American Free Trade Agreement (NAFTA) Legislation signed in 1993 that removed tariff barriers between the United States, Mexico, and Canada (p. 546)

World Trade Organization (WTO) International agency designed to resolve disputes between trading partners and advocate free trade (p. 546)

term limits Legal restriction that limits the number of terms a person may serve in political office (p. 548)

Contract with America Document released by the Republican Party during the 1994 congressional elections promising to reform government, impose term limits, reduce taxes, increase military spending, and loosen regulations on businesses (p. 548)

28-2 **Discuss the technological revolution that took place in the 1990s, and describe the social and economic changes that took place as a result of this revolution.** Recovering from the Reagan recession, America was poised to move forward into the information age. America led the world in its number of cell phones, personal computers, and other devices. Speculation in dot-com companies made millionaires overnight—even as it hinted at major problems. Computers helped most economic sectors, streamlining jobs (and also replacing many with machines). The Internet sped communications so much that marketplace globalization became noticeable. Though at first these innovations created more jobs in America, as the decade progressed many companies moved factories overseas and American jobs were actually lost.

28-3 **Discuss the new focus on multiculturalism during the latter part of the twentieth** century. After 1965's Immigration Act, the main immigration source areas became Latin America and Asia. Today, more than 1 million immigrants arrive in America each year. The demographic breakdown is more varied, too, with 64% of the country listing themselves as white, 16.4% as Latino or Hispanic, 12.6% as African American, and 5% as Asian. Hispanics are the fastest-growing population (including an estimated 10 million who arrived illegally). Some states have tried a variety of means to curb illegal border-crossing, with mixed results. Calls for accepting America as a nation of many colors and cultures are termed "multiculturalism." Many embrace this concept, but others see the problems of dealing with newcomers who find solace in their previous cultures and ways of life.

28-4 **Explain the kinds of homegrown terrorism that shocked many Americans in the** 1990s. The Oklahoma City bombing illuminated Timothy McVeigh's hatred of the strong-arm tactics used against an antigovernment group at Ruby Ridge, Idaho, and the Branch Davidian sect at Waco, Texas. In 1998, white supremacists in Jasper, Texas, murdered a black man and dragged his body for miles. In a Wyoming bar, Matthew Shepard was savagely attacked and killed because he was gay. In 1999, two students at Colorado's Columbine High School murdered 14 before killing themselves.

28-5 **Describe how the political, cultural, and economic polarization of the nation came to a head in the presidential election of 2000.** A strong economy and peaceful world should have helped Clinton's vice president Al Gore win in 2000. But America reeled from homegrown terrorism and began to question what it meant to their world. Conservatives blamed liberals for their leniency; liberals blamed conservatives for lacking compassion. A divided U.S. saw the Supreme Court finally decide the contested 2000 election for George W. Bush.

What Else Was Happening

2000 Reality TV shows experience an explosion of popularity, beginning with *Big Brother* and *Survivor*.

2001 Republican Congress passes Bush's $1.3 trillion tax cut.

September 11: Terrorists fly hijacked planes into World Trade Center, Pentagon; over 3,000 die.

October: United States invades Taliban-controlled Afghanistan to hunt down al Qaeda and bin Laden.

Bush forms fifteenth cabinet position for Department of Homeland Security.

Apple launches the iPod, revolutionizing the music industry.

2002 Enron bankruptcy begins series of corporate scandals of fraud and corruption.

2003 **March 19:** United States preemptively invades Iraq for harboring weapons of mass destruction.

April: United States armed forces march into Baghdad.

Saddam Hussein captured.

August: Hurricane Katrina devastates Mississippi Gulf Coast and parts of New Orleans, kills 1,900, reveals poor disaster response and the prevalence of race-based poverty.

2004: April: *News about torture in U.S.-run Abu Ghraib prison shocks Americans and world.*

November: *George W. Bush prevails over Democratic challenger John Kerry in presidential race.*

A partially eaten, ten-year-old grilled cheese sandwich said to bear the image of the Virgin Mary sells on eBay for $28,000.

2005: *Iraqis elect members of constitutional convention.*

Video-sharing website YouTube is launched by three former PayPal employees.

2006: *Saddam Hussein is found guilty of crimes against humanity in Iraqi court and executed.*

2008 Barack Obama becomes the first black presidential nominee for a major political party.

Crisis in global financial markets prompts governmental "bailout."

November: Barack Obama defeats John McCain in presidential election.

Democratic primaries led by first woman and African American candidates.

Dramatic increases in oil and food prices.

2010 Using support from the emerging Tea Party Movement, Republicans win control of the House of Representatives.

2011 The Occupy Wall Street movement takes over Zucotti Park, adjacent to Wall Street, in New York City. The Occupy Movement, under the banner of "We Are the 99%," spreads nationwide.

2012 **February:** George Zimmerman's killing of an unarmed African American teenager named Trayvon Martin sparks nationwide protests against violence perpetrated against the African American community.

November: Barack Obama is elected to his second term as president, defeating Republican opponent Mitt Romney.

2015 In the case of *Obergefell* v. *Hodges*, the U.S. Supreme Court legalized same-sex marriage throughout the nation.

2016 **November:** Election of Donald J. Trump as 45th president of the United States of America.

29-1 **Describe the advent of the War on Terror and how George W. Bush handled the initial events.** Bush quickly began implementing his conservative agenda, starting with a large tax cut for the wealthy. Control of the Senate unexpectedly shifted to the Democrats, checking any advantage he had. After September 11, a stunned America allowed Bush carte blanche to go after Osama bin Laden. With an international coalition, American troops surged into Afghanistan and ousted the Taliban. The "Bush doctrine" declared America's right to initiate war anytime it was deemed necessary. He pushed through a new Department of Homeland Security, the USA PATRIOT Act, and more tax cuts. As many began to question his methods, Bush maintained that his actions would curtail terrorism.

al Qaeda A global militant Islamic organization founded in 1988 or 1989 by Osama bin Laden to advocate through publicity and violence a strict interpretation of Islamic law and to prohibit the penetration of the Middle East by Western and other outside influences (p. 560)

Bush doctrine Political principle articulated by President George W. Bush in which he declared America's right to fight a "preemptive war" against any nation that, one day, might threaten the United States (p. 560)

USA PATRIOT Act Act passed in October 2001 allowing the federal government greater latitude in surveillance of its citizens in order to monitor for potential acts of terrorism (p. 561)

29-2 **Describe George W. Bush's plans for democracy in the Middle East, including his declaration of a "War on Terror," and assess the degree of his success.** Bush believed that every country in the world, given an educated choice, would choose democracy. He started in the Middle East, where those who planned the September 11 attacks had come from. Critics, with some justification, accused America of trying to remake the world in its image. After Afghanistan, Bush sought war in Iraq, on the pretext of its weapons of mass destruction (WMDs). America invaded Iraq, and Hussein was ousted and put to death for committing crimes against humanity.

29-3 **Discuss the domestic problems that America faced during George W. Bush's second term.** An economic slump combined with record oil company profits embittered ordinary Americans. Scandals in the business world led to a rising anger, as some 20,000 employees lost jobs and pensions. In fall 2005, the U.S. experienced its worst natural disaster ever, Hurricane Katrina. In Mississippi's and Louisiana's coastal areas, storm surges wiped out whole communities. In New Orleans, the waters fatally weakened aging levees, causing massive and deadly floods. The world watched as people huddled and waited for help that was much too slow to arrive. In his final months, Bush faced a deepening crisis prompted by a large number of home loan defaults. This created severe cash shortages, which made creditors more reluctant to loan money. A tightened credit market deeply affected the American economy, especially the stock market. The market lost roughly 40 percent of its value by the end of 2008.

29-4 **Explain some of the hopes and frustrations of Barack Obama's two terms in office, and some of the persistent divisions within the United States.** With domestic problems and war weariness, Americans flocked to a message of "change." Barack Obama, a junior senator, became the first African American president of the United States. As president, Obama confronted a host of challenges: the enormously expensive war on terror; Middle East instability; and a "Great Recession" that weakened the foundations of the American economy. Obama has had some success, notably passing the nation's first comprehensive health care bill. Predictably, a conservative backlash emerged, as Republicans protested expansion of the federal government, a complaint made against Democrats since the New Deal. Obama, meanwhile, continued to target thorny issues like banking regulation, immigration reform, and gay rights. The 2012 election revealed demographic shifts, and gains in the political power of racial minorities, women, and gay rights advocates. Indeed, in June 2015, with the U.S. Supreme Court's decision in *Obergefell v. Hodges*, the United States became the largest country in the world to legalize same-sex marriage. Nonetheless, continued racialized violence, economic inequality, and political polarization mean the future will likely be just as contested as the past.

ISIL a jihadist militant group that follows a fundamentalist doctrine of Sunni Islam and uses violence and terrorism in its attempts to return an Islamic caliphate (p. 567)

Affordable Care Act A federal statute signed into law by President Barack Obama on March 23, 2010, designed to increase health insurance quality and affordability, and increase the number of Americans covered by health insurance. Opponents derisively called it "Obamacare," a name President Obama eventually adopted himself. (p. 568)

29-5 **Explain the rise of Donald J. Trump and the increased political polarization within the U.S.** In November 2016, after a highly contested and incredibly divisive campaign, Donald J. Trump, a businessman and reality television star, became President of the United States, defeating Sen. Hilary Clinton, despite the fact that Clinton won the popular vote by more than 3 million votes. With his victory in the Electoral College, Trump has waded into one controversy after another, the most lasting of which seems to be his connections to Russia and their disputed role in his election. Nonetheless, several of his major campaign promises, including repealing the Affordable Care Act and building a wall across the nation's southern border, have been stymied by both the right and the left as cost-prohibitive and unnecessarily divisive.